Moral Anthropology

This Reader is the first anthology to cover the growing field of moral anthropology and will be an essential resource for students and scholars interested in exploring the important issues involved. Morality and ethics are increasingly invoked in the most diverse domains, from politics to economics, from war to sexuality, and from international justice to biological research. To interpret this phenomenon from a critical standpoint, anthropology offers unique perspectives. This volume includes classical as well as recent material and sheds light on continuing debates about relativism and universalism, values and emotions, moral duty and ethical freedom, human rights and humanitarianism, the responsibility of the researcher and the regulation of research. The carefully chosen texts are contextualised with lucid editorial material, including a substantial introduction.

Didier Fassin is the James D. Wolfensohn Professor of Social Science at the Institute for Advanced Study, Princeton, and Director of Studies at the École des Hautes Études en Sciences Sociales, Paris.

Samuel Lézé is an Assistant Professor at the École Normale Supérieure, Lyon.

Praise for this volume:

'*Moral Anthropology: A Critical Reader* is a stunning achievement. It is uniquely suited to introduce the genealogical depth and contemporary relevance of ethical and moral questions in the terrain of social sciences and humanities. Fassin and Lézé show a superb command over a complex literature as they present each chapter with a clear and concise description of its relevance for what they call the "moral question". The main introduction and conclusion will help students to navigate the chapters but also signal contributions to the issues that have arisen to the center of concern in the public sphere.'
Veena Das, *Johns Hopkins University, USA*

'Now that the compilers of this creative collection have satisfied the need they identify, it becomes almost inconceivable to think of the anthropological horizon without it. Care, thoughtfulness and considerable imagination have gone into the compilation. The result is a work that is surprisingly fresh and vigorous. More than all the "uses" to which it can be put, this is also going to be – and not for anthropologists alone – a real source of intellectual stimulus.'
Marilyn Strathern, *University of Cambridge, UK*

'This compendium is an essential tool for anyone interested in the study of morality in the social sciences and the humanities. The texts, classical and recent, are judiciously chosen and give an unparalleled perspective on a range of burning questions. The editors have done us a great service in assembling them in a single volume.'
Michèle Lamont, *Harvard University*

Moral Anthropology

A critical reader

**Edited by
Didier Fassin and Samuel Lézé**

LONDON AND NEW YORK

First published in 2014
by Routledge
2 Park Square, Milton Park, Abingdon, Oxon OX14 4RN

and by Routledge
711 Third Avenue, New York, NY 10017

Routledge is an imprint of the Taylor & Francis Group, an informa business

© 2014 Didier Fassin and Samuel Lézé for selection and editorial matter; individual chapters, the contributors

The right of the editors to be identified as the authors of the editorial material, and of the authors for their individual chapters, has been asserted in accordance with sections 77 and 78 of the Copyright, Designs and Patents Act 1988.

All rights reserved. No part of this book may be reprinted or reproduced or utilised in any form or by any electronic, mechanical, or other means, now known or hereafter invented, including photocopying and recording, or in any information storage or retrieval system, without permission in writing from the publishers.

Trademark notice: Product or corporate names may be trademarks or registered trademarks, and are used only for identification and explanation without intent to infringe.

British Library Cataloguing in Publication Data
A catalogue record for this book is available from the British Library

Library of Congress Cataloging in Publication Data
Moral anthropology : a critical reader / [edited by] Didier Fassin, Samuel Leze.
page cm
1. Anthropological ethics. I. Fassin, Didier. II. Leze, Samuel.
GN33.6.M67 2013
301–dc23
2013022376

ISBN: 978-0-415-62726-9 (hbk)
ISBN: 978-0-415-62727-6 (pbk)

Typeset in Baskerville
by GreenGate Publishing Services, Tonbridge, Kent

Contents

Acknowledgements ix

Introduction: The moral question in anthropology 1
DIDIER FASSIN

PART I
Foundations 13
Introduction 13
DIDIER FASSIN

Legacies of moral philosophies

1 Of cannibals 19
   MICHEL DE MONTAIGNE

2 Groundwork of the metaphysic of morals 23
   IMMANUEL KANT

3 On the genealogy of morality 29
   FRIEDRICH NIETZSCHE

4 Critique of ethics 33
   ELIZABETH ANSCOMBE

5 Morality and practice of the self 40
   MICHEL FOUCAULT

6 A dialogue to come 46
   ABRAHAM EDEL

Premises of a science of morality

7 Notes and queries 53
   EDWARD BURNETT TYLOR

8 The determination of moral facts 56
   ÉMILE DURKHEIM

9	The ethic of capitalism MAX WEBER	64
10	Emotions and judgements EDWARD A. WESTERMARCK	69
11	Crime and punishment BRONISLAW MALINOWSKI	75
12	Primitive man as philosopher PAUL RADIN	82

PART II
Positions — 87

Introduction — 87
DIDIER FASSIN

The location of the moral

13	The structure of a moral code JOHN LADD	95
14	An ethics of freedom JAMES LAIDLAW	100
15	An ethics of the act MICHAEL LAMBEK	111
16	Deontology and consequentialism JOEL ROBBINS	118

Ethical relativism in question

17	Anti-relativism CLYDE KLUCKHOHN	127
18	Anti anti-relativism CLIFFORD GEERTZ	135
19	Ambivalence and contradictions BRADD SHORE	141
20	The universal and the relative STEVEN LUKES	148

PART III
Descriptions   **155**

Introduction   155
DIDIER FASSIN

Local ethics

21   The moral person in context   163
KENNETH READ

22   The moral basis of hierarchy   173
LILA ABU-LUGHOD

23   Honour and shame   182
MICHAEL HERZFELD

24   Sentiments and consciousness   192
STEVEN M. PARISH

Moral economies

25   The moral economy of the crowd   201
EDWARD PALMER THOMPSON

26   The ethic of subsistence   205
JAMES C. SCOTT

27   The logics of corruption   212
JEAN-PIERRE OLIVIER DE SARDAN

28   The values of science   221
LORRAINE DASTON

PART IV
Confrontations   **231**

Introduction   231
DIDIER FASSIN

Critical situations

29   Facing cruelty   239
COLIN M. TURNBULL

30   Representing poverty   244
OSCAR LEWIS

31   Understanding suicide bombers   249
GHASSAN HAGE

32   Assessing the new bioethics   256
ARTHUR KLEINMAN

Practical tensions

33 Culpability and reparation 265
NANDINI SUNDAR

34 Development and assistance 273
ERICA BORNSTEIN

35 Selfhood and prayer 279
GREGORY M. SIMON

36 Compassion and accountability 288
OMRI ELISHA

PART V
Prescriptions **297**

Introduction 297
DIDIER FASSIN

Moralising the world?

37 Whose side are we on? 305
HOWARD S. BECKER

38 The primacy of the ethical 313
NANCY SCHEPER-HUGHES

39 The empire of suffering 321
LESLIE BUTT

40 The immunity of humanitarianism 328
DIDIER FASSIN

Codifying the discipline?

41 Anthropologists as spies 341
DAVID PRICE

42 The moral ordeals of anthropology 347
PETER PELS

43 The new bureaucracies of virtue 357
CHARLES L. BOSK

44 Ethical code 365
AMERICAN ANTHROPOLOGICAL ASSOCIATION

Conclusion: Towards a *hauntology* of the moral question 373
SAMUEL LÉZÉ

Index 377

Acknowledgements

The preparation of this volume has benefited from the financial contribution of the European Research Council, as part of an Advanced Grant. We are extremely grateful to Linda Garat for her invaluable assistance in this process, to Lucy Garnier for her faithful translation of the introductions of the volume, parts and texts, to Patrick Brown for his meticulous copyediting and to Lesley Riddle for her warm support of the project at Routledge.

We thankfully acknowledge the participation of our colleagues in the presentations of authors and texts: Yasmine Bouagga for Omri Elisha and Peter Pels; Jean-Sébastien Eideliman for Arthur Kleinman; Fabrice Fernandez for Howard Becker and Steven Parish; Nicolas Fischer for Charles Bosk and Bradd Shore; Carolina Kobelinsky for Erica Bornstein and Nandini Sundar; Chowra Makaremi for Michael Herzfeld; Sarah Mazouz for Hassan Hage and James Scott; and Sébastien Roux for Nancy Scheper-Hughes and Gregory Simon.

Every effort has been made to trace copyright holders and obtain permission to reproduce material. Any errors or omissions brought to the attention of the publisher will be remedied in future editions.

1 Michel de Montaigne (2007), Of Cannibals, in *The Complete Essays of Montaigne*, trans. by Donald M. Frame, Stanford: Stanford University Press. Excerpts from pp. 150–159. © 1943, Donald Frame, 1948, 1958 Stanford University, renewed 1971, 1976. All rights reserved. Used with permission of Stanford University Press.
2 Immanuel Kant (2005), *The Moral Law: Groundwork of the Metaphysic of Morals*, trans. by H. J. Paton, Abingdon: Routledge. Excerpts from pp. 64–76.
3 Friedrich Nietzsche (1994), *On the Genealogy of Morality*, trans. by Carol Diethe, New York: Cambridge University Press. Excerpts from pp. 4–40.
4 Elizabeth Anscombe (1958), Modern Moral Philosophy, *Philosophy*, 33 (124). Excerpts from pp. 1–17.
5 Michel Foucault (1990), 'Forms of Problematization' and 'Morality and Practice of the Self', in *The Use of Pleasure: Volume 2 of The History of Sexuality*, trans. by Robert Hurley, New York: Vintage Books. Excerpt pp. 24–32. Used with permission of Penguin Books and Georges Borchardt, Inc.
6 Abraham Edel (1962), Anthropology and Ethics in Common Focus, *The Journal of the Royal Anthropological Institute of Great Britain and Ireland*, 92 (1). Excerpts from pp. 56–70.
7 Edward Burnett Tylor (1892), Morals, in *Notes and Queries on Anthropology*, second edition, London: The Anthropological Institute. Excerpt XXXII, pp. 146–149.

8 Émile Durkheim (2010), The Determination of Moral Facts, in *Sociology and Philosophy*, trans. by D. F. Pocock, Abingdon: Routledge. Excerpts from pp. 16–26.
9 Max Weber (2001), The Spirit of Capitalism, in *The Protestant Ethic and the Spirit of Capitalism*, trans. by Talcott Parsons, Abingdon: Routledge. Excerpts from pp. 14–38.
10 Edward A. Westermarck (1906), *The Origin and Development of the Moral Ideas*, Vol. I, London: Macmillan. Excerpts from pp. 4–20.
11 Bronislaw Malinowski (1926), *Crime and Custom in Savage Society*, London: Routledge & Kegan Paul. Excerpts from pp. 72–105.
12 Paul Radin (2002), Right and Wrong, in *Primitive Man as Philosopher*, Mineola, NY: Dover Publications. Excerpt pp. 63–72.
13 John Ladd (2004), *The Structure of a Moral Code*, Eugene, OR: Wipf and Stock. Excerpts from pp. 1–12. Used with permission of Wipf and Stock Publishers.
14 James Laidlaw (2002), For an Anthropology of Ethics and Freedom, *The Journal of the Royal Anthropological Institute*, 8 (2). Excerpts from pp. 311–327. Reproduced with permission of Wiley–Blackwell Publishing.
15 Michael Lambek (2010), Toward an Ethics of the Act, in *Ordinary Ethics*, Michael Lambek (ed.), Bronx, NY: Fordham University Press. Excerpts from pp. 39–63. Used with permission of Fordham University Press.
16 Joel Robbins (2010), On the Pleasures and Dangers of Culpability, *Critique of Anthropology*, 30 (1). Excerpt pp. 122–128.
17 Clyde Kluckhohn (1955), Ethical Relativity: Sic et Non, *The Journal of Philosophy*, 52 (23). Excerpts from pp. 663–674.
18 Clifford Geertz (1984), Anti Anti-Relativism, *American Anthropologist*, 86 (2). Excerpts from pp. 263–278. Reproduced by permission of the American Anthropological Association. Not for sale or further reproduction.
19 Bradd Shore (1990), Human Ambivalence and the Structuring of Moral Values, *Ethos*, 18 (2). Excerpts from pp. 165–179. Reproduced by permission of the American Anthropological Association. Not for sale or further reproduction.
20 Steven Lukes (2008), The Universal and the Relative, in *Moral Relativism*, New York: Picador. Excerpts from pp. 129–159. Reprinted by permission of Picador.
21 Kenneth Read (1955), Morality and the Concept of the Person among the Gahuku-Gama, *Oceania*, 25 (4). Excerpts from pp. 254–265.
22 Lila Abu-Lughod (2000), Honor and the Virtues of Autonomy, in *Veiled Sentiments: Honor and Poetry in a Bedouin Society*, Berkeley, CA: University of California Press. Excerpts from pp. 78–110. Courtesy of University of California Press.
23 Michael Herzfeld (1980), Honour and Shame: Problems in the Comparative Analysis of Moral Systems, *Man*, New Series 15 (2). Excerpts from pp. 339–351. Reproduced with permission of Wiley–Blackwell Publishing.
24 Steven M. Parish (1991), The Sacred Mind: Newar Cultural Representations of Mental Life and the Production of Moral Consciousness, *Ethos*, 19 (3). Excerpts from pp. 313–351. Reproduced by permission of the American Anthropological Association. Not for sale or further reproduction.
25 Edward Palmer Thompson (1971), The Moral Economy of the English Crowd in the Eighteenth Century, *Past & Present*, 50 (1). Excerpts from pp. 76–79. Courtesy of Oxford University Press.
26 James C. Scott (1976), *The Moral Economy of the Peasant: Rebellion and Subsistence in Southeast Asia*, New Haven, CT: Yale University Press. Excerpts from pp. 4–167.

27 Jean-Pierre Olivier de Sardan (1999), A Moral Economy of Corruption in Africa? *Journal of Modern African Studies*, 37 (1). Excerpts from pp. 25–52. Courtesy of Cambridge University Press.

28 Lorraine Daston (1995), The Moral Economy of Science, *Osiris*, 10. Excerpts from pp. 3–12.

29 Colin M. Turnbull (1972), *The Mountain People*, New York: Simon & Schuster. Excerpts from pp. 11–295.

30 Oscar Lewis (1966), *La Vida*, New York: Random House, pp. xlii–xlviii.

31 Ghassan Hage (2003), 'Comes a Time We are All Enthusiasm': Understanding Palestinian Suicide Bombers in Times of Exighophobia, *Public Culture*, 15 (1). Excerpts from pp. 65–89. All rights reserved. Republished by permission of Duke University Press.

32 Arthur Kleinman (1999), Moral Experience and Ethical Reflection: Can Ethnography Reconcile Them? A Quandary for 'The New Bioethics', *Daedalus*, 128 (4). Excerpts from pp. 70–92. © American Academy of Arts and Sciences. Courtesy of MIT Press Journals.

33 Nandini Sundar (2004), Toward an Anthropology of Culpability, *American Ethnologist*, 31 (2). Excerpts from pp. 145–163. Reproduced by permission of the American Anthropological Association. Not for sale or further reproduction.

34 Erica Bornstein (2001), The Verge of Good and Evil: Christian NGOs and Economic Development in Zimbabwe, *PoLAR: Political and Legal Anthropology Review*, 24 (1). Excerpts from pp. 59–77. Reproduced by permission of the American Anthropological Association. Not for sale or further reproduction.

35 Gregory M. Simon (2009), The Soul Freed of Cares? Islamic Prayer, Subjectivity, and the Contradictions of Moral Selfhood in Minangkabau, Indonesia, *American Ethnologist*, 36 (2). Excerpts from pp. 258–265. Reproduced by permission of the American Anthropological Association. Not for sale or further reproduction.

36 Omri Elisha (2008), Moral Ambitions of Grace: The Paradox of Compassion and Accountability in Evangelical Faith-Based Activism, *Cultural Anthropology*, 23 (1). Excerpts from pp. 155–189. Reproduced by permission of the American Anthropological Association. Not for sale or further reproduction.

37 Howard S. Becker (1967), Whose Side Are We On?, *Social Problems*, 14 (3): 239–247. Excerpts from presidential address delivered at the annual meeting of the Society for the Study of Social Problems, Miami Beach, 1966. © Society for the Study of Social Problems. Courtesy of University of California Press.

38 Nancy Scheper-Hughes (1995), The Primacy of the Ethical: Propositions for a Militant Anthropology, *Current Anthropology*, 36 (3). Excerpts from pp. 409–420. Courtesy of University of Chicago Press.

39 Leslie Butt (2002), The Suffering Stranger: Medical Anthropology and International Morality, *Medical Anthropology*, 21 (1). Excerpts from pp. 2–18. Courtesy of Taylor & Francis Group.

40 Didier Fassin (2011), *Noli Me Tangere*: The Moral Untouchability of Humanitarianism, in *Forces of Compassion: Humanitarianism Between Ethics and Politics*, Erica Bornstein and Peter Redfield (eds.), trans. by Amy Jacobs, Santa Fe: School of Advanced Research Press. Excerpts from pp. 35–52. Courtesy of School of Advanced Research Press.

41 David Price (2000), Anthropologists as Spies, *The Nation*, 271 (16): 24–27. Reprinted with permission from *The Nation*.

xii   *Acknowledgements*

42 Peter Pels (1999), Professions of Duplexity: A Prehistory of Ethical Codes in Anthropology, *Current Anthropology*, 40 (2). Excerpts from pp. 101–111. Courtesy of University of Chicago Press.
43 Charles L. Bosk (2007), The New Bureaucracies of Virtue or When Form Fails to Follow Function, *PoLAR : Political and Legal Anthropological Review*, 30 (2). Excerpts from pp. 197–206. Reproduced by permission of the American Anthropological Association. Not for sale or further reproduction.
44 American Anthropological Association (2009), *Code of Ethics*, approved February 2009 (unabridged version), www.aaanet.org/issues/policy-advocacy/Code-of-Ethics.cfm. Courtesy of the American Anthropological Association.

Introduction

The moral question in anthropology

Didier Fassin

> There is nothing either good or bad, but thinking makes it so.
> William Shakespeare, *Hamlet*

> Under what conditions did man invent the value judgements good and evil? and what value do they themselves have?
> Friedrich Nietzsche, *On the Genealogy of Morality*

Over recent decades, morality and ethics have been increasingly called upon in the most varied and sometimes unexpected fields. We now expect politicians to behave morally in their public and private lives, and both spheres are subject to a degree of scrutiny to which such agents had previously not been accustomed. Tyrants and torturers are held accountable for their actions in the context of international tribunals that judge war crimes and crimes against humanity. When dictatorships fall, commissions are then set up in the name of truth and reconciliation, thus replacing the silence or revenge that was usual in the past. The world of banking no longer finds its justification simply in expanding capitalism and speculators' wealth; savers and stockholders prefer to invest in ethical funds that claim to adhere to principles of solidarity or ecology. Wars no longer represent simply a power struggle between nations defending their interests; when they are carried out by Western powers, they are often declared to be humanitarian. People affected by natural disasters, violence and discrimination are no longer abandoned to their fate or to local systems of aid; their suffering now grants them the status of victim. Sexual abuse carried out by close relations, sports coaches or priests is no longer subject to the veil of silence that was long the case in families, teams and churches; such actions are now debated in the public sphere and sanctioned by law. Physicians can no longer rely on their opinion alone when deciding whether their methods for testing new medication are valid; ethics committees check that their clinical trials respect the norms protecting their test subjects. Biologists can no longer monitor their research on their own; bioethics laws regulate what they can and cannot do. The increasing prevalence in all fields of human activity of the discourse of human rights, but also of the rights of minority groups, patients, children and animals, is the expression of the values and affects that are characteristic of contemporary societies. Finally, attentive observers of current affairs will not fail to note the extent to which the language of morality and references to ethics permeate both the representation of events and situations – from the most tragic to the most banal – and the comments to which they give rise.

This list, composed in the manner of Jorge Luis Borges's famous apocryphal Chinese encyclopaedia, should not, however, mislead. The intention is not to suggest that morality and ethics were, until recently, absent from our debates or from our lives. Nor is it to state that the changes described here reflect a sort of moral progress or ethical revolution, as some would have it. Finally, it is not to suppose that all these phenomena derive from a common logic, whether it be a return to moral conservatism or the emergence of social ethics. Rather it is a question of approaching what Michel Foucault would refer to as a problematisation or, in J. G. A. Pocock's terms, a moment; in other words, a historical configuration marked by an increase in preoccupations, expectations and doubts surrounding morality and ethics, and also characterised by the way in which related words, images and practices have become commonplace. The manner by which these two layers – the profound and the superficial – are combined and superimposed in the public sphere, to the point of becoming inseparable, constitutes what we could call the moral question. Just as the social question grasps the reality of economic inequalities and the discourses that construct it, so too does the moral question bring together moral problems and how they are dealt with in the public sphere. And again, much like the social question, the accumulation of elements referred to above could be described as the new moral question, characteristic of current times.

While the reason for this book lies in the contemporary nature of these changes and in the thought that they require, the aim here is not to analyse their signs and uncover their meaning. It is rather to allow the reader to distance himself or herself, and the distance in question is twofold. First, it is temporal and spatial insofar as reference is made to other times and places where many of our current worries and questions were already subject to analysis and discussion. Second, it is theoretical and critical insofar as it leads the reader onto the domain of the social sciences and the humanities, beginning with philosophy – a discipline that has been dealing with the moral question for over 2000 years. In our view, anthropology is at the heart of this project because its aim has always been to adopt a distant perspective, whether in order to discover faraway societies or to explore worlds closer to home. Reading and rereading the texts of anthropologists, as well as the thinkers who inspired them, is a way of revisiting the moral question afresh, via historical, geographical and intellectual detours, returning to the origins of the discipline and retracing its genealogy, travelling from exotic horizons to more familiar climes, and facing the certitude of some and the scepticism of others. However, as we embark upon this journey, a remarkable fact must be underlined from the outset.

* * *

The moral question presents the historian of anthropology with a surprising paradox: it has been omnipresent within the discipline since its inception, to the extent that it could almost be said to haunt anthropology's quest for human truth, and yet, at the same time, it is absent both from the numerous summaries provided by those chronicling the progress of the field and by encyclopaedia and dictionary authors, thus posing the question of whether it is not a blind spot or a shameful blot. Indeed, a common trait of the studies focusing on this question over the past fifty years has been to commence by deploring the lack of research in the field, while noting the rise in concerns on the subject – although the longevity of such statements is questionable, given how often they are repeated. In this way, in their pioneering work May Edel and Abraham Edel (1968/1959), an anthropologist and a philosopher respectively, observed with regret the lack of collaboration between their disciplines and gave concrete proof of the lack of scientific output by identifying the only four articles that had focused on morals or ethics in more than fifty years of publication of the discipline's official journal, *American Anthropologist*. Four decades later, James Laidlaw (2002), an ethnologist of the Indian world, offered a similar opinion when he claimed that there was no anthropology of ethics, in the sense of a systematic effort to understand morality in the same way as kinship or religion.

Of course, it makes rhetorical sense to justify one's own contribution to the field by underscoring both its novelty and imperative necessity. In this perspective, we might express some surprise that British anthropologists are so rarely cited by most anthropologists of morality, from Bronislaw Malinowski (1967/1926), who through an analysis of crime and punishment laid down the foundations for a study of the norms upon which the law is based, to Raymond Firth (1964/1953), who made the study of values one of the three main orientations of anthropology alongside social structure and social organisation, not to mention the debates raised by E. E. Evans-Pritchard's lecture (1963/1950) and its implications for the conception of 'society as a moral system' (Evens 1982). Nonetheless, rhetorical strategies aside and a few significant omissions notwithstanding, the disparity between the proliferation of moral questionings and judgements in anthropological literature, and the limited degree to which, at least until recently, they have been conceived as a moral question, warrants reflection. The reasons for this neglect are principally of two types: cognitive and political.

On the one hand, within the Durkheimian tradition, morality has often been viewed as the set of rules that lead to sanctions when they are transgressed and that therefore determine the moral obligation regulating life in society; or else, in a Boasian perspective, as the whole of the customs that are subject to social approval and that therefore take different shapes depending on cultural entities. In the former case, morality is none other than the social; in the latter, it is hardly distinguishable from culture. Consequently, morality becomes difficult to identify and is not seen to warrant separate examination. Norms and mores, values and usages have been the objects of anthropological study since the beginnings of the discipline, and in this perspective there is no need to isolate morality as a subject or field of enquiry. Even today, this objection is often raised in the face of attempts to study morality in and of itself; it is either subsumed within an existing field, such as religion or law, or else it is considered simply as another, and indeed suspicious, name for the social or for culture.

On the other hand, anthropologists have generally viewed morality with a certain amount of scepticism and mistrust due to the normative and judgemental aspects it frequently entails. While their cultural relativism protected them from giving in to the conquering universalism of the colonial project of yesteryear or the progressive ideologies of today, the concern has been that the analysis of moral facts might in fact drag banished forms of judgement in through the back door. Condemning representations and practices rejected in the name of natural law, human rights, women's rights, or children's rights could prompt the resurrection of the savages and barbarians of evolutionary or even racist models of thinking, albeit couched in more socially acceptable terms. Studying morality, and particularly the morality of others, would therefore mean running the risk of turning anthropology into a moral enterprise, as it had been in the past. It is true, indeed, that the debates surrounding moral relativism have generated confusion between describing value differences among cultures and judging these cultures according to a hierarchy based on their values.

Interestingly, this dual obstacle, both cognitive and political, seems to have been at stake from anthropology's very inception. Edward Tylor's book *Primitive Culture* (1871: 1–2 and 1874: 453), often considered the first treatise of the discipline, opened with a definition of 'culture' that may have included morality but considered it extensively in opposition to 'natural things' and concluded by invoking a 'science of culture' that would characterise its vocation of reform, in other words, bring progress 'for the good of mankind'. On the one hand, morality disappears, subsumed by culture, and on the other, it reappears in its moralising form. It is easy to see the difficulties and challenges that anthropology faced in escaping this double bind.

* * *

These two objections to morality as an anthropological object are serious. They have not, however, prevented the recent rise of a veritable research field, which has seen the publication of collective volumes, the holding of debates in journals of the discipline, and the organisation of special panels at international conferences. If we take the Bourdieusian reference to the notion of a scientific field seriously, it is necessary to describe the social space in which researchers position themselves according to their school of thought and in which the theoretical stakes regarding morality as a topic of study are defined. Carrying out this task means identifying not only the most visible part of the domain of enquiry regarding morality, namely the part that defines and promotes itself as such, but also various areas that are less obviously identifiable because the moral stakes are not necessarily explicit or recognised. At the heart of this field, in its most legitimate section, as it were, a tension has arisen between two main approaches. The first emphasises the moral constraints that society places upon individuals – which can take the positive form of obligations or the negative form of sanctions – whereas the second highlights the ability of the individual to produce ethical reasoning and judgements with a certain freedom from the pervasive nature of the social.

The first approach follows on from Émile Durkheim (2010/1924), and through him from Kant's ethics of duty, and elaborates an ethnography of moralities (Howell 1997). It looks at the values and norms that – in a given society at a given time – define, on the one hand, what is right or good and what is wrong or bad, and, on the other, what one should or should not do. This perspective is not new. John Ladd's (1957) 'descriptive ethics' pieces together the 'moral code' of the Navajo, i.e. the 'collection of rules and principles' that enable individuals to determine what is a matter of duty or what is right, while Kenneth Read's (1955) 'comparative ethics' opposes Western Christian morality and the morality of the Gahuku-Gama of New Guinea from the point of view of 'notions of duty and the ideal, of obligation and intrinsic desirability'. Whether descriptive or comparative, the study of local morality implies a relativism that is twofold: first, recognising moral systems as the result of abstract measures and not simply the product of emotions and drives; second, suspending judgement about the values and norms observed in contrast with more or less explicit forms of evaluation and hierarchical ranking. However, through ethnographic and linguistic studies, subsequent research has enabled a more refined understanding of both the values underpinning local moralities and their concrete inclusion in daily life. This is the case for Michelle Rosaldo's (1980) survey of anger and pain among the Ilongot hunters of the Philippines and for Lila Abu-Lughod's (1986) study of honour and modesty in an Egyptian Bedouin society. More recently, research has focused on the conflicts that can develop when different, or even conflicting, local moralities come into contact: traditional values versus a Christian ethos in the Urapmin people of Papua New Guinea (Robbins 2004), orthodox asceticism versus Socialist atheism among a community of Old Believers in the Urals (Rogers 2009), and medical morals versus Islamic ethics in the practice of kidney transplants in Egypt (Hamdy 2012). By placing value on a certain cultural unity – that of the group being analysed, even if this unity is constructed through opposing value systems – the idea is that above and beyond individual variations there exists a certain coherency allowing local moralities to be defined with precision, even when history has also had its impact.

The second approach, inspired by Michel Foucault (1990/1984) and more distantly by Aristotle's ethics of virtue, deploys an anthropology of ethics (Faubion 2011). It endeavours to give subjects back their individual leeway and to reveal their ability to escape the ascendancy of the social, to debate moral dilemmas and to produce ethical subjectivities. In the line of Talal Asad's (1993) work, the experience of religion, and in particular of prayer, as a mode of self-transformation, has become central to this approach whether examining the experience of women engaged in Islamist movements in Egypt (Mahmood 2005) or AIDS sufferers in Christian rehabilitation centres in Russia (Zigon 2011). This attention to agents' subjectivities manifested itself in reaction to the traditional vision of norms imposed by the fear of sanctions, on the one hand, and of collectively produced values, on the other. However, it takes a variety of different forms depending on whether the focus is on expressions of emotion, explicit judgements or ordinary actions. Some highlight the sentiments motivating individuals and especially the experience of 'this dialectic of suffering and compassion' (Throop 2010: 37). Others consider the reasoning developed by agents regarding moral stakes, revealing the dynamics and arrangements at work and even establishing 'paradox and contradiction as conscious aspects of human experience' (Sykes 2009: 24). Still others pay attention to everyday interactions or decisions in such a way as to 'show the centrality of ethical practice in life' (Lambek 2010: 1). The stakes surrounding this shift from social constraints to individual freedom and from local morality to ethical subjectivities concern a certain reformulation of universalism – not the universalism of moral values, generally rejected by anthropologists, but rather that of ethical skills. It is no longer a question of defending a particular moral meaning in a given society, but rather of recognising that all human beings are capable of acting like ethical subjects.

The reader who is well versed in the debates of moral philosophy will not fail to note that while the two theoretical strands composing the anthropological landscape on the moral question today borrow more or less freely from two of the paradigms of ethics, namely duty and virtue, a third seems to have been left aside, that of consequentialist ethics. According to this approach, morality is not to be judged according to the rules of behaviour to which one must conform in practice or by the personal endeavour involved in sentiments, reasoning and actions, but rather according to the consequences of what one says and does. An expression of this theoretical approach can be found in Max Weber's work, although less so in his book *The Protestant Ethic and the Spirit of Capitalism* than in his lecture on 'Politics as a Vocation' (Weber 2004/1919) in which he creates an opposition precisely between an ethics of conviction founded on applying principles absolutely and an ethics of responsibility attentive to the consequences of actions. Some recent research fits in with this line, such as that focusing on moral panic in the United States (Lancaster 2011), neoliberal programmes in Italy (Muehlebach 2012), human rights in Africa (Englund 2006), and humanitarian government in international relations (Fassin 2011). Unlike the two previous approaches, this perspective does not isolate morality and ethics as the product of society or of subjectivity, but rather historicises and politicises them. It is necessary to consider the contemporary developments of discourse and practice claiming to pertain to morality and ethics as being the result of a historical past, essentially that of the West and its relation to the 'rest', and as having political significance that reaches beyond the generous values and benevolent sentiments displayed.

* * *

The lines of research mentioned above prevail in contemporary anthropological studies on the moral question and have largely contributed to renewing the latter. They have not, however, exhausted the wealth of approaches and questions surrounding this issue. Other perspectives must be discussed, not only for their own interest, but also for what they can bring to our understanding of the moral stakes of our world.

First, anthropology has a long-standing tradition of debates regarding relativism or moral universalism (Westermarck 2000/1932). While there is a consensus regarding the empirical existence of diverse moral standards according to culture and period, the question remains of knowing whether, on the one hand, common foundations exist across all societies – elementary structures of morality, in a sense – and whether, on the other hand, it is possible to establish procedures determining the superiority of one set of values and norms over another – a hierarchy of morality, as it were, even though in general it is rarely officially framed as such (Lukes 2008). Today this debate has been launched again on both fronts for very different reasons, some strictly scientific, others sociological. On the first front, neurocognitive approaches to morality, whether originating in evolutionary biology (Baumard 2010) or experimental psychology (Gazzaniga 2005), suggest that all human beings are equipped with the same neurological and cognitive tools through which they process moral objects on the basis of a common grammar, which would not be contradictory with observed cultural variations but would allow a universal ethics to be envisaged (Haidt 2003). On the second front, the recurrent controversies on sensitive topics such as the excision of young girls in African countries (Boddy 2007) or honour crimes in Muslim societies (Wikan 2008) give rise to radically opposing positions of either categorical condemnation or lenient understanding, which divide the public space (Shweder et al. 2002). Having their origins deeply entrenched in the founding questions of anthropology, relativism, and universalism are thus regularly called upon and reformulated according to new knowledge and societal debates.

Second, anthropology has always been confronted with the moral problems posed by its own practice, or rather the practice of its members – the very founder of the discipline in the United States found himself expelled from the professional association he had created following a disagreement concerning mutual accusations of deontological breaches (Price 2008). Ever since, anthropologists have incessantly questioned their good practice and the loyalty and responsibility they have towards the people they study but also towards the entities that fund their research, and of course towards their discipline itself, leading to sometimes difficult ethical choices (Pels 1999). In certain cases, moral questions have emerged in a controversial fashion in the context of scandals involving, for example, collaboration between researchers and intelligence corps or armies, from the Camelot project in Chile in the 1960s to the Human Terrain System in Iraq in the 2000s, which largely contributed to the production and transformation of ethical codes for anthropology, particularly in the United States (Fluehr-Lobban 2003). In a whole other rationale, the discipline has also faced deontological issues raised by the ever-increasing pressure of ethics committees in the evaluation and follow-up of research. Once again, this seems most prevalent in North America, in the form of Institutional Review Boards initially designed to protect 'human subjects' involved in the life sciences (Lederman 2006). A product of the constraints of events or systems in place, but also – and above all – of its members' considerations regarding their own practice, anthropology is therefore shaped by moral issues related to the very particular nature of its topics, fields, methods and engagements.

Third, anthropology itself is often practised as a moral discipline, in the normative sense, that is, with a vocation to make the world a better place. This tendency, which raises sensitive questions, is related to the two previous points – the debate regarding relativism and universalism, and the deontological issues surrounding professional practice. This is neither new nor specific to anthropology. From the inception of the social sciences, the aim of understanding society has gone hand-in-hand with the aim of changing it, and among both European sociologists and North American anthropologists, moral liberalism has often been concomitant with the attempt to make morality into a subject of scientific knowledge. Nonetheless, it would seem that this trend has recently intensified, and it is Nancy Scheper-Hughes (1995: 409) who posed the question of the researcher's moral engagement with the most clarity in a famous text wherein she declared herself in favour of 'militant anthropology'. More recently, eschewing the anthropological tradition of studying the 'abstruse customs of out-of-the-way tribes' and 'extraordinary ceremonies in exotic settings', Jeremy MacClancy (2002: 1 and cover) claimed that 'more and more anthropologists are dedicating themselves to addressing matters of public concern and to understanding and helping solve social problems wherever they occur', while Michael Carrithers (2005: 433), in an article on 'anthropology as a moral science', suggested that the discipline be used 'for sceptical and therapeutic criticism of rhetoric exercised in pursuit of empire' in the United States. Of this constantly revisited moral orientation to anthropology, Wiktor Stoczkowski (2008) offers a critical reading, inviting researchers to use greater rigour in examining the conflicts that can arise from the confrontation between ethical and epistemological norms.

Finally, following this discussion and within the context of a reflexive approach to the discipline, the need remains to question why the social sciences show such interest in the moral question today. For it is not enough to simply suggest that researchers content themselves with studying existing social reality and therefore consider this issue because it is raised by or within society; this would raise the question as to why they did not do it sooner. In fact, research in general is constructed in relative autonomy from the world that surrounds it: it develops its own questions and problematics. This observation is valid for the humanities. That a new scientific field be formed is consequently not a response to a hypothetical social demand nor, conversely, pure coincidence regarding the developments observed in the public space. The rise of a moral question in anthropology calls for the same anthropological analysis as the rise of a moral question in the contemporary world. It is in particular a question of thinking through what it reveals and what it evades, the facts it enlightens and the problems it conceals, the discourses it enables or prevents. In sum, the issue is to provide a critique of moral anthropology.

* * *

The aim of this anthology is to present an account of the remarkable wealth of these discussions surrounding the moral question in anthropology, a wealth that renders the relative absence of these issues in the treatises of the discipline all the more surprising, and that makes it all the more necessary to attempt to bring together texts defining this new scientific space. The energy of a nascent scientific field, with the stakes and perimeters that we have just outlined, would in itself justify our project to make these texts available and to explain the related debates. However, above and beyond this interest, which concerns a relatively specialised audience, it seems to us that this literature can also prove relevant to anyone who is concerned about moral and ethical problems and who wishes to delve into the topic by going beyond the emotional reactions and categorical judgements to which these issues often give rise. The anthropological 'detour' referred to by Georges Balandier (1985) comes fully into play here.

The book is structured around five themes. The first part examines the foundations of the moral question in anthropology. We call upon, on the one hand, the writers and philosophers whose thought has proved especially enlightening for the social sciences of morality, and, on the other, the anthropologists and sociologists who were the first to venture onto this domain, and who thus provided a lasting definition of its perimeters. The second part outlines the different positions, as they progressively crystallised. We initially present the different theoretical approaches that supply ways of considering morality, between obligation and freedom, and then outline the debates which the diversity of moral systems have elected, between relativism and universalism. The third part offers descriptions of moral frameworks. We bring together studies on local moralities, focusing on the norms, values and affects present in specific cultural contexts, and on moral economies, illustrating the progressive shifts of this polymorphous concept. The fourth part concerns the confrontation of different moralities. We look, on the one hand, at the difficulties encountered by anthropologists themselves when faced with this gap in their fieldwork and, on the other, at the ambiguities present in the deployment of benevolent politics in the name of human rights and humanitarianism. The final part addresses the way in which anthropology has found itself alternately in the position of producing and of receiving moral prescriptions. Notably, we take up the discussion surrounding the researcher's involvement and detachment, as well as the attempts to codify the deontological rules of the discipline in the face of its possible excesses.

While the texts that we present here reflect the scope of anthropology and its history, they offer only fragments of this diversity. Inevitably, choices had to be made allowing certain inexplicably forgotten texts back into the limelight but also setting interesting studies aside, and although we may refer to them in our comments, it is in the knowledge that this cannot fully compensate for their absence. In particular, with a view to avoiding repetition, with two exceptions, we chose not to include texts by authors who had also been invited to contribute previously unpublished chapters to a book being published in parallel on moral anthropology (Fassin 2012). Moreover, despite our eclectic approach, we abandoned the idea of including research carried out in cognitive science, analytical philosophy, evolutionary biology, experimental psychology and neuroimaging, not because it did not seem relevant to the moral question, but rather because we would only have been able to deal with them superficially and this would have been all the more problematic since other collections provide thorough presentations and discussions of these approaches (Sinnot-Armstrong 2008). Ultimately, we preferred a coherent rather than exhaustive selection of texts. The works that we put forward here for readers to discover or rediscover therefore only represent a portion of the moral field. This is inevitably the lot of any anthology, and the present volume should be considered less a definitive and comprehensive survey than as an invitation to pursue further reading.

Although this editorial endeavour was mainly conducted by two authors, Samuel Lézé and myself, it is also the result of a project carried out over four years bringing together the following researchers: Yasmine Bouagga, Jean-Sébastien Eideliman, Fabrice Fernandez, Nicolas Fischer, Carolina Kobelinsky, Chowra Makaremi, Sarah Mazouz, and Sébastien Roux. Within the framework of the European Research Council's scientific programme 'Towards a Critical Moral Anthropology', which I supervised between 2009 and 2013, this pluri-disciplinary team composed of anthropologists, sociologists, and political scientists tackled the substantial task of preparing the ground for exploring a little-known field. As well as a large-scale empirical survey on the moral treatment of precarious populations by public institutions (Fassin et al. 2013), we tried to account for the main theoretical strands of approaches to the moral question – within anthropology, of course, but also within related disciplines. In doing so, we attempted to widen our horizons regarding the structure that the field had begun to assume over recent years and returned to older and rarely cited texts, while including contemporary authors who are likewise seldom referred to. Considering this volume was also intended for a non-specialist audience, we provided a short introduction to each author and text as part of the collective enterprise that I coordinated.

As this intellectual journey draws to a close, we hope that the resulting book will shed light on this moral question that our societies tend all too often to consider passionately and intuitively, at the risk of oversimplification and ethnocentrism. Anthropology can bring complexity and relativism to the table – it is reproached often enough for both these things. But, contrary to what is said, neither is an obstacle to judgement or action. Quite the opposite – they render the first better informed and the second better equipped. Intellectual engagement and scientific distance are often set in opposition to one another. And yet the latter should be seen as a prerequisite for the former. Spinoza's maxim, according to which, rather than to mock, lament, or execrate, it is crucial to understand, is well known. There is no domain in which it can be better applied than that addressing the moral question.

References

Abu-Lughod, Lila (1986), *Veiled Sentiments: Honor and Poetry in a Bedouin Society*, Berkeley, CA: University of California Press.
Asad, Talal (1993), *Genealogies of Religion: Discipline and Reasons of Power in Christianity and Islam*, Baltimore, MD: The Johns Hopkins University Press.
Balandier, Georges (1985), *Le Détour: Pouvoir et modernité*, Paris: Fayard.
Baumard, Nicolas (2010), *Comment nous sommes devenus moraux*, Paris: Odile Jacob.
Boddy, Janice (2007), *Civilizing Women: British Crusades in Colonial Sudan*, Princeton, NJ: Princeton University Press.
Carrithers, Michael (2005), Anthropology as a Moral Science of Possibilities, *Current Anthropology*, 46 (3): 433–456.
Durkheim, Émile (2010), The Determination of Moral Facts, in *Sociology and Philosophy*, New York: Routledge, first French publication 1924.
Edel, May and Abraham Edel (1968), *Anthropology & Ethics: The Quest for Moral Understanding*, Cleveland, OH: Press of Case Western Reserve University, first edition 1959.
Englund, Harri (2006), *Prisoners of Freedom: Human Rights and the African Poor*, Berkeley, CA: University of California Press.
Evans-Pritchard, E. E. (1963), Social Anthropology: Past and Present, in *Essays in Social Anthropology*, New York: The Free Press of Glencoe, pp. 13–29, Marett Lecture 1950.
Evens, T. M. S. (1982), Two Concepts of 'Society as a Moral System': Evans-Pritchard's Heterodoxy, *Man*, 17: 205–218.
Fassin, Didier (2011), *Humanitarian Reason: A Moral History of the Present*, Berkeley, CA: University of California Press.
Fassin, Didier ed. (2012), *A Companion to Moral Anthropology*, Malden, MA: Wiley Blackwell.
Fassin, Didier et al. (2013), *Juger, réprimer, accompagner. Essai sur la morale de l'État*, Paris: Seuil.
Faubion, James (2011), *An Anthropology of Ethics*, Cambridge: Cambridge University Press.
Firth, Raymond (1964), The Study of Values by Social Anthropologists, in *Essays on Social Organization and Values*, London: The Athlone Press, pp. 206–224, Marett Lecture 1953.
Fluehr-Lobban, Carolyn ed. (2003), *Ethics and the Profession of Anthropology: Dialogue for Ethically Conscious Practice*, Walnut Creek, CA: Altamira Press.
Foucault, Michel (1990), *The Use of Pleasure*, New York: Vintage Books, pp. 24–32, first French publication 1984.
Gazzaniga, Michael (2005), *The Ethical Brain: The Science of our Moral Dilemmas*, New York: Harper.
Haidt, Jonathan (2003), The New Synthesis in Moral Psychology, *Science*, 316: 998–1002.
Hamdy, Sherine (2012), *Our Bodies Belong to God: Organ Transplants, Islam, and the Struggle for Human Dignity in Egypt*, Berkeley, CA: University of California Press.
Howell, Signe ed. (1997), *The Ethnography of Moralities*, London: Routledge.
Ladd, John (1957), *The Structure of a Moral Code: A Philosophical Analysis of Ethical Discourse Applied to the Ethics of the Navaho Indians*, Cambridge, MA: Harvard University Press.
Laidlaw, James (2002), For an Anthropology of Ethics and Freedom, *Journal of the Royal Anthropological Institute*, 8 (2): 311–332.
Lambek, Michael ed. (2010), *Ordinary Ethics: Anthropology, Language, and Action*, New York: Fordham University Press.
Lancaster, Roger (2011), *Sex Panic and the Punitive State*, Berkeley, CA: University of California Press.

Lederman, Rena (2006), Anxious Borders Between Work and Life in a Time of Bureaucratic Ethics Regulation, *American Ethnologist*, 33 (4): 477–481.

Lukes, Steven (2008), *Moral Relativism*, New York: Picador.

MacClancy, Jeremy ed. (2002), *Exotic No More: Anthropology on the Front Lines*, Chicago, IL: University of Chicago Press.

Mahmood, Saba (2005), *The Politics of Piety: The Islamic Revival and the Feminist Subject*, Princeton, NJ: Princeton University Press.

Malinowski, Bronislaw (1967), *Crime and Custom in Savage Society*, London: Routledge & Kegan Paul, first edition 1926.

Muehlebach, Andrea (2012), *The Moral Neoliberal: Welfare and Citizenship in Italy*, Chicago, IL: University of Chicago Press.

Pels, Peter (1999), Professions of Duplexity: A Prehistory of Ethical Codes in Anthropology, *Current Anthropology*, 40 (2): 101–136.

Price, David (2008), *Anthropological Intelligence: The Deployment and Neglect of American Anthropology during the Second World War*, Durham: Duke University Press.

Read, Kenneth (1955), Morality and the Concept of the Person Among the Gahuku-Gama, *Oceania*, 25 (4): 233–282.

Robbins, Joel (2004), *Becoming Sinners: Christianity and Moral Torment in a Papua New Guinea Society*, Berkeley, CA: University of California Press.

Rogers, Douglas (2009), *The Old Faith and the Russian Land: A Historical Ethnography of Ethic in the Urals*, Ithaca, NY: Cornell University Press.

Rosaldo, Michelle (1980), *Knowledge and Passion: Ilongot Notions of Self and Social Life*, Cambridge: Cambridge University Press.

Scheper-Hughes, Nancy (1995), The Primacy of the Ethical: Propositions for a Militant Anthropology, *Current Anthropology*, 36 (3): 409–440.

Shweder, Richard, Martha Minow and Hazel Rose Markus eds. (2002), *Engaging Cultural Differences: The Multicultural Challenge in Liberal Societies*, New York: Russell Sage.

Sinnot-Armstrong, Walter ed. (2008), *Moral Psychology, 1. The Evolution of Morality; 2. The Neuroscience of Morality; 3. The Cognitive Sciences of Morality*, Cambridge: The MIT Press.

Stoczkowski, Wiktor (2008), The 'Fourth Aim' of Anthropology: Between Knowledge and Ethics, *Anthropological Theory*, 8 (4): 345–356.

Sykes, Karen ed. (2009), *The Ethnographies of Moral Reasoning: Living Paradoxes in a Global Age*, New York: Palgrave Macmillan.

Throop, Jason (2010), *Suffering and Sentiment: Exploring the Vicissitudes of Experience and Pain in Yap*, Berkeley, CA: University of California Press.

Tylor, Edward B. (1871 and 1874), *Primitive Culture: Researches into the Development of Mythology, Philosophy, Religion, Language, Art, and Customs*, Volumes 1 and 2, London: John Murray.

Weber, Max (2004), Politics as a Vocation, in *The Vocation Lectures: 'Science as a Vocation'; 'Politics as a Vocation'*, Cambridge: Hackett Publishing, pp. 32–94, first German publication 1919.

Westermarck, Edvard (2000), *Ethical Relativity*, London: Routledge, first English publication 1932.

Wikan, Unni (2008), *In Honor of Fadime: Murder and Shame*, Chicago, IL: University of Chicago Press, first Norwegian publication 2003.

Zigon, Jarrett (2011), *'HIV is God's Blessing': Rehabilitating Morality in Neoliberal Russia*, Berkeley, CA: University of California Press.

Part I
Foundations

Introduction

Didier Fassin

Morality was long the preserve of religion, for most people, and of philosophy, for the happy few – although the distinction between the two should definitely be put into perspective given their numerous interactions, from the Early Church Fathers to Hume and Kant, to consider only the Christian world. Whether for religion or philosophy, the main concern was normative: What is right? What is a good life? What virtues should be developed? What code of conduct should be adopted in a given situation? This prescriptive approach certainly presupposed, for the philosophers, a corresponding descriptive questioning: How can morality be defined? How can it be distinguished from etiquette, law, or religion? How can it be grounded objectively in reason or subjectively in emotion? Nonetheless, the final aim of morality resided in what it allowed humanity or the individual to achieve and in the improvement of society or the elevation of the subject that it encouraged, whatever the doctrine or theory defended.

The social sciences of morality were principally formed in opposition to this perspective.[1] Their scientific project, inspired by that of the natural sciences, gave preference to the laws of the social world rather than the rules of good conduct, and to the principles of living as a community rather than the precepts of living a good life – in other words, to description rather than prescription. It was a matter of analysing and understanding the way in which men and women, in a given context, decide what is right or wrong, just or unjust, desirable or reprehensible. For anthropology in particular, it fell to this discipline to account for the diverse 'mores' and 'customs' that were reported from different places in the world by travellers' narratives, missionary reports and the pioneer studies of ethnographers. Of course this learned aim did not preclude the expression of judgements, far from it – although more often than not, to defend exotic beliefs or practices rather than condemn them. Nor did it preclude the desire to reform – usually the researcher's own society rather than others. However, the primary intention was to study morality just like any other dimension of human life in society, from kinship to witchcraft or politics. And yet achieving this aim proved far more problematic than imagined, which explains the recent and slow emergence of the domain.

However, the opposition outlined here between the approaches of philosophy and social science warrants further qualification, for reasons that are relatively specific to morality. On this topic, far more than on the others tackled by anthropologists and sociologists, the debt to philosophy is substantial. To take only a few examples from this anthology, we can cite Nietzsche and Foucault for James Laidlaw, Wittgenstein and Austin for Michael Lambek, or Kant and Aristotle for Steven Lukes. This is why it seemed essential to us that this part on the foundations of the moral question in anthropology include a set of philosophical texts. The first, Michel de Montaigne's 'Of Cannibals', falls rather within the province of humanist meditation and is often cited, along with 'Of Customs' by the same author, as the precursor to modern thought on culture and the Other. The moralist's complexity and even ambiguity prefigures in many ways the fluctuations and equivocations of anthropology – his relativism leads him to assert that 'each man calls barbarism whatever is not his own practice', reducing morality to a question of tradition, whereas his universalism is belied by the judgements he makes about others and his own society 'in respect to the rules of reason', thus presupposing the existence of superior moral criteria.[2] As for the last text of this short series, a programmatic article by the philosopher Abraham Edel, it can be seen rather as initiating a demanding dialogue in which anthropology is expected to consider morality and ethics with a conceptual and ethnographical rigour that the author considers to be sorely lacking in general.

From the immense corpus of moral philosophy, we chose to retain four texts due to their particular importance for the way in which anthropology has formed around the moral question. Immanuel Kant's *Groundwork for the Metaphysic of Morals* established the principles on which a universal morality could be built based on the good will and the categorical imperative: the human being acts morally when he acts by obligation rather than inclination, in other words when he respects natural law; the maxim to which he refers in doing so should be valid for all human beings; in this way he is his own legislator. Kantian deontology can be seen to influence the social sciences in two main fashions: on the one hand, the ethics of duty paved the way for the Durkheimian approach that defines morality by the rules that one must or one wishes to obey; on the other, the universal law that it promulgates served, in parallel, as a foundation for the critical social sciences that claim implicitly or explicitly to draw on human rights. In his work *On the Genealogy of Morality*, Friedrich Nietzsche formulated what is probably the most radical critique by showing that what we refer to as morality is neither an absolute nor a universal given, but rather a historical product of Judaeo-Christian origin, and by then asking the question of the value of our values, that is, of the relevance of our distinction between good and evil. This dual questioning of the bedrock of morality can be found in two different lines of anthropological studies: on the one hand, those that reject Western moral hegemony, whether or not they are labelled as post-colonial; on the other, those that explore cultures in which the foundations of ethics do not rest upon any of the premises of Christian morality, which often serves as a tacit point of reference for anthropological analysis. Elizabeth Anscombe, with her article on 'Modern Moral Philosophy', holds a very particular position within this intellectual landscape. By attacking what she calls the law conception of ethics, in other words a Kantian conception in reference to his universal law, and the theories for which she creates the label 'consequentialist', in other words the assessment of the value of an act according to its effects, and by advocating a return to Aristotle's thought, less bound up with absolute good and bad than with cultivated virtues, she clarified the ethical trio according to which most anthropologists position themselves today. Finally, Michel Foucault, with his short introductory text to *The Use of Pleasure*, appears to have inspired a recent renewal of the anthropology of ethics. The third form of morality that interests him, the first and second referring respectively to rules and obeying rules, concerns conduct and more specifically the way in which individuals constitute themselves as ethical subjects just as much through ordinary actions as through ritual practices. From charismatic or evangelical Christians to Muslim worshippers and Jain renouncers, the study of subjective ethics has enriched not only religious anthropology but also more widely our understanding of the experience of morality.

If we turn now to the works of social science that laid the foundations for the study of the moral question,[3] it is remarkable that Edward Burnett Tylor, whose *Primitive Culture* was the first great anthropological synthesis, devoted a brief article to this question in one of the editions of the famous *Notes and Queries*, which, from the mid-nineteenth century onwards, served as a communication tool in the scientific world: this little-known text was technical rather than epistemological and testifies to the author's early interest in a methodological perspective neglected by contemporary anthropologists of morality. However, it is of course to Émile Durkheim that we owe the first theoretical endeavour to produce a systematic analysis of morality, first in his large-scale works, particularly *The Division of Labour in Society*, and then in his lectures, beginning with 'The Determination of Moral Facts'. The description he gives of these, linking the obligation to obey rules with the desire to pursue good, in other words norms and values, is continued by an exploration of its foundations that he sees residing not in the human freedom of Kantian theory, but in the existence of the collective that forms society. This reading of morality as a socially produced code went on to fuel many ethnological studies. In contrast, Max Weber's influence has no doubt been underestimated. First, *The Protestant Ethic and the Spirit of Capitalism* made an important contribution to the analysis of the relationship between religion and economy, from the point of view of moral doctrines and practices upon which many studies in the anthropology of religion are dependent. Second, the distinction that he puts forward in 'Politics as Vocation' between an ethics of conviction and an ethics of responsibility offers a consequentialist reading in counterpoint to absolutist approaches, that provides a way of thinking the relationship between morality and politics. Where anthropology is concerned, the foundations seem less sound. Of course, Edward A. Westermarck's impressive *The Origin and Development of the Moral Ideas*, which offers a rich collection of theoretical discussions and empirical illustrations regarding morality, generated genuine interest when it was published; however, its influence remained limited in time and, due to its mixture of professed moral subjectivism and relativism, for many it tends now to be relegated to the status of a relic. As for Bronislaw Malinowski's *Crime and Custom in Savage Society*, more modest in size but more decisive for the discipline, it is considered a founding text for legal anthropology. This, however, runs the risk of passing over the fact that the work sets out a very novel principle according to which members of primitive societies, as they were called at the time, far from contenting themselves with obeying strict rules, violations of which would result in automatic sanctions, adapted these rules and sanctions in an interpretation that is far removed from the Durkheimian paradigm. In parallel, Paul Radin opened up a productive path for a comparative anthropology of morality with his work *Primitive Man as Philosopher*, in which he affirmed that 'primitive thought' was perfectly capable of abstraction and that traditional societies grounded their morality in superior values, not only practical rules, just like modern societies.

Ultimately, while it is true, as Albert Hirschman writes, that in order to grasp the relationships between morality and the social sciences we must take into account the fact that the latter have only been able to study the former by freeing themselves from traditional teachings on the subject, that is, from the normative conceptions that prevailed for centuries, it should also be noted that anthropologists and sociologists – while striving to produce autonomous scientific work – were fuelled by philosophical theories and discussions as they formed the moral field. But the contribution of these classical authors to such debates was already essential in three complementary ways: bringing empirical recognition of cultural diversity, thus rocking universalistic certitudes; observing the flexibility of practices, thus forcing law-based conceptions to be revised; and providing evidence of the social, thus calling individualistic approaches into question. Nonetheless, it took anthropology no less than a century – long after sociology – to draw substantial benefit from these promising beginnings.

Notes

1 The dual model presented here should be expanded by including another essential aspect that developed in France in the Early Modern period, i.e. the tradition of moralists. As Johan Heilbron shows, moral thinking developed in the literary field at the edges of religion and alongside philosophy through the writings of Montaigne, La Rochefoucauld, Pascal, Nicole, La Bruyère, Madame de Staël, Chamfort, and others. These moralists, who were often concerned with questions of conventions and behaviour defining courtly life, also expressed interest in more general questions regarding human beings and the qualities one could expect from them. They focused more on concrete ethos than on abstract ethics. See Johan Heilbron (1995), *The Rise of Social Theory*, Cambridge: Polity Press.
2 Montaigne's fluctuation between relativism and universalism, and the more general questions that it raises for Western thinking, have often been discussed. See Tzvetan Todorov (1994/1989), *On Human Diversity: Nationalism, Racism, and Exoticism in French Thought*, Cambridge, MA: Harvard University Press; and Richard Handler (1986), Of Cannibals and Custom: Montaigne's Cultural Relativism, *Anthropology Today*, 5 (2): 12–14.
3 As well as the numerous recent works provided by collective projects on specific approaches to morality, which will be mentioned further on, several overviews exist, notably, Jarrett Zigon (2008), *Morality: An Anthropological Perspective*, Oxford: Berg; Steven Hitlin and Stephen Vaisey eds. (2010), *Handbook of the Sociology of Morality*, New York: Springer; and Didier Fassin ed. (2012), *Moral Anthropology: A Companion*, Malden: Wiley-Blackwell.

Legacies of moral philosophies

1 Of cannibals

Michel de Montaigne

Michel de Montaigne (1533–1592) was a magistrate at the Court of Périgueux and counsellor at the Parliament of Bordeaux and, in this capacity, responsible for various diplomatic and political missions for the king. After having left his official functions and retired to the family estate at the age of thirty-seven, he devoted his time to his major work, the *Essays*, interrupting this only after being elected Mayor of Bordeaux, a position he held for four years. When it was published, composed only of books I and II, it met with great success and, until his death, Montaigne continued to work on correcting it and writing a third volume.

Although the *Essays* are rightfully considered a long work of introspection – 'And therefore, Reader, I myself am the subject of my book,' wrote Montaigne in the foreword – books I and II are presented rather as a series of short compositions on diverse subjects about which the author brings together erudition, experience and reflection. The themes are varied, ranging from notes on Cicero, Cato the Younger, the punishment of cowardice, and the force of imagination to considerations on friendship, sorrow, death, inequality, moderation, and cruelty. The most famous of these essays, and probably the most influential in Western thinking, is entitled 'Of Cannibals' and was inspired by an encounter in Rouen with three men presented to the King by an explorer returned from Brazil. It was the first modern text to explicitly pose the question, within the context of the recent discovery of the New World, not only of cultural relativism (recognising the existence of different beliefs and customs) but also of moral relativism (recognising the worthiness of other systems of norms and values). By reversing the facts considered as self-evident at the time, Montaigne calls on his contemporaries to revise their disparaging judgements on the mores of 'savages' and to consider with more severity their own supposedly 'civilised' practices. The author even concludes his essay by criticising French society, having one of his unexpected foreign interlocutors question the arbitrary nature of power and the inequalities tolerated.

When King Pyrrhus passed over into Italy, after he had reconnoitered the formation of the army that the Romans were sending to meet him, he said: 'I do not know what barbarians these are' (for so the Greeks called all foreign nations), 'but the formation of this army that I see is not at all barbarous.' The Greeks said as much of the army that Flamininus brought into their country, and so did Philip, seeing from a knoll the order and distribution of the Roman camp, in his kingdom, under Publius Sulpicius Galba. Thus we should beware of clinging to vulgar opinions, and judge things by reason's way, not by popular say.

I had with me for a long time a man who had lived for ten or twelve years in that other world which has been discovered in our century, in the place where Villegaignon landed, and which he called Antarctic France. [...]

This man I had was a simple, crude fellow – a character fit to bear true witness; for clever people observe more things and more curiously, but they interpret them; and to lend weight and conviction to their interpretation, they cannot help altering history a little. They never show you things as they are, but bend and disguise them according to the way they have seen them; and to give credence to their judgement and attract you to it, they are prone to add something to their matter, to stretch it out and amplify it. We need a man either very honest, or so simple that he has not the stuff to build up false inventions and give them plausibility; and wedded to no theory. Such was my man; and besides this, he at various times brought sailors and merchants, whom he had known on that trip, to see me. So I content myself with his information, without inquiring what the cosmographers say about it. [...]

Now, to return to my subject, I think there is nothing barbarous and savage in that nation, from what I have been told, except that each man calls barbarism whatever is not his own practice; for indeed it seems we have no other test of truth and reason than the example and pattern of the opinions and customs of the country we live in. *There is always the perfect religion, the perfect government, the perfect and accomplished manners in all things.* Those people are wild, just as we call wild the fruits that Nature has produced by herself and in her normal course; whereas really it is those that we have changed artificially and led astray from the common order, that we should rather call wild. The former retain alive and vigorous their genuine, their most useful and natural, virtues and properties, which we have debased in the latter in adapting them to gratify our corrupted taste. And yet for all that, the savor and delicacy of some uncultivated fruits of those countries is quite as excellent, even to our taste, as that of our own. It is not reasonable that art should win the place of honor over our great and powerful mother Nature. We have so overloaded the beauty and richness of her works by our inventions that we have quite smothered her. Yet wherever her purity shines forth, she wonderfully puts to shame our vain and frivolous attempts. [...]

These nations, then, seem to me barbarous in this sense, that they have been fashioned very little by the human mind, and are still very close to their original naturalness. The laws of nature still rule them, very little corrupted by ours; and they are in such a state of purity that I am sometimes vexed that they were unknown earlier, in the days when there were men able to judge them better than we. I am sorry that Lycurgus and Plato did not know of them; for it seems to me that what we actually see in these nations surpasses not only all the pictures in which poets have idealized the golden age and all their inventions in imagining a happy state of man, but also the conceptions and the very desire of philosophy. They could not imagine a naturalness so pure and simple as we see by experience; nor could they believe that our society could be maintained with so little artifice and human solder. This is a nation, I should say to Plato, in which there is no sort of traffic, no knowledge of letters, no science of numbers, no name for a magistrate or for political superiority, no custom of servitude, no riches or poverty, no contracts, no successions, no partitions, no occupations but leisure ones, no care for any but common kinship, no clothes, no agriculture, no metal, no use of wine or wheat. The very words that signify lying, treachery, dissimulation, avarice, envy, belittling, pardon – unheard of. How far from this perfection would he find the republic that he imagined. [...]

They drink several times a day and to capacity. Their drink is made of some root, and is of the color of our claret wines. They drink it only lukewarm. This beverage keeps only two or three days; it has a slightly sharp taste, is not at all heady, is good for the stomach, and has a laxative effect upon those who are not used to it; it is a very pleasant drink for anyone who is accustomed to it. In place of bread they use a certain white substance like preserved coriander. I have tried it; it tastes sweet and a little flat.

The whole day is spent in dancing. The younger men go to hunt animals with bows. Some of the women busy themselves meanwhile with warming their drink, which is their chief duty. Some one of the old men, in the morning before they begin to eat, preaches to the whole barnful in common, walking from one end to the other, and repeating one single sentence several times until he has completed the circuit (for the buildings are fully a hundred paces long). He recommends to them only two things: valor against the enemy and love for their wives. [...]

It is astonishing what firmness they show in their combats, which never end but in slaughter and bloodshed; for as to routs and terror, they know nothing of either. Each man brings back as his trophy the head of the enemy he has killed, and sets it up at the entrance to his dwelling. After they have treated their prisoners well for a long time with all the hospitality they can think of, each man who has a prisoner calls a great assembly of his acquaintances. He ties a rope to one of the prisoner's arms, by the end of which he holds him, a few steps away, for fear of being hurt, and gives his dearest friend the other arm to hold in the same way; and these two, in the presence of the whole assembly, kill him with their swords. This done, they roast him and eat him in common and send some pieces to their absent friends. This is not, as people think, for nourishment, as of old the Scythians used to do; it is to betoken an extreme revenge. And the proof of this came when they saw the Portuguese, who had joined forces with their adversaries, inflict a different kind of death on them when they took them prisoner, which was to bury them up to the waist, shoot the rest of their body full of arrows, and afterward hang them. They thought that these people from the other world, being men who had sown the knowledge of many vices among their neighbors and were much greater masters than themselves in every sort of wickedness, did not adopt this sort of vengeance without some reason, and that it must be more painful than their own; so they began to give up their old method and to follow this one.

I am not sorry that we notice the barbarous horror of such acts, but I am heartily sorry that, judging their faults rightly, we should be so blind to our own. I think there is more barbarity in eating a man alive than in eating him dead; and in tearing by tortures and the rack a body still full of feeling, in roasting a man bit by bit, in having him bitten and mangled by dogs and swine (as we have not only read but seen within fresh memory, not among ancient enemies, but among neighbors and fellow citizens, and what is worse, on the pretext of piety and religion), than in roasting and eating him after he is dead.

Indeed, Chrysippus and Zeno, heads of the Stoic sect, thought there was nothing wrong in using our carcasses for any purpose in case of need, and getting nourishment from them; just as our ancestors, when besieged by Caesar in the city of Alésia, resolved to relieve their famine by eating old men, women, and other people useless for fighting. 'The Gascons once, 'tis said, their life renewed by eating such food' (Juvenal). And physicians do not fear to use human flesh in all sorts of ways for our health, applying it either inwardly or outwardly. But there never was any opinion so disordered as to excuse treachery, disloyalty, tyranny, and cruelty, which are our ordinary vices. So we may well call these people barbarians, in respect to the rules of reason, but not in respect to ourselves, who surpass them in every kind of barbarity. [...]

Three of these men, ignorant of the price they will pay some day, in loss of repose and happiness, for gaining knowledge of the corruptions of this side of the ocean; ignorant also of the fact that of this intercourse will come their ruin (which I suppose is already well advanced: poor wretches, to let themselves be tricked by the desire for new things, and to have left the serenity of their own sky to come and see ours!) – three of these men were at Rouen, at the time the late King Charles IX was there. The king talked to them for a long time; they were shown our ways, our splendor, the aspect of a fine city. After that, someone asked their opinion, and wanted to know what they had found most amazing. They mentioned three things, of which I have forgotten the third, and I am very sorry for it; but I still remember two of them. They said that in the first place they thought it very strange that so many grown men, bearded, strong, and armed, who were around the king (it is likely that they were talking about the Swiss of his guard) should submit to obey a child, and that one of them was not chosen to command instead. Second (they have a way in their language of speaking of men as halves of one another), they had noticed that there were among us men full and gorged with all sorts of good things, and that their other halves were beggars at their doors, emaciated with hunger and poverty; and they thought it strange that these needy halves could endure such an injustice, and did not take the others by the throat, or set fire to their houses.

I had a very long talk with one of them; but I had an interpreter who followed my meaning so badly, and who was so hindered by his stupidity in taking in my ideas, that I could get hardly any satisfaction from the man. When I asked him what profit he gained from his superior position among his people (for he was a captain, and our sailors called him king), he told me that it was to march foremost in war. How many men followed him? He pointed to a piece of ground, to signify as many as such a space could hold; it might have been four or five thousand men. Did all his authority expire with the war? He said that this much remained, that when he visited the villages dependent on him, they made paths for him through the underbrush by which he might pass quite comfortably.

All this is not too bad – but what's the use? They don't wear breeches.

2 Groundwork of the metaphysic of morals

Immanuel Kant

Immanuel Kant (1724–1804) was a German philosopher whose critical works, which broached most aspects of philosophy, have been essential to modern thinking, particularly in the field of morals. Born in Königsberg, capital of Prussia at the time, he spent his life there as he was appointed to the city's university, where he remained throughout his career. While his initial studies focused on physics, logic and aesthetics, his most decisive work was completed relatively late, with the publication over a decade of *Critique of Pure Reason, Critique of Practical Reason*, and *Critique of Judgment* as well as his major works of moral philosophy: *Groundwork of the Metaphysic of Morals, The Metaphysics of Morals*, and *Anthropology from a Pragmatic Point of View*. In the different domains he explored, Kant endeavoured to create the foundations for a system of critical thinking that, in his view, marked the distinctive rupture of the Enlightenment.

In *Groundwork of the Metaphysic of Morals*, Kant does not seek to prescribe a particular morality, but rather to understand what defines morals in general or, better yet, upon what it is grounded – according to him, 'good will'. An act is not moral because it seeks to be good, but because it conforms to a principle of moral duty. It is therefore not personal inclination, such as the sympathy one feels for the suffering of others, according to the theory of moral sentiments, nor the effect produced, for example the happiness one causes, according to utilitarian theory, that makes a kind action moral: it is the fact that one undertakes it in order to respect a moral law – even if one does not want to and no matter what the intended effect. This is what Kant calls the 'categorical imperative'. But what is this moral law? For him, it is general, rather than specific to a given context. It implies acting according to a maxim that one would also wish to see become a universal law, that is, a law of nature. It follows that humanity should always be considered not simply as a means, but as an end in itself, whether in ourselves or in others: that is why this theory is so attractive to those looking for universal foundations to ethics, in human rights for instance. Kantian moral philosophy is generally qualified as a deontology or an ethics of obligation. In the social sciences, it has notably influenced the whole Durkheimian approach to morality and the anthropological trends that claim to adhere to it.

The good will

It is impossible to conceive anything at all in the world, or even out of it, which can be taken as good without qualification, except a *good will*. Intelligence, wit, judgement, and any other *talents* of the mind we may care to name, or courage, resolution, and constancy of purpose, as qualities of *temperament*, are without doubt good and desirable in many respects; but they can also be extremely bad and hurtful when the will is not good which has to make use of these gifts of nature, and which for this reason has the term *'character'* applied to its peculiar quality. It is exactly the same with *gifts of fortune*. Power, wealth, honour, even health and that complete well-being and contentment with one's state which goes by the name of *'happiness'*, produce boldness, and as a consequence often over-boldness as well, unless a good will is present by which their influence on the mind—and so too the whole principle of action—may be corrected and adjusted to universal ends; not to mention that a rational and impartial spectator can never feel approval in contemplating the uninterrupted prosperity of a being graced by no touch of a pure and good will, and that consequently a good will seems to constitute the indispensable condition of our very worthiness to be happy. [...]

The good will and duty

We have now to elucidate the concept of a will estimable in itself and good apart from any further end. This concept, which is already present in a sound natural understanding and requires not so much to be taught as merely to be clarified, always holds the highest place in estimating the total worth of our actions and constitutes the condition of all the rest. We will therefore take up the concept of *duty*, which includes that of a good will, exposed, however, to certain subjective limitations and obstacles. These, so far from hiding a good will or disguising it, rather bring it out by contrast and make it shine forth more brightly.

The motive of duty

I will here pass over all actions already recognized as contrary to duty, however useful they may be with a view to this or that end; for about these the question does not even arise whether they could have been done *for the sake of duty* inasmuch as they are directly opposed to it. I will also set aside actions which in fact accord with duty, yet for which men have *no immediate inclination*, but perform them because impelled to do so by some other inclination. For there it is easy to decide whether the action which accords with duty has been done *from duty* or from some purpose of self-interest. This distinction is far more difficult to perceive when the action accords with duty and the subject has in addition an *immediate* inclination to the action. For example, it certainly accords with duty that a grocer should not overcharge his inexperienced customer; and where there is much competition a sensible shopkeeper refrains from so doing and keeps to a fixed and general price for everybody so that a child can buy from him just as well as anyone else. Thus people are served *honestly*; but this is not nearly enough to justify us in believing that the shopkeeper has acted in this way from duty or from principles of fair dealing; his interests required him to do so. We cannot assume him to have in addition an immediate inclination towards his customers, leading him, as it were out of love, to give no man preference over another in the matter of price. Thus the action was done neither from duty nor from immediate inclination, but solely from purposes of self-interest.

On the other hand, to preserve one's life is a duty, and besides this everyone has also an immediate inclination to do so. But on account of this the often anxious precautions taken by the greater part of mankind for this purpose have no inner worth, and the maxim of their action is without moral content. They do protect their lives *in conformity with duty* but not *from the motive of duty*. When on the contrary, disappointments and hopeless misery have quite taken away the taste for life; when a wretched man, strong in soul and more angered at his fate than faint-hearted or cast down, longs for death and still preserves his life without loving it—not from inclination or fear but from duty; then indeed his maxim has a moral content.

To help others where one can is a duty, and besides this there are many spirits of so sympathetic a temper that, without any further motive of vanity or self-interest, they find an inner pleasure in spreading happiness around them and can take delight in the contentment of others as their own work. Yet I maintain that in such a case an action of this kind, however right and however amiable it may be, has still no genuinely moral worth. It stands on the same footing as other inclinations—for example, the inclination for honour, which if fortunate enough to hit on something beneficial and right and consequently honourable, deserves praise and encouragement, but not esteem; for its maxim lacks moral content, namely, the performance of such actions, not from inclination, but *from duty*. Suppose then that the mind of this friend of man were overclouded by sorrows of his own which extinguished all sympathy with the fate of others, but that he still had power to help those in distress, though no longer stirred by the need of others because sufficiently occupied with his own; and suppose that, when no longer moved by any inclination, he tears himself out of this deadly insensibility and does the action without any inclination for the sake of duty alone; then for the first time his action has its genuine moral worth. Still further: if nature had implanted little sympathy in this or that man's heart; if (being in other respects an honest fellow) he were cold in temperament and indifferent to the sufferings of others—perhaps because, being endowed with the special gift of patience and robust endurance in his own sufferings, he assumed the like in others or even demanded it; if such a man (who would in truth not be the worst product of nature) were not exactly fashioned by her to be a philanthropist, would he not still find in himself a source from which he might draw a worth far higher than any that a good-natured temperament can have? Assuredly he would. It is precisely in this that the worth of character begins to show—a moral worth and beyond all comparison the highest—namely, that he does good, not from inclination, but from duty.

To assure one's own happiness is a duty (at least indirectly); for discontent with one's state, in a press of cares and amidst unsatisfied wants, might easily become a great *temptation to the transgression of duty*. But here also, apart from regard to duty, all men have already of themselves the strongest and deepest inclination towards happiness, because precisely in this Idea of happiness all inclinations are combined into a sum total. The prescription for happiness is however, often so constituted as greatly to interfere with some inclinations, and yet men cannot form under the name of 'happiness' any determinate and assured conception of the satisfaction of all inclinations as a sum. Hence it is not to be wondered at that a single inclination which is determinate as to what it promises and as to the time of its satisfaction may outweigh a wavering Idea; and that a man, for example, a sufferer from gout, may choose to enjoy what he fancies and put up with what he can—on the ground that on balance he has here at least not killed the enjoyment of the present moment because of some possibly groundless expectations of the good fortune supposed to attach to soundness of health. But in this case also, when the universal inclination towards happiness has failed to determine his will, when good health, at least for him, has not entered into his calculations as so necessary, what remains over, here as in other cases, is a law—the law of furthering his happiness, not from inclination, but from duty; and in this for the first time his conduct has a real moral worth.

It is doubtless in this sense that we should understand too the passages from Scripture in which we are commanded to love our neighbour and even our enemy. For love out of inclination cannot be commanded; but kindness done from duty—although no inclination impels us, and even although natural and unconquerable disinclination stands in our way—is *practical*, and not *pathological*, love, residing in the will and not in the propensions of feeling, in principles of action and not of melting compassion; and it is this practical love alone which can be an object of command.

The formal principle of duty

Our second proposition is this: An action done from duty has its moral worth, *not in the purpose* to be attained by it, but in the maxim in accordance with which it is decided upon; it depends therefore, not on the realization of the object of the action, but solely on the *principle of volition* in accordance with which, irrespective of all objects of the faculty of desire, the action has been performed. That the purposes we may have in our actions and also their effects considered as ends and motives of the will can give to actions no unconditioned and moral worth is clear from what has gone before. Where then can this worth be found if we are not to find it in the will's relation to the effect hoped for from the action? It can be found nowhere but *in the principle of the will*, irrespective of the ends which can be brought about by such an action; for between its *a priori* principle, which is formal, and its *a posteriori* motive, which is material, the will stands, so to speak, at a parting of the ways; and since it must be determined by some principle, it will have to be determined by the formal principle of volition when an action is done from duty, where, as we have seen, every material principle is taken away from it.

Reverence for the law

Our third proposition, as an inference from the two preceding, I would express thus: *Duty is the necessity to act out of reverence for the law*. For an object as the effect of my proposed action I can have an *inclination*, but *never reverence*, precisely because it is merely the effect, and not the activity, of a will. Similarly for inclination as such, whether my own or that of another, I cannot have reverence: I can at most in the first case approve, and in the second case sometimes even love—that is, regard it as favourable to my own advantage. Only something which is conjoined with my will solely as a ground and never as an effect—something which does not serve my inclination, but outweighs it or at least leaves it entirely out of account in my choice—and therefore only bare law for its own sake, can be an object of reverence and therewith a command. Now an action done from duty has to set aside altogether the influence of inclination, and along with inclination every object of the will; so there is nothing left able to determine the will except objectively the *law* and subjectively *pure reverence* for this practical law, and therefore the maxim[1] of obeying this law even to the detriment of all my inclinations.

Thus the moral worth of an action does not depend on the result expected from it, and so too does not depend on any principle of action that needs to borrow its motive from this expected result. For all these results (agreeable states and even the promotion of happiness in others) could have been brought about by other causes as well, and consequently their production did not require the will of a rational being, in which, however, the highest and unconditioned good can alone be found. Therefore nothing but the *idea of the law* in itself, *which admittedly is present only in a rational being*—so far as it, and not an expected result, is the ground determining the will—can constitute that pre-eminent good which we call moral, a good which is already present in the person acting on this idea and has not to be awaited merely from the result.[2]

The categorical imperative

But what kind of law can this be the thought of which, even without regard to the results expected from it, has to determine the will if this is to be called good absolutely and without qualification? Since I have robbed the will of every inducement that might arise for it as a consequence of obeying any particular law, nothing is left but the conformity of actions to universal law as such, and this alone must serve the will as its principle. That is to say, I ought never to act except in such a way *that I can also will that my maxim should become a universal law*. Here, bare conformity to universal law as such (without having as its base any law prescribing particular actions) is what serves the will as its principle, and must so serve it if duty is not to be everywhere an empty delusion and a chimerical concept. The ordinary reason of mankind also agrees with this completely in its practical judgements and always has the aforesaid principle before its eyes.

Take this question, for example. May I not, when I am hard pressed, make a promise with the intention of not keeping it? Here I readily distinguish the two senses which the question can have—Is it prudent, or is it right, to make a false promise? The first no doubt can often be the case. I do indeed see that it is not enough for me to extricate myself from present embarrassment by this subterfuge: I have to consider whether from this lie there may not subsequently accrue to me much greater inconvenience than that from which I now escape, and also—since, with all my supposed *astuteness*, to foresee the consequences is not so easy that I can be sure there is no chance, once confidence in me is lost, of this proving far more disadvantageous than all the ills I now think to avoid—whether it may not be a *more prudent* action to proceed here on a general maxim and make it my habit not to give a promise except with the intention of keeping it. Yet it becomes clear to me at once that such a maxim is always founded solely on fear of consequences. To tell the truth for the sake of duty is something entirely different from doing so out of concern for inconvenient results; for in the first case the concept of the action already contains in itself a law for me, while in the second case I have first of all to look around elsewhere in order to see what effects may be bound up with it for me. When I deviate from the principle of duty, this is quite certainly bad; but if I desert my prudential maxim, this can often be greatly to my advantage, though it is admittedly safer to stick to it. Suppose I seek, however, to learn in the quickest way and yet unerringly how to solve the problem 'Does a lying promise accord with duty?' I have then to ask myself 'Should I really be content that my maxim (the maxim of getting out of a difficulty by a false promise) should hold as a universal law (one valid both for myself and others)? And could I really say to myself that every one may make a false promise if he finds himself in a difficulty from which he can extricate himself in no other way?' I then become aware at once that I can indeed will to lie, but I can by no means will a universal law of lying; for by such a law there could properly be no promises at all, since it would be futile to profess a will for future action to others who would not believe my profession or who, if they did so over-hastily, would pay me back in like coin; and consequently my maxim, as soon as it was made a universal law, would be bound to annul itself.

Thus I need no far-reaching ingenuity to find out what I have to do in order to possess a good will. Inexperienced in the course of world affairs and incapable of being prepared for all the chances that happen in it, I ask myself only 'Can you also will that your maxim should become a universal law?' Where you cannot, it is to be rejected, and that not because of a prospective loss to you or even to others, but because it cannot fit as a principle into a possible enactment of universal law. For such an enactment reason compels my immediate reverence, into whose grounds (which the philosopher may investigate) I have as yet no *insight*, although I do at least understand this much: reverence is the assessment of a worth which far outweighs all the worth of what is commended by inclination, and the necessity for me to act out of *pure* reverence for the practical law is what constitutes duty, to which every other motive must give way because it is the condition of a will good *in itself*, whose value is above all else.

Notes

1 A *maxim* is the subjective principle of a volition: an objective principle (that is, one which would also serve subjectively as a practical principle for all rational beings if reason had full control over the faculty of desire) is a practical law.
2 It might be urged against me that I have merely tried, under cover of the word *'reverence'*, to take refuge in an obscure feeling instead of giving a clearly articulated answer to the question by means of a concept of reason. Yet although reverence is a feeling, it is not a feeling *received* through outside influence, but one *self-produced* by a rational concept, and therefore specifically distinct from feelings of the first kind; all of which can be reduced to inclination or fear. What I recognize immediately as law for me, I recognize with reverence, which means merely consciousness of the *subordination* of my will to a law without the mediation of external influences on my senses. Immediate determination of the will by the law and consciousness of this determination is called *'reverence'*, so that reverence is regarded as the *effect* of the law on the subject and not as the cause of the law. Reverence is properly awareness of a value which demolishes my self-love. Hence there is something which is regarded neither as an object of inclination nor as an object of fear, though it has at the same time some analogy with both. The *object* of reverence is the *law* alone—that law which we impose *on ourselves* but yet is necessary in itself. Considered as a law, we are subject to it without any consultation of self-love; considered as self-imposed it is a consequence of our will. In the first respect it is analogous to fear, in the second to inclination. All reverence for a person is properly only reverence for the law (of honesty and so on) of which that person gives us an example. Because we regard the development of our talents as a duty, we see too in a man of talent a sort of *example of the law* (the law of becoming like him by practice), and this is what constitutes our reverence for him. All moral *interest*, so-called, consists solely in *reverence* for the law.

3 On the genealogy of morality

Friedrich Nietzsche

Friedrich Nietzsche (1840–1900) was a German philosopher and philologist whose work called the moral presuppositions of the Western world firmly into question, particularly their Christian foundations. The son of a Lutheran pastor, he studied theology and philology, but the most decisive influences of his formative years on his philosophical thought and musical sensibility were his reading of Arthur Schopenhauer and his encounter with Richard Wagner. Appointed Professor at the University of Basel at the age of twenty-four, he published *The Birth of Tragedy*, which met with little enthusiasm from the academic world, as well as *Untimely Meditations* and *Human, All too Human*. Serious health problems led him to resign from his position after only ten years of his academic career. Thus began a decade of travelling throughout Europe during which, having renounced his German nationality, he was officially stateless. However, this period was most fruitful in terms of publications, which included *Thus Spoke Zarathustra, Beyond Good and Evil*, and *On the Genealogy of Morality*. In 1889, he had a stroke that left him an invalid for the last eleven years of his life.

The subtitle of *On the Genealogy of Morality – A Polemic –* gives a clear indication of the author's intention. The text opens with a radical questioning of the origin and values of notions of good and evil. According to Nietzsche, the moral apprehension of the world, which is generally held to be self-evident, should be called into question by a relativism that is twofold: first, by considering it as historically constituted by Christianity, and second, by contesting it politically from the point of view of its effects on humanity. For him, Christian morality transformed the opposition between good and bad into one between good and evil. By putting down the 'masters' and elevating the 'slaves', this morality reverses the order of values and places the oppressed, the humiliated, the weak and the poor at the pinnacle of the moral hierarchy. It extols compassion and altruism, sin and bad conscience, and finally, not without hypocrisy, it brings about the triumph of a morality of ressentiment that leads to the weakening of humanity. By the strength with which it questions the moral facts considered as self-evident in the contemporary world, this impassioned and controversial text remains relevant and topical. Nietzsche's thought has been of considerable influence upon twentieth-century humanities and social sciences, from Max Scheler to Gilles Deleuze.

3. With a characteristic scepticism to which I confess only reluctantly – it relates to *morality* and to all that hitherto on earth has been celebrated as morality –, a scepticism which sprang up in my life so early, so unbidden, so unstoppably, and which was in such conflict with my surroundings, age, precedents and lineage that I would

almost be justified in calling it my '*a priori*', – eventually my curiosity and suspicion were bound to fix on the question of *what origin* our terms good and evil actually have. Indeed, as a thirteen-year-old boy, I was preoccupied with the problem of the origin of evil: at an age when one's heart was 'half-filled with childish games, half-filled with God',[1] I dedicated my first literary childish game, my first philosophical essay, to this problem – and as regards my 'solution' to the problem at that time, I quite properly gave God credit for it and made him the *father* of evil. Did my '*a priori*' want *this* of me? That new, immoral, or at least immoralistic '*a priori*' and the oh-so-anti-Kantian, so enigmatic 'categorical imperative'[2] which spoke from it and to which I have, in the meantime, increasingly lent an ear, and not just an ear? ... Fortunately I learnt, in time, to separate theological from moral prejudice and I no longer searched for the origin of evil *beyond* the world. Some training in history and philology, together with my innate fastidiousness with regard to all psychological problems, soon transformed my problem into another: under what conditions did man invent the value judgments good and evil? *and what value do they themselves have?* Have they up to now obstructed or promoted human flourishing? Are they a sign of distress, poverty and the degeneration of life? Or, on the contrary, do they reveal the fullness, strength and will of life, its courage, its confidence, its future? [...]

6. This problem of the *value* of compassion and of the morality of compassion (– I am opposed to the disgraceful modern softness of feeling –) seems at first to be only an isolated phenomenon, a lone question mark; but whoever pauses over the question and *learns* to ask, will find what I found: – that a vast new panorama opens up for him, a possibility makes him giddy, mistrust, suspicion and fear of every kind spring up, belief in morality, all morality, wavers, – finally, a new demand becomes articulate. So let us give voice to this *new demand*: we need a *critique* of moral values, *the value of these values should itself, for once, be examined* – and so we need to know about the conditions and circumstances under which the values grew up, developed and changed (morality as result, as symptom, as mask, as tartuffery, as sickness, as misunderstanding; but also morality as cause, remedy, stimulant, inhibition, poison), since we have neither had this knowledge up till now nor even desired it. People have taken the *value* of these 'values' as given, as factual, as beyond all questioning; up till now, nobody has had the remotest doubt or hesitation in placing higher value on 'the good man' than on 'the evil', higher value in the sense of advancement, benefit and prosperity for man in general (and this includes man's future). What if the opposite were true? What if a regressive trait lurked in 'the good man', likewise a danger, an enticement, a poison, a narcotic, so that the present *lived at the expense of the future*? Perhaps in more comfort and less danger, but also in a smaller-minded, meaner manner? ... So that morality itself were to blame if man, as species, never reached his *highest potential power and splendour*? So that morality itself was the danger of dangers? [...]

First essay: Good and evil, good and bad

13. The problem of the *other* origin of 'good', of good as thought up by the man *of ressentiment*, demands its solution. – There is nothing strange about the fact that lambs bear a grudge towards large birds of prey: but that is no reason to blame the large birds of prey for carrying off the little lambs. And if the lambs say to each other, 'These birds of prey are evil; and whoever is least like a bird of prey and most like its

opposite, a lamb, – is good, isn't he?', then there is no reason to raise objections to this setting-up of an ideal beyond the fact that the birds of prey will view it somewhat derisively, and will perhaps say: 'We don't bear any grudge at all towards these good lambs, in fact we love them, nothing is tastier, than a tender lamb.' – It is just as absurd to ask strength *not* to express itself as strength, *not* to be a desire to overthrow, crush, become master, to be a thirst for enemies, resistance and triumphs, as it is to ask weakness to express itself as strength. A quantum of force is just such a quantum of drive, will, action, in fact it is nothing but this driving, willing and acting, and only the seduction of language (and the fundamental errors of reason petrified within it), which construes and misconstrues all actions as conditional upon an agency, a 'subject', can make it appear otherwise. And just as the common people separate lightning from its flash and take the latter to be a *deed*, something performed by a subject, which is called lightning, popular morality separates strength from the manifestations of strength, as though there were an indifferent substratum behind the strong person which had the *freedom* to manifest strength or not. But there is no such substratum; there is no 'being' behind the deed, its effect and what becomes of it; 'the doer' is invented as an afterthought, – the doing is everything. Basically, the common people double a deed; when they see lightning, they make a doing-a-deed out of it: they posit the same event, first as cause and then as its effect. The scientists do no better when they say 'force moves, force causes' and such like, – all our science, in spite of its coolness and freedom from emotion, still stands exposed to the seduction of language and has not rid itself of the changelings foisted upon it, the 'subjects' (the atom is, for example, just such a changeling, likewise the Kantian, 'thing-in-itself'): no wonder, then, if the entrenched, secretly smouldering emotions of revenge and hatred put this belief to their own use and, in fact, do not defend any belief more passionately than that *the strong are free* to be weak, and the birds of prey are free to be lambs: – in this way, they gain the right to make the birds of prey *responsible* for being birds of prey ... When the oppressed, the downtrodden, the violated say to each other with the vindictive cunning of powerlessness: 'Let us be different from evil people, let us be good! And a good person is anyone who does not rape, does not harm anyone, who does not attack, does not retaliate, who leaves the taking of revenge to God, who keeps hidden as we do, avoids all evil and asks little from life in general, like us who are patient, humble and upright' – this means, if heard coolly and impartially, nothing more than: 'We weak people are just weak; it is good to do nothing *for which we are not strong enough*' – but this grim state of affairs, this cleverness of the lowest rank which even insects possess (which play dead, in order not to 'do too much' when in great danger), has, thanks to the counterfeiting and self-deception of powerlessness, clothed itself in the finery of self-denying, quiet, patient virtue, as though the weakness of the weak were itself – I mean its *essence*, its effect, its whole unique, unavoidable, irredeemable reality – a voluntary achievement, something wanted, chosen, a *deed*, an *accomplishment*. This type of man *needs* to believe in an unbiased 'subject' with freedom of choice, because he has an instinct of self-preservation and self-affirmation in which every life is sanctified. The reason the subject (or, as we more colloquially say, *the soul*) has been, until now, the best doctrine on earth, is perhaps because it facilitated that sublime self-deception whereby the majority of the dying, the weak and the oppressed of every kind could construe weakness itself as freedom, and their particular mode of existence as an *accomplishment*. [...]

Second essay: Guilt, bad consciousness

4. How, then, did that other 'dismal thing', the consciousness of guilt, the whole 'bad conscience', come into the world? – And with this we return to our genealogists of morality. I'll say it again – or maybe I haven't said it yet? – they are no good. No more than five spans of their own, merely 'modern' experience; no knowledge and no will to know the past; still less an instinct for history, a 'second sight' so necessary at this point – and yet they go in for the history of morality: of course, this must logically end in results that have a more than brittle relationship to the truth. Have these genealogists of morality up to now ever remotely dreamt that, for example, the main moral concept '*Schuld*' ('guilt') descends from the very material concept of '*Schulden*' ('debts')? Or that punishment, as *retribution*, evolved quite independently of any assumption about freedom or lack of freedom of the will? – and this to the point where a *high* degree of humanization had first to be achieved, so that the animal 'man' could begin to differentiate between those much more primitive nuances 'intentional', 'negligent', 'accidental', 'of sound mind' and their opposites, and take them into account when dealing out punishment. That inescapable thought, which is now so cheap and apparently natural, and which has had to serve as an explanation of how the sense of justice came about at all on earth, 'the criminal deserves to be punished *because* he could have acted otherwise', is actually an extremely late and refined form of human judgment and inference; whoever thinks it dates back to the beginning is laying his coarse hands on the psychology of primitive man in the wrong way. Throughout most of human history, punishment has *not* been meted out *because* the miscreant was held responsible for his act, therefore it was *not* assumed that the guilty party alone should be punished: – but rather, as parents still punish their children, it was out of anger over some wrong that had been suffered, directed at the perpetrator, – but this anger was held in check and modified by the idea that every injury has its *equivalent* which can be paid in compensation, if only through the *pain* of the person who injures. And where did this primeval, deeply-rooted and perhaps now ineradicable idea gain its power, this idea of an equivalence between injury and pain? I have already let it out: in the contractual relationship between *creditor* and *debtor*, which is as old as the very conception of a 'legal subject' and itself refers back to the basic forms of buying, selling, bartering, trade and traffic.

Notes

1 Goethe, *Faust* I. 3781f.
2 Immanuel Kant gives a number of different formulations of what he takes to be the basic principle of morality in his two major works on ethics, *The Groundwork of the Metaphysic of Morals* (1785) and the *Critique of Practical Reason* (1788). The first formulation of the 'categorical imperative' in *The Groundwork of the Metaphysic of Morals* reads: 'Act only on that maxim through which you can at the same time will that it become a universal law' (*Groundwork*, section 1).

4 Critique of ethics

Elizabeth Anscombe

Elizabeth Anscombe (1919–2001) is one of the major philosophers of the twentieth century. As Ludwig Wittgenstein's student and friend, she later became his literary executor, translated his *Philosophical Investigations* and followed in his footsteps as Professor of Philosophy at Cambridge University. While her focus was on metaphysics, particularly the problem of causality, and on action theory, developed notably in her classic book *Intention*, she also exerted a considerable influence on contemporary moral philosophy. She was involved herself in various ethical causes, protesting against the honorary degree conferred upon Harry Truman, whom she considered to be responsible for mass murders in Hiroshima and Nagasaki, and showing her support for the Catholic Church's position on reproduction by publicly opposing contraception and joining protests against the legalisation of abortion.

The text presented here is a turning point in the history of contemporary moral philosophy. In a sense, it marks the return to Aristotle that Alisdair MacIntyre would go on to champion in *After Virtue*. Elizabeth Anscombe radically attacks the two main philosophical trends in ethics: Kantianism, and its definition of morality in terms of obligation and duty, which she designates as the 'law conception of ethics'; and utilitarianism, above all its revised version in which the morality of an act is judged not according to whether or not rules have been respected but according to the effects produced. She labels this theory 'consequentialism', thus forging the term that would become the official designation of this approach of ethics. In strong and often ironic terms, she criticises the poverty of moral philosophy of her time, berating Kantian ethics for the theoretical confusion created by the expression 'ought' that does not differentiate between practical and moral necessity, and consequentialism as developed by Henry Sidgwick for the ethical indeterminacy consisting in not distinguishing between intended and foreseen consequences. According to her, Christianity, with its all-encompassing notions of good and evil defined by divine law, has made the moral question unthinkable. It is therefore necessary to return to more specific concepts, using terms such as 'untruthful', 'unchaste', or 'unjust' rather than 'wrong' and refounding ethics on the basis of psychology by looking at concepts such as action, intention, wanting, and eventually virtue.

I will begin by stating three theses which I present in this paper. The first is that it is not profitable for us at present to do moral philosophy; that should be laid aside at any rate until we have an adequate philosophy of psychology, in which we are conspicuously lacking. The second is that the concepts of obligation, and duty – *moral* obligation and *moral* duty, that is to say – and of what is *morally* right and wrong, and of the *moral* sense of "ought," ought to be jettisoned if this is psychologically possible; because they are survivals, or derivatives from survivals, from an earlier conception of ethics which no longer generally survives, and are only harmful without it. My third thesis is that the differences between the well-known English writers on moral philosophy from Sidgwick to the present day are of little importance. [...]

That I owe the grocer such-and-such a sum would be one of a set of facts which would be "brute" in relation to the description "I am a bilker." "Bilking" is of course a species of "dishonesty" or "injustice." (Naturally the consideration will not have any effect on my actions unless I want to commit or avoid acts of injustice.)

So far, in spite of their strong associations, I conceive "bilking," "injustice" and "dishonesty" in a merely "factual" way. That I can do this for "bilking" is obvious enough; "justice" I have no idea how to define, except that its sphere is that of actions which relate to someone else, but "injustice," its defect, can for the moment be offered as a generic name covering various species. E.g.: "bilking," "theft" (which is relative to whatever property institutions exist), "slander," "adultery," "punishment of the innocent."

In present-day philosophy an explanation is required how an unjust man is a bad man, or an unjust action a bad one; to give such an explanation belongs to ethics; but it cannot even be begun until we are equipped with a sound philosophy of psychology. For the proof that an unjust man is a bad man would require a positive account of justice as a "virtue." This part of the subject-matter of ethics is, however, completely closed to us until we have an account of what *type of characteristic* a virtue is – a problem, not of ethics, but of conceptual analysis – and how it relates to the actions in which it is instanced: a matter which I think Aristotle did not succeed in really making clear. For this we certainly need an account at least of what a human action is at all, and how its description as "doing such-and-such" is affected by its motive and by the intention or intentions in it; and for this an account of such concepts is required.

The terms "should" or "ought" or "needs" relate to good and bad: e.g. machinery needs oil, or should or ought to be oiled, in that running without oil is bad for it, or it runs badly without oil. According to this conception, of course, "should" and "ought" are not used in a special "moral" sense when one says that a man should not bilk. (In Aristotle's sense of the term "moral" (ἠθικός), they are being used in connection with a *moral* subject-matter: namely that of human passions and (non-technical) actions.) But they have now acquired a special so-called "moral" sense – i.e. a sense in which they imply some absolute verdict (like one of guilty/not guilty on a man) on what is described in the "ought" sentences used in certain types of context: not merely the contexts that *Aristotle* would call "moral" – passions and actions – but also some of the contexts that he would call "intellectual."

The ordinary (and quite indispensable) terms "should," "needs," "ought," "must" – acquired this special sense by being equated in the relevant contexts with "is obliged," or "is bound," or "is required to," in the sense in which one can be obliged or bound by law, or something can be required by law.

How did this come about? The answer is in history: between Aristotle and us came Christianity, with its *law* conception of ethics. For Christianity derived its ethical notions from the Torah. (One might be inclined to think that a law conception of ethics could arise only among people who accepted an allegedly divine positive law; that this is not so is shown by the example of the Stoics, who also thought that whatever was involved in conformity to human virtues was required by divine law.)

In consequence of the dominance of Christianity for many centuries, the concepts of being bound, permitted, or excused became deeply embedded in our language and thought. The Greek word "ἁμαρτάνειν," the aptest to be turned to that use, acquired the sense "sin," from having meant "mistake," "missing the mark," "going wrong." The Latin *peccatum* which roughly corresponded to ἁμάρτημα was even apter for the sense "sin," because it was already associated with "culpa" – "guilt" – a juridical notion. The blanket term "illicit," "unlawful," meaning much the same as our blanket term "wrong," explains itself. It is interesting that Aristotle did not have such a blanket term. He has blanket terms for wickedness – "villain," "scoundrel"; but of course a man is not a villain or a scoundrel by the performance of one bad action, or a few bad actions. And he has terms like "disgraceful," "impious"; and specific terms signifying defect of the relevant virtue, like "unjust"; but no term corresponding to "illicit." The extension of this term (i.e. the range of its application) could be indicated in his terminology only by a quite lengthy sentence: that is "illicit" which, whether it is a thought or a consented-to passion or an action or an omission in thought or action, is something contrary to one of the virtues the lack of which shows a man to be bad *qua* man. That formulation would yield a concept co-extensive with the concept "illicit."

To have a *law* conception of ethics is to hold that what is needed for conformity with the virtues failure in which is the mark of being bad *qua* man (and not merely, say, *qua* craftsman or logician) – that what is needed for *this*, is required by divine law. Naturally it is not possible to have such a conception unless you believe in God as a lawgiver; like Jews, Stoics, and Christians. But if such a conception is dominant for many centuries, and then is given up, it is a natural result that the concepts of "obligation," of being bound or required as by a law, should remain though they had lost their root; and if the word "ought" has become invested in certain contexts with the sense of "obligation," it too will remain to be spoken with a special emphasis and a special feeling in these contexts.

It is as if the notion "criminal" were to remain when criminal law and criminal courts had been abolished and forgotten. [...]

I should judge that Hume and our present-day ethicists had done a considerable service by showing that no content could be found in the notion "morally ought"; if it were not that the latter philosophers try to find an alternative (very fishy) content and to retain the psychological force of the term. It would be most reasonable to drop it. It has no reasonable sense outside a law conception of ethics; they are not going to maintain such a conception; and you can do ethics without it, as is shown by the example of Aristotle. It would be a great improvement if, instead of "morally wrong," one always named a genus such as "untruthful," "unchaste," "unjust." We should no longer ask whether doing something was "wrong," passing directly from some description of an action to this notion; we should ask whether, e.g., it was unjust; and the answer would sometimes be clear at once.

I now come to the epoch in modern English moral philosophy marked by Sidgwick. There is a startling change that seems to have taken place between Mill and Moore. Mill assumes, as we saw, that there is no question of calculating the particular consequences of an action such as murder or theft; and we saw too that his position was stupid, because it is not at all clear how an action *can* fall under just one principle of utility. In Moore and in subsequent academic moralists of England we find it taken to be pretty obvious that "the right action" is the action which produces the best possible consequences (reckoning among consequences the intrinsic values ascribed to certain kinds of act by some "Objectivists").[1] Now it follows from this that a man does well, subjectively speaking, if he acts for the best in the particular circumstances according to his judgment of the total consequences of this particular action. I say that this follows, not that any philosopher has said precisely that. For discussion of these questions can of course get extremely complicated: e.g. it can be doubted whether "such-and-such is the right action" is a satisfactory formulation, on the grounds that things have to exist to have predicates – so perhaps the best formulation is "I am obliged"; or again, a philosopher may deny that "right" is a "descriptive" term, and then take a roundabout route through linguistic analysis to reach a view which comes to the same thing as "the right action is the one productive of the best consequences" (e.g. the view that you frame your "principles" to effect the end you choose to pursue, the connexion between "choice" and "best" being supposedly such that choosing reflectively means that you choose how to act so as to produce the best consequences); further, the roles of what are called "moral principles" and of the "motive of duty" have to be described; the differences between "good" and "morally good" and "right" need to be explored, the special characteristics of "ought" sentences investigated. Such discussions generate an appearance of significant diversity of views where what is really significant is an overall similarity. The overall similarity is made clear if you consider that every one of the best known English academic moral philosophers has put out a philosophy according to which, e.g., it is not possible to hold that it cannot be right to kill the innocent as a means to any end whatsoever and that someone who thinks otherwise is in error. [...]

From the point of view of the present enquiry, the most important thing about Sidgwick was his definition of intention. He defines intention in such a way that one must be said to intend any foreseen consequences of one's voluntary action. This definition is obviously incorrect, and I dare say that no one would be found to defend it now. He uses it to put forward an ethical thesis which would now be accepted by many people: the thesis that it does not make any difference to a man's responsibility for something that he foresaw, that he felt no desire for it, either as an end or as a means to an end. Using the language of intention more correctly, and avoiding Sidgwick's faulty conception, we may state the thesis thus: it does not make any difference to a man's responsibility for an effect of his action which he can foresee, that he does not intend it. Now this sounds rather edifying; it is I think quite characteristic of very bad degenerations of thought on such questions that they sound edifying. We can see what it amounts to by considering an example. Let us suppose that a man has a responsibility for the maintenance of some child. Therefore deliberately to withdraw support from it is a bad sort of thing for him to do. It would be bad for him to withdraw its maintenance because he didn't want to maintain it any longer; *and* also bad for him to withdraw it because by doing so he would, let us say, compel someone else to do something. (We may suppose for the sake of argument that compelling that person to do that thing is in itself quite admirable.) But now he has to choose between doing something disgraceful and going to prison; if he goes to prison, it will follow that he withdraws support from the child. By Sidgwick's doctrine, there is no difference in his responsibility for ceasing to maintain the child, between the case where he does it for its own sake or as a means to some other purpose, and when it happens as a foreseen and unavoidable consequence of his going to prison rather than do something disgraceful. It follows that he must weigh up the relative badness of withdrawing support from the child and of doing the disgraceful thing; and it may easily be that the disgraceful thing is in fact a less vicious action than intentionally withdrawing support from the child would be; if then the fact that withdrawing support from the child is a side effect of his going to prison does not make any difference to his responsibility, this consideration will incline him to do the disgraceful thing; which can still be pretty bad. And of course, once he has started to look at the matter in this light, the only reasonable thing for him to consider will be the consequences and not the intrinsic badness of this or that action. So that, given that he judges reasonably that no *great* harm will come of it, he can do a much more disgraceful thing than deliberately withdrawing support from the child. And if his calculations turn out in fact wrong, it will appear that he was not responsible for the consequences, because he did not foresee them. For in fact Sidgwick's thesis leads to its being quite impossible to estimate the badness of an action except in the light of *expected* consequences. But if so, then *you* must estimate the badness in the light of the consequences *you* expect; and so it will follow that you can exculpate yourself from the *actual* consequences of the most disgraceful actions, so long as you can make out a case for not having foreseen them. Whereas I should contend that a man is responsible for the bad consequences of his bad actions, but gets no credit for the good ones; and contrariwise is not responsible for the bad consequences of good actions.

The denial of *any* distinction between foreseen and intended consequences, as far as responsibility is concerned, was not made by Sidgwick in developing any one "method of ethics"; he made this important move on behalf of everybody and just on its own account; and I think it plausible to suggest that *this* move on the part of Sidgwick explains the difference between old-fashioned Utilitarianism and that *consequentialism*, as I name it, which marks him and every English academic moral philosopher since him. [...]

But – is it not clear that there are several concepts that need investigating simply as part of the philosophy of psychology and, – as I should recommend – *banishing ethics totally* from our minds? Namely – to begin with: "action," "intention," "pleasure," "wanting." More will probably turn up if we start with these. Eventually it might be possible to advance to considering the concept "virtue"; with which, I suppose, we should be beginning some sort of a study of ethics.

I will end by describing the advantages of using the word "ought" in a non-emphatic fashion, and not in a special "moral" sense; of discarding the term "wrongs" in a "moral" sense, and using such notions as "unjust."

It is possible, if one is allowed to proceed just by giving examples, to distinguish between the intrinsically unjust, and what is unjust given the circumstances. To arrange to get a man judicially punished for something which it can be clearly seen he has not done is intrinsically unjust. This might be done, of course, and often has been done, in all sorts of ways; by suborning false witnesses, by a rule of law by which something is "deemed" to be the case which is admittedly not the case as a matter of fact, and by open insolence on the part of the judges and powerful people when they more or less openly say: "A fig for the fact that you did not do it; we mean to sentence you for it all the same." What is unjust given, e.g., normal circumstances is to deprive people of their ostensible property without legal procedure, not to pay debts, not to keep contracts, and a host of other things of the kind. Now, the circumstances can clearly make a great deal of difference in estimating the justice or injustice of such procedures as these; and these circumstances may *sometimes* include expected consequences; for example, a man's claim to a bit of property can become a nullity when its seizure and use can avert some obvious disaster: as, e.g., if you could use a machine of his to produce an explosion in which it would be destroyed, but by means of which you could divert a flood or make a gap which a fire could not jump. Now this certainly does not mean that what would ordinarily be an act of injustice, but is not intrinsically unjust, can always be rendered just by a reasonable calculation of better consequences; far from it; but the problems that would be raised in an attempt to draw a boundary line (or boundary area) here are obviously complicated. And while there are certainly some general remarks which ought to be made here, and some boundaries that can be drawn, the decision on particular cases would for the most part be determined κατὰ τὸν ὀρθὸν λόγον "according to what's reasonable", – e.g. that *such-and-such* a delay of payment of a *such-and-such* debt to a person *so* circumstanced, on the part of a person so circumstanced, would or would not be unjust, is really only to be decided "according to what's reasonable"; and for this there can *in principle* be no canon other than giving a few examples. That is to say, while it is because of a big gap in philosophy that we can give no general account of the concept of virtue and of the concept of justice, but have to proceed, using the concepts, only by giving examples; still there is an area where it is not because of any gap, but is in principle the case, that there is no account except by way of examples: and that is where the canon is "what's reasonable": which of course is *not* a canon.

That is all I wish to say about what is just in some circumstances, unjust in others; and about the way in which expected consequences can play a part in determining what is just. Returning to my example of the intrinsically unjust: if a procedure is one of judicially punishing a man for what he is clearly understood not to have done, there can be absolutely no argument about the description of this as unjust. No circumstances, and no expected consequences, which do *not* modify the description of the procedure as one of judicially punishing a man for what he is known not to have done can modify the description of it as unjust. Someone who attempted to dispute this would only be pretending not to know what "unjust" means: for this is a paradigm case of injustice.

And here we see the superiority of the term "unjust" over the terms "morally right" and "morally wrong." For in the context of English moral philosophy since Sidgwick it appears legitimate to discuss whether it *might* be "morally right" in some circumstances to adopt that procedure; but it cannot be argued that the procedure would in any circumstances be just.

Now I am not able to do the philosophy involved – and I think that no one in the present situation of English philosophy *can* do the philosophy involved – but it is clear that a good man is a just man; and a just man is a man who habitually refuses to commit or participate in any unjust actions for fear of any consequences, or to obtain any advantage, for himself or anyone else. Perhaps no one will disagree. But, it will be said, what is unjust is sometimes determined by expected consequences; and certainly that is true. But there are cases where it is not: now if someone says, "I agree, but all this wants a lot of explaining," then he is right, and, what is more, the situation at present is that we can't do the explaining; we lack the philosophic equipment. But if someone really thinks, *in advance*,[2] that it is open to question whether such an action as procuring the judicial execution of the innocent should be quite excluded from consideration – I do not want to argue with him; he shows a corrupt mind.

Notes

1 Oxford Objectivists of course distinguish between "consequences" and "intrinsic values" and so produce a misleading appearance of not being "consequentialists." But they do not hold – and Ross explicitly denies – that the gravity of, e.g., procuring the condemnation of the innocent is such that it cannot be outweighed by, e.g., national interest. Hence their distinction is of no importance.

2 If he thinks it in the concrete situation, he is of course merely a normally tempted human being. In discussion when this paper was read, as was perhaps to be expected, this case was produced: a government is required to have an innocent man tried, sentenced, and executed under threat of a "hydrogen bomb war." It would seem strange to me to have much hope of so averting a war threatened by such men as made this demand. But the most important thing about the way in which cases like this are invented in discussions, is the assumption that only two courses are open: here, compliance and open defiance. No one can say in advance of such a situation what the possibilities are going to be – e.g. that there is none of stalling by a feigned willingness to comply, accompanied by a skillfully arranged "escape" of the victim.

5 Morality and practice of the self

Michel Foucault

Michel Foucault (1926–1984) was a philosopher, social theorist and historian of ideas. After holding posts in Lille, Uppsala, Warsaw, Hamburg, Clermont-Ferrand, Tunis and Paris Vincennes, he went on to follow in his tutor Jean Hippolyte's footsteps with a Chair at the Collège de France under the title 'History of Systems of Thought'. His works *Madness and Civilization* and *The Birth of the Clinic*, followed by *The Order of Things* and *The Archaeology of Knowledge*, brought him international recognition. With *Discipline and Punish*, which retraces the genesis of the modern prison and disciplinary society, and *The Will to Knowledge*, the first volume of his *History of Sexuality* at the end of which he introduced the concepts of biopower and biopolitics, he moved from an archaeological to a genealogical approach. During the 1960s and 1970s, in the context of great political agitation within intellectual circles, he was involved in substantial militant activity, particularly with the Prison Information Group that he founded. The last years of his life, much of it spent on American campuses, notably at Berkeley, were marked by the continuation of his project of the history of sexuality and developing his teaching on governmentality and subjectivation.

Reflection on morality and ethics came relatively late in Michel Foucault's work: until the end of the 1970s, the latter was practically never mentioned while the former was only referred to negatively, assimilated to a form of soft domination. It was while working on his study on sexuality reading the Greek and Roman philosophers, examining techniques of the self and the government of others, and developing an interest in the hermeneutics of the subject, and in courage and truth (the title of his last lectures at the Collège de France), that he turned to morality and ethics. The text presented here appeared first as a journal article before becoming part of the introduction to *The Use of Pleasure*. Although only relatively recent, its influence has been considerable, notably in the anthropology of religion with the work of Talal Asad, Saba Mahmood, and James Laidlaw, and in the anthropology of ethics with the work of James Faubion and Carlo Caduff. For Michel Foucault, morality can be considered on three levels: as 'a moral code', i.e. a prescriptive ensemble regarding what should or should not be done in a given culture; 'the morality of behaviours', i.e. the way in which individuals act with regard to these rules and norms, complying more or less willingly to them or transgressing them more or less openly; and finally, 'the manner in which one ought to form oneself as an ethical subject', in other words how individuals work upon themselves, independently of the moral codes of society and the ways in which their behaviour conforms to these. Michel Foucault's interest is in these 'practices of the self' and the tension between subjection and subjectivation from which they derive, situated between external impositions and internal transformations.

It was logical to ask why the four great domains of relations in which it seemed that a free man in classical societies was able to develop and display his activity without encountering any major prohibition, were precisely the loci of an intense problematization of sexual practice. Why was it in those areas – apropos of the body, of the wife, of boys, and of truth – that the practice of pleasures became a matter for debate? Why did the bringing of sexual activity into these relations occasion anxiety, discussion, and reflection? Why did these axes of everyday experience give rise to a way of thinking that sought to rarefy sexual behavior, to moderate and condition it, and to define an austere style in the practice of pleasures? How did sexual behavior, insofar as it implied these different types of relations, come to be conceived as a domain of moral experience?

In order to answer this question, some methodological considerations need to be brought in; more specifically, it is best to reflect on the object one has in view when one undertakes to study the forms and transformations of a "morality."

Everyone is aware of the word's ambiguity. By "morality," one means a set of values and rules of action that are recommended to individuals through the intermediary of various prescriptive agencies such as the family (in one of its roles), educational institutions, churches, and so forth. It is sometimes the case that these rules and values are plainly set forth in a coherent doctrine and an explicit teaching. But it also happens that they are transmitted in a diffuse manner, so that, far from constituting a systematic ensemble, they form a complex interplay of elements that counterbalance and correct one another, and cancel each other out on certain points, thus providing for compromises or loopholes. With these qualifications taken into account, we can call this prescriptive ensemble a "moral code." But "morality" also refers to the real behavior of individuals in relation to the rules and values that are recommended to them: the word thus designates the manner in which they comply more or less fully with a standard of conduct, the manner in which they obey or resist an interdiction or a prescription; the manner in which they respect or disregard a set of values. In studying this aspect of morality, one must determine how and with what margins of variation or transgression individuals or groups conduct themselves in reference to a prescriptive system that is explicitly or implicitly operative in their culture, and of which they are more or less aware. We can call this level of phenomena "the morality of behaviors."

There is more. For a rule of conduct is one thing; the conduct that may be measured by this rule is another. But another thing still is the manner in which one ought to "conduct oneself" – that is, the manner in which one ought to form oneself as an ethical subject acting in reference to the prescriptive elements that make up the code. Given a code of actions, and with regard to a specific type of actions (which can be defined by their degree of conformity with or divergence from the code), there are different ways to "conduct oneself" morally, different ways for the acting individual to operate, not just as an agent, but as an ethical subject of this action. Take, for example, a code of sexual prescriptions enjoining the two marital partners to practice a strict and symmetrical conjugal fidelity, always with a view to procreation; there will be many ways, even within such a rigid frame, to practice that austerity, many ways to "be faithful." These differences can bear on several points worth considering.

They concern what might be called the *determination of the ethical substance*; that is, the way in which the individual has to constitute this or that part of himself as the prime material of his moral conduct. Thus, one can relate the crucial aspects of the practice of fidelity to the strict observance of interdictions and obligations in the very acts one accomplishes. But one can also make the essence of fidelity consist in the mastery of desires, in the fervent combat one directs against them, in the strength with which one is able to resist temptations: what makes up the content of fidelity in this case is that vigilance and that struggle. In these conditions, the contradictory movements of the soul – much more than the carrying out of the acts themselves – will be the prime material of moral practice. Alternatively, one can have it consist in the intensity, continuity, and reciprocity of feelings that are experienced vis-à-vis the partner, and in the quality of the relationship that permanently binds the two spouses.

The differences can also have to do with the *mode of subjection (mode d'assujettissement)*; that is, with the way in which the individual establishes his relation to the rule and recognizes himself as obliged to put it into practice. One can, for example, practice conjugal fidelity and comply with the precept that imposes it, because one acknowledges oneself to be a member of the group that accepts it, declares adherence to it out loud, and silently preserves it as a custom. But one can practice it, too, because one regards oneself as an heir to a spiritual tradition that one has the responsibility of maintaining or reviving; one can also practice fidelity in response to an appeal, by offering oneself as an example, or by seeking to give one's personal life a form that answers to criteria of brilliance, beauty, nobility, or perfection.

There are also possible differences in the forms of *elaboration*, of *ethical work (travail éthique)* that one performs on oneself, not only in order to bring one's conduct into compliance with a given rule, but to attempt to transform oneself into the ethical subject of one's behavior. Thus, sexual austerity can be practiced through a long effort of learning, memorization, and assimilation of a systematic ensemble of precepts, and through a regular checking of conduct aimed at measuring the exactness with which one is applying these rules. It can be practiced in the form of a sudden, all-embracing, and definitive renunciation of pleasures; it can also be practiced in the form of a relentless combat whose vicissitudes – including momentary setbacks – can have meaning and value in themselves; and it can be practiced through a decipherment as painstaking, continuous, and detailed as possible, of the movements of desire in all its hidden forms, including the most obscure.

Other differences, finally, concern what might be called the *telos* of the ethical subject: an action is not only moral in itself, in its singularity; it is also moral in its circumstantial integration and by virtue of the place it occupies in a pattern of conduct. It is an element and an aspect of this conduct, and it marks a stage in its life, a possible advance in its continuity. A moral action tends toward its own accomplishment; but it also aims beyond the latter, to the establishing of a moral conduct that commits an individual, not only to other actions always in conformity with values and rules, but to a certain mode of being, a mode of being characteristic of the ethical subject. Many differences are possible here as well: conjugal fidelity can be associated with a moral conduct that aspires to an ever more complete mastery of the self; it can be a moral conduct that manifests a sudden and radical detachment vis-à-vis the world; it may strain toward a perfect tranquillity of soul, a total insensitivity to the agitations of the passions, or toward a purification that will ensure salvation after death and blissful immortality.

In short, for an action to be "moral," it must not be reducible to an act or a series of acts conforming to a rule, a law, or a value. Of course all moral action involves a relationship with the reality in which it is carried out, and a relationship with the self.

The latter is not simply "self-awareness" but self-formation as an "ethical subject," a process in which the individual delimits that part of himself that will form the object of his moral practice, defines his position relative to the precept he will follow, and decides on a certain mode of being that will serve as his moral goal. And this requires him to act upon himself, to monitor, test, improve, and transform himself. There is no specific moral action that does not refer to a unified moral conduct; no moral conduct that does not call for the forming of oneself as an ethical subject; and no forming of the ethical subject without "modes of subjectivation" and an "ascetics" or "practices of the self" that support them. Moral action is indissociable from these forms of self-activity and they do not differ any less from one morality to another than do the systems of values, rules, and interdictions.

These distinctions are bound to have effects that are not confined to theory. They also have consequences for historical analysis. Anyone who wishes to study the history of a "morality" has to take into account the different realities that are covered by the term. A history of "moral behaviors" would study the extent to which actions of certain individuals or groups are consistent with the rules and values that are prescribed for them by various agencies. A history of "codes" would analyze the different systems of rules and values that are operative in a given society or group, the agencies or mechanisms of constraint that enforce them, the forms they take in their multifariousness, their divergences and their contradictions. And finally, a history of the way in which individuals are urged to constitute themselves as subjects of moral conduct would be concerned with the models proposed for setting up and developing relationships with the self, for self-reflection, self-knowledge, self-examination, for the decipherment of the self by oneself, for the transformations that one seeks to accomplish with oneself as object. This last is what might be called a history of "ethics" and "ascetics," understood as a history of the forms of moral subjectivation and of the practices of self that are meant to ensure it.

If it is true, in fact, that every morality, in the broad sense, comprises the two elements I have just mentioned: codes of behavior and forms of subjectivation; if it is true that they can never be entirely dissociated, though they may develop in relative independence from one another – then we should not be surprised to find that in certain moralities the main emphasis is placed on the code, on its systematicity, its richness, its capacity to adjust to every possible case and to embrace every area of behavior. With moralities of this type, the important thing is to focus on the instances of authority that enforce the code, that require it to be learned and observed, that penalize infractions; in these conditions, the subjectivation occurs basically in a quasi-juridical form, where the ethical subject refers his conduct to a law, or set of laws, to which he must submit at the risk of committing offenses that may make him liable to punishment. It would be quite incorrect to reduce Christian morality – one probably should say "Christian moralities" – to such a model; and yet it may not be wrong to think that the organization of the penitential system at the beginning of the thirteenth century, and its development up to the eve of the Reformation, brought about a very strong "juridification" – more precisely, a very strong "codification" – of the moral experience. It was against this codification that many spiritual movements reacted before the Reformation.

On the other hand, it is easy to conceive of moralities in which the strong and dynamic element is to be sought in the forms of subjectivation and the practices of the self. In this case, the system of codes and rules of behavior may be rather rudimentary. Their exact observance may be relatively unimportant, at least compared with what is required of the individual in the relationship he has with himself, in his different actions, thoughts, and feelings as he endeavors to form himself as an ethical subject. Here the emphasis is on the forms of relations with the self, on the methods and techniques by which he works them out, on the exercises by which he makes of himself an object to be known, and on the practices that enable him to transform his own mode of being. These "ethics-oriented" moralities (which do not necessarily correspond to those involving "ascetic denial") have been very important in Christianity, functioning alongside the "code-oriented" moralities. Between the two types there have been, at different times, juxtapositions, rivalries and conflicts, and compromises.

Now, it seems clear, from a first approach at least, that moral conceptions in Greek and Greco-Roman antiquity were much more oriented toward practices of the self and the question of *askesis* than toward codifications of conducts and the strict definition of what is permitted and what is forbidden. If exception is made of the *Republic* and the *Laws*, one finds very few references to the principle of a code that would define in detail the right conduct to maintain, few references to the need for an authority charged with seeing to its application, few references to the possibility of punishments that would sanction infractions. Although the necessity of respecting the law and the customs – the *nomoi* – was very often underscored, more important than the content of the law and its conditions of application was the attitude that caused one to respect them. The accent was placed on the relationship with the self that enabled a person to keep from being carried away by the appetites and pleasures, to maintain a mastery and superiority over them, to keep his senses in a state of tranquillity, to remain free from interior bondage to the passions, and to achieve a mode of being that could be defined by the full enjoyment of oneself, or the perfect supremacy of oneself over oneself.

This explains the choice of method I have kept to throughout this study on the sexual morality of pagan and Christian antiquity; that is, I had to keep in mind the distinction between the code elements of a morality and the elements of *ascesis*, neglecting neither their coexistence, their interrelations, their relative autonomy, nor their possible differences of emphasis. I had to take into account everything, in these moralities, that seemed to have to do with the privileged status of the practices of the self and the interest that may have been accorded them; with the effort that was made to develop them, perfect them, and teach them; and with the debate that went on concerning them. Consequently, the question that is so often raised regarding the continuity (or break) between the philosophical moralities of antiquity and Christian morality had to be reformulated; instead of asking what were the code elements that Christianity may have borrowed from ancient thought, and what were those that it added in its own right, in order to define what was permitted and what forbidden within a sexuality assumed to be constant, it seemed more pertinent to ask how, given the continuity, transfer, or modification of codes, the forms of self-relationship (and the practices of the self that were associated with them) were defined, modified, recast, and diversified.

I am not supposing that the codes are unimportant. But one notices that they ultimately revolve around a rather small number of rather simple principles: perhaps men are not much more inventive when it comes to interdictions than they are when it comes to pleasures. Their stability is also rather remarkable; the notable proliferation of codifications (concerning permitted or forbidden places, partners, and acts) occurred rather late in Christianity. On the other hand, it appears – at any rate this is the hypothesis I would like to explore here – that there is a whole rich and complex field of historicity in the way the individual is summoned to recognize himself as an ethical subject of sexual conduct. This will be a matter of seeing how that subjectivation was defined and transformed, from classical Greek thought up to the formulation of the Christian doctrine and pastoral ministry regarding the flesh.

6 A dialogue to come

Abraham Edel

Abraham Edel (1908–2007) was a philosopher who specialised in morality and ethics, and taught during his entire academic career at the City College of the City University of New York (CUNY), which was renowned at the time for its radical orientation and even its socialist leanings. His initial training was in ancient philosophy, but he then turned to the study of ethics and questioned the issue of moral relativism. His response, particularly in *Ethical Judgment: The Use of Science in Ethics*, was fundamentally rationalist, even positivist: while he recognised the diversity and variability of moral precepts, he claimed that it was possible to determine ethical principles through reason. He pursued this reflection in *Anthropology and Ethics*, which he co-authored with his second wife May Mandelbaum Edel, an anthropologist in African studies. It is one of the rare endeavours to systematically develop a comparative anthropology of morality.

The text presented here, published a few years after this book, takes up its subject again in a programmatic vein. Noting the lack of anthropological studies devoted to examining morality, Abraham Edel attempts to account for this without contenting himself with the usual explanations that the common understanding of morality is self-evident, or that it is abstract, or that it is heterogeneous. He states that it is necessary to work on the basis of a strong concept of morality, not by laying it out as a priori knowledge, which would lead to a form of ethnocentrism, but rather by building it on the basis of empirical data collected in different cultures. Under these conditions, it is possible to formulate a concept of morality that meets the triple necessity of being able to describe, of being a generalised value and of being independent from the other aspects of human life.

How are we to explain this lack of a well-articulated concept to serve as guide to enquiry? Three preliminary answers suggest themselves. One is that it is assumed that we all know what morality is and no explicit account need be given. If this is so, it is an unsatisfactory state of affairs. It runs the risk of ethno-centrism in our working conception of morality—for example, looking everywhere for pangs of conscience as a mark of the moral. Explicitness has been sought in mapping equally 'obvious' fields—legal or religious. Why not in the case of the moral?

A second path of explanation is to stress the practical difficulties in locating the moral. Morality is so abstractly ideational. There are no moral institutions or moral products to lay hold of, no priests or quasi-courts, or pictures and books. Perhaps we are still in the stage indicated by *Notes and Queries* when it says: 'The first rule in all investigations is to advance from the concrete and tangible to the abstract. Social events must be recorded as they happen. Accounts of how natives "think" or "feel" are of little value without information as to how they actually behave in concrete situations.'[1] I do not want to argue here the question whether morality is largely a matter of thought and feeling or how far in a Deweyan vein the moral situation is to be construed as one of the conflict of habits necessitating decision. But even thoughts and feelings have to be tackled in the long run, if the culture is to be understood. And interestingly enough, when John Ladd, a philosopher, worked among the Navaho specifically on questions of moral discourse, his major informant expressed to Kluckhohn[2] a genuine delight that here at last he was being asked really important questions! (But, of course, he was a sophisticated informant, and practically sent Kluckhohn grade reports on the different anthropological workers who kept coming to consult him.)

A third possible explanation is that there is some theoretical difficulty in the concept of the moral itself. It may, after all, be a residual or again a miscellaneous class of sanctions or motivations. Perhaps we only really discover a moral sanction by stripping off what is not definitely religious, or legal, or fear of violent action, and seeing that something is left moving people. Obviously, however, once this is located, we should want to pursue deliberately the identification of such motives. Even the miscellaneous invites itemization and the breaking up of the problem. But this third line of explanation does raise the possibility that in principle little more can be done anthropologically in the delineation of the moral than has so far been done practically. It is therefore important to probe for the implicit conceptions of the nature, scope, role, and relations of morality in the work of anthropologists, and to differentiate what may be different assumptions influencing the operation of research and the formulation of results. [...]

I turn finally to the concept of morality which we elaborated in *Anthropology and Ethics*, considered as a scientific construct for theoretical analysis and descriptive research. It is clear that anthropology has not furnished a systematic concept. It is perhaps not equally clear that philosophy has not furnished a systematic concept that can serve the anthropological purpose of descriptive investigation. Philosophy has many concepts, tied to different theoretical approaches. Some today talk of morals in terms of the apprehension of phenomenological qualities of fitness or requiredness. Some begin with distinctively ethical terms. Some prefer distinctive ethical uses of terms, such as to express certain emotions, or to decide, to commend, or persuade or subscribe. Some delimit a set of behaviourally or phenomenally described activities or states, such as being pleased by, or interested in, or approving of, or desiring for its own sake, or reflectively appraising, or ascribing obligations, recognizing claims, evaluating, and so on. The very wealth of candidates prevents us from committing ourselves antecedently to any one of them. From a descriptive point of view they provide us with a set of varying phenomena on the linguistic, psychological, phenomenological, interpersonal, and social level. We may suspect that in the long run any choice among them will rest not on initial presuppositions but on the results of empirical study of these kinds of phenomena and their interrelations in human life. But the study itself requires a guiding concept of what a morality is. What form, then, shall it take at the outset?

I indicated at the beginning that the concept of morality we proposed was descriptively oriented, that it was a generalized concept, and that it treated morality as relatively independent. It is possible now, in the light of our analyses in the preceding parts, to sketch the justification of these features.

The descriptive orientation is, of course, required for an anthropological comparative investigation. To show that it is a desirable orientation from the point of view of ethical theorizing is a large and difficult question. Its obvious advantages are that it would furnish a more or less demarcated domain of phenomena to which propositions about morality would refer, where verifying observations for factual assertions relevant to ethics could be identified and the assertions put to the test. The fuller justification of this orientation, however, could come only from taking stubborn issues in theoretical ethics and showing in detail how they can be reanalysed, paradoxes minimized, and familiar controversies at an impasse give way to specific tasks.[3] The analysis of the Kantian example above can serve as one illustration.

Our decision to fashion a generalized concept was guided by both anthropological and philosophical considerations. Three conditions may be set down for a contemporary descriptive concept of morality. (1) It must avoid ethnocentrism, that is, it must not choose such initial marks of the moral as would rule out in advance materials that might make a bid for inclusion. The policy to be followed is: better too much at first than too little. For example, we cannot say that it must deal with concepts of right and wrong, since it may turn out in some peoples to deal with what is safe and dangerous, or what is folk and un-folk. (2) The very marks of the moral must allow for the widest variety of possible cultural specialization. If one of the marks, for example, is a kind of individual feeling correlated with transgression, it must be so formulated as not to prejudge that it be a remorse type or a shame type, but must allow in advance for varied cultural patterning as a theoretic possibility. (3) It must make possible its own refinement as the systematic data on moralities are accumulated, as comparative empirical generalizations grow, or as established knowledge from other disciplines (e.g. psychology) casts light on the moral materials. The aim is, of course, eventual embodiment, within the marks, of knowledge that is acquired about moralities: for example, if there should turn out to be invariant feeling–responses to transgression, or if all injunctions turn out to be addressed directly or indirectly to the problem of interpersonal aggression (as Freud seemed to think), or if the social functions of moralities prove to be limited to a specific set of control aims. In short, we expect eventual revision in the concept of morality just as there has been revision in the concepts of religion and of law in anthropological investigation. But this is *after* comparative investigation.

A concept of morality satisfying these conditions could embrace all the phenomena pointed to by varying philosophical approaches and provide a field in which these approaches themselves could be put to the test. Accordingly, in *Anthropology and Ethics*, the generalized concept was explicated through an inventory of constituents. The constituents were partly types of content, and partly features of the way the content is organized in the life and consciousness of a people. A morality is thus taken to contain: selected rules enjoining or forbidding (e.g. a set of commandments), character-traits cultivated or avoided (virtues and vices), patterns of goals and means (ideals and instrumental values); a bounding concept of the moral community and a set of qualifications for a responsible person; a more or less distinctive selection of linguistic terms and rules for moral discourse; some patterns of systematization; some selected modes of justification; some selection from the range of human feelings which in complex ways is tied into the regulative procedures; and, involved in all of these, some specific existential perspective or view of man, his equipment, his place in nature, the human condition and predicament.

Such an approach uncovered many clues for understanding the integrated pattern of a morality, both the kinds of configurations to be looked for and the interrelations of morality with other phases of human life. It also pointed to ways in which each of the constituents might be sharpened in further research. Take, for example, a configurational feature like stringency in a morality. Comparatively, we found it could appear in: specific obligation-content where many acts are ruled in or ruled out; virtues, where firm adherence to rule is made the mark of appropriate character; ideals, where peace of mind in doing one's duty is a dominating goal; organization of moral discourse, where morality is cast in absolute rules rather than probability judgments; systematization, where deductive certainty is the garb that morality takes; sanctions, where punishment is heavy for simple violation; moral feelings, where the weight of guilt finds no ready expiation. Thus the identification of the one modality in a multitude of expressions made it possible to push further questions about causal and functional relations—where stringency is to be attributed to a traditional personality type, to social pressures and continuing tensions, and so on. It seemed to us, therefore, that the generalized concept 'paid off' rapidly in opening up more clearly areas for investigation.

As for the feature of relative independence for morality, I have in part argued for this by showing that the reassurances on behalf of a specific institutional location or on behalf of a dispersed concept of morality are inadequate. In part, of course, the proposed construct has to justify itself by how it works out in anthropological and philosophical enquiry. One of its special advantages is that it prevents morality from being narrowly construed in terms of some initial hypothesis about its nature, causes and functions—as has happened so often in wholesale social theories. The stress on independence makes the search for antecendent data a primary goal. Hypotheses about what morality can be correlated with stand out separately, instead of being built into initial definitions. Independently establishing the data thus serves the methodological role of widening the range of evidence for social theories.

Notes

1 *Notes and Queries on Anthropology* (1951, sixth edition). London: Royal Anthropological Institute, p. 37.
2 Ladd, John (1957), *The Structure of a Moral Code*, Cambridge, MA: Harvard University Press, p. xiv.
3 See Edel, Abraham (1963), *Method in Ethical Theory*, Indianapolis, IN: Bobbs-Merrill, chapter 10 for a sampling of such analysis.

Premises of a science of morality

7 Notes and queries

Edward Burnett Tylor

Edward Burnett Tylor (1832–1917) was a British anthropologist, considered as one of the founders of the discipline. Educated by Quakers, he became an eclectic autodidact who broached many themes of the nascent field focusing on faraway societies, calling upon ethnographic data and even statistics far more than his contemporaries, such as James Frazer. Influenced by the evolutionist theories of his time, he developed his own version of cultural evolutionism. After an initial empirical study of Mexican society, in 1871 he published his theoretical masterpiece, *Primitive Culture*, which opens with the now famous definition: 'Culture, or civilization, taken in its broad, ethnographic sense, is that complex whole which includes knowledge, belief, art, morals, law, custom, and any other capabilities and habits acquired by man as a member of society.' After having been curator of the University Museum at Oxford, he became the first professor of anthropology at the university.

The brief text presented here testifies to this empirical concern. It can be read as the first attempt to grasp the cultural diversity of value systems in ethnographical terms. *Notes and Queries on Anthropology*, four volumes of which were published between 1870 and 1920 under the aegis of the British Association for the Advancement of Science and the Royal Anthropological Institute, was the ideal locus for publishing these short articles mixing theoretical intuitions and methodological orientations, notably the famous ethnographic questionnaires aimed at providing guidelines for fieldwork. Edward Tylor begins by rejecting any external moral judgement of other societies' morality before setting out the epistemological principle consisting in understanding a system of values from the perspective of the social group in question. This would become a distinctive principle of anthropology. He continues by putting forward a series of general statements about these systems of value, which are in fact a set of relativist statements, since each society adopts its own norms, which are sometimes in contradiction with those of the neighbouring group: there is therefore a universality of morality without there being moral universals. The questionnaire aims to reach an understanding of this essential dual hypothesis through the use of precise queries.

The imperfection of our accounts of morals among savage and barbarous peoples is in a great measure due to travellers supposing the particular system of morals in which they themselves were educated to be the absolute system; thus they have merely approved or condemned what corresponded with, or opposed their own notions, but have scarcely ever appreciated the fact that every tribe has its own system of morality, based on its own principles of right and wrong. It is necessary to place ourselves at the point of view of the particular tribe, to understand its moral scheme. The leading ideas to be borne in mind are especially the following: That every tribe makes a distinction between right and wrong, but hardly two tribes exactly agree on what acts are right and what wrong; in fact, there is hardly any act considered wicked and abominable by some men, that is not somewhere or other looked on as harmless or virtuous, e.g., infanticide, treachery, &c. Next, that in all peoples, civilized or not, there exists an ideal high standard of morals, while public opinion tolerates or approves a lower practical standard: it is desirable to obtain a definition of both. Also the moral standard varies from age to age, as our own has changed in the last thousand years; all records of such variations are important. Lastly, the moral standard differs, as between members of a family, members of a nation, or tribe, or alliance, and aliens and enemies; among many nations it may be held right and even glorious to cheat, plunder, illuse, or even murder a stranger, or foreigner, or one of another religion, but wrong to act thus towards a kinsman, fellow-citizen, or co-religionist.

1. What words are used to express right and wrong, virtuous and vicious?
2. Do terms such as good and bad also denote this distinction when a man is described as good or bad? what characters correspond to this description?
3. Are there well-known precepts as to what acts are right or wrong? are these taught to children, or inculcated in any ceremonial act by elders or priests?
4. Do popular legends, &c., set up heroic ideals of virtue?
5. What is the practical judgment of public opinion as to what conduct is admirable and glorious? What is required of every man on pain of public disapprobation? And what conduct is held wicked, vile, despicable?
6. What distinction is drawn between punishable crimes and wrong acts only to be visited by public reprobation?
7. What acts of oppression or cruelty may be done by the father in his family or the chief in his tribe, without its being any one's place to condemn him?
8. What acts are considered wrong when done against a tribesman, but right when done against an alien (e.g., theft, deceit, &c.)?
9. Is any moral code ascribed to an ancient lawgiver, hero, or deity?
10. Is religious influence brought to bear on moral conduct? Are gods or spirits considered to punish certain acts by afflicting the doer or his family?
11. Is any moral or immoral conduct considered to affect the state of a man's soul during life or after death?
12. Is it wrong to do harm to the person or property of a non-tribesman or member of a hostile tribe? Are there exceptional cases?
13. Is wanton ill-treatment of wives, children, and slaves wrong? And who may protest?
14. Is hospitality inculcated toward tribesmen or all men? Is it wicked to refuse it and mean to stint it?
15. Is giving away or sharing of food and other property a duty or a virtuous act? What is the notion of liberality and generosity?
16. Is covetousness condemned? And is the accumulation of property regarded as an avaricious act?
17. Is it wrong to steal from one's friends and tribesmen?
18. Is it wrong to rob strangers?
19. Is cheating approved or condemned? And what difference does it make whether the person cheated is a friend or stranger?

20. Is lying wrong in itself, or under particular circumstances?
21. Is the breaking of solemn engagements or oaths condemned? And what is the usual judgment as to treachery?
22. Is abstemiousness in eating, and temperance in, or abstinence from, use of intoxicating drink approved?
23. Are gluttony, laziness, dirtiness, gossipping, tale-bearing, &c., condemned?
24. Is reverence to the aged a duty or virtue? And is its neglect condemned?
25. Is general courtesy and kindness inculcated and rudeness condemned?
26. What are the rules of right and wrong as to unchastity in either sex before marriage?
27. After marriage, are acts of unchastity offences which public opinion takes account of as wrong?
28. Is adultery a personal injury, or an offence against morals, or both?
29. How does public opinion judge of unnatural crimes?
30. Is selfishness considered a vice?
31. How is cowardice judged of?
32. Are bravery, ferocity, tenacity of revenge, endurance of pain and hardship, and other warlike qualities looked on as the chief virtues?
33. How are such warlike virtues accounted of in comparison with the milder virtues of kindness, generosity, &c.?
34. Can offences against public feeling be atoned for by courageous acts?

8 The determination of moral facts

Émile Durkheim

Émile Durkheim (1858–1917) was one of the founders of sociology, which he sought to establish as an autonomous science grounded in a positivist approach. Born to a family of rabbis, and trained in philosophy in Paris, he was a professor at the University of Bordeaux before taking up a chair in pedagogy at the Sorbonne, where he taught generations of teachers. His books *The Division of Labor in Society*, *Suicide*, and *The Elementary Forms of the Religious Life* implemented his famous 'rules of the sociological method' with the dual affirmation that 'social facts' should be treated 'as things' and that 'the determining cause of a social fact must be sought among antecedent social facts and not among the states of the individual consciousness'. The school of thought that he built around him through the publication of the journal *L'Année Sociologique*, with Célestin Bouglé, Henri Hubert, Robert Hertz, Marcel Mauss and François Simiand, played a key role in the structuring of French sociology in the first half of the twentieth century.

According to Émile Durkheim, the general principles of sociology could be perfectly applied to the study of morality and he was writing a book on this subject when he died. The text presented here, initially published in the *Bulletin de la Société Française de Philosophie* and discussed at the institution's meeting on 2 February 1906, brings together the main elements of his thinking on what he calls the 'moral fact'. Rejecting the normative study of morality, as carried out by religion, he suggests an analytical approach. First, taking inspiration from Kantian deontology, he defines morality as rules of conduct imposed upon individuals by a sense of duty and also by the desirability of what is 'good'. Second, seeking the sources of morality, he locates them not in the individual but rather in the collective. In this way, his moral theory is part of a wider theory of society. This sociological reading of morality has had a profound influence on the anthropology of morality, leading in particular to the development of research surrounding the moral codes specific to each society.

Theses

Moral reality, like all reality, can be studied from two different points of view. One can set out to explore and understand it and one can set out to evaluate it. The first of these problems, which is theoretical, must necessarily precede the second, and it is the only one with which we shall deal here. In closing, however, we shall show that the methods followed and the solutions adopted leave the field clear for the treatment of the practical problem.

For the theoretical study of moral reality we must determine beforehand the nature of moral facts. In order to observe them we must know their characteristics so that we can recognize them. This is the first question we shall deal with. Later we shall see if it is possible to give a satisfactory explanation of these characteristics.

I. What are the distinctive characteristics of a moral fact?
All morality appears to us as a system of rules of conduct. But all techniques are equally ruled by maxims that prescribe the behaviour of the agent in particular circumstances. What then is the difference between moral rules and other rules of technique?

(i) We shall show that moral rules are invested with a special authority by virtue of which they are obeyed simply because they command. We shall reaffirm, as a result of a purely empirical analysis, the notion of duty and nevertheless give a definition of it closely resembling that already given by Kant. Obligation is, then, one of the primary characteristics of the moral rule.
(ii) In opposition to Kant, however, we shall show that the notion of duty does not exhaust the concept of morality. It is impossible for us to carry out an act simply because we are ordered to do so and without consideration of its content. For us to become the agents of an act it must interest our sensibility to a certain extent and appear to us as, in some way, *desirable*. Obligation or duty only expresses one aspect abstracted from morality. A certain degree of desirability is another characteristic no less important than the first.

Something of the nature of duty is found in the desirability of morality. If it is true that the content of the act appeals to us, nevertheless its nature is such that it cannot be accomplished without effort and self-constraint. The *élan*, even the enthusiasm, with which we perform a moral act takes us outside ourselves and above our nature, and this is not achieved without difficulty and inner conflict. It is this *sui generis* desirability which is commonly called *good*.

Desirability and obligation are the two characteristics which it is useful to stress, without necessarily denying the existence of others. It will be our main intention to show that all moral acts have these two characteristics, even though they may be combined in different proportions.

In order to give some idea of these two partly contradictory aspects of moral facts, we shall compare them to the idea of *sacredness*, which has the same duality. The sacred being is in a sense forbidden; it is a being which may not be violated; it is also good, loved and sought after. The association of these two qualities will be justified: (i) historically by an examination of the filiation which links them; (ii) by examples taken from contemporary morality. The human personality is a sacred thing; one dare not violate it nor infringe its bounds, while at the same time the greatest good is in communion with others.

II. Having determined these characteristics, we should try to discover a means of understanding how it is that certain precepts are obeyed because they command, and also cause us to perform those acts which are desirable in the sense that we have noted above. A methodical reply to this question would call for as exhaustive a study as possible of the particular rules, the sum total of which constitutes our morality. But instead of such a study, which is impossible in these circumstances, it is possible to use more summary means to arrive at results of some value.

By examining the contemporary moral consciousness (and checking our findings by what we know of the moralities of all known peoples) we can agree upon the following points: (i) The qualification 'moral' has never been given to an act which has individual interests, or the perfection of the individual from a purely egotistic point of view, as its object; (ii) if I as an individual do not constitute *in myself* a moral end, this is also true of the other individuals who are more or less like me; (iii) from which we conclude that, *if a morality exists*, it can only have as object the group formed by the associated individuals—that is to say, society, *with the condition that society be always considered as being qualitatively different from the individual beings that compose it*. Morality begins with membership of a group, whatever that group may be. When this premise is accepted the characteristics of the moral fact become explicable. First, we shall show how society is good and desirable for the individual who cannot exist without it or deny it without denying himself, and how at the same time, because society surpasses the individual, he cannot desire it without to a certain extent violating his nature as an individual.

Secondly, we shall show that society, while being good, constitutes a moral authority which, by manifesting itself in certain precepts particularly important to it, confers upon them an obligatory character.

We shall endeavour further to establish that certain ends—devotion between individuals, the devotion of a scientist to his work—which are not in themselves moral ends, participate of morality indirectly and by derivation.

Finally, an analysis of collective sentiments will explain the characteristic of *sacredness* which is attributed to moral facts; an analysis which will, however, only serve to confirm the preceding analysis.

III. The objection has been made to this conception that it subjugates the mind to the prevailing moral opinion. This is not so. The society that morality bids us desire is not the society as it *appears* to itself, but the society as it is or is really becoming. The consciousness which society may have of itself which is expressed in general opinion (*dans et par l'opinion*) may be an inadequate view of the underlying reality. It is possible that opinion, weighed down by survivals, lags behind the real condition of the society. It is also possible that, under the effect of passing circumstances, certain principles, even though essential to the existing morality, may for a time be relegated to the unconscious and so appear not to exist. The science of morality will allow us to rectify these errors, of which we shall later give examples.

But we shall maintain that it is impossible to desire a morality other than that endorsed by the condition of society at a given time. To desire a morality other than that implied by the nature of society is to deny the latter and, consequently, oneself.

The question remains: Should a man deny himself? This is a legitimate question, but we shall not examine it. We shall postulate that we are right in wishing to live. [...]

Discussion

I. Moral reality appears to us under two different aspects that must be clearly distinguished: the objective and the subjective.

Each people at a given moment of its history has a morality, and it is in the name of this ruling morality that tribunals condemn and opinion judges. For a given group there is a clearly defined morality. I postulate, then, supported by the facts, that there is a general morality common to all individuals belonging to a collectivity.

Now, apart from this morality there is an indefinite multitude of others. Each individual moral conscience expresses the collective morality in its own way. Each one sees it and understands it from a different angle. No individual can be completely in tune with the morality of his time, and one could say that there is no conscience that is not in some ways immoral. Each mind, under the influence of its milieu, education or heredity sees moral rules by a different light. One individual will feel the rules of civic morality keenly, but not so strongly the rules of domestic morality, or inversely. Another who feels only very slightly the duties of charity may have a profound respect for contract and justice. The most essential aspects of morality are seen differently by different people.

I do not intend to treat here of both these two sorts of moral reality, but only of the first. I shall deal with objective moral reality, that common and impersonal standard by which we evaluate action. The diversity of individual moral consciences shows how impossible it is to make use of them in order to arrive at an understanding of morality itself. Research into the conditions that determine these individual variations of morality would, no doubt, be an interesting psychological study, but would not help us to reach our particular goal.

Just as I am not concerned with the manner in which this or that particular individual sees morality, I also leave on one side the opinions of philosophers and moralists. I have nothing whatever to do with their systematic attempts to explain or construct moral reality except in so far as one can find in them a more or less adequate expression of the morality of their time. A moralist has a far greater sensibility than the average man to the dominant moral trends of his time, and consequently his consciousness is more representative of the moral reality. But I refuse to accept his doctrines as explanations, as scientific expressions of past or present moral reality. […]

The first question that confronts us, as in all rational and scientific research, is: By what characteristics can we recognize and distinguish moral facts?

Morality appears to us to be a collection of maxims, of rules of conduct. But there are also other rules that prescribe our behaviour. All utilitarian techniques are governed by analogous systems of rules, and we must find the distinguishing characteristics of moral rules. If we consider all the rules that govern conduct we shall be able to see whether there are not some that have peculiar and specific characteristics. If we agree that the rules that show these characteristics conform to the popular conception of moral rules, we shall be able to apply to them the usual title and to say that here we have the characteristics of moral reality.

To achieve any result at all in this research there is only one method of proceeding. We must discover the intrinsic differences between these moral rules and other rules through their apparent and exterior differences, for at the beginning this is all that is accessible to us. We must find a reagent that will force moral rules to demonstrate their specific character. The reagent we shall employ is this: We shall put these various rules to the test of violation and see whether from this point of view there is not some difference between moral rules and rules of technique.

The violation of a rule generally brings unpleasant consequences to the agent. But we may distinguish two different types of consequence: (i) The first results mechanically from the act of violation. If I violate a rule of hygiene that orders me to stay away from infection, the result of this act will automatically be disease. The act, once it has been performed, sets in motion the consequences, and by analysis of the act we can know in advance what the result will be. (ii) When, however, I violate the rule that forbids me to kill, an analysis of my act will tell me nothing. I shall not find inherent in it the subsequent blame or punishment.

There is complete heterogeneity between the act and its consequence. It is impossible to discover *analytically* in the act of murder the slightest notion of blame. The link between act and consequence is here a *synthetic* one.

Such consequences attached to acts by synthetic links I shall call *sanctions*. I do not as yet know the origin or explanation of this link. I merely note its existence and nature, without at the moment going any further.

We can, however, enlarge upon this notion. Since sanctions are not revealed by analysis of the act that they govern, it is apparent that I am not punished *simply because* I did this or that. It is not the intrinsic nature of my action that produces the sanction which follows, but the fact that the act violates the rule that forbids it. In fact, one and the same act, identically performed with the same material consequences, is blamed or not blamed according to whether or not there is a rule forbidding it. The existence of the rule and the relation to it of the act determine the sanction. Thus homicide, condemned in time of peace, is freed from blame in time of war. An act, intrinsically the same, which is blamed today among Europeans, was not blamed in ancient Greece since there it violated no pre-established rule.

We have now reached a deeper conception of sanctions. A sanction is the consequence of an act that does not result from the content of that act, but from the violation by that act of a pre-established rule. It is because there is a pre-established rule, and the breach is a rebellion against this rule, that a sanction is entailed.

Thus there are rules that present this particular characteristic: We refrain from performing the acts they forbid simply because they are forbidden. This is what is meant by the obligatory character of the moral rule. We rediscover by a rigorously empirical analysis the idea of *duty* and obligation almost as Kant understood it.

We have so far only considered negative sanctions (blame, punishment), since in these the characteristic of obligation is most apparent. There are sanctions of another kind. Acts that conform to the moral rule are praised and those who accomplish them are honoured. In this case the public moral consciousness reacts in a different way and the consequence of the act is favourable to the agent, but the mechanism of this social phenomenon is the same. As in the preceding instance the sanction comes, not from the act itself, but from its conformity to a rule that prescribes it. No doubt this type of obligation differs slightly from the former in degree, but we have here two varieties of the same group. There are not two kinds of moral rules, negative and positive commands; both are but two classes within the same category. [...]

So far we have followed Kant fairly closely. But if his analysis of moral acts is in part correct, it is nevertheless incomplete and insufficient, since it shows us only one aspect of moral reality. We cannot perform an act which is not in some way meaningful to us simply because we have been commanded to do so. It is psychologically impossible to pursue an end to which we are indifferent—i.e. that does not appear to us as *good* and does not affect our sensibility. Morality must, then, be not only obligatory but also desirable and desired. This *desirability* is the second characteristic of all moral acts.

This desirability peculiar to moral life participates of the preceding characteristic of obligation, and is not the same as the desirability of the objects that attract our ordinary desires. The nature of our desire for the commanded act is a special one. Our *élan* and aspiration are accompanied by discipline and effort. Even when we carry out a moral act with enthusiasm we feel that we dominate and transcend ourselves, and this cannot occur without a feeling of tension and self-restraint. We feel that we do violence to a part of our being. Thus we must admit a certain element of eudemonism and one could show that desirability and pleasure permeate the obligation. We find charm in the accomplishment of a moral act prescribed by a rule that has no other justification than that it is a rule. We feel a *sui generis* pleasure in performing our duty simply because it is our duty. The notion of good enters into those of duty and obligation just as they in turn enter into the notion of good. Eudemonism and its contrary pervade moral life.

Duty, the Kantian Imperative, is only one abstract aspect of moral reality. In fact, moral reality always presents simultaneously these two aspects which cannot, in fact, be isolated. No act has ever been performed as a result of duty alone; it has always been necessary for it to appear in some respect as good. Inversely there is no act that is purely desirable, since all call for some effort.

Just as the idea of obligation, the first characteristic of moral life, gave us the opportunity to criticize utilitarianism, the second characteristic, that of goodness, shows us the insufficiency of Kant's explanation of moral obligation. Kant's hypothesis, according to which the sentiment of obligation was due to the heterogeneity of reason and sensibility, is not easy to reconcile with the fact that moral ends are in one aspect objects of desire. If to a certain extent sensibility has the same end as reason, it cannot be humbled by submitting to the latter.

Are these, then, the only two characteristics of moral reality? They are not, and I could demonstrate others. The two that I have just noted appear to me to be the most important, constant and universal. I know of no moral rule or morality where they are not found. However, in different instances they combine in varied proportions. There are acts which are accomplished almost exclusively by enthusiasm, acts of moral heroism where the element of obligation is at a minimum and where the idea of goodness predominates. There are others also where the idea of duty finds a minimum of support in the sensibility. The relation between these two elements also varies with time; thus in antiquity it would "appear that the notion of duty was on the wane; in the systems of morality, and perhaps in the everyday life of the people, the idea of the Sovereign Good predominated. Generally speaking, I believe it is the same wherever morality is essentially religious. In the same epoch the relation of the two elements may vary in the extreme in different individuals. Different persons feel in different degrees the attraction of one or other of these elements, and it is very rarely indeed that both exert an equal attraction. Each one of us has his moral blind spots. There are those for whom moral acts are above all good and desirable; there are those with a greater feeling for the rule itself who enjoy discipline, loathe anything indeterminate, and wish their lives to follow a rigid programme and their conduct to be constantly controlled by inflexible rules." [...]

Further, there is another idea that presents the same duality: the idea of the *sacred*. The sacred object inspires us, if not with fear, at least with respect that keeps us at a distance; at the same time it is an object of love and aspiration that we are drawn towards. Here, then, is a dual sentiment which seems to be self-contradictory but does not for all that cease to be real.

The human personality presents a notable example of this apparent duality which we have just distinguished. On the one hand, it inspires us with a religious respect that keeps us at some distance. Any encroachment upon the legitimate sphere of action of our fellow beings we regard as a sacrilege. It is, as it were, sacrosanct and thus apart. But at the same time human personality is the outstanding object of our sympathy and we endeavour to develop it. It is an ideal to be realized in ourselves as completely as possible.

If I compare the idea of the sacred with that of the moral, it is not merely in order to draw an interesting analogy. It is because it is very difficult to understand moral life if we do not relate it to religious life. For centuries morals and religion have been intimately linked and even completely fused. Even today one is bound to recognize this close association in the majority of minds. It is apparent that moral life has not been, and never will be, able to shed all the characteristics that it holds in common with religion. When two orders of facts have been so closely linked, when there has been between them so close a relationship for so long a time, it is impossible for them to be dissociated and become distinct. For this to happen they would have to undergo a complete transformation and so change their nature. There must, then, be morality in religion and elements of the religious in morality. In fact, present moral life abounds in the religious. These religious elements do not remain unchanged and it is certain that the religious sentiment of morality tends to become quite a different thing from that of theology. The characteristic of the sacred in morality does not lift it above criticism, as it does religion. But this is only a difference of degree and scarcely recognized by the majority even today. We may cite as proof the repugnance shown to any attempt to apply to morality the ordinary methods of science.

It would seem that in presuming to think of it and study it with the procedures of profane science we are *profaning* morality itself and threatening its dignity. Our contemporaries do not willingly admit that moral reality may, with all other realities, be submitted to discussion.

II. I have now reached the second part of my exposition, and it is here most of all that I feel certain scruples. Having determined the characteristics of moral reality, I wish to attempt some explanation of them. [...]

Morality begins with life in the group, since it is only there that disinterestedness and devotion become meaningful. I speak of the life of the group generally; there are different groups—the family, the corporation, the city, the nation and the international group. A hierarchy could be established for these various groups and one would find corresponding degrees of moral activity according to the field concerned, according to the size of the society, its degree of complexity and specialization. At the moment there is little point in discussing these problems. It is enough that we mark the point where the domain of moral life appears to begin, without introducing a differentiation. Moral life begins with membership of a group, however small the group may be.

We can see now how certain acts that we have left on one side during our discussion can take on, indirectly, a moral character. The interests of others can have, we noted, no more intrinsic moral value than our own. In so far, however, as another participates in the life of the group and in so far as he is a member of the collectivity to which we are attached, he tends to take on some of its dignity and he becomes an object of our affection and interest. To be a member of the society is, as we shall shortly show, to be bound to the social ideal. There is a little of this ideal in each one of us. It is then natural that each individual participates to some extent in the religious aspect which this ideal inspires. Attachment to a group implies a necessary, if indirect, attachment to individuals. When the social ideal is a particular form of the ideal of humanity, when the type of citizen blends to a great extent with the generic type of man, it is to man as such that we find ourselves bound. This explains the moral character which is attributed to feelings of sympathy between individuals and the acts which they inspire. It is not that they themselves constitute the intrinsic elements of the moral temperament, but they are so closely—if indirectly—bound to the most essential moral attitudes that we may take their absence as very probably an index of a lesser morality. When one loves one's country or humanity one cannot see one's fellows suffer without suffering oneself and without feeling a desire to help them. But what binds us morally to others is nothing intrinsic in their empirical individuality; it is the superior end of which they are the servants and instruments.

We are now in a position to understand how it is that there are rules called moral rules which we must obey because they command and which direct our actions to ends that transcend us while at the same time appearing desirable. We have just seen that society is the end of all moral activity. Now (i) while it transcends the individual it is immanent in him; (ii) it has all the characteristics of a moral authority that imposes respect.

9 The ethic of capitalism

Max Weber

Max Weber (1864–1920) was a German sociologist whose work was seminal for the social sciences in general. His contribution to the understanding of modernity through the concepts of rationalisation and disenchantment has been essential, as has his contribution to epistemology with the development of his method of comprehensive interpretation. Brought up in a family of intellectuals, he studied law at Heidelberg and Berlin. He became a lawyer while continuing an academic career in history and taking an interest in social policy. After the publication of his research on the 'Polish question', he was appointed professor of economics at the University of Freiburg and then the University of Heidelberg, which he left a few years later due to health problems. This withdrawal from academic life was compensated by a position as associate editor for the *Archives for Social Science and Social Welfare*, which allowed him to devote his time to academic writing, most of his work being published posthumously, in particular the monumental *Economy and Society*. Having always been involved in contemporary public life, he became more actively engaged against German expansionism during the First World War and at the end of the conflict became an important political figure with the German Democratic Party. After a brief return to the academic world as a professor in Vienna and then in Munich, during which period he gave the two famous lectures translated into English under the titles *Science as a Vocation* and *Politics as a Vocation*, he died of the Spanish flu.

The extract presented here is taken from the beginning of *The Protestant Ethic and the Spirit of Capitalism*. The book was conceived of as an introduction to a much more ambitious work aiming to found a sociology of religion and include studies of the Indian, Chinese, and Jewish religions. Concerning more specifically the Protestant ethic, Max Weber shows that it played a crucial role in the development of the capitalist economy because of the values it promoted and the conduct it legitimised. The concept of *Beruf*, translated by vocation and meaning both profession and calling, is central because it links work and meaning, the perspective of profit and that of salvation. Max Weber's interest is more in the behaviour that the Protestant ethos makes socially useful and morally necessary than in a religious doctrine producing – or simply justifying – the yearning to possess an ascetic practice. How has one come to consider that the material belongings of this world no longer need to be rejected in order to conform to one's faith, but rather need to be cultivated and valued in order to better obey divine law, or even God's calling? That is the question this text attempts to answer, rejecting the Marxist vision that reduces religion to an ideology and institutions to a superstructure.

If we try to determine the object, the analysis and historical explanation of which we are attempting, it cannot be in the form of a conceptual definition, but at least in the beginning only a provisional description of what is here meant by the spirit of capitalism. Such a description is, however, indispensable in order clearly to understand the object of the investigation. For this purpose we turn to a document of that spirit which contains what we are looking for in almost classical purity, and at the same time has the advantage of being free from all direct relationship to religion, being thus, for our purposes, free of preconceptions.

> "Remember, that *time* is money. He that can earn ten shillings a day by his labour, and goes abroad, or sits idle, one half of that day, though he spends but sixpence during his diversion or idleness, ought not to reckon *that* the only expense; he has really spent, or rather thrown away, five shillings besides.
>
> Remember, that *credit* is money. If a man lets his money lie in my hands after it is due, he gives me the interest, or so much as I can make of it during that time. This amounts to a considerable sum where a man has good and large credit, and makes good use of it.
>
> Remember, that money is of the prolific, generating nature. Money can beget money, and its offspring can beget more, and so on. Five shillings turned is six, turned again it is seven and threepence, and so on, till it becomes a hundred pounds. The more there is of it, the more it produces every turning, so that the profits rise quicker and quicker. He that kills a breeding-sow, destroys all her offspring to the thousandth generation. He that murders a crown, destroys all that it might have produced, even scores of pounds.
>
> Remember this saying, *The good paymaster is lord of another man's purse.* He that is known to pay punctually and exactly to the time he promises, may at any time, and on any occasion, raise all the money his friends can spare. This is sometimes of great use. After industry and frugality, nothing contributes more to the raising of a young man in the world than punctuality and justice in all his dealings; therefore never keep borrowed money an hour beyond the time you promised, lest a disappointment shut up your friend's purse for ever."[1] [...]

It is Benjamin Franklin who preaches to us in these sentences, the same which Ferdinand Kürnberger satirizes in his clever and malicious *Picture of American Culture*[2] as the supposed confession of faith of the Yankee. That it is the spirit of capitalism which here speaks in characteristic fashion, no one will doubt, however little we may wish to claim that everything which could be understood as pertaining to that spirit is contained in it. Let us pause a moment to consider this passage, the philosophy of which Kürnberger sums up in the words, "They make tallow out of cattle and money out of men." The peculiarity of this philosophy of avarice appears to be the ideal of the honest man of recognized credit and above all the idea of a duty of the individual toward the increase of his capital, which is assumed as an end in itself. Truly what is here preached is not simply a means of making one's way in the world, but a peculiar ethic. The infraction of its rules is treated not as foolishness but as forgetfulness of duty. That is the essence of the matter. It is not mere business astuteness, that sort of thing is common enough, it is an ethos. *This* is the quality which interests us.

When Jacob Fugger, in speaking to a business associate who had retired and who wanted to persuade him to do the same, since he had made enough money and should let others have a chance, rejected that as pusillanimity and answered that "he (Fugger) thought otherwise, he wanted to make money as long as he could,"[3] the spirit of his statement is evidently quite different from that of Franklin. What in the former case was an expression of commercial daring and a personal inclination morally neutral, in the latter takes on the character of an ethically coloured maxim for the conduct of life. The concept spirit of capitalism is here used in this specific sense, it is the spirit of modern capitalism. For that we are here dealing only with Western European and American capitalism is obvious from the way in which the problem was stated. Capitalism existed in China, India, Babylon, in the classic world, and in the Middle Ages. But in all these cases, as we shall see, this particular ethos was lacking.

Now, all Franklin's moral attitudes are coloured with utilitarianism. Honesty is useful, because it assures credit; so are punctuality, industry, frugality, and that is the reason they are virtues. A logical deduction from this would be that where, for instance, the appearance of honesty serves the same purpose, that would suffice, and an unnecessary surplus of this virtue would evidently appear to Franklin's eyes as unproductive waste. And as a matter of fact, the story in his autobiography of his conversion to those virtues, or the discussion of the value of a strict maintenance of the appearance of modesty, the assiduous belittlement of one's own deserts in order to gain general recognition later, confirms this impression. According to Franklin, those virtues, like all others, are only in so far virtues as they are actually useful to the individual, and the surrogate of mere appearance is always sufficient when it accomplishes the end in view. It is a conclusion which is inevitable for strict utilitarianism. The impression of many Germans that the virtues professed by Americanism are pure hypocrisy seems to have been confirmed by this striking case. But in fact the matter is not by any means so simple. Benjamin Franklin's own character, as it appears in the really unusual candidness of his autobiography, belies that suspicion. The circumstance that he ascribes his recognition of the utility of virtue to a divine revelation which was intended to lead him in the path of righteousness shows that something more than mere garnishing for purely egocentric motives is involved.

In fact, the *summum bonum* of this ethic, the earning of more and more money, combined with the strict avoidance of all spontaneous enjoyment of life, is above all completely devoid of any eudaemonistic, not to say hedonistic, admixture. It is thought of so purely as an end in itself, that from the point of view of the happiness of, or utility to, the single individual, it appears entirely transcendental and absolutely irrational. Man is dominated by the making of money, by acquisition as the ultimate purpose of his life. Economic acquisition is no longer subordinated to man as the means for the satisfaction of his material needs. This reversal of what we should call the natural relationship, so irrational from a naïve point of view, is evidently as definitely a leading principle of capitalism as it is foreign to all peoples not under capitalistic influence. At the same time it expresses a type of feeling which is closely connected with certain religious ideas. If we thus ask, *why* should "money be made out of men," Benjamin Franklin himself, although he was a colourless deist, answers in his autobiography with a quotation from the Bible, which his strict Calvinistic father drummed into him again and again in his youth: "Seest thou a man diligent in his business? He shall stand before kings" (Prov. xxii. 29). The earning of money within the modern economic order is, so long as it is done legally, the result and the expression of virtue and proficiency in a calling; and this virtue and proficiency are, as it is now not difficult to see, the real Alpha and Omega of Franklin's ethic, as expressed in the passages we have quoted, as well as in all his works without exception.

And in truth this peculiar idea, so familiar to us today, but in reality so little a matter of course, of one's duty in a calling, is what is most characteristic of the social ethic of capitalistic culture, and is in a sense the fundamental basis of it. It is an obligation which the individual is supposed to feel and does feel towards the content of his professional[4] activity, no matter in what it consists, in particular no matter whether it appears on the surface as a utilization of his personal powers, or only of his material possessions (as capital).

Of course, this conception has not appeared only under capitalistic conditions. On the contrary, we shall later trace its origins back to a time previous to the advent of capitalism. Still less, naturally, do we maintain that a conscious acceptance of these ethical maxims on the part of the individuals, entrepreneurs or labourers, in modern capitalistic enterprises, is a condition of the further existence of present-day capitalism. The capitalistic economy of the present day is an immense cosmos into which the individual is born, and which presents itself to him, at least as an individual, as an unalterable order of things in which he must live. It forces the individual, in so far as he is involved in the system of market relationships, to conform to capitalistic rules of action. The manufacturer who in the long run acts counter to these norms, will just as inevitably be eliminated from the economic scene as the worker who cannot or will not adapt himself to them will be thrown into the streets without a job.

Thus the capitalism of today, which has come to dominate economic life, educates and selects the economic subjects which it needs through a process of economic survival of the fittest. But here one can easily see the limits of the concept of selection as a means of historical explanation. In order that a manner of life so well adapted to the peculiarities of capitalism could be selected at all, i.e. should come to dominate others, it had to originate somewhere, and not in isolated individuals alone, but as a way of life common to whole groups of men. This origin is what really needs explanation. Concerning the doctrine of the more naïve historical materialism, that such ideas originate as a reflection or superstructure of economic situations, we shall speak more in detail below. At this point it will suffice for our purpose to call attention to the fact that without doubt, in the country of Benjamin Franklin's birth (Massachusetts), the spirit of capitalism (in the sense we have attached to it) was present before the capitalistic order. There were complaints of a peculiarly calculating sort of profit-seeking in New England, as distinguished from other parts of America, as early as 1632. It is further undoubted that capitalism remained far less developed in some of the neighbouring colonies, the later Southern States of the United States of America, in spite of the fact that these latter were founded by large capitalists for business motives, while the New England colonies were founded by preachers and seminary graduates with the help of small bourgeois, craftsmen and yeomen, for religious reasons. In this case the causal relation is certainly the reverse of that suggested by the materialistic standpoint. [...]

Now, how could activity, which was at best ethically tolerated, turn into a calling in the sense of Benjamin Franklin? The fact to be explained historically is that in the most highly capitalistic centre of that time, in Florence of the fourteenth and fifteenth centuries, the money and capital market of all the great political Powers, this attitude was considered ethically unjustifiable, or at best to be tolerated. But in the backwoods small bourgeois circumstances of Pennsylvania in the eighteenth century, where business threatened for simple lack of money to fall back into barter, where there was hardly a sign of large enterprise, where only the earliest beginnings of banking were to be found, the same thing was considered the essence of moral conduct, even commanded in the name of duty. To speak here of a reflection of material conditions in the ideal superstructure would be patent nonsense. What was the background of ideas which could account for the sort of activity apparently directed toward profit alone as a calling toward which the individual feels himself to have an ethical obligation? For it was this idea which gave the way of life of the new entrepreneur its ethical foundation and justification. [...]

In fact, one may—this simple proposition, which is often forgotten, should be placed at the beginning of every study which essays to deal with rationalism—rationalize life from fundamentally different basic points of view and in very different directions. Rationalism is an historical concept which covers a whole world of different things. It will be our task to find out whose intellectual child the particular concrete form of rational thought was, from which the idea of a calling and the devotion to labour in the calling has grown, which is, as we have seen, so irrational from the standpoint of purely eudaemonistic self-interest, but which has been and still is one of the most characteristic elements of our capitalistic culture. We are here particularly interested in the origin of precisely the irrational element which lies in this, as in every conception of a calling.

Notes

1 Franklin, Benjamin, *Advice to a Young Tradesman*, written 1748, Sparks edition, II, pp. 87 ff. The italics in the text are Franklin's.
2 *Der Amerikamüde*, Frankfurt, 1855, well known to be an imaginative paraphrase of Lenau's impressions of America. As a work of art, the book would today be somewhat difficult to enjoy, but it is incomparable as a document of the (now long since blurred-over) differences between the German and the American outlook, one may even say of the type of spiritual life which, in spite of everything, has remained common to all Germans, Catholic and Protestant alike, since the German mysticism of the Middle Ages, as against the Puritan capitalistic valuation of action.
3 Werner Sombart has used this quotation as a motto for his section dealing with the genesis of capitalism. *Der modern Kapitalismus*, first edition, I, p. 193. See also p. 390.
4 The two terms profession and calling I have used in translation of the German *Beruf*, whichever seemed best to fit the particular context. Vocation does not carry the ethical connotation in which Weber is interested. It is especially to be remembered that profession in this sense is not contrasted with business, but it refers to a particular attitude towards one's occupation no matter what that occupation may be. This should become abundantly clear from the whole of Weber's argument. – Translator's Note.

10 Emotions and judgements

Edward A. Westermarck

Edward A. Westermarck (1852–1939) was a Finnish philosopher and sociologist who looked at a number of anthropological questions, from the incest taboo to the rules of marriage and particularly the rationales of exogamy. He was Professor at the Universities of Helsinki and London and conducted his empirical research in Morocco, where he studied 'beliefs', ritual practices and wedding ceremonies. Critical of Christian dogmatism, he became renowned for his liberal moral positions regarding gender and sexuality. His main anthropological contribution was his voluminous study *The Origin and Development of the Moral Ideas*, in which he developed a relativist reading that he later took up again in a shorter essay entitled *Ethical Relativity*. While Edward Westermarck's legacy remains relatively limited, his study of morality was the first of its kind in the social sciences and was widely disseminated during his lifetime, although it did not lead to research that would have followed his systematic attempt to build a science of morality grounded in an almost culturalist approach to ethics.

The text presented here is the beginning of his magnum opus and delineates its general argument. Against utilitarian ideas, which give a rational basis to the meaning of good and bad, i.e. maximising happiness, and more generally against objectivist approaches to morality that would have it rest upon forms of rationality, Edward Westermarck considers morality to be the product not of intellect but rather of emotions and therefore offers a subjectivist reading of ethics: in the last instance, moral judgements correspond to reactions of indignation or approval regarding situations with which individuals are confronted. It is society that teaches us to distinguish right from wrong, and customs that guide us through this learning process. In this schema, which only seems to leave room for the social reproduction of morality, changes are nonetheless possible when disagreements arise and open up the possibility for common values to be contested. In these conditions, morality has no rational foundation and therefore no ultimate truth.

That the moral concepts are ultimately based on emotions either of indignation or approval, is a fact which a certain school of thinkers has in vain attempted to deny. The terms which embody these concepts must originally have been used—indeed they still constantly are so used—as direct expressions of such emotions with reference to the phenomena which evoked them. Men pronounced certain acts to be good or bad on account of the emotions those acts aroused in their minds, just as they called sunshine warm and ice cold on account of certain sensations which they experienced, and as they named a thing pleasant or painful because they felt pleasure or pain. But to attribute a quality to a thing is never the same as merely to state the existence of a particular sensation or feeling in the mind which perceives it. Such an attribution must mean that the thing, under certain circumstances, makes a certain impression on the mind. By calling an object warm or pleasant, a person asserts that it is apt to produce in him a sensation of heat or a feeling of pleasure. Similarly, to name an act good or bad ultimately implies that it is apt to give rise to an emotion of approval or disapproval in him who pronounces the judgment. Whilst not affirming the actual existence of any specific emotion in the mind of the person judging or of anybody else, the predicate of a moral judgment attributes to the subject a tendency to arouse an emotion. The moral concepts, then, are essentially generalisations of tendencies in certain phenomena to call forth moral emotions.

However, as is frequently the case with general terms, these concepts are mentioned without any distinct idea of their contents. The relation in which many of them stand to the moral emotions is complicated; the use of them is often vague; and ethical theorisers, instead of subjecting them to a careful analysis, have done their best to increase the confusion by adapting the meaning of the terms to fit their theories. Very commonly, in the definition of the goodness or badness of acts, reference is made, not to their tendencies to evoke emotions of approval or indignation, but to the causes of these tendencies, that is, to those qualities in the acts which call forth moral emotions. Thus, because good acts generally produce pleasure and bad acts pain, goodness and badness have been identified with the tendencies of acts to produce pleasure or pain. The following statement of Sir James Stephen is a clearly expressed instance of this confusion, so common among utilitarians: "Speaking generally, the acts which are called right do promote, or are supposed to promote general happiness, and the acts which are called wrong do diminish, or are supposed to diminish it. I say, therefore, that this is what the words 'right' and 'wrong' mean, just as the words 'up' and 'down' mean that which points from or towards the earth's centre of gravity, though they are used by millions who have not the least notion of the fact that such is their meaning, and though they were used for centuries and millenniums before any one was or even could be aware of it."[1] So, too, Bentham maintained that words like "ought," "right," and "wrong," have no meaning unless interpreted in accordance with the principle of utility[2]; and John Stuart Mill was of the opinion that "the very morality" of the act lies, not in the sentiments raised in the breast of him who perceives or contemplates it, but in "the consequences of the act, good or evil, and their being within the intention of the agent."[3] He adds that a rational assertor of the principle of utility approves of an action "because it is good," and calls it good "because it conduces to happiness."[4] This, however, is to invert the sequence of the facts, since, properly speaking, an act is called good because it is approved of, and is approved of by an utilitarian in so far as it conduces to happiness.

Such confusion of terms cannot affect the real meaning of the moral concepts. It is true that he who holds that "actions are right in proportion as they tend to promote happiness, wrong as they tend to produce the reverse of happiness,"[5] may, by a merely intellectual process, pass judgment on the moral character of particular acts; but, if he is an utilitarian from conviction, his first principle, at least, has an emotional origin. The case is similar with many of the moral judgments ordinarily passed by men. They are applications of some accepted general rule: conformity or non-conformity to the rule decides the rightness or wrongness of the act judged of. But whether the rule be the result of a person's independent deductions, or be based upon authority, human or divine, the fact that his moral consciousness recognises it as valid implies that it has an emotional sanction in his own mind.

Whilst the import of the predicate of a moral judgment may thus in every case be traced back to an emotion in him who pronounces the judgment, it is generally assumed to possess the character of universality or "objectivity" as well. The statement that an act is good or bad does not merely refer to an individual emotion; as will be shown subsequently, it always has reference to an emotion of a more public character. Very often it even implies some vague assumption that the act must be recognised as good or bad by everybody who possesses a sufficient knowledge of the case and of all attendant circumstances, and who has a "sufficiently developed" moral consciousness. We are not willing to admit that our moral convictions are a mere matter of taste, and we are inclined to regard convictions differing from our own as errors. This characteristic of our moral judgments has been adduced as an argument against the emotionalist theory of moral origins, and has led to the belief that the moral concepts represent qualities which are discerned by reason.

Cudworth, Clarke, Price, and Reid are names which recall to our mind a theory according to which the morality of actions is perceived by the intellect, just as are number, diversity, causation, proportion. "Morality is eternal and immutable," says Richard Price. "Right and wrong, it appears, denote what actions are. Now whatever any thing is, that it is, not by will, or degree, or power, but by nature and necessity. Whatever a triangle or circle is, that it is unchangeably and eternally ... The same is to be said of right and wrong, of moral good and evil, as far as they express real characters of actions. They must immutably and necessarily belong to those actions of which they are truly affirmed."[6] And as having a real existence outside the mind, they can only be discerned by the understanding. It is true that this discernment is accompanied with an emotion: "Some impressions of pleasure or pain, satisfaction or disgust, generally attend our perceptions of virtue and vice. But these are merely their effects and concomitants, and not the perceptions themselves, which ought no more to be confounded with them, than a particular truth (like that for which Pythagoras offered a hecatomb) ought to be confounded with the pleasure that may attend the discovery of it."[7]

According to another doctrine, the moral predicates, though not regarded as expressions of "theoretical" truth, nevertheless derive all their import from reason— from "practical" or "moral" reason, as it is variously called. Thus Professor Sidgwick holds that the fundamental notions represented by the word "ought" or "right," which moral judgments contain expressly or by implication, are essentially different from all notions representing facts of physical or psychical experience, and he refers such judgments to the "reason," understood as a faculty of cognition. By this he implies "that what ought to be is a possible object of knowledge, i.e., that what I judge ought to be, must, unless I am in error, be similarly judged by all rational beings who judge truly of the matter." The moral judgments contain moral *truths*, and "cannot legitimately be interpreted as judgments respecting the present or future existence of human feelings or any facts of the sensible world."[8]

Yet our tendency to objectivise the moral judgments is no sufficient ground for referring them to the province of reason. If, in this respect, there is a difference between these judgments and others that are rooted in the subjective sphere of experience, it is, largely, a difference in degree rather than in kind. The aesthetic judgments, which indisputably have an emotional origin, also lay claim to a certain amount of "objectivity." By saying of a piece of music that it is beautiful, we do not merely mean that it gives ourselves aesthetic enjoyment, but we make a latent assumption that it must have a similar effect upon everybody who is sufficiently musical to appreciate it. This objectivity ascribed to judgments which have a merely subjective origin springs in the first place from the similarity of the mental constitution of men, and, generally speaking, the tendency to regard them as objective is greater in proportion as the impressions vary less in each particular case. If "there is no disputing of tastes," that is because taste is so extremely variable; and yet even in this instance we recognise a certain "objective" standard by speaking of a "bad" and a "good" taste. On the other hand, if the appearance of objectivity in the moral judgments is so illusive as to make it seem necessary to refer them to reason, that is partly on account of the comparatively uniform nature of the moral consciousness.

Society is the school in which men learn to distinguish between right and wrong. The headmaster is Custom, and the lessons are the same for all. The first moral judgments were pronounced by public opinion; public indignation and public approval are the prototypes of the moral emotions. As regards questions of morality, there was, in early society, practically no difference of opinion; hence a character of universality, or objectivity, was from the very beginning attached to all moral judgments. And when, with advancing civilisation, this unanimity was to some extent disturbed by individuals venturing to dissent from the opinions of the majority, the disagreement was largely due to facts which in no way affected the moral principle, but had reference only to its application. [...]

The presumed objectivity of moral judgments thus being a chimera, there can be no moral truth in the sense in which this term is generally understood. The ultimate reason for this is, that the moral concepts are based upon emotions, and that the contents of an emotion fall entirely outside the category of truth. But it may be true or not that we have a certain emotion, it may be true or not that a given mode of conduct has a tendency to evoke in us moral indignation or moral approval. Hence a moral judgment is true or false according as its subject has or has not that tendency which the predicate attributes to it. If I say that it is wrong to resist evil, and yet resistance to evil has no tendency whatsoever to call forth in me an emotion of moral disapproval, then my judgment is false.

If there are no general moral truths, the object of scientific ethics cannot be to fix rules for human conduct, the aim of all science being the discovery of some truth. It has been said by Bentham and others that moral principles cannot be proved because they are first principles which are used to prove everything else.[9] But the real reason for their being inaccessible to demonstration is that, owing to their very nature, they can never be true. If the word "Ethics," then, is to be used as the name for a science, the object of that science can only be to study the moral consciousness as a fact.[10]

Ethical subjectivism is commonly held to be a dangerous doctrine, destructive to morality, opening the door to all sorts of libertinism. If that which appears to each man as right or good, stands for that which is right or good; if he is allowed to make his own law, or to make no law at all; then, it is said, everybody has the natural right to follow his caprice and inclinations, and to hinder him from doing so is an infringement on his rights, a constraint with which no one is bound to comply provided that he has the power to evade it. This inference was long ago drawn from the teaching of the Sophists,[11] and it will no doubt be still repeated as an argument against any theorist who dares to assert that nothing can be said to be truly right or wrong.

To this argument may, first, be objected that a scientific theory is not invalidated by the mere fact that it is likely to cause mischief. The unfortunate circumstance that there do exist dangerous things in the world, proves that something may be dangerous and yet true. Another question is whether any scientific truth really is mischievous on the whole, although it may cause much discomfort to certain people. I venture to believe that this, at any rate, is not the case with that form of ethical subjectivism which I am here advocating. The charge brought against the Sophists does not at all apply to it. I do not even subscribe to that beautiful modern sophism which admits every man's conscience to be an infallible guide. If we had to recognise, or rather if we did recognise, as right everything which is held to be right by anybody, savage or Christian, criminal or saint, morality would really suffer a serious loss. But we do not, and we cannot, do so. My moral judgments are my own judgments; they spring from my own moral consciousness; they judge of the conduct of other men not from their point of view but from mine, not with primary reference to their opinions about right and wrong, but with reference to my own. Most of us indeed admit that, when judging of an act, we also ought to take into consideration the moral conviction of the agent, and the agreement or disagreement between his doing and his idea of what he ought to do. But although we hold it to be wrong of a person to act against his conscience, we may at the same time blame him for having such a conscience as he has. Ethical subjectivism covers all such cases. It certainly does not allow everybody to follow his own inclinations; nor does it lend sanction to arbitrariness and caprice. Our moral consciousness belongs to our mental constitution, which we cannot change as we please. We approve and we disapprove because we cannot do otherwise. Can we help feeling pain when the fire burns us? Can we help sympathizing with our friends? Are these phenomena less necessary or less powerful in their consequences, because they fall within the subjective sphere of experience? So, too, why should the moral law command less obedience because it forms part of our own nature?

Far from being a danger, ethical subjectivism seems to me more likely to be an acquisition for moral practice. Could it be brought home to people that there is no absolute standard in morality, they would perhaps be somewhat more tolerant in their judgments, and more apt to listen to the voice of reason. If the right has an objective existence, the moral consciousness has certainly been playing at blindman's buff ever since it was born, and will continue to do so until the extinction of the human race. But who does admit this? The popular mind is always inclined to believe that it possesses the knowledge of what *is* right and wrong, and to regard public opinion as the reliable guide of conduct. We have, indeed, no reason to regret that there are men who rebel against the established rules of morality; it is more deplorable that the rebels are so few, and that, consequently, the old rules change so slowly. Far above the vulgar idea that the right is a settled something to which everybody has to adjust his opinions, rises the conviction that it has its existence in each individual mind, capable of any expansion, proclaiming its own right to exist, and, if need be, venturing to make a stand against the whole world. Such a conviction makes for progress.

Notes

1 Stephen, James Fitzjames (1873), *Liberty, Equality, Fraternity*, London: Cambridge University Press, p. 338.
2 Bentham, Jeremy (1789), *An Introduction to the Principles of Morals and Legislation*, Oxford: Clarendon Press, p. 4.
3 Mill, James (1835), *A Fragment on Mackintosh*, London: Baldwin & Cradock, pp. 5, 376.
4 Ibid., p. 368.
5 Mill, John Stuart (1895), *Utilitarianism*, London: Routledge, p. 9 *sq.*
6 Price, Richard (1787), *A Review of the Principal Questions in Morals*, London: Thomas Cadell, pp. 63, 74 *sq.*
7 Ibid., p. 63.
8 Sidgwick, Henry (1901), *The Methods of Ethics*, London: Macmillan, pp. 25, 33 *sq.*
9 Bentham (1789), *An Introduction to the Principles of Morals and Legislation*, op. cit.
10 Simmel, Georg (1892–1893), *Einleitung in die Moralwissenschaft*, Volume I, p. iii. *sq.*; Westermarck, Edward A. (1897), Normative und psychologische Ethik, in *Dritter Internationaler Congress für Psychologie in München*, Munich: Verlag von J. F. Lehmann, p. 428 *sqq.*
11 Zeller, Eduard (1881), *A History of Greek Philosophy from the Earliest Period to the Time of Socrates*, Volume II, trans. by S. F. Alleyne, London: Longmans, Green, and Co., p. 475.

11 Crime and punishment

Bronislaw Malinowski

Bronislaw Malinowski (1884–1942) was a British anthropologist of Polish origin who played a major role in the history of the discipline, particularly by establishing the method of participant observation inaugurated during his study in the Trobriand Isles during the 1920s. He studied at the London School of Economics under Charles Seligman and Edward Westermarck, and went on to become a professor of anthropology there, with notable students including E. E. Evans-Pritchard, Meyer Fortes, and Edmund Leach, before finishing his career at Yale University. Above and beyond the functionalism with which his name is associated and which is probably his most controversial contribution to anthropology, his theoretical contribution has also been essential in a variety of fields ranging from generalised exchange, which inspired Marcel Mauss's work on the gift, and psychological development, contesting the universality of Freud's concept of the Oedipus complex. As well as his major book, *Argonauts of the Western Pacific*, he was also the author of many works on myth, sexuality and marriage.

Crime and Custom in Savage Society, a short essay that examines traditional law, has been a founding work in legal anthropology. While usual representations of the customs of the societies designated at the time as 'primitive' or 'savage' focused on the strangest, most disturbing or spectacular aspects from the Western viewpoint, Bronislaw Malinowski looks rather at the ordinary, that is, the way law is respected as opposed to broken in the everyday. Far from the typical presentation of rules as rigid fetters obliging members of the group to behave in a certain fashion, he shows them to be flexible with individuals able to adapt to them and even sanctions being adjustable. In fact, magical practices themselves offer solutions when the law is broken, thus avoiding more dramatic responses such as murders or suicides, including after cases of incest. Bronislaw Malinowski therefore sheds light on an important aspect of morality, namely the relation to the social norm, as well as the principles of justice and the regulation procedures that are implemented when it is transgressed, thus revealing the pragmatic responses to deviance.

Anthropology, still a young science, is now on the way to free itself from the control of pre-scientific interest, though certain recent attempts at offering extremely simple and, at the same time, sensational solutions of all the riddles of Culture are still dominated by crude curiosity. In the study of primitive law we can perceive this sound tendency in the gradual but definite recognition that savagery is not ruled by moods, passions, and accidents, but by tradition and order. Even then there remains something of the old 'shocker' interest in the over-emphasis of criminal justice, in the attention devoted to the breaches of the law and their punishment.

Law in modern Anthropology is still almost exclusively studied in its singular and sensational manipulations, in cases of blood-curdling crime, followed by tribal vendetta, in accounts of criminal sorcery with retaliation, of incest, adultery, breach of taboo or murder. In all this, besides the dramatic piquancy of the incidents, the anthropologist can, or thinks he can, trace certain unexpected, exotic, astonishing features of primitive law: a transcending solidarity of the kindred group, excluding all sense of self-interest; a legal and economic Communism; a submission to a rigid, undifferentiated tribal law.

As a reaction against the method and the principles just stated, I have tried to approach the facts of primitive law in the Trobriands from the other end. I have started with the description of the ordinary, not the singular; of the law obeyed and not the law broken; of the permanent currents and tides in their social life and not its adventitious storms. From the account given, I have been able to conclude that contrary to most established views civil law—or its savage equivalent—is extremely well developed, and that it rules all aspects of social organization. We also found that it is clearly distinguishable, and distinguished by the natives, from the other types of norm, whether morals or manners, rules of art or commands of religion. The rules of their law, far from being rigid, absolute or issued in the Divine Name, are maintained by social forces, understood as rational and necessary, elastic and capable of adjustment. Far also from being exclusively a group affair, his rights and his duties are in the main the concern of the individual, who knows perfectly well how to look after his interests and realizes that he has to redeem his obligations. We found indeed that the native's attitude towards duty and privilege is very much the same as in a civilized community—to the extent in fact that he not only stretches but also at times breaks the law. And this subject, not yet discussed, will claim our attention in these chapters. It would be a very one-sided picture indeed of the law in the Trobriands, if the rules were shown only in good working order, if the system were only described in equilibrium! That law functions only very imperfectly, that there are many hitches and breakdowns, I have now and again indicated, but a full description of the criminal and dramatic issues is necessary, though, as I have said, it should not be unduly emphasized.

There is still one reason why we must have a close look at native life in disorder. We found that in the Trobriands, social relations are governed by a number of legal principles. The most important of these is Mother-right, which rules that a child is bodily related and morally beholden by kinship to its mother and to her only. This principle governs succession to rank, power and dignities, economic inheritance, the rights to soil and to local citizenship and membership in the totemic clan. The status between brother and sister, the relations between the sexes and most of their private and public social intercourse is defined by rules forming part of matriarchal law. The economic duties of a man towards his married sister and her household constitute a strange and important feature of this law. The whole system is based on mythology, on the native theory of procreation, on certain of their magico-religious beliefs and it pervades all the institutions and customs of the tribe.

But, side by side with the system of Mother-right, in its shadow so to speak, there exist certain other, minor systems of legal rules. The law of marriage, defining the status of husband and wife, with its patrilocal arrangements, with its limited but clear bestowal of authority on the man and of guardianship over his wife and children in certain specified matters, is based on legal principles independent of Mother-right, though on several points intertwined with it and adjusted to it. The constitution of a village community, the position of the headman in his village and of the chief in his district, the privileges and duties of the public magician—all these are independent legal systems.

Now since we know that primitive law is not perfect, the problem emerges: how does this composite body of systems behave under the strain of circumstances? Is each system well harmonized within its own limits? Does such a system, moreover, keep within its limits or has it a tendency to encroach upon alien ground? Do the systems then come into conflict, and what is the character of such conflict? Here once more we have to appeal to the criminal, disorderly, disloyal elements of the community to furnish us with material from which we can answer our questions.

In the accounts to which we now proceed—and which will be given concretely and with some detail—we shall keep before us the main problems still unsolved: the nature of criminal acts and procedure and their relation to civil law; the main factors active in the restitution of the disturbed equilibrium; the relations and the possible conflicts between the several systems of native law.

While engaged in my field-work in the Trobriands, I used always to live right among the natives, pitching my tent in the village, and being thus forcibly present at all that happened, trivial or solemn, hum-drum or dramatic. The event which I now proceed to relate happened during my first visit in the Trobriands, a few months only after I had started my field-work in the archipelago.

One day an outbreak of wailing and a great commotion told me that a death had occurred somewhere in the neighbourhood. I was informed that Kima'i, a young lad of my acquaintance, of sixteen or so, had fallen from a coco-nut palm and killed himself.

I hastened to the next village where this had occurred, only to find the whole mortuary proceedings in progress. This was my first case of death, mourning, and burial, so that in my concern with the ethnographical aspects of the ceremonial, I forgot the circumstances of the tragedy even though one or two singular facts occurred at the same time in the village which should have aroused my suspicions. I found that another youth had been severely wounded by some mysterious coincidence. And at the funeral there was obviously a general feeling of hostility between the village where the boy died and that into which his body was carried for burial.

Only much later was I able to discover the real meaning of these events: the boy had committed suicide. The truth was that he had broken the rules of exogamy, the partner in his crime being his maternal cousin, the daughter of his mother's sister. This had been known and generally disapproved of, but nothing was done until the girl's discarded lover, who had wanted to marry her and who felt personally injured, took the initiative. This rival threatened first to use black magic against the guilty youth, but this had not much effect. Then one evening he insulted the culprit in public—accusing him in the hearing of the whole community of incest and hurling at him certain expressions intolerable to a native.

For this there was only one remedy; only one means of escape remained for the unfortunate youth. Next morning he put on festive attire and ornamentation, climbed a coco-nut palm and addressed the community, speaking from among the palm leaves and bidding them farewell. He explained the reasons for his desperate deed and also launched forth a veiled accusation against the man who had driven him to his death, upon which it became the duty of his clansmen to avenge him.

Then he wailed aloud, as is the custom, jumped from a palm some sixty feet high and was killed on the spot. There followed a fight within the village in which the rival was wounded; and the quarrel was repeated during the funeral.

Now this case opened up a number of important lines of inquiry. I was here in the presence of a pronounced crime: the breach of totemic clan exogamy. The exogamous prohibition is one of the cornerstones of totemism, Mother-right, and the classificatory system of kinship. All females of his clan are called sisters by a man and forbidden as such. It is an axiom of Anthropology that nothing arouses a greater horror than the breach of this prohibition, and that besides a strong reaction of public opinion, there are also supernatural punishments, which visit this crime. Nor is this axiom devoid of foundation in fact. If you were to inquire into the matter among the Trobrianders, you would find that all statements confirm the axiom, that the natives show horror at the idea of violating the rules of exogamy and that they believe that sores, disease, and even death might follow clan incest. This is the ideal of native law, and in moral matters it is easy and pleasant strictly to adhere to the ideal—when judging the conduct of others or expressing an opinion about conduct in general.

When it comes to the application of morality and ideals to real life, however, things take on a different complexion. In the case described it was obvious that the facts would not tally with the ideal of conduct. Public opinion was neither outraged by the knowledge of the crime to any extent, nor did it react directly—it had to be mobilized by a public statement of the crime and by insults being hurled at the culprit by an interested party. Even then he had to carry out the punishment himself. The 'group-reaction' and the 'supernatural sanction' were not therefore the active principles. Probing further into the matter and collecting concrete information, I found that the breach of exogamy—as regards intercourse and not marriage—is by no means a rare occurrence, and public opinion is lenient, though decidedly hypocritical. If the affair is carried on *sub rosa* with a certain amount of decorum, and if no one in particular stirs up trouble—'public opinion' will gossip, but not demand any harsh punishment. If, on the contrary, scandal breaks out—every one turns against the guilty pair and by ostracism and insults one or the other may be driven to suicide.

As regards the supernatural sanction, this case led me to an interesting and important discovery. I learned that there is a perfectly well established remedy against any pathological consequences of this trespass, a remedy considered practically infallible, if properly executed. That is to say the natives possess a system of magic consisting of spells and rites performed over water, herbs, and stones, which when correctly carried out, is completely efficient in undoing the bad results of clan incest.

That was the first time in my field-work that I came across what could be called a well-established system of evasion and that in the case of one of the most fundamental laws of the tribe. Later on I discovered that such parasitic growths upon the main branches of tribal order exist in several other cases, besides the counteraction of incest. The importance of this fact is obvious. It shows clearly that a supernatural sanction need not safeguard a rule of conduct with an automatic effect. Against magical influence there may be counter-magic. It is no doubt better not to run the risk—the counter-magic may have been imperfectly learned or faultily performed—but the risk is not great. The supernatural sanction shows then a considerable elasticity, in conjunction with a suitable antidote.

This methodical antidote teaches us another lesson. In a community where laws are not only occasionally broken, but systematically circumvented by well-established methods, there can be no question of a 'spontaneous' obedience to law, of slavish adherence to tradition. For this tradition teaches man surreptitiously how to evade some of its sterner commands—and you cannot be *spontaneously* pushed forwards and pulled back at the same time! [...]

Primitive law is not a homogeneous, perfectly unified body of rules, based upon one principle developed into a consistent system. So much we know already from our previous survey of legal facts in the Trobriand Islands. The law of these natives consists on the contrary of a number of more or less independent systems, only partially adjusted to one another. Each of these—matriarchy, father-right, the law of marriage, the prerogatives and duties of a chief and so on—has a certain field completely its own, but it can also trespass beyond its legitimate boundaries. This results in a state of tense equilibrium with an occasional outbreak. The study of the mechanism of such conflicts between legal principles, whether overt or masked, is extremely instructive and it reveals to us the very nature of the social fabric in a primitive tribe. I shall therefore proceed now to the description of one or two occurrences and then to their analysis.

I shall describe first a dramatic event which illustrates the conflict between the main principle of law, Mother-right, and one of the strongest sentiments, paternal love, round which there clusters many usages, tolerated by custom, though in reality working against the law.

The two principles Mother-right and Father-love are focused most sharply in the relation of a man to his sister's son and to his own son respectively. His matrilineal nephew is his nearest kinsman and the legal heir to all his dignities and offices. His own son on the other hand is not regarded as a kinsman; legally he is not related to his father, and the only bond is the sociological status of marriage with the mother.

Yet in the reality of actual life the father is much more attached to his own son than to his nephew. Between father and son there obtains invariably friendship and personal attachment; between uncle and nephew not infrequently the ideal of perfect solidarity is marred by the rivalries and suspicions inherent in any relationship of succession.

Thus the powerful legal system of Mother-right is associated with a rather weak sentiment, while Father-love, much less important in law, is backed by a strong personal feeling. In the case of a chief whose power is considerable, the personal influence outweighs the ruling of the law and the position of the son is as strong as that of the nephew.

That was the case in the capital village of Omarakana, the residence of the principal chief, whose power extends over the whole district, whose influence reaches many archipelagoes, and whose fame is spread all over the eastern end of New Guinea. I soon found out that there was a standing feud between his sons and nephews, a feud which assumed a really acute form in the ever recurrent quarrels between his favourite son Namwana Guya'u and his second eldest nephew Mitakata.

The final outbreak came when the chief's son inflicted a serious injury on the nephew in a litigation before the resident government official of the district. Mitakata, the nephew, was in fact convicted and put to prison for a month or so.

When the news of this reached the village, the short exultation among the partisans of Namwana Guya'u was followed by a panic, for everyone felt that things had come to a crisis. The chief shut himself up in his personal hut, full of evil forebodings of the consequences for his favourite, who was felt to have acted rashly and in outrage of tribal law and feeling. The kinsmen of the imprisoned young heir to chieftainship were boiling with suppressed anger and indignation. As night fell, the subdued village settled down to a silent supper, each family over its solitary meal. There was nobody on the central place—Namwana Guya'u was not to be seen, the chief To'uluwa hid in his hut, most of his wives and their families also remained indoors. Suddenly a loud voice rang out across the silent village. Bagido'u, the heir apparent, and eldest brother of the imprisoned man, standing before his hut, spoke out, addressing the offender of his family: "Namwana Guya'u, you are a cause of trouble. We, the Tabalu of Omarakana, allowed you to stay here, to live among us. You had plenty of food in Omarakana, you ate of our food, you partook of the pigs brought to us as a tribute and of the fish. You sailed in our canoe. You built a hut on our soil. Now you have done us harm. You have told lies. Mitakata is in prison. We do not want you to stay here. This is our village! You are a stranger here. Go away! We chase you away! We chase you out of Omarakana."

These words were uttered in a loud piercing voice, trembling with strong emotion, each short sentence spoken after a pause, each like an individual missile, hurled across the empty space to the hut where Namwana Guya'u sat brooding. After that the younger sister of Mitakata also arose and spoke, and then a young man, one of the maternal nephews. Their words were almost the same as in the first speech, the burden being the formula of chasing away, the *yoba*. The speeches were received in deep silence. Nothing stirred in the village. But, before the night was over, Namwana Guya'u had left Omarakana for ever. He had gone over and settled in his own village, in Osapola the village whence his mother came, a few miles distant. For weeks his mother and sister wailed for him with the loud lamentations of mourning for the dead. The chief remained for three days in his hut, and when he came out looked older and broken up by grief. All his personal interest and affection were on the side of his favourite son, of course. Yet he could do nothing to help him. His kinsmen had acted in complete accordance with their rights and, according to tribal law, he could not possibly dissociate himself from them. No power could change the decree of exile. Once the 'Go away'—(*bukula*), 'we chase thee away'—(*kayabaim*), were pronounced, the man had to go. These words, very rarely uttered in dead earnest, have a binding force and almost ritual power when pronounced by the citizens of a place against a resident outsider. A man who would try to brave the dreadful insult involved in them and remain in spite of them, would be dishonoured for ever. In fact, anything but immediate compliance with a ritual request is unthinkable for a Trobriand Islander.

The chief's resentment against his kinsmen was deep and lasting. At first he would not even speak to them. For a year or so, not one of them dared to ask to be taken on overseas expeditions by him, although they were fully entitled to this privilege. Two years later in 1917, when I returned to the Trobriands, Namwana Guya'u was still resident in the other village and keeping aloof from his father's kinsmen, though he frequently paid visits to Omarakana in order to be in attendance on his father, especially when To'uluwa went abroad. The mother had died within a year after the expulsion. As the natives described it: "She wailed and wailed, refused to eat, and died." The relations between the two main enemies were completely broken and Mitakata, the young chieftain who had been imprisoned, had sent away his wife who belonged to the same subclan as Namwana Guya'u. There was a deep rift in the whole social life of Kiriwina.

The incident was one of the most dramatic events which I have ever witnessed in the Trobriands. I have described it at length, as it contains a clear illustration of Mother-right, of the power of tribal law and of the passions which work in spite of it.

12 Primitive man as philosopher

Paul Radin

Paul Radin (1883–1959) was an American anthropologist of Polish origin. A member of the first generation of Franz Boas's students at Columbia University, he taught at the universities of California, Chicago, and finally Brandeis. A renowned specialist of the Winnebago of the Great Lakes region, about whom he published a long monograph entitled *The Winnebago Tribe*, he developed an interest in the biographical method within anthropology and, more specifically, in individual variations within one society: *Crashing Thunder: The Autobiography of an American Indian* was a leading work of the golden age of cultural anthropology in the United States. However, he owes his – late – recognition to his comparative study of a mythical figure, the 'divine trickster' in *The Trickster: A Study in Native American Mythology*.

In *Primitive Man as Philosopher*, prefaced by the philosopher John Dewey, Paul Radin explicitly attacks Lucien Lévy-Bruhl's argument concerning the existence of a prelogical mentality in primitive people, which would be different in nature to our own. The general issue of rationality, central to anthropology, is therefore broached here from the point of view of the capacity for abstract thinking and the moral control of emotions. The primitive philosopher that he seeks to foreground is in fact a moralist who attains the same truths as our moral philosophers. Paul Radin uses his own ethnographic work to illustrate the moral sense of the Winnebago through a series of maxims, showing that they are not applied simply out of fear of facing sanctions if they were to be transgressed but rather in the name of higher values. However, according to him, the difference between Western morality and Winnebago morality is that the former is often expressed in the language of intention while the latter is evaluated in daily actions and behaviour.

On no subject connected with primitive people does so much confusion exist in the mind of the general public and have so many ill-considered statements been made as on the nature of their behavior to one another. The prevalent view today among laymen is that they are at all times the plaything of their passions, and that self-control and poise are utterly alien to their character, if not, indeed, quite beyond their reach. Even so open-minded and sympathetic a scholar as Jung apparently still accepts this view.[1] That an example like the one used by Jung should in all good faith be given as representative of the normal or even the abnormal reaction of a primitive man to a given emotional situation, shows the depth of ignorance that still exists on this subject. Now quite apart from the manifest absurdity involved in the belief that any parent in a primitive group would wreak his rage at his lack of success in hunting, in this murderous fashion upon the first object that came within his reach, even if it be his innocent and beloved child, there are a hundred and one reasons that would have deterred him, even had he been the uncontrolled animal the illustration assumes him to have been. However, let that pass. The illustration has its uses, for it permits the contrast between the generally accepted belief and the true nature of the facts to emerge all the more definitely. Actually the situation is quite different.

Briefly stated, the underlying ideal of conduct among most primitive tribes is self-discipline, self-control and a resolute endeavor to observe a proper measure of proportion in all things. I am well aware that in some tribes this is more definitely expressed than in others and that not infrequently certain excrescences in their ceremonial life seem to contradict this assertion. Yet I think most field ethnologists would agree with me. Since in the face of so formidable a body of opinion apparently to the contrary, incontrovertible evidence will be demanded of me to substantiate so broad and explicit a statement, I shall confine myself in my presentation of the facts to a tribe which I know personally and where the material which I use can be definitely controlled. The data upon which I rely come from the Winnebago Indians of Wisconsin and Nebraska and are to be found in two monographs published by me. Only statements made by the Winnebago themselves in accounts either actually written by themselves or contained in verbatim descriptions of the rituals obtained in the original Winnebago are used in order to obviate all inaccuracy.

I can think of no better method of introducing the subject than by quoting appropriate passages from the Winnebago texts secured and then discussing them in the light of the knowledge they throw upon the system of ethics enunciated and, more specifically, upon the type of self-control implied. For facility of reference I shall number these passages:[2]

1. It is always good to be good.
2. What does life consist of but love?
3. Of what value is it to kill?
4. You ought to be of some help to your fellow men.
5. Do not abuse your wife; women are sacred.
6. If you cast off your dress for many people, they will be benefitted by your deed.
7. For the good you do every one will love you.
8. Never do any wrong to children.
9. It is not good to gamble.
10. If you see a helpless old man, help him if you have anything at all.
11. If you have a home of your own, see to it that whoever enters it obtains something to eat. Such food will be a source of death to you if withheld.
12. When you are recounting your war deeds on behalf of the departed soul, do not try to add to your honor by claiming more for yourself than you have actually accomplished. If you tell a falsehood then and exaggerate your achievements you will die beforehand. The telling of truth is sacred. Tell less than you did. The old men say it is wiser.
13. Be on friendly terms with every one and then every one will love you.
14. Marry only one person at a time.
15. Do not be haughty with your husband. Kindness will be returned to you and he will treat you in the same way in which you treat him.
16. Do not imagine that you are taking your children's part if you just speak about loving them. Let them see it for themselves.

17. Do not show your love for other people so that people notice it. Love them but let your love be different from that for your own.
18. As you travel along life's road, never harm any one or cause any one to feel sad. On the contrary, if at any time you can make a person feel happy, do so. If at any time you meet a woman away from your village and you are both alone and no one can see you, do not frighten her or harm her.
19. If you meet any one on the road, even if it is only a child, speak a cheering word before you pass on.
20. If your husband's people ever ask their own children for something when you are present, assume that they had asked it of you. If there is anything to be done, do not wait till you are asked to do it but do it immediately.
21. Never think a home is yours until you have made one for yourself.
22. If you have put people in charge of your household, do not nevertheless act as though the home were still yours.
23. When visiting your husband's people, do not act as if you were far above them.

Obviously we are here in the presence of a fairly well elaborated system of conduct. To those who consistently deny to primitive man any true capacity for abstract thinking or objective formulation of an ethical code and their number is very large both among scholars and laymen the injunctions given above would probably be interpreted as having a definitely concrete significance. That is, they are not to be regarded as attempts at generalization in any true sense of the word but merely as inherently wise laws and precepts of a practical and personal application. Now there is sufficient justification for such a view to warrant our discussing it before we proceed any further.

A number of the precepts given avowedly allow a concrete practical and personal application. In 5, for example, we are told, "If you abuse your wife you will die in a short time. Our grandmother Earth is a woman and in abusing your wife you will be abusing her. Since it is she who takes care of us, by your actions you will be practically killing yourself." To precept 10 is added the following: "If you happen to possess a home, take him (the old man) there and feed him for he may suddenly make uncomplimentary remarks about you. You will be strengthened thereby."

We thus do indeed seem to obtain the impression that a Winnebago in being good to a helpless old man is guided by motives secondary to those implied in the precept as quoted. And what follows would seem to strip our apparently generous precept of whatever further altruistic value still attaches to it, for there it is stated that perhaps the old man is carrying under his arm a box of medicines that he cherishes very much and which he will offer to you. Similarly in precept 11 we find, "If you are stingy about giving food someone may kill you." Indeed I think we shall have to admit that in the majority of cases none of the Winnebago virtues or actions are extolled for their own sake, and that in every instance they have reference to and derive their validity from whatever relation they possess to the preponderatingly practical needs of human intercourse. "Don't be a fool," precept 5 seems to imply, "and treat your wife badly, because if you do, you'll run the risk of having the woman's protecting deity, the Earth, punish you." I should not even be surprised if, in concrete instances, the moral was further emphasized by giving examples of how men were punished who had abused their wives. We are fairly obviously told to be guided by the practical side of the question, i.e., take no risks and get the most out of every good action you perform.

Now all this sounds extremely cynical and practical. But we must be fair and not too hasty in drawing our inferences. First of all it should be asked if the Winnebago in actual practice give the impression of always being guided by egotistical and ulterior motives, and second it should be borne in mind that if we can really prove that the ideal of human conduct is on a high plane, we need not concern ourselves needlessly with the apparent nature of the motives prompting individual acts. As a matter of fact primitive people are much less guided by consciously selfish and ulterior motives than we are, not because of any innate superiority over ourselves in this regard but because of the conditions under which they live. But, quite apart from this consideration, ought we in fact to lay undue stress on illustrations following what is clearly a general principle? Are we not after all, in our illustrations, merely dealing with a statement of what happens when some general principle of the ethical code is transgressed, and not primarily with an explanation of the principle? I do not feel, therefore, that even those instances which seem superficially to corroborate the prevalent assumption of primitive man's inability to formulate an abstract ethical creed, actually bear out, when more carefully examined, the contention of its advocates.

Now the question of the capacity of the Winnebago to formulate an ethical code in a fairly abstract fashion is of fundamental importance for the thesis of this chapter and that is why I am laying so much stress on it; for if it were not true our precepts would have to be regarded in the nature of mere proverbs and practical folk wisdom, as nothing higher indeed than crystallized maxims of conduct.

There are, however, in our list certain precepts where the abstract formulation is undeniable, where, in fact, reference to the particular context in which the precepts occur not only shows no secondary concrete significance, but, on the contrary, a reinforcement of their abstract and general connotation. In precept 1 the full statement is this: "If you hear of a person traveling through your country and you want to see him, prepare your table and send for him. In this manner you will do good and it is always good to do good, it is said." Similarly in precept 2. Here it is in the course of a speech delivered at a ceremony that the phrase occurs: "what does life consist of but love?" "All the members of the clan have given me counsel," the speaker says, "and all the women and children have pleaded in my behalf with the spirits. What love that was! And of what does life consist but of love?"

Here we have no concrete practical implications. The statements are meant to be taken as general propositions. They are very remarkable enunciations and we may legitimately draw from their existence the inference that even in so-called "primitive" tribes, certain individuals have apparently felt within themselves the same moral truths that are regarded as the glory of our great moralists, and that they have formulated these truths in general terms.

So much for the actual formulation. What, however, does this Winnebago creed tell us about the ideal of conduct itself? Does it teach us that love and forbearance are to be practiced for their own sake and is the love of which they speak identical with or even comparable to our idea of love?

When a Western European speaks of love, forbearance, remorse, sorrow, etc., he generally understands by these terms some quality belonging to an individual and for the possession of which he is to be honored and praised. We do not ask whether the love or the virtue in question is of an intelligent nature, whether it does harm or good, or whether we have any right to it. Who among us would speak of an individual not being entitled to his remorse or sorrow? We assume that the mere expression of remorse and sorrow is somehow ethically praiseworthy. If we see a man of manifestly weak character but of a loving disposition, even if his actions are inconsistent with a true love for his fellow men, insist that he loves them, while we may condemn him, we are inclined to overlook much in recognition of his enunciation of the principle that love of mankind is the highest ideal of life. In much the same way do we look upon any manifestation of sincere remorse or sorrow. We simply regard love, remorse, sorrow, etc., as inalienable rights of man, quite independent of any right, as it were, he may possess to express them. In other words, the Western European ethics is frankly egocentric and concerned primarily with self-expression. The object toward which love, remorse, repentance, sorrow, is directed is secondary. Christian theology has elevated them all to the rank of virtues as such, and enjoins their observance upon us because they are manifestations of God's, if not of man's, way.

Among primitive people this is emphatically not true. Ethics there is based upon behavior. No mere enunciation of an ideal of love, no matter how often and sincerely repeated, would gain an individual either admiration, sympathy, or respect. Every ethical precept must be submitted to the touchstone of conduct. The Winnebago moralist would insist that we have no right to preach an ideal of love or to claim that we love, unless we have lived up to its practical implications. That is the fundamental basis of all primitive education and is unusually well expressed among the Winnebago. "When you are bringing up children," runs the injunction to a young mother, "do not imagine that you are taking their part if you merely speak of loving them. Let them see it for themselves; let them know what love is by seeing you give away things to the poor. Then they will see your good deeds and then they will know whether you have been telling the truth or not." An exactly similar attitude is taken toward remorse. "If you have always loved a person, then when he dies you will have the right to feel sorrow." No amount of money spent upon the funeral of a person with whom you had been quarreling will make amends.

Notes

1 Jung, Carl (1976), *Psychological Types*, Princeton, NJ: Princeton University Press, p. 295.
2 All these passages, with the exception of 3, 18, 19 and 20, come from *Crashing Thunder: the Autobiography of an American Indian*, edited by Paul Radin; 3 comes from the myth given on pages 79 ff. of this book, and the others from the *37th Annual Report of the Bureau of American Ethnology*.

Part II
Positions

Introduction

Didier Fassin

Anthropologists whose research focuses on moral issues generally ask themselves one of two big questions. First, what is morality? How can it be described theoretically? How can it be studied empirically? Second, what should be made of the diversity of morality? Does it exclude any universal criteria? Is it compatible with common foundations? These two series of questions give rise to different, even contradictory, answers that are the result of distinct and sometimes opposed philosophical and ideological positions. However, these do not only concern anthropologists: they cross societies as a whole and often divide them.

Take, for example, the so-called 'question of the veil' in France, where the issue at stake was whether wearing ostensible Muslim religious signs in certain public spaces was to be tolerated or penalised. The first question – defining the nature of morality – is relevant for both interpreting the facts and drawing conclusions from them. We can take the view that young Muslim women who wear a veil do so to obey a rule that is imposed upon them as part of a religious law that legitimises masculine domination, whether they are aware of this or not. In this case, we would be tempted to ban the veil to protect them. Or we can consider that they are acting in a lucid and voluntary fashion, according to what they believe to be a virtuous practice in line with their faith. Accordingly, we will respect their choice in the name of their freedom of conscience. Or else we can find ourselves unable to decide between the two interpretations, or think that it is not essential to do so, because the important point is understanding what consequences each option – prohibition or freedom – will entail for those concerned, for example in terms of social marginalisation if they become excluded from public spaces. As a result, we will try to choose the solution most beneficial to them. And it just so happens that these three options correspond approximately to the three main anthropological – and philosophical – positions regarding morality.

As for the second question – the status of the truth of morality – it is just as central here, but this time not from the point of view of the young Muslim women but rather from the point of view of those commenting on the practice of wearing the veil, whether journalists, intellectuals, feminist activists, political leaders, religious representatives or anyone who has an opinion on the matter. The relativist would claim that different religious cultures exist and that they are all equally respectable: this is the multiculturalist argument. The universalist would believe that a superior principle must prevail, which makes public space unsuited to the expression of religious belief: this is the secular stance. And finally, one would probably also find pragmatists who would recognise that sectarianism should not be encouraged but who would also express surprise that Republican values had only been called upon regarding Muslim religious signs whereas this had never posed a problem in the past for Christians or Jews. While they would not wish to choose between relativism and universalism, they would mention the risks of stigmatising a group and of creating societal tensions. Once again, these three orientations correspond to three main anthropological – and ideological – positions regarding the relationships between morality and politics. This means that anthropological discussions can shed light on the issues at stake in the contemporary world. Shed light on, but not resolve, because, as we can see in this example, anthropologists bring different answers to the question.

The first question – what is morality? – is the most directly scientific of the two, in principle.[1] Like any social science, anthropology must define its object. The response that first appeared to researchers working in societies culturally distant from their own consisted in showing that the members of these societies obeyed a set of rules concerning behaviour, which dictated what they should and should not do. This was an adaptation of the Kantian or, more precisely, Durkheimian approach. This moral code was not only composed of prescriptions and prohibitions, it also referred to more general and more abstract principles corresponding to what some would label a local ethics. The most far-reaching work in this perspective is the study carried out by John Ladd. Claiming to adhere to descriptive ethics as opposed to the usual normative ethics of philosophers, this author retraced the moral code of the Navajo in an exhaustive and precise fashion thanks to one of their most famous native moralists.[2] However, no matter how subtle it might be, such an approach tends, on the one hand, to reduce morality to a particular ideology, namely a set of ideas and ideals that are explicitly disconnected from practice, and, on the other, to adopt an essentialist sociological reading of norms and values, that is, to place the emphasis on the collective genesis of ethics to the detriment of the individual level.

This criticism has been made in particular by certain anthropologists of religion working in Muslim or Indian societies, whose observations of practices of confession, prayer or renunciation did not fit well with the idea of rules imposed upon individuals. Their ethnography made them more attentive to how agents work on their selves in order to transform them, to improve their conduct and to bring themselves closer to the divine ideal: here we can see the Aristotelian paradigm, or more precisely, its Foucauldian reformulation. From this viewpoint, morality does not reside in external norms and values that the individual would simply seek to respect. Rather, it is expressed in techniques of the self and actions towards others. Ethics is a subjective process. One of the first anthropologists to have stated and illustrated this perspective is James Laidlaw, who in a theoretical text asserted the importance of approaching ethics from the point of view of freedom, even when subject to the strongest of constraints. He provides the example of practising Jains, whose most radical asceticism leads to a form of spiritual liberation.[3] However, this approach tends to valorise specific and sometimes extreme expressions of moral subjectivation, expressions that are situated within a particular universe in which religion exalts and produces ethics.

And yet do daily life and the secular world not also offer examples of moral attitudes and ethical behaviour? This question has led certain anthropologists to focus on the category of the ordinary, on those everyday actions that reveal moral considerations and on those familiar situations in which ethical practices unfold. This is notably Michael Lambek's project. He is interested more in the ethical act itself than in the subject performing it. The question is knowing how to determine what, when carried out, is a matter of intention (for example, the intention of doing good) and what is a matter of performance (that is, actually doing good). The answer, in which Wittgenstein's influence can be discerned, is that in general there are no pre-existing values according to which we would position ourselves in order to decide how to act; rather, there is a permanent tension and constant adjustment between action and its evaluation. It is by acting in a way that we and others recognise as moral that we produce ordinary ethics.[4] While studies on the ethical subject tend to emphasise the relationship to the self, those focusing on the ethical act concentrate on the relationship to others.

These different definitions of morality and ethics, whether they originate in norms and values, or in concern for the self and others, nonetheless overlook an important dimension that utilitarian and subsequently consequentialist philosophers have considered to be the ultimate criteria for enabling decisions regarding good or bad actions: the effects produced. It is no longer a matter of asking oneself whether one is obeying a moral obligation or accomplishing an ethical act, but rather whether the consequences are positive. Little anthropological research takes this line, seeming to implicitly consider that agents ground their morality in duty or virtue rather than in calculations that anticipate the results of their actions. It is true that, in general, theories regarding the rational actor have fallen out of favour as regards their ethnographic relevance.[5] Joel Robbins considers this absence to be the result of the uncertainty of the contemporary world in which individuals are incapable of predicting the near future and therefore take refuge in an ethics of duty and equally, one might add, in moralities of the subject. He presents the paradigm of the martyr carrying out a suicide bombing, which can be linked here to the renouncer who withdraws from the world. He then asks whether researchers would not do well to rediscover the importance of the ethics of responsibility. In both their observations and commitments, they would be attentive to consequences.

The second question – what should we make of the diversity of morality? – might seem at first glance to be a political question, and indeed it is. It has nevertheless mobilised anthropologists in perspectives that, while rarely escaping a certain normativity, still testify to a concern with taking a rational approach to the tensions between relativism and universalism.[6] The stakes are important because anthropologists have often been criticised for recognising differences between value systems to such an extent that they suspend all judgement regarding societies other than their own, thus justifying any practice on the basis of its meaning within its cultural setting: polygamy, female circumcision, corporal punishment, honour crimes and Islamic law are just some of the topics thus supposed to test the limits of tolerance.[7] In reality, these criticisms are rarely borne out by specific texts or facts, and the supposed relativism bringing anthropologists to the brink of nihilism is in fact the exception rather than the rule in what they write as well as in the claims they make. Nonetheless, this remains a sensitive issue that is subject to debate both within the discipline and within society.

One could say that it all began with the culturalist theory surrounding and following on from Franz Boas. By stating the idiosyncratic and incommensurable nature of cultures, and by going so far as to define morality as 'a convenient term for socially approved habits', Ruth Benedict did not fail to provoke reactions of incomprehension. In reality, the relativism thus professed was already a response to the dominant evolutionist model of the time and to the hierarchy of cultures that it established: universalism had fired the first shot. And the reaction was not long in coming, with Clyde Kluckhohn's attack against relativism, to which Clifford Geertz responded at a distance and not without irony in an article against anti-relativism.[8] What sense can be made of this crossfire, where controversy often outweighs argumentative rigour? Two responses, among others, are put forward here: a differentiated form of relativism and a well-tempered universalism.

The first, offered by Bradd Shore, is based on an ethnographical study and shows us that, contrary to the claims of the culturalist theory, a society does not define a coherent moral system. On the contrary, different norms and values exist, the very validity of which is relative because they can enter into tension or even conflict. We would therefore be wrong to make generalisations regarding what we erroneously consider to be a homogeneous culture. Instead, it would be preferable to consider norms and values as resources called upon by agents according to the type of problems and situations they encounter. In sum, rather than focusing on intercultural diversity, much would be gained from also considering intracultural diversity, which could provide a means of escaping the ideological power relations between local ethics and Western morality. The second answer, suggested by Steven Lukes, rests on an eclectic philosophical approach that makes use of both the Kantian and Aristotelian legacies. On the one hand, the existence of all possible varieties of moral and ethical principles is noted, along with the recognition that all these principles and practices necessarily suppose that they can be justified before others, which is a variant of the Kantian 'categorical imperative': in other words, there is indeed a common foundation that one could label justifiably to others. On the other hand, this approach accepts that different societies, or one society at different times, can have distinct norms and values leading them to judge distinctly between what is good or bad for human beings, but nonetheless considers that it is possible to ascribe objectively a general aim to all these norms and values, that is, the idea of a successful life, which is a possible translation of Aristotle's 'eudaimonia'. One can therefore invoke both the universal and the relative.

These questions have particular political relevance at a time when some speak of the clash of cultures or proclaim the death of multiculturalism, and when many see human rights as a universal value that should be applied to all, while others contest their foundations or the conditions in which they are applied. But they also have remarkable scientific pertinence as new knowledge from cognitive science, analytical philosophy, experimental philosophy, biological evolutionism, and neuroimaging herald the return of a universalism that brings together, for the first time in such a clearly combined form, the two approaches that have so often been presented in opposition: naturalism and rationalism. These challenges, as political as they are scientific, fully justify the need for the citizen as well as the researcher to be equipped with the necessary intellectual tools to address them.

Notes

1 This presentation of the different answers to this fundamental question obviously cannot account for the full wealth of research developed over recent years. However, the reader will find an insight into these in the second part of the book edited by Didier Fassin (2012), *Moral Anthropology: A Companion*, Malden: Wiley-Blackwell, with the contributions by Joel Robbins on cultural values, Veena Das on ordinary ethics, Jason Throop on moral sentiments, Karen Sykes on moral reasoning, Thomas Widlok on virtues and Jarrett Zigon on narratives.

2 In a somewhat different perspective, this is also the approach taken by Kenneth Read in Papua New Guinea. However, this line of analysis can also be linked to classical studies carried out in societies of the Mediterranean region on honour and shame, to which we refer later. See Kenneth Read (1955), Morality and the Concept of Person Among the Gahuku-Gama, Eastern Highlands, New Guinea, *Oceania*, 25 (4): 233–282.

3 In this line of research, we can also mention Saba Mahmood and Charles Hirschkind's work on the Islamic world, Jarrett Zigon and Omri Elisha's work on the Christian world, and Talal Asad's pioneering research looking at the parallels between the two. See Saba Mahmood (2005), *Politics of Piety: The Islamic Revival and the Feminist Subject*, Princeton, NJ: Princeton University Press; Charles Hirschkind (2006), *The Ethical Soundscape: Cassette Sermons and Islamic Counterpublics*, New York: Columbia University Press; Jarrett Zigon (2010), *HIV is God's Blessing: Rehabilitating Morality in Neoliberal Russia*, Berkeley, CA: University of California Press; Omri Elisha (2011), *Moral Ambition: Mobilization and Social Outreach in Evangelical Megachurches*, Berkeley, CA: University of California Press; Talal Asad (1993), *Genealogies of Religion: Discipline and Reasons of Power in Christianity and Islam*, Baltimore, MD: The Johns Hopkins University Press.

4 Veena Das was one of the first to pay this attention to the ordinary dimension of ethics in (2006), *Life and Words: Violence and the Descent into the Ordinary*, Berkeley, CA: University of California Press. However, it would also be justified to link this approach with another, stemming from a very different philosophical line of thinking, carried by feminism, and in particular by Carol Gilligan, which is known as the ethics of care. This theory specifically aims to identify and recognise, in maternal actions and in care giving, a concern for others and an attention to their needs, expectations, and suffering that has long been ignored by theory. See Joan Tronto (1993), *Moral Boundaries: A Political Argument for an Ethic of Care*, London: Routledge, as well as Sandra Laugier, Pascale Molinier and Patricia Paperman eds. (2009), *Qu'est-ce que le care? Souci des autres, sensibilité, responsabilité*, Paris: Payot.

5 An exception to this observation exists in the shape of the research recently developed around the question of moral reasoning, on the basis of studies of Melanesian societies. See Karen Sykes ed. (2009), *Ethnographies of Moral Reasoning: Living Paradoxes of a Global Age*, New York: Palgrave Macmillan.

6 Anthropologists are not alone on this ground. While philosophers have long ignored the cultural diversity of values, reducing them to a simple plurality of customs that in no way affected the unique nature of morals or ethics, over the last two decades some have begun to show interest in this question. See, for example, from the point of view of political theory, Michael Walzer (1994), *Thick and Thin: Moral Argument at Home and Abroad*, Notre Dame: University of Notre Dame Press, in an anthropological perspective, John Cook (2002), *Morality and Cultural Differences*, Oxford: Oxford University Press, and from the approach of moral philosophy, Kwame Anthony Appiah (2006), *Cosmopolitanism: Ethics in a World of Strangers*, New York: W. W. Norton.

7 Numerous examples can be found at the intersection of anthropology and law in the collective volume by Richard Shweder, Martha Minow and Hazel Rose Markus eds. (2002), *Engaging Cultural Differences: The Multicultural Challenge of Liberal Democracies*, New York: Russell Sage Foundation.

8 In the article cited, Clifford Geertz opposes what he states are often presented as two factions: on the one hand, the relativists, with Boas, Benedict, Herskovits and before them Westermarck, and on the other, the universalists, with Kroeber, Kluckhohn, Redfield, and after them Lévi-Strauss. It goes without saying that Clifford Geertz situated himself in the first group. It is not uninteresting, however, to note that in *Race and History* Claude Lévi-Strauss, legitimately considered as belonging to the second group given some of his writings, still presented a point of view on the singular and incommensurable nature of cultures that would not be rejected by a true culturalist.

The location of the moral

13 The structure of a moral code

John Ladd

John Ladd (1917–2011) was a professor at Brown University, where he founded and directed the programme of biomedical ethics and the Center for the Study of Race and Ethnicity in America. The research he conducted for his doctoral dissertation in philosophy led to a famous monograph published a few years later under the title *The Structure of a Moral Code*. Chiefly the result of a dialogue with Son of Many Beads, a Navajo who became his main informant as he was for other anthropologists, the text endeavoured to reconstitute the set of rules and norms that formed the moral code of this group. Paradoxically, what is often seen as the first systematic ethnography of morality was thus written by a philosopher. Following this pioneering work, John Ladd published mainly articles on general issues of moral philosophy, which are brought together in two volumes: *Ethical Relativism* and *Ethical Issues Relating to Life and Death*.

In the introduction to his book on the Navajo, extracts of which are presented here, John Ladd outlines with precision what he calls 'descriptive ethics' as opposed to 'normative ethics'. The point is not to enunciate general moral principles, as philosophers tend to, but rather to collect and analyse the specific moral precepts of a given society. This endeavour implies benefiting from the empirical approach of the anthropological method, grounded particularly in case studies, but also going beyond the theoretical inadequacies of available anthropological works that, for him, do not sufficiently conceptualise their object. In this regard, he defines the moral code of a society as the ensemble of moral rules: among the corpus of ideas, which he qualifies as ideology, those which are part of ethics of this society can be recognised by the fact they are formulated around the term 'ought'. Two statements are therefore made: first, that it is possible to separate the moral sphere from the other spheres of social life; second, that it is necessary to distinguish ideals, which constitute the moral code, from actual practice, which can deviate from this. In this way, like others before him, John Ladd shows that members of a traditional society are moralists capable of a sophisticated ethical system, but he does so with a rigour that is both ethnographic and philosophical. His study, though, could be subject to the same critical discussion that arose around Griaulian anthropology, namely whether one source, no matter how well informed, can suffice to represent the ideology of a whole society.

The object of *The Structure of a Moral Code* is to explore the problems involved in describing the ethics of societies other than our own. I shall call the investigation of the moral code and accompanying ethical conceptions of a person or group *descriptive ethics*. The kind of description sought would be a part of the more general description of the culture to which the people in question belong, and so descriptive ethics is a branch of cultural anthropology. Accordingly, it is a social science and should aim at conforming as closely as possible to the canons of the empirical sciences. In this book I shall develop a general theory of descriptive ethics, which will show how to formulate rigorously testable hypotheses about a people's ethics, and in this sense I hope to demonstrate that a scientific descriptive ethics is possible. In order to illustrate how this general theory can be used in actual anthropological research, I shall offer a detailed application of it to the ethics of the Navaho Indians.

At the outset, it is important to note the differences between descriptive ethics and what philosophers have called "normative ethics." These two disciplines are distinguished from each other in two respects, namely, in the kind of questions which they ask and in the subject matter with which they are concerned. Normative ethics asks such questions as: What ought I to do? What kinds of action are right or wrong? What is the good life? The answers to these questions are intended to provide guidance for conduct and for the evaluation of it. The act of accepting them *ipso facto* involves a commitment to living in accordance with them, and to counseling others to do so as well. In this sense, normative ethics has traditionally been understood by philosophers to be practical. Descriptive ethics, on the other hand, asks for a description of someone's answers to these questions. Thus, although its findings may be relevant to practice, its goal is theoretical in that it is possible to accept these findings without committing oneself to any kind of action. It follows that the subject matter of these two disciplines is entirely different; descriptive ethics is about someone's opinions while normative ethics is about conduct itself. Accordingly, the former might be said to be at a second-level or twice-removed from the actual actions of men. Indeed, the normative ethical activities of any person might well constitute the subject matter for an inquiry in descriptive ethics.

I do not wish to deny that there is any relation between descriptive and normative ethics. Obviously, the procedures and findings of the one may have relevance for those of the other; although the other parts of anthropology and the social sciences are probably more important than descriptive ethics for normative ethics. What I wish to deny is that the answers to the questions of descriptive ethics are also answers to those of normative ethics, and conversely. To assume that they are is either to commit a logical fallacy or to introduce a questionable premise. Thus, for instance, a fact about the ethical opinions of a people has no consequences with respect to the rightness or wrongness of their conduct, unless an additional premise in normative ethics is granted, namely, that the moral quality of actions is determined by people's opinions about it. This doubtful premise could be established only by arguments within normative ethics, and so cannot be derived from descriptive ethics alone. Conversely, the inferring of facts about people's opinions from the rightness or wrongness of their actions is also obviously a fallacy; unless, again, it is assumed that if an action is right people will think it is right. This, in turn, is an assumption which belongs to descriptive ethics and would in principle be capable of empirical confirmation or disconfirmation. In sum, the failure to distinguish between these two fields of inquiry has wrought confusion in both; and the result has been much inconsequential reasoning about what is right and wrong as well as about people's opinions about what is right and wrong. Unfortunately, it is an error which has not infrequently been committed by philosophers and anthropologists alike—a fact which readily becomes apparent if their arguments are subjected to rigorous logical analysis.

Although we cannot deduce our own ethical theories from the fact of agreement or disagreement with the majority of man's cultures, the study of descriptive ethics may make some contribution to the advancement of normative ethics. Philosophers usually suppose that non-literate peoples have little to offer in the way of insight into moral problems. But this view is a survival of an already outdated anthropological view which held such people to be "primitive" and to have an undeveloped "primitive mentality." From my own experience in talking to a Navaho moralist, I am convinced that his ideas are as rationally coherent and systematic as any of those to be found in the moral codes of our own culture, although before I visited the Southwest I had no preconceptions one way or the other. The evidence seems to confirm the Greek conception of man as a rational animal—whether he can write or not, and whether he believes in witches or angels.

The study of other moral codes may suggest various new ways of approaching and solving moral problems, and call our attention to some modes of ethical reasoning which have not been "dreamed of in our philosophy." It may also help us to become aware of our own presuppositions about ethics, and thus make us more critical of our own approach to ethical problems. Finally, although information about the ethical ideas of other cultures cannot be used to prove or disprove the universal validity of our own principles, it may entail certain consequences with respect to their universal applicability, and as such may indirectly affect the tenability of a proposed ethical theory.

Many contemporary philosophers have been concerned not so much with normative ethics as with what may be called "theoretical" or "analytical" ethics, that is, a kind of second level analysis of moral judgments and ethical discourse. However, they have limited their discussion to those moral judgments which are accepted in our society and to which they themselves are committed. Perhaps an acquaintance with moral codes outside the Greek and Judaic–Christian tradition will help them to gain some perspective on their own theories and thus have a broadening effect on these analytical inquiries.

In sum, descriptive ethics should be carefully distinguished from philosophical ethics, whether it be normative or theoretical ethics, since its subject matter is cross-cultural, its aim is descriptive and its method is scientific.

Descriptive ethics must also be distinguished from other types of anthropological inquiry. Its subject matter does not include the more general range of cultural and social phenomena to which anthropologists have generally devoted their attention, but only the informant's ethical ideas as a system of ideas. The wider ramifications of ethics for social and personality systems are, of course, legitimate and important fields of inquiry; but there is more reason to hope for success in descriptive ethics if we approach the subject matter directly, and formulate its methods and findings in such a way that they are not logically dependent on these other inquiries.

Despite the fact that interest in the ethical opinions of other peoples goes back at least as far as Herodotus, there seems to have been little effort made to render the descriptions of these opinions scientific. A generation ago some writers concerned themselves with what was then called "comparative ethics," another name for descriptive ethics. However, the perfunctory character of their methods and data, as well as subsequent developments in the social sciences and philosophy have rendered their theories almost completely obsolete. In recent years, anthropologists and philosophers have paid relatively little attention to descriptive ethics.

Most of the available accounts of the ethics of non-literate societies seem to me to lack the precision and subtlety that are required to make them scientifically reliable and philosophically interesting. These inadequacies are due in part to the absence of any detailed analysis of basic concepts. Terms like "moral judgment," "moral sentiment," "obligations," "sanctions," "moral standards," and "ethics" are used with great abandon and little explication. There is rarely any awareness of what type of evidence would be relevant to the proof or disproof of the theories offered, and often no clear-cut distinction has been made between the evidence for a people's ethics and the evidence for other cultural and social phenomena. Indeed, it is possible to find descriptions of a people's ethics where no evidence whatsoever is offered, and we are supposed to accept them on the basis of the investigator's intuitions. [...]

A moral code is a collection of moral rules and principles relating to what ought or ought not to be done—what is right or wrong. An ethics includes both the moral code and all the ethical conceptions and argumentation which are associated with it. It is with these meanings that the terms "moral code" and "ethics" are ordinarily used, and they correspond not only to the primary senses of the words listed in the dictionary but to traditional philosophical usage as well. It follows from the very meaning of the terms that both the moral code and the ethics of a particular person or group are part of their ideology.

The word "ethics," however, has been used by many writers on the ethics of non-literate societies to include also actual conduct. Admittedly there is a way in which the English word "ethics" is popularly employed as a synonym for "morals," in the sense in which "morals" refers to an agent's actual conduct rather than to the principles he espouses. For instance: we sometimes hear people speak of someone's "unethical" behavior. (It should be noted that this meaning of the word does not appear in the *Oxford English Dictionary*.) But even admitting the possibility of this use of "ethics," such use is clearly derivative, since in order to determine whether someone's behavior is unethical we not only have to know the facts about his behavior but must also have a body of ethical ideals by which to evaluate them. Thus, all uses of "ethics" presuppose the meaning in which it refers to a body of ideas or principles.

The ethics of a particular person or group is distinguishable from other systems of ideas, such as beliefs about natural events, in that it is primarily concerned with what *ought* to be done, rather than with what is done, has been done, or will be done. In this sense, it is a system of ideals or norms. It is obvious that people do not always do what they think they ought to do; therefore, moral ideal and practice cannot be expected always to coincide. It has frequently been pointed out that one of the striking differences between moral laws and scientific laws is that the former can be violated, while the latter cannot be, except in the Pickwickian sense in which a statistical law allows for the possibility of negative instances. Hence, the fact of violability, or the logical possibility of nonconforming behavior, is an essential element in the conception of a moral code. It is this fact that makes possible the use of such terms as "transgression," "crime," "sin," "doing wrong," "temptation," or "remorse." [...]

Thus, in some accounts of non-literate ethics where behavioral evidence is adduced, I suspect that the writers may be employing their own ethical principles as the standard of reference, and that their reports are often descriptions of the degree to which the conduct of non-literate peoples conforms or does not conform to these principles. This reflects a use of the term "ethics" which is perfectly legitimate. But from this use it follows that there is just one ethical system for all of mankind, and that the actions of all individuals must be evaluated by these universal standards. It is misleading, however, to claim that by using such a definition of "ethics," we can provide an account of a people's moral code. In actuality it is an account of their moral practice based on standards of which the people in question may not be aware.

Still other writers have explicitly identified the ethics of a person with his overt conduct or some aspect of it. If this identification is regarded as a stipulative definition, there can be no objection to it on theoretical grounds. If such a stipulation is made, however, it must be expressly stated so that the usual connotations of the term "ethics" will not be assumed by the reader, and the investigator himself must scrupulously adhere to the stipulated meaning and avoid using "ethics" in the ordinary sense. If he fails to do so, his argument is bound to be based upon an equivocation. Nevertheless, we find examples of such illegitimate argumentation in anthropological literature. For example, one writer contends that in a certain non-literate society theory and practice do not diverge as greatly as they do in American society, and there are insinuations that Americans are more hypocritical than simpler folk. But, as soon as we note that the "ethics" of the non-literate society is defined at least partially in behavioral terms, the statement about the non-literate society becomes true by definition and has no scientific value. And, since the statement about Americans is based on the usual meaning of "ethics," the two sets of facts are not comparable because they employ different definitions of "ethics."

The use of stipulative definitions of "ethics" in terms of behavior or some aspect of it has certain methodological consequences of its own. By employing such definitions the investigator automatically deprives himself of the opportunity both to investigate the extent to which people conform to their standards and to inquire into the functional relationships between moral codes and social organization or social mechanisms, for any inference made about the efficacy or function of a moral standard would be circular, and true by definition. Thus, if a behavioral definition of "ethics" is adopted, it would follow that every ethics has objective consequences, to the extent to which the actions of individuals have such consequences. Hence, any investigation of the function of moral codes, in this sense, would be of no empirical value because "moral code" has been so defined as to exclude any parts of it which could be nonfunctional as a result of having no objectively observable consequences.

It should be noted that in maintaining that a moral code is part of an ideology, and that it is to be distinguished from actual observable behavior, I do not wish to deny that there is any relation between them, such as a mutual causal dependence of the one on the other. Not only is a moral code supposed to influence conduct, it obviously often does influence it; conversely, the elements and general character of a moral code are dependent on situational factors and social functions. But if these dependencies are made true by definition, as the denial of the distinction would entail, an empirical investigation of them would become impossible.

In sum, there are two reasons for regarding a moral code (or an ethics) as part of an ideology, and, thus, as distinct from practice or observed behavior. First, this is an obvious consequence of the meaning of the term "moral code" as ordinarily understood; and if we depart from this usage we can no longer claim to be discussing a people's moral code in the usual sense. Second, by adopting a definition which will in some way enable us to distinguish between a people's moral code and their overt conduct or some aspect or pattern of their behavior, we will make a noncircular investigation of the causal dependencies between them logically possible.

14 An ethics of freedom

James Laidlaw

James Laidlaw (born in 1963) is a director of studies at King's College, Cambridge. A specialist in the anthropology of religion, he carried out most of his ethnographical work in India on Jainism but has recently also analysed Buddhist practices in East Asia. In both cases, he reflects on the ethical work carried out on the self in the context of ritual practices and ascetic behaviours, which he presents in his monograph on the Jains: *Riches and Renunciation*. Recently, James Laidlaw has also developed theoretical research inspired by the cognitive science of religion, notably in two books that he co-edited with Harvey Whitehouse: *Ritual and Memory* and *Religion, Anthropology and Cognitive Science*.

The text presented here, which reproduces the Malinowski Memorial Lecture that he gave in 2001, is often cited as having opened up new perspectives within the anthropology of ethics. Noting, like others before him, the almost complete absence of ethnological studies focusing explicitly on ethics, James Laidlaw lays the responsibility on Durkheim and his successors. And indeed, paradoxically, by making morality a question of rules and obligation and by grounding it in the collective, the French sociologist makes it impossible to think through the individual's freedom to act ethically, which did exist in Kant's work. It is this 'ethics of freedom' that, for James Laidlaw, should be brought back to analysis – something that the concept of agency does not allow because it means only taking into account expressions of autonomy or resistance that researchers themselves evaluate positively. Two philosophers guide the author in this endeavour: Nietzsche, with his *Genealogy of Morals* which situates morality historically and therefore allows a distinction to be made between the particular morality of Judaeo–Christian society and non-moral forms of ethics such as that of the Jains; and Michel Foucault, in that he defines ethics as a 'conscious practice of freedom' and that the parallel between techniques of the self in the Catholic monastic world and Jain practices of confession and renunciation prove heuristic. Within what is imposed upon the subject, there is an expression of and a claim to freedom or even liberation. This theoretical approach thus offers a clear alternative to the anthropology of moral codes by providing an ethnography of ethics that escapes the various forms of moral ethnocentrism.

The argument I present here begins from the observation that despite the interest shown in the matter by some of the very greatest anthropologists our discipline has not developed a body of theoretical reflection on the nature of ethics. I shall assume that this is a deficiency, and that it would therefore be an advance if it could be rectified. And my claim will be that in order to do so we shall need a way of describing the possibilities of human freedom: of describing, that is, how freedom is exercised in different social contexts and cultural traditions. However, freedom is a concept about which anthropology has had strikingly little to say. Malinowski was an honourable exception here – both in his insistence, in *Crime and Custom* (1926), that the Trobriander in particular and the 'savage' in general is not an unthinking slave of custom but a free agent exercising his own judgement and choice; and also in his posthumously published book, *Freedom and Civilisation* (1947), where he considers the social conditions of political freedom. As Ernest Gellner remarked,[1] the case of Malinowski illustrates that it is possible to be a believer in freedom – in its existence and in its value – without necessarily subscribing to an atomistic social ontology, and without denying the importance of the social or cultural in human flourishing.

I have said that there is no anthropology of ethics, and I am aware that viewed in a certain light this may seem controversial. I do not mean of course that no anthropologists have ever written about morality. What I mean is that there is no sustained field of enquiry and debate. There is no connected history we can tell ourselves about the study of morality in anthropology, as we do for a range of topics such as kinship, the economy, the state, or the body. There is no history, that is to say, that includes sustained debate on specific interpretive problems, or distinctive concepts contributed by particular authors or schools, or which reflects changes in general theoretical orientation, as one 'ism' gives way to the next. There are no equivalents of descent theory and alliance theory, no formalism and substantivism, no instrumentalism and primordialism, no symbolist and phenomenological approaches.

It is also striking that no serious dialogue has developed with moral philosophy.[2] There, as in more general public debate, the usual way in which our discipline appears in discussion is where someone cites, as being what 'anthropologists say,' the basically incoherent position that the facts of cultural variation lend 'empirical support' to moral relativism.[3] Less frequently, but perhaps increasingly, studies of hunter-gatherer co-operation and reciprocity are cited by utilitarian animal liberation theorists, to help bridge the gap between human and other species.[4] Probably most anthropologists are not entirely comfortable with either of these representations, but in the absence of sustained argument within the discipline we are more entitled to regret than to complaint.

This unhappy situation persists even though there have unquestionably been some individually brilliant discussions of morality by anthropologists. Some of the greatest ethnographies are dominated by the explication of moral concepts and reasoning. And several anthropologists have recognized that sustained theoretical reflection on ethics would enrich the discipline.[5] And then, of course, there is Durkheim.

As is well known, Durkheim's later work announced the ambition of subsuming what had been moral philosophy into an empirically grounded science of 'moral facts.' Indeed, given the extent to which Durkheim set the intellectual agenda for twentieth-century anthropology, it might seem at first sight surprising that an anthropology of morality does not stand at the centre of the discipline (and at the core of every undergraduate course). Durkheim, after all, understood society to be based on moral obligation, and indeed defined it as being a system of moral facts.

But this, I want to suggest, is part of the problem. Durkheim's conception of the social so completely identifies the collective with the good that an independent understanding of ethics appears neither necessary nor possible. There is no conceptual space for it. His subsequent influence on anthropologists and others has waxed and waned, and in some respects it is unfair to single out Durkheim for criticism. He did not invent the collectivist conception of society (though he does remain one of its most eloquent exponents). But just because he devoted so much explicit attention to morality, and seems at first sight to have achieved its integration into the study of society, his writings reveal the disabling consequences of identifying the social with the moral as he did. Durkheim's 'social' is, effectively, Immanuel Kant's notion of the moral law, with the all-important change that the concept of human freedom, which was of course central for Kant, has been neatly excised from it. The category of the moral has, accordingly, almost invariably collapsed in the hands of anthropologists into whatever other terms we have been enthusiastically using to explain collectively sanctioned rules, beliefs, and opinions: sometimes 'culture,' sometimes 'ideology,' sometimes 'discourse.' The questions that then get asked are ones that are appropriate for these other concepts. If these are the rules, how and by whom are they formulated? How are they re-enforced and transmitted through time, and how and by whom are they challenged? Who gets to say what counts as a breach of them? And so on. In this situation the concept of the moral means everything and nothing. It does no distinctive conceptual work and therefore it is not surprising that, despite occasional attempts to arouse some interest in it, it keeps going out of focus and fading away.[6] [...]

I want therefore to argue that an anthropology of ethics will only be possible – will only be prevented from constantly collapsing into general questions of social regularity and social control – if we take seriously, as something requiring ethnographic description, the possibilities of human freedom.

Why will the concept of 'agency' not do just as well? It is necessary briefly to address this question because this concept is so routinely cited these days as if it were the mandatory solution to nearly every problem, with self-evident virtues that are moral and political as well as theoretical. The problem with this, of course, is that perspicuous description can easily give way to wishfulfilment: it is a temptation to describe the world as we would like it to be, rather than as it is. In any case, even if it is accepted that agency is a good thing, and worth describing, where it is present, it is not the only good thing, and not the same good thing as is freedom.

What the concept of agency, as it has become popularized in anthropology, picks out is a matter of the effectiveness of action – specifically its effectiveness in producing, reproducing, or changing the structures within which people act. Agency is therefore a means of pinpointing whose acts are, to various degrees, structurally or transformatively important, or powerful. In so far as talk of agency raises the question of whether persons' choices are genuinely their choices – in so far, that is, as it points to questions of freedom – it does so in a way that is necessarily and systematically conflated with the question of the capacity or power which their choices have in causal terms. This means that, as an index of freedom, the concept of agency is pre-emptively selective. Only actions contributing towards what the analyst sees as structurally significant count as instances of agency. Put most crudely, we only mark them down as agency when people's choices seem to us to be the right ones.

So I want to insist that there is important conceptual work that 'agency' cannot do, and it remains therefore to try to show how the concepts of ethics and freedom might enrich the anthropological understanding of human conduct. I am going to look for help, in doing this, to two perhaps initially surprising authors, namely Nietzsche and Foucault. Both of these authors have been fashionable recently, although only the latter in anthropology, and he for reasons that are different from those that interest me here. I shall also draw, perhaps less surprisingly, on the writings of the moral philosopher Bernard Williams.

Nietzsche[7] may seem a surprising choice, because apart from his (or anyway his 'madman's') declaration of the death of God,[8] the thing for which he is perhaps most celebrated is declaring himself to be an immoralist.[9] However, this does not mean that he rejects all ways of evaluating human conduct as more or less admirable. On the contrary his concern is critically to assess the *value* of the values we think of as morality.[10] What he does is to identify, and try to explain, what is distinctive about moral as distinct from other non-moral values, claiming that there have been in the past and could be in the future systems of values other than 'morality.'[11] [...]

How far does Nietzsche's account of the genealogy of morality – of the relation between morality and other ethical values – apply to the case of the Jains? I have written elsewhere about how lay followers of this religion – the people who do not actually give up all their material possessions, abandon their families, and take to a life of wandering barefoot in emulation of these ascetic exemplars – combine a partial participation in this strong example of self-denying asceticism with adherence also to quite different values, in the pursuit of wealth, prestige, personal fulfilment, fecundity, and so on. Living in the light of such starkly conflicting values, Jain communities have developed religious practices that can make them seem compossible, but individuals still have to make choices.[12] The asceticism prescribed in Jain religious teaching is plainly a powerful influence in everyday life. But only to a limited degree does it make itself felt through moral rules. For the most part, instead, people voluntarily place themselves under ascetic obligations by taking temporary vows, though they may also do so permanently. We do have here a version of the general problem situation with which Nietzsche is concerned. How well then does his account of the genesis of ascetic morality illuminate the Jain case?

Nietzsche often refers to the transvaluation of values that gives rise to morality as the 'slave revolt.' The expression is somewhat misleading since he is not imagining a violent uprising but the process whereby everyone, including the nobles in what had been pre-moral heroic societies, come to subscribe to the values espoused and promoted initially by the lowest in the society. The source of the creativity that makes this possible lies in the powerful resentment – Nietzsche says '*ressentiment*' – articulated for them by their priests.[13] *Ressentiment* 'turns creative' and gives rise to new values.[14] In place of the nonchalant and even pitying disdain of the nobles for their inferiors, the slaves regarded their superiors as dangerous enemies. So was born the concept of evil. What had been good characteristics were now 're-touched, re-interpreted, and re-viewed through the poisonous eye of *ressentiment*'.[15] They were seen not just in a negative light but as the malevolent expression of an unseen agency. So where force, vitality, and formidableness had been inseparable natural expressions of strength, they are now seen, as if strength had the choice of not being strong, as 'aggression.' Correspondingly, being weak was also represented as if it were from choice, and therefore as an accomplishment. Weakness now becomes, in the new moral sense, good. [...]

Jainism appears to lack the idea that any of these debts are owed to God. The perfected souls worshipped by Jains do observe the continuing *karmik* drama of everyone else's good and bad deeds being rewarded and punished, but it is not they who make or carry out these judgements, and nor are the judgements in any sense made for their sake or on their behalf. They are instead the automatic doing of the uncreated universe. This means that asceticism in the Jain case is not so much a matter of obedience to God's law or commands as it is of enlightened self-interest, where the 'self' whose interest is at stake is not that of the living person but the imagined future purified soul one could become after enlightenment and death.[16] What would have to be the case for this hypothetical possibility to give rise to definite moral obligations, as Nietzsche envisages?

If one were finally to achieve liberation, one would become a pure soul, devoid of all the characteristics of one's present self, and identical to those souls one now worships. As the Jains say, one would 'become God.' As they also say, it is already your soul's inherent nature to achieve this goal: your soul already in some sense 'wants' to be free of everything that makes you the person you are. You could be said then, in Nietzsche's terms, to owe it to the God you might become to practise ascetic morality. Someone for whom the idea of a pure and liberated soul was present, not just as a believed-in ideal, but as the 'I' that stands at the centre of his sense of self, such a person's body, identity, thoughts, acts, and character – his *karma* – would be debts he owed to himself and, indistinguishably, to God. For such a person Jain asceticism would be, in Nietzsche's and Williams's terms, a matter of moral obligation.

So we can pose Nietzsche's question about the genealogy of morality – of the relation between morality and non-moral ethics – as a question, for the case of Jainism, of how such a person could come to be. What would make it the case that 'I' was not James Laidlaw, thirty-eight years old, five foot nine and a half, and so on, but a pure and perfect soul somehow trapped in that person and fundamentally alien to everything that makes him up?

An anthropology of ethics – of which the anthropology of morality would be a part – would seek to answer this question; and to show what an answer might look like, I want to turn now to the later writings of Michel Foucault. From him I want to take two things. The first is a way of writing about the aspects of ethical life that cannot be captured in a history of moral codes or social rules. Like Williams, Foucault insists that the domain of ethics is wider than the following of socially sanctioned moral rules, in Durkheimian terms. It also includes our response to invitations or injunctions to make oneself into a certain kind of person. Self-fashioning of this kind is described by Foucault, in my view rightly, as a practice of freedom. So the second point I want to take from Foucault is a way of studying ethical freedom ethnographically. For Foucault, freedom is exercised in different ways in different historical circumstances, and so studying it involves describing the ethical practices – Foucault calls them also 'techniques of the self' – through which this may be done.

Foucault may seem to be as unlikely an ally for me in the argument I have been pursuing as was Nietzsche. His works have been enormously influential in anthropology, but the Foucault who has had this influence has been the advocate of a bleakly totalizing vision of societies as systems of power/knowledge, where domination and resistance are necessary, pervasive, and mutually implicating aspects of all social relations.[17] There is some warrant for this reading of Foucault, especially in *Discipline and Punish*. But Foucault himself spent the remaining years of his life, from the moment that book was delivered to its publisher, thinking himself out of that conception.[18] Among antiFoucauldians, Foucault was the original, and in many ways the best. [...]

The notion of freedom is central to this project, and it is important to note how this contentious term appears in Foucault's writings. He does not propose a prescriptive account of human freedom, or offer criteria for its full realization. He speaks not of achieving but of exercising freedom, and does so to refer to the extent to which and the ways in which people can exercise choice or are subject to coercion. One can have more or less freedom, and it takes different forms, in different historical situations. This is consistent with his view that human nature is not fixed, and waiting to be discovered and realized, but instead perpetually reinvented through human choice and action: hence his hostility to the rhetoric of 'liberation', with its implication of releasing a formerly suppressed true nature.[19] Thus, while Foucault remains studiedly non-committal with respect to a philosophical characterization of freedom, he does persistently distance himself from two utopian ideas about freedom (ideas which, being utopian, often lead in practice to the opposite of freedom): the idea that to act freely is to act in conformity with reason (or one's 'true' interests – this is the idea that lurks behind much anthropological use of 'agency'), and the idea that freedom is only possible in the total absence of constraint or relations of power. This latter idea, of freedom as something akin to randomness or being uncaused, finds expression in many articulations of morality, where moral judgement attaches only to the will, and therefore only to actions in so far as they are, in a very strong sense, voluntary.[20] It is only in so far as acts are voluntary that the idea of peculiarly moral responsibility – responsibility that can inspire moral guilt because, as Williams puts it, it 'goes all the way down' – has purchase. This means that morality tends to take a particularizing view of human actions. It looks at specific, singular acts and choices and, taking the agent and his or her character as given, assigns praise or blame to what he or she decides to do. If one looks outside the singular act, one sees that the agent and his or her character are not givens, but respond instead to what Williams describes as 'practices of encouragement and discouragement, acceptance and rejection, which work on desire and character to shape them into the requirements and possibilities of ethical life.' These practices provide the context in which an agent can exercise some 'freedom to have chosen some other character.'[21] Foucault is making the same point when he says that, when 'the subject constitutes itself in an active fashion through practices of the self,' these practices are 'models that he finds in his culture and are proposed, suggested, imposed upon him by his culture, his society, his social group.'[22] This does not mean that his doing so is not an exercise of freedom, but that the freedom he exercises is of a definite, historically produced kind. There is no other kind.

'Ethics,' Foucault writes, 'is the conscious (*réfléchie*) practice of freedom.' It is 'the considered form that freedom takes when it is informed by reflection.'[23] The 'reflection' in this formulation is equivalent to 'thought,' as Foucault used the word in the designation he chose for himself as Professor of the History of Systems of Thought at the College de France. What does he mean by 'thought'? He describes it as 'not just representations that inhabit conduct,' so not the stuff in which anthropology often deals, the taken-for-granted cultural representations, or habitus, or 'discourse.' Instead: 'it is what allows one to step back from this way of acting or reacting, to present it to oneself as an object of thought and to question it as to its meaning, its conditions, and its goals. Thought is freedom in relation to what one does, the motion by which one detaches oneself from it, establishes it as an object, and reflects on it as a problem.'[24]

(Note that it is possible to exercise 'agency' without doing any of this.) Elsewhere, he says that thought is 'what establishes the relation with oneself and with others, and constitutes the human being as an ethical subject.'[25] Therefore the freedom of the ethical subject, for Foucault, consists in the possibility of choosing the kind of self one wishes to be. Actively answering the ethical question of how or as what one ought to live is to exercise this self-constituting freedom.

Foucault's great achievement in my view was to see, and to show, how we can have a history of this: that by describing the different techniques of the self, one can tell the story of different ways in which people have purposefully made themselves into certain kinds of persons, and therefore of the historically specific and definite (and of course always limited) forms which that ethical freedom has taken.

Foucault never puts the matter in the way I have here, and indeed he never raises the question in quite this way, but I think that his analysis of ethics and his notion of techniques of the self enable us to describe, in more detailed and intricate terms than does Nietzsche's language about values and theological ideas, how certain ethical projects can become that very singular thing – a self-denying morality. A late seminar by Foucault includes an analysis of two kinds of Christian monastic techniques of confession and penance – called the *exomologenesis* and *exagoreusis* – the latter especially as set out in the writings of the fifth-century monastic writer Cassian.[26] I shall use this discussion as a sounding-board for some brief and programmatic remarks on the most important confessional rite in Jainism, a practice called *pratikraman*.

Foucault remarks that techniques of the self generally involve some kind of obligation to truth.[27] In Christianity, there is a double truth obligation. There is an obligation to affirm 'the Truth' as revealed by God and as contained in scripture; and there is the obligation to discover the truth about yourself. This double obligation is also found, he observes, in Buddhism, but he insists upon a difference.[28] In Buddhism, the truth you discover about the self is that the self is an illusion. This is not so in Christianity, where the self that you discover is a real one. Actually, Foucault's point about Buddhism (which anyway he does not pursue) is not without its difficulties, but, however the case may be there, in Jainism it is clear. The self is emphatically not an illusion – it is the very real result of all one's former actions, in this and in previous lives. Actions have this effect because they give rise to karma: matter which attaches to and pollutes the soul with the definite, substantive characteristics one has made for oneself through one's various lives: caste and kin identity, longevity and health, body, mind, emotions, habits, and dispositions. In Jainism as in Christianity there is the idea that in order to purify the soul, one must not only affirm the truth of scripture, but also establish the truth about oneself, and come to live by and act upon that truth. Knowing oneself is a centrally important means of self-transformation. And in both cases – and this I think is the crucial thing – the process of discovering the truth about the self leads to a cumulative and increasingly intense renunciation of that self. One becomes, in Nietzsche's terms, moral. How does this come about?

In Cassian, as it comes to be in Christianity in general, the self that must be known comes to be seen increasingly as a self with secret desires – paradigmatically and most persistently sexual desires. Unlike the Pagan world (as Foucault describes it), the way sex was problematized for Cassian and his Christian monastic contemporaries focused hardly at all on actual sex acts or sex relations between persons.[29] Abstention from sexual intercourse did not in itself constitute chastity, which required in addition the progressive stilling of all even involuntary stirrings of the flesh. This required the dissociation of the mind and the disengagement of the will from any sexual desire, and was pursued through techniques of self-analysis. Confession therefore tended towards the verbalization not just of specified sins, but of all one's thoughts and impulses, to bring them to scrutiny so that their source and nature could be divined – does this thought come from God? Or does it come from the Devil?

The Jain confessional practice of *pratikraman* is performed every morning and evening by renouncers, and by lay people as often as they choose – this varies radically between individuals depending on the extent to which they take on the ethical project of making themselves truly Jain.[30] *Pratikraman* involves a long, complex series of prostrations and other bodily postures, which are understood to be penances for the sins being enumerated. These sins are listed in a recitation which continues during the whole performance (which can take up to three hours) and this involves not a spelling out of what you, individually, have done that day or that week or that month. Instead, it is a comprehensive catalogue of all the things that could ever be done. All the emotions and passions that can be felt, all the actions that can be undertaken, and, crucially, all the kinds of living things there are, and which you might have harmed or killed, whether by thought, word, or deed, intentionally or unintentionally: all are catalogued. By performing the penances, you acknowledge that you will, even in spite of yourself, necessarily have committed these acts; you declare that you cast off the unaware and careless or wanton self that did so. And because the air is inhabited by uncountable millions of invisible living things, you must necessarily have killed a great many of these, even in the course of performing this very confession and penance. Here, knowledge of the self includes knowledge, derived from religious teaching but experienced in bodily practice, of the destructive effects your living, breathing, and acting have on other living things. So the confession itself contains within it confession and penance for the sins committed in the course of it.

In the Christian practice of *exagoreusis*, you piece together the truth about yourself by registering all the ways in which that self makes itself felt, even in the merest stirrings of the flesh or the most indistinct thoughts and desires. The injunction to find the truth of oneself is therefore part of a self-forming and self-transforming practice in which, as Foucault puts it, 'self-revelation is at the same time self-destruction.'[31] In *pratikraman* and in Jain ascetic practice a similar dynamic of self-revelation and self-destruction is generated, in a different but related way. The self that is discovered and renounced includes all one's kinship and other social relations, and it is not principally about sexual desire. It is again the case that the cause of sin is desire, and desires must again be enumerated, identified, repudiated, and extinguished, so that again the self is renounced even as it is discovered. This is clearly expressed in the Jain idiom according to which one 'casts off' the self that committed the sin. But the way in which desire makes itself known is not so much in sex, as in all the carelessness of physical motion – motion that causes one routinely to slaughter one's fellow creatures. It is violence, rather than sex, that is the unavoidable sin, the sin that can only finally come to an end with the end of one's physical life. So the techniques by which one purifies the self involve minute care about how one moves, walks, sits and stands, speaks, washes, and defecates; then learning to remain absolutely still in one's sleep, learning to regulate and limit what one eats, to fast for long periods, and in the end to give up eating entirely.[32]

The Jain ascetic treats his life, in Nietzsche's vivid phrase, as a wrong path that he has to walk along backwards.[33] Progressively, the constituents of the person, from one's caste and family relations, to one's name and personal identity, one's habits and mannerisms, preferences and sentiments, and finally one's bodily needs, are all by degrees known and renounced, leaving in the end only the pure soul, which is, finally, identical with every other purified soul.

The pursuit of this project of self-knowledge and self-renunciation may seem to be a very singular thing to do with one's freedom. But if the word 'freedom' is reserved only for choices one approves, then it loses its meaning. So the project's singularity should not prevent us from acknowledging that an exercise of freedom is indeed what it is. The adoption of even this extremely severe and literally self-destructive asceticism is a voluntary ethical project. Moral obligation is its end-point, not its beginning; and although it is pursued through instituted social practices, it is not a socially imposed code of rules.

Of course, some such rules deriving from this ethical project are to be found in Jain communities: for people brought up in a Jain milieu vegetarianism is a more-or-less compulsory rule, for example. And for people who take the most serious permanent vows and become Jain renouncers, quite a lot of their daily routine becomes prescribed. It would be reasonable to call both of these kinds of rules 'Jain morality,' and to understand that expression in the way Durkheim would have done. But nothing in the content of the rules would make sense without understanding the ethical project from which they derive. And to think that they encompassed the ethical lives of practising Jains would be an error.

In formalized religious techniques of the self such as *exagoreusis* or *pratikraman* the ambition of shaping the self is explicit, and is informed by sophisticated theoretical reflection, as it is not, perhaps, when people join a voluntary association of some kind, or change the way they dress, or take to buying recycled washing powder. They are doubtless much more powerful techniques of the self than these more do-it-yourself activities. But these, too, may be instances of the exercise of ethical freedom.

Wherever and in so far as people's conduct is shaped by attempts to make of themselves a certain kind of person, because it is as such a person that, on reflection, they think they ought to live, to that extent their conduct is ethical and free. And to the extent that they do so with reference to ideals, values, models, practices, relationships, and institutions that are amenable to ethnographic study, to that extent their conduct becomes the subject matter for an anthropology of ethics.

Notes

1 Gellner, E. (1998), *Language and Solitude: Wittgenstein, Malinowski and the Habsburg Dilemma*, Cambridge: Cambridge University Press, p. 141.
2 It is odd, for instance, that MacIntyre (MacIntyre, A., 1981, *After Virtue*, London: Duckworth; 1988, *Whose Justice? Which Rationality?* London: Duckworth; 1990, *Three Rival Versions of Moral Enquiry*, London: Duckworth) and Taylor (Taylor, C., 1985, *Philosophical Papers*. 2 vols. Cambridge: Cambridge University Press; 1989, *Sources of the Self*, Cambridge: Cambridge University Press; 1997, *Philosophical Arguments*, Cambridge, MA: Harvard University Press), who have argued in their different ways that morality can only be understood through a study of concrete social arrangements, have not found themselves engaged in fruitful dialogue by anthropologists. A recent exception, with respect to MacIntyre, is the interesting paper by Lambek (Lambek, M., 2000, The Anthropology of Religion and the Quarrel between Poetry and Philosophy, *Current Anthropology*, 41: 309–320).
3 Williams (Williams, B., 1972, *Morality*, Cambridge: Cambridge University Press, pp. 34–39) provides a classic discussion of what he calls the 'anthropologist's heresy.'
4 Examples of this include Singer (Singer, P., 1981, *The Expanding Circle: Ethics and Sociobiology*, Oxford: Clarendon Press).
5 See, for instance, Firth (Firth, R., 1951, Moral Standards and Social Organization, in *Elements of Social Organization*, Firth, R. (ed.), London: Athlone, pp. 206–224; Firth, R., 1953, The Study of Values by Social Anthropologists, *Journal of the Royal Anthropological Institute*, 53: 146–153).
6 Howell's *The Ethnography of Moralities* (Howell, S. (ed.), London: Routledge, 1997) may serve as a recent illustration. The editor, in an attempt in the introduction to draw some

general theoretical themes from the ethnographic contributions to the volume, notes that the Edels' (Edel, M. and A. Edel, *Anthropology and Ethics*, Cleveland, OH: Case Western, 1959) notion of 'ethics wide' is basically equivalent to traditional anthropological conceptions of culture. She defends the latter against some recent criticisms, and suggests that the use of the concept of morality is equally defensible, without saying what if anything she takes the difference between the two to be, or why we might need both.

7 Many editions/translations of Nietzsche's works are in use. I shall follow standard scholarly practice and refer to them using conventional abbreviations and paragraph/section numbers.
8 *The Gay Science*, B. Williams (ed.), Cambridge: Cambridge University Press, 2001 [1882, 1887], pp. 125, 343.
9 *Beyond Good and Evil*, M. Tanner (ed.), Harmondsworth, Penguin, 1990 [1886], pp. 23, 32, 226.
10 *On the Genealogy of Morality*, K. Ansell-Pearson (ed.), Cambridge: Cambridge University Press, 1994 [1887], p. 1.6.
11 See *Ecce Homo* 1968 [1888], in *Basic Writings of Nietzsche*, W. Kaufmann (ed.), New York: Modern Library, pp. 768–769. Sometimes Nietzsche distinguishes the morality he attacks from a prospective future 'higher' kind (BGE: 202) or 'wider' morality (BGE: 32). He also distinguishes morality in this sense from 'the morality of custom,' which is 'much older and more primitive' (OGM: 4).
12 Laidlaw (Laidlaw, J., *Riches and Renunciation: Religion, Economy, and Society among the Jains*, Oxford: Clarendon, 1995). The excellent ethnographies by Babb (Babb, L. A., *Absent Lord: Ascetics and Kings in a Jain Ritual Culture*, Berkeley, CA: University of California Press, 1996) and Cort (Cort, J., *Jains in the World: Religious Values and Ideology in India*, New York: Oxford University Press, 2001) are organized around the same issue. See also Chapple (Chapple, C., Pushing the Boundaries of Personal Ethics: The Practice of Jaina Vows, in *Ethics in the World Religions*, Runzo, J. and N. M. Martin (eds.), Oxford: Oneworld, 2001).
13 Nietzsche emphasizes in fact that the priestly proponents of ascetic values have come from all classes (OGM: 3.11).
14 *On the Genealogy of Morality*, 1.10.
15 *On the Genealogy of Morality*, 1.10; see also 3.14.
16 The difference is nowhere near absolute, however, for just as versions of Pascal's wager have always been a part of popular Christian moral thinking, so too in Jainism there are subordinate deities – deities in the sense of being supernatural beings possessed of miraculous powers – who do as it were make it a rule for their devotees to observe Jain moral precepts and will only confer the worldly benefits their miraculous power makes possible on people who venerate and follow the teachings of the Jinas. They may even punish those who do not. But these deities, unlike the Christian God, enjoy limited moral authority themselves. In some Jain traditions they are of almost no importance, and even in the traditions where they are a prominent part of popular religious practice, those who most strenuously practise Jain asceticism are generally those who worship these deities least.
17 This style of analysis, as Sahlins (Sahlins, M. [1993], *Waiting for Foucault*, Cambridge: Prickly Pear Press; [1999] Two or Three Things that I Know about Culture, *Journal of the Royal Anthropological Institute* [N.S.] 5: 399–421) has been insisting, is really just a modified crude functionalism.
18 See the intriguing discussion in Miller (Miller, J. [1993], *The Passion of Michel Foucault*, London: HarperCollins).
19 Foucault, M. (1981), *The History of Sexuality*, Vol. 1: An Introduction, Harmondsworth: Penguin; Foucault (1984), On the Genealogy of Ethics: An Overview of Work in Progress, in *The Foucault Reader*, Rabinow, P. (ed.), New York: Pantheon, pp. 340–372 [also in Foucault 2000, *Essential Works of Michel Foucault*, Vol. 1: *Ethics: Subjectivity and Truth* (P. Rabinow, ed.), London: Allen Lane, pp. 253–280]; Foucault (1984), The Ethics of the Concern of the Self as a Practice of Freedom, in *Philosophy and Social Criticism*, 12 (2–3): 1121–1131 [also in Foucault 2000, pp. 281–301].
20 Williams, B. (1985), *Ethics and the Limits of Philosophy*, London: Fontana; Williams (1995), *Making Sense of Humanity*, Cambridge: Cambridge University Press, pp. 3–76, 241–247; see also Nietzsche 1990 [1886], Beyond Good and Evil, op. cit., p. 21. One of Williams's purposes in *Shame and Necessity* is to show that the ancient Greeks operated with a more

realistic notion of responsibility (*Shame and Necessity*, Berkeley, CA: University of California Press, 1993, pp. 50–74). He shows that they had notions of cause, intention, state, and response – the basic elements of a conception of responsibility – but did not try to give the notion of the voluntary 'metaphysical depth' (p. 55). 'Just as there is a "problem of evil" only for those who expect the world to be good, there is a problem of free will only for those who think that the notion of the voluntary can be metaphysically deepened' (p. 68).

21 Williams (1985), *Ethics and the Limits of Philosophy*, op. cit., p. 194.
22 Foucault (1984 [2000]), The Ethics of the Concern of the Self, op. cit., p. 291.
23 Ibid., p. 284.
24 Ibid., p. 117.
25 Foucault, M. (1984 [2000]), Preface to the History of Sexuality, Vol. 2, in *The Foucault Reader*, Rabinow, P. (ed.), New York: Pantheon, p. 200 [also in Foucault 2000: 199–205].
26 Cassian, J. (2000), *The Institutes* (trans. by B. Ramsey), New York: Newman Press; Foucault, M. (1988), Technologies of the Self, in *Technologies of the Self: A Seminar with Michel Foucault*, Martin, L. H., H. Gutman and P. H. Hutton (eds.), Amherst, MA: University of Massachusetts Press, pp. 9–15 [expanded version in Foucault 2000, pp. 223–251]; see also Foucault 2000, pp. 81–86.
27 Foucault (1981), Sexuality and Solitude, *London Review of Books*, 3: 9, 21 May–5 June, 3–6 [also in Foucault 2000: 177–178]; Foucault (1988 [2000]), Technologies of the Self, op. cit., p. 223.
28 Foucault (1981 [2000]), Sexuality and Solitude, op. cit., p. 178.
29 Ibid.; Foucault, M. (1985), The Battle for Chastity, in *Western Sexuality*, Ariès, P. and A. Béjin (eds.), Oxford: Blackwell, pp. 14–25 [also in Foucault 2000: 185–197]; Foucault (1988), Technologies of the Self, op. cit.
30 Laidlaw (1995), *Riches and Renunciation*, op. cit., pp. 204–215. See also Cort (2001), *Jains in the World*, op. cit., pp. 122–127, Dundas, P. (1992), *The Jains*, London: Routledge, pp. 146–149, Jaini, P. S. (1979), *The Jaina Path of Purification*, Berkeley, CA: University of California Press, pp. 189–191, 209–217, and Williams, R. (1963), *Jaina Yoga: A Survey of the Mediaeval Sravakacaras*, London: Oxford University Press, pp. 203–207.
31 Foucault (1988 [2000]), Technologies of the Self, op. cit., p. 245.
32 On the way in which Jain asceticism and specifically non-violence requires comprehensive bodily control and fasting, see Laidlaw (1995), *Riches and Renunciation*, op. cit., pp. 151–172, 216–229. On the practice of fasting to death, see Dundas (1992), *The Jains*, op. cit., pp. 155–156, Jaini (1979), *The Jaina Path of Purification*, op. cit., pp. 227–240, and Settar, S. (1990), *Pursuing Death: Philosophy and Practice of Voluntary Termination of Life*, Dharwad: Institute of Indian Art History, Karnataka University.
33 Nietzsche (1994 [1887]), *On the Genealogy of Morality*, op. cit., 3.11.

15 An ethics of the act

Michael Lambek

Michael Lambek (born in 1950) is a professor of anthropology at the University of Toronto where he holds the Canada Research Chair in 'Anthropology of Ethical Life'. A specialist of religion, he has been president of the Society for the Anthropology of Religion and has published a *Reader in the Anthropology of Religion*. He mainly conducted his ethnographic studies in Madagascar and Mayotte, focusing on possession, trance and Islam, on which he has published *Human Spirits: A Cultural Account of Trance in Mayotte* and *Knowledge and Practice in Mayotte: Local Discourses of Islam, Sorcery and Spirit Possession*. He is also interested in the anthropology of the body and illness, on which he has co-edited *Bodies and Persons* and *Illness and Irony*. His recent research includes a set of reflections on memory and trauma, presented in *Tense Past* and *The Weight of the Past*.

In *Ordinary Ethics*, which he edited, Michael Lambek begins with a statement of fact: in their research, anthropologists encounter agents who try to conduct themselves morally, who evaluate the moral qualities of others and who discuss moral questions — and yet their publications bear little trace of this, as if the only issues that mattered were those relating to structure, power and interest. The collective project of this book is therefore to provide an account of this ordinary ethics. How? In his own contribution to the volume, extracts from which are presented here, he answers this question by situating ethics within action, that is, in the performance of acts and the practice of judgement. In other words, it is not located in codes or values, but in the movement back and forth between acts and judgement, and in the limitations revealed by both. The ethical theory developed by Michael Lambek is rooted in the philosophy of ordinary language as developed by Ludwig Wittgenstein and John Langshaw Austin, and taken further by Stanley Cavell: the meaning of the words that we use is to be found in everyday language, rather than in definitions of substance; it is the same for actions. On the basis of anthropologist Roy Rappaport's work on rituals, Michael Lambek shows that the latter constitute moments when we make commitments, for example when marriage confers not only a new moral status (that of spouse), but also relevant criteria according to which the behaviour of newlyweds will be judged (fidelity, sincerity, responsibility). More generally, he strives to account for both the regularity of actions, without reducing it to the application of restrictive rules, and the reflexivity of agents, without reducing this to the total freedom of conscience.

Where is the ethical located? I shall argue that it is intrinsic to action. I look at action in two related ways—as specific acts (performance) and ongoing judgment (practice)—and show that ethics is a function of each. Criteria for practical judgment are established and acknowledged in performative acts, while acts emerge from the stream of practice. Performance draws on previously established criteria, or felicity conditions, in order to produce its effects. These effects can be understood as committing performers to one particular alternative or set of alternatives out of many, and these commitments in turn inform subsequent evaluations of practice, and thus practical judgment itself, but do not determine practice. A simple illustration: insofar as the performance of a wedding instantiates the state of marriage, it provides criteria for evaluating the actors' subsequent practice as spouses. The act of marriage does not determine whether people remain "faithful" or practice "adultery," but it entails that their actions fall under such descriptions. If practice is rendered possible and meaningful through performative acts, practice also inevitably reveals the inadequacy of such acts and the limits of criteria and descriptions, especially their vulnerability to skepticism, and hence the need to start anew. Ethics, then, is not only about executing acts, establishing criteria, and practicing judgment, but also about confronting their limits, and ours. [...]

Ethics entails judgment (evaluation)[1] with respect to situations, actions, and, cumulatively, actors, persons, or character. The exercise of judgment is prospective (evaluating what to do, how to live), immediate (doing the right thing, drawing on what is at hand, jumping in), and retrospective (acknowledging what has been done for what it was and is). Articulated more strongly as forms of action, these can be epitomized, respectively, as promising, beginning, and forgiving.[2] Judgment is both of others, thus social and conventional, and for oneself, thus linked to freedom and self-fashioning, but also to responsibility, care, guilt, forgiveness, and insight, and to recognizing the limits of what one can know or do or understand.

In order to exercise judgment, there must be criteria. Whence come criteria? I assume some come from mind and some from experience. But criteria are also instantiated through human speech and action. Ethics is intrinsic because there are always criteria already in place, because speaking entails and generates criteria, and because there are always places where disagreement over criteria or their absence is troubling. Criteria serve as the basis for judging how to conduct oneself, whether to commit or exercise specific acts, to what ends and in what manner—but also for deciding what constitutes a given act or kind of act, where specific acts begin and end, whether acts have in fact been committed correctly, completely, and legitimately (Austin's felicity conditions), and how to evaluate one's own and others' actions. In the ordinary course of events, criteria are implicit, internal to judgment itself, but they are also available for conscious discernment and deliberation. It should be evident that criteria are not rules for using words that can guarantee the correctness or success of our claims but 'rather, criteria bring out what we claim by using the words we do ... in making claims to knowledge, undertaking actions, and forming interpersonal relationships.'[3] As Cavell notes,[4] if in ordinary usage (as in prize juries or admissions committees) agreement over criteria makes possible agreement over judgments, for Wittgenstein it appears that the ability to establish criteria is based on prior agreement in judgment. Wittgenstein's "appeal to criteria is meant, one might say, exactly to call to consciousness the astonishing fact of the astonishing extent to which we *do* agree in judgment; eliciting criteria goes to show therefore that our judgments *are* public, that is, shared."[5] However, for that reason, criteria do not often need to be publicly enunciated; we appeal to criteria only when the sense of mutual attunement is threatened.[6] As Shiner helpfully explicates, for Cavell, Wittgenstein's criteria are in the nature of things, not a matter of imposed convention. "Criterial rules ... are not external to, but *internal to* the human form of life."[7] To call them conventional, "alienates us from them, and thus from ourselves, for our form of life and our criteria are one."[8]

I take this to indicate the fundamental givenness of ethics. Nevertheless, while certain criteria are continuous or perduring, others are contingent. If criteria define contexts of action, there must be the means to transform the context and hence the relevant criteria. There are times when new criteria must be brought into effect or applied to new persons or new contexts and hence when they must be made relatively explicit. Rappaport[9] shows how ritual operates as a central means through which this happens. Among Tsembaga Maring of highland Papua New Guinea, rituals effect—bring into being—particular states of war and peace. These can be considered ethical states, since any aggressive or non-aggressive act is interpreted and evaluated as such in their light (that is, differently according to whether the current state is one of peace or war). Likewise, acts may be discerned as cooperative or uncooperative among those constituted as allies by having undergone the ritual together. More generally, rituals effect states of ethical personhood and relation, transforming a biological infant into a named social person, a man and woman into a married couple, a novice into a monk, a profane condition into one of blessing, a breach into a reconciliation, and so forth. To each of these persons, relationships, and states, criteria departing or renewed from or additional to what has hitherto been the case apply.

Whereas Austin argued that criteria of truth and falsity do not apply to illocutionary statements, Rappaport showed that in a sense they do, but in an inverted fashion. A locutionary statement is judged true or false according to whether it is in conformity with the state of affairs that it purports to describe or refer to (it is raining, Sarah Palin is president). However, following a felicitously enacted illocutionary utterance, it is the state of affairs or the subsequent actions that are to be judged as true or false according to whether they are in conformity with the utterance (you are false not to keep your promise or the peace; the drought is false once the rain magic has been performed). These are faults—falsehoods, lies, errors, sins, etc.—insofar as they are not in conformity with the moral condition that has been brought into effect. When the state of affairs is in conformity with the performative act, then the state can be said to be "true" (or correct, right, or good). Once I am inaugurated as president, my conduct is judged with respect to my status as an office holder and no longer as a contender. It is my conduct that is in question, not the act of inauguration or the office. If I serve as witness to a marriage, I cannot henceforward deny that the couple are married, nor act toward them or evaluate their actions as if they were not. To undergo a ritual is to commit, says Rappaport, both to the specific effects or conditions it produces (thereby agreeing to apply to them the relevant criteria) and to commit more generally to the relevance of the criteria that the ritual underwrites or reproduces, as well as the means of producing them (the nature of marriage, the legitimacy of weddings). Thus, the performance of a ritual initiates or transforms a specific moral state or condition relative to the participants, while also reproducing the felicity conditions or criteria that apply to such a transformation. Hence Rappaport says that ritual is simultaneously performative and meta-performative.[10]

The performance of a ritual, argues Rappaport, is characterized by the conjunction of indexical and canonical dimensions—that it is me undergoing it here and now ("indexical"), and that it is these previously inscribed and relatively unchangeable ("canonical") utterances and acts, part of a perduring liturgical order, that I hereby repeat. Rappaport argues that, by their submission to its bodily demands (of presence, posture, endurance, etc.), the participants performing or undergoing a ritual demonstrate to others and to themselves their acceptance of both its message and its form. They do so whether or not they "believe" in any specific propositions associated with it; hence the outward, public consequences prevail irrespective of the inner states of the participants. This evades the problem of recursiveness inherent to theories of intentionality, as well as the instability of subjectivity. In these respects Rappaport is very close to Austin and somewhat akin to what Derrida means by "tethering" or avowal, or Cavell means by acknowledgment, and quite distinct from what is commonly meant by sincerity. I can pray effectively, for example, without being certain that I believe in God, that I want to do so, or that prayer is the means to address God; I can successfully ask for forgiveness without feeling particularly contrite.[11]

Indeed, in Rappaport's view, I am *likely* to be uncertain; the point of ritual is to substitute public clarity for private obscurity or ambiguity, that is, to establish beyond question the relevant criteria. The central criterion—being accountable for what one says and does—is virtually universal, by contrast to the substantive criteria put into effect by specific rituals. Definitive ethical commitments and criteria are thus produced publicly and irrespective of personal doubt.

Rappaport begins his book not by acknowledging the universality of acknowledgment but by asserting that recognizing lies is a human problem. Insofar as symbols form the basis for human language and culture, hence for creativity, speculation, and so forth, hence, following Kant, for freedom from immediate sensations and circumstance, thought and communication by means of symbols raise two enormous problems. These are the problem of the lie and the problem of the alternative. The problem of the alternative can be seen as the flip side to Geertz's observation that culture always manifests itself as particular;[12] it is always in some specific form and thereby in contrast to alternative forms. This raises the following questions. On what basis should I follow one alternative rather than another? Is the choice mutually exclusive? (Does the acceptance of one entail the rejection of all others?[13]) How do I indicate which alternative I have chosen? How do I come to accept that I have made the (right) choice and hence stick to it? Rappaport attends more explicitly in his subsequent argument to the way ritual addresses the problem of the lie (How can we be reasonably sure that we are not lying to each other or establish commitments in the face of possible insincerity?) than to how it addresses alternatives. But in a sense the lie is a subspecies of alternative, and the focus in the subsequent argument on how ritual produces (relative) certainty is a way of reducing alternatives and specifying a particular path or set of criteria as much as it is one of assuring the truthfulness of any given utterance or set of propositions or, as noted above, of moving from the assertion's conformity to the facts to the facts' conformity to the assertion.[14] Rituals commit their performers to taking up specific alternatives and therefore rejecting competing or contradictory ones (you cannot be simultaneously married and unmarried or alternate between these states at will) and to ignoring incommensurable ones (alternative views of what constitutes "marriage"). Moreover, they render such acts of commitment difficult, and sometimes impossible, to take back, as in acts of scarification, circumcision, and other forms of sacrifice.[15] (Cavell's problem of finding a voice is thus partially obviated by inhabiting and suffering a body.) A critical point here is that, while the unfolding of events enables us to reinterpret earlier events in light of subsequent ones through the ongoing construction of narrative, it is more difficult to reinterpret after the fact the commitments entered into and the moral conditions brought into effect through the performance of rituals and, indeed, of everyday performative utterances of all kinds. [...]

By contrast to those who have seen the substance of ethics as either values or rules, or as the freedom to break away from the obligation of adhering to rules, I have argued that the ethical is intrinsic to human action, to meaning what one says and does and to living according to the criteria thereby established. Ethics is a property of speech and action, as mind is a property of body (or, action is a manifestation of ethics as body is an extension of mind). Ethics is not a discrete object, not best understood as a kind or set of things. Taking such an approach has avoided explaining ethics in universal rational, instrumental, psychological, or biological terms. And while acknowledging cultural difference, it has equally avoided depicting such difference according to distinctive values and thus stumbling over problems of relativism.

If I have advocated the exercise of practical judgment at the expense of following (or rejecting) rules, that is in large part because it is a more accurate description of how we live. And if I have taken up the concept of virtue at the expense of values, that is largely because virtue pertains to the qualities of acts and practical judgment rather than to the depiction of discrete objects or cultures. The substance of a virtue is never fixed but is a function of contingent circumstances; virtues are attributions in context, not things in themselves.[16] Whether a specific act is to be described as virtuous is a matter not of adherence to a rule but of the quality of judgment it exhibits. The judgments entailed in ongoing practice (when and in what manner to act), no less than the judgments entailed in evaluating acts and character after the fact, are rendered possible by the criteria at hand. Criteria are embedded in our use of language or established by means of the relatively formal orders of acts and utterances that anthropologists describe as ritual and that have as their core the illocutionary function of speech acts.[17] Criteria can be found in a hierarchy or continuum—from the fundamental, constant, comprehensive, or certain to those specific to the moral states, persons, and relations that have been brought into effect (under description) through immediate performances and acts of commitment. Criteria shape but do not determine how we act. We are never free insofar as we are always already spoken, spoken to, and spoken for; we are always free insofar as we are always already responsible for exercising our practical judgment.

Aristotle's conception of virtue as a function of ongoing practical judgment (*phronesis*) needs to be supplemented with an understanding of how criteria are established and how they come to apply to specific circumstances, contingencies, subjects, objects, and means of action. It is in the definitive acts and utterances we refer to as ritual that particular criteria are simultaneously established, acknowledged in principle, and rendered applicable in practice. To establish criteria is to acknowledge them both as valid generally and as relevant and relative to particular persons and circumstances. To live ethically is to accept specific criteria and nominations, to acknowledge such acceptance, to live in accord with such acceptance, to recognize the fragility of that acceptance and those criteria, and, finally, in the least felicitous circumstances, to acknowledge when one has failed and to forgive others their failures. Among the most significant and pervasive criteria are those that establish the basic humanity of persons—as beings mutually subject to criteria and hence to be acknowledged as ethical subjects in their own right, thereby, as Kant put it, having dignity, not price. However, this is also an area both subject to abuse and vulnerable to skepticism.

Speaking and acting entail the predication and appropriation of voice—speaking and acting as oneself (to someone, in the sight or hearing of someone, with reference to someone …)—and as such are intrinsically constitutive of ethical subjects and relations. We must (in this sense) mean what we say and do. In addition, we are required to acknowledge what we have said and done. And yet, at the same time, we cannot always mean what we say, insofar as we do not fully know the consequences of our actions, the depths of our intentions, the specificity of our path, or even that it is we who are called upon to speak and act now. We must speak and act seriously and commit to the paths we have begun, to which we are held (and hold ourselves) accountable—and also recognize that full certainty and consistency are not possible. Ethics is vulnerable to—but also achieved in the face of—rupture, erosion, and skepticism.

Speech and action, understood as illocutionary performance, establish the criteria according to which practice, understood as the ongoing exercise of judgment, takes place. We are judged and we judge according to the commitments we make and have made (including those that others have made on our behalf). Ritual acts establish moral states in which new or renewed criteria apply. Ritual serves to increase clarity, certainty, consistency and completeness in what is accomplished in speech and action. Yet it can never fully overcome skepticism or the work of time.

Since every utterance entails a commitment to our words, we are continually put to the test to keep, as it were, our promises. But in the face of circumstance this is often hard to do, and so we are also faced with the challenges of acknowledging our failures, thoughtlessness, misdeeds, infelicities, and changes of heart—and forgiving those of others. It might be said, then, that promising, acknowledging, and forgiving are meta-ethical acts. Such acts are intrinsically temporal and historical. Indeed, insofar as taking responsibility, rather than apportioning blame, serves as the motor of history, it not inconsequentially produces a subject position of agent rather than victim (except insofar as one is victim to one's own acts).

Insofar as these are features intrinsic to human speech and action, criteria of being human, they will be culturally recognized, a part of the store of human wisdom transmitted in distinctive traditions, cultivated through forms of discipline, embedded in the fine discriminations of ordinary language, and enunciated more explicitly in proverbs and narratives, and sometimes in the rationalized bodies of argument we call philosophy, theology, and even "ethics."

Notes

1 I use "judgment" to similar ends but in virtually the opposite sense from Veena Das, for whom "the crucial requirement is that we should be able to take an abstract, nonsubjective vantage position from which we can orient ourselves to the world." My usage is thus not that of the definitive attributive actions of the courts.
2 Arendt, Hannah (1998 [1958]), *The Human Condition*, 2nd ed., Chicago, IL: University of Chicago Press, pp. 237–246.
3 Guyer, Paul (1999), Cavell, Stanley Louis, in *The Cambridge Dictionary of Philosophy*, Cambridge: Cambridge University Press, p. 128.
4 Cavell, Stanley (1979), Criteria and Judgment, in *The Claim of Reason*, Oxford: Oxford University Press, p. 30.
5 Ibid., p. 31.
6 Ibid., p. 34.
7 Shiner, Roger (1986), Canfield, Cavell and Criteria, in *Criteria*, Canfield, John (ed.), London: Garland, p. 364, italics in original.

8 Ibid. The depth of human agreement is acknowledged in Cavell's phrase "the conventionality of human nature itself" (1979: 111, as cited by Hammer, Espen [2002], *Stanley Cavell: Skepticism, Subjectivity, and the Ordinary*, Cambridge: Polity, p. 28).
9 Rappaport, Roy (1999), *Ritual and Religion in the Making of Humanity*, Cambridge: Cambridge University Press.
10 Here and below I severely condense what is actually a highly elaborated and systematic argument (Rappaport 1999).
11 The matter of sincerity has been the subject of considerable debate, especially over the interpretation of Austin's citation of the words Euripides gives to Hippolytus, "my tongue swore to, but my heart did not" (Austin, J. L. 1965 [1955], *How to Do Things with Words*, New York: Oxford University Press, pp. 9–10; Cavell [1995], What Did Derrida Want of Austin?, in *Philosophical Passages: Wittgenstein, Emerson, Austin, Derrida*, Oxford: Blackwell, pp. 42–65; Cavell [1996], *A Pitch of Philosophy*, Cambridge, MA: Harvard University Press). Presumably its salience as a felicity condition depends on the "semiotic ideology" in place (Keane, Webb [2007], *Christian Moderns: Freedom and Fetish in the Mission Encounter*, Berkeley, CA: University of California Press; compare Lambek, Michael [2007], On Catching Up with Oneself: Learning to Know That One Means What One Does, in *Learning Religion*, Berliner, David and Ramon Sarró [eds.], Oxford: Berghahn, pp. 65–81). Mahmood (Mahmood, Saba [2004], *Politics of Piety: The Islamic Revival and the Feminist Subject*, Princeton, NJ: Princeton University Press) and Hirschkind (Hirschkind, Charles [2006], *The Ethical Soundscape: Cassette Sermons and Islamic Counter-Publics*, New York: Columbia University Press) have pointed interestingly to an ideology in which the "inside" of a person is part of the context that is expected to be transformed by performative acts and utterances. Here, then, is the reverse of the idea that a "good" or "true" utterance corresponds to an existing interior state. Rather, a person becomes better insofar as his interior state is appropriately shaped by the right acts and utterances: for example, contrition would follow from rather than precede an act of apology. Prevalent among pious Muslims in Cairo, such an argument draws from (and elaborates) Aristotle's ideas about the cultivation of character through education and good deeds.
12 Geertz, Clifford (1973 [1966]), *The Interpretation of Cultures*, New York: Basic Books.
13 Alternatives thus come in the form of either/or and both/and. The tension between them exemplifies a central feature of human thought (Lambek, Michael [1998], Body and Mind in Mind, Body and Mind in Body: Some Anthropological Interventions in a Long Conversation, in *Bodies and Persons: Comparative Perspectives from Africa and Melanesia*, Lambek, M. and A. Strathern [eds.], Cambridge: Cambridge University Press, pp. 103–123; Lambek [2007], Provincializing God? Provocations from an Anthropology of Religion, in *Religion: Beyond a Concept*, de Vries, Hent [ed.], New York: Fordham University Press, pp. 120–138).
14 The most salient and succinct form of the question of commitment is that of making a pledge or promise, a matter that, as noted, in the Introduction, is central to and often materialized as the gift.
15 Lambek, Michael (2007), Sacrifice and the Problem of Beginning: Reflections from Sakalava Mythopraxis, *Journal of the Royal Anthropological Institute*, 13 (1): 19–38.
16 Of course, they often do become objectified as values. For an earlier and somewhat different attempt to articulate the relation of virtue to value, see Lambek (Lambek, Michael [2008], Value and Virtue, *Anthropological Theory*, 8 (2): 133–157).
17 I have not addressed the place of criteria established through law, and hence the tension between ritual performance and legal act.

16 Deontology and consequentialism

Joel Robbins

Joel Robbins (born in 1961) is a professor of social anthropology at the University of Cambridge, and co-editor of the journal *Anthropological Theory*. A specialist in the anthropology of religion, he has been conducting a study among the Urapmins for numerous years. This society of Papua New Guinea only became Christianised a few decades ago, officially rejecting their traditional religion in favour of the Baptist doctrine. Joel Robbins describes this conversion and the tensions to which it gives rise in *Becoming Sinners: Christianity and Moral Torment in a Papua New Guinea Society*. His contribution to anthropology, inspired by Louis Dumont's works, is situated at the intersection of an approach considering moral codes – showing their possible conflict within one society – and considering ethical subjectivities – uncovering the dilemmas on the occasion of confessions or rituals of redemption.

In the text presented here, Joel Robbins extends this dual reading, first by including a consequentialist approach, and second by including anthropologists themselves in his analysis. Why, he asks, are Charismatic and Pentecostal Churches, which advocate moral rigour, meeting with such success worldwide? Why, more generally, are agents tending to consider morality in terms of absolute duty rather than in terms of foreseeable consequences, or, to use Weber's terms, why are they opting for an ethics of conviction rather than an ethics of responsibility? According to Joel Robbins, the contemporary period is filled with uncertainty concerning the near future, for which it is no longer possible to predict anything. This leads individuals to concentrate on the present, where their acts are concerned, and to project themselves into a mystical faraway future, with the former guaranteeing the latter. The religions that produce guilt and redemption as the source of salvation both relate and contribute to these anxieties and aspirations. For those who adopt them, respecting principles prevails over predicting effects – and anthropology, surprisingly, does not escape this temptation, showing a certain reliance on deontological reasoning that Joel Robbins criticises.

The rubric under which this article on moral reasoning unfolds is that of culpability. This represents a particular kind of constraint, one that would not have been in place had a related rubric such as that of responsibility been chosen. Responsibility is certainly one aspect of culpability, but culpability only encompasses that kind of responsibility one has for wrongdoing. Taken on its own terms, responsibility can refer to good things one ought to do, and can shade into notions of positive duty. But when responsibility is absorbed within culpability, it cannot point to the prospect of moral accomplishment, but only to that of moral guilt. A preoccupation with culpability thus leads to a style of moral reasoning that invests itself in worrying primarily about the possibility of being guilty and about how to avoid becoming so. Moral excellence in this frame is more about what one avoids than about what one accomplishes. Constrained as the view from culpability thus appears, I would still contend that at this time it is an inspired rubric under which to consider some of the prospects for an anthropological approach to moral reasoning. I say this because I think that many moral reasoners in the world today, including many anthropologists, do focus on culpability and operate within its constraints. In what follows I will try to back up this claim and to ask how we might begin to explain why concerns about culpability are so important to so many people's moral lives today.

In order to provide a sketch of what I have in mind when I refer to what we might call culpable moral reasoning, let me briefly consider the case of Pentecostal and charismatic Christianity. These kinds of Christianity, which I will call simply 'Pentecostal' in what follows to make for easier reading, are those in which believers are understood to be able to receive the gifts of the Holy Spirit; gifts which allow them to speak in tongues, heal, prophesy, sometimes prosper, and struggle with some (though not perfect) success to lead moral lives, among other things. They are the fastest growing kinds of Christianity in the world today. *The Economist*[1] has recently reported that there are 500 million Pentecostals worldwide, a figure that accords well with the high end of social scientific estimates of a few years ago.[2] Pentecostalism's growth has been particularly impressive in Africa, Latin America and Asia, but it is also spreading quickly in the Pacific and in the post-Soviet world. In light of the huge influence this version of Christianity has come to exercise on so many people in so many parts of the world, few would quibble with historian Mark Noll's[3] claim that its emergence at the beginning of the 20th century is an event that 'has had world historical significance'.

In this article, the aspect of that significance I want to examine is the style of moral reasoning Pentecostalism tends to encourage among its converts. This style, which is recognizable among Pentecostals from all of the myriad places where the faith has taken root, focuses on the human propensity to sin and the need to combat it. For Pentecostals, temptations to sin are everywhere. These temptations can follow from the nature of human desire, but they can also be the result of the deceptive enticements of various kinds of evil beings. In order to achieve their primary goal of salvation, Pentecostals have to resist these temptations. Left to their own devices, they stand little chance of success in this project, but with the help of the Holy Spirit in their hearts, they can hope to follow God's laws and live good Christian lives that are at least relatively free of sin. Toward this end, they spend a lot of time dwelling on the sins they have committed and those they feel tempted to commit, and they frequently engage in rituals such as prayer and church attendance that are designed to solicit the Spirit's help in their endeavor to avoid sin in the future.

The content of Pentecostal moral reasoning is far more complex than I can do justice to in this short article. I have explored it in detail elsewhere, both in a single ethnographic case and comparatively, and will not take it up further here.[4] But even without saying more about its content, the brief sketch I have given is enough to provide us with a sense of the most important outlines of its general style. This is a style focused on individual culpability (one has to recognize that one has sinned in order to convert) and on the need to control one's own propensity to sin. Those who follow it tend to adopt more or less ascetic lifestyles in relation to worldly pleasures – usually forgoing alcohol, violence, sexual relations outside of marriage and public displays of whatever counts locally as conspicuous consumption. Often, though not always, they also withdraw from politics both in the local and broader arenas; to engage politically is to court falling into lying, anger and other sinful behaviors. Overall, Pentecostalism promotes a moral style that turns an overwhelming concern with personal culpability into a single-minded effort to follow a strict set of rules in order to move toward a state of spiritual purity. Its followers are people who have a strong sense of personal guilt and a burning desire to avoid or alleviate it.

In order to define this style of moral reasoning in a way that makes it useful for asking comparative questions, I want to characterize in very general terms two different ways people can approach moral questions. The two different ways of taking up moral questions that I have in mind are what in Western philosophy are distinguished as deontological and consequentialist approaches to moral reasoning. Roughly speaking, in deontological approaches, one focuses on knowing and intentionally following appropriate rules and not on the consequences of one's rule-governed actions. Having understood and intentionally followed the rules is enough to ensure that one is free of moral guilt. In a consequentialist framework, by contrast, one's actions are judged by their results, not by how closely they conform to a given rule. In such systems, it is possible with good intentions to follow a rule by performing an action that in the context in which it is performed turns out to have bad consequences and be culpable for those consequences. In the terms of this distinction it is clear that Pentecostals fall on the deontological side. As Soeffner[5] has put it for Luther, so too for Pentecostals, they live in a moral system so concerned with following the rules and purifying one's inner life that it has to be described as one based on an 'impractical' reason that 'is under no obligation to the logic of action' and its consequences. If some manner of withdrawal from the world is the cost Pentecostals and others who follow this course pay for attaining deontological security, then such withdrawal is justified.

Having characterized the Pentecostal approach to moral reasoning as predominantly deontological, I want to ask why so many people in the world today (at least most of those 500 million Pentecostals, but also, I would argue, many others as well) would want to adopt such a style of moral reasoning. Focused as it is on the tendency for individuals to do wrong and the need for vigilance to combat this tendency, it is on the face of things one of the 'harsher' versions of moral reasoning from which one might choose. What accounts for its current appeal?

By way of exploring a potential answer to this question, let me start with the claim that different styles of moral reasoning are embedded in different kinds of social circumstances, and that forms of moral reasoning only flourish in those social circumstances that are well suited to them. Consequentialist moral reasoning, for example, only works where people have a sense that the social world they inhabit is relatively predictable, such that the probable consequences of an action appear relatively easy to gauge with certainty. Where such conditions do not hold, deontological approaches make much more sense – even in situations in which one cannot control the consequences of one's actions, one can control whether or not they conform to a rule or set of rules. Devji[6] makes a similar argument, and one that has inspired my own, in his account of the self-understanding of Al-Qaeda. As he analyzes Al-Qaeda, its members do not see themselves as engaged in instrumental politics because they find it impossible, under current global conditions, to predict the exact political effects their actions will have. Instead, they evaluate their actions in terms of an ethics of duty, one in which it is having done the right thing that counts, not the consequences of one's act.[7] I would suggest that a similar argument can be made for the Pentecostals I have discussed (though the content of the set of rules they adhere to is quite different): they find the world too chaotic and unpredictable to support consequentialism as a dominant style of moral reasoning (which is not to say they never have recourse to it, only that it is not the primary way in which they understand themselves morally), and instead find a kind of security in the promises deontological schemes make to guarantee the moral value of every act at the moment it is undertaken.

Should one want to expand this examination of the attraction of deontological reasoning far more broadly than I have here, a good place to start would be Guyer's[8] very stimulating recent article on what she calls 'the evaporation of the near future in theory and public representations' in the contemporary United States. Focusing on monetarist macro-economic policy and evangelical Christian discourse (a larger discourse within which that of Pentecostalism is located), she shows how a combined emphasis on the immediate present and the very long run have put the near future out of play as a temporal framework. What is lost in this move is the provision of a temporal space for the kinds of consequentialist reasoning Guyer sees as having dominated the politics of the 1950s and 1960s, at least in Britain.[9] Although it goes unsaid in the article, what takes the place of this kind of reasoning is a turn to deontological forms that do not need to refer to the near future world of demonstrable consequences to reckon the value of actions. Working deftly across a wide range of materials, Guyer's discussion provides a sense of some of the conceptual infrastructure, particularly as regards time, that allows for the shift to deontological styles of moral reasoning I have tried to track here.

One of the virtues of an analysis of something as abstract as a 'style of moral reasoning' is that it allows one to see connections between cases one might have missed had one stayed a bit closer to the ground. In this spirit, I want, in closing, to consider the extent to which Pentecostals and contemporary anthropologists might, from this abstract point of view, sit more closely together than one would have thought. Few would contest the claim that anthropology is full of moral passion at the moment, and that such passion often steers not only the kinds of analyses anthropologists perform, but even the kinds of research they take up. Rather than try to prove such a general claim here, I want simply to ask if this moral passion, assuming it exists, has not itself lately taken on a deontological cast. And to start to answer this question in the brief compass of this article, I want to approach it by looking at one unusually eloquent and self-aware article that suggests that it has.

The article in question is by Speed,[10] and it presents an account and critical analysis of her 'critically engaged activist research', aimed, among other things, at helping the Nicolás Ruiz community of Chiapas to present a case before the International Labour Organization (ILO). If won, the case would help the majority of the community's members in their struggle to define themselves as indigenous, retrieve lost lands and protect their right to maintain their customary consensual political process by refusing land usage to community members who did not join the majority decision to become a 'Zapatista base community'.[11] Speed's account of her collaborative, engaged work in this divided community is exemplary for its clear-sighted presentation both of a very complex social situation and of the ethical and political issues it raises for the politically involved anthropologist. Moreover, toward the end of the article she takes a turn that is directly relevant to my concerns in this article. Having reported that the ILO refused to hear the case she prepared with the people of Nicolás Ruiz on the basis of a technicality, Speed[12] asks how activist research such as hers should be judged – should the court's refusal to hear the case be counted as a failure of the research? In response, she notes that she is 'wary' of the '"practical effectiveness" criteria' that would lead us to answer yes to that question. 'Might not,' she wonders, 'an outcome that seems negative in the short run contribute to a situation that generates a positive result in the medium or long run (or vice versa for that matter)?'[13] She then goes on to suggest that 'perhaps a better criterion for evaluating the success of activist research undertakings would be to ask ourselves whether they address the critical questions directed at the discipline. Do they address neocolonial power dynamics in our research processes? Do they seek to engage rather than to protect our research subjects? Do they maintain a critical focus even as they make explicit political commitments, thus creating a productive tension in which critical analysis meets (and must come to terms with) day-to-day political realities?'[14] The shift from consequentialist to deontological moral reasoning is clear here. In a world where we are unable to gauge the practical consequences of our actions (and note that neither the 'medium' nor the 'long' run in Speed's argument represent Guyer's practical space of the near future), we best lay down clear deontological rules for what constitutes good practice and make sure to follow them, finding our sense of moral security in the fact of our having done so.

I cannot imagine any reader who would come away from Speed's article without a good deal of admiration for the thoughtful, self-critical voice with which she presents her research. But her openness to the complexity of the situation both she and her 'research subjects' find themselves in only makes this last minute turn to deontology seem that much more symptomatic of a strong trend in this direction within anthropology more generally. Weber[15] long ago took up the dangers of relying solely on deontological moral reasoning in his lecture on 'Politics as a Vocation'. Calling the deontological style an 'ethic of conviction', and counter-posing it to a more consequentialist 'ethic of responsibility', he comes down squarely in favor of the latter. He even at one point suggests that it is dangerous to give any quarter to the ethics of conviction by aiming to reconcile both kinds of moral reason.[16] Yet in some of the most potent words of his famous conclusion, he does acknowledge that, when carried out well, such reconciliation may be possible: 'I find it immeasurably moving when a mature human being – whether young or old in actual years is immaterial – who feels the responsibility he bears for the consequences of his own actions with his entire soul and who acts in harmony with an ethics of responsibility reaches the point where he says, "Here I stand, I can do no other". That is authentically human and cannot fail to move us. For this is a situation that may befall any of us at some point, if we are not inwardly dead. In this sense an ethics of conviction and an ethics of responsibility are not absolute antitheses but are mutually complementary, and only when taken together do they constitute the authentic human being who is capable of having a "vocation for politics".'[17]

These are words worth recalling at a time in which anthropologists, as much as the people among whom they work, confront a world terrain so broken and hazardous that it appears navigable only with the aid of a deontological crutch. For the costs of achieving the feeling of steady progress that a sole reliance on deontological reasoning affords are surely too high to be worth paying.

Notes

1 Christianity Reborn, *The Economist*, 23 December 2006, p. 48.
2 Robbins, Joel (2004), The Globalization of Pentecostal and Charismatic Christianity, *Annual Review of Anthropology*, 33: 117–143.
3 Noll, Mark A. (2004), Foreword: American Past and World Present in the Search for Evangelical Identity, in *Pilgrims on the Sawdust Trail: Evangelical Ecumenism and the Quest for Christian Identity*, George, Timothy (ed.), Grand Rapids, MI: Baker Academic, p. 12.
4 Robbins (2004), The Globalization, op. cit.; Robbins, Joel (2004), *Becoming Sinners: Christianity and Moral Torment in a Papua New Guinea Society*, Berkeley, CA: University of California Press.
5 Soeffner, Hans-Georg (1997), *The Order of Rituals: The Interpretation of Everyday Life*, trans. by Maria Luckmann, New Brunswick, NJ: Transaction Publishers, p. 41.
6 Devji, Faisal (2005), *Landscapes of the Jihad: Militancy, Morality, Modernity*, Ithaca, NY: Cornell University Press.
7 Ibid., pp. 3–4.
8 Guyer, Jane I. (2007), Prophecy and the Near Future: Thoughts on Macroeconomic, Evangelical, and Punctuated Time, *American Ethnologist*, 34 (3): 410.
9 Ibid., pp. 410, 418.
10 Speed, Shannon (2006), At the Crossroads of Human Rights and Anthropology: Toward a Critically Engaged Activist Research, *American Anthropologist*, 108 (1): 71.
11 Ibid., p. 68.
12 Ibid., p. 73.
13 Ibid., p. 74.
14 Ibid.
15 Weber, Max (2004), *The Vocation Lectures*, trans. by R. Livingstone, Indianapolis, IN: Hackett, pp. 83–94.
16 Ibid., p. 86.
17 Ibid., p. 92, emphases in original.

Ethical relativism in question

17 Anti-relativism

Clyde Kluckhohn

Clyde Kluckhohn (1905–1960) was an American anthropologist whose ethnographic work focused mainly on the Navajo. His first two books, published when he was still a student, *To the Foot of the Rainbow* and *Beyond the Rainbow*, met with considerable success among the general public. After a short period at the University of New Mexico, he became a professor of anthropology, then later of social relations at Harvard University where he was also curator at the Peabody Museum and director of the Center for Russian Studies which focused on research in the Soviet world. As well as being President of the American Anthropological Association and Director of the Institute of Ethnic Affairs, he also held various official positions including that of consultant to the American government. His main scientific works concern general questions of anthropology, particularly *Mirror for Men*, which makes a plea for the discipline to contribute to 'personal happiness and world peace'.

Published in a philosophy journal, the text presented here is a manifesto against moral relativism. The tone is set by Clyde Kluckhohn's opening comment about Ruth Benedict's statement on the 'co-existing and equally valid patterns of life which mankind has carved for itself from the raw materials of existence', which he infers would mean suspending any judgement on slavery or Nazism. The argument unfolds essentially through a series of quotes from psychologists, sociologists, psychoanalysts, philosophers and anthropologists in favour of the existence of universals, including of a moral nature. For Clyde Kluckhohn, 'the human parade has many floats, but, when one strips off the cultural symbolism, the ethical standards represented are akin': he speaks of the cultural 'wrapping' of ethics. The author gives two explanations for this universality, which he does not see as exclusive: diffusion and evolution. Finally, contrary to the impression that the title could give – 'Sic et non' (yes and no), a reference to Abelard's scholastic text looking to go beyond a series of contradictory affirmations by the Church Fathers by using a form of dialectics – Clyde Kluckhohn chooses, in spite of a few final concessions, the side of the 'no' to relativism.

Few anthropologists[1] would today defend without important qualification Ruth Benedict's[2] famous statement: "the co-existing and equally valid patterns of life which mankind has carved for itself from the raw materials of existence." In part, I think we must admit, the abandonment of the doctrine of untrammeled cultural relativity is a reaction to the observation of social consequences. If one follows out literally and logically the implications of Benedict's words, one is compelled to accept any cultural pattern as vindicated precisely by its cultural status: slavery, cannibalism, Nazism, or Communism may not be congenial to Christians or to contemporary Western societies, but moral criticism of the cultural patterns of other people is precluded.

Emotionally and practically, this extreme position is hardly tolerable—even for scholars—in the contemporary world.

But actually the trend of strictly scientific enquiry had shifted before there was general awareness of the more immediate implications of extreme relativism. During the nineteenth century anthropologists had tended to stress the unity of mankind and the diversity of the inanimate environment. At about the turn of the century, however, this emphasis came largely to be reversed. This was due in considerable part to Franz Boas. He stated explicitly that anthropology was interested in historically created diversities, leaving to psychology the exploration of common human nature. For at least a generation American anthropology (and, to a considerable degree, anthropology in the world in general) concentrated its attention upon the differences between peoples, neglecting the similarities. Recently, the balance has been righted somewhat. This occurred, no doubt, under the influence of factors of the sort studied by sociologists of knowledge. This is not, however, the whole story. Also significant was the breakdown of the isolation of anthropology from psychology and sociology. Since the present anthropological stance on relativity can be grasped only in the light of the inter-disciplinary thinking that has flourished of late, I shall briefly review some of the most relevant facts and theories of psychology and sociology. I shall turn then to a more extended consideration of the field where I can speak with more competence.

The psychological contribution

During the phase of the predominance of radical behaviorism, most American psychologists eschewed the realm of values and everything immediately pertinent to ethics. By 1935, however, E. L. Thorndike gave his presidential address to the American Association for the Advancement of Science on Values.[3] In 1945 even Clark Hull published a paper on values.[4] And over the past fifteen years Allport, Ames, Cantril, Frenkel-Brunswik, Hastorf, Maslow, and Woodruff—to name only a few—have discussed at considerable length the implications of psychological findings about human nature to values and specifically to ethics.

To summarize quickly this considerable literature is impossible. I shall therefore limit myself to some representative points from the writings of academic and of medical psychologists. Maslow, for example, wrote:[5] "Once granted reliable knowledge of what man *can* be under 'certain-conditions-which-we-have-learned-to-call-good,' and granted that he is happy, serene, self-accepting, unguilty, and at peace with himself only when he is fulfilling himself and becoming what he can be, then it is possible and reasonable to speak about good and right and bad and wrong and desirable and undesirable. ... The key concepts in the newer dynamic psychology are spontaneity, release, naturalness, self-acceptance, impulse-awareness, gratification. They *used* to be control, inhibition, discipline, training, shaping, on the principle that the depths of human nature were dangerous, evil, predatory, and ravenous." [...]

Flugel[6] sketches a "psychology of moral progress": from egocentricity to sociality; from autism to realism, moral inhibition to spontaneous "goodness"; aggression to tolerance and love, fear to security, heteronomy to autonomy, oretic (moral) judgment to cognitive (psychological) judgment. Dicks[7] refers with approval to Money-Kyrle's concept of "natural morality" and adds: "In simplest, proto-mental ways the rudiments of love rooted in the social–biological dependence on protective, nourishing objects, are clearly present and capable of flowering and maturation in human beings."

Contemporary psychologists and psychiatrists differ, of course, in their views on many of the issues with which we are here concerned. Yet there appears to be a growing trend toward agreement on two fundamentals: (1) an insistence that psychological fact and theory must be taken into account in dealing with ethical problems; (2) there are pan-human universals as regards needs and capacities that shape, or could rightly shape, at least the broad outlines of a morality that transcends cultural difference.

The sociological contribution

The sociologists have similarly been placing greater emphasis upon the universals. Kolb[8] writes: "The basic field conditions for the emergence of the human psyche have been relatively the same since man has been man: society, culture, symbolic interaction, and the potentialities of the biological organism interacting in the basic process of socialization. All social psychologists recognize these universal conditions and processes. Yet, impressed by the facts of social and cultural differences among societies, they have failed to inquire into the qualities of the universal emergent: human nature. ... Surely it is probable that psychic systems the world over have certain identical basic structures and functions organized around universal psychic needs. The methodological arguments advanced against universal psychic needs attest only to the difficulty of determining their nature, not to their absence."

In American sociology at least as far back as Cooley there has been a current of stress upon universals that cut across all cultures. The fact that every human being, irrespective of culture, has had the experience of intimate association with "the primary group" upon whom he was emotionally and otherwise dependent has been held to lead to the so-called universal sentiments: love, jealousy, respect, need for respect, and the like. All moralities, if not built upon these sentiments, must at least take account of them. This total conception, although arising from a different perspective, comes out at about the same place as the psychoanalytic view. The universal sentiments leading to a "natural morality" have a biological basis but the resultant is sociological rather than biological.

Parsons and Shils,[9] in rejecting radical relativism, point to functional interdependences and to the limitations of possibilities: "The exhaustive character of the classification of pattern variables has far-reaching implications for the analysis of systems of moral standards; it provides a determinate range of variability and it allows only a number of combinations of alternatives which—on this level of generality at least—is sufficiently small to permit analysis with the resources we possess at present. There has been a tendency, under the impact of insight into the wider range of differences among cultures, to think, implicitly at least, of a limitlessly pluralistic value-universe. In its extreme form, the proponents of this view have even asserted that every moral standard is necessarily unique. There is much aesthetic sensibility underlying and justifying this contention, but it is neither convincing logically nor fruitful scientifically. If carried to its logical conclusions, it denies the possibility of systematic analysis of cultural values. In fact, of course, all patterns of moral standards are interdependent with all the other factors which operate in the determination of action."

Once again, although the language used and the data cited are different, there is a marked congruence between certain recent sociological and psychoanalytic views. Roheim[10] argues the limitation of possibilities in the light of the facts that human infants invariably are dependent, have two parents of opposite sex, face the emotional problems of being in competition with their siblings for the attention of these parents, and possess basically similar neurological mechanisms for defenses and otherwise dealing with their dilemmas. He (along with Rank, Abraham, Marie Bonaparte, and other psychoanalysts) mobilizes evidence for psychic universals in myths and other culture forms. Roheim maintains that in addition to demonstrable universals there are many other "potential universals." Erich Fromm takes the same general line in many recent writings.

Cultural relativity

Edel[11] begins his discussion of this subject with a subhead, "The Vagueness of the Concept." Certainly it has been employed, by anthropologists and by others, in importantly different senses. [...] No anthropologist, however, doubts that the theory of cultural relativity is in some sense forced by the facts and meaningful. There is an exuberant variation in ethical codes, and surely a satisfactory interpretation of morality must be able to account for the moral judgments found in all cultures. Where anthropologists are not in full agreement is as to the extent to which this variation is basic or comparatively superficial. Is ethical *intent* very similar if not identical the world over? Are variations largely related to means rather than ends? Are means and some of the more proximate ends determined by historical accident and local circumstance? Is the whole picture needlessly confused by the local symbolisms for expressing ultimate goals and enforcing ultimate standards that are universal or near-universal?

Universals. From the anthropological viewpoint, the question as to whether there are ethical universals is a part of a larger question: Are there universals or near-universals of any sort that cut across cultural boundaries? There is good agreement that there are—in some form or other. In the 1911 edition of *The Mind of Primitive Man* Boas called Chapter VI "The Universality of Culture Traits." In the 1938 edition[12] he wrote: "The dynamic forces that mould social life are the same now as those that moulded life thousands of years ago. We can follow the intellectual and emotional drives that actuate man at present and that shape his actions and thoughts." While Boas held, as do most psychologists and psychiatrists, that the needs of men and their "thought processes" are essentially the same throughout the world in time and space and hence give rise to similar cultural forms such as values, Wissler was almost the only one of his associates or students who devoted empirical attention to this question. In *Man and Culture*[13] Wissler wrote a chapter on "The Universal Culture Pattern" in which he showed that the "ground plan" of all cultures is very similar. More recently, Murdock,[14] Kluckhohn,[15] and Trimborn[16] have examined these issues both conceptually and empirically. And Leslie White,[17] Gordon Childe,[18] and Julian Steward[19] have looked specifically at environmental, technological, and economic "determination" of cultural similarities.

That music, graphic arts, dancing, parallels in linguistic structure, standards of personal excellence, kinship terminology, such categories as age grading and many other formal similarities exist in all known cultures no one questions. Nor, on the other hand, does anyone dispute that such resemblances as approach universality are broad likenesses rather than concrete identities. Argument centers on three questions: (1) How numerous are these similarities? (2) Are they just "empty frames" which do not enable us to escape from the impasse of complete cultural relativity? (3) Are they cultural or subcultural or the "conditions for culture"? On the first question not much can be said at present beyond the fact that not enough research has been done to give more than an impressionistic answer.

The next two questions can be considered together. Professor Kroeber writes:[20] "such more or less recurrent near-regularities of form or process as have to date been formulated for culture are actually mainly subcultural in nature. They are limits set to culture by physical or organic factors. The so-called "cultural constants" of family, religion, war, communication, and the like appear to be biopsychological frames variably filled with cultural content." Since cultures include organization as well as content, I myself would include these "frames" as part of culture. They are incorporated—admittedly with variable content in detail—into ways of life and socially transmitted as part of the total tradition. In any case whether these phenomena are cultural or subcultural is, for purposes of the present paper, an academic haggle.

What is significant is that such categories remove cultures from the status of completely isolated monads and make some valid comparisons possible. While scientific analysis commonly unites what the lay mind distinguishes and separates what "common sense" groups together, these broad similarities at very least provide a starting point for valid comparison. Here I stand with Lévi-Strauss[21] in his reply to some earlier strictures of Kroeber's upon "fake universals": "Indeed, if behind such broad categories as Sacrifice, or Gifts, or Suicide, there are not at least some characters which are common to all forms—among, of course, many others which are different—, and if this does not allow the use of those categories as starting points for the analysis, then sociology may as well abandon every pretention to become scientific, and the sociologist must be resigned to pile up descriptions of individual groups, without any hope that the pile shall ever become of any use, except, perhaps, to cultural history. ... When Durkheim studies division of labor, it is in order to reach such abstract, hidden categories as 'organic solidarity' and 'mechanical solidarity'; when he analyzes suicide, he formulates the notion of integration of individual to the group; when Mauss undertakes a comparison between the different types of gifts, it is to discover, behind the more diversified types, the fundamental idea of reciprocity; when he follows the transformation of the psychological conceptions of the 'Ego,' it is in order to establish a relation between social forms and the concept of personality. These categories may be good or bad; they may prove useful or be wrongly chosen but ... they do not resemble the categories of 'long,' 'flat,' or 'round,' but rather such categories as 'dilation,' 'ondulation,' or 'viscosity,' of which the physicist has precisely made his study." Linton[22] is squarely in the mainstream of contemporary anthropological opinion when he says: "Behind the seemingly endless diversity of culture patterns there is a fundamental uniformity."

Ethical Universals. The first thing to note is the universality of moral standards in general. To the philosopher and social scientist this generalization may appear too commonplace to require comment. But the universality may not strike the general zoologist as so obvious. Not only is *human* social life inevitably a moral life in theory and to a large extent in practice, but ethical principles are the fundament of most of the rest of the culture. Fortes[23] remarks: "Every social system presupposes such basic moral axioms ... these axioms are rooted in the direct experience of the inevitability of interdependence between men in society. ... The focal field of kinship is also the focal field of moral experience."

Every culture has a concept of murder, distinguishing this from execution, killing in war, and other "justifiable homicides." The notions of incest and other regulations upon sexual behavior, of prohibitions upon untruth under defined circumstances, of restitution and reciprocity, of mutual obligations between parents and children— these and many other moral concepts are altogether universal. The philosopher James Feibleman[24] goes a bit further than most anthropologists would in saying: "the context of ethical values as of other values, changes constantly; but the values have a striking similarity and even, we strongly suspect, an identity." Anthropologists are more comfortable with a treatment like Linton's,[25] which emphasizes that the likenesses are primarily conceptual and that variation rages rampant as to details of prescribed behavior, instrumentalities, and sanctions. This is important as is also the fact that universality as such is not transmutable into a categorical imperative. Pascal's suggestion that moral canons exist in spite of such empirical universals may be correct in certain instances.

Universality may be due, or largely due, to diffusion or other historical accident. Universality may reflect the general moral immaturity of the human species. That is, present agreements may in some instances indicate no more than that human cultures have thus far evolved only to a roughly similar moral stage. Near-universality in other cases may mean only that there are many "sick societies." Nor does the fact that the simple but basic wants of all men are similar lead us inevitably to sweetness and light. It has made and can continue to make for bitter struggles for scarce goods. Similarly, as everyone knows, some of the worst wars in history have been fought not over "final" goals but rather over "means." Nevertheless the universalities in wants[26] and the universals and near-universals in moral concepts do generate two fairly cheerful propositions. First, the similarities in human needs and human response-potentialities across cultures do at any rate greatly heighten the possibilities of cross-cultural communication once these core likenesses have been somewhat disentangled from their cultural wrappings. Second, while we must not glibly equate universals with absolutes, the existence of a universal certainly raises this question: If, in spite of biological variation and historical and environmental diversities, we find these congruences, is there not a presumptive likelihood that these moral principles somehow correspond to inevitabilities, given the nature of the human organism and of the human situation? They may at any rate lead us to "conditional absolutes" or "moving absolutes," not in the metaphysical but in the empirical sense.

Discussion

Psychology, psychiatry, sociology, and anthropology in different ways and on somewhat different evidence converge in attesting to similar human needs and psychic mechanisms.[27] These, plus the rough regularities in the human situation regardless of culture, give rise to widespread moral principles which are very much alike in concept—in "intent." These considerations make the position of radical cultural relativity untenable. Indeed this view when pressed to its logical extreme soon reaches absurdity. If one is to evaluate an act or a moral judgment *entirely* by its context, it is inescapable that no two contexts are literally identical. And yet the brute fact is that the members of all societies create and are influenced by principles of some generality, by moral abstractions. Human beings generalize as well as discriminate. The human parade has many floats, but, when one strips off the cultural symbolism, the ethical standards represented are akin. The ostensible self-effacement of the Zuni and the exhibitionism of the Kwakiutl affirm the same moral value: allegiance to the norms of one's culture.

To be sure, there must be room left for relativity as regards specific moral rules—for what Macbeath calls the "operative ideals" of each distinct culture. Zuni and Kwakiutl behavior manifest at least one generic value in common. The variations in ideal–typical behavior in the two cases also, of course, reflect certain other values distinctive of the two cultures. The indeterminacy here may well appreciably diminish as science spreads throughout the whole world. If there is any "pan" movement in the world today, sweeping behind both "curtains" and into the "uncommitted third," this is science. And, as Hocking has remarked, if there is to be a common science in the world there will also arise, to some extent, a common conscience. Even then, however, *both* within[28] and between cultures moral behavior in specific instances and in all its details must be judged within a wide context *but with reference to principles which are not relative*. This combines what R. B. Perry and P. B. Rice have called virtuous relativism and virtuous absolutism, though I much prefer "virtuous relativity" because the word "relativism" seems to imply the utter incommensurability of the entities.

Notes

1 M. J. Herskovits is a partial exception; *Man and His Works*, New York: A. A. Knopf, 1948, pp. 76–77.
2 Benedict, Ruth (1934), *Patterns of Culture*, New York: Houghton Mifflin, p. 278.
3 Thorndike, E. L. (Jan. 3, 1936), *Science*, 83 (2140). For a significant discussion of the psychological aspect from the philosophical side see Karl Duncker (1939), Ethical Relativity? (An Enquiry into the Psychology of Ethics), *Mind*, 48: 39–57.
4 Hull, Clark (1945), Moral Values, Behaviorism, and the World Crisis, *Transactions of the New York Academy of Sciences*, Section of Psychology, Series II, Vol. 7: 90–94.
5 Maslow, Abraham (1954), Psychological Progress in Understanding Human Nature and a Scientific Ethics, *Main Currents*, 10: 75–81.
6 Flugel, John (1945), *Man, Morals and Society*, New York: Duckworth.
7 Dicks, Henry V. (1950), In Search of Our Proper Ethic, *British Journal of Medical Psychology*, 23 (1–2): 1–14.
8 Kolb, W. L. (1953), Social–Psychological Conception of Human Freedom, *Ethics*, 63: 180–189.
9 Parsons, Talcott and Shils, Edward (1951), *Toward a General Theory of Action*, Cambridge, MA: Harvard University Press, p. 171.
10 Roheim, Geza (1950), *Psychoanalysis and Anthropology*, New York: International Universities Press. On p. 435 Roheim says firmly: "the psychic unity of mankind is more than a working hypothesis, it is so obvious that it hardly requires proof." Cf. the statement by a French psychologist, Octave Mannoni (1950), L'Unité Humaine, in *Psychologie de la Colonisation*, Paris: Seuil, Chapter VIII.
11 Edel, Abraham (1955), *Ethical Judgment*, Glencoe, IL: Free Press, p. 205.
12 Boas, Franz (1938), *The Mind of Primitive Man*, New York: Macmillan, p. 195.
13 Wissler, Clark (1923), *Man and Culture*, New York: Thomas Y. Crowell Company.
14 Murdock, George Peter (1945), The Common Denominator of Cultures, in *The Science of Man in the World Crisis*, Linton, R. (ed.), New York: Columbia University Press.
15 Kluckhohn, Clyde (1953), Universal Categories of Culture, in *Anthropology Today: An Encyclopedic Inventory*, Kroeber, A. L. (ed.), Chicago, IL: University of Chicago Press.
16 Trimborn, Hermann (1949), *Das Menschliche ist Gleich im Urgrund aller Kulturen*, Braunschweig (Beitrage zum Geschichtsunterricht, No. 9).

17 See, for example, Leslie A. White (1943), Energy and the Evolution of Culture, *American Anthropologist*, 45 (3): 335–356.
18 See, for example, V. Gordon Childe (1951), *Social Evolution*, London: Watts & Co.
19 See, for example, Julian H. Steward (1949), Cultural Causality and Law, *American Anthropologist*, 51 (1): 1–27.
20 Kroeber, A. L. (1949), The Concept of Culture in Science, *Journal of General Education*, 3 (3): 188.
21 Lévi-Strauss, Claude (1945), French Sociology, in *Twentieth Century Sociology*, Gurvitch, Georges and Moore, Wilbert (eds.), New York: Philosophical Library, pp. 525–526.
22 Linton, Ralph (1952), Universal Ethical Principles: An Anthropological View, in *Moral Principles of Action*, Anshen, Ruth (ed.), New York: Harper & Brothers, p. 646.
23 Fortes, Meyer (1949), *The Web of Kinship Among the Tallensi*, London: Oxford University Press, p. 346.
24 Feibleman, James K. (1955), Introduction to an Objective, Empirical Ethics, *Ethics*, 65 (2): 106.
25 Linton, Ralph (1954), The Problem of Universal Values, in *Method and Perspective in Anthropology*, Spencer, R. F. (ed.), Minneapolis, MN: University of Minnesota Press, pp. 150–152, 166.
26 Feibleman (1955), Introduction to an Objective, Empirical Ethics, op. cit., pp. 106, 110.
27 It has often been noted that, while culturally patterned behavior varies regularly, responses to totally new and unfamiliar situations may be fundamentally the same (i.e., at "raw human" level) in societies of quite diverse type.
28 Because each culture must allow for the differentiation of individuals, tolerating and indeed supporting psychological minorities as long as this pluralism does not violate universal morality.

18 Anti anti-relativism

Clifford Geertz

Clifford Geertz (1926–2006) is generally considered the most important American anthropologist of the second half of the twentieth century. He taught first at the University of Chicago and ended his career at the Institute for Advanced Study in Princeton where he founded the School of Social Science. His empirical research was carried out in Morocco and Indonesia. Taking inspiration from the philosophy of Gilbert Ryle – from whom he borrowed the famous concept of 'thick description' – and Ludwig Wittgenstein – taking up his notion of 'family resemblance' – he developed a symbolic approach to human activity, notably in the series of essays brought together under the title *The Interpretation of Cultures*, published in 1973, and completed by *Local Knowledge* in 1983. His numerous works, including anthropological investigations on religion, such as *Islam Observed*, historical studies of theatre, such as *Negara*, and reflections on the discipline and its authors, such as *Works and Lives*, or on philosophy and its uses, such as *Available Light*, have exercised a profound influence throughout the humanities in North America and beyond.

The article presented here is representative of Clifford Geertz's brilliant and ironic style and broaches a subject he felt strongly about: the anti-relativism rife within the discipline and even more so surrounding it. Rather than a relativist manifesto, we could say that this is an anti-anti-relativism pamphlet, criticising the presuppositions and over-simplifications of the attacks against this straw man all too quickly likened to nihilism. These attacks, which concern all forms of relativism implying a normative dimension – whether regarding knowledge, beauty or morality – is not without consequences because it contributes to discrediting the discipline: according to their authors, anthropologists would be quick to consider that everything is equal and that all differences should be respected; their cultural relativism could thus lead them irresistibly down the slippery slope of ethical relativism; renouncing all judgement they would thus abdicate from all values, whether cognitive, aesthetic or moral. Clifford Geertz therefore endeavours to unpick the two universalising tendencies in the sciences, namely naturalism, whether sociobiology or other branches of the life sciences, and rationalism, whether structuralism or numerous other approaches to ways of thinking. For him, whatever the quality and potential of these works, they present the danger of inferring that there is a unity to human nature or the human mind, independent of any historical, cultural, or social context. Three decades after the text was written, in a period during which an alliance seems to have been formed between experts of the brain and specialists of language, Clifford Geertz's critical reflection has lost none of its relevance, although there has been a shift in some of the issues at stake.

A scholar can hardly be better employed than in destroying a fear. The one I want to go after is cultural relativism. Not the thing itself, which I think merely there, like Transylvania, but the dread of it, which I think unfounded. It is unfounded because the moral and intellectual consequences that are commonly supposed to flow from relativism—subjectivism, nihilism, incoherence, Machiavellianism, ethical idiocy, esthetic blindness, and so on—do not in fact do so and the promised rewards of escaping its clutches, mostly having to do with pasteurized knowledge, are illusory.

To be more specific, I want not to defend relativism, which is a drained term anyway, yesterday's battle cry, but to attack anti-relativism, which seems to me broadly on the rise and to represent a streamlined version of an antique mistake. Whatever cultural relativism may be or originally has been (and there is not one of its critics in a hundred who has got that right), it serves these days largely as a specter to scare us away from certain ways of thinking and toward others. And, as the ways of thinking away from which we are being driven seem to me to be more cogent than those toward which we are being propelled, and to lie at the heart of the anthropological heritage, I would like to do something about this. Casting out demons is a praxis we should practice as well as study. [...]

So lumbering an approach to the matter, explaining and excusing itself as it goes, is necessary because, as the philosopher–anthropologist John Ladd[1] has remarked, "all the common definitions of ... relativism are framed by opponents of relativism ... they are absolutist definitions." (Ladd, whose immediate focus is Edward Westermarck's famous book, is speaking of "ethical relativism" in particular, but the point is general: for "cognitive relativism" think of Israel Scheffler's attack on Thomas Kuhn, for "aesthetic relativism," Wayne Booth's on Stanley Fish.[2]) And, as Ladd also says, the result of this is that relativism, or anything that at all looks like relativism under such hostile definitions, is identified with nihilism. To suggest that "hard rock" foundations for cognitive, esthetic, or moral judgments may not, in fact, be available, or anyway that those one is being offered are dubious, is to find oneself accused of disbelieving in the existence of the physical world, thinking pushpin as good as poetry, regarding Hitler as just a fellow with unstandard tastes, or even, as I myself have recently been—God save the mark—"[having] no politics at all."[3] The notion that someone who does not hold your views holds the reciprocal of them, or simply hasn't got any, has, whatever its comforts for those afraid reality is going to go away unless we believe very hard in it, not conduced to much in the way of clarity in the anti-relativist discussion, but merely to far too many people spending far too much time describing at length what it is they do *not* maintain than seems in any way profitable.

All this is of relevance to anthropology because, of course, it is by way of the idea of relativism, grandly ill-defined, that it has most disturbed the general intellectual peace. From our earliest days, even when theory in anthropology—evolutionary, diffusionist, or *elementargedankenisch*—was anything but relativistic, the message that we have been thought to have for the wider world has been that, as they see things differently and do them otherwise in Alaska or the D'Entrecasteaux, our confidence in our own seeings and doings and our resolve to bring others around to sharing them are rather poorly based. This point, too, is commonly ill-understood. It has not been anthropological theory, such as it is, that has made our field seem to be a massive argument against absolutism in thought, morals, and esthetic judgment; it has been anthropological data: customs, crania, living floors, and lexicons. The notion that it was Boas, Benedict, and Melville Herskovits, with a European assist from Westermarck, who infected our field with the relativist virus, and Kroeber, Kluckhohn, and Redfield, with a similar assist from Lévi-Strauss, who have labored to rid us of it, is but another of the myths that bedevil this whole discussion. After all, Montaigne[4] could draw relativistic, or relativistic-looking, conclusions from the fact, as he heard it, that the Caribs didn't wear breeches; he did not have to read *Patterns of Culture*. Even earlier on, Herodotus, contemplating "certain Indians of the race called Callatians," among whom men were said to eat their fathers, came, as one would think he might, to similar views.[5]

The relativist bent, or more accurately the relativist bent anthropology so often induces in those who have much traffic with its materials, is thus in some sense implicit in the field as such; in cultural anthropology perhaps particularly, but in much of archeology, anthropological linguistics, and physical anthropology as well. One cannot read too long about Nayar matriliny, Aztec sacrifice, the Hopi verb, or the convolutions of the hominid transition and not begin at least to consider the possibility that, to quote Montaigne again, "each man calls barbarism whatever is not his own practice ... for we have no other criterion of reason than the example and idea of the opinions and customs of the country we live in."[6] That notion, whatever its problems, and however more delicately expressed, is not likely to go entirely away unless anthropology does.

It is to this fact, progressively discovered to be one as our enterprise has advanced and our findings grown more circumstantial, that both relativists and anti-relativists have, according to their sensibilities, reacted. The realization that news from elsewhere about ghost marriage, ritual destruction of property, initiatory fellatio, royal immolation, and (Dare I say it? Will he strike again?) nonchalant adolescent sex naturally inclines the mind to an "other beasts other mores" view of things has led to arguments, outraged, desperate, and exultant by turns, designed to persuade us either to resist that inclination in the name of reason, or to embrace it on the same grounds. What looks like a debate about the broader implications of anthropological research is really a debate about how to live with them.

Once this fact is grasped, and "relativism" and "anti-relativism" are seen as general responses to the way in which what Kroeber once called the centrifugal impulse of anthropology—distant places, distant times, distant species ... distant grammars—affects our sense of things, the whole discussion comes rather better into focus. The supposed conflict between Benedict's and Herskovits's call for tolerance and the intolerant passion with which they called for it turns out not to be the simple contradiction so many amateur logicians have held it to be, but the expression of a perception, caused by thinking a lot about Zunis and Dahomeys, that, the world being so full of a number of things, rushing to judgment is more than a mistake, it's a crime. Similarly, Kroeber's and Kluckhohn's pan-cultural verities—Kroeber's were mostly about messy creatural matters like delirium and menstruation, Kluckhohn's about messy social ones like lying and killing within the in-group—turn out not to be just the arbitrary, personal obsessions they so much look like, but the expression of a much vaster concern, caused by thinking a lot about *anthropōs* in general, that if something isn't anchored everywhere nothing can be anchored anywhere. Theory here—if that is what these earnest advices as to how we must look at things if we are to be accounted decent should be called—is rather more an exchange of warnings than an analytical debate. We are being offered a choice of worries.

What the relativists, so-called, want us to worry about is provincialism—the danger that our perceptions will be dulled, our intellects constricted, and our sympathies narrowed by the overlearned and overvalued acceptances of our own society. What the anti-relativists, self-declared, want us to worry about, and worry about and worry about, as though our very souls depended upon it, is a kind of spiritual entropy, a heat death of the mind, in which everything is as significant, thus as insignificant, as everything else: anything goes, to each his own, you pays your money and you takes your choice, I know what I like, not in the south, *tout comprendre, c'est tout pardonner.*

As I have already suggested, I myself find provincialism altogether the more real concern so far as what actually goes on in the world. [...]

These moves toward restoring culture-free conceptions of what we amount to as basic, sticker-price homo and essential, no additives sapiens take a number of quite disparate forms, not in much agreement beyond their general tenor, naturalist in the one case, rationalist in the other. On the naturalist side there is, of course, sociobiology and other hyper-adaptationist orientations. But there are also perspectives growing out of psychoanalysis, ecology, neurology, display-and-imprint ethology, some kinds of developmental theory, and some kinds of Marxism. On the rationalist side there is, of course, the new intellectualism one associates with structuralism and other hyper-logicist orientations. But there are also perspectives growing out of generative linguistics, experimental psychology, artificial intelligence research, ploy and counterploy microsociology, some kinds of developmental theory, and some kinds of Marxism. Attempts to banish the specter of relativism whether by sliding down The Great Chain of Being or edging up it—the dog beneath the skin, a mind for all cultures—do not comprise a single enterprise, massive and coordinate, but a loose and immiscible crowd of them, each pressing its own cause and in its own direction. The sin may be one, but the salvations are many.

It is for this reason, too, that an attack, such as mine, upon the efforts to draw context-independent concepts of "Human Nature" or "The Human Mind" from biological, psychological, linguistic, or for that matter cultural (HRAF and all that) inquiries should not be mistaken for an attack upon those inquiries as research programs. Whether or not sociobiology is, as I think, a degenerative research program destined to expire in its own confusions, and neuroscience a progressive one (to use Imre Lakatos's[7] useful epithets) on the verge of extraordinary achievements, anthropologists will be well advised to attend to, with various shades of mixed, maybe, maybe not, verdicts for structuralism, generative grammar, ethology, AI, psychoanalysis, ecology, microsociology, Marxism, or developmental psychology in between, is quite beside the point. It is not, or anyway not here, the validity of the sciences, real or would-be, that is at issue. What concerns me, and should concern us all, are the axes that, with an increasing determination bordering on the evangelical, are being busily ground with their assistance. [...]

Looking into dragons, not domesticating or abominating them, nor drowning them in vats of theory, is what anthropology has been all about. At least, that is what it has been all about, as I, no nihilist, no subjectivist, and possessed, as you can see, of some strong views as to what is real and what is not, what is commendable and what is not, what is reasonable and what is not, understand it. We have, with no little success, sought to keep the world off balance; pulling out rugs, upsetting tea tables, setting off firecrackers. It has been the office of others to reassure; ours to unsettle. Australopithicenes, Tricksters, Clicks, Megaliths—we hawk the anomalous, peddle the strange. Merchants of astonishment.

We have, no doubt, on occasion moved too far in this direction and transformed idiosyncrasies into puzzles, puzzles into mysteries, and mysteries into humbug. But such an affection for what doesn't fit and won't comport, reality out of place, has connected us to the leading theme of the cultural history of "Modern Times." For that history has indeed consisted of one field of thought after another having to discover how to live on without the certainties that launched it. Brute fact, natural law, necessary truth, transcendent beauty, immanent authority, unique revelation, even the in-here self facing the out-there world have all come under such heavy attack as to seem by now lost simplicities of a less strenuous past. But science, law, philosophy, art, political theory, religion, and the stubborn insistences of common sense have contrived nonetheless to continue. It has not proved necessary to revive the simplicities.

It is, so I think, precisely the determination not to cling to what once worked well enough and got us to where we are and now doesn't quite work well enough and gets us into recurrent stalemates that makes a science move. […]

In this move away from old triumphs become complacencies, one-time breakthroughs transformed to roadblocks, anthropology has played, in our day, a vanguard role. We have been the first to insist on a number of things: that the world does not divide into the pious and the superstitious; that there are sculptures in jungles and paintings in deserts; that political order is possible without centralized power and principled justice without codified rules; that the norms of reason were not fixed in Greece, the evolution of morality not consummated in England. Most important, we were the first to insist that we see the lives of others through lenses of our own grinding and that they look back on ours through ones of their own. That this led some to think the sky was falling, solipsism was upon us, and intellect, judgment, even the sheer possibility of communication had all fled is not surprising. The repositioning of horizons and the decentering of perspectives has had that effect before. The Bellarmines you have always with you; and as someone has remarked of the Polynesians, it takes a certain kind of mind to sail out of the sight of land in an outrigger canoe.

But that is, at least at our best and to the degree that we have been able, what we have been doing. And it would be, I think, a large pity if, now that the distances we have established and the elsewheres we have located are beginning to bite, to change our sense of sense and our perception of perception we should turn back to old songs and older stories in the hope that somehow only the superficial need alter and that we shan't fall off the edge of the world. The objection to anti-relativism is not that it rejects an it's-all-how-you-look-at-it approach to knowledge or a when-in-Rome approach to morality, but that it imagines that they can only be defeated by placing morality beyond culture and knowledge beyond both. This, speaking of things which must needs be so, is no longer possible. If we wanted home truths, we should have stayed at home.

Notes

1 Ladd, John (1982), The Poverty of Absolutism, in Edward Westermarck: Essays on His Life and Works, *Acta Philosophica Fennica* (Helsinki), 34: 161 and 158.
2 Scheffler, Israel (1967), *Science and Subjectivity*, Indianapolis, IN: Bobbs-Merrill; Booth, Wayne (1983), A New Strategy for Establishing a Truly Democratic Criticism, *Daedalus*, 112: 193–214.

3 Rabinow, P. (1983), Humanism as Nihilism: The Bracketing of Truth and Seriousness in American Cultural Anthropology, in *Social Science as Moral Inquiry*, Haan, N., R. M. Bellah, P. Rabinow and W. M. Sullivan (eds.), New York: Columbia University Press, p. 70.
4 Montaigne, Michel de (1978 [1st French publication 1580]), *Les Essais*, Villey, P. (ed.), Paris: Presses Universitaires de France, pp. 202–214. [Actually, Montaigne explains he has met (not heard of) Indians from Brazil (not Caribs) and his final sentence about the breeches ironically refers to the comment of an imaginary interlocutor trying to disqualify them (not to his own view) – Translator's note.]
5 Herodotus (1859–61), *History of Herodotus*, Bk. 3 Chapter 38, New York: Appleton.
6 See Todorov, T. (1983) Montaigne, Essays in Reading, *Yale French Studies*, 64: 113–144, for general discussion of Montaigne's relativism from a position similar to mine.
7 Lakatos, Imre (1976), *The Methodology of Scientific Research*, Cambridge, England: Cambridge University Press.

19 Ambivalence and contradictions

Bradd Shore

Bradd Shore (born in 1945) is a professor of anthropology at Emory University in Atlanta where he is also director of the MARIAL (Myth and Ritual in American Life) centre. His early research, published in the monograph *Sala'ilua: A Samoan Mystery*, aimed to grasp the cultural models of person and conflict in the Samoan Islands from the perspective of interpretive anthropology developed by Clifford Geertz. His later work, presented in the book *Culture in Mind: Cognition, Culture and the Problem of Meaning*, attempts to combine the benefits of the ethnographic approach with those of cognitive psychology.

In this text, the author poses the problem of moral relativism as a logical question (it is a paradox that relativism should become the only absolute) and personal issue (it is disconcerting to think that the diversity of value systems would allow no ethical common ground). How can we avoid the dual trap of reductionism, which either misunderstands or minimises differences between cultures, and contextualism, which makes each value system into a coherent and unique ensemble? Bradd Shore suggests a way out of this apparent aporia that is original and yet perfectly congruent with the anthropological method because, on the one hand, it rejects culturalist essentialisation by stating that societies are not morally homogeneous entities, and, on the other hand, it uses the ethnographic method to establish empirically that in a given society and even for a specific individual contradictions arise between different ethical systems. Indeed, acting morally does not consist in applying a norm to a situation without any reflection: rather, on a daily basis, actors are confronted with concrete ethical conflicts bringing together norms that are opposed, and yet of equal value. This statement, which appears simple, means considering the question of relativism differently, as well as altering our perspective on moral values and the cultural systems underpinning them. Envisaged as practical resources for resolving a conflict, moral values are always of relative validity, according to the concrete situations that lead them to prevail or not. By concluding with this strategic reading of ethics, Bradd Shore manages to extract the debate on moral relativism from its theoretical deadlock.

Ethical relativism is only a special case of cultural relativism, but it is a particularly troublesome case. We might take comfort in what Geertz[1] has called "the repositioning of horizons and the decentering of perspectives" afforded by a confrontation with exotic world views and diverse cultural symbolisms. Yet it is somewhat alarming to contemplate the irreducible relativity of moral reasoning or ethical axioms among human communities. Geertz's assurances that such expanded horizons will actually enlarge our moral sensibilities are comforting but, in the end, do not allay the suspicion that such an enterprise might uproot the foundations of moral discourse.

The discussion of ethical relativism is beset by several problems. The first is rhetorical. A sophisticated argument leveled against all relativisms is that their very articulation rests on an irresolvable paradox: relativism as a doctrine proposes itself as an absolute. All truths are held to be relative, except this one. On the face of it, this argument denies only the possibility of a coherent logical defense of relativism. It is merely a paradox of discourse with no necessary bearing on the truth or falsehood that local ethical standards are ultimately local fictions and thus incommensurable.

The second difficulty is more personal. The possibility that ethical discourse is just that, a discourse, rooted in a particular time and place, is disconcerting, relativizing the foundations of our moral judgment. Of course the desirability of ethical relativism is a separate issue from its existence or nonexistence. Whether we find the prospect of an irreducible multiplicity of moral horizons invigorating or alarming cannot be allowed to shape our perceptions of what is out there. The wish for transcendent grounding for values does not make it so.

Yet such a desire does point to an important if unspoken motive in the pursuit of cultural anthropology: the possibility that the otherness of those we study might eventually transform the way we understand ourselves, yielding unsuspected congruences as well as the anticipated differences between remote human communities. The rarely questioned "psychic unity of mankind" might possibly encompass a moral dimension. This possibility is anticipated in the enterprise of ethnography in the act of what Roy Wagner[2] has called the "bridging" of cultures that inevitably underlies the creation of sensitive ethnography. Such bridging presupposes an intellectual footing in both the observer's culture and that of the observed, as well as a link between them, in the same way as any translation of a foreign tongue must necessarily point beyond the prisonhouse view of language.[3]

Some who study exotic ethics are motivated by more than a dispassionate goal of cataloging new species of human thought and diversity of moral fictions. To the extent that the comparative study of ethics is a philosophical as well as a scientific enterprise, it has as its proper goal not only the pursuit of information, but also the refinement of our ethical sensibilities: something akin to the pursuit of wisdom.

The problem, I think, is to reconcile two apparently contradictory perceptions. The first is the evident fact of important local differences in moral systems—whether viewed as systems of local differences in specific values or in the formal structure of moral reasoning. Thus, Ladd[4] describes for the Navajo what he terms a "negative ethics of constraint" whereby virtue is understood as the containment of evil, rather than the assertion of goodness. Kluckhohn argues that Navajo ethical discourse justifies actions less on the basis of abstract principles than on pragmatic and situational grounds.[5]

I have suggested that Samoan ethical discourse evaluates behaviors more in terms of their social effects than in terms of causes or personal motivations.[6] Moreover, despite a century-and-a-half of strong Christian influence, much day-to-day ethical discourse in Samoa seems to lack an "objective" moral viewpoint outside of any social context.[7] For the Baktaman of Highland New Guinea, the moral calculus underlying social interaction is made according to the perception of the immediate emotional state of a particular individual, rather than in terms of some general moral principles or long-term calculation of balance or fairness.[8] Barth argues that, whereas Westerners have their notion of an almighty and all-knowing god as the basis for moral judgment, the Baktaman "have only their ancestral spirits, which are entirely human in their capriciousness and subjectivity."[9]

The second observation is that, despite such differences in ethical discourse, it is nonetheless possible to bridge such cultural chasms and eventually to find alien ethical systems comprehensible and even credible. We can often eventually find our footing on what had seemed to be impossibly slippery terrain. Our dilemma, then, is to save the phenomenon of culture from two opposite sorts of misrepresentation. On the one hand, there is the trivial reductionism in which genuine differences among value systems—which we, ourselves, have experienced in fieldwork—are explained away in the interest of insipid and ultimately trivial universals. On the other hand, there is the danger of total contextualism, a form of extreme aestheticism in which each moral system is assumed to define a unique and irreducible system of thought and in which considerations of common human experience, evolutionary history, and nature have no place. Since neither of these positions strikes me as either empirically defensible or desirable, we need to seek a way out of this impasse.

There is, I think, a way out, though it leads us into other, less compliant dilemmas. Ethics involves the evaluation of actions on some moral scale. As such, ethics presupposes some system of moral values. The putative differences among ethical systems assume value differences between cultures. The elucidation of *contrasting values* has been a specialty of cultural anthropologists. The comparativist perspective, with its attraction to maximal contrast, lies behind much ethnography, though often it is only an implicit bias. Societies seem to reveal their value systems most clearly when these values contrast with those of another society. As Melville Herskovits, one of the more ardent defenders of cultural relativism, once argued: "The very core of cultural relativism is the social discipline that comes with respect for differences—or mutual respect. Emphasis on the worth of many ways of life, not one, is an affirmation of the values of each culture."[10] The consequence of this dependence on contrastive analysis has been the frequent flattening of our renderings of the cultures we describe and the acceptance of a homogenized conception of what a value or value system is that we would not accept as intuitively real for ourselves.[11] Such characterizations are a form of stereotyping. They are useful in delineating differences in emphasis *between* societies. Yet, they also tend to mask complexity and variation existing not only within a given culture but also within individuals *for whom ethics is realized more commonly as dilemma than as the simple mobilization of values.*

An example from my own fieldwork in Samoa illustrates the complexity of ethical discourse. During my stay in a large village, my host, a distinguished senior chief of the village, was shot to death by another village chief following an argument over a card game. Any such violent event would normally create extreme tension within a village, but given the status of the two men involved, and the prominence of their respective families in village politics, this murder threatened to tear the fabric of the village and to precipitate a chain of increasing violence that, once begun, would be hard to stop. Both the village chiefs and the local pastors of the churches in the village played important roles in trying to minimize the threat to village peace, often with appeals to both traditional Samoan and Christian ideals of harmony, patience, forgiveness, and so forth.

One such appeal that I heard was in the form of a homily delivered by a local pastor to the eldest son of the murder victim the day after the shooting. The pastor counseled forbearance to the young man and recommended that, in the spirit of Christian love, he turn the other cheek to this assault on his father and on his family. The message was conveyed both explicitly in content and implicitly through several rhetorical devices. First, the homily was delivered in a polite and formal phonological register which Samoans call "good-speaking" and which uses the phones [t] and [n].[12] It is a speech register associated with church, school, and other Western-introduced institutions, and is linked for Samoans with delicacy of subject matter, personal reserve, social distance, and subordination of personal impulses to social propriety. The other rhetorical strategy was the frequent use of the first-person-plural, "inclusive" pronoun *tatou* (all of us, including you), a form of verbal co-opting in which potential rifts in an assembly are verbally masked and the organic unity of the assembly is stressed.

This kind of advice from the pastor to the distraught young man was, perhaps, to be expected under the circumstances. What is surprising is the private conversation I witnessed between them a day later. Here the pastor, sotto voce, told the youth, "If you don't avenge the death of your father, you are not your father's son." The next day, the boy attacked his father's murderer with a machete while the prisoner was being escorted through the village by a local constable. Although the prisoner survived the attack, he was badly wounded and had to be rushed to a hospital. The pastor's advice this time was conveyed to the lad in the colloquial phonological register, in which the phonemes /t/ and /n/ are realized as [k] and [ng]. This register is linked in Samoan conception to both traditional, fully Samoan institutions (such as traditional oratory) and also to the expression of aggressive or angry impulses.

How do we make sense of the apparently contradictory behavior of the pastor? Do we conclude that he is a hypocrite? That he didn't really mean what he said in at least one of the reported conversations? That Samoans are confused, or amoral? What I think was going on in this case was simply the expression of alternative Samoan ethical norms, each relegated to a distinct set of contexts, masking their incompatibility. These contexts pattern the expression of different aspects of Samoan ethos. On the one hand there is a set of Samoan values emphasizing cooperation, harmony, deference to authority, and the subordination of antisocial impulses to the needs of the group. On the other hand there is another set of Samoan values emphasizing personal heroism, boldness, competitiveness, fierce loyalty to one's own group at the expense of social harmony, and personal touchiness at perceived attacks on personal or family honor.[13]

Several observers of Samoa have noted these contradictory tendencies in Samoan ethos. Felix and Marie Keesing observed that in the anthropological literature on Samoa there has been an emphasis on "'security,' 'conformity,' and 'group responsibility' and the symmetrical balancing of social structures on the one hand … [and] 'divisiveness,' 'deviousness,' 'turbulence,' and the potential of 'violence' on the other."[14] Margaret Mead, whose understanding of Samoan ethos tended to stress the cooperative and passive aspects of ethos, also noted these two tendencies in terms of Samoan social organization, stressing: "the tendency to place each individual, each household, each village, even (in Western Samoa) each district in a hierarchy, wherein each is dignified only by its relationship to the whole, each performs tasks which contribute the honor and well-being of the whole, and competition is completely impossible. The other tendency, the rebellion of units against subordination to a plan and their use of a place within the component unit to foment trouble and rivalry with other units, while not so strong, is always present."[15]

Freeman has characterized the Samoan ethos in terms of "a susceptibility to dissociated reactions" of a sort in which "the emotionally impulsive is split off from the socially acceptable," leading to considerable ambivalence about authority.[16]

Although it is true that one dimension of Samoan ethos is associated with the socially acceptable, it is misleading to understand this dichotomy as opposing the ethical to the unethical. As the case study described above suggests, both sides of Samoan ethos have ethical implications, suggesting, in different contexts, appropriate kinds of action. Thus, Samoan children are taught publicly by parents to value submission to authority, while at the same time they are often encouraged to defend their honor and that of their family even at the expense of social harmony and hierarchy. Both heroic assertiveness in the interest of personal or local group status and deference to an encompassing social order are legitimate Samoan values, and the fact that they often conflict means that Samoan ethical discourse involves competing and mutually exclusive claims.

The analysis of ethics in Samoa, then, cannot be limited to the enumeration of a set of coherent Samoan ethical values and their application in action. It necessarily involves the fine-grained analysis of how conflicting moral or ethical claims are resolved in practice. Ethical discourse, thus, is not just the enunciation of moral values; it often involves a rhetorical struggle to legitimize one course of action and depreciate an alternative, even though both possibilities exist as ethical alternatives.

Contradictions in ethical discourse are not, of course, just Samoan. A little introspection suggests the lines along which such conflicted discourse might proceed in our own society. Is it really possible to subscribe *both* to the right of a human fetus to be preserved from an untimely death and also to the rights of women to control their own bodies? This was the ethical dilemma faced by Geraldine Ferraro in the 1986 presidential elections. Can we appeal to the principle of human equality and still support the right of an individual to the fruits of his or her own labor? What is the relation between equality of opportunity and equality at the finish line? Does the sacred value of the individual human life, upheld by those opposed to capital punishment, have no reasonable, if painful, dialogue with the rights of the victim and society to avenge a violent crime? How is the moral authority of the Old Testament affirmation of vengeance to be weighed against the New Testament value of forgiveness? If we favor the right of the State to take a human life, can we also oppose—on the principle of the inviolable sacredness of life—abortion, suicide, or euthanasia? Is the general principle of patriotism making it noble to die for one's country really different from the justifications that motivate young Muslim fanatics to wrap themselves in funerary shrouds and drive explosive-laden trucks into American embassies? [...]

In transforming ethics from the realm of value propositions to that of contradictions, have I really transcended the dilemma of ethical relativism? In part, I think I have. For many of the contradictions that generate ethical discourse in human life are themselves transcultural in origin and emerge from contradictions inherent in the human condition. The Samoan mother is caught in a dilemma in which the attachment of mother and infant and all of the moral associations of nurturing one's offspring are incompatible with the social virtues of sharing. Both positions are represented, though unequally, in Samoan ethical discourse. We can recognize the pastor's appeals to the twin virtues of filial piety and community harmony as based upon moral imperatives that have become mutually exclusive in a particular context. Moreover, neither of these values is a Samoan invention, and both are understandable as potential human values. What is Samoan, however, is the particular handling of the dilemma, by dissociating the imperatives and assigning the one to a very personal linguistic register and the other to a more fully socialized and sublimated form of discourse.

What accounts for the cultural variability of ethical systems? If, as I suggest, the hidden agenda of ethical discourse is not the choice between good and evil but that between competing virtues or competing vices, then ethics must be experienced as saturated by considerable anxiety and ambivalence. In this view, ethical discourse would suggest the polyphonous garble of contradictory voices. Yet, with the exception of philosophers and other specialists in subtle reasoning, most ethical reasoning requires some help by reducing complex and inconclusive evaluations to clear terms and simple choices. Culture provides us with rhetorical strategies for making such choices in the form of clichés, proverbs, heroic models in myth, and other such cultural resources that help provide partial and temporary resolutions to what may be ultimately irresolvable predicaments. In this view, *cultural systems do not invent values so much as they orchestrate rhetorical strategies, organizing the perception of value-laden situations with standardized and culturally acceptable formulations.*

At their most extreme, value systems can render certain moral positions shadowy and inarticulate, as in the cases of the Japanese or Samoan apprehension of the rights of the individual or the American understanding of the irreducible moral status of certain forms of personal subordination and dependency. Such inchoate positions remain potentially problematic areas of conflict experienced by individuals privately, but not always given public articulation. Here, ethical relativism appears *between* cultures. In other instances, as in Fiske's illuminating analysis of contrasting and context-dependent Moose (Mossi) ethical norms,[17] contradictions are rationalized by contextual dissociation. Culture can orchestrate alternative justifications for contradictory positions to be invoked by competing interest groups or by a single group on different occasions. Thus, the irreducible value of the individual life is invoked by some American groups to attack abortion on ethical grounds, yet many of the same individuals would not choose to invoke this same value in relation to capital punishment, shifting instead to an alternative stress on the right of society to exact vengeance or to deter future crimes. In these cases ethical relativism may be said to exist *within* a culture.

The cultural variability of ethical systems is linked to the very conditions that generate coherent ethical systems. We have noted that the anxiety surrounding ethically relevant situations is linked to the fact that underlying ethical principles are often conflicting virtues (or vices) where tough decisions have to be made. To perceive clearly such dilemmas, to see all sides of an issue all the time, would make action difficult at best. Hamlet's near paralysis in the face of such an ethical dilemma well illustrates the weakness of the philosopher-king. In normal circumstances, cultural systems *partly* resolve such dilemmas for us by reducing ambiguity, rendering certain choices cognitively more salient and emotionally more acceptable than others.

Yet the relation between cultural systems and individual experience is never simple or fully determinate, which is why ethical situations are so emotionally provocative. Not only do cultures fail to eliminate completely the anxiety inherent in ethical dilemmas, but, as we have seen, this ambivalence is frequently linked to the fact that ethical systems themselves usually contain principles that are bound to collide in any given situation.

Notes

1 Geertz, Clifford (1984), Anti Anti-Relativism, *American Anthropologist*, 86: 276.
2 Wagner, Roy (1975), *The Invention of Culture*, Chicago, IL: University of Chicago Press.
3 Shore, Bradd (1987), Is Language a Prisonhouse?, *Cultural Anthropology*, 2: 115–136.
4 Ladd, John (1957), *The Structure of a Moral Code*, Cambridge: Cambridge University Press.
5 Kluckhohn, Clyde (1974), *The Navaho*, Cambridge: Harvard University Press, p. 297.
6 Shore, Bradd (1982), *Sala'ilua: A Samoan Mystery*, New York: Columbia University Press, pp. 182–183.
7 Ibid., p. 190.
8 Barth, Fredrik (1975), *Ritual and Knowledge Among the Baktaman of New Guinea*, New Haven, CT: Yale University Press, pp. 134–135.
9 Ibid., p. 134.
10 Quoted in Elvin Hatch (1983), *Culture and Morality: The Relativity of Values in Anthropology*, New York: Columbia University Press, p. 64.
11 The most famous paradigm for this kind of contrastive model of cultures is Ruth Benedict's *Patterns of Culture* (New York: Houghton Mifflin, 1934). The explicit model for cultural configuration or what came to be known as "ethos" was the gestalt concept from the psychology of perception then in some vogue (Koffka). Since the hallmark of this configurationist model of culture was internal coherence, contradiction or contrast came to characterize differences between cultures or else the gap between deviant individuals and the larger pattern. It was only in *The Chrysanthemum and the Sword* (New York: Houghton Mifflin, 1946) that Benedict came to recognize the importance of patterned contradiction within a cultural configuration.
12 Shore, op. cit.; *A Samoan Theory of Action: Social Order and Social Control in a Polynesian Paradox*, Doctoral thesis, University of Chicago, 1977; Ochs, Elinor (1988), *Culture and Language Development: Language Acquisition and Language Socialization in a Samoan Village*, Cambridge: Cambridge University Press; Duranti, Allesandro (1981), *The Samoan Fono: A Sociolinguistic Study*, Pacific Linguistics Series B, No. 80, Canberra: Australian National University, pp. 165–169.
13 These apparently contradictory aspects of Samoan ethos were a central factor in the notorious controversy over Margaret Mead's early characterization of Samoa (Mead [1928], *Coming of Age in Samoa: A Psychological Study of Primitive Youth for Western Civilization*, New York: Morrow; Mead [1928], The Role of the Individual in Samoan Society, *Journal of the Royal Anthropological Institute*, 58: 481–495; and Mead 1969 [1930] *The Social Organization of Manu'a*, Honolulu: Bishop Museum Press) provoked by the publication in 1983 of Derek Freeman's *Margaret Mead and Samoa: The Making and Unmaking of an Anthropological Myth* (Cambridge: Harvard University Press). Freeman's "refutation" of Mead's characterization focused on, among other things, the stress Mead placed on the casualness of Samoan ethos and the emphasis on gentleness and cooperation. Freeman takes issue with the characterization, arguing in almost every instance that Mead got it virtually backwards. In his chapter entitled "Cooperation and Competition" Freeman documents the highly competitive and aggressive Samoan ethos, manifesting what Freeman calls, quoting an early European observer of Samoa, "ungovernable pride" (Freeman p. 151; see also Chapter 11, "Aggressive Behavior and Warfare"). What is, to me, most striking in this controversy is not so much the differences between Mead's and Freeman's readings of Samoan ethos and values but, rather, their similarity. Both anthropologists mute the apparent contradictions in Samoan culture in favor of a self-consistent and one-dimensional portrait. Focusing on complementary aspects of a complex culture, and downplaying the dualisms that pervade Samoans' own understanding of their ethos (Shore 1982), both Freeman and Mead present partial visions as if they constituted the whole.
14 Keesing, Felix M. and Marie M. Keesing (1956), *Elite Communication in Samoa*, Stanford: Stanford University Press, p. 8.
15 Mead, Margaret (1965), The Samoans, in *Peoples and Cultures of the Pacific*, Vayda, A. (ed.), New York: Natural History Press, p. 262.
16 Freeman (1983), *Margaret Mead and Samoa*, op. cit., p. 223.
17 Fiske, A. P. (1990), Relativity within Moose ("Mossi") Culture: Four Incommensurable Models for Social Relationships, *Ethos* (18) 2: 180–204.

20 The universal and the relative

Steven Lukes

Steven Lukes (born in 1941) is a professor of sociology and politics at New York University. He previously taught at the University of Sienna, the European University Institute in Florence and the London School of Economics. Expert in the sociology of Durkheim, which was the focus of his doctoral dissertation, he has provided critical editions in English of several of Durkheim's works as well as authoring *Emile Durkheim: His Life and Work* and *Durkheim and the Law*. Among his research in political theory, inspired by Marxism, the most well known puts forward, in *Power: A Radical View*, a three-dimensional approach to power comprising the power to decide, the power to determine the political agenda and the ideological power to influence individuals, including against their best interests. A substantial part of his work has focused on moral questions, developed in *Marxism and Morality*, then in *Moral Conflict and Politics*, and finally in *Moral Relativism*. A politically engaged theorist, Steven Lukes always attempts to situate his reflection on the border between scientific analysis and civic engagement.

The text on moral relativism presented here is situated precisely in this perspective. Throughout the book, Steven Lukes endeavours to lay out in the most explicit terms the tensions between relativism and universalism, recognising the intellectual logic and even political relevance of the positions on both sides. In the conclusion, he summarises his argument. Moral diversity is a fact that everyone can acknowledge. However, using this observation to infer that there is no grounding to morality, because there is no ultimate truth, equates to moving from objective fact to moral relativism. For Steven Lukes, this inference is not self-evident. In fact it is possible, whilst still recognising the existing diversity, to consider that there are foundations for a universal morality. Two paths are then possible. The first, in a Kantian legacy, tries to find an underlying common principle beneath multiple moralities, and is what Thomas Scanlon describes as that which we are able to justify before others. The second, of Aristotelian inspiration, concentrates on identifying an objective foundation that would go beyond subjective values, what Martha Nussbaum and Amartya Sen name capabilities, that is, the aptitude for full self-realisation. Steven Lukes therefore calls his reader to a certain form of universalism, one that is respectful of local ethics insofar as they do not contradict the principle of justifiability nor impede capabilities.

The journey down the road to moral relativism begins from the observation of the facts of diversity. As an observer you note that there are many moralities. More precisely, moral norms and systems of such norms are seen as diverging across time and space, in both content and scope of application. What people value in their practices and the conduct of their lives diverges both within and across what we call cultures, sometimes incommensurably. The relativistic turn comes when you transfer these observations into the first-person perspective of a moral agent—you are now a person with moral views and making moral judgments—and you conclude that therefore there is no one true morality but many, and that no value perspective is privileged over others, and none from which all can be evaluated, and so you conclude that your judgments apply only to adherents of your morality.

The first thing to notice is that the *therefore* in the last sentence is entirely misleading. There is no logical entailment here: the relativist conclusion does not follow inexorably from the observations of factual diversity. Indeed, until the nineteenth century few even contemplated drawing this conclusion. Pascal wrote that "what is truth on one side of the Pyrenees is error on the other" and "three degrees of latitude reverse all jurisprudence; a meridian decides the truth."[1] But it never occurred to him to suppose that the truths of Christianity might be limited in scope. "Mahomet," he wrote, "does not prophesy; Jesus prophesies." For no religion "other than ours has taught that man is born in sin, no sect of philosophers has said it: none has therefore spoken the truth."

Ever since the discoveries at the time of Montaigne, awareness of cross-cultural differences has become ever more vivid and involving, but these were widely seen in the West, even until the end of colonialism, within the framework that opposed the less to the more civilized peoples. Today many people accept the facts about diversity while remaining firmly absolutist and objectivist in their moral views and judgments—among their number Pope Benedict and Allan Bloom. […]

I cite these two examples, not for their representativeness but to illuminate, by contrast, what it is that motivates many people to think it natural to move toward relativist conclusions. For them, scientific and "modern" thinking does indeed exclude from reality not just Christian but all religious faith. They do not expect such faith to "guide" their reason or establish "grounds" for their values. Rather, they seek rational grounds for those values. Nor do they understand how there could be "true or superior" opinions about good and bad, let alone *knowledge* about "the nature of the good," and they can make little sense of phrases like "essential being" and "the only real common good." We live, it is often said, in a "post-metaphysical age" in which our moral views are "without foundations." Or rather (which is to say the same thing) there are too many foundations. For, as Anthony Appiah understates the case, in real life "judgments about right and wrong are intimately tied up with metaphysical and religious belief and with beliefs about the natural order. And these are matters about which agreement may be difficult to achieve."[2]

Moreover, those whose views do rest on religious or metaphysical foundations may disagree about moral issues, so what is the probability that any one denomination or school of thought will have attained knowledge of the truth, and how, lacking belief in such foundations, would one know? And so it seems entirely natural to wonder what authority any given set of moral norms can claim and on what basis we can arrive at our value judgments. Thus we arrive at the idea, that the answer is that the authority is *social* and the basis emotional; that custom is indeed lord of all and that what we call our reasoning in matters of morals is but a mere coloring of local tribal customs, calculated, as Westermarck thought, to give moral values an objectivity they do not possess. This movement of thought has found sustenance in the context of multiculturalism. It is also sustained by identity politics, which encourages attitudes of exclusivity and pride and calls for respect and the recognition of collective identities. [...]

If these are the considerations that draw people toward moral relativism, we must next ask what can lead them away from it. How, in a postmetaphysical and foundationless world, can one justify subscribing to universal moral norms and values, that is, norms and values that apply to all human beings in relevantly similar circumstances? That is the first of two questions I shall address, and in doing so I shall suggest that there are two promising approaches to answering it, one in the spirit of Kant, the other in the spirit of Aristotle. Once it has been addressed, we can turn to the second question, namely, what scope remains for a relativistic approach within the moral domain?

In order to consider both questions, we need to return to the question of how to define the moral domain, something I earlier attempted in a provisional way. I offered a very broad and loose definition, suggesting that moral norms cover matters of importance in people's lives where they are faced with distinguishing right from wrong. Such norms are directed at promoting good and avoiding evil, at encouraging virtue and discouraging vice, at avoiding harm to others and promoting their well-being or welfare. In general, they are concerned with the interests of others or the common interest rather than just with the individual's self-interest, and they are distinct from the rules of etiquette, law, and religion (though the conduct they require may overlap with what these require). I also suggested that what counts as "moral" is disputed and that the dispute matters. We now need to see why.

I first introduced the provisional definition just cited as an account of moral norms, but morality at its broadest encompasses both norms and values: both rules that impose obligations, on the one hand, and values, or conceptions of the good, on the other. Durkheim captured this duality when he characterized morality as incorporating both rules imposing obligations and ends that are "desired and desirable": "moral reality," he wrote, "always presents simultaneously these two aspects which cannot be isolated empirically."[3] No act, he wrote, "has ever been performed out of duty alone; it has always been necessary for it to appear in some respect as good."[4] This duality has a long history within philosophy, distinguishing "the right" from "the good" as elements of morality in the broad sense and debating which has priority over the other, which comes first and shapes the other. Here the distinction is between rules that implement and values that express morality as broadly defined in the previous paragraph.

But there is another traditional way of marking this distinction. "The moral" can also be distinguished from "the ethical." This latter way (which descends from Hegel's distinction between *Moralität* and *Sittlichkeit*) involves postulating a different and narrower sense of "moral" that derives from Kant. In this view, morality denotes something that is both more severe and more abstract; and it is seen as applying anywhere and everywhere. It directs attention to the duties or obligations I have to other human beings viewed, from the standpoint of justice, as possessors of rights. The ethical, by contrast, refers to the values and ideals that inhere in one or another specific way of life—and these will, of course, be multiple and sometimes mutually incompatible. Ronald Dworkin, the legal theorist, captured the core of this distinction when he wrote that "ethics includes convictions about which kinds of lives are good or bad for a person to lead, and morality includes principles about how a person should treat other people."[5]

This narrow sense of morality is the focus of Kant's philosophy: for Kant a moral principle indicating what is right and wrong is one that moral agents could will as a universal law. In the same spirit the philosopher Thomas Scanlon, who focuses on this narrow sense of morality, holds that if a moral norm is to be valid it must be justifiable such that *no one* could reasonably reject it. The key idea here is that "what we owe to each other" (the title of his book[6]) is *justification*. Deciding what is right and wrong requires making a judgment about what others could or could not reasonably reject. Justifiability to others is the key to moral motivation and "must be recognized in, and shape, any morally defensible form of life."

This key idea of justifiability is also at the center of the universalistic moral theory of Karl-Otto Apel, the German philosopher, and Jürgen Habermas, the German sociologist–philosopher (a theory that Habermas has considerably modified over the years and that he used to call "discourse ethics" but now calls "discourse morality")—a theory that defends a morality of equal respect and solidaristic responsibility for everybody.[7] The original motivating idea behind this theory was that in the very practice of human communication, or "rational discourse," there is implicit the commitment to mutual justification among persons on a free and equal basis in unrestricted deliberation. The central idea is what Habermas calls "the discursive principle," according to which only those norms can claim validity that could meet with the agreement of all those concerned, in their capacity as participants in a practical discourse: for a norm to be valid, "the consequences and side-effects of its observance for the satisfaction of each person's particular interests must be acceptable to all."[8] Habermas criticizes Kant for supposing, as a child of the eighteenth century, that "in making moral judgments each individual can project himself into the situation of everyone else *through his own imagination*." In today's world, "when the participants can no longer rely on a transcendental preunderstanding grounded in more or less homogeneous conditions of life and interests, the moral point of view can only be realized under conditions of communication that ensure that *everyone* tests the acceptability of a norm, implemented in a general practice, also from the perspective of his own understanding of himself and of the world."[9] [...]

I suggested above that, in distinguishing the moral from the ethical, we view morality as applying anywhere and everywhere and directing attention to the duties or obligations I have to other human beings viewed, from the standpoint of justice, as possessors of rights. The ethical, by contrast, refers to the values and ideals that inhere in one or another specific way of life—and these will, of course, be multiple and sometimes, as we have seen, mutually incompatible. But now a further question arises. Values are subjective (and intersubjective). They indicate how people view their choices and their lives—their conceptions of what can make these good rather than bad, what they count as important or worthwhile. But can values also be *objective*? Can one identify components of well-being that are present within any life that goes well rather than badly: conditions of human flourishing? The question comes from Aristotle and, though she does not give Aristotle's answer, it has been addressed in the writings of Martha Nussbaum.

Together with the economist Amartya Sen, Nussbaum has developed what they have both called "the capabilities approach." Sen's interest is in how to compare and even measure "the quality of life"; Nussbaum's is in finding principles to provide constitutional guarantees and guide law and public policy. Both were dissatisfied with standard economic approaches to questions of justice that focused either on the distribution of resources or on utility, or preference satisfaction. They were also impelled to go beyond John Rawls's theory of justice, which also focuses on resources and thus fails to consider that individuals differ in their needs for resources and in their capacities to convert resources into valued ways of living, or what Nussbaum and Sen call "functioning." For instance, "women who begin from a position of traditional deprivation and powerlessness will frequently require special attention and aid to arrive at a level of capability that the more powerful can easily attain."[10] What really matters, after all, is how people are actually enabled to live their lives: what they are actually able to do and be.

Nussbaum's key idea is that there is a range of distinctively human abilities that "exert a moral claim that they should be developed." Of course, not all human abilities exert such a claim (for example, the capacity for cruelty): only those that "have been evaluated as valuable from an ethical viewpoint." There is thus a set of "core human entitlements that should be respected and implemented by the governments of all nations, as a bare minimum of what respect for human dignity requires."[11] [...]

The latest version of the list identifies ten central human capabilities under these headings: life; bodily health; bodily integrity; senses, imagination, and thought; emotions; practical reason; affiliation; other species; play; and control over one's environment. The assumption is that all individuals, provided with the right educational and material support, can become fully capable of all of them and that the state's role is to do what can be done to remedy unequal starting points due to natural endowments, luck, and power. [...]

The very idea of universalism in ethics and political thought is sometimes criticized as inherently ethnocentric,[12] and so the project of establishing and transplanting human rights across the globe comes to seem like a further case of Western, or rather Northern, ideological hegemony.

In her fine study *Human Rights and Gender Violence: Translating International Law into Local Justice*,[13] the anthropologist Sally Merry comments on the parallels and, indeed, continuities here. As with colonial legal transplants, human rights law is "dedicated to transforming family structure, land and labor relations and the tie between the individual and the state." Moreover the proponents of human rights are the very same colonial powers, and their targets are the ex-colonies. Often the old imperialist habits of contrasting more with less advanced societies, civilization with barbarism, creep back into the debates, and the move to human rights establishes "the terrain of social justice as the law and the state, not religion or community. At the same time it imports through the back door assumptions about oppositions between rights and culture that were fundamental during imperialism and are still embedded in human rights rhetoric." And finally, the "human rights system is deeply shaped by power and resource inequalities between the global North and the global South, as was the imperial system." This determines the flow of funding, the recognition of NGOs (non-governmental organizations), and the selection of projects, avoiding structural changes that would reduce global inequality and capitalist expansion.

And yet the differences are decisive. The generation of human rights laws, declarations, and other documents is a global process of transnational consensus building. As such it is highly imperfect, in the ways indicated and others, but it incorporates the very standards by which it can be criticized and improved. Moreover it is, as Merry observes, "being appropriated around the globe by national and local actors who see the potential benefits of a human rights framework and redefine their agendas in these terms" and offers "a new cultural framework that breaks with past ways of understanding behavior." Such a break, she writes, "is critical in changing behavior such as wife battering that was long accepted as normal but must be redefined as offensive in order to diminish its frequency. This is a process of appropriation rather than imposition." […]

Acknowledging the surviving truth in moral relativism—that there are multiple best ways for human beings to live—can be combined with making moral judgments and thus recognizing the authority of moral standards and the reality of moral disagreements. As suggested above, one can take the Kantian line of asking whether a given practice can be justified to all those affected, or one can take the Aristotelian line of asking whether it drags those involved in it below the threshold of one or more of the central human capabilities. Many ways of life—involving different forms of marriage and gender relations, for example[14]—may pass these tests, but wife-battering certainly will not.

Notes

1. Pascal, Blaise, *Pensées*, Secs. 294.
2. Appiah, Kwame Anthony (2005), *The Ethics of Identity*, Princeton, NJ: Princeton University Press, pp. 252–253.
3. Durkheim, Émile (1951 [1925]), *Moral Education: A Study in the Theory and Application of the Sociology of Education*, trans. Everett K. Wilson and Herman Schnurer, ed. Everett K. Wilson, New York: Free Press of Glencoe, p. 45. See the discussion of Durkheim's view in Hans Joas (2000), *The Genesis of Values*, trans. Gregory Moore, Cambridge: Polity, p. 66.
4. Durkheim (1951 [1925]), *Moral Education*, op. cit., p. 45.
5. Dworkin, Ronald (2000), *Sovereign Virtue: The Theory and Practice of Equality*, Cambridge, MA: Harvard University Press, 485n1.
6. Scanlon, T. M. (1998), *What We Owe to Each Other*, Cambridge, MA: Belknap Press of Harvard University Press (quotation p. 338).
7. Habermas, Jürgen (1998), *The Inclusion of the Other: Studies in Political Theory*, Ciaran Cronin and Pablo De Greiff (eds.), Cambridge, MA: MIT Press, Chapters 1, 39.
8. Habermas, Jürgen (1990), *Moral Consciousness and Communicative Action*, trans. C. Lenhart and S. W. Nicholsen, Cambridge, MA: MIT Press, p. 197.
9. Habermas (1998), *The Inclusion of the Other*, op. cit., p. 33.
10. Nussbaum, Martha C. (2000), *Women and Human Development: The Capabilities Approach*, Cambridge: Cambridge University Press, pp. 69 and 83.
11. Nussbaum, Martha C. (2006), *Frontiers of Justice: Disability, Nationality, Species Membership*, Cambridge, MA: Belknap Press of the Harvard University Press, p. 70.
12. See my essay: Is Universalism Ethnocentric? in Steven Lukes (2003), *Liberals and Cannibals: The Implications of Diversity*, London: Verso, and Seyla Benhabib (1999), "Nous" et "les Autres": The Politics of Complex Cultural Dialogue in a Global Civilization, in *Multicultural Questions*, Christian Joppke and Steven Lukes (eds.), Oxford: Oxford University Press, reprinted in modified form in her *The Claims of Culture*, Chapter 2.
13. Merry, Sally Engle (2006), *Human Rights and Gender Violence: Translating International Law into Local Justice*, Chicago, IL: University of Chicago Press (quotations pp. 225–227).
14. For evidence and discussion of such diversity within the United States alone, see *Handbook of Family Diversity*, David H. Demo, Katherine R. Allen, and Mark A. Fine (eds.), New York: Oxford University Press, 1999.

Part III
Descriptions

Introduction

Didier Fassin

Anthropologists have always dealt with morality in their ethnographical studies, write those who contest the novelty of moral anthropology. And they are not wrong. Much like Molière's Monsieur Jourdain who realises that, unbeknown to him, he has been speaking 'prose' all his life, many anthropologists have written about morality without realising it – or admitting it. In fact, when they described in their monographs the prevailing norms of a society or the values that its members took as a reference, it was often a matter of morality even when all the norms and values in question were not necessarily of a moral nature. At the very least, protesters must concede that these authors studied morality without saying so. Therefore what is actually new is the use within anthropology of the term itself – long considered problematic and irrelevant – and the reflection that this has entailed. This lexical innovation, albeit relative, has allowed unprecedented descriptions of the social world. Two particular types will be retained here: first, local moralities, that is, descriptions of systems of norms and values that are specific to a given society; second, moral economies, that is, descriptions considering the relationships between these systems and other aspects of social life.

Over the past decade, the study of local moralities has seen remarkable development.[1] Anthropologists have endeavoured to describe configurations of norms, values and emotions in often faraway societies (particularly the Indian and Oceanic worlds), basing themselves on a variety of theoretical models, some giving more importance to affects, others to reasoning, others still to practice. These scholars have sometimes used the term 'morality', sometimes preferred instead to refer to 'ethics', or sometimes claimed that the two terms are interchangeable. However, the reader will not find these authors here, but rather those who preceded them. Without speaking of ethnographies of morality or the anthropology of ethics, they also produced surveys of the norms and values of the societies they studied, sometimes including an emotional dimension.[2] Retaining some of their texts here is not simply a matter of recognising their pioneering role but also of providing a better account of the continuities and changes at work in both the questions raised by anthropologists in the field, and the answers they provide, without presupposing that introducing the terms 'morality' and 'ethics' sufficed to lead to innovative research issues.

In this regard, Kenneth Read's long article on the Gahuku-Gama of Papua New Guinea is an exception in that the author explicitly states from the very title that the subject is 'morality' and speaks in the text of his project for a 'comparative ethics'. Contrasting his subjects' conceptions in this domain with those of the Christian tradition, he shows that, in the group he is studying, obligations and sanctions are not the same for everyone: there is a social distribution of morality according to the status of individuals, implying therefore that human beings are not equal before ethical principles. This can be understood from the different ways that homicide is considered – even 'human life is given a variable value'. It is a question of understanding an ideology rather than a set of rules imposed more less or less efficiently upon members of society. This is also what Lila Abu-Lughod accomplishes in her study of an Egyptian Berber group: she seeks to identify what legitimises the hierarchical system based on sex, age and status. Whether individuals are honourable or not is grounded in the idea that they do or do not have superior virtues enabling them to demonstrate their autonomy. The code that must be obeyed is honour, for some, and modesty, for others; this is then demonstrated in haughty and self-assured attitudes for the former, and humble and embarrassed attitudes for the latter. This recalls Nietzsche's expression: become what you are. Individuals must act in accordance with what society prescribes for them, depending on their social qualities, which are considered as being ethical ones.

This question of honour in Mediterranean and Muslim societies has given rise to a substantial body of literature and it is surprising that this is rarely cited in contemporary studies on morality and ethics, as if the coherency of cultural areas were more important than that of the issues addressed.[3] Michael Herzfeld, who carried out studies of Greek society over many years, can be seen as fitting into this line of thinking, although he does criticise the tendency towards geographical over-generalisations. Through very precise ethnography, he shows that conceptions of honour and shame, central to social life, differ greatly even from one village to the next: moralities therefore become hyper-local. Conversely, however, we could also say that they extend much further than simply across the geographical and cultural zones generally associated with honour and shame. This can be inferred from Steven M. Parish's work on the Newars in Nepal. Given that he considers affects as 'embodied' social judgements, and this is where the originality of his approach lies, he centres his analysis on shame, which he considers to be a 'moral emotion'. It is obviously not a question of suggesting hasty parallels between emotions felt in very different cultural contexts – in this case, the Mediterranean world and the Indian peninsula – but rather of suggesting the heuristic value of using different lenses when carrying out comparative studies of local morals ranging from the most close-up detailed analysis to the widest possible perspective.

The concept of moral economies encourages a similar reflection. It has a very different genealogy, however, including as a scientific discipline. The difficulty it presents comes from the multiplicity of meanings that it covers and the frequently approximate use that is made of the notion.[4] It is therefore necessary to retrace this genesis and above all to clarify the various meanings that this concept has taken on. Originally, moral economies were the theoretical innovation of historians. The plural is most important here, particularly given how most analysts ignore the reason for it. There are indeed two main theoretical lines.

The first, which is the best known, was initiated by Marxist historian Edward Palmer Thompson. He introduced the term in his penetrating study of the making of the English working class and developed it in a famous article on the moral economy of the crowd. His aim was to establish that the nineteenth-century working classes, just like the eighteenth-century farmers before them, were not provoked solely by material concerns, but also by moral ones, that is, a system of principles, obligations and expectations regulating social relationships and economic life. The fact that the capitalist logics and market economy did not respect this system led to riots that were not provoked by misery and hunger but rather by the breaking of a moral contract. Although this theory is a matter of dispute among historians, it was rapidly adopted by anthropologists via the political scientist James C. Scott. His study on Southeast Asian peasants endeavours to understand their rationales of production. Although he uses the expression 'moral economy', including in the title of his book, he refers rather to the idea of a 'subsistence ethic' consisting in a series of values that determine the behaviour of the peasants with a view not to maximising their possible revenue but rather to minimising the potential risks. Here again the economy is moral – the things at stake are not competition and the quest for profit, as market law would have it, but reciprocity within the community and the duties of the landlord towards his tenants. This approach, whether it concerns moments of crisis, such as for the British farmers, or daily survival, such as for the Burmese peasants, has inspired many ethnological studies. Jean-Pierre Olivier de Sardan's use of the concept of moral economy is paradoxical, as he explains himself, because he applies it to a practice generally considered to be immoral: corruption. However, and this is precisely the value of a set of recent works in this vein, the practices grouped together under this generic term are often part of an ensemble of norms and values, particularly in African societies, which the author does not seek to justify or culturalise, yet which can explain why actions condemned by international organisations are not only tolerated locally, but often considered to be good.

The second theoretical line, less often referred to but just as fundamental for its influence in the anthropology of science and of medicine in particular, has its origin in an article by Lorraine Daston, a historian of Renaissance and Classical Age science. Taking inspiration from Bachelardian philosophy, she defines a moral economy as a network of values underpinned by affects and applies this to scientific activity, showing that the work of scientists rests not only on using reason, as they tend to think and as the social sciences long imagined, but also on moral principles and emotions that are crystallised around concepts such as objectivity or methods such as quantification. In this interpretation economy no longer refers to the production and exchange of goods and services but to an arrangement presenting regularities, and morality is no longer the preserve of the dominated, as was the case in the previous approach.[5] The question therefore arises of whether it is reasonable to retain the same term, given that what it refers to is not the same. Of course, it is researchers who replied to this question, and did so, as we have seen, by adopting one or other of the two paradigms, often with little knowledge of the other. Is it possible to move beyond this confused situation, which is somewhat unusual for the scientific world? If so, it would not be a case of trying to find some sort of compromise between two models that are too dissimilar, but rather of making the most of the originality of each.

In this perspective, one can say, in parallel with the traditional definition of political economy, that a moral economy is the production, distribution, circulation, and use of affects and values in the social space.[6] On the one hand, such a definition avoids the normative dimension implicit when applying the concept to peasants: their economy was defined as moral because it was considered to be built upon values seen to be positive and affects regarded as legitimate. This then made the market economy appear as lacking morals, grounded solely in rationality and interest; and yet giving a moral connotation to the adjective 'moral' necessarily entails reducing its analytical incisiveness. On the other hand, the definition proposed also introduces a dynamic dimension that was lacking in the way the concept was used to talk about science: in the meaning suggested here, it is no longer a matter of focusing on affects and values that are part of networks, which amounts to fixing them in what could also be described as an ethos, but rather of looking at how they are produced at given moments, how they circulate between groups, how they are taken on board by agents and how they change over time; henceforth, moral economies necessarily fall within the scope of both a history and a sociology. Thus redefined, the concept offers a means of thinking through the evolutions of moral configurations (for example, the emergence over the recent decades of human rights and humanitarian reason as a mode of representation and of legitimisation of politics in the global public space), of analysing their modalities, tensions, and contradictions, and of observing how agents adopt, modify, or contest them.

Local moralities and moral economies are two ways of describing affects and values in the social world. The former tend to be limited to a group, a society or even a cultural area, placing emphasis on its permanence – on what founds and feeds a culture. The latter can be used to describe a field or an issue, placing emphasis on its evolution – and therefore on what links morality to politics.

Notes

1 Signe Howell's book can be viewed as the point of departure for this trend. Its title clearly indicates its intention and it was also significant due to its institutional links, as it was the continuation of a conference organised by the European Association of Social Anthropologists. See Signe Howell ed. (1997), *The Ethnography of Moralities*, London: Routledge. Many collective volumes have been published since and, even if not all the texts refer to local moralities as a concept, they all draw on them for their subject matter. John Barker ed. (2007), *The Anthropology of Morality in Melanesia and Beyond*, Aldershot: Ashgate; Karen Sykes ed. (2009), *The Ethnographies of Moral Reasoning: Living Paradoxes in a Global Age*, New York: Palgrave Macmillan; Monica Heinz ed. (2009), *The Anthropology of Moralities*, New York: Berghahn Books; Michael Lambek ed. (2010), *Ordinary Ethics: Anthropology, Language, and Action*, New York: Fordham University Press.

2 It would be interesting to analyse how the anthropology of emotions anticipated the ethnography of moralities. Michelle Rosaldo, who carried out pioneering work in this area with her studies of the Ilongot headhunters in the Philippines, refers to guilt and shame as 'moral affects'. See Michelle Rosaldo (1983), The Shame of Headhunters and the Autonomy of the Self, *Ethos*, 11 (3): 135–151; as well as Catherine Lutz and Lila Abu-Lughod eds. (1990), *Language and the Politics of Emotion*, Cambridge: Cambridge University Press. In a perspective of a comparative history of the two fields, but also of a multidisciplinary approach to these questions, we can note that the current development of moral anthropology is concomitant with the inception of a field of literary studies on emotions. See Sara Ahmed (2004), *The Cultural Politics of Emotion*, New York: Routledge; and Melissa Gregg and Gregory Seighworth eds. (2010), *The Affect Theory Reader*, Durham: Duke University Press.

3 To mention only the two most influential authors, see in particular: John G. Peristiany ed. (1965), *Honour and Shame: The Values of Mediterranean Society*, Athens: Weidenfeld and Nicolson; Julian Pitt-Rivers (1977), *The Fate of Shechem, or The Politics of Sex: Essays in the Anthropology of the Mediterranean*, Cambridge: Cambridge University Press; John G. Peristiany and Julian Pitt-Rivers (1992), *Honor and Grace in Anthropology*, Cambridge: Cambridge University Press.

4 To give an idea if not of the diversity of meanings of the phrase 'moral economy', at least of the variety of uses to which it is put, a few titles of works calling upon this term can be mentioned: Benjamin Orlove (1997), Meat and Strength: The Moral Economy of a Chilean Food Riot, *Cultural Anthropology*, 12 (2): 234–268; Philippe Bourgois (1998), The Moral Economies of Homeless Heroin Addicts, *Substance Use and Misuse*, 33 (11): 2323–2351; Kuhn Eng Kuah (1999), The Changing Moral Economy of Ancestor Worship in a Chinese Emigrant District, *Culture, Medicine and Psychiatry*, 23 (1): 99–132; Gilbert Quintero (2002), Nostalgia and Degeneration: The Moral Economy of Drinking in Navajo Society, *Medical Anthropology Quarterly*, 16 (1): 3–21; John Tresch (2007), The Daguerreotype's First Frame: François Arago's Moral Economy of Instruments, *Studies in History and Philosophy of Science* (38): 445–476; Sangeeta Chattoo and Waqar Ahmad (2008), The Moral Economy of Selfhood and Caring: Negotiating Boundaries of Personal Care as Embodied Moral Practice, *Sociology of Health and Illness*, 30 (4): 550–564; David Griffith (2009), The Moral Economy of Tobacco, *American Anthropologist*, 111 (4): 432–442.

5 Over recent years, we have seen the scientific, and probably political, value in not limiting the moral question to the dominated, with the work of political scientist Nicolas Guilhot (2004), *Financiers, philanthropes: Vocations éthiques et reproduction du capital à Wall Street depuis 1970*, Paris: Raisons d'agir; of neuro-economist Paul Zak (2008), *Moral Markets: The Critical Role of Values*, Princeton, NJ: Princeton University Press; of anthropologist Karen Ho (2009), *Liquidated: An Ethnography of Wall Street*, Durham: Duke University Press; of sociologist Viviana Zelizer (2010), *Economic Lives: How Culture Shapes the Economy*, Princeton, NJ: Princeton University Press; and of historian Olivier Zunz (2012), *Philanthropy in America: A History*, Princeton, NJ: Princeton University Press.

6 This idea is developed in Didier Fassin (2009), Les économies morales revisitées, *Annales: Histoire, Sciences Sociales*, 64 (6): 1237–1266; and in Didier Fassin and Jean-Sébastien Eideliman eds. (2012), *Économies morales contemporaines*, Paris: La Découverte.

Local ethics

21 The moral person in context

Kenneth Read

Kenneth Read (1917–1995) was an American anthropologist of Australian origin. During the Second World War he was posted to Papua New Guinea, where he discovered what was to be his main locus for fieldwork. Under the direction of Siegfried Frederick Nadel, who had founded the anthropology department at the Australian National University, he undertook the study of the Gahuku-Gama people, making him the first ethnographer to carry out long-term research in the Highlands. His initial work gave rise to a series of articles which went on to become classics and, above all, to his major book *The High Valley*, praised not only for its ethnographic subtlety but also for its personal tone and literary style: far from British positivism, the book announced a reflexive turning point in anthropology. Later, Kenneth Read became a professor at Washington University in Seattle and conducted a study in a gay bar: *Other Voices: The Style of a Male Homosexual Tavern*, thus opening up anthropology to the study of homosexuality – he was also the first president of what became the Society for Lesbian and Gay Anthropology. After he retired, he returned to his initial terrain on several occasions and produced one final work entitled *Return to the High Valley*.

The article presented here is a long and dense text often cited as a pioneering work due to its comparative approach to ethics. He draws a parallel between the morality of the Gahuku-Gama and Christian morality, not to judge one with regard to the other, or even to suggest that they have equal value, but rather to establish their differences and thus better grasp the local ethics that form the subject of his study. Going against the general trend of theories of the time, he rejects the reduction of morality to a system of rules. Similarly, he refuses the formalism of the functionalist or structuralist approaches, as well as the relativism of culturalist readings. Basing himself on rigorous ethnography, he uses a series of examples (attitudes towards homicide and adultery, towards property and theft) to establish that the Gahuku-Gama's categories of obligation and moral individuals are distributive: they vary according to the situation and the social status of the individuals and do not lead to entities with universal meaning or value, such as life or the human being. This research paved the way for subsequent studies examining local moralities from the point of view of individuals, considered in their cultural context, rather than through the codes supposed to define a moral community.

Morality is an aspect of evaluation. All social life, as Nadel has pointed out, may be said to implicate or to involve the idea of value, in that being aimful it expresses preferences, ideas of worth, of what is desirable or undesirable.[1] Clearly, however, the concept of value in this generic sense covers many forms of conduct which are not equivalent; worth, desirability or undesirability possess differences of degree as well as referring to different qualities in things. Conduct which is moral is conduct which involves the notions of duty and the ideal, of obligation and intrinsic desirability. It is conduct judged in terms of such qualities as good and bad, right and wrong – goodness and rightness being here conceived in an absolute sense; indeed, it is the absolute nature of the good which gives to moral values their particular requiredness. Although all social behaviour is not invested with a moral quality, moral values tend to pervade the greater part of social life, forming a relatively autonomous system whose influence is sought and felt by most individuals and institutions. From the sociological point of view, moral norms are, above all, directives for action. Possessing requiredness, they lead to conformity, ensuring, for example, that in specific situations certain choices are normally made and that behaviour is thus channelled in certain directions. In other words, moral values are one of the principal regulative mechanisms of culture. Indeed, in small scale, undifferentiated societies which rely to a large extent on self-regulation – where, for example, there are few *sui generis* legal institutions – the social order may be seen to depend quite largely on the requiredness of moral values which are simply held.[2] It follows that in these societies there is usually a close consistency between the norms which constitute the moral system and the social structure.

To be effective, it is obvious that moral values must be internalized and generally accepted by the majority of those who constitute the group. It is equally obvious that they must be capable of generalized expression, for moral judgments are the criticism of conduct in terms of generally accepted notions of the good. Such judgments, as Firth has said, are notable for the ease with which they tend to be uttered: "they cost so little."[3] But we do them an injustice if, for this reason, we regard them simply as the expression of states of emotion. They possess, too, an intellectual component which, though present in varying degrees, bears on the nature of the good and of obligation as these are conceived by a particular people. Thus, a majority of our own moral judgments imply the Christian ethic of personal freedom and responsibility, the transcendent and objective nature of the good and our common obligations in a moral universe. By way of contrast, the moral judgments of other peoples may be couched in terms of practicality; they may eschew the speculative and abstract and they may stress the immediate claims of interpersonal relationships. The assertion of right and wrong is in each case not only emotionally but also ideologically founded. The good is not simply what people feel to be right but also what they think or believe to be right, and we may thus regard their moral judgments as the expression of a particular ethic, as involving, among other things, some conception of human nature, of man's relationship to man and of the obligations which devolve on him through certain presupposed conditions of existence.

Among the Gahuku-Gama, people do not normally appeal to abstract principles but rather emphasize the practical consequences of moral deviation. Instead of saying it is "good" or "right" to help others, they state quite simply that "if you don't help others, others won't help you." Indeed, in a possible majority of instances, the practical consequences of disregarding moral norms is fairly readily apparent, if not as obviously direct as in this particular illustration. Thus, disrespect for elders, lack of regard for age mates, failure to support fellow clansmen, incest or breaking the rules of clan exogamy all involve practical penalties, not explicitly stated in each case but undoubtedly understood by the individuals who assert that the norms concerned are right. Sociologically, in fact, the right must frequently be regarded as the cognitive counterpart of what Nadel refers to as an instrumental nexus, the extent, that is, to which a norm or activity is the focal centre of a series of activities which may be impeded if it is impeded by variation.[4] At the same time, this is not quite the same thing as saying that Gahuku-Gama ethics are avowedly utilitarian, for although in most instances the right is that course which can be proved pragmatically to offer the most satisfaction, or to result in the least dislocation, the agent also conceives it to be right intrinsically. He is in varying degrees aware of the pragmatic effects, but rightness is itself an aspect of his awareness, being, as it were, an irreducible value which he attaches to certain things in certain situations. In short, moral norms are not merely instrumental imperatives. They possess an ontological element, and I shall try to show that for the Gahuku-Gama this is bound up with a particular conception of man which does not allow for any clearly recognized distinction between the individual and the status which he occupies. This is the theme I wish to develop now, and I shall approach it by way of a description of Gahuku-Gama morality. I cannot, however, attempt a complete account of all the occasions and events which are made the subject of moral judgments and shall confine myself to those which seem to me to be most critical.

As an introduction to the subject, a few additional remarks on the general form of Gahuku-Gama moral assertions may be appropriate. They frequently express moral statements as universals on the pattern of "help others so they will help you," or "give food to those who visit you so they will think well of you." But the practical rider may be omitted, and the moral directive then takes the simple form of "it is good to obey your elders"; "it is bad for brothers to quarrel"; "it is right for a man to fence his wife's garden"; "it is good to think of your sister and her children"; "it is bad to slander your fellow clansman," or "it is good to be friendly with your age mates." We may note, however, that people do not assert that "it is wrong to kill," or that "it is right to love everyone," while of the other universal commands of Christianity a large number are conspicuously absent. The Gahuku-Gama, for example, do not say that one should practice forbearance in all circumstances; indeed, their injunctions against adultery, against lying, thieving and slander should not be accepted as applying to all the situations in which the individual may find himself. There is nothing unusual in this. It is simply another way of saying that we are dealing with a tribal morality as distinct from the universal morality of Christian teaching. In other words, Gahuku-Gama assertions of what is right or wrong, good or bad, are not intended to apply to all men; they are stated from the position of a particular collectivity outside of which the moral norm ceases to have any meaning. Thus, the manner in which people behave who are outside the tribal system of inter-group and inter-personal relationships is virtually a matter of indifference. More than this, the individual does not regard himself as being bound to them by any moral obligation: it is justifiable to kill them, to steal from them and to seduce their women.

There is a more important point, namely, that within the group itself there is what might be called a "distributive" recognition of moral obligation. For, while the moral assertions are clearly the expression of values acknowledged by all members of the group, the individual is not bound to all his fellows in like degree. As a moral agent his responsibilities vary considerably according to the positioning of other individuals within the system of inter-personal and inter-group relationships. Any particular moral norm may therefore have a more or less relevance or requiredness according to the individuals involved in a specific situation. In other words, it is not simply that the applicability of a certain norm may be temporarily affected by particular circumstances. The distributive character of Gahuku-Gama morality lies rather in the fact that each agent recognizes that his moral obligations to others are differentially apportioned.

We may express this in an alternative way. From the standpoint of the group at large the Gahuku-Gama recognize common moral obligations. Certain values are acknowledged, recognized and espoused by all members of the group: they are held in common. Obligations may also be said to be common in a second sense, when a relationship between any two or more individuals entails reciprocal moral duties which are identical or complementary. Thus, we may speak of the common obligations of husband and wife, of brothers, age mates, of parents and children, of members of linked clans and so on. But there is a sense in which we cannot use the term, as implying, that is, that every individual recognizes an identical moral responsibility towards all other individuals. The Christian ethic, on the other hand, requires us to do just this. It is our responsibility to regard every individual in the same moral terms; all make the same moral demands of us. We may argue, of course, that the historical forms of Western European morality have also been distributive. The ideal, nevertheless, has achieved expression in many of our most cherished institutions, and the Western conception of individuality, of personal integrity and obligation, as well as many of our grounds for social and political criticism, are quite clearly derived from it. The contrast is, therefore, significant, and fundamentally ethical, being concerned with different ontological conceptions of man and of human relationships and with the nature of moral obligation. The distributive morality of the Gahuku-Gama explicitly recognizes significant differences in the individual's moral obligations and responsibilities to other people, and while these differences are closely related to a particular social structure, they imply, too, an ethical outlook which in itself is of considerable importance. Thus, to return to my original phrasing of the question, this distributive character involves what is from the Western point of view a basic failure to distinguish an ethical category of the person. It is a failure to separate the individual from the social context and, ethically speaking, to grant him an intrinsic moral value apart from that which attaches to him as the occupant of a particular status. I will be citing other evidence to support this view, but for the moment we need to examine more closely the distributive nature of the moral system.

The morality of kinship provides an obvious starting point, for not only is the pattern of each individual's daily life, from birth to death, quite largely determined by kinship, but it is also that subject on which the anthropologist may justifiably claim to speak with most authority. Disregarding the treatment given to it by earlier historical and evolutionary schools, the study of kinship by anthropologists in this century has taken two principal directions: some have been primarily concerned with a socio-functional analysis while others have been mainly interested in the study of kinship structure. For some time, too, these different approaches tended to keep apart, the formal and essentially static structural analysis becoming for some the principal aim and sole end of social anthropology. More reasonable counsels – which, indeed, appear to be gathering the greater following – stress, however, that the two are inter-dependent and that structure is not a reality *sui generis* to which all activities contribute. It is argued, rather, that structure appears only within the context of specific aims, interests and activities, and that it is from these that it derives its meaning and significance. As we might expect, those who have adopted the socio-functional approach have been more ready to give explicit recognition to the moral character of kinship relationships.[5] Yet on the whole they have taken this quality as given and have concerned themselves primarily with analysing the relationship between kinship and other aspects of social organization. This is not said in disparagement, for in a sense we can take this nature for granted. Firth, for example, has remarked that "the transmutation of biological relations into social relations is intelligible for the ordinary member of society only in terms of appeal to customary notions of what is right," and for kinship to be the effective organizing principle it is, it must be firmly grounded in the moral order.[6] Thus, in the analysis of economic or political organization we do not need to give separate consideration to the moral aspect of kinship relationships. The fact that such relationships channel behaviour, that they determine the choices made, implies that they are felt to be right.

It is hardly worth saying that different patterns of behaviour, different social rights and obligations are enjoined between an individual and his different categories of kinsmen. What is of more importance, however, is that these differences also possess a moral quality. Thus, we may speak of the reciprocal moral duties of elder and younger brothers, and we may compare the ideal in this instance with the kind of behaviour enjoined between kinsmen who are age mates. A younger brother, for example, is expected to be mindful at all times of his elder brother's superior status. He is required to show the latter respect, to accept his criticism, to heed his wishes and to obey his commands. There are moral duties on the side of the elder brother too, for he has to see that his younger brother does not want. The latter looks to him for assistance in obtaining a wife, for pigs with which to start his household and for a fair share of their father's property. From the younger brother's point of view, however, the moral quality of the relationship is primarily one of constraint, of obedience and the acceptance of discipline. It contrasts, therefore, with the moral relationship between kinsmen who are the same age. Here, the ideals of friendship and equality are stressed. Mutual help, frankness, a comradeship which is expressed in sharing one another's secrets and in freely asking and giving – all these add their measure to the moral quality of the age-mate relationship. The comparison could be carried further, to take in, one by one, all the categories of kin which a man recognizes. The moral quality, of the individual's relationship with his mother's brother is, for example, quite different from the moral quality of the ties he has with his father's brothers, different again from those which he recognizes with his wife's parents and her brothers, and, different again from his responsibilities towards his sister's husband. Finally, we could extend the examination to the various groups of which a man is a member, contrasting his moral rights and responsibilities towards members of his sub-clan with those towards members of his clan and these with his obligations towards members of other clans of the same tribe.

These characteristics are sufficiently commonplace to stand without elaboration. Indeed, it could be said that our own moral system possesses many comparable features. Thus, we might point to the different moral obligations of a father to his children, of an employer to his employees, of the members of a club or other association to one another, in fact of any of the thousand and one socially recognized relationships between two or more individuals. Closer examination suggests, however, that the diversity in our moral obligations is more apparent than real, for we recognize that there is – or at least that there should be – a certain common measure of ethical content in all our relationships. Ideally, we may say that certain duties are felt to be independent of status. There are minimum responsibilities which apply to all the circumstances in which the individual finds himself, and there are actions and attitudes which are considered wrong in all situations.

Ultimately, this common measure of rights and responsibilities depends on the intrinsic ethical value which we attach to the individual. We recognize, that is, that all men, in virtue of this intrinsic worth, have a valid claim to be treated as moral equals; they make identical demands which, as moral agents, we are required to respect. Needless to say, moral reality shows varying degrees of approximation to or departure from the ideal, but we cannot, for that reason, deny that the ideal has any influence. Many, if not all, of the social reforms of the past one and a half centuries could be viewed as attempts to correct conditions in which practice has seemed to obscure or to depart too far from it. Similarly, many feel bound at times to criticize and to oppose political movements which show a calculated or cynical disregard for the moral rights of the individual. In other words, while our moral system possesses some distributive features, I suggest that these also embody certain common principles. Ideally, in our moral relationships we operate, as it were, from a fixed ethical perspective, the perspective of the person and his moral claim, regardless of social ties or status, to a certain minimum consideration. That this claim is frequently couched in different terms does not alter the issue; nor is it affected materially by the fact that the ideal has seldom, if ever, received complete expression. The essential point is that we acknowledge that all men, in virtue of their nature as such, make certain basic and invariant moral demands of us.

It is in the absence of any comparable conception of obligation that the distributive character of Gahuku-Gama morality is most clearly revealed. Contrasted with our own fixed ethical perspective, that of the Gahuku-Gama is continually changing. Men, in other words, are not conceived to be equals in a moral sense: their value does not reside in themselves as individuals or persons; it is dependent, rather, on the position they occupy within a system of inter-personal and inter-group relationships. Moral obligation, therefore, is distributive in the sense that it is also dependent on and varies with this social positioning of individuals. This does not mean simply that certain relationships obviously involve or charge the individual with differential duties. In our own society, for example, a father has specific duties towards his own children which he is not called upon to assume in respect of others. In like manner among the Gahuku-Gama the parent–child relationship involves specific obligations which we would not expect to find between, say, a man and the children of his wife's brothers. I refer, however, to a fundamental difference between the two systems, the distributive character of Gahuku-Gama morality issuing from the fact that there is no common measure of ethical content which should serve as a guide for the moral agent in whatever situations he finds himself.

Stated as sharply as possible, moral obligations are primarily contingent on the social positioning of individuals. They are not derived from, neither do they refer to anything which is intrinsic to the nature of the agent himself or to the nature of other human beings as such. Thus, in a way which is quite different from our own traditional point of view, the differential duties associated with status are the principal constituents of moral obligation, and this is therefore seen to change or vary according to the individuals or groups involved. The result may be described as a continual narrowing or contraction of the moral judgment, due to the fact that the right, in any given instance, has basically a social connotation. This, of course, is also true of ourselves, for our moral norms refer to what we consider to be the appropriate form for human relationships. But rightness is nevertheless an independent and invariable quality which transcends any given social context, whereas with the Gahuku-Gama it is the social context itself which largely determines the moral character of a particular action. It is not, then, simply that we can observe a distributive apportionment of duties at the descriptive level, but rather that this distributive element is the expression of basic ethical principles.

Evidence is not lacking to support this interpretation. Thus, from the Western point of view, it is significant that in the situations which normally arise moral judgments are not phrased in terms of what is appropriate or inappropriate in the relationships of men considered simply as human beings. This does not mean that the Gahuku-Gama have no conception of behaviour which is becoming or, conversely, unbecoming to men as such. They say, for example, that "men are not dogs," quite clearly meaning to imply that there is a certain minimum of behaviour which is considered appropriate to human beings.[7] Indeed, any culturally standardized pattern of behaviour could be said to possess this particular "rightness." From the individual's point of view, there are therefore minimum standards which can be said to apply to him as a human being. The important point is that these basic or generic conceptions of rightness and wrongness are not universalized: the Gahuku-Gama do not go on to argue or to assert that because man *is* a human being – because, that is, of some inherent quality which distinguishes him from other animals – there are invariable standards which he must apply in his relationships with all other human beings. [...]

This attitude is not unusual, and its sociological implications are fairly obvious. I have brought it in merely to illustrate, at one extreme, the Gahuku-Gama failure to universalize a concept of human nature and moral obligation, which they nevertheless possess. Unlike ourselves, in other words, human nature as such does not necessarily establish a moral bond between individuals, nor does it provide a standard against which all actions can be judged and either approved or disapproved. We are confronted instead with what I have referred to as a continually changing moral perspective. The moral judgment operates, as it were, at a number of different levels. At one level, certain things are approved for men as men. At other levels the rightness or wrongness of an action varies according to the status of those who are involved. Homicide provides us with an obvious example. Stated briefly: it is wrong for an individual to kill a member of his own tribe, but it is commendable to kill members of opposed tribes, always provided that they are not related to him. Thus a man is expected to avoid his maternal kinsmen in battle though other members of his own clan have no such moral obligation towards these individuals. Within the tribe, too, homicide is regarded with varying degrees of moral reprehension, according to whether the individuals involved are, for example, members of the same sub-clan, of different sub-clans of the same clan, or of different clans. Our own attitude towards parricide or fratricide may be cited as comparable, but there is this difference. The Christian attitude towards homicide is indissolubly linked with the intrinsic personal value of the individual and our traditional teaching emphasizes that it is the taking of innocent human life as such that is wrong. With us, the individual life has, in other words, an absolute value which is greater than and quite sharply distinguished from a value which is conferred by a specific social tie or by membership of a particular social group. With the Gahuku-Gama, however, it is clear that the value of an individual life is primarily dependent on these social criteria. Thus, the reaction to homicide emphasizes the moral nature of the social bonds between individuals and groups of individuals rather than the inviolability of human life itself.

Considered as they bear upon the theory of primitive law, these remarks have a familiar ring. I refer to what Nadel has called the "social range" of offences.[8] Thus, he has pointed out that among the Nuba the evaluation of a crime such as homicide, and the sanctions which it provokes, varies according to whether it occurs "within the clan or outside it, in or outside the political unit." Homicide within the Nuba kinship group or clan is an unpunishable offence, in the sense that it does not provoke forceful retaliation by the members of the clan or its segments. Between clans, however, punishment is exacted in the form of blood feud and revenge. The sociological explanation for the unpunishable nature of intra-clan homicide is seen to lie in the principle of self-help on which the law is based. Homicide within the clan affects a group which is so closely knit that although its unity has been violated by the act, it would be violated in even greater measure by retaliation. Punishment is therefore left to supernatural agencies or it is excluded altogether. There is a comparable situation among the Gahuku-Gama and, since Gahuku-Gama law is also founded on self-help, the same sociological explanation may be advanced to account for the absence of forceful retaliation following homicide within the sub-clan. But, as Nadel has also stressed, the failure to take retaliatory action implies a moral attitude wherein this particular act is regarded with such abhorrence that it is unthinkable, beyond the realm of human sanction. Indeed, Nadel prefers to speak of the "sin" of intra-clan homicide as compared with the crime of homicide between clans. My own point is that human life is given a variable value, depending on the social positioning of different individuals. It is unthinkable to kill in certain contexts, wrong in others, right in others, and a matter of indifference in others. In each case, the moral nature of particular social bonds is the important factor rather than anything intrinsic to man as such. To sum up: morality is primarily contextual. The moral judgment does not operate from the fixed perspective of universal obligation for the moral assessment of behaviour varies in different social contexts, according, that is, to the different values placed on different individuals in different contexts.

I regard this failure to universalize a concept of moral obligation – and to grant an invariant ethical value to the individual – as the most important characteristic of the moral system. I have referred in passing to homicide as a case in point, but lest this should be thought a special or exceptional instance, it could be shown that the vast majority of moral norms are similarly restrictive or distributive. A few examples must suffice to clarify this position.

Christian teaching holds that man, as person, has a moral duty to himself and to others to tell the truth. To lie is to act in a manner which is contrary to his true nature, a denial of the transcendent value which he embodies. To the Gahuku-Gama, on the other hand, the value of truth is not absolute, nor is it related to intrinsic human nature. The prudent individual is truthful, because "lying makes people angry; it causes trouble," and most people wish to retain the good opinion of those with whom they are in close daily association. But there are circumstances in which deceit is not considered wrong. Thus, men have frequently asked me to hide their personal possessions in my house and to take charge of their cash for them, so that they may plead poverty if their affinal kin demand any of the ceremonial payments to which they are entitled. Nor does anyone expect an individual to admit his guilt if he is charged with some offence by a member of another clan. Similarly, the truth is not expected from members of other groups if, in the event of some claim or quarrel, there is the possibility of gaining a greater advantage by concealing it. To lie and to be deceitful may be regarded as bad, but almost in the same breath people joke about the manner in which they have either misled others or have escaped the consequences of some of their actions. An examination of all these occasions shows that the moral evaluation is primarily contextual, dependent, that is, on the nature of specific social ties rather than on the recognition of a moral absolute.

Turning to the morality of property-holding, we find a similar situation. Firth has pointed out the difficulty of making a sharp distinction between borrowing and stealing in many primitive communities, instancing the fact that theft involves more than taking an article without having obtained the prior permission of its owner.[9] Kinship ties, he says, "may give a moral umbrella to the abstraction of the article," and he concludes that "the classification and the moral evaluation of the act depend in part on the moral evaluation of the ties between the participants." This is a neat expression of the situation among the Gahuku-Gama. Theft, or converting another's property to one's own use, is considered wrong, but kinsmen – in virtue of the moral quality of the social ties between them – are permitted a large measure of freedom with one another's goods. Generally speaking, a man is not expected to be angry if a kinsman appropriates something belonging to him provided the latter tells him what he has done, and even if the owner is not notified he seldom regards the act as theft. He is angry. He chides his kinsman for omitting to inform him of the action, but he does not feel as injured as if it had been a member of another clan or someone to whom he was not related. Moreover, theft is regarded as more or less reprehensible according to whether it involves members of the same clan, of different clans of the same tribe, of friendly clans of different tribes, or of groups without any recognized social ties. In the past, for example, pig stealing was considered a legitimate way of scoring off a rival group; and even between friendly clans or between different clans of the same tribe, a good deal is condoned provided it is not found out. The Gahuku-Gama remark quite casually that "everyone steals," and they have no compunction about keeping some item of property which they come by accidentally, even if there is no doubt as to the rightful owner's identity. In short, the moral nature of specific social ties is primarily responsible for defining the limits within which the appropriation of the property of another is right or wrong. Respect for property, like the virtue of truth, is not a moral absolute.

Finally, we may turn to the attitude towards adultery. Here again the moral evaluation of adultery depends primarily on the moral evaluation of the ties between the parties concerned.[10] Adultery within the sub-clan and the clan is strongly condemned, for the anger and the enmity which it creates are contrary to the moral ideal that the members of these groups should assist and support each other. People will even deny that it occurs, and though they recognize that a man who has been wronged in this way has cause to show anger, and to seek redress for the injury, they invariably express resentment for the informant whose tattling has been responsible for bringing the matter into the open. Action has to be taken if the offence is brought to the wronged husband's notice and he, in turn, makes a public issue of it; but the general attitude is that it would have been better for all concerned if the offence had passed unnoticed. At the opposite extreme, adultery with women of different tribes is regarded lightly, as hardly worthy, in fact, of moral censure. It is necessary to conceal it, but men boast a good deal about their own affairs and they will quite proudly display the scars left on their thighs by the arrows of irate husbands. They are less ready to admit adultery with women of different clans of the same tribe, but here too one receives the impression that if a man can get away with it, no great moral blame attaches to him. Moral disapproval is more pronounced than in the previous instance, but it is far less emphatic than in cases of adultery within the clan or sub-clan. In other words, moral evaluation is again contextual. Adultery is not wrong universally and intrinsically, that is in the sense of being contrary to man's moral constitution. The wrongness of the act depends on the evaluation of the social ties between the individuals involved.

We are brought back, then, to the ground on which a moral obligation is felt to rest. With our own traditional teaching, I have tried to show that this ground is ultimately the person, and since all men, irrespective of status, are also persons, they are bound by a common measure of obligation. The source of moral authority, moreover, is seen to lie outside the system of social relationships which bind men to one another as members of society. Moral duty is never simply synonymous with social duty, for the moral agent is required to look beyond the form of particular relationships and the differential rights which they involve, and to measure these against the invariable and inherent value which he and all other men possess. It will be clear by now that the Gahuku-Gama conception of obligation is based on a fundamentally different view of human beings. We will look in vain, for example, for any comparable concept that men, as men, are bound to one another by a moral tie which is wider than, and subsumes, the ties that link them socially. In short, my examination has tended to show that men are not primarily persons, in the moral sense, but social individuals. The analysis, however, is not complete, for we have yet to see what ideas of man's nature are held by the Gahuku-Gama and what ethical consequences, if any, they involve.

Notes

1. Nadel, S. F. (1953), Social Control and Self-Regulation, *Social Forces*, 31 (3): 265–273.
2. Ibid.
3. Firth, Raymond (1951), *Elements of Social Organization*, New York: Philosophical Library, p. 184.
4. Nadel (1953), Social Control and Self-Regulation, op. cit., p. 267.
5. Meyer Fortes' *The Web of Kinship Among the Tallensi* (Oxford, 1949) is a notable exception among studies of kinship structure. To Fortes, the essence of the Tale kinship system is "its function as the primary mechanism through which the basic moral axioms of a society of the type represented by the Tallensi are translated into the concrete give and take of social life" (p. 346).
6. Firth (1951), *Elements of Social Organization*, op. cit., p. 210.
7. Sexual behaviour is a case in point, though even here disapproval is rarely expressed in terms of a particular practice being contrary to human nature. Thus, the attitude towards masturbation is not that it is intrinsically wrong, but rather that it is unnecessary. Homosexuality, too, is foolish rather than immoral. People denied any knowledge of it, but they were not morally affronted by the idea, taking the more practical view that it would be silly, as well as undignified, to indulge in it.
8. Nadel, S. F. (1947), *The Nuba*, London, New York: Oxford University Press, pp. 501–504.
9. Firth (1951), *Elements of Social Organization*, op. cit., p. 196.
10. Hogbin, H. Ian (1938) draws attention to this fact in his paper "Social Reaction to Crime," *Journal of the Royal Anthropological Institute*, Vol. LXVIII, pp. 226–248. The situations which he describes for Wogeo are in most respects similar to those which arise among the Gahuku-Gama.

22 The moral basis of hierarchy

Lila Abu-Lughod

Lila Abu-Lughod (born in 1952) is a professor of social science at Columbia University. An anthropologist of Palestinian origin, she is a renowned specialist of the Arab world. Her research on the women of a Bedouin community in Egypt resulted in a pioneering study in the anthropology of emotions: *Veiled Sentiments: Honor and Poetry in a Bedouin Society*. Her later works, also based on an ethnographic study carried out in the Egyptian world, have mainly concentrated on gender issues, which she addressed in *Writing Women's Words*, and media politics, which she analysed in *Dramas of Nationhood*. In the context of increasing hostility towards Islam on an international level, notably through the denunciation of the oppression of women, she has recently focused on a critique of the universalist ideology of human rights and on re-establishing the complexity of the ethical and political issues at stake in a feminist approach to Muslim societies.

The text presented here deals with the local morality of the Bedouin community of the Awlad 'Ali, showing the centrality of honour and modesty. The paradox of this society is that it combines strict social hierarchy with formal egalitarianism and relations of domination with the affirmation of autonomy, both within the family unit and within the tribe as a whole. This inequality rests not upon the use or threat of force, but rather on a moral argument of honour. Some members of the community, due to their age, sex, wealth or genealogy, are regarded as having superior virtues and therefore enjoy a superior status, which they must however maintain by conforming to the prescribed code of honour and by deserving the respect they are shown; conversely, others, because they cannot attain independence, must display the habitus of discomfort and shame in their code of modesty. Based on a detailed description of Bedouin culture and its moral codes, the analysis avoids the various forms of culturalism or indeed sociologism by revealing the social tensions within this culture and showing the practical dilemmas faced by its agents.

"Blood," the central concept in the definition of both Bedouin cultural identity and individual identity is seen as closely tied to moral nature. And Awlad 'Ali believe that morality is what most distinguishes them from and makes them superior to other peoples. At the heart of their moral system are the values of honor and modesty. What these values are and how they shape individual actions, interpretations of others' actions, and even the life of sentiment must be explored.

This system of morality is especially important to understand because it is the basis for the hierarchical social divisions that exist in the Bedouin social system. Although this social system is often touted as highly egalitarian, and is indeed more egalitarian than many, the realities of power differences are inescapable, especially within the family and lineage. What is intriguing is how, through several ideological means, Awlad 'Ali reconcile their basic value of equality with the hierarchical system by which they live. First, they view as ultimately moral the bases of greater status, control over resources, and such control as people can exercise over others. Individuals must achieve social status by living up to the cultural ideals entailed by the code of honor, in which the supreme value is autonomy. The weak and dependent, who cannot realize many of the ideals of the honor code, can still achieve respect and honor through an alternative code, the modesty code. Second, Awlad 'Ali mediate the contradiction between the ideals of equality and the realities of hierarchy by considering relations of inequality not antagonistic but complementary. They invest independence with responsibility and a set of obligations and dependency with the dignity of choice.

Autonomy or freedom is the standard by which status is measured and social hierarchy determined. It is the consistent element shaping the Bedouin ideology of social life, in which equality is nothing other than equality of autonomy—that is, equality of freedom from domination by or dependency on others. This principle is clear in Bedouin political organization, the segmentary lineage model. Although anthropologists disagree about many other aspects of this system, there is consensus that the system has as its central feature the maximization of unit autonomy.[1] Each tribal segment is theoretically equal to every other through opposition. No leader is given authority over the whole confederation of tribal segments, and there are no offices or titles, although there is informal leadership at various levels of segmentation. The value of political autonomy to Awlad 'Ali is even borne out by their continuing resistance to the imposition of state authority, first by the colonial powers and later by the Egyptian government.

The relationship between autonomy and hierarchy is manifested in the broadest social division in the Western Desert, between the Sa'ādi tribes, the true Awlad 'Ali, and their traditional client tribes, the Mrābtīn. The Sa'ādi are known as the "free" (*ḥurr*) tribes, and the word *mrābit* means "tied"—in this case, tied by obligations of clientage. In the past the Mrābtīn paid tribute to their Awlad 'Ali patrons, had no tribal territorial rights, and depended on their patrons for the right to use land, wells, and pastures. Although the Mrābtīn are now independent, able to own land, and no longer paying tribute, the distinction of freedom remains a source of social differentiation because of the moral implications of their ancestry.

Despite the rhetoric regarding the jural equivalence and equality of agnates, tremendous inequalities of status and authority exist within the lineage or tribe as well. These amount to differences in degree of autonomy and are linked, like the distinction between the Sa'ādi and Mrābtīn, to control of resources. The primary distinction is between elders and juniors, involving primarily a differential authority to make decisions. Lineage elders control resources such as tribally owned wells and land. (Livestock is individually owned and is a separate matter.) Senior men make decisions and arrange marriages for junior men. In fact, this relationship is modeled on the extended family, where the father and his brothers (paternal uncles) have authority over sons and nephews. By extension, all older men, as important figures in their own lineages, are deferred to by younger men, who are less important. Junior members serve senior men and sit quietly on the fringes, listening but rarely speaking at gatherings.

Within the family itself, the inequality of patriarch and dependents—in the nuclear family, the man and his wife and children (who are known collectively as his *washūn*)—is similarly an inequality in relative independence. The family is the prototype of hierarchical relationships. The patriarch controls resources; his dependents are weaker, younger, and control no resources independently. But other relationships within the family are also unequal, for instance that between older and younger siblings, older siblings having precedence. The relationship of inequality between the sexes is usually a function of the familial relationships obtaining between them. Fathers have authority over daughters, as over sons. Older brothers have authority over younger sisters, although, as children, older sisters care for younger brothers and can order them around.

Familial relationships alone do not determine relationships of inequality between the sexes, however. Women are always dependents, as the most common term of reference for women, *wliyya* (under the protection), indicates. The hierarchical relationship between male and female in general is somewhat independent of particular roles. For example, advantages of age and responsibility for younger siblings are erased in the case of older sisters and younger brothers. As adults, even younger brothers are responsible for their older sisters and have authority over them. Similarly, the relationship between mother and son, in which initially the mother is all-powerful, controlling access to food and other resources and having the authority to tell sons what to do, equalizes with time. Husband and wife, although both adults and ideally from tribes and lineages of equal standing, are also never equal. There may be severe limits on the husband's ability to impose his will on his wife, yet she remains dependent and subordinate. [...]

Honor: the moral basis of hierarchy

Those who would have social precedence have more than just a responsibility to care for dependents. In Bedouin ideology, the tension between the ideals of equality and independence on the one hand and the reality of status differentials on the other is mediated through the notion that authority derives neither from the use of force nor from ascribed position, but from moral worthiness. Hierarchy is legitimated through beliefs about the disparate possession of certain virtues or moral attributes. Furthermore, Bedouins act as though authority must be earned. Because authority is achieved, it can also be lost. This is where the analogy to kinship breaks down. In the family, the roles of provider and dependent and the prerogatives and duties associated with each are more or less fixed or ascribed; certainly the positions of family members are unchangeable. But in social life at large there is more flexibility and room for achievement.

Individuals must earn the respect on which their positions rest through the embodiment of their society's moral ideals. Although the regularities of status distinction expressed in principles of the precedence of genealogy, greater age and wealth, and gender might seem to contradict any notion of achievement, Awlad 'Ali view these principles as being generally associated with, and hence rough indices of, the moral virtues described below. Insofar as persons demonstrate these virtues, they are entitled to the respect that validates, if not establishes, the social precedence and authority generally associated with these principles. But, as I will illustrate, the principles themselves are not sufficient to determine status. In other words, greater age or wealth, better genealogy or ancestry, or even gender does not necessarily guarantee greater authority or social precedence.

The ideals or moral virtues of Bedouin society together constitute what I refer to as the Bedouin code of honor. The honor code is, despite (or perhaps because of) the tremendous amount of anthropological attention devoted to it in studies of both Christian and Muslim circum-Mediterranean cultures, strangely difficult to define.[2] Friedrich provides the most attractive way of thinking about it: "Honor is a code for both interpretation and action: in other words, with both cognitive and pragmatic components." In its first aspect it is "a system of symbols, values, and definitions in terms of which phenomena are conceptualized and interpreted." In the second, honor guides and motivates acts "organized in terms of categories, rules, and processes that are, to a significant degree, specific to a given culture." Friedrich then goes on to outline the structure of Iliadic honor as a "network" of propositions about honor and "honor-linked values" that he considers specific to Homeric Greek culture.[3]

The values of the Bedouin honor complex are not those of the Iliad, nor those of the complex as found in Spain, Sicily, Algeria, or any other Mediterranean society. The critical term in the Awlad 'Ali honor code is *aṣl* (ancestry/origin/nobility), a term expressive of a range of ideas. It is the basis for the proud differentiation of Bedouin from non-Bedouin. Drawing on the genealogical notion of roots, or the pure and illustrious bloodline, it also implies the moral character believed to be passed on through this line. Thus *aṣl* is the primary metaphor for virtue or honor.

What is the Awlad 'Ali network of honor-linked values? And how do these values legitimate greater social standing? First, there are the values of generosity, honesty, sincerity, loyalty to friends, and keeping one's word, all implied in the term usually translated as honor (*sharaf*). Even more important, however, is the complex of values associated with independence. Being free (*ḥurr*) implies several qualities, including the strength to stand alone and freedom from domination. This freedom with regard to other people is won through tough assertiveness, fearlessness, and pride, whereas with regard to needs and passions, it is won through self-control. Failings or weaknesses in any of these areas disqualify one for positions of responsibility and respect and put one in a position of dependency or vulnerability to domination by others.

Applied in numerous contexts to distinguish both individual Bedouins and families and lineages, the qualities associated with *aṣl* are apparent in the way the differences between Sa'ādis and Mrābṭīn are characterized. Technically, only the Sa'ādi tribes are known as the Awlad 'Ali, or sons of 'Ali. Their ability to trace their genealogical connection to a single eponymous ancestor is a matter of pride, as is the corresponding ability to find a relationship of kinship between any two individuals, lineages, segments, or tribes. By contrast, the Mrābṭīn are considered an unrelated conglomeration of tribes with no overarching genealogical unity. This absence of genealogy implies lesser moral worth.[4] Sa'ādis describe Mrābṭīn as lacking in the virtues of honor, such as generosity (Mrābṭīn are said to be stingy), ability to fight and resolve disputes, and efficaciousness in the world (Mrābṭīn are described as "all talk," or as "a pot that boils and boils"). In fact, even Mrābṭīn view themselves as inferior to the Sa'ādi. One Mrābiṭ explained to me, "We are weak, humble. It is not a matter of money, because some Mrābṭīn are wealthy. But a Si'dāwi [sing.] has 'standing,' pride, boldness, and goodness. He has a 'face in front of people' [respect, reputation]."

Sometimes Mrābiṭ individuals are recognized as noble, as displaying the moral qualities associated with *aṣl*; but people explained that in such cases, if one probed, one always discovered the existence of some Sa'ādi blood in the family line—a Sa'ādi maternal uncle or grandfather, perhaps—which indicates how closely the Bedouins associate blood and character.

The ideals of Bedouin manhood highlight the importance of freedom to *aṣl*. One man explained, "A real man stands alone and fears nothing. He is like a falcon [*shahīn*]. A falcon flies alone. If there are two in the same territory, one must kill the other." Freedom and fearlessness are coupled in another word for falcon, "free bird" (*ṭēr ḥurr*). The courage of the warrior ethic applies not just to matters of war or fighting, as described in the contrast between Bedouin and Egyptian and between Sa'ādi and Mrābiṭ, but to the interactions of everyday life. The "real man" is not afraid of being alone at night, despite the risk of confrontation with wild animals and spirits (*'afārīt*) in the open desert where there are no lights and few humans. Fear of anyone or anything implies that it has control over one. [...]

The correspondence between these qualities of assertiveness and the quality of potency, as described by Bourdieu of a Kabyle man of honor, are striking.[5] Bourdieu sees the "rules of honour" as those of the logic of challenge and riposte, in which a challenge both validates an individual's honor by recognizing him as worth challenging and serves as a "provocation to reply." Inability to reply and counter the challenge results in a loss of honor. As he notes, "Evil lies in pusillanimity, in suffering the offence without demanding amends." In both the Awlad 'Ali and the Kabyle codes, men of honor share a general orientation toward assertiveness and efficacy.

The final element in the Bedouin network of honor-linked values is self-mastery, one aspect of which is physical stoicism. Bedouins think physical pain and discomfort should be borne without complaint.[6] When a youth from our community underwent a serious operation in Cairo, I visited him in the hospital. His non-Bedouin roommates, all of whom had undergone the same operation, remarked on the fact that he had not complained once, whereas they had suffered terribly, moaning and complaining to all who would listen. The young man's father turned to me with pride, glad that his son had confirmed the Bedouin ideal in practice. It may well be that people disapproved of my continual complaints about my flea bites for the same reason. They always told me to try to be tougher.

The stoic acceptance of emotional pain is another aspect of self-mastery. To weep is a sign of weakness, so men of *aṣl* do not cry, regardless of the intensity of their grief. In describing his reaction to the death of a favorite aunt, one young man said, "Men don't cry. I got a terrible headache because the death was so hard on me [*ṣa'bat 'alayy*]." Mastery of needs for and passions toward others—the true sources of that dependency so antithetical to honor—seems to be related to the development of *'agl*, a complex concept, fundamental in most Muslim cultures, from Morocco to Afghanistan,[7] that can be glossed as reason or social sense. It is said that angels have only *'agl*, whereas Adam was a combination of *'agl* and passion, or carnal appetite (*shahwa*). Animals are at the other extreme from angels, having no *'agl*.

Children are born with almost no *'agl* but develop it in the process of maturing,[8] as is clear in the Awlad 'Ali description of the four stages in the male life cycle. First is childhood, a time of no responsibility when a boy merely gratifies his needs and plays. On reaching majority (*sinn ir-rushd*), when fasting and praying begin in earnest and a man becomes responsible for blood-payments of his tribe, he begins the years of youth (*shabāb*). The Bedouins have mixed feelings about this period, which lasts until about age forty. These are the great years of love and life; yet because he is governed by his passions, a man is considered flawed in religious and social terms. At forty, however, he begins to be "wise" or "reasonable" (*'āgil*). He is said to know right from wrong and to be complete. The last stage, old age (*shēkhūkha*) can be merely a continuation of the period of being *'āgil*, unless senility sets in. *'Agl*, then, is an aspect of maturity.

The value of self-control, or the possession of *'agl*, is especially apparent in the political realm. The most respected men in the Western Desert are those called on to mediate disputes. The person who does not anger easily, who is even-tempered and patient, dispassionate and fair, is "asked for in tribal hearings" (*maṭlūb fil-mi'ād*). Mediators are usually drawn from the ranks of the leaders of the smallest sociopolitical units, the *byūt* or residential sections, and referred to by the term *'awāgil*, the plural of the adjectival form of *'agl*.[9] Reason and age are embedded in this title, since most section leaders are the most senior men in a group of agnates. [...]

Ḥasham: honor of the weak

Most analyses of honor take the perspective of those at the top of the hierarchy who are able to realize the social ideals. Yet it is important to ask how those at the bottom resolve the contradiction between their acceptance of these ideals and their own limited position, which rarely allows them to realize the ideals themselves. The tensions between Bedouin cultural ideals for the individual and the realities of hierarchy are most acute for these people. As Bedouins, they share with their superiors a high regard for autonomy and equality, the values of honor. Individuals of lower status, especially young persons and women, may have *aṣl*, or noble origins, through their tribal affiliations or merely as Bedouins, in contrast to Egyptians. But as dependents, the extent to which they can realize the ideals of behavior that validate *aṣl* is limited. Their lack of control over resources handicaps them with regard to the generosity and ability to provide that lie at the heart of power (*gadr*). By definition, their independence and capacity to stand alone are minimal, and they can assert their wills only in highly circumscribed social situations. Moreover, opposition to those who provide for them and have authority over them is only successful when their superiors' decisions are clearly unreasonable or their treatment of dependents disrespectful.

One way those at the bottom resolve the contradiction between their positions and the system's ideals is by appearing to defer to those in authority voluntarily. This situation is merely the obverse of the point made earlier, that a person in authority must earn respect through moral worthiness: the free consent of dependents is essential to the superior's legitimacy. What is voluntary is by nature free and is thus also a sign of independence. Voluntary deference is therefore the honorable mode of dependency. [...]

In daily parlance, words from the root *ḥashama* are used in various grammatical forms, each having a slightly different sense. The two poles of meaning around which usage clusters are those referring to an internal state and those referring to a way of acting; thus, *ḥasham* involves both feelings of shame in the company of the more powerful and the acts of deference that arise from these feelings. In the first instance, *ḥasham* is conceptualized as an involuntary experience (we might even call it an emotion); in the second, as a voluntary set of behaviors conforming to the "code of modesty." The experience is one of discomfort, linked to feelings of shyness, embarrassment, or shame, and the acts are those of the modesty code, a language of formal self-restraint and effacement. The cultural repertoire of such behaviors includes the most extreme and visible acts of veiling and dressing modestly (covering hair, arms, legs, and the outlines of the body) as well as more personal gestures such as downcast eyes, humble but formal posture, and restraint in eating, smoking, talking, laughing, and joking.

Ḥasham is closely tied to the concept of 'aql, the social sense and self-control of honorable persons. Just as the possession of 'aql enables persons to control their needs and passions in recognition of the ideals of honor, so it also allows them to perceive the social order and their place within it. Children, who are said not to have much 'aql, must be taught to taḥashsham; the primary goal of socialization is to teach them to understand social contexts and to act appropriately within them—which means knowing when to taḥashsham. Mothers often scold their children with the imperative, which can be translated as "behave yourself" or "act right" and which implies, "have some shame."[10] The dual connotations of appropriate ways of feeling and voluntary behavior control are apparent here.

The concepts of ḥasham and 'aql are closely wedded in notions of the ideal woman. The woman who is 'āgla (reasonable, characterized by 'aql) is well-behaved; she acts properly in social life, highly attuned to her relative position in all interactions. There is also a spillover into general comportment, which should conform to the behavior appropriate to modesty. People say of a woman who is 'āgla that she knows when to speak and when to listen. This description draws attention to the fact that she is deferential, since in Bedouin society the superior speaks and the inferior listens. A leader or important person is one said to have the "word" (kilma). The ideal woman is described as having a soft voice (ḥissha waṭī), not a "long tongue."

The negative case of the woman who lacks 'aql or does not taḥashsham can take one of two forms: she can be described either as willful (gāwya) or as slutty (qḥaba). The second aspect refers specifically to sexuality. I argue that conformity to sexual norms is merely an aspect of deference to those who more closely represent the social ideals. The first, gāwya—from the root qwy, to be strong or powerful—clearly pertains to hierarchical relations. The Bedouins use this particular adjectival form in reference only to females. It means something like "overly strong" and suggests excessive assertiveness. The negative connotations of this sort of assertiveness derive from its inappropriateness for those in positions of dependency or social inferiority. For example, the word is applied to a woman or girl who is contrary or argumentative with her elders, who refuses to do what she is told, talks back, or does things without permission. Grown women who refuse requests or disobey husbands or in-laws are also labeled willful and are perceived as lacking in ḥasham. Those who "talk too much" invite disciplinary action.

Bedouins attribute such disrespectful behavior to improper upbringing, specifically overindulgent treatment. Although mothers threaten and discipline boys as much as girls, they say that girls should be treated with less indulgence lest they become willful, and boys should not be disciplined as much lest they become fearful. Boys should also be indulged, presumably so they will gain a sense of power, rather than weakness, in interactions with others. Women rationalize their belief that boys should be breastfed longer than girls through these ideas. One old woman said, "The more willful the boy, the better."

The different beliefs about the value of assertiveness for boys and girls correspond to their future positions in the hierarchy. Even though ḥasham really applies only to specific social situations involving persons of unequal status, women are so often in such positions that they must be trained to be modest in general demeanor—to be deferential, soft-spoken, obedient, and cooperative—or at least to be more sensitive to the social contexts in which modesty would be appropriate. Girls will grow up to be dependents, perhaps exchanging their positions as daughters for those as wives. At best, women, as matriarchs, can come to control some property and have influence over those men, usually sons, on whom they must depend to negotiate business and deal with the world of non-kin. Boys will nearly always grow up to become providers, if not for large groups of dependents, then at least for their own wives and children, and thus will not need to defer to many.

Notes

1 See Eickelman, Dale (1981), *The Middle East: An Anthropological Approach*, Englewood Cliffs, NJ: Prentice-Hall; Lancaster, William (1981), *The Rwala Bedouin Today*, Cambridge: Cambridge University Press; and Meeker, Michael (1979), *Literature and Violence in North Arabia*, Cambridge: Cambridge University Press.
2 The literature is quite extensive. The volume edited by Peristiany (Peristiany, Jean G. [1966], *Honour and Shame: The Values of Mediterranean Society*, Chicago: University of Chicago Press) remains a classic. Davis, J. (1977, *People of the Mediterranean: An Essay in Comparative Social Anthropology*, London: Routledge & Kegan Paul) and Gilmore (Gilmore, David [1982], Anthropology of the Mediterranean Area, *Annual Review of Anthropology*, 11: 175–205) summarize some of the diverse materials in their recent reviews of Mediterranean anthropology. On the Christian side, Campbell (Campbell, John K. [1964], *Honour, Family, and Patronage*, Oxford: Oxford University Press) provides some of the most thorough ethnographic description, while Blok (Blok, Anton [1981], Rams and Billy-Goats: A Key to the Mediterranean Code of Honour, *Man*, n.s. 16: 427–440), Brandes (Brandes, Stanley [1980], *Metaphors of Masculinity: Sex and Status in Andalusian Folklore*, Philadelphia: University of Pennsylvania Press), Gilmore (1980, *The People of the Plain: Class and Community in Lower Andalusia*, New York: Columbia University Press), Herzfeld (Herzfeld, Michael [1980], Honour and Shame: Problems in the Comparative Analysis of Moral Systems, *Man*, n.s. 15: 339–351), and Pitt-Rivers (Pitt-Rivers, J. A. [1977], *The Fate of Shechem, or the Politics of Sex: Essays in the Anthropology of the Mediterranean*, Cambridge: Cambridge University Press) each make significant arguments. Meeker, M. [1976] Meaning and Society in the Near East: Examples from the Black Sea Turks and the Levantine Arabs, *International Journal of Middle East Studies*, 7: 43–70, 383–422) and Bourdieu (Bourdieu, Pierre [1966], The Sentiment of Honour in Kabyle Society, in *Honour and Shame: The Values of Mediterranean Society*, pp. 191–241; [1977], *Outline of a Theory of Practice*, Cambridge: Cambridge University Press; and [1979], The Sense of Honour, Chap. 2 in *Algeria 1960*, Cambridge: Cambridge University Press) present the most stimulating discussions of honor on the Islamic side of the Mediterranean. For a more traditional approach to the honor code in the Islamic world, see Abou-Zeid (Abou-Zeid, Ahmed M. [1966], Honour and Shame Among the Bedouins of Egypt, in *Honour and Shame: The Values of Mediterranean Society*, pp. 243–259) on Awlad 'Ali. Most recently, Wikan (Wikan, Unni [1984], Shame and Honour: A Contestable Pair, *Man*, n.s. 19: 63552) has made the important point, which my own analysis certainly confirms, that the concepts of honor and shame should not be seen as binary opposites. Herzfeld (1984, The Horns of the Mediterraneanist Dilemma, *American Ethnologist*, 11: 439–454) warns of the dangers of reifying the Mediterranean culture area.
3 Friedrich, Paul (1977), Sanity and the Myth of Honor, *Ethos*, 5: 281–305.
4 This matter of the moral worth of Mrābṭīn is complicated by the facts that certain tribes are associated with religious piety and that most saints and healers come from Mrābiṭ tribes. Awlad 'Ali associate Islam with morality, sometimes even noting how their ideas about honor are against Islamic principles.
5 I have chosen to refer to the recent version of this paper, which first appeared in Peristiany (1966), because the translation is better and the author has made a few modifications.

See Bourdieu, Pierre (1966), The Sentiment of Honour in Kabyle Society, in *Honour and Shame*, Peristiany, Jean G. (ed.), Chicago, IL: The University Press of Chicago, pp. 191–241.

6 Lancaster (1981, p. 67) describes the same stoicism in the face of physical pain as characteristic of the Rwala Bedouins.

7 There do seem to be differences in usage for the word *'agl*, however. Eickelman interprets it for the Moroccan case in terms similar to those I use for the Bedouin instance. He argues that "reason is the capacity to discern realistically existing, if ephemeral, patterns of dominance and deference in the social order and to act appropriately" (1976, *Moroccan Islam: Tradition and Society in a Pilgrimage Center*, Austin: University of Texas Press, p. 141). He notes that "reason grows in a person with his ability to perceive the social order and to discipline himself to act effectively within it" (1976, p. 138). Anderson (Anderson, Jon [1982], Social Structure and the Veil: Comportment and the Composition of Interaction in Afghanistan, *Anthropos*, 77: 405) argues that for the Pakhtun in Afghanistan, *'agl* is "sense" or "reason" and "is manifest as cooperation and composure and is acquired by learning in society, most especially in public worship." A systematic comparison.

8 According to Dwyer (Dwyer, Daisy H. [1978], *Images and Self-Images: Male and Female in Morocco*, New York: Columbia University Press) Moroccans hold similar beliefs. She notes, "Given the uncertain origins of male responsibility, it is not surprising that most men are said to reach their quota of *'aqel* (intelligence, responsibility) relatively late in life. Its flowering is believed to begin at the earliest at age forty, when a context that is maximally conducive to the development of responsibility tends to take place" (1978, p. 101).

9 See Mohsen (Mohsen, Safia Kassem [1975], *Conflict and Law Among Awlad 'Ali of the Western Desert*, Cairo: National Center for Social and Criminological Research, p. 39) for more on the *'awāgil* of the Western Desert.

10 Davis, Susan (1983, *Patience and Power: Women's Lives in a Moroccan Village*, Cambridge, MA: Schenkman, pp. 156–157) notes similar uses of the term in Morocco.

23 Honour and shame

Michael Herzfeld

Michael Herzfeld (born in 1947) is a professor of anthropology at Harvard University. A specialist in contemporary Greece and Italy, with a focus ranging from village life and the arts to political issues and urban issues in Europe, he is the author of *Anthropology Through the Looking-Glass: Margins of Europe* and *Cultural Intimacy: Social Poetics of the Nation-State*. Putting forward the emotions and values of modern bureaucracy, his work *The Social Production of Indifference: Exploring the Symbolic Roots of Western Bureaucracy* renewed the Weberian approach by adding a moral dimension. His recent book, *Evicted from Eternity: The Restructuring of Modern Rome*, examines the physical and social transformations of the Italian capital.

In the text presented here, Michael Herzfeld examines the moral values of rural Greek society. He calls into question anthropological generalisations based on notions of cultural zones, such as 'the Mediterranean' as constructed around notions of 'honour' and 'shame' popularised by anthropologists such as Julian Pitt-Rivers and J. G. Peristiany in the 1960s. Rather than studying 'systems of values', he analyses the 'moral taxonomy', that is, the classification according to which elements are organised and placed in relation one to another. The notions that order the moral sphere are not absolute and should not be essentialised; they are relative and allow the behaviour of each member of the group to be evaluated regarding a specific horizon of expectation. To establish this, Michael Herzfeld compares two villages in Crete and uses ethnographic examples to underline how behaviour that is judged to be positive or negative is in fact relative to the more general values that define each society. The question of cultural and moral relativism is displaced and renewed as he establishes that before being relative between one society and another, moral evaluations are already in fact relative within each society. However, while moral values are therefore doubly relative, the mechanism by which behaviour is evaluated with regard to a horizon of expectation is a permanent feature within the different societies of the Mediterranean regions. The value attributed to behaviour depends on the way it maintains or threatens social cohesion. According to this functionalist reading, the particular horizon of expectations according to which group members are evaluated can be explained by its cohesive function: in a word, its 'social virtue'. The relativism shown throughout the ethnography is thus anchored in an analysis offering a clear framework for cultural comparison.

Since the beginning of systematic anthropological research in the Mediterranean lands, the terms 'honour' and 'shame' have been used to represent an enormous variety of local social, sexual, economic and other standards. The significance of these values in each culture should not be minimized. It is, however, reduced and obscured by the apriorism, circularity and ethnocentrism inherent in the use of such inefficient English-language glosses for the purposes of cross-cultural analysis.

To date, little effort has been directed towards the comparison of usages within each linguistic tradition, or towards a critical appraisal of the assumption that indigenous terms mean much the same thing wherever they occur. Yet without a series of such internal perspectives, the cross-cultural comparison of concepts to which our only effective access is through local usage makes little sense. It would therefore be useful to attempt a comparative analysis of local usage within one language area, and this I do for the Greek-speaking world, after first setting out some theoretical issues in more detail.

The earliest systematic collection of essays on Mediterranean value-systems[1] avoided facile correlations through its scrupulous attention to the details of particularistic ethnographic description. The question of cross-cultural comparison was addressed, not begged. Mediterranean anthropology has nevertheless been faulted for its 'failure' to adopt a comparativist position.[2] Such a criticism raises the logical difficulty which the ethnographic accounts largely escaped: it presupposes that there exists within the circum-Mediterranean region something which is both worthy of cross-cultural examination and yet somehow 'less' characteristic of other areas.[3]

While this criticism does not necessarily require the adoption of a crudely undifferentiated culture-area concept, the overall impression of homogeneity is attributed to 'contact ... for millennia'. That a primarily geographical entity has to be defined by historical criteria, however, only compounds the difficulty of fitting so nebulous a concept as 'honour' to it. Another approach[4] has the Mediterranean as 'all regions surrounding the [Mediterranean] sea in which great emphasis is placed on the chastity and virginity of women'. Here, however, since the defence of female chastity is equated with 'honour', any attempt to correlate 'honour' with a geographical distribution must necessarily be circular. Once again, the definition relies on an implicit quantification of the unquantifiable – this time, the 'emphasis' on chastity.[5]

Moreover, whether 'honour' is defined as an index of female chastity or of economic stratification,[6] such concentration on a single well-defined variable suggests that the term 'honour' may itself be redundant. Its use has already introduced an element of nominalism. This is especially apparent in Davis's complaint that Bailey,[7] who prefers the unambiguously etic 'reputation', does not then explain why 'honour' might be 'inappropriate'. If most of the behaviour described by Bailey as 'competing to remain equal' is in fact 'honour-oriented behavior',[8] that fact originates in Davis's definition of 'honour' rather than in the indigenous categories.

Many of the local terms for moral values correspond closely to English-language cognates; obvious examples include *onore, rispetto* and *egoismos*. Similarities of this sort, which are not necessarily matched in the semantic domain, make it particularly hard to abandon the habit of assuming virtual equivalence. In fact, the semantic disparity between English and Mediterranean cognates is often obvious from the careful descriptions of ethnographers. A single instance will suffice to make the point here. Some of Brögger's south Italian informants 'maintained that honour (*onore*) only concerned the sexual conduct of the female members of the household as reflected on its male members, and they would use the term respect (*rispetto*) in other contexts'.[9] This statement only makes sense when we realize that the 'translations' of the Italian terms are unavoidably inexact. South Italian *onore* clearly operates in a manner markedly different from the Victorian English sense of 'honour' as a man's ideal comportment towards unrelated women.[10]

Peristiany, Bailey and their collaborators similarly avoided linguistic reductionism by reporting each terminological usage in its own ethnographic context. They have in effect provided moral taxonomies – systems, that is, for the ranking of one's fellow-citizens according to a set of ethical criteria. Treating these taxonomies collectively as 'stratification' reduces the non-material aspects of social classification to reflections of an economic ordering.

Nor must alternative interpretations necessarily be expressed in terms of 'belief'. Davis decries the early emphasis on moral criteria as merely 'a technique which treats beliefs as *sui generis* phenomena'.[11] But all the authors just cited correlate local terminologies with several variables (including wealth), without awarding any single variable an unwarranted logical priority. Nor were those writers primarily concerned with 'belief' in the strict sense of the word. Moral taxonomies have to do with the public evaluation of behaviour, with degrees of conformity to a social code, rather than with hypothetical inner states.

Thus a Greek *egoistis* is not really demonstrating the rugged individualism which has for so long been upheld (e.g. d'Istria[12]) as the cornerstone of his 'national character'. On the contrary, by his very insistence on having respect paid to him, he is exhibiting conformity to a socially sanctioned ideal.[13] *Egoismos* is neither a form of belief nor a condition of social isolation, but an evaluative description of public behaviour. As such, it may have much less to do with a person's actual wealth than with the extent to which he is treated as a privileged individual. Since the other indigenous terms which have been translated as 'honour' and 'shame' are similarly categories of public evaluation, it may be no less inappropriate to refer to them as indices of absolute economic standing. [...]

Ethnographic amplification: Pefko, Glendi

We now turn to field data from Pefko (Rhodes) and Glendi (Western Crete) for further ethnographic illustration from within the Greek-speaking world.[14] The most striking difference between these two communities lies in their respective attitudes to the law. While the Pefkiots pride themselves on their sobriety and their respect for the law – they managed a total of one suspected and one confirmed case of theft over an eight-year period (1967–74) – the Glendiots engage in systematic sheep-stealing, illegally gamble for high stakes in public, carry and use firearms, and indulge in a wide assortment of petty infractions which the local police usually consider it politic to overlook. It is only to be expected that these two communities will also differ radically in their use of morally evaluative terms; Pefkiot values harmonize, at least superficially, with those of the civil and religious authorities, while the Glendiot attitude is perhaps best summarized in the assertion that 'we're free Greece here!'

In both communities, social 'worth' is denoted by *timi*, the specific referents of which may be provisionally listed as social responsibility, female chastity, and commercial value. A proverb ('*timi* has no *timi* / and joy to him who has it!') plays on its double meaning as something supremely 'valued' and as the definitively 'invaluable'. A 'love of *timi*', the *filotimo* so familiar from the ethnographic literature,[15] is thought in both communities to be particularly well expressed through hospitality. *Filotimo* means not so much the financial ability to entertain lavishly as the clearly communicated desire to do so as best one can. Indeed, *noblesse oblige*: a wealthier man's *filotimo* may actually be at greater risk than that of his economic inferiors. *Filotimo* is demonstrated through the adequate recognition of a social obligation. It is thus shown, for example, by a foreign visitor who later sends a postcard to thank for a villager's hospitality. At every turn, *filotimo* is assessed in terms of a changeable context of expectations.

Filotimo is revealed, above all, in socially appropriate behaviour. In a settled village community, where overt aggression is often perceived as disruptive, the term is used in connection with dignified self-restraint. Where self-restraint is seen as tantamount to cowardice, however, *filotimo* is not the appropriate term. Just what constitutes appropriate behaviour is, of course, open to debate in each situation as it arises. '*Filotimithika* (I've done all that you can reasonably expect of me),' remarked the son of a Pefko coffee-house proprietor when he made my order of coffee but chose not to bring it over to my table. Other villagers did not see his general behaviour in such flattering terms, and criticized his habitual indolence.

This aspect of fulfilling expectations is crucial to the definition of *filotimo*. In both Pefko and Glendi, it is particularly apparent in regard to the 'word' (*logos*) or verbal assurance which a man gives of his eventual intentions, especially where these concern a woman's chastity (*timi*). Nowhere else is one's *filotimo* so clearly offered for judgement, because it is here that one has the greatest control over the expectations which one creates about oneself. While a jilted woman is thought 'adulterated' through her betrothal, and consequently may never get another chance to marry, her ex-fiancé is regarded as lacking in *filotimo*. Usually the only strategy open to him for dealing with such opprobrium is to claim that the woman had herself turned out to be morally flawed.

Sometimes expectations originate less in a voluntary 'word' than in the role of co-villager. When a water-shortage became acute in Pefko, villagers were asked to exercise restraint in their use of irrigation-water. When two or three individuals nevertheless continued to take more than their fair share, the village mayor told the entire community (over the public-address system) to 'show *filotimo* [verb]' by subordinating selfish to collective interests. *Filotimo* was again enjoined upon all villagers when the State agricultural authorities failed to deliver sufficient sulphur-dust, urgently needed for treating the vines against a recurrent pest. Those who persisted in taking all they could get were condemned as 'anti-social' (*grousouzis*: see below). *Filotimo* here emerges as a 'brake' (*freno*) on aggressively competitive behaviour. But if competition and the 'word' are predominantly male modes in rural Greece, a woman may also be regarded as *filotimi* in so far as she lives up to her social and moral obligations. Conversely, *dropi*, which is conventionally glossed as 'shame', may be regarded as a positive virtue in men as well as in women under appropriate circumstances. As a sense of restraint, a 'brake', it can indeed be equivalent to *filotimo*, rather than its opposite as the honour–shame dichotomy implies.

Egoismos, the self-regard which the Sarakatsani and the Glendiots view as a manly virtue, is treated by law-abiding Pefkiots as a virtual antonym of *filotimo*. As an aggressive form of social disruptiveness, *egoismos* may differ from *filotimo* 'as the day from the night'. The Pefko villager who drew this analogy, and who also described both *filotimo* and *dropi* as a 'brake', was an in-marrying husband with a strong sense of his dependence upon the locally born Pefkiots' sufferance. His viewpoint underlines a facet of rural Greek morality which seldom appears in the ethnographic accounts,[16] and which is doubtless attenuated in the more dramatically competitive communities.

Given the great variety of ecological conditions, economic patterns and forms of social organization to be found in rural Greece, some degree of variation is only to be expected in the moral code also. *Egoismos* has obvious virtues when, as among the Sarakatsani, each household has only to defend its particular interests against all comers. When, however, there are recurrent practical reasons for communal responsibility and solidarity, the positive sense of *egoismos* becomes more questionable. The distaste felt for those who take more than their fair share of water or sulphur may then extend to others who indulge in more harmless forms of self-aggrandizement. A Pefkiot schoolteacher was criticized as an *egoistis*, for example, because his lofty affectations violated the egalitarian pretensions of the community. Only in the entirely hypothetical case of blood-vengeance for close kin might some Pefkiots assimilate *egoismos* with *filotimo*.

In Glendi, few reservations are entertained about the positive sense of *egoismos*. The Glendiots, some of whom are still transhumant pastoralists, sanction displays of aggressive male behaviour as well as the brazen flouting of official authority. Just as a man may be *kala kleftis*, 'good at [animal-] rustling', so, more generally, may he be *kala egoistis*. The adverbial *kala* ('well') implies performative ability, rather than simply an innate capacity. Echoing urban prejudices, a few self-conscious Glendiots decry the Cretans' notorious, collective *egoismos*, but this conceit is evidently tailored to external consumption. Most Glendiots, most of the time, proudly describe *egoismos* as one of their definitive traits. They associate it, not only with the defence of household and village, but also with the assertiveness that goes with being a member of one of the larger agnatic lineages which still, uncharacteristically for Greece as a whole, play a large part in the conduct of municipal elections and of feuds. Like the familial notion of self-interest,[17] *egoismos* is not egocentric in the sense suggested by its English cognate. Indeed, its effectiveness actually increases with the size of the solidary unit on which the actor can count: the expectations which he raises about himself are correspondingly safe from challenge.

Privatives

This public and relative aspect of moral evaluation is perhaps more strikingly evident in the negation of *timi* and *filotimo*. A Pefko field warden claimed that his absentee-landowner brother was lacking in *filotimo* because the latter would not pay him in cash for tending his vines. Actually, although brothers do engage in commercial relations in the extremely fragmented social nexus of Pefko, 'lack of *filotimo*' is not something which a man who himself possessed *filotimo* would attribute to his immediate kin before outsiders. It was thus consistent for the field warden to be regarded as a notorious *grousouzis* – a co-villager who nevertheless lacked the ordinary decency meant by *filotimo*. Here lies the rub: *atimia*, the definitive and total absence of *filotimo*, is something which may only be attributed to outsiders – criminals, Turks, political enemies, and in some contexts, non-kin within the community, but most certainly never one's own brother! The warden, by thus inverting normative usage, was living up to his unenviable reputation as a *grousouzis* – one who is 'without luck' (Turkish *uğursiz*), hence a socially polluting agent of misfortune, a morally defective insider.

An insider (defined according to context) cannot be *atimos*. On the other hand, both *atimia* and *grousouzia* are, in their respective contexts, antonyms of *filotimo*.

One characteristic form of *grousouzia* is the alleged possession of the evil eye. This is a mark of jealousy or overweening curiosity; since it is mostly one's fellow-villagers who have the sustained opportunity for prying, the evil eye is rarely if ever attributed to outsiders. An envious man negates fortune, and this affects those around him. Evil eye accusations thus attach to those whom one 'knows', people who are in some clear sense fellow-insiders, but whose behaviour suggests 'outsider-like' tendencies. The field warden, for example, was a locally born Pefkiot, but his position gave him a discomfiting licence to interfere in the affairs of his fellow-villagers, while his inquisitive mien and (by local standards) excessive friendliness to visiting tourists violated conventional boundaries.

More generally, *grousouzia* is a moral taint within the community. A Glendiot regards stealing a co-villager's sheep as *grousouzia* (or *(o)goursouza*); yet he will condone, perhaps participate in, a raid on flocks from another village. The East Cretan lowlander, by contrast, may use this label of distaste for *all* forms of animal-stealing. Not only is he nowadays only the victim and never the beneficiary of such raids, but he views them as an internally destructive force; 'the community' is here the whole island of Crete, rather than just the speaker's village.

While the *grousouzis* is deficient, he is at least known to be so. By contrast, the *atimos*, as an outsider, is inherently unpredictable. The Turk is described as *atimos*, because he lies in wait 'like a wolf' to pounce on the unsuspecting Greek. There are other uses of the term in which unfulfilled expectations seem to be the key component, rather than the absence of 'honour'. Hence, for example, the *atimo* die or card which lets one down in a game; the '*atimo* weed' of tobacco, which is capable of doing one inestimable harm; the *atimo* garlic crop, which rewards hard work with an uncertain yield; *atimo* vetch, which sometimes spoils before it can be harvested; and *atimo* frozen chicken, which has an insipid taste because it has been force-fed with hormones. The logic which unites these highly varied usages is that what comes from outside the range of one's immediate social control is by definition unpredictable, perhaps harmful; it therefore lacks that certainty of repute which is essential to *timi*.

Filotimo, the presence of *timi*, thus has two distinct antonyms, and the resultant discriminations can be expressed formally: *atimia*, unpredictable danger of outsider; *grousouzia*, predictable taint of insider. The 'honour–dishonour' gloss does indeed 'gloss over' these essential properties of social demarcation.

Conscience or custom?

Filotimo is often equated with *sinidhisi*, 'conscience' according to the formal lexicon, in both Pefko and Glendi. The grounds for this are that 'you feel for' (*sinesthanese*) those to whom your behaviour shows *filotimo*. More often, however, the /dh/ of *sinidhisi* is devocalized, giving a term (*sinithisi*) which suggests 'custom' rather than 'conscience'.[18] Such a semantic shift is fully consistent with rural Greeks' habitual reluctance to judge a person's inner state, *filotimo* itself being largely concerned with the protective concealment of everything internalized in a person or society.

In Glendi, *sinithisi* is cited as a reason for not reporting sheep-stealing incidents to the State authorities; for repaying the generosity which others show one in the coffee-houses; and for voting in municipal elections for one's lineage or sub-lineage representative according to segmentary principles of choice. Theoretically, ballot-boxes are secret, so that this last use of the term would seem to refer to conscience *qua* inner state. In fact, however, one's personal voting habits are usually well known in the home community, although intentional deceit (*tapa*) is retrospectively invoked to explain failure at the polls.

More generally, moreover, a man whose public actions violate village canons is said to lack *sinithisi*, or even *sinithio* (the usual word for 'custom'). Since *filotimo* is often explicitly equated with *sinithisi*, both terms clearly refer to public evaluation. 'Having a weight (*varos*) on one's soul', the closest analogue of 'bad conscience' in both Pefko and Glendi, is not directly associated with *sinithisi* by informants.

In Glendi, *sinithisi* is rarely far from *egoismos*: by showing hospitality to a guest one brings credit on one's entire household, while a vote for one's lineage-mate is a similarly sanctioned index of reliability. In Pefko, by contrast, *sinithisi* is clearly antithetical to *egoismos*, since it demands a measure of cooperation among households. In contrast both to this participatory ideal and to its deliberate violation, *grousouzia* signifies abstention through some innate condition; this may be incapacitating sickness (as when a deaf and blind old man is called a *grousouzis* in commiserating tones), or it may be miserliness, or the possession of malign properties such as the evil eye. One is thought to cast the evil eye 'without intent' (*athela tou*); it cannot be admitted that insiders would intentionally harm their fellows. Yet the effects of *grousouzia* are no less disruptive for all that. One Pefkiot who was accredited with an outstandingly dangerous eye was so stingy that he would not even provide his labourers with clean food; his behaviour was thus both socially and physically unclean. The eventual result was that he could not find labourers in Pefko itself any more, and so had to recruit them elsewhere, thereby transgressing the introverted Pefkiot social code. He was thus an internal deviant, rather than an external threat; he was a villager without *filotimo* or *sinithisi*.

This man was relatively wealthy by the pre-war Pefkiot standards by which he was judged. The higher one is raised, the harder one may fall; such is the ambiguous relationship between material and spiritual worth encapsulated in the word *timi*. Once a *grousouzis*, always a *grousouzis*; or, as the villagers say, 'it's better to lose your eye (lit.: that your eye come out) than your [good] name.'

The evidence for this damning condition, moreover, may be perceived in more than behaviour alone. '*Grousouzia* from God', for example, is the Pefkiots' label and explanation for childlessness, a punishment for sins assumed to have occurred in the past. Pefkiots also say that 'many children are wealth', despite the fact that a large progeny reduces the property available for each child. In the Pefkiot context, therefore, it makes poor logic to argue for a literal interpretation of the proverb, although the earning-power of male children has seemed a persuasive factor in other contexts. The proverb seems, rather, to state a *moral* equivalence, since both wealth and children potentially raise one's *timi*. Conversely, a wealthy miser and poorly raised progeny both immediately invite the charge of *grousouzia*. Economic factors are thus relevant to *timi* in terms of the expectations which they generate. It is only in a person's repetitive, predictable and normatively acceptable behaviour that peers can discern *filotimo* and *sinithisi*, and can thereby attribute high *timi* to the individual and his family alike.

Conclusions and implications

The evidence presented in this article demonstrates that the precise interpretation of moral-value terms requires a clear perception of their linguistic and social context in each community. If there is indeed a 'false coherence'[19] in the study of Mediterranean values, it lies not in the indigenous terminologies nor in the conceptual schemata which these represent but in their summary conflation as 'honour' and 'shame'.

The Greek taxonomy of values outlined here expresses the matching of performance with expectations. Italian peasants, too, apparently employ a usage which departs significantly from the chivalrous and psychological implications of the English word 'honour': 'To maintain his honour intact a Pisticcese has to conform to the expectations his neighbours have about his domestic behaviour.'[20] The Pisticcesi thus share the Greeks' concern with relative and changing expectations. Reputation is clearly the common theme.

The present analysis has thus become more general. At the same time, however, freed from the presuppositions which the glosses of 'honour' and 'shame' demand, we can more fully appreciate the significance of intra-cultural and intra-linguistic variation. The reading suggested here for *filotimo*, as the quality of conformity to socially positive expectations, lends itself to a comparison of behavioural norms within a common terminological tradition. To the concepts of *filotimo*, *sinithisi* and *egoismos* can be added the demonstrative eccentricity known as *khoui*, which is treated with disdain by the Sarakatsani and by settled villagers who use the term, but which Glendiots view as a possibly extreme form of *egoismos* and therefore as something to be highly valued. The various concepts are arranged here in terms of their locally perceived equivalences:

Glendi: $\quad khoui = egoismos = filotimo = sinithisi$
Sarakatsani: $\quad khoui \neq egoismos = (filotimo)\ (?)$
Pefko: $\quad (khoui) \neq egoismos \neq filotimo = sinithisi$

The three communities represent points on a continuum. The relationship between them is further strengthened by the fact that the Glendiots and Sarakatsani share a predominantly pastoral mode of subsistence, whereas the Sarakatsani and the Pefkiots place greater emphasis on the cognatic kindred (as opposed to the agnatic lineage) in the domain of kinship modes.

Thus, a Glendiot of powerful lineage need not fear the consequences of eccentric self-aggrandizement (*khoui*). In the Sarakatsan social universe, with its greater fragmentation, such flamboyance is more dangerous and therefore discouraged. The Pefkiots adhere to an extreme avoidance of conflict, preferring covert malice to open aggression under any circumstances.

Interestingly, this schema resonates with J. Schneider's[21] proposed continuum between pastoral communities with large, politically independent groups at one end, and fragmented, sedentary agricultural societies at the other. The present analysis, however, has been kept within a single language-tradition, through a strategy of matching local patterns to a base term (*filotimo*) denoting socially appropriate behaviour. There does seem to be a systematic connexion between moral, ecological and kinship variables, and it is easier to demonstrate this within the specific limits of a single language-area in the first instance. More such localized analyses are needed, and there seems to be no good reason to confine these to the Mediterranean lands.

Massive generalizations of 'honour' and 'shame' have become counterproductive; their continued use elevates what began as a genuine convenience for the readers of ethnographic essays to the level of a theoretical proposition. When indigenous terminologies are taken from a single language, as in the data discussed above, we may be reasonably sure that they are in some sense comparable. When they are taken from different language-traditions, however, that comparability has to be demonstrated before it can be used as an analytic base. The summation of our understanding in the form of 'translated' terms offers no such assurance. It is rather in ethnographic particularism that we should seek, without any sense of paradox, those theoretical insights which the reductionist generalization of glossing can never yield.

Notes

1 Peristiany, J. G. (ed.) (1965), *Honour and Shame: The Values of Mediterranean Society*, London: Weidenfeld & Nicolson.
2 Davis, J. (1977), *People of the Mediterranean: An Essay in Comparative Social Anthropology*, London: Routledge & Kegan Paul, p. 5.
3 Clarke's (Clarke, David L. [1968], *Analytical Archaeology*, London: Methuen, pp. 28–29) strictures on the careless use of notions of typicality in archaeology are also extremely germane to social anthropology.
4 Schneider, Jane (1971), Of Vigilance and Virgins: Honor, Shame and Access to Resources in Mediterranean Societies, *Ethnology*, 10 (1): 1–24.
5 For a more recent and significantly modified statement, however, see Jane and Peter T. Schneider (1976), *Culture and Political Economy in Western Sicily*, New York: Academic Press, pp. 86–102.
6 Davis, J. (1977), *People of the Mediterranean*, op. cit., pp. 89–101, and Davis, J. (1978), The Value of the Evidence [Correspondence], *Man*, 13 (3): 472.
7 Bailey, Frederick George (ed.) (1971), Gifts and Poison, in *Gifts and Poison: The Politics of Reputation*, New York: Schocken Books.
8 Davis, J. (1977), *People of the Mediterranean*, op. cit., p. 99.
9 Brögger, J. (1968), Conflict Resolution and the Role of the Bandit in Peasant Society, *Anthropology Quarterly*, 41: 228–240.
10 Pitt-Rivers' insight (Pitt-Rivers, J. [1977], *The Fate of Shechem, or the Politics of Sex: Essays in the Anthropology of the Mediterranean*, Cambridge: Cambridge University Press, p. 13) that 'the early anthropologists might well have translated the word *mana* as *honour*'.
11 Davis, J., Honour and Politics in Pisticci, *Proceedings of the Royal Anthropological Institute of Great Britain and Ireland for 1969*, p. 69.
12 d'Istria, D. (1867), La nationalité hellénique d'après les chants populaires, *Revue des deux Mondes*, 37: 584–627.
13 Nor does *egoismos* denote an *innate* selfishness; Greek moral terminology, as will emerge later in this account, is little concerned with inner states. Cf. the use of *khristianos* ('Christian'), which means, not a 'believer', but a socially acceptable human being, one who observes the appropriate social and ritual norms (see Kenna, M. E. [1976], Houses, Fields, and Graves: Property and Ritual Obligation on a Greek Island, *Ethnology*, 15: 33). Italian usage is very similar (Boissevain, J. [1966], Patronage in Sicily, *Man*, 1(3): 19; Davis, J. [1973], *Land and Family in Pisticci*, London: Athlone Press, p. 93).
14 Pefko is a depopulated, prescriptively (i.e. normatively) endogamous, agricultural community of some 160 inhabitants in the coastal lowlands of western Rhodes. Since houses form a part of the bridal endowment, there is a tendency to matrifocal clustering. Glendi is situated in the foothills of Mt Ida, in western Crete; it has a fluctuating population of approximately one thousand, including a now dwindling proportion of transhumant shepherds. Village and large-lineage endogamy is preferred, but not mandatory, although there have been many exceptions in the last decade. At marriage, a house is provided by the groom's father. Fieldwork was conducted in Pefko between December 1973 and July 1974, and in Glendi between December 1974 and May 1975, in July 1976, and between August 1977 and May 1978. 'Pefko' and 'Glendi' are pseudonyms.

15 Campbell, J. K. (1964), *Honour, Family, and Patronage: A Study of Institutions and Moral Values in a Greek Mountain Community*, Oxford: Clarendon Press, pp. 294–295; Dubisch, J., Honor and Shame in Complex Society. Ms., paper read at the 1974 Annual Meeting of the American Anthropological Association, Mexico City.
16 See, however, du Boulay, J. (1974), *Portrait of a Greek Mountain Village*, Oxford: Clarendon Press, pp. 75–76; Dubisch (1974), Honor and Shame in Complex Society, op. cit.
17 Loizos, P. (1975), *The Greek Gift: Politics in a Cypriot Village*, Oxford: Blackwell, p. 66.
18 Significantly, the form *sinithisi* does not appear in any standard dictionary of Modern Greek. Cf. *sinithia*, 'custom, habit' (Glendiot *sinithio*), (Classical Greek *syn + ethos*); *sinithizo*, 'become accustomed (to)'; *sinidhisi*, 'conscience', = New Testament *syneidesis*, < *syn + oida* ('know') (Latin *conscientia*, < *con + scio*).
19 Davis, J. (1969), Honour and Politics in Pisticci, op. cit., p. 69.
20 Ibid., p. 80.
21 Schneider, J. (1971), Of Vigilance and Virgins, op. cit., pp. 11, 22.

24 Sentiments and consciousness

Steven M. Parish

Steven M. Parish (born in 1953) is a professor of anthropology at the University of California, San Diego, a centre renowned for psychological anthropology. Trained in psychiatry, he explores the boundary between the anthropology of subjectivity and the anthropology of religion. His research, conducted in Nepal and India, focuses on Hinduism and Buddhism, endeavouring to understand how ritual practices produce subjectivities. Breaking with the Durkheimian tradition of analysing the moral codes of given societies, *Moral Knowing in a Hindu Sacred City: An Exploration of Mind, Self and Emotion* is one of the pioneering works of the ethnography of morality on the basis of consciousness and affects. Continuing this exploration within American society, *Subjectivity and Suffering in American Culture: Possible Selves* has recourse to life narratives at moments of extreme experiences due to illness or bereavement.

In the text presented here, Steven Parish attempts to understand the 'inner life' of the Newars, a Nepalese ethnic group, in other words their 'self' and their 'mental life'. In order to do this, he distances himself from two universalistic perspectives: the first focusing on the psycho-physiological mechanisms of emotions, the second examining the socio-cognitive processes of judgement. In both cases, culture seems to be neglected as if it were possible to understand the production of 'moral consciousness' without it. Basing his analysis on an ethnography that is attentive to the description of norms and affects surrounding shame, Steven Parish considers emotions as embodied social judgements that contribute to producing a culturally defined moral knowledge. The Newars experience the emotion linked to shame passively and the reflection on its ethical significance actively, with both contributing to forming the moral person.

For the Newars of Nepal, mind, self, and emotion are sacred and moral; the "inner" world is absorbed in a religious ethos. This sacralization of mental life in Newar culture is consistent with the way religious forms—sacred beings and symbols and a moral order based on a religious worldview—provide the fundamental grounds for the Newar construction of reality. Newar life has not been secularized; the world and the mind have not been disenchanted.

The concept of mind Newars bring to the experience of an "inner" life, of mental existence, helps Newars create themselves as moral beings. As Newars evaluate and experience themselves in terms of cultural theories of mental life, they produce states of moral consciousness, ways of knowing themselves as moral agents. Their concepts of mind, formed within a religious and ethical worldview, mediate the development of a "moral self." Their vision of mind sensitizes them to "moral" emotion, shapes insight into self, and structures efforts to alter self. In sum, their cultural concept of mind helps generate what I would term "moral knowing."

My discussion of these processes—the sacralization and ethicization of mind and the production of moral consciousness—will underscore the need for more flexible and less reductive accounts of mind, self, and emotion. Some theorists, reacting to a tradition in academic psychology that reduces feeling to a material entity or psychophysiological process, have played down the importance of affective experience, of feeling as a core aspect of emotion, emphasizing instead the way emotions are cognitive and social judgments.[1] While I also view emotions as judgments about the relationship of self to world, and reject theories of emotions that reduce them to nothing but physiological processes, I think we miss something vital if we treat emotions as nothing but discourse. Emotions are social judgments, but judgments embodied reflexively in affective experience.[2] That emotions are affective rather than discursive judgments makes a difference: I may use emotion concepts without feeling them, but when I feel an emotion I am more completely and powerfully engaged with my world. Emotions prepare people to be agents. The experience of emotion mediates engagement with life, priming social actors to find meaning in events and experiences, preparing them to know themselves in certain ways, and readying them to act.

Other theorists ignore the role of culture, stressing instead psychological processes. They view cultural models of psychological experience as unrelated to the processes that generate that experience. For example, the psychologist George Mandler[3] has argued that people's beliefs and intuitions about how minds work have little to do with how minds actually work. He argues that "folk theories" fundamentally misrepresent psychological processes. Indeed, experimental psychologists should probably not look to ordinary language or to culture for "concepts and distinctions" that can stand as "ultimate descriptions" of mind from the point of view of academic psychology. In contrast, it is people's beliefs about mental life that pose fundamental questions for anthropologists. Ethnographic research makes it clear that emotional experience is culturally embedded; it is more than a set of psychophysiological processes.[4] Since emotion has cultural meaning, we are compelled to ask: What place do "folk theories" of mind and emotion have in people's lives and experience? Although cultural concepts of mind may not be "true," from the perspective of experimental psychology, neuroscience, or analytical philosophy, they may reflect significant aspects of social, cultural, and personal reality.

Thus, the ethnographic data to be presented here point out the need to bridge the gap between two opposed approaches to emotion. These opposing approaches force the analyst either to decontextualize emotion or to disembody it. Both strategies are reductive; one severs the connection of emotion with sensation and feeling, with the actual self-experience of human bodies, while the other eliminates the need to explore cultural and social context. As useful as these strategies may be for very limited purposes, I believe the Newar material presented here makes it clear how emotional life is both intricately embedded in culture and dynamically embodied in affective experience. Since people make their lives within the world created by the interaction and interpenetration of culture and experience, it is there that the analysis of emotional *life* should begin.

The Newars are the indigenous inhabitants of the Kathmandu Valley; the Newar cities of Patan, Bhaktapur, and Kathmandu were independent city-states, ruled by

Hindu kings, until their conquest by another ethnic group in the 16th century. The basis for the Newar economy is irrigated rice agriculture, which supports a complex division of labor. A range of occupational specialists—Brahman and Tantric priests, artisans and craftsmen, merchants, untouchable sweepers, and others—is organized into a complex caste system. The informants cited and quoted here are Saivite Hindus, but other Newars are Buddhists. For descriptions and interpretation of Newar culture, society, and religion, see Levy, Toffin, and Nepali.[5]

Here I will describe Newar concepts of mind by presenting and interpreting data from open-ended interviews with Hindu Newar informants. The goal is to show some of the ways in which Newars ethicize and sacralize mind, emotion, and self and come to know themselves as moral beings. [...]

The cultural experience of feelings or emotions—feelings structured in cultural ways—also helps create moral orientations. Newars sometimes say: If you are a person, through shame you must bind yourself (*Manu kha: sā tha: yāta lajyā(n) cī-mā*).

This Newar maxim says something important about the morality of everyday life in Newar society and about the sort of person required by that everyday morality: being a moral person means regulating the self through *sensitivity* to the emotion *lajyā*. Self-control requires the capacity to experience *lajyā*, an emotion embracing the kinds of emotional experiences and contexts usually designated by the English words "shyness," "embarrassment," and "shame." Although a number of "moral emotions" play a significant role in the everyday morality of the Newars, I will focus primarily on *lajyā*, as it is especially important as a moral control.[6]

Lajyā combines feeling and evaluation; it is an emotion and a moral state. The noun *lajyā* is used with the verb *cay-gu*, "to feel." Informants report that the feeling of *lajyā* may be associated with blushing, sweating, altered pulse, and similar psychophysiological phenomena, which are general signs of emotional arousal or anxiety. However, experienced emotion in a physiological sense is not always present. The term may be used coherently in the absence of such states, since *lajyā* has, as a moral concept, evaluative and social-regulative uses. By showing the contexts in which Newars speak of *lajyā*, I will show that this emotion—like emotion in general and moral emotion in particular—cannot be reduced to states of physiological arousal. The perceived connection with experienced feeling is, however, central to the larger, evaluative sense of the concept. To disembody *lajyā*—by identifying it with cognitive and social judgments and treating it as a moral discourse alone, while ignoring the feelings that energize and ground it—would deeply distort what *lajyā* is for Newars.

The connection with "energizing" feeling seems critical. Even though an actual state of "raw" feeling—the emotional experience—may not always be present, the affiliation of *lajyā* with feeling is crucial to the understanding of the concept in general. A feeling may be understood to supply motive and to animate action. Because feeling is central to *lajyā*, and relates it to action, *lajyā* can be used to assert a number of things about moral behavior and moral personhood. The person with *lajyā* (the self, that is, who possesses the capacity to experience shame, who is sensitive to the possibilities of shame) is seen as motivated by *lajyā* (as feeling) to act in a manner consistent with moral norms. A person who lacks the capacity to experience *lajyā* is, as Newars often put it, "like an animal." The idea is that animals have no moral standards and do not live in conformity to a moral order. They will "do anything."

Thus, one of the central features of the Newar cultural concept of the moral person is the idea that all people are subject to *lajyā* as a feeling or emotion. They are potentially sensitive to it. But the capacity to experience *lajyā*—the disposition to know shame—is conceived to be more developed in some people than in others. A greater degree of *lajyā* is held to be inherent in the personalities or natures of women, children, and youths. The assumption is not only that they do have more *lajyā* than adult males, but that they *should* have more.

As an evaluative concept that expresses disapproval, *lajyā* is used to point out violations of norms and to affirm standards of behavior in contrast to the violation. When a person does something wrong, disapproval may be expressed by saying that the violator is without *lajyā* (*lajyā marumha manu*). This assumes that *lajyā* (as sensitivity to shame) would cause a person to behave in conformity to norms: if one had *lajyā*, one would behave in a proper way. There are degrees of sensitivity to *lajyā*. One person might be moved by feelings of shame to stop behaving in a way that violates a community standard. Another would never have begun to behave in a way that would inevitably elicit disapproval, because he or she would anxiously anticipate that such acts would be greeted with shame-inducing criticism.

The kinds of behavior subject to evaluation in terms of *lajyā* are diverse. One can be ashamed, for example, because one is poor. [...] The "shame" of being a have-not has to do, I think, with perceived failure to be the kind of person who is socially valued. It is not just that he is poor, but that being poor points out, for others to see, that he is inadequate, a "failure" as a person—or as I heard other Newars put it, that he has not yet "become a person"—and that he knows others see this.

Lajyā is said by informants to be elicited as well by the following: 1. To be caught in a lie or deception. 2. To be forced to beg for a living. 3. To be seen eating at the door of a house. 4. For certain parts of the body to be exposed or mentioned. 5. For an unmarried woman to be seen in the company of men. 6. To make a mistake or misspeak in the presence of others. 7. To be seen urinating or defecating. 8. Obscene, rude, or improper language. 9. To fail to show proper respect in speech or action. 10. To be rebuked in front of others.

One basic criterion for inclusion in this list is being seen, being in view, publicity: in each instance, something becomes known to others. Each act is publicly in violation of a norm. The feeling of *lajyā* is triggered (or at least is most acute) when others become cognizant of or confront a person with a breach. The norms or standards, themselves, are not of equal importance and have different sorts of meaning; social mistakes and inadvertent mishaps, as well as moral offenses, are grounds for *lajyā*.

Lajyā has to do with intersubjective integration into public life: *lajyā* is felt when a person knows that others know that a breach has been committed. When asked if *lajyā* would be felt if no one would see, a high-caste man replied, "If no one sees, why would they feel *lajyā*?" [...] *Lajyā* applies not only to social mistakes and lapses or inadequacies in the presentation of self, but also to serious cases of wrongdoing.

How do Newars experience *lajyā*? Let me take the case, not of minor social mistakes or lapses in the presentation of self, but of serious transgressions. By violating important moral norms, people risk their social identities, and they may seriously complicate their views of themselves. A high-caste informant makes this point by describing a hypothetical scenario, a situation to which *lajyā* applies both as evaluation and as an emotion: "Let's say that I told you that you owe me money. But you don't owe me money. But what I say is, you owe me money. Will you pay or not? An argument starts. You do not owe me any money. Without justification, I say, 'Give the money to me.' While we argue, having no proof, our friends will ask, 'What money?'[That is, they demand an explanation.] Since I lied, I now have to make something else up: isn't it *lajyā*? This is a very low thing. If I could, I would have taken your money. If I could, I would have taken it by fighting. I would try to get it by taking your watch. If I'm stronger than you, I'd take it. But my friends and neighbors will ask, 'What money?' If I can make up some proof, whether it is true or not, I can take the money. So I would be a liar. One without *lajyā*. If someone then says, 'He is a liar,' then I will have *lajyā*. I am as good as dead [literally, I am equal to dead]. A person who lives by lying may as well die, no?"

This account shows how *lajyā* is central to moral discourse. "Shame" is not only a feeling here; it also organizes and animates moral judgment, helping to define the wrongfulness of co-coercion, force, and intimidation. It is thus a moral–psychological concept—the evaluative and the psychological senses of the term support each other. The violation the informant gives as an example here is serious; the stakes are high. *Lajyā* is conceived of as a basic standard of conduct, closely associated with right and wrong (a person with *lajyā* does what is right, while the person without *lajyā* does wrong); it is viewed as a motive for moral behavior (a person who lies has no *lajyā*, while, by implication, a person with *lajyā* will not lie, steal, or do "low things"); and it is conceived of as an experienced feeling (a person caught in a lie feels *lajyā*).

The thread I want to pursue here is the expression "as good as dead," or "the same as dead." By using this expression, Newars say something about the organization and meaning of the experience of *lajyā*.

Another high-caste informant, commenting on this expression, suggested that persons who lied would feel "as good as dead" because of the "raw" experience of great *lajyā*. "When people say you have no *lajyā*, you feel *lajyā*." The notion of a kind of social death seems appropriate. Newars who ignore standards of conduct risk loss of social standing and prestige (*ijjat*). They may face ostracism, which can have devastating social and economic consequences. The threat of social death, like the threat of physical death, is a shock; it can cause a derealization of the self, experienced as a loss of meaning, as emptiness, withdrawal, and confusion.

Yet another high-caste informant elaborated on the ideas that a person shamed is "as good as dead" or "already dead" by speaking of the way he experienced *lajyā*. He said that *lajyā* felt "cold—like you did not exist." This indicates that *lajyā* may, in certain situations, have a cold, withdrawn dimension, drawing on, or providing an experiential base for, the death metaphor.

This contrasts with hot, flushed, red-faced feelings of embarrassment that are also part of the experience of *lajyā*. When the presentation of self as a proper social person slips, not coldness, but blurred perception, a red face, and blushing are attributed to the experience. [...]

D'Andrade[7] suggests that even if parts of cultural models of mind are based on universal psychological experience, other parts may be related to the ecological and social structure of a community, and still others may be "legacies from the past"— historical formations unrelated either to current conditions of life or to universals of psychological experience. The Newar case leads to similar conclusions. Some elements of the Newar conception of mind seem to be due to social and political factors, while others can be seen as reflecting the cultural history of the Newars, especially the way they have made cultural and religious developments in South Asia part of their own worldview—and cultural selves. Other aspects of the Newar concept of mind seem to reflect universals, near universals, or probable forms, of mental experience.

The Newar material suggests that fully understanding how people understand mind (and use their beliefs about mind to understand themselves and others) will involve a range of approaches. It will certainly require examining the local organization of mental life and the way mental experience is grounded in specific historical conditions and cultural frames. In the Newar case, this includes attention to religious and moral ideas. I believe it will also require that this body of data and theory be related to more universal perspectives on mind, which take account of the way mental life reflects transcultural existential, ethical, psychological, and linguistic experiences.

It is easy to slip into a cultural determinism that is as one-dimensional and limiting as psychological reductionism. The fact that emotions are socially and culturally constituted does not necessarily entail the view that social actors are simply "programmed" by culture to have certain emotions. Social actors are not merely passive receivers of emotional discourse, incapable of acting on and restructuring that discourse in any way. They are biographical individuals and cultural selves at the same time—thinking, feeling, *and* cultural subjects all at once. The social and cultural structuring of emotion does not rule out the psychological and biographical structuring of emotion. These can be complementary perspectives.

To point out that models found in different cultures make similar assumptions about the categories or organization of mental experience is not to say that the ways in which these assumptions are fleshed out, represented, and reconstructed in particular cultures do not make a difference. They do. The Newar concept of mind takes forms of experience and knowing that may be universals and fuses them with culture, developing and shaping them into local forms of experience and knowing. Newar concepts of a psychologically active and morally sensitive "heart," their vision of a moral god animating and inhabiting this heart-mind, and their cultural experience of moral emotions, all help articulate a concept of the moral person. These ideas build on, and elaborate, the notion that "self" can passively experience—and yet actively evaluate—thoughts and feelings originated by other parts of self. This "self" integrates a capacity for self-knowledge and self-control (however problematic) with sensitivity to moral emotions. Newar ethnopsychology thus articulates a concept of person as, at once, an agent and a passive experiencer within a complex internal world and places this concept of the person in a religious and ethical context. Newar concepts of mind help Newars know that "the person" is constituted as a moral being, with an "inner" life that participates in the moral and the sacred.

Notes

1 Solomon, Robert (1984), Getting Angry: The Jamesian Theory of Emotion, in Shweder, Richard A. and Robert A. Le Vine (eds.), *Culture Theory: Essays on Mind, Self, and Emotion*, New York: Cambridge University Press, pp. 238–254; Myers, Fred (1986), *Pintupi Country, Pintupi Self: Sentiment, Place, and Politics among the Western Desert Aborigines*, Washington, DC: Smithsonian Institution Press.
2 Rosaldo, Michelle (1984), Toward an Anthropology of Self and Feeling, in Shweder and Le Vine, *Culture Theory*, op. cit., pp. 137–157; Levy, Robert (1984), Emotion, Knowing, and Culture, in Shweder and Le Vine, *Culture Theory*, pp. 214–237.
3 Mandler, George (1975), *Mind and Emotion*, New York: John Wiley, pp. 5–10.
4 Emotion, mind, and self have become important subjects of culture theory, and ethnographic studies have shown how deeply and fundamentally psychological life is embedded

in culture (cf. Levy, R. [1973], *Tahitians: Mind and Experience in the Society Islands*, Chicago, IL: University of Chicago Press; Levy, R. [1984], Emotion, Knowing, and Culture, op. cit.; Lutz, Catherine [1988], *Unnatural Emotions*, Chicago, IL: University of Chicago Press; Lutz, Catherine and Geoffrey White [1986], The Anthropology of Emotions, *Annual Review of Anthropology*, 15: 405–436; Myers, Fred [1979], Emotions and the Self: A Theory of Personhood and Political Order among Pintupi Aborigines, *Ethos*, 7: 343–370; Myers, F. [1986], *Pintupi Country, Pintupi Self: Sentiment, Place, and Politics among the Western Desert Aborigines*, Washington, DC: Smithsonian Institution Press; Obeyesekere, Gananath [1981], *Medusa's Hair: An Essay on Personal Symbols and Religious Experience*, Chicago, IL: University of Chicago Press; White, Geoffrey and John Kirkpatrick [1985] (eds.), *Person, Self, and Experience: Exploring Pacific Ethnopsychologies*, Berkeley, CA: University of California Press). Moral phenomena are also receiving increasing scrutiny in anthropology. Cf. Fiske, Alan (1990) (ed.), Special Issue Devoted to Moral Relativism, *Ethos*, 18.
5 Levy, R. (1990), *Mesocosm*, Berkeley, CA: University of California Press; Toffin, Gérard (1994), *Société et religion chez les Newar du Nepal*, Paris: Centre National de la Recherche Scientifique; Nepali, Gopal Singh (1965), *The Newars*, Bombay: United Asia Publications.
6 There is a fair amount of work on "shame," dating from early attempts to identify and contrast "shame cultures" and "guilt cultures" (Benedict, Ruth [1946], *The Chrysanthemum and the Sword*, Boston, MA: Houghton Mifflin). Singer (Piers, Gerhart and Milton Singer [1971], *Shame and Guilt: A Psychoanalytic and a Cultural Study*, New York: Norton) argued that such contrasts were overdrawn. See also Spiro (Spiro, Melford [1965], *Children of the Kibbutz*, New York: Schocken Books, Chapter 15) and DeVos (DeVos, George [1973], *Socialization for Achievement: Essays on the Cultural Psychology of the Japanese*, Berkeley, CA: University of California Press, Chapter 5). In South Asia, Obeyesekere (Obeyesekere, Gananath [1984], *The Cult of the Goddess Pattini*, Chicago, IL: University of Chicago Press, pp. 499–508). Other recent discussions of shame-like emotion include Geertz (Geertz, Clifford [1973], *The Interpretation of Cultures*, New York: Basic Books), Keeler (Keeler, Ward [1983], Shame and Stage Fright in Java, *Ethos*, 11: 152–165), and Rosaldo (Rosaldo, Michelle [1983], The Shame of Headhunters and the Autonomy of the Self, *Ethos*, 11: 135–151). For future inquiry, I would suggest that the relationship of shame and empathy deserves attention. Both seem to involve a dialectical, culturally mediated relationship of self and other (Sartre, Jean-Paul [1963], *Saint Genet*, New York: Pantheon; Obeyesekere, G. [1984], *The Cult of the Goddess Pattini*, op. cit., pp. 502–503). On empathy, see Eisenberg and Strayer (Eisenberg, Nancy and Janet Strayer [1987], *Empathy and Its Development*, Cambridge: Cambridge University Press).
7 D'Andrade, Roy (1987), A Folk Model of the Mind, in *Cultural Models in Language and Thought*, Holland, D. and N. Quinn (eds.), New York: Cambridge University Press, pp. 112–148.

Moral economies

25 The moral economy of the crowd

Edward Palmer Thompson

Edward Palmer Thompson (1924–1993) was a British Marxist historian. He taught at the University of Leeds and then the University of Warwick, but pursued his career on the edges of the traditional academic world, preferring intellectual and political engagement. After the Second World War he created with Eric Hobsbawm, George Rudé and a few others the Communist Party Historian's Group, which was behind the journal *Past and Present*. Shocked by the Soviet Union's repression of the Hungarian revolution in 1956, he resigned from the British Communist Party and, along with other left-wing political figures, founded the New Left, which gave rise to *The New Left Review*. In parallel to this intellectual and political work, which later led him to become a pacifist and antinuclear activist in the context of the Cold War, he pursued academic research that culminated in the publication of *The Making of the English Working Class*. In this study of the development of the British working class, he criticised the materialist, quantitative and determinist approach of traditional Marxist historiography, foregrounding instead the initiative, imagination and commitment of the proletariat in the formation of its class identity and defending a bottom-up history.

It is in this book that he first coined the expression 'moral economy', albeit almost furtively, which he took up again in a long article entitled 'The Moral Economy of the English Crowd in the Eighteenth Century' focusing on the 'food riots' in eighteenth-century England. According to him, this violence was not simply a primary reaction to physiological needs leading to looting: they expressed a feeling of injustice when speculation put too much pressure on the price of food and they revealed the breaking of a moral contract which had, until then, allowed the agricultural world to be maintained despite profound inequalities. The notion of moral economy therefore refers to norms and obligations present in peasant society and called into question by the excesses of liberalism. As he went on to clarify in a chapter of *Customs in Common*, which gave him the opportunity to return to the concept twenty years later, moral economies do not include values, but affects do play an important role: indignation and anger are the moral emotions that lead to acts of political significance.

We have been warned in recent years, by George Rudé and others, against the loose employment of the term "mob". I wish in this article to extend the warning to the term "riot", especially where the food riot in eighteenth-century England is concerned.

This simple four-letter word can conceal what may be described as a spasmodic view of popular history. According to this view the common people can scarcely be taken as historical agents before the French Revolution. Before this period they intrude occasionally and spasmodically upon the historical canvas, in periods of sudden social disturbance. These intrusions are compulsive, rather than self-conscious or self-activating: they are simple responses to economic stimuli. It is sufficient to mention a bad harvest or a down-turn in trade, and all requirements of historical explanation are satisfied.

Unfortunately, even among those few British historians who have added to our knowledge of such popular actions, several have lent support to the spasmodic view. They have reflected in only a cursory way upon the materials which they themselves disclose. Thus Beloff comments on the food riots of the early eighteenth century: "this resentment, when unemployment and high prices combined to make conditions unendurable, vented itself in attacks upon corn-dealers and millers, attacks which often must have degenerated into mere excuses for crime".[1] But we search his pages in vain for evidence as to the frequency of this "degeneration". Wearmouth, in his useful chronicle of disturbance, allows himself one explanatory category: "distress".[2] Ashton, in his study of food riots among the colliers, brings the support of the paternalist: "the turbulence of the colliers is, of course, to be accounted for by something more elementary than politics: it was the instinctive reaction of virility to hunger".[3] The riots were "rebellions of the belly", and there is a suggestion that this is somehow a comforting explanation. The line of analysis runs: elementary – instinctive – hunger. Charles Wilson continues the tradition: "Spasmodic rises in food prices provoked keelmen on the Tyne to riot in 1709, tin miners to plunder granaries at Falmouth in 1727." One spasm led on to another: the outcome was "plunder".[4]

For decades systematic social history has lagged in the rear of economic history, until the present day, when a qualification in the second discipline is assumed to confer, automatically, proficiency in the first. One cannot therefore complain that recent scholarship has tended to sophisticate and quantify evidence which is only imperfectly understood. The dean of the spasmodic school is of course Rostow, whose crude "social tension chart" was first put forward in 1948.[5] According to this, we need only bring together an index of unemployment and one of high food prices to be able to chart the course of social disturbance. This contains a self-evident truth (people protest when they are hungry): and in much the same way a "sexual tension chart" would show that the onset of sexual maturity can be correlated with a greater frequency of sexual activity. The objection is that such a chart, if used unwisely, may conclude investigation at the exact point at which it becomes of serious sociological or cultural interest: being hungry (or being sexy), what do people do? How is their behaviour modified by custom, culture, and reason? And (having granted that the primary stimulus of "distress" is present) does their behaviour contribute towards any more complex, culturally-mediated function, which cannot be reduced – however long it is stewed over the fires of statistical analysis – back to stimulus once again?

Too many of our growth historians are guilty of a crass economic reductionism, obliterating the complexities of motive, behaviour, and function, which, if they noted it in the work of their Marxist analogues, would make them protest. The weakness which these explanations share is an abbreviated view of economic man. What is perhaps an occasion for surprise is the schizoid intellectual climate, which permits this quantitative historiography to co-exist (in the same places and sometimes in the same minds) with a social anthropology which derives from Durkheim, Weber, or Malinowski. We know all about the delicate tissue of social norms and reciprocities which regulates the life of Trobriand islanders, and the psychic energies involved in the cargo cults of Melanesia; but at some point this infinitely complex social creature, Melanesian man, becomes (in our histories) the eighteenth-century English collier who claps his hand spasmodically upon his stomach, and responds to elementary economic stimuli.

To the spasmodic I will oppose my own view.[6] It is possible to detect in almost every eighteenth-century crowd action some legitimizing notion. By the notion of legitimation I mean that the men and women in the crowd were informed by the belief that they were defending traditional rights or customs; and, in general, that they were supported by the wider consensus of the community. On occasion this popular consensus was endorsed by some measure of licence afforded by the authorities. More commonly, the consensus was so strong that it overrode motives of fear or deference.

The food riot in eighteenth-century England was a highly-complex form of direct popular action, disciplined and with clear objectives. How far these objectives were achieved – that is, how far the food riot was a "successful" form of action – is too intricate a question to tackle within the limits of an article; but the question can at least be posed (rather than, as is customary, being dismissed unexamined with a negative), and this cannot be done until the crowd's own objectives are identified. It is of course true that riots were triggered off by soaring prices, by malpractices among dealers, or by hunger. But these grievances operated within a popular consensus as to what were legitimate and what were illegitimate practices in marketing, milling, baking, etc. This in its turn was grounded upon a consistent traditional view of social norms and obligations, of the proper economic functions of several parties within the community, which, taken together, can be said to constitute the moral economy of the poor. An outrage to these moral assumptions, quite as much as actual deprivation, was the usual occasion for direct action.

While this moral economy cannot be described as "political" in any advanced sense, nevertheless it cannot be described as unpolitical either, since it supposed definite, and passionately held, notions of the common weal – notions which, indeed, found some support in the paternalist tradition of the authorities; notions which the people re-echoed so loudly in their turn that the authorities were, in some measure, the prisoners of the people. Hence this moral economy impinged very generally upon eighteenth-century government and thought, and did not only intrude at moments of disturbance. The word "riot" is too small to encompass all this.

Notes

1 Beloff, Max (1938), *Public Order and Popular Disturbances, 1660–1714*, London: Oxford University Press, p. 75.
2 Wearmouth, R. F. (1945), *Methodism and the Common People of the Eighteenth Century*, London: Epworth Press, esp. Chapters 1 and 2.
3 Ashton, T. S. and J. Sykes (1929), *The Coal Industry of the Eighteenth Century*, Manchester University Press, p. 131.
4 Wilson, Charles (1965), *England's Apprenticeship, 1603–1763*, London: Longman, p. 345. It is true that the Falmouth magistrates reported to the duke of Newcastle (16 Nov. 1727) that "the unruly tinners" had "broke open and plundered several cellars and granaries of corn". Their report concludes with a comment which suggests that they were no more able than some modern historians to understand the rationale of the direct action of the tinners: "the occasion of these outrages was pretended by the rioters to be a scarcity of corn in the county, but this suggestion is probably false, as most of those who carried off the corn gave it away or sold it at quarter price". Public Record Office (hereafter P.R.O.), S.P., 36/4/22.

5 Rostow, W. W. (1948), *British Economy of the Nineteenth Century*, Oxford: Clarendon Press, esp. pp. 122–125. Among the more interesting studies which correlate prices, harvests, and popular disturbance are: Hobsbawm, E. J. (1964 [1951]), Economic Fluctuations and Some Social Movements Since 1800, in *Labouring Men*, Hobsbawm, E. J., London: Weidenfeld & Nicolson, and Ashton, T. S. (1959), *Economic Fluctuations in England, 1700–1800*, Oxford: Clarendon Press.
6 I have found most helpful the pioneering study by R. B. Rose (1961), Eighteenth Century Price Riots and Public Policy in England, *International Review of Social History*, vi; and George Rudé (1964), *The Crowd in History*, New York: John Wiley & Sons.

26 The ethic of subsistence

James C. Scott

James C. Scott (born in 1936) is a professor of political science and anthropology at Yale University where he is director of the programme in agrarian studies. His research focuses on dominance and forms of resistance, on the comparative approach to agrarian systems and on peasant peoples' modes of political action, particularly in Southeast Asia. Following the tradition of American Marxist anthropology, which produced work on the rural Third World that played an important role in the 1960s and 1970s, particularly with Eric Wolf and Sidney Mintz, he has notably published *Weapons of the Weak: Everyday Forms of Peasant Resistance*, *Domination and the Arts of Resistance: Hidden Transcripts* and, more recently, *The Art of Not Being Governed: An Anarchist History of Upland Southeast Asia*. His work has had a deep and lasting influence on critical anthropology of imperialism and development that is sensitive to forms of local resistance and collective mobilisation in the Third World.

The first book of this series, *The Moral Economy of the Peasant: Rebellion and Subsistence in Southeast Asia*, was published in 1976. Although the title referred to the concept put forward by British historian E. P. Thompson, there is little trace of it in the book. In fact, James Scott speaks rather of an ethics of subsistence, in other words economic practices grounded in social relations and moral values that involve caution regarding the vagaries of rural life, solidarity towards other members of the community, and dependence on the powerful. The poor peasants, confronted with precarious situations, do not seek to maximise their profits but rather to minimise their risks of food shortage. These are the norms and moral values that they put forward against the State, big landowners or international institutions when tax on their harvest brings them to the brink of extreme poverty. But the notion of moral economy is used more directly to examine the conditions rendering the peasants' revolts possible, not because their needs are no longer met but because their rights are violated. Affects such as resentment and emotions such as indignation thus become catalysts for rebellion. However, in the continuation of his research, James Scott moved away from these exceptional moments of crisis leading to rebellions to examine instead ordinary modes of resistance.

The basic idea upon which my argument rests is both simple and, I believe, powerful. It arises from the central economic dilemma of most peasant households. Living close to the subsistence margin and subject to the vagaries of weather and the claims of outsiders, the peasant household has little scope for the profit maximization calculus of traditional neoclassical economics. Typically, the peasant cultivator seeks to avoid the failure that will ruin him rather than attempting a big, but risky, killing.

In decision-making parlance his behavior is risk-averse; he minimizes the subjective probability of the maximum loss. If treating the peasant as a would-be Schumpeterian entrepreneur misses his key existential dilemma, so do the normal power-maximizing assumptions fail to do justice to his political behavior. To begin instead with the need for a reliable subsistence as the primordial goal of the peasant cultivator and then to examine his relationships to his neighbors, to elites, and to the state in terms of whether they aid or hinder him in meeting that need, is to recast many issues.

It is this "safety-first" principle which lies behind a great many of the technical, social, and moral arrangements of a precapitalist agrarian order. The use of more than one seed variety, the European traditional farming on scattered strips, to mention only two, are classical techniques for avoiding undue risks often at the cost of a reduction in average return. Within the village context, a wide array of social arrangements typically operated to assure a minimum income to inhabitants. The existence of communal land that was periodically redistributed, in part on the basis of need, or the commons in European villages functioned in this way. In addition, social pressures within the precapitalist village had a certain redistributive effect: rich peasants were expected to be charitable, to sponsor more lavish celebrations, to help out temporarily indigent kin and neighbors, to give generously to local shrines and temples. As Michael Lipton has noted, "many superficially odd village practices make sense as disguised forms of insurance."[1]

It is all too easy, and a serious mistake, to romanticize these social arrangements that distinguish much of peasant society. They are not radically egalitarian. Rather, they imply only that all are entitled to a *living* out of the resources within the village, and that living is attained often at the cost of a loss of status and autonomy. They work, moreover, in large measure through the abrasive force of gossip and envy and the knowledge that the abandoned poor are likely to be a real and present danger to better-off villagers. These modest but critical redistributive mechanisms nonetheless do provide a minimal subsistence insurance for villagers. Polanyi claims on the basis of historical and anthropological evidence that such practices were nearly universal in traditional society and served to mark it off from the modern market economy. He concludes, "It is the absence of the threat of *individual* starvation which makes primitive society, in a sense, more human than market economy, and at the same time less economic."[2]

The provision of subsistence insurance was not confined to the village sphere; it also structured the moral economy of relations to outside elites. As Eric Wolf observed: "It is significant, however, that before the advent of capitalism ... social equilibrium depended in both the long and short run on a balance of transfers of peasant surpluses to the rulers and the provision of minimal security for the cultivator. Sharing resources within communal organizations and reliance on ties with powerful patrons were recurrent ways in which peasants strove to reduce risks and to improve their stability, and both were condoned and frequently supported by the state."[3] Again, we must guard against the impulse to idealize these arrangements. Where they worked, and they did not always work, they were not so much a product of altruism as of necessity. Where land was abundant and labor scarce, subsistence insurance was virtually the only way to attach a labor force; where the means of coercion at the disposal of elites and the state was sharply limited, it was prudent to show some respect for the needs of the subordinate population.

Although the desire for subsistence security grew out of the needs of cultivators—out of peasant economics—it was socially experienced as a pattern of moral rights or expectations. Barrington Moore has captured the normative tone of these expectations: "This experience [of sharing risks within the community] provides the soil out of which grow peasant mores and the moral standards by which they judge their own behavior and that of others. The essence of these standards is a crude notion of equality, stressing the justice and necessity of a minimum of land [resources] for the performance of essential social tasks. These standards usually have some sort of religious sanction, and it is likely to be in their stress on these points that the religion of peasants differs from that of other social classes."[4] The violation of these standards could be expected to provoke resentment and resistance—not only because needs were unmet, but because rights were violated.

The subsistence ethic, then, is rooted in the economic practices and social exchanges of peasant society. As a moral principle, as a right to subsistence, I believe I can show that it forms the standard against which claims to the surplus by landlords and the state are evaluated. The essential question is who stabilizes his income at whose expense. Since the tenant prefers to minimize the probability of a disaster rather than to maximize his average return, the stability and security of his subsistence income are more critical to his evaluation of the tenure system than either his average return or the amount of the crop taken by the landlord. A tenure system which provides the tenant with a minimal guaranteed return is likely to be experienced as less exploitative than a system which, while it may take less from him on the average, does not rate his needs as a consumer as primary. The same reasoning may be applied to the claim of the state. To the extent that the claim is a fixed charge which does not vary with the peasant's capacity to pay in any given year, it is likely to be viewed as more exploitative than a fiscal burden which varies with his income. The test for the peasant is more likely to be "What is left?" than "How much is taken?" The subsistence test offers a very different perspective on exploitation than theories which rely only on the criterion of surplus value expropriated. While the latter may be useful in classifying modes of expropriation, it is my contention that they are less likely to be an adequate guide to the phenomenology of peasant experience than the subsistence test. For it is the question of subsistence that is most directly related to the ultimate needs and fears of peasant life. [...]

The problem for the peasantry during the capitalist transformation of the Third World, viewed from this perspective, is that of providing for a *minimum income*. While a minimum income has solid physiological dimensions, we must not overlook its social and cultural implications. In order to be a fully functioning member of village society, a household needs a certain level of resources to discharge its necessary ceremonial and social obligations as well as to feed itself adequately and continue to cultivate. To fall below this level is not only to risk starvation, it is to suffer a profound loss of standing within the community and perhaps to fall into a permanent situation of dependence.

The precapitalist community was, in a sense, organized around this problem of the minimum income—organized to minimize the risk to which its members were exposed by virtue of its limited techniques and the caprice of nature. Traditional forms of patron–client relationships, reciprocity, and redistributive mechanisms may be seen from this perspective. While precapitalist society was singularly ill-equipped to provide for its members in the event of collective disaster, it did provide household social insurance against the "normal" risks of agriculture through an elaborate system of social exchange.

In more recent times, of course, the state itself has assumed the role of providing for a minimum income with such devices as countercyclical fiscal policy, unemployment compensation, welfare programs, social medicine, and the negative income tax. One effect of these guarantees, incidentally, has been to make it more rational for individuals to engage in profit-maximizing behavior.

The colonial period in Southeast Asia, and elsewhere for that matter, was marked by an almost total absence of any provision for the maintenance of a minimal income while, at the same time, the commercialization of the agrarian economy was steadily stripping away most of the traditional forms of social insurance.[5] Far from shielding the peasantry against the fluctuations of the market, colonial regimes were likely to press even harder in a slump so as to maintain their own revenue. The result was something of a paradox. In the midst of a booming export economy, new fortunes for indigenous landowners, officeholders, and moneylenders and, occasionally, rising average per capita income, there was also growing concern with rural indebtedness and poverty and an increasing tempo of peasant unrest. It was not unlike the discovery of pauperism in the midst of England's industrial revolution.[6] The explanation for this paradox is to be sought in the new insecurities of subsistence income to which the poorer sector of the population was exposed. Although the average wage rate might be adequate, employment was highly uncertain; although the average prices for peasant produce might be buoyant, they fluctuated dramatically; although taxes might be modest, they were a steady charge against a highly variable peasant income; although the export economy created new opportunities, it also concentrated the ownership of productive resources and eroded the leveling mechanisms of the older village economy.

The moral economy of the subsistence ethic can be clearly seen in the themes of peasant protest throughout this period. Two themes prevailed: first, claims on peasant incomes by landlords, moneylenders, or the state were never legitimate when they infringed on what was judged to be the minimal culturally defined subsistence level; and second, the *product* of the land should be distributed in such a way that all were guaranteed a subsistence niche. The appeal was in almost every case to the past—to traditional practices—and the revolts I discuss are best seen as defensive reactions. Such backward-looking intentions are by now a commonplace in the analysis of peasant movements. As Moore, citing Tawney puts it, "the peasant radical would be astonished to hear that he is undermining the foundations of society; he is merely trying to get back what has long been rightfully his."[7] The revolts were, by the same token, essentially the revolts of consumers rather than producers. Except where communal land had been appropriated by local notables, the demand for the redistribution of land itself was strikingly absent. Protests against taxes and rents were couched in terms of their effect on consumption; what was an admissible tax or rent in a good year was inadmissible in a bad year. It was the smallness of what was left rather than the amount taken (the two are obviously related, but by no means are they identical) that moved peasants to rebel. [...]

The justification for assuming that "social norms of fairness" exist apart from actual terms of exchange seems substantial. Durkheim reminds us that "in every society and in all ages, there exists a vague but lively sense of the value of the various services used in society and of the value of things that are the subject of exchange."

This "true" price "very rarely coincides with the real price, but these [real prices] cannot go beyond a certain range in any direction without seeming abnormal."[8] The existence of a "fair price" or "true value" is implicit whenever bargains that have been made under duress give offense. A man who surrenders his child for a loan or who sells his birthright for a mess of pottage are extreme examples. The needs of the weaker party have allowed the stronger to impose an exchange that violates the true value of things; the bargain is thus unjust and extortionary. Even contracts that have been freely consented to may not be considered fair if one party has been driven to pay a price that offends a shared sense of fair value. Minimum wage laws, as Durkheim notes, arise from just such sentiments of fair value. They are designed precisely to preclude employers from taking advantage of their power to force "unjust" bargains.

Evidence for the notion of fair value comes not only from such reflections on moral sentiments but also from concrete historical movements. The venerable tradition of *taxation populaire* and hunger riots in France and England is a striking case in point. There was a shared popular notion of what constituted a fair price for bread that, when it was exceeded, provoked moral indignation and the seizure of markets. "The central action in this pattern is not the sack of granaries and the pilfering of grain and flour, but the action of 'setting the price.'"[9] It was not uncommon for "rioters" to pay what they regarded as a just price in lieu of the market price. Such crowds and agrarian rioters often saw themselves as law-givers (one group called itself "the regulators") who enforced a popular moral consensus.

In any particular agrarian order there is likely to be a similar moral consensus among tenants. Some balance between what tenants provide in goods and services to landlords and what they receive in return will be seen as reasonable and any substantial departure from that norm in the landlord's favor will appear exploitative. Naturally, such norms will vary from place to place and from one period to the next. Despite these variations, however, there are some constants. First, a single interclass dyad is being dealt with here that everywhere originates in an exchange of land-use rights for rent. Second, if only tenants near the subsistence level are involved, it is likely that the common problems of welfare and security that they all face may foster common moral expectations about landlord behavior.

Any viable analysis of exploitation must, then, encompass at least three elements. It must be attentive to the relational or exchange quality of social relations; it must seek out the shared human needs that social actors expect from these relationships; and, in this context, it must work from the actual notions of "fair value" that prevail.

The discussion of the norm of fairness brings us directly up against the fact that our approach to exploitation has thus far been too one-sidedly materialistic. An analysis that begins, as this one has, with the givens of the peasant household budget, and deduces peasant needs and interests from them, runs the risk of what one writer has aptly called "methodological individualism."[10] That is, it risks treating the peasant purely as a kind of marketplace individualist who amorally ransacks his environment so as to reach his personal goal—that is, the stabilization of his subsistence arrangements. The individual and society are set apart from this perspective and society is simply the milieu in which he must act.

To be sure, the goal of assuring subsistence exists as an irreducible given in the lives of most peasants. But to stop there is to miss the critical social context of peasant action. It is to miss the central fact that the peasant is born into a society and culture that provide him with a fund of moral values, a set of concrete social relationships, a pattern of expectations about the behavior of others, and a sense of how those in his culture have proceeded to similar goals in the past. The same might be said for any goal of man in society. The need to mate, for example, might also be "given," but the forms of marriage, their meaning, and the mutual expectations of the spouses are essentially cultural and historical creations. To say that people are born into society is not to deny their capacity to create new forms and break old ones; it is merely to recall that they do not walk out on an empty stage and make up their lines at random.

We are thus in the presence of cultural values and forms in all peasant social action. A villager whose harvest has failed does not respond randomly. He has a clear idea of those from whom he might appropriately ask help and what he might justifiably expect from each. He acts, moreover, in the expectation that his social map is more or less accurate, that his notion of the structure of moral claims conforms with the sense of obligation felt by others. Similarly, the widespread confiscation of grain from wealthy landowners and its communal division in Nghe-An and Ha-Tinh can only have come from a widely shared sentiment of what was justifiable under the circumstances. When Saya San urged the cultivators of Lower Burma to refuse to pay the capitation tax, he was likewise appealing to a common perception of the conditions under which the tax claim of the state was inadmissible. His appeal rested on the new hardships such taxes imposed in the midst of a depression and on the fact that the British had taxed what the Burmese took to be free gifts of nature.

Woven into the tissue of peasant behavior, then, whether in normal local routines or in the violence of an uprising, is the structure of a shared moral universe, a common notion of what is just. It is this moral heritage that, in peasant revolts, selects certain targets rather than others, certain forms rather than others, and that makes possible a collective (though rarely coordinated) action born of moral outrage.

To speak of righteous anger is, in the same breath, to speak of standards of justice, or moral values. Thus we are not dealing merely with a theory of peasant income or a theory of "relative deprivation" when we treat the peasant's subsistence ethic. Such theories by themselves tell us only that the peasant has a problem. How the peasant perceives that problem, whom—if anyone—he sees as responsible for his plight, what he expects from those around him, how he reacts, are beyond the scope of any analysis centered exclusively on his level of material well-being.

How, then, can we understand the moral passion that is so obviously an integral part of the peasant revolts we have described? How can we grasp the peasant's sense of social justice? We can begin, I believe, with two moral principles that seem firmly embedded in both the social patterns and injunctions of peasant life: the *norm of reciprocity* and the *right to subsistence*. There is good reason for viewing both the norm of reciprocity and the right to subsistence as genuine moral components of the "little tradition." Reciprocity serves as a central moral formula for interpersonal conduct. The right to subsistence, in effect, defines the minimal needs that must be met for members of the community within the context of reciprocity. Both principles correspond to vital human needs within the peasant economy; both are embodied in many concrete social patterns that owe their strength and longevity to the force of moral approval or disapproval that villagers can bring to bear.

Notes

1 Michael Lipton (1968), The Theory of the Optimising Peasant, *Journal of Development Studies*, 4 (3): 341, cited in Wolf, Eric R. (1969), *Peasant Wars of the Twentieth Century*, New York: Harper and Row, p. 279.
2 Karl Polanyi (1957), *The Great Transformation*, Boston: Beacon Press, pp. 163–164. Even the term seminal, applied as it is without discretion, is too weak a tribute for this book. His analysis of premarket and market economies has been formative for my own work. The emphasis in this quote has been added.
3 Wolf (1969), *Peasant Wars*, op. cit., p. 279.
4 Barrington Moore (1966), *Social Origins of Dictatorship and Democracy: Lord and Peasant in the Making of the Modern World*, Boston, MA: Beacon Press, pp. 497–498. I believe the emphasis in most peasant societies is not so much on land per se as on the right to a share of the product of land; hence I have added "resources" in brackets.
5 A possible exception to this rule was the Dutch East Indies where, at least on Java, colonial policy was bent to extracting a marketable surplus while at the same time preserving—not to say fossilizing—as much of rural society as possible.
6 See Wolfram Fischer (1966–67), Social Tensions at the Early Stages of Industrialization, *Comparative Studies in Society and History*, 9: 64–83.
7 Moore (1966), *Social Origins*, op. cit., p. 498 (see R. H. Tawney [1966], *Land and Labor in China*, Boston, MA: Beacon Press).
8 Émile Durkheim (1957), *Professional Ethics and Civic Morals*, London: Routledge and Kegan Paul, pp. 209–210.
9 Edward Palmer Thompson (1971), The Moral Economy of the English Crowd in the Eighteenth Century, *Past and Present*, 50: 108.
10 Hamza Alavi (1973), Peasant Classes and Primordial Loyalties, *Journal of Peasant Studies*, 1 (1): 22–62. Alavi is particularly criticizing the analysis of factions in anthropology but his point is applicable here too. His usage of the term, I should add, is somewhat different than its usage in social science methodology.

27 The logics of corruption

Jean-Pierre Olivier de Sardan

Jean-Pierre Olivier de Sardan (born in 1941) is a director of research at the Centre national de la recherche scientifique and at the École des hautes études en sciences sociales. He has devoted most of his anthropological work to the Songhay-Zarma in Niger, published in the book *Les Sociétés songhay-zarma*. In parallel, he has developed a political anthropology of development in Africa, a field to which he has made a significant contribution with *Anthropology and Development* and a collective volume *Everyday Corruption and the State*. His incursion in the field of medical anthropology focuses on ordinary forms of knowledge on illness and treatment, and the everyday activities in health-care institutions. A substantial part of his writings emphasizes the epistemological and methodological challenges of ethnographic research. Very involved in collective programmes, he has created a network of social science researchers working on Africa.

The text presented here is a pioneering study on corruption in Africa, analysing practices that are usually simply denounced. For Jean-Pierre Olivier de Sardan, it is a question of accounting for a phenomenon that, while not specific to Africa, has a remarkable presence there, both on a qualitative and quantitative level, for reasons that are not cultural but historical. Indeed, the 'complex of corruption' is part of the processes through which African societies and economies function and these are both a legacy of the colonial period and an expression of the post-colonial era. The arguments and rationales analysed here allow a distinctive understanding of corruption by re-situating it within a network of mundane and legitimate practices, and by avoiding the dual trap of condemnation or relativism. E. P. Thompson's concept of moral economy is loosely interpreted here in such a way as to render intelligible the system of norms and values upon which, paradoxically, these conducts that are condemned – but also tolerated, and even encouraged – rest.

The rampant corruption affecting the totality of African countries has scarcely become a bona fide object in the sociological or anthropological study of Africa, in which corruption is barely mentioned except in the course of studies dealing with other themes, usually African political systems. The types of corruption in West Africa, characterised by their conspicuousness and their generality, and which obviously bear some resemblance to the Asiatic and Latino-American types, deserve particular attention because of the specific nature of contemporary African states, and the depth of the crisis which affects them. Besides, international organizations, investors and public opinion are often reminded of the scope of this problem, which is currently considered to be fundamental to 'good governance'. Unfortunately, beyond declarations of principle, pathetic or exasperated acknowledgements and moralistic condemnations, the social mechanisms of corruption are scarcely explored, nor are its processes of legitimation *seen from the actors' point of view*. This is why this article uses the term: *moral economy*, which may appear surprising when attached to a term as unanimously stigmatised as amoral or immoral. The intention here is to insist on as subtle as possible a restitution of the value systems and cultural codes, which permit a justification of corruption by those who practise it (and who do not necessarily consider it to be such – quite the contrary), and to anchor corruption in ordinary everyday practice.

However, the use of the expression 'moral economy', which makes an obvious reference to a certain intellectual tradition,[1] does not imply any intention to adopt a 'culturalist' point of view. Although reference is made to the *cultural embeddedness* of corruption, this is not done in the name of any monolithic or determinist theory of culture. Our intention is rather to pinpoint certain *social norms* widely represented in modern Africa, which 'communicate' with or influence the practices of corruption. It is, in a manner of speaking, a question of 'slants' which leave a certain room for manoeuvre to the actors who operate within or around certain 'logics', often combining them, sometimes dissociating or refuting them. These logics seem to have a 'family resemblance', a certain relation of affinity with 'corruption'-type practices, but are not in themselves corruption. Their role is simply to provide a better understanding of the reasons why corruption finds, in contemporary Africa, such a favourable ground for its extension and generalisation, in short for its banalisation.[2]

Needless to say, this moral economy is 'post-colonial'[3] and fundamentally syncretic. It in no way reflects on 'traditional' or pre-colonial culture, even though ancient cultural elements, transformed and recombined, are undeniably amalgamated with numerous elements inherited from the colonial period, as well as others produced during the independence era. The process of state-apparatus building during the twentieth century, a process that is far from being achieved,[4] is obviously fundamental not only for the production of corruption itself, but also for the production of a cultural embeddedness of corruption.

Before entering into these diverse logics in which corruption appears to be embedded, some extended preliminary remarks will be made in the guise of six general theses on corruption in Africa.

Six theses on corruption in Africa

Thesis 1: The moral economy of corruption in Africa does not merely concern corruption in the strict sense of the word, but rather the 'corruption complex' in a wider sense, which covers a number of illicit practices, technically distinct from corruption, all of which none the less have in common with corruption their association with state, parastatal or bureaucratic functions, and also contradict the official ethics of 'public property' or 'public service', and likewise offer the possibility of illegal enrichment, and the use and abuse to this end of positions of authority. [...]

Thesis 2: Corruption (that is to say the 'corruption complex') has become, in almost all African countries, a common and routine element of the functioning of the administrative and para-administrative apparatus, from top to bottom. This being the case, corruption is neither marginal nor sectoralised or repressed, but is generalised and banalised. [...]

Thesis 3: The stigmatisation of corruption, as well as recriminations against it, are a central element of all discourses, public or private, at all levels of society, and have punctuated all the political phases since independence. Corruption is therefore as frequently denounced in words as it is practised in fact. But the verbal stigmatisation of corruption rarely leads to legal proceedings or sanctions. If there is officially a 'public domain', there is almost no 'practical ethic of the public service'. [...]

Thesis 4: Corruption is a cumulative and expansionist process, which is hardly reversible and mostly spreads from the top down. The factors favouring its diffusion cannot be reversed so as to produce its regression. [...]

Thesis 5: There is no obvious correlation between the extent of corruption, on the one hand, and the types of political regime, their degree of despotism and their economic effectiveness on the other. [...]

Thesis 6: The practices that come under the complex of corruption, while being legally culpable and widely reproved, are none the less considered by their perpetrators as being legitimate, and often as not being corruption at all. In other words, the real borderline between what is corruption and what is not fluctuates, and depends on the context and on the position of the actors involved. [...]

At this point, one could easily fall into a mere relativism, thus legitimising any act of delinquency. This relativism can be looked at from two sociological perspectives:

First, a description of the universe of legitimation peculiar to a given subculture in a given space–time: this will include, for example, an identification of the way in which a 'delinquent' subculture – corrupted civil servants, or elsewhere gangs of young burglars, drug dealers, mafiosi, computer pirates – produce specific forms of self-justification.[5]

Second, an analysis over time of the fluctuations in official as well as in practical norms.[6] That is, how formerly legal practices now fall under the rigours of the law (such as the sale of public offices in eighteenth-century Europe); how formerly tolerated actions are currently 'repressed' (such as the prosecution of enterprise managers in modern France for abuse of public property); or how the clandestine practices of yesterday are now carried out in the light of day (such as bribing a traffic policeman in Niger).

But I would like to propose yet another perspective, which will depart for a while from the ambiguous 'stigmatisation/self-justification' dichotomy. It consists in pinpointing a number of current social *practices* which, in themselves, have nothing to do with corruption, but none the less provide a favourable ground for its generalisation and banalisation. It will then be possible to reintegrate the practices of corruption, defined a priori in a negative light, in terms of illegality, into the larger fabric of everyday practices, expressing positive logics from the perspective of habitual local social norms.

The cultural embeddedness of the corruption complex

Five logics, profoundly engrained in current social life, and underlying a number of common behavioural traits, seem to influence the complex of corruption. Others surely exist. We will subsequently consider the existence of two 'facilitators', which cut across these logics and accelerate their effects.

The logics of negotiation

Corruption has, of course, long since been analysed as a transaction, and, as such, the cost of the transaction is obviously a subject of 'bargaining', that is a commodified form of negotiation regulating almost all forms of current exchange in Africa. But we would like to go beyond this particular aspect of the matter. Bargaining is not only pertinent to the pricing of commercial transactions. It enters into the larger configuration of everyday negotiations, commodified or not, which does not only concern a simple matter of negotiation within the limits of a set of stable rules, accepted on all sides, but is extended to a negotiation of the rules themselves.[7]

Marriage provides a significant example, especially in the urban, lower-middle-class or aristocratic milieus: not only is there constant negotiation on the expenditure that the prospective husband has to face (as well as the sum that must be given in return), but there is also permanent negotiation between both families and within each, on the very nature of the dues to be taken into account. There is no consensus on many of the rules of this 'game', which are selected, arranged, modified and reinvented along the way.[8]

The history of African countries obviously provides for an understanding of the current instability of these norms. This is evident in the juridical domain, where there is a superimposition of various types of law, inherited over several eras: pre-colonial (common law, Muslim law, for example), colonial ('customary law', 'indigenous law', French law), and post-independence (national law, constantly modified). None of these legal forms, however, is completely 'abolished' in practice, and all can be called into service according to need. The same holds true in the political domain, successive forms of political power having been piled one upon the other, and reorganised in relation to one another, without there being any question of substitution (coexistence of politico-religious authorities of pre-colonial origin with administrative chiefdoms, regional administrators of colonial origin, mayors and representatives of political parties and other mass structures of post-colonial origin, and so forth). [...]

The logics of gift-giving

In Sahelian countries one would say 'kola' (*goro*). The giving of 'little gifts' is one of the thousands of actions of everyday life, mostly as thanks for service rendered. This 'kola nut' is not a fixed or negotiated price of remuneration, nor is it a brokerage commission; it is above all a moral duty. The beneficiary of whatever kind of aid has the duty to make some gesture of thanks. This duty to give a 'kola' goes even beyond the mere rendering of service. Aren't the inevitable gifts given to *griots* who flatter one a contributing factor to the extension of the field of application of these logics of gift-giving? There exists an entire crop of names designating one type or another of these common, more or less solicited gifts. Is it not right to offer a gift to the bearer of good news (cf. *tukunci* in Hausa and Songhay-Zarma: symbolic gifts to a bearer of glad tidings), or to the witness of an important transaction, the purchase of a car or a house, for example (*alaada nooru*, 'customary money')? Shouldn't someone who goes to the market bring back 'something' to his relatives (*habiize*: 'a market product'), who have the right to claim this in case of non-execution? Doesn't this also apply to the traveller who returns home? Shouldn't the passer-by or visitor give something to women encountered in the act of hair braiding (*turguru nooru*: 'braiding money') or engaged in collective work (*yuubi*)?

Gift-giving is practised equally in the direction of 'superiors', equals or 'inferiors'. The holders of traditional power, for example, are receivers as well as donors. In Niger (where chiefs retain official entitlement to local power and are paid by the Ministry of Home Affairs), a gift is brought to the customary chief when one goes to greet him, even in the absence of any precise request; this is the 'done thing', and has the additional value of entering into his good graces or assuring his goodwill in the future. For an enthroning (as for a marriage or baptism) everyone brings his 'contribution' (*kambu-zaa*, which means, more or less, 'to give a hand').

Nowadays gift-giving is usually a question of money. The general monetarisation of everyday life has transformed the giving of kola into the giving of money. One must constantly have one's hand on one's purse. Many practices of petty corruption enter into this 'gift' category: one owes a 'little something' by way of thanks to a compliant or helpful civil servant. If, out of kindness, he has refrained from applying in one's disfavour the rigours of the law, doesn't he typically become one of those to whom one is obliged to give something, out of good manners? He himself will not forget to claim his 'kola' or rightful 'part', as occurs when the potential donor seems distracted or recalcitrant. [...]

The logics of the solidarity network

There are a multitude of solidarity networks in Africa. These are of course far from being negligible in Europe, where, however, their extension is clearly inferior: factors such as the withdrawal of the nuclear family, confinement of friends and close acquaintances to limited circles, the absence of relations between neighbours, among others, result in a weaker sociability in the North than in the South. The importance of these networks of sociability in Africa, in particular in urban areas, goes far beyond the family framework, which is, however, as we all know, widely extended and replete with pressures and solicitations which can hardly be ignored. Links created within peer groups (primary school, secondary school and college friends) last until retirement. Comradeship, good neighbourliness and work relationships also multiply this 'strength of weak ties'.[9] Solidarities that arise from adherence to a common association, church or confraternity, to the same party, to the same faction within a party, also play their role, as does the fact of originating from the same region or district.

However, not only are these various forms of interrelations particularly extended, providing each person with a capital of social relations far exceeding that of other continents, they also include an almost general obligation of mutual assistance. One cannot refuse a service, a favour, a bit of string-pulling or compliance to a relative, neighbour, party comrade or friend. Nor ought one to refuse the same to someone who is 'sent' by any of the above. The circle of individuals to whom one feels obliged to render services is thus astonishingly wide. One must add the converse, that there is also a great number of persons to call upon. The system thus becomes one of a 'generalised exchange' of services, big or small, often in the shape of an officially illicit favour.

Let us employ the conventional term 'network' to qualify these multiple forms of belonging.[10] Each individual is integrated into various networks, each of which entails solidarities and therefore corresponding pressures. The problem is that the solidarity exacted by the network is so rigorous that anyone who fails to respect his obligations to a member of one of the networks to which he belongs suffers reproach, and becomes the object of considerable and sustained pressure from all members of the network. Should he persist, he becomes the cause of scandal, and his reputation soon becomes detestable. […]

The logics of predatory authority

While the preceding logics share obvious elements of complementarity, and concern just about everyone, the two that follow are somewhat different, and are linked to functions of authority. The first concerns the right that many persons holding positions of power accord themselves to proceed to various types of extortion, to the detriment of their 'subjects', that is to those who must toady to them. These royal prerogatives, which their victims describe as rackets, appear in the eyes of the beneficiaries, not simply as a matter of personal choice, but rather as a rightful aspect of their office. The latter therefore 'naturally' entails a predatory dimension. A policeman has the right to deduct his dues from transporters, in the same way that a *directeur de cabinet* has the right to dip into special funds, or the customary judge the right to exact fees from offenders.

Bankruptcy of the state and non-payment of salaries explain in part why public servants holding the slightest bit of authority fatten themselves on the other man's back. But one can go further in history in search of more general causes. Might one not consider the banalisation of despotic extortion as a prolongation of certain pre-colonial habits (raids, tributes of war which were at the time a part of the social landscape)? But the current context is so different (the modern African state has little or no resemblance, whatever may be said to the contrary, to the chiefdoms, kingdoms and emirates of yesterday) that one needs to turn instead towards colonial customs, from the military conquest and the all-powerful 'commandant', to administrative chiefs appointed by colonialism and to indigenous auxiliaries, who have always enjoyed a wide margin for arbitrary actions.[11] As for post-colonial regimes, these have propelled into existence and into sudden omnipotence a local elite wearing the boots of the European dominators, flattered by both camps of the Cold War, without any counterbalance to their despotic or predatory temptations.[12] From the top to the bottom of the state apparatus, the assimilation of positions of power with the right to levy tribute has undergone rapid extension (despite the existence of a few remarkable exceptions, whose exceptional character is thus noted by one and all). The change to democracy seems, in this regard, merely to have introduced the possibility of openly attacking practices (by means of a denunciation of 'prebend' and 'racket'), without modifying them; those who criticise them today, when in opposition or without power, will adopt them tomorrow when in power or possessing influence. […]

The logics of redistributive accumulation

A civil servant who accedes to a prestigious position, a post of responsibility, and of course to an appointment considered to be 'juicy', must, in the sight of his relatives, profit from this and spread the benefit around. It is obviously a question of making a fortune, that is of displaying the outward signs of wealth (villas, luxurious cars, private schools for the children, jewels for the wives, etc.), and at the same time making this of benefit to his extended family, his acquaintances, his village, his dependants by means of numerous and visible signs of largesse. To refuse to grab such an opportunity to make a fortune is to make oneself an object of reproach in some cases or of mockery in others. Illegal enrichment and nepotism are definitely supported by positive social values, namely the necessity to seize all opportunities allowing for a manifestation of cardinal virtues, such as generosity, largesse and gratitude to all those who in the past, when you were unimportant, weak, in need, provided help, encouragement and support. Now, for a civil servant, positions of power provide the only means of coming into any kind of wealth. To refuse them is to make a simultaneous show of ingratitude, egoism, pride, naiveté and even stupidity. Social pressure is very strong in the direction of the accumulation of wealth in view of redistribution.[13]

This cultural logic, like others mentioned, does not come down directly from the past. It is clear, particularly so in the present case, that the factors originating in pre-colonial culture of ostentation are of some importance;[14] the pre-colonial chief was obliged to show largesse to all, and thus to allow for public praise of his generosity. Here the capacity to redistribute was of course founded on patrimonialism, which regulated traditional power in the context of a confusion between the wealth of the state and that of the sovereign. But these customs had to be recycled under colonial and post-colonial periods, in order to come down to us in the present day, while retaining their power in a world which has undergone such enormous transformation. [...]

Culture and corruption

The role played by all these logics in the banalisation of corrupt practices seems undeniable. They are usually combined, thus dissolving juridically reprehensible practices into the fabric of similar and socially commonplace practices, which happen to be accepted and even esteemed.[15] Of course corruption is not produced as such by these logics – except perhaps, to some extent, by the last two. Neither permanent negotiation nor the prevalence of brokerage, nor the practice of frequent gift-giving, nor solidarity with the social networks to which one belongs, *automatically* give rise to illicit practices, and there are examples of particularly vigilant, and relatively atypical public servants, who, at least for the most part, refuse to indulge. However, these logics, while exerting continuous pressure on social actors, help to accord a cultural acceptability to corruption. Should one therefore impute corruption in Africa to some kind of 'African culture'? Nothing would be more absurd. The notion of culture is extremely polysemic, and many of its interpretations are, to my mind, unacceptable. Nowhere is there any Value System, soaring above the populations and inducing their deportment, be it on an 'ethnic', national or 'African' level. 'Culturalism', to the extent that it occasions an excessive homogenisation of the way in which practices are perceived, to the extent that it transforms the abstract construction of the researcher into a Subject, to the extent that it deduces from social actions a kind of cultural 'tablet of the law', is indefensible. On the other hand, the converse, denial of the existence of common normative pressures exerted on actors, or a refusal to take into account shared social codes which act as a foundation for modes of social recognition or modes of intelligibility of interrelations, would imply falling into the opposite excess. The logics here enumerated thus attempt an avoidance of both of these opposed and symmetrical stumbling blocks: an explanation by 'culture', or the denial of any 'cultural factor' whatsoever. 'Cultural factor' is as vague an expression as one may encounter. The notion of logics therefore seems to be more analytically operational, in that it refers to normative configurations which influence actors' strategies. All these logics are syncretic, none is 'traditional', none comes directly from any so-called pre-colonial culture.

This brings us to the following proposition: in the modern process of its generalisation, induced to a great extent by the bankruptcy of the political elite, corruption benefits from a favourable terrain for its routinisation and banalisation, owing to an encounter with widespread behavioural logics within post-colonial societies.

Notes

1 Thompson, E. P. (1971), The Moral Economy of the English Crowd During the Eighteenth Century, *Past & Present*, 50: 76–117; Scott, J. (1976), *The Moral Economy of the Peasant: Rebellion and Subsistence in Southeast Asia*, New Haven, CT and London: Yale University Press.
2 Although reference is made to general tendencies, which seem quite widespread on the African continent, this does not imply an ignorance of specific national and sectarian distinctions. Each country (and in some instances each administration) obviously has its own 'style' of corruption, in the same way that it has its own political culture (the examples here refer to West African countries in general and to Niger in particular). The forms assumed by its generalisation and banalisation are also variable and can present more or less obvious exceptions.
3 See Mbembe, A. (1992), Provisional Notes on the Post-Colony, *Africa*, 62 (1): 3–37.
4 See Olivier de Sardan, J. P. and T. Bierschenk (1998), *Les pouvoirs au village: Le Benin rural entre democratisation et décentralisation*, Paris: Karthala.
5 See Whyte, W. (1955), *Street Corner Society*, Chicago, IL: Chicago University Press; or Becker, H. (1963), *Outsiders: Studies in the Sociology of Deviance*, New York: Free Press, on gangs in the USA.
6 The official norms in question are those defining corruption in terms of illegality; the practical norms are those that regulate practices that are illegal but which are culturally legitimate or tolerated. Generalised cultural legitimacy corresponds to what Heidenheimer (Heidenheimer, A. [1989], Perspectives on the Perception of Corruption, in *Political Corruption: A Handbook*, A. Heidenheimer, M. Johnston and V. Le Vine [eds.], New Brunswick, NJ: Transaction Publishers, p. 161) calls 'white corruption'.
7 Cf. Berry (Berry, S. [1994], *No Condition is Permanent: The Social Dynamics of Agrarian Change in Sub-Saharan Africa*, Madison, WI: University of Wisconsin Press) who has pointed out this particularity of contemporary Africa. Lund (Lund, C. [1998], *Law, Power and Politics in Niger*, Hamburg: Lit. Verlag), for his part, develops an example on the subject of property conflicts. It has already been noted (e.g. Padioleau, J. [1975], De la corruption dans les oligarchies pluralistes, *Revue Française de Sociologie*, 17: 33–58) that the coexistence of several systems of norms is a factor favourable to corruption.
8 There is of course a general agreement on certain usages which remain or have become unavoidable, for example the bride price and 'suitcase' in Niger (the latter being a tradition of recent invention); but beyond these scant guidelines, the notable variations in local custom and the numerous changes that have intervened over the years, have opened up the list of possible references, thus leaving elbow room that 'uncles' and 'aunts' do not ignore, each in their own interest.
9 Granovetter, M. (1973), The Strength of Weak Ties, *American Journal of Sociology*, 78 (6): 1360–1380.
10 Though the term is vague, it seems preferable to excessively rigid anthropological designations such as 'corporate groups' or 'primary solidarities'.
11 Wangrin obviously comes to mind, a scarcely fictive hero of the well-known book by Amadou Hampate Ba. For a sociopolitical analysis of colonial despotism in western Niger based on the accounts of peasant victims, see Olivier de Sardan (1984, *Les Sociétés songhay-zarma: Chefs, Esclaves, Guerriers, Paysans*, Paris: Karthala).
12 See Darbon, D. (1990), L'Etat prédateur, *Politique Africaine*, 39: 37–45.
13 Chinua Achebe's novels *A Man of the People* and *No Longer at Ease* are remarkable illustrations of this.

14 See Nicholas, G. (1986), *Don Rituel et Échange Marchand dans une Société Sahélienne*, Paris: Institut d'ethnologie.
15 Several authors have already pointed out this characteristic; note, for example, Heidenheimer (1989, *Political Corruption*, op. cit., p. 159): 'all the activities considered "routine corruption" by official Western standards are standard practices deeply rooted in more general social relationships and obligations'.

28 The values of science

Lorraine Daston

Lorraine Daston (born in 1951) is a historian of science. After having taught at Harvard, Princeton and Brandeis Universities, she became executive director of the Max Planck Institute for the History of Science in Berlin and Visiting Professor in the Committee on Social Thought at the University of Chicago. She is a specialist in the Early Modern period and her research has focused on probability, with *Classical Probability and the Enlightenment*, on the limits of the natural world, with *Wonders and the Order of Nature*, on objects of scientific inquiry, with *Biographies of Scientific Objects*, and on animals, with *Thinking with Animals*. At the intersection of the social studies of science and the history of science, but also close to the literary and philosophical reflection developed within the journal *Critical Inquiry* for which she serves on the editorial board, she has developed an original multidisciplinary approach. Her recent research has led her to study in particular the moral dimension of scientific activity and the relationship between the moral and natural orders.

The seminal article presented here should be situated within this perspective. Lorraine Daston formulates a concept that has gone on to prove most fruitful for the history of science, that of moral economy, specifying in a footnote that it has been pointed out to her that this concept had been largely developed before her by E. P. Thompson and his followers. However, the use that she makes of it is very different from that of her predecessors. Economy, here, does not correspond to what economists study, but rather to the classical sense of organisation according to explicable regularities. Moral economies are 'networks of values charged with affects' that, in this instance, provide a way of accounting for a side to scientific work that had thus far been neglected by the sociological approach, whether in Robert Merton's ideal norms or Pierre Bourdieu's strategic perspective. Taking inspiration from Gaston Bachelard and Ludwig Fleck, she shows that scholars from the Early Modern period had a moral vision of their work, which rested on values such as objectivity, empiricism or precision measurement, which were inextricably linked to their concomitant affects. This reading of moral economies has known interesting developments in medical anthropology, in particular by Margaret Lock on local biologies and Allan Young on the post-traumatic stress disorder.

What is a moral economy?

We are heirs to an ancient tradition that opposes the life of the mind to the life of the heart, and to a more recent one that opposes facts to values. Because science in our culture has come to exemplify rationality and facticity, to suggest that science depends in essential ways upon highly specific constellations of emotions and values has the air of proposing a paradox. Emotions may fuel scientific work by supplying motivation, values may infiltrate scientific products as ideology or sustain them as institutionalized norms, but neither emotions nor values intrude upon the core of science—such are the boundaries that these habitual oppositions would seem to dictate. The ideal of scientific objectivity, as currently avowed, insists upon the existence and impenetrability of these boundaries. I will nonetheless claim that not only does science have what I will call a moral economy (indeed, several); these moral economies are moreover constitutive of those features conventionally (and, to my mind, correctly) deemed most characteristic of science as a way of knowing. Put more sharply and specifically: certain forms of empiricism, quantification, and objectivity itself are not simply compatible with moral economies; they require moral economies.[1]

What exactly is a moral economy? Although several recent studies in the history of science testify to the existence and significance of moral economies, such studies have yet to crystallize around a common rubric, much less to rally around a common standard.[2] Part of my work here will be to extrapolate implications and tendencies that seem to me to unite these scattered studies, and to clarify their contributions to a nascent investigation of moral economies in science.[3] What I mean by a moral economy is a web of affect-saturated values that stand and function in well-defined relationship to one another. In this usage, "moral" carries its full complement of eighteenth- and nineteenth-century resonances: it refers at once to the psychological and to the normative. As Gaston Bachelard decades ago remarked, to imbue objects or actions with emotion is almost always thereby to valorize them, and vice versa.[4] Here *economy* also has a deliberately old-fashioned ring: it refers not to money, markets, labor, production, and distribution of material resources, but rather to an organized system that displays certain regularities, regularities that are explicable but not always predictable in their details. A moral economy is a balanced system of emotional forces, with equilibrium points and constraints. Although it is a contingent, malleable thing of no necessity, a moral economy has a certain logic to its composition and operations. Not all conceivable combinations of affects and values are in fact possible. Much of the stability and integrity of a moral economy derives from its ties to activities, such as precision measurement or collaborative empiricism, which anchor and entrench but do not determine it.

It may help to etch the outlines of the notion of moral economy more crisply to point out what it is *not*. It is not a matter of individual psychology. Whatever and however vehement their other confessional differences, historians, sociologists, and philosophers of science share a certain horror of the psychological, properly so-called, and I confess I am no exception to this general hostility. The historians glare in distrust at the purported eternal verities of the mind, just because they are alleged to be eternal; the sociologists, recalling the warnings of Auguste Comte and Émile Durkheim, bare their teeth at the isolated individualism of much current psychology, including that labeled "social psychology"; the philosophers, post-Frege, take the word "psychological" into their mouths only as an epithet, as *ipso facto* proof that the problem or explanation at hand has nothing to do with genuine philosophy.[5] Although moral economies are about mental states, these are the mental states of collectives, in this case collectives of scientists, not of lone individuals. To extend Ludwik Fleck's terminology, what is meant here is a *Gefühls-* as well as a *Denkkollektiv*.[6] Apprenticeship into a science schools the neophyte into ways of feeling as well as into ways of seeing, manipulating, and understanding. This is a psychology at the level of whole cultures, or at least subcultures, one that takes root within and is shaped by quite particular historical circumstances.⁷ I hope that the collectivity and particularity of mental economies will go some way in assuaging the suspicions of the sociologists and historians, respectively; I shall return to the worries of the philosophers in the conclusion.

Nor is a moral economy confined to the level of motivation, whether in spurring individuals into scientific careers or in persuading society that science is worthy of encouragement and support. Since motivations of both sorts have been one of the principal loci for the discussion of values in science studies, it may be tempting to assimilate moral economies to them. However, this temptation should be resisted. The classical studies of how values, predominantly religious values, motivate both individuals and societies to pursue science grant such values at best a neutral and at worst a negative role with respect to the forms and content of scientific methods and assertions. Robert Merton's pioneering study *Science, Technology and Society in Seventeenth-Century England,* as well as his subsequent work in the sociology of science, advances the neutral alternative: the fervent desire of a seventeenth-century Englishman to glorify God through the investigation of His works might steer him toward a career in natural philosophy; the equally fervent desire of his twentieth-century counterpart to win the good opinion of a select circle of peers might propel him toward a scientific career. At the macrosocial level, utilitarianism, piety, or other cultural values may bolster the prestige and funding of science and even elevate some kinds of science above others. But none of these values impinges on scientific ways of knowing. As Steven Shapin points out in a lucid recent essay on the reception of the Merton thesis: "For Merton, the explanandum was emphatically not scientific method or scientific knowledge: it was the dynamics and social standing of a scientific enterprise that was itself conceived of as a black box."⁸ Moral economies belong to the interior of Merton's black box. The outstanding example of the negative alternative also treats religion and science in seventeenth-century England, and it provides what are still some of the most exquisitely sensitive readings of how the Christian virtuoso's frame of mind and soul inclined him toward natural philosophy. R. S. Westfall was concerned, however, not only with the shading of religious reverence into scientific dedication, but also with the interaction of theological with natural philosophical doctrines. When these doctrines clashed, as Westfall believed they did on the topics of miracles and providences, the only role that values could play was to veil contradictions and foment inconsistencies.⁹ Values could mix with scientific knowledge, but only as a contaminant. Moral economics, in contrast, are integral to science: to its sources of inspiration, its choice of subject matter and procedures, its sifting of evidence, and its standards of explanation.

Much the same might be said apropos of the relationship between moral economies and ideology in science. This is the other classical locus of how and why values enter science, this time opening the black box of scientific assumptions and assertions, and treating it very much as Pandora's box.¹⁰ Whereas moral economies moralize scientists, ideologies moralize nature in the service of social interests. The numerous case studies in this genre run the gamut from piecemeal attempts to unmask this or that scientific claim as a piece of political interest tricked out as neutral fact, to more systematic exposés of all of science as a "social construction," laboriously if clandestinely built up out of interests, resources, and negotiations. Because it in principle encompasses all science, not just this or that ideologically tainted claim, the social-constructionist program comes closest to acknowledging the integral role of values in scientific work and its products: values do not distort science; they are science. This is why the annals of this program supply some of the most intriguing insights for the study of the moral economy of science.

However, because social constructionism focuses primarily on interests, be they political, social, or economic, and on (hidden) labor, it retains some of the muckraking character of more conventional revelations about ideology in science.[11] In contrast, to examine a moral economy of science may render familiar scientific procedures such as quantification strange, but seldom devious. Insofar as the study of moral economies in science is about power, it is power of the microscopic, internalized Foucauldian sort, rather than of the political (or martial), externalized kind.[12] In other words, the moral economy of science is more about self-discipline than coercion. Moreover, because social constructionists generally understand values as veiled interests, they are seldom concerned to explore the links between values and affects, unless these affects have an overtly societal character or influence. The stressed "social" in the social constructionist program refers not only to the disguised social components of which science is purportedly assembled, but also to the social uses to which science is put. Traffic flows in both directions across the science–society divide. Moral economies, however, tend to be one-way affairs. Although moral economies in science draw routinely and liberally upon the values and affects of ambient culture, the reworking that results usually becomes the peculiar property of scientists. Traces of the original cultural models—for example, the simplicity, dedication, and humility of Christian saints or the unworldly innocence of the pastoral idyll—lie ready to hand, and can be evoked by the spokesmen of science to win public approval and support. But the ultimate forms that moral economies assume within science, and the functions that they serve, are science's own.[13]

Finally, moral economies are not Mertonian norms, although here again there is a certain fleeting resemblance. Merton defines the "ethos of science" as: "that affectively toned complex of values and norms which is held to be binding on the man of science. ... These imperatives, transmitted by precept and example and reenforced by sanctions, are in varying degrees internalized by the scientist, thus fashioning his scientific conscience or, if one prefers the latter-day phrase, his super-ego."[14] However, the well-known norms of universalism, communism, disinterestedness, and organized skepticism, although "procedurally efficient," represent for Merton "one limited aspect of science as an institution," as carefully cordoned off from the "characteristic methods" and the "stock of accumulated knowledge" of science as motivations had been in his historical work. Moreover, these norms were, once established, immune to the vagaries of history and the pressures of context, for they were ultimately enforced not by human conscience but by nature. Scientists might violate the norms of universalism or communism, but only at their peril, for they were underwritten not simply by human sanctions but also by uniform, inexorable natural laws. Despite this alleged metaphysical grounding, a handful of scientific exposés, followed by a generation's worth of contextual studies in the history of science, apparently presented empirical refutation of Merton's norms, for here was candid testimony that violations could produce science of the first magnitude.[15] In contrast to Mertonian norms, moral economies are historically created, modified, and destroyed; enforced by culture rather than nature and therefore both mutable and violable; and integral to scientific ways of knowing.

To define an entity either directly or by contradistinction as I have tried to do above offers little proof that such entities exist, much less of their significance. Do moral economies of science really exist, and if so, what are they good for? These are challenges that can be met only by instantiation, not definition. In the next section I examine three examples of how moral economies have structured key aspects of how scientists come to know: quantification, empiricism, and objectivity.

What is a moral economy good for? Quantification

Quantification is a portmanteau term that holds a multitude of meanings. It is part of our number fetishism that we seldom distinguish among them. Historians of science routinely use it to refer to abstract mathematical models that may or may not be tethered to measurements or even observations (e.g., Nicole Oresme's doctrine of the latitude of forms, or Jakob Bernoulli's probabilities of legal evidence); measurements that may or may not connect to a mathematical model of the phenomena under scrutiny (e.g., the physiological researches of Stephen Hales); straightforward counting (e.g., almost all of descriptive statistics); estimates grounded neither in measurement nor theory (e.g., many of William Petty's figures in his political arithmetic); methods of data representation and analysis (e.g., graphs and tables or the method of least squares); and the creation of new entities (e.g., index numbers such as the gross national product). The common denominator (so to speak) of all of these usages is not even numbers, for many historical instances of quantification in the sciences have been purely geometrical: when Galileo claimed in *Il Saggiatore* (1623) that the book of nature was written in the characters of "triangles, circles, and other geometric figures," he probably meant it quite narrowly.

Amidst this plurality of forms that scientific quantification has assumed, only some have aspired to accuracy, that is, to a close fit between mathematics and a select set of phenomena, although this is the virtue most heeded and praised by historians. Other mathematical virtues touted by quantifiers of various stripes have included precision, communicability, and impartiality, all of which can be cleanly detached from accuracy. For example, when in 1699 the English mathematician John Craig calculated the date of the millennium (AD 3150, when the credibility of the New Testament decays completely) on the basis of assumptions about the probability of human testimony, or when G. W. Leibniz proclaimed (with breathtaking optimism) that it would take a team of scholars less than five years to construct a Universal Characteristic by matching numbers to ideas and arithmetic operations to thought processes, they aimed primarily at precise knowledge, and only secondarily at accurate knowledge.[16] Accuracy concerns the fit of numbers or geometrical magnitudes to some part of the world and presupposes that a mathematical model can be anchored in measurement; precision concerns the clarity, distinctness, and intelligibility of concepts, and, by itself, stipulates nothing about whether and how those concepts match the world. Although striving for precision as a goal in and of itself is distinctive of much early modern quantification, in part because of a largely psychological account of the grounds for mathematical certainty, it is by no means extinct among latter-day quantifiers.[17]

The cults of communicability and impartiality—again, with or without accuracy— also have an almost unbroken history in the sciences as well as in public life from the seventeenth century to the present. These quantifying virtues have often worked in tandem, usually to the end of damping controversy and compelling consensus.

Even when neither measurements nor statistics were available, quantifiers of, say, the productivity of Holland or of the efficacy of smallpox inoculation pleaded for the superior clarity and communicability of numbers, favorably contrasted to "only comparative and superlative Words, and intellectual Arguments."[18] Leibniz contended that lack of clarity was at the root of almost all controversy and could therefore be cured by a goodly dose of numbers: "We need not be surprised then that most disputes arise from the lack of clarity in things, that is, from the failure to reduce them to numbers."[19] Although these attempts to silence dissent through quantification were (and still are) occasionally parasitic upon the vaunted certainty of mathematical demonstrations and operations, their dominant appeal was to consensus achieved through communication and thereby shared understanding, rather than through the necessity of demonstration. Even when the truth of the matter was not to be had, numbers could be invented, dispersed to correspondents at home and abroad, and, above all, mentally shared: you and I may disagree about the accuracy and the implications of a set of numbers, but we understand the same thing by them.

The moral economy of this form of quantification is sociable but intolerant of deviations, and it is not surprising that it flourishes under conditions of weak or confused authority—for example, the contested intellectual authority of sixteenth- and seventeenth-century natural philosophy, or, as Theodore Porter has recently argued, the contested political authority of twentieth-century pluralistic democracies.[20] In both cases the aim of quantification is not to secure individual conviction, but rather to secure the acquiescence of a diverse and scattered constituency. That is, the scientific polity that cherishes quantification is not only a collective, but also one whose members may differ from one another in nationality, skill, training, assumptions, or material resources such as laboratory equipment or statistical bureaus. It is quite possible to imagine, and to instantiate historically, scientific ideals and practices that preferred the solitary sage to the collective, or a more local and homogeneous collective that need not resort to the minimalist, information-losing techniques of quantification in order to communicate and persuade. For quantification, no matter how thorough and detailed, is necessarily a sieve: if it did not filter out local knowledge such as individual skill and experience, and local conditions such as this brand of instrument or that degree of humidity, it would lose its portability.[21] The moral commitment to a certain form of sociability among colleagues who may never meet face to face must be strong in order to countenance the loss of so much hard-won detail.[22] It is in part the systematic erasure of these details in the service of extended sociability that creates the impression of the uniformity of nature: to turn Merton on his head, the uniformity of nature presupposes universalism among scientists, rather than the reverse.

Among the preconditions for this far-flung sociability are the oft-remarked impartiality and impersonality of quantified results and procedures. These qualities may flourish even in the absence of accuracy, and are indeed all the more highly valued when accuracy seems unattainable. Impartiality is first and foremost a judicial rather than a scientific virtue, and at most a prerequisite for rather than a guarantee of the truth of a verdict. Similarly, there is no a priori reason to believe that the elimination of all that is idiosyncratic will clear a path to the "really real": if the idiosyncrasy in question is skill, one might expect just the opposite. The point here is that impersonality and impartiality are cultivated by quantifiers as much for moral as for functional reasons. It is proverbial that both require dutiful self-abnegation so as to repress individuality and interest, and neither accrues automatically to quantified procedures and results. "Faceless numbers" fairly radiate personality in the hands of numerologists and cabalists; the chicaneries practiced with statistics are all too familiar. Abstraction alone never eliminates all traces of individuality and interest, and the history of applied mathematics, particularly social mathematics, is strewn with examples of partial impartiality.[23] Impersonality and impartiality in quantification might be better conceived as a continuum, more or less achieved by an effort of self-imposed restraint, rather than as properties inherent in the numbers themselves. To practice the form of quantification that breaches the boundaries of language, confession, nationality, and theoretical allegiance demands that the quantifiers voluntarily restrict their sphere of discretion. They must also sacrifice some of the meanings attached to numbers and techniques: Johannes Kepler's successors stripped his "laws" of their Pythagorean halo; Adolphe Quetelet's successors jettisoned his normative understanding of the normal curve. In other words, the choice of an extended form of scientific sociability incurs certain forms of moral obligation and discipline: the reining in of judgment, the submission to rules, the reduction of meanings—what Bachelard once called "that asceticism that is abstract thought."[24] The affinities and arguably the origins of this ethos are bureaucratic, appealing to the rigid rationality of rules, conscientiously blind to variations of person or situation.[25] This is one moral economy of the several varieties of quantification.

When concerns for precision and accuracy combine in the enterprise of precision measurement, the moral economy takes another form. Whereas the quantification of precision alone aims at impersonality in the service of a collectivity, the quantification of precision measurement aims at integrity, sometimes in defiance of the collectivity. The more precise the measurement, the more it stands as a solitary achievement of the measurer, rather than as the replicable common property of the group. Not all scientific measurement aspires to precision: Robert Hooke, for example, recommended mathematics to the natural philosopher because it "accustoms the Mind to a more strict way of Reasoning, to a more nice and exact way of examining, and to a much more accurate way of inquiring into the Nature of things." But he did not require "Mathematical Exactness" of his measurements, "for we find that Nature it self does not so exactly determine its operations, but allows a Latitude almost to all its Workings, though ... it seems to be restrain'd within certain Limits." The belief in the sharp-edged determinacy of nature grew slowly, and the scientific cult of precision measurement, with its rites of instrument making and error analysis, emerged only in the nineteenth century.[26]

With precision measurement emerged a quite different moral economy of quantification, one just as stern in its call for self-discipline, but self-discipline channeled to different ends. This is the self-discipline of caution and fastidious attention to detail, the painstaking prudence of the account ledger. In her fine recent study of Franz Neumann's physics seminar (established 1834) at Konigsberg, Kathryn Olesko shows how the "ethos of exactitude" evolved in German astronomy, geodesy, and experimental physics, and how it was inculcated by the practices, particularly that of error analysis, taught in Neumann's seminar. The initiates of Konigsberg scrupled to graph their measurements, for they distrusted the unobserved interpolated values. They warily sifted the results of colleagues, according to the known diligence and care of the experimenter. They balked at theoretical generalizations, unpersuaded that the data had been sufficiently purged of errors. In contrast to the moral economy of precision *tout court*, that of precision measurement cultivated certain personal idiosyncrasies, namely those of skill and, especially, the character traits of diligence, fastidiousness, thoroughness, and caution. Nor did scientific sociability figure prominently in their creed. Although the devotees of precision measurement never meant to withdraw from the scientific community, the rigor of their faith effectively isolated them even from other experimentalists, not to mention theorists, for all measurements were in principle subject to revision, correction, improvement. To pursue the "duty" of perfecting precision led to the perceived incommensurability of experimental results.[27]

This is perhaps a pathological expression of the moral economy of precision measurement, but like so many pathologies, simply an exaggeration of the same values and affects that sustained precision measurement under more normal conditions. Olesko correctly identifies integrity as the cardinal virtue of precision measurement, simultaneously applied to the character of the measurers and to the quality of the measurements.[28] Yet paradoxically integrity sometimes teetered on the edge of disintegration: the disintegration of a smooth curve into discrete data points, the disintegration of a set of apparently uniform measurements, the disintegration of the bonds between experiment and theory, the disintegration of the scientific collectivity.

Notes

1 I am grateful to John Carson and Nathan Reingold for pointing out that my use of the term *moral economy* diverges significantly from E. P. Thompson's (1971) in The Moral Economy of the English Crowd in the Eighteenth Century, *Past and Present*, 50: 76–136, reprinted in Thompson (1991), *Customs in Common: Studies in Traditional Popular Culture*, New York: New Press, pp. 185–258, along with replies to critics and later reflections, The Moral Economy Reviewed, pp. 259–351. My appeal here to "economies" of affects and values has little to do with Thompson's accounts of corn markets and the tradition of "setting the price" by persuasion or riot, although it does appeal to a broader sense of "legitimizing notion."

2 See, e.g. (this list is by no means exhaustive), Hannaway, Owen (1986), Laboratory Design and the Aim of Science: Andreas Libavius versus Tycho Brahe, *Isis*, 77: 585–610; Porter, Theodore M. (1992), Objectivity as Standardization: The Rhetoric of Impersonality in Measurement, Statistics, and Cost-Benefit Analysis, *Annals of Scholarship*, 9: 19–60; Porter (1992), Quantification and the Accounting Ideal in Science, *Social Studies of Science*, 22: 633–652; Schaffer, Simon (1988), Astronomers Mark Time: Discipline and the Personal Equation, *Science in Context*, 2: 115–145; Schaffer (1992), A Manufactory of Ohms: The Integrity of Victorian Values, in *Invisible Connections: Instruments, Institutions, and Science*, Bud, Robert and Susan Cozzens (eds.), Bellingham, WA: SPIE Press, pp. 23–56; Shapin, Steven (1988), The House of Experiment in Seventeenth-Century England, *Isis*, 79: 373–404; Shapin (1991), "The Mind in Its Own Place": Science and Solitude in Seventeenth-Century England, *Science in Context*, 4: 191–217; Daston, Lorraine and Peter Galison (1992), The Image of Objectivity, *Representations*, 40: 81–128; and Daston (1992), Objectivity and the Escape from Perspective, *Social Studies of Science*, 22: 597–618. I am grateful to authors who made prepublication versions of this recent work available to me when I was preparing this essay.

3 I undertake this task with considerable diffidence, given the obvious risks of misinterpretation and misappropriation. The studies I shall treat here have served as inspiration for my analysis, but their authors are wholly innocent of any responsibility for that analysis.

4 See, e.g., Gaston Bachelard (1989), Libido et connaissance objective, in *La Formation de l'esprit scientifique* [1938], 14th edition, Paris: Vrin, pp. 183–209.

5 Among the notable exceptions to this general disdain of the psychological within the history of science is Ryan D. Tweney (1985), Faraday's Discovery of Induction: A Cognitive Approach, in *Faraday Rediscovered: Essays on the Life and Work of Michael Faraday, 1791–1867*, Gooding, David and Frank James (eds.), London: Macmillan, pp. 189–209. The recent

surge of interest among philosophers of science in approaches imported from cognitive science does not contradict their general dislike of psychology. Philosophers were repelled earlier not only because psychology smacked of the "irrational," but also because the psychological perspective seemed to them oozily invertebrate, lacking all coherent structure. Although cognitive science has done little to rehabilitate the mind's rationality, it offers structures aplenty.

6 Fleck in fact emphasized that emotions as well as concepts were shared by members of scientific thought collectives, and suggested that it was just this unanimity of feeling that created the illusion of freedom from emotions: Fleck, Ludwik (1979), *Genesis and Development of a Scientific Fact*, Trenn, Thaddeus and Robert K. Merton (eds.), trans. Fred Bradley and Thaddeus Trenn, Chicago/London: University of Chicago Press [1st German edition 1935], p. 49.

7 I have in mind a gradual shaping of a collective personality akin (and, as will be seen below, sometimes identical) to Norbert Elias's "civilizing process": see Elias (1982), Synopsis: Towards a Theory of Civilizing Processes, in *Power and Civility*, Vol. II of *The Civilizing Process*, trans. Edmund Jephcott, New York: Pantheon [1st German edition 1939], pp. 229–333.

8 Shapin, Steven (1988), Understanding the Merton Thesis, *Isis*, 79: 594–605, on p. 595. Merton's work was originally published in 1938 in *Osiris*, 4: 360–632; rpt. New York: Harper Torchbooks, 1970.

9 Westfall, Richard S. (1958), *Science and Religion in Seventeenth-Century England*, New Haven: Yale University Press, pp. 90 et passim; for the sensitive readings see, e.g., pp. 27–28.

10 Perhaps the most challenging of the current wave of ideology-and-science studies are those which address scientific accounts of gender: see, e.g., Lloyd, G. E. R. (1983), *Science, Folklore, and Ideology*, Cambridge: Cambridge University Press; Jordanova, Ludmilla (1989), *Sexual Visions: Images of Gender in Science and Medicine between the Eighteenth and Twentieth Centuries*, Madison, WI: University of Wisconsin Press; Schiebinger, Londa (1989), *The Mind Has No Sex? Women in the Origins of Modern Science*, Cambridge, MA: Harvard University Press; and Russett, Cynthia Eagle (1989), *Sexual Science: The Victorian Construction of Womanhood*, Cambridge, MA: Harvard University Press.

11 For a more sanguine view of how ideology-laden or socially constructed science can sometimes count as an intellectual achievement rather than as a distortion, see M. Norton Wise (1988), Mediating Machines, *Science in Context*, 2: 77–113.

12 See Michel Foucault (1977), *Discipline and Punish: The Birth of the Prison*, trans. A. Sheridan, New York: Pantheon [1st French edition 1975]; Elias (1982), *The Civilizing Process*, op. cit., pp. 240–242. For the coercive, indeed bellicose view of power in science see Bruno Latour (1987), *Science in Action: How to Follow Scientists and Engineers through Society*, Cambridge, MA: Harvard University Press.

13 On the evocation of these models in French academic éloges see Dorinda Outram (1978), The Language of Natural Power: The Éloges of Georges Cuvier and the Public Language of Nineteenth-Century Science, *History of Science*, 16: 153–178; see also Suzanne Delorme (1937), La vie scientifique à l'époque de Fontenelle après les éloges des savants, *Archeion*, 19: 217–235; and Charles B. Paul (1980), *Science and Immortality: The Éloges of the Paris Academy of Sciences (1699–1791)*, Berkeley, CA: University of California Press, esp. pp. 90–94.

14 Merton, Robert K. (1973), The Normative Structure of Science, rpt. in *The Sociology of Science: Theoretical and Empirical Investigations*, Storer, Norman (ed.), Chicago/London: University of Chicago Press, pp. 267–278, on pp. 268–269. Originally published in 1942 as Science and Technology in a Democratic Order, *Journal of Legal and Political Sociology*, 1: 115–126.

15 The most spectacular of these exposés was James D. Watson (1968), *The Double Helix: A Personal Account of the Discovery of the Structure of DNA*, New York: New American Library; for reactions see Watson (1980), *The Double Helix*, including text, commentary, reviews, original papers, Stent, Gunther (ed.), New York: W. W. Norton, pp. 161–234. See also Stehr, Nico (1978), The Ethos of Science Revisited: Social and Cognitive Norms, in *The Sociology of Science: Problems, Approaches, and Research*, Gaston, Jerry (ed.), San Francisco, CA: Jossey-Bass, pp. 172–196.

16 Craig, John (1699), *Theologiae christianae principia mathematica*, London, and Leibniz, Gottfried Wilhelm (1677), Towards a Universal Characteristic, in *Leibniz Selections*, Wiener, Philip (ed.), New York: Scribners, 1951, pp. 22–23.

17 See, e.g., René Thom (1982), Mathématique et théorisation scientifique, in *Penser les mathématiques*, Guénard, François and Gilbert Lelièvre (eds.), Paris: Editions de Seuil, pp. 252–273.
18 Petty, William (1690), *Political Arithmetick*, London, preface.
19 Leibniz (1677), Towards a Universal Characteristic, op. cit., p. 24; cf. his plans for a language with "no equivocations or amphibolies," Preface to the General Science, p. 16.
20 Porter (1992), Objectivity as Standardization, op. cit.
21 Ibid. The same is true, mutatis mutandis, of the conditions for replicating empirical results: on the discord that ensues when aspects of local knowledge (e.g., a certain kind of glass prism) are not omitted see Simon Schaffer (1989), Glass Works: Newton's Prism and the Uses of Experiment, in *The Uses of Experiment: Studies in the Natural Sciences*, Gooding, David, Trevor Pinch, and Simon Schaffer (eds.), Cambridge: Cambridge University Press, pp. 67–104. On the ideal of the solitary intellectual see Shapin (1991), The Mind in Its Own Place, op. cit.; see also Martin Warnke (1987), Das Bild des Gelehrten im 17. Jahrhundert, in *Res publica litteraria: Die Institutionen der Gelehrsamkeit in der frühen Neuzeit*, Neumeister, Sebastien and Conrad Wiedemann (eds.), Wolfenbüttler Arbeiten zur Barockforschung, 14, Wiesbaden: Otto Harrasowitz, Part I, pp. 1–34. For one collective that valued details over replicability or communicability see Lorraine Daston (1997), The Cold Light of Facts and the Facts of Cold Light: Luminescence and the Transformation of the Scientific Fact, 1600–1750, in *Early Modern France*, Charlottesville: Rookwood Press; see also Steven Shapin (1988), Robert Boyle and Mathematics: Reality, Representation, and Experimental Practice, *Science in Context*, 2: 23–58.
22 On the origins of this form of sociability among European intellectuals see Lorraine Daston (1991), The Ideal and Reality of the Republic of Letters in the Enlightenment, *Science in Context*, 4: 367–386.
23 See, e.g., Donald A. Mackenzie (1981), *Statistics in Britain, 1865–1930: The Social Construction of Scientific Knowledge*, Edinburgh: Edinburgh University Press.
24 Bachelard (1989) [1938], Les obstacles de la connaissance quantitative, in *La formation de l'esprit scientifique*, op. cit., pp. 211–238, on p. 237.
25 Gigerenzer, Gerd et al. (1989), *The Empire of Chance: How Probability Changed Science and Everyday Life*, Cambridge: Cambridge University Press, pp. 236–237; see also Porter (1992), Objectivity as Standardization, op. cit.
26 Hooke, Robert (1969) [1705], A General Scheme of the Present State of Natural Philosophy, and How its Defects may be Remedied by a Methodical Proceeding in the Making Experiments and Collecting Observations, in *The Posthumous Works of Robert Hooke*, Waller, Richard (ed.), with an introduction by Richard S. Westfall, New York/London: Johnson Reprint, pp. 19, 38. On the instrumental preconditions for, and relative indifference to, precision measurement in eighteenth-century science see Maurice Daumas (1963), Precision of Measurement and Physical and Chemical Research in the Eighteenth Century, in *Scientific Change*, Crombie, A. C. (ed.), London: Heinemann, pp. 418–430.
27 Olesko, Kathryn M. (1991), *Physics as a Calling: Discipline and Practice in the Konigsberg Seminar for Physics*, Ithaca, NY/London: Cornell University Press, pp. 250–252, 287, 392–393, 378–386. On precision measurement as a matter of character see Schaffer (1988), Astronomers Mark Time, op. cit. On the constraints practical and economic considerations could place upon the atomizing tendencies of precision measurement see Smith, Crosbie and M. Norton Wise (1989), *Energy and Empire: A Biographical Study of Lord Kelvin*, Cambridge: Cambridge University Press, pp. 684–722.
28 On the integrity of values, in both senses of both words, see Schaffer (1992), A Manufactory of Ohms, op. cit.

Part IV
Confrontations

Introduction

Didier Fassin

Anthropology is an encounter born of another encounter. At the very beginning, there was the encounter of the Greeks and the Barbarians, followed by a series of other encounters between the Romans and the Numidians, the Spanish and the Natives, the French and the Africans, the British and the Indians, the Jesuits and the Chinese, and, more generally, the Europeans and the Non-Europeans. Each time, they gave rise to renewed experiences of difference, which ended more or less badly, often in conquests, predations, massacres or simply exploitation, but always generated a certain curiosity, yet more or else tarred by condescension. Then came a second kind of encounter, initiated by historians, explorers, missionaries or geographers going by the name of Herodotus or Tacitus, James Cook or Mungo Park, Bartolomé de Las Casas or Jean-Baptiste Labat, Alexander Von Humboldt or Henrich Barth, and who discovered new lands and cultures about which they then provided tales and analyses. Anthropologists are the last in this long historical line and they are also, or at least were at the outset, Westerners discovering non-Westerners. Consequently, there was something structurally but also historically determined in the relationship to the Other that was established in the field. It is this dual encounter, and the resulting moral confrontations, that should be considered here.

The first of the two encounters – between anthropologists and those they study – was initially the encounter of the Western world and of societies framed by the latter in terms of radical difference.[1] It is in terms of this 'great divide' that it was initially considered. Everything that was not 'us' was 'them' and, even when it sometimes proved difficult to lump together under the same umbrella of 'difference' so-called 'primitive' societies with oral traditions and the societies with written traditions studied by Orientalists, it was nonetheless always a case of 'the West and the Rest'. It is not a matter of saying, of course, that the history and pre-history of the social sciences are limited to the European world and its North American extensions. To make such a claim would mean forgetting the great Arab, Indian, and Chinese chroniclers of otherness who wrote about their own societies and about other peoples, and were read and commented upon by European authors whom they often influenced. It would also mean neglecting to mention the modern and contemporary historiographical, sociological, and anthropological contributions that have developed on other continents and that are rarely accounted for in the textbooks. Nonetheless, for the most part, the genealogy of these disciplines is essentially Western.[2] This is particularly the case for anthropology as we understand it, and as it is practised and taught throughout the world. This heritage, which is notably that of humanism and the Enlightenment, of Rousseau and of Hegel, is expressed – often unwittingly – in the writings of anthropologists, through their manner of representing the world or sometimes in the moral evaluations that they seem to let slip.

In this regard, the posthumous publication of Bronislaw Malinowski's diary in 1967 appears as a moment of truth, even though the principle of making public something that had been intended to remain private gave rise to reservations and criticism within the field. The text showed emotional reactions and moral positions that were sometimes very violent and filled with surprising hostility on the part of the ethnographer who invented participant observation, and thus promoted long-term presence in the field among the people being studied so as to allow relationships of trust to be built and a deeper knowledge of their culture to be acquired.[3] However, many anthropological studies published by the authors themselves rather than their legatees, and sometimes intended to reach a wide audience, also include frequent comments that are just as judgemental as they are analytical. Certain chapters of Claude Lévi-Strauss's *Tristes Tropiques*, which was published twelve years before the field notes of the British anthropologist, may not have provoked quite the same debates, but they nonetheless expressed the author's disenchantment with the direction taken by the world, his disapproval of the evolution of certain societies and his dislike of the way of being of their members: this is a far cry from the scientific objectivity and moral neutrality that we imagine of the founder of structuralism, and yet this personal stance shows that behind the scholar lies the man who liked to describe himself as a man of the eighteenth century, which also implied a Rousseauist conception of the Amazonian societies he chose to study.[4] The subjective presence of the author is even more manifest in the book written by Colin M. Turnbull about the Iks: *The Mountain People*. Badly affected by several years of food shortages due to the forced displacement they suffered at the hands of the Ugandan government, this society is described as dehumanised and having lost all solidarity, friendship and affection, even within families. When it came out, the book gave rise to controversy, with critics describing it as a caricature of reality and an expression of the aversion that the author had progressively developed towards the group. This figure of the anthropologist as a moralist is far from the exception. It shows the distress of the researcher confronted in the field with cultural, and therefore moral, difference. Other versions of this figure are less tragic, though, and it is interesting to reconsider from this perspective Oscar Lewis's study of a Puerto Rican family, *La Vida*, in which he develops the controversial concept of a culture of poverty. Beyond the debates provoked by the application of the culturalist paradigm to the disadvantaged, this approach can also be regarded as a moralistic reflexion on the supposed shared norms and values of the poor, which reveals the anthropologist's implicit judgement.

However, confrontation, and the resulting confusion, can also be of a different nature. It is possible for anthropologists to be faced not only with the society they are studying and its members and their practices, but also with their own society. The unease is no longer that of not understanding others, but that of one's 'own' society, as it were, not understanding them. Such a situation is frequent, and the anthropologist often plays the role of righter of the wrongs of common understanding, contesting prejudice about or against cultures seen as being foreign, or more precisely against those to whom those cultures are ascribed – what we could call ordinary culturalism.[5] This common understanding can take on radical forms. The experience that Ghassan Hage recounts regarding the reactions of colleagues and students to his analysis of the practices of Palestinian suicide bombers against Israeli civilians is a case in point. In this example, it is the very attempt at analysing these practices that is rejected, as if rendering them intelligible meant presenting them as justifiable. The researcher is confronted with a refusal to understand and with the rejection of any social explanation for the acts committed, as if moral judgement should obliterate all forms of reflection. This common understanding can also take on paradoxical forms. The criticism formulated by Arthur Kleinman against ethicists focuses on the fact that, by wanting to defend and impose a certain idea of what is right and good practice, they often display a lack of comprehension of the realities of local ethics, that is, both the social conditions that could make universalist frameworks impossible to apply and the specific forms that morality takes in this context. And he calls for an 'ethnographic moment' that would make it possible to consider local 'moral experiences'.

The second encounter – between the Western world and other societies – was of course much larger in scale. It played out against a backdrop of wars and crusades, trading posts and imperial conquests, religious missions and scientific institutions. And it took the shape of both bloody confrontation and charitable practice, domination relationships and civilising projects, colonial oppression and post-colonial cooperation. These evocations indicate to what extent it was made up of contradictions and compromises.[6] In the contemporary period, this ambivalence is also apparent in the combination of military operations and humanitarian aid, or even in the existence of so-called humanitarian military interventions, in the name of the responsibility to protect, which is now a constitutive element of international law.[7] And through both global and local transitional justice, from tribunals to commissions, this law puts into place mechanisms and procedures that administrate post-crisis situations. Linking together the different elements of this system, Nandini Sundar questions the political rationales underpinning the contemporary international moral order. She underlines in particular how procedures and mechanisms implemented – and sometimes imposed – in the name of justice, truth, forgiveness, reparation and, more widely, human rights allow Western values to be celebrated and Western responsibility to be eschewed.

The moral ambiguity of the encounter with the Other is also expressed in the field of development and aid in poor countries. States, international agencies and non-government organisations find themselves caught between their own aims and paradigms, on the one hand, and the representations and practices of the populations they are supposed to be helping, on the other. Religious institutions, or institutions strongly imbued with a religious ethos, are subject to very specific tensions. As Erica Bornstein illustrates, taking inspiration from Weberian analysis, this is the case for evangelical associations such as World Vision and Christian Care whose actions in Zimbabwe she examines. In keeping with the Protestant ethos, their aid programmes valorise personal economic success whereas, in traditional morality, the success of an individual generates jealousy and suspicion. There is also a confrontation between a discourse of what is right, built around the idea of progress, and an ideology of what is wrong, expressed in accusations of witchcraft. Just as much as a confrontation between the self and others, the ethical tensions here reveal an internal confrontation of the self, caught between contradictory principles within Protestant morality. In a very different configuration, this tension can also be found in Gregory Simon's study of a

Muslim group in Sumatra. The members of this group often find themselves caught between diverging obligations, and in particular between respect for the values of social integration and the ethos of the autonomous actor. This dialectic is expressed in the economic field, where both social conventions and individual endeavour are celebrated. The encounter with the Other does not, however, only concern the relationship between the Western world and the African, Asian or Latin-American continents. The moral dilemmas involved in the relationships between different social classes present many similarities with those that arise in relationships between different national cultures. This is what Omri Elisha's survey of charitable work by members of Protestant megachurches in Tennessee revealed. Devoted to the cause of helping the poor, these people experience a distance that is twofold – both social and racial – which crystallises around the ethical aporia between, on the one hand, the affirmation of a disinterested gift and, on the other, the expectation of a response in terms of gratitude and determination: those receiving help should prove themselves to be grateful and enterprising. However, the reality is quite different, thus generating 'compassion fatigue', to use the accepted expression qualifying the negative consequences of these moral conflicts.

Anthropology is still a matter of encounters – between worlds and between individuals. And the moral dimension of these encounters and the inevitable resulting ethical confrontations have no doubt been underestimated. These confrontations, which cut across both the relationship between anthropologists and their subjects, and the relationship between societies themselves, are part of a long history. And in this history, morality is inextricably linked to politics.

Notes

1 The very particular relationship between anthropologists and their subjects – in reality often a colonial 'subject' – has been analysed in Talal Asad (ed.) (1973), *Anthropology and the Colonial Encounter*, London: Ithaca Press. Wendy James's text in the collection describes the anthropologist as 'a reluctant imperialist'. The great divide is discussed in Jack Goody (1977), *The Domestication of the Savage Mind*, Cambridge: Cambridge University Press, and in Bruno Latour (1993), *We Have Never Been Modern*, Cambridge, MA: Harvard University Press.
2 Cofounder of Indian Subaltern Studies, which contested the hegemony of Western social sciences, Dipesh Chakraborty underlines himself that it is impossible to consider these disciplines, in the South Asian context, independently of the influence of European thought, including in the very way of conceiving of social science. See Dipesh Chakraborty (2000), *Provincializing Europe: Postcolonial Thought and Historical Difference*, Princeton, NJ: Princeton University Press. Achille Mbembe, one of the main representatives of the Postcolonial Studies, has expressed similar reflections regarding the African context. See Achille Mbembe (2000), *De la postcolonie: Essai sur l'imagination politique dans l'Afrique contemporaine*, Paris: Karthala.
3 We can read, for example: 'As for ethnology: I see the life of the natives as utterly devoid of interest or importance, something as remote from me as the life of a dog.' See Bronislaw Malinowski (1967), *A Diary in the Strict Sense of the Term*, London: Routledge & Kegan Paul.
4 We can think of the chapters 'Crowds' and 'Markets', remarkably forgotten in the first English translation of the book by John Russell in 1961, but reintegrated in the second one by John and Doreen Weightman in 1973. Here is for instance what Claude Lévi-Strauss writes about India, after having described its population: 'In the light of this, the term "subcontinent", which is often applied to India in India itself, takes on a new meaning. Instead of simply signifying a part of the Asiatic continent, it seems to imply a world hardly deserving of the name of continent, since disintegration, carried to the extreme limit of its cycle, has destroyed the structure which in the past maintained a few hundred million human particles within organized frameworks; they have now been set loose in a void created by

history, and are being driven in all directions by the most elementary motivations of fear, suffering and hunger'; Claude Lévi-Strauss (1973), *Tristes Tropiques*, New York: Atheneum Publishers, 1st French edition 1955. Interesting light is shed on Claude Lévi-Strauss's moral thought in Wiktor Stoczkowski (2008), *Anthropologies rédemptrices: Le monde selon Lévi-Strauss*, Paris: Hermann.

5 This expression, which aims to differentiate culturalism as an ideology from culturalism as a scientific theory, was analysed and illustrated in Didier Fassin (2001), Culturalism as Ideology, in *Cultural Perspectives on Reproductive Health*, Carla Makhlouf-Obermeyer (ed.), Oxford: Oxford University Press, pp. 300–317, and (2011), La médecine entre culture et culturalisme, in *Aux origines de la médecine*, Didier Sicard and Georges Vigarello (ed.), Paris: Fayard, pp. 324–337.

6 This moral ambiguity is the subject of the two volumes of the book by John and Jean Comaroff (1991 and 1997), *Of Revelation and Revolution*, Chicago, IL: The University of Chicago Press, on South Africa. A good illustration of the power dialectics underpinning the meeting of the Western world and imperial subject can be provided by bringing together the works of Michael Taussig (1987), *Shamanism, Colonialism, and the Wild Man: A Study in Terror and Healing*, Berkeley, CA: University of California Press, on the economy of terror and racism in the Colombian Amazon, and of Ann Laura Stoler (2002), *Carnal Knowledge and Imperial Power: Race and the Intimate in the Colonial Rule*, Berkeley, CA: University of California Press, on the politics of sexuality and race in Indonesia.

7 The combination of these two registers – the military and the humanitarian – is discussed in the following collective volume: Didier Fassin and Mariella Pandolfi (2010), *Contemporary States of Emergency: The Politics of Military and Humanitarian Interventions*, New York: Zone Books. For a history of the relationship between the two, see Michael Barnett (2011), *Empire of Humanity: A History of Humanitarianism*, Ithaca, NY: Cornell University Press.

Critical situations

29 Facing cruelty

Colin M. Turnbull

Colin M. Turnbull (1924–1994) was a British anthropologist who followed an atypical career path. After having studied religion in an Indian university, he travelled in the Democratic Republic of Congo, worked with Sam Spiegel on the film *The African Queen*, began specialising in anthropology at Oxford, conducted research in Uganda and finally settled in the United States as curator at the American Museum of Natural History. His work on the BaMbuti pygmies gave rise not only to an important book, *The Forest People*, but also to one of the first studies in ethnomusicology. However, it was above all his book on the Iks, *The Mountain People*, that brought him celebrity, due to the controversy that surrounded it.

To a large extent a matter of circumstance, the research that brought Colin Turnbull to study the Ik in Uganda led him to discover a population decimated by famine after having been displaced by the government in order to create a national park on the group's hunting territory. As described by the author, the villagers were reduced to a form of competition for survival in which the values and affects attributed to human beings – and which, according to testimonies, existed prior to this ordeal – seemed to have disappeared. There was no longer any solidarity, compassion or any other tie. In a tragic meditation, Colin Turnbull describes a collective group in which, for him, individualism has destroyed all social life and whose cruelty reveals the decline of humanity. As soon as it came out, the book gave rise to virulent criticism of both its methodology (the many factual errors and more generally the non-respect of the usual rules of the discipline) and its analysis (other observers, including the author's colleague and partner Joseph Towles, contested the dehumanisation described). The narrative nonetheless met with success beyond the academic sphere and Peter Brook directed a stage adaptation of the text. In this regard, Thomas Beidelman's review – in which he stated that 'Rather than being a study of the Ik, this is an autobiographical portrait of the author utilizing the Ik as counters for expressing his personal feelings and experiences in the field' – invites us to consider, beyond this extreme case, the emotional and moral projections anthropologists and their readership can make, often unknowingly, in worlds both far away and closer to home.

In what follows, there will be much to shock, and the reader will be tempted to say "how primitive … how savage … how disgusting" and, above all, "how inhuman." In living the experience I said all those things over and over again. The first judgments are typical of the kind of ethno- and egocentrism from which we can never quite escape, however much we try, and are little more than reaffirmations of standards that are different in circumstances that are different. But the latter judgment, "how inhuman," is of a different order, and supposes that there are certain standards common to all humanity, certain values inherent in humanity itself, from which the people described in this book seem to depart in a most drastic manner. In living the experience, however, and perhaps in reading it, one finds that it is oneself one is looking at and questioning; it is a voyage in quest of the basic human and a discovery of his potential for inhumanity, a potential that lies within us all. [...]

Society and belief

Villages were villages of the dead and dying, and there was little difference between the two. People crawled rather than walked—the very young and the very old all crawled. The usual method was to squat and raise the buttocks off the ground by pressing down on the fists, then swinging the body forward on the arms, like a pendulum, dropping it to the ground again a few inches ahead. After a few feet some would lie down to rest, but they could not be sure of ever being able to sit up again, so they mostly stayed upright until they reached their destination. It was their destination that intrigued me, for really they were going nowhere, these semi-animate bags of skin and bone, they just wanted to be with others, and they stopped whenever they met. Perhaps it was the most important demonstration of sociality I ever saw among the Ik. They just gathered during the morning and stayed until late afternoon. Once together they neither spoke nor did anything together, they were together and that seemed enough. The skin hung from their bones in such wrinkled folds, especially at the joints, that when they raised their backsides off the ground the skin folds that had been buttocks flapped along underneath. In places it was drawn tight, a patchy red, but the overall impression was the blotchy look of a corpse that has been smoked. The fact that these corpses moved and smiled did not make them any easier to live with.

One afternoon I had been trying to feed some of them, in a moment of weakness, when the first of the youths returning from Kasilé arrived, laughing and shouting. One man carried a spear broken off halfway down, for they had been attacked by a buffalo on the way and it had made off with the blade and part of the shaft in its side. Children followed and were promptly sent to get water; they were the older children, almost ready to move into adulthood, and it was yet another contradiction that made no sense to see them fetching water for their "families." They laughed as they splashed in the filthy, muddy pool beneath the sacred tree, and, that done, they set to teasing the old skeletons who by then were dragging their way back to the villages. One girl had fastened a white flower onto a piece of vine, and swung it prettily around her head as she danced around Ngorok and blocked his progress whichever way he turned. Lokwam almost looked attractive; he had adorned himself handsomely with broad bands of grass tied tightly around his calves, his arms and his forehead. But he was more active and liked to push the crawlers lightly so that they teetered and then toppled. It was a time of fun and laughter for all.

In the midst of this conviviality it was mentioned that Jana's wife had not come back. Jana said she had been lagging behind, the fool had been trying to carry some *posho*—much good that would do her if she ever got it as far as Pirre. Someone else said they had seen her fall, but had not bothered to wait and see if she got up again. By then it was getting dark and the high spirits were wearing low, and everyone, including Jana, felt tired and wanted to go to sleep. The next morning this brief surge of good humor had vanished, and children no longer went to fetch water at their elders' behest. Jana announced that he was going up the mountainside to see if there was any of his wife's *posho* left; it was assumed she had died during the night, for she had not come back, and it had been bitterly cold with a strong wind. But someone had been there before him, he angrily told us on his return, and had taken both the *posho* and the skin bag she had been carrying it in. He carried two necklaces his wife had been wearing, one of dark red nuts and the other of bright blue glass beads, and her stick. I wondered why those had not been taken too. She must have died near where Kauar had died, but I could find no mound of stones. Maybe Jana just pushed her over the edge; she would have rolled well out of sight unless the body got stuck in a thorn bush.

Then there was a bad night's raiding in which the police and we were all awakened by shrill ululations and people blowing signal horns as some Dodos pursued Turkana who had stolen their cattle, passing close to Atum's village. Nobody was killed, but there were more injuries, and I for one felt no less unsafe with the police blasting off their rifles in the middle of the night than if they had been Turkana. Even before dawn every single household was at work dismantling what it could, moving possessions down the hillside and choosing new sites for new villages more easily protected by the police and less likely to be in the path of raiders. It was easier for me; all I had to do was to load up the Land Rover and drive back to my old camping site, but the others had to move their belongings and build some sort of shelter for the night. In some cases whole roofs were lifted off and carried, but this required at least four people. More often the thatch was removed and carried in long bundles. Rough shelters were erected of stick frames covered with skins, and thorn scrub served as a temporary outer stockade. In the midst of this hive of activity moved the aged and the crippled, some of whom I had never seen before, like slugs, in danger of being trampled underfoot but seemingly unaware of it, concentrating only on covering the next few feet of ground ahead of them.

It was then that I saw Loiangorok for the first time. He had managed to get out of the ruins of his village by late afternoon, when most of the moving was over for the day, and had started down the hill. But he could not even raise his frail bones off the ground, and was dragging himself along on his side, as though he were swimming. Loiamukat, the *niampara* of that village, came out with a bundle of sticks and stepped right over the old man and continued down the path. I shouted to him to find out who it was, and he replied, "Loiangorok—don't worry, he's my father." Which, knowing Loiamukat, I thought was the best of reasons for worrying. My nerves were still on edge from the confusion and uncertainty of the night before, and my threats, combined with bribes, were so effective that Loiamukat put down his sticks and returned to pick up his father, who had barely enough strength to put his arms around his son's neck. But when we got in sight of the temporary camp, Niangasir, Loiamukat's younger brother and the old man's youngest son, shrieked with derision to see Loiamukat carrying such a useless bundle. Loiamukat promptly deposited Loiangorok on the ground and told me I could carry him myself, which I did, feeling sick, not at the unkindness, but at the feel of those bones as they wrapped themselves around me.

I carried him past where his sons and daughter were busy setting up their new compounds, to where Atum's village was taking shape. Kinimei and Lotuköi had put up a rough shelter for themselves within what was to be Yakuma's compound, and I paid them to let me use it for the old man. Sensing that food would be in the offing as well as money, they readily agreed and started building another for themselves.

Atum had chosen a site closer to the Police Post than any of the others, and I found I could get the Land Rover there without much difficulty. It was there, while I was nursing Loiangorok, that there was a sudden exodus from the village, distant shouts of laughter, and then someone running back to tell me to come quickly. At first I thought it was a trick to get me away from the old man while in the middle of feeding him, so I finished that first and then went to see what the excitement was about. It was someone else whom I had never seen before, dead Lolim's widow, Lo'ono. She too had been abandoned, and had tried to make her way down the mountainside. But she was totally blind and had tripped and rolled to the bottom of the *oror a pirre'i*, and there she lay on her back, her legs and arms thrashing feebly, while a little crowd standing on the edge above looked down at her and laughed at the spectacle.

At this time Joseph Towles was with me and had brought fresh medical supplies. He stayed with her and kept the others away, while I ran back to get medicine and food and water, for Lo'ono was obviously nearly dead from hunger and thirst as well as from the fall. Then a really terrible thing happened. We treated her and fed her, and asked her to come back with us, thinking we might as well start a whole village for the old and abandoned. But she refused, and said she wanted to go on, if we would just point her in the direction of her son's new village. Her son was the same one who had driven old Lolim out so that Lolim died outside, not more than a few yards away. I said I did not think she would get much of a welcome there, and she replied that she knew it but at least she wanted to be near him when she died: perhaps when Longoli saw the food we had given her he might let her into the compound. So we gave her more food and made her eat and drink all she could, put her stick in her hand and pointed her the way she wanted to be pointed, and she suddenly cried. Thinking she was afraid or wanted us to go with her, I asked, and she said no; she was crying, she said, because all of a sudden we had reminded her that there had been a time when people had helped each other, when people had been kind and good. Still crying, she set off. […]

The world that is

It is, of course, guesswork when we try to say what the Ik were like before all this happened, for there are no records. However, the guesswork is not entirely without foundation, for we can use our knowledge of other hunting peoples for comparison, and we have the remnants of past traditions, customs and beliefs, and something of their own oral tradition, all of which indicate that they were, much like other hunters and gatherers, an easy-going, loosely organized people whose fluid organization enabled them to respond with sensitivity to the ever changing demands of their environment. There is ample evidence in their language that they once held values which they no longer hold, that they understood by "goodness" and "happiness" something very different from what those words have come to mean now. It is reasonable to suppose that the Ik were much like any other human society in terms of how firmly they held to their values and put their beliefs into practice, and it is by no means unreasonable, by comparison with other hunting societies, to suppose that very likely they were rather more faithful to their stated beliefs than we have become. Fidelity was possible for them; it is becoming impossible for us. And now, in one dramatic generation, they have leaped ahead and given us a taste of things to come.

In evidence, too, of how recently the Ik knew goodness, and of how rapidly we could lose it, are not only the stories told by the old who remembered it, but their lives. There was Nangoli and her family, who still wanted to be a family, yet who also still wanted to be part of the larger family of mountain people, the *kwarikik*. And Lolim, who wanted to die as a father should, in what should have been his *asak* shared with his son, but had become his son's *asak* from which he was turned away. Lomeraniang, Amuarkuar, Loiangorok—they all died without complaint, long before their time, because of the end of goodness; and goodness died with them. They died without complaint because the chill dispassion that is the Ik's new weapon against the world, their world, had touched them. Only Lo'ono remembered in full, when we reminded her, and made her cry and die in grief. [...]

The Ik teach us that our much vaunted human values are not inherent in humanity at all, but are associated only with a particular form of survival called society, and that all, even society itself, are luxuries that can be dispensed with. That does not make them any the less wonderful or desirable, and if man has any greatness it is surely in his ability to maintain these values, clinging to them to an often very bitter end, even shortening an already pitifully short life rather than sacrificing his humanity. But that too involves choice, and the Ik teach us that man can lose the will to make it. That is the point at which there is an end to truth, to goodness and to beauty; an end to the struggle for their achievement, which gives life to the individual while at the same time giving strength and meaning to society. The Ik have relinquished all luxury in the name of individual survival, and the result is that they live on as a people without life, without passion, beyond humanity. We pursue those trivial, idiotic technological encumbrances and imagine *them* to be the luxuries that make life worth living, and all the time we are losing our potential for social rather than individual survival, for hating as well as loving, losing perhaps our last chance to enjoy life with all the passion that is our nature and being.

30 Representing poverty

Oscar Lewis

Oscar Lewis (1914–1970) is an American anthropologist best known for his work on the poor in Mexico and the United States. After teaching at Brooklyn College and Washington University, he created the anthropology programme at the University of Illinois at Champagne-Urbana. His first research, on a Mexican village, Tepoztlan, roused controversy: indeed, contesting the results of the study carried out in the same location by Robert Redfield, he shows the importance of social change, economic precariousness, political conflicts and inequalities whereas his predecessor had been more attentive to the permanence and homogeneity of the village society. His most famous monographs, *Five Families: Mexican Case Studies in the Culture of Poverty* (1959), *The Children of Sanchez* (1961) and especially *La Vida: A Puerto Rican Family in the Culture of Poverty* (1966), share the same structure: a brief introduction presenting the theoretical frame, essentially the culture of poverty, followed by lengthy narratives about individuals, initially Mexicans and later Puerto Ricans, situated in the socio-economic context of their family life.

The concept of the culture of poverty first appears in his family study, but at the end of his life, Oscar Lewis would take it up again in his books and articles without substantially renewing it. The empirical material on which he grounds this concept is principally qualitative, based on his ethnography, but he would also mobilise in his later work large statistical surveys on the poor in the United States. The general idea is to interpret the production and reproduction of poverty through a series of norms and values, attitudes and practices that constitute a subculture, which can be found in various places of the world, almost independently of each specific context. Although he is resolutely a culturalist, Lewis has a paradoxically universalist aspiration. Because he fixes the poor in this culture of poverty and renders it responsible for the transmission of inequalities from one generation to the next, at the risk of blaming the victim, he has been used by conservative policymakers and criticised by progressive social scientists. Interestingly, four decades after his death, sociologists now rehabilitate if not his model, at least the necessity to approach poverty in its cultural aspects. However, in the discussion of the concept, its moral dimension has probably been overlooked. The starting point of Lewis is to avoid the dual pitfalls of denouncing and idealising the poor by presenting a sort of objective portrait of them. But in his very endeavour, the insistence on the sole negative traits of their culture in opposition to the norms and values of mainstream society boils down to validating a form of moral disqualification of the disadvantaged.

Although a great deal has been written about poverty and the poor, the concept of a culture of poverty is relatively new. I first suggested it in 1959 in my book *Five Families: Mexican Case Studies in the Culture of Poverty*. The phrase is a catchy one and has become widely used and misused. Michael Harrington used it extensively in his book *The Other America* (1961), which played an important role in sparking the national antipoverty program in the United States. However, he used it in a somewhat broader and less technical sense than I had intended. I shall try to define it more precisely as a conceptual model, with special emphasis upon the distinction between poverty and the culture of poverty. The absence of intensive anthropological studies of poor families from a wide variety of national and cultural contexts and especially from the socialist countries, is a serious handicap in formulating valid cross-cultural regularities. The model presented here is therefore provisional and subject to modification as new studies become available.

Throughout recorded history, in literature, in proverbs and in popular sayings, we find two opposite evaluations of the nature of the poor. Some characterize the poor as blessed, virtuous, upright, serene, independent, honest, kind and happy. Others characterize them as evil, mean, violent, sordid and criminal. These contradictory and confusing evaluations are also reflected in the in-fighting that is going on in the current war against poverty. Some stress the great potential of the poor for self-help, leadership and community organization, while others point to the sometimes irreversible, destructive effect of poverty upon individual character, and therefore emphasize the need for guidance and control to remain in the hands of the middle class, which presumably has better mental health.

These opposing views reflect a political power struggle between competing groups. However, some of the confusion results from the failure to distinguish between poverty per se and the culture of poverty and the tendency to focus upon the individual personality rather than upon the group—that is, the family and the slum community.

As an anthropologist I have tried to understand poverty and its associated traits as a culture or, more accurately, as a subculture with its own structure and rationale, as a way of life which is passed down from generation to generation along family lines. This view directs attention to the fact that the culture of poverty in modern nations is not only a matter of economic deprivation, of disorganization or of the absence of something. It is also something positive and provides some rewards without which the poor could hardly carry on.

Elsewhere I have suggested that the culture of poverty transcends regional, rural–urban and national differences and shows remarkable similarities in family structure, interpersonal relations, time orientation, value systems and spending patterns. These cross-national similarities are examples of independent invention and convergence. They are common adaptations to common problems.

The culture of poverty can come into being in a variety of historical contexts. However, it tends to grow and flourish in societies with the following set of conditions: (1) a cash economy, wage labor and production for profit; (2) a persistently high rate of unemployment and underemployment for unskilled labor; (3) low wages; (4) the failure to provide social, political and economic organization, either on a voluntary basis or by government imposition, for the low-income population; (5) the existence of a bilateral kinship system rather than a unilateral one; and finally, (6) the existence of a set of values in the dominant class which stresses the accumulation of wealth and property, the possibility of upward mobility and thrift, and explains low economic status as the result of personal inadequacy or inferiority.

The way of life which develops among some of the poor under these conditions is the culture of poverty. It can best be studied in urban or rural slums and can be described in terms of some seventy interrelated social, economic and psychological traits. However, the number of traits and the relationships between them may vary from society to society and from family to family. For example, in a highly literate society, illiteracy may be more diagnostic of the culture of poverty than in a society where illiteracy is widespread and where even the well-to-do may be illiterate, as in some Mexican peasant villages before the revolution.

The culture of poverty is both an adaptation and a reaction of the poor to their marginal position in a class-stratified, highly individuated, capitalistic society. It represents an effort to cope with feelings of hopelessness and despair which develop from the realization of the improbability of achieving success in terms of the values and goals of the larger society. Indeed, many of the traits of the culture of poverty can be viewed as attempts at local solutions for problems not met by existing institutions and agencies because the people are not eligible for them, cannot afford them, or are ignorant or suspicious of them. For example, unable to obtain credit from banks, they are thrown upon their own resources and organize informal credit devices without interest.

The culture of poverty, however, is not only an adaptation to a set of objective conditions of the larger society. Once it comes into existence it tends to perpetuate itself from generation to generation because of its effect on the children. By the time slum children are age six or seven they have usually absorbed the basic values and attitudes of their subculture and are not psychologically geared to take full advantage of changing conditions or increased opportunities which may occur in their lifetime.

Most frequently the culture of poverty develops when a stratified social and economic system is breaking down or is being replaced by another, as in the case of the transition from feudalism to capitalism or during periods of rapid technological change. Often it results from imperial conquest in which the native social and economic structure is smashed and the natives are maintained in a servile colonial status, sometimes for many generations. It can also occur in the process of detribalization, such as that now going on in Africa.

The most likely candidates for the culture of poverty are the people who come from the lower strata of a rapidly changing society and are already partially alienated from it. Thus landless rural workers who migrate to the cities can be expected to develop a culture of poverty much more readily than migrants from stable peasant villages with a well-organized traditional culture. In this connection there is a striking contrast between Latin America, where the rural population long ago made the transition from a tribal to a peasant society, and Africa, which is still close to its tribal heritage. The more corporate nature of many of the African tribal societies, in contrast to Latin American rural communities, and the persistence of village ties tend to inhibit or delay the formation of a full-blown culture of poverty in many of the African towns and cities. The special conditions of apartheid in South Africa, where the migrants are segregated into separate "locations" and do not enjoy freedom of movement, create special problems. Here the institutionalization of repression and discrimination tend to develop a greater sense of identity and group consciousness.

The culture of poverty can be studied from various points of view: the relationship between the subculture and the larger society; the nature of the slum community; the nature of the family; and the attitudes, values and character structure of the individual.

1. The lack of effective participation and integration of the poor in the major institutions of the larger society is one of the crucial characteristics of the culture of poverty. This is a complex matter and results from a variety of factors which may

include lack of economic resources, segregation and discrimination, fear, suspicion or apathy, and the development of local solutions for problems. However, "participation" in some of the institutions of the larger society—for example, in the jails, the army and the public relief system—does not per se eliminate the traits of the culture of poverty. In the case of a relief system which barely keeps people alive, both the basic poverty and the sense of hopelessness are perpetuated rather than eliminated.

Low wages, chronic unemployment and underemployment lead to low income, lack of property ownership, absence of savings, absence of food reserves in the home, and a chronic shortage of cash. These conditions reduce the possibility of effective participation in the larger economic system. And as a response to these conditions we find in the culture of poverty a high incidence of pawning of personal goods, borrowing from local moneylenders at usurious rates of interest, spontaneous informal credit devices organized by neighbors, the use of second-hand clothing and furniture, and the pattern of frequent buying of small quantities of food many times a day as the need arises.

People with a culture of poverty produce very little wealth and receive very little in return. They have a low level of literacy and education, usually do not belong to labor unions, are not members of political parties, generally do not participate in the national welfare agencies, and make very little use of banks, hospitals, department stores, museums or art galleries. They have a critical attitude toward some of the basic institutions of the dominant classes, hatred of the police, mistrust of government and those in high position, and a cynicism which extends even to the church. This gives the culture of poverty a high potential for protest and for being used in political movements aimed against the existing social order.

People with a culture of poverty are aware of middle-class values, talk about them and even claim some of them as their own, but on the whole they do not live by them. Thus it is important to distinguish between what they say and what they do. For example, many will tell you that marriage by law, by the church, or by both, is the ideal form of marriage, but few will marry. To men who have no steady jobs or other sources of income, who do not own property and have no wealth to pass on to their children, who are present-time oriented and who want to avoid the expense and legal difficulties involved in formal marriage and divorce, free unions or consensual marriage makes a lot of sense. Women will often turn down offers of marriage because they feel it ties them down to men who are immature, punishing and generally unreliable. Women feel that consensual union gives them a better break; it gives them some of the freedom and flexibility that men have. By not giving the fathers of their children legal status as husbands, the women have a stronger claim on their children if they decide to leave their men. It also gives women exclusive rights to a house or any other property they may own.

2. When we look at the culture of poverty on the local community level, we find poor housing conditions, crowding, gregariousness, but above all a minimum of organization beyond the level of the nuclear and extended family. Occasionally there are informal, temporary groupings or voluntary associations within slums. The existence of neighborhood gangs which cut across slum settlements represents a considerable advance beyond the zero point of the continuum that I have in mind. Indeed, it is the low level of organization which gives the culture of poverty its marginal and anachronistic quality in our highly complex, specialized, organized society. Most primitive peoples have achieved a higher level of sociocultural organization than our modern urban slum dwellers.

In spite of the generally low level of organization, there may be a sense of community and *esprit de corps* in urban slums and in slum neighborhoods. This can vary within a single city, or from region to region or country to country. The major factors influencing this variation are the size of the slum, its location and physical characteristics, length of residence, incidence of home and landownership (versus squatter rights), rentals, ethnicity, kinship ties, and freedom or lack of freedom of movement. When slums are separated from the surrounding area by enclosing walls or other physical barriers, when rents are low and fixed and stability of residence is great (twenty or thirty years), when the population constitutes a distinct ethnic, racial or language group, is bound by ties of kinship or *compadrazgo*, and when there are some internal voluntary associations, then the sense of local community approaches that of a village community. In many cases this combination of favorable conditions does not exist. However, even where internal organization and *esprit de corps* is at a bare minimum and people move around a great deal, a sense of territoriality develops which sets off the slum neighborhoods from the rest of the city. In Mexico City and San Juan this sense of territoriality results from the unavailability of low-income housing outside the slum areas. In South Africa the sense of territoriality grows out of the segregation enforced by the government, which confines the rural migrants to specific locations.

3. On the family level the major traits of the culture of poverty are the absence of childhood as a specially prolonged and protected stage in the life cycle, early initiation into sex, free unions or consensual marriages, a relatively high incidence of the abandonment of wives and children, a trend toward female- or mother-centered families and consequently a much greater knowledge of maternal relatives, a strong predisposition to authoritarianism, lack of privacy, verbal emphasis upon family solidarity which is only rarely achieved because of sibling rivalry, and competition for limited goods and maternal affection.

4. On the level of the individual the major characteristics are a strong feeling of marginality, of helplessness, of dependence and of inferiority. I found this to be true of slum dwellers in Mexico City and San Juan among families who do not constitute a distinct ethnic or racial group and who do not suffer from racial discrimination. In the United States, of course, the culture of poverty of the Negroes has the additional disadvantage of racial discrimination, but as I have already suggested, this additional disadvantage contains a great potential for revolutionary protest and organization which seems to be absent in the slums of Mexico City or among the poor whites in the South.

Other traits include a high incidence of maternal deprivation, of orality, of weak ego structure, confusion of sexual identification, a lack of impulse control, a strong present-time orientation with relatively little ability to defer gratification and to plan for the future, a sense of resignation and fatalism, a widespread belief in male superiority, and a high tolerance for psychological pathology of all sorts.

People with a culture of poverty are provincial and locally oriented and have very little sense of history. They know only their own troubles, their own local conditions, their own neighborhood, their own way of life. Usually they do not have the knowledge, the vision or the ideology to see the similarities between their problems and those of their counterparts elsewhere in the world. They are not class conscious, although they are very sensitive indeed to status distinctions.

31 Understanding suicide bombers

Ghassan Hage

Ghassan Hage (born in 1957) is a professor of anthropology and social theory at the University of Melbourne. He had previously worked with Pierre Bourdieu at the École des Hautes Études en Sciences Sociales and later at the University of Sydney within the anthropology department. His work, which is based on a comparative approach, focuses on globalisation, nationalism, racism and multiculturalism. In particular his two books *White Nation and Against Paranoid Nationalism* offer a critical and engaged reading of the long history and recent evolution of Australian society. The subject of his recent research is political emotions and their circulation among migrants. Focusing particularly on the experiences of members of the Lebanese diaspora and their relationship to the Israeli–Palestinian conflict, Ghassan Hage endeavours to highlight both how individuals' migratory or transnational experiences transform these emotions and how the changes that occur play a role in the integration, or lack of integration, of these populations in the countries in which they live.

The text presented here is part of this reflection on 'political imaginaries'. Based on a dual personal experience of his interlocutors' incomprehension in face of his efforts to 'understand' Palestinian suicide bombings in response to the occupation of the West Bank by the Israeli army, Ghassan Hage offers a theoretical and political reflection upon the conditions in which anthropological discourse is possible when focusing on subjects considered to only call for moral condemnation. By analysing the asymmetrical terms of the public debate in this way, he affirms the need for a discourse in the social sciences to unveil and criticise what is generally accepted as self-evident. In particular, he attempts to show that rejecting social explanations, which has become commonplace, also means rejecting the humanity of the Other, preferring to reduce him or her to essentialist interpretations of evil. Ghassan Hage thus puts forwards two neologisms – exighophobia, the fear of explanation, and homoiophobia, the fear of the same – to account for this post 9/11 political imaginary, both in the United States and in Australia. There is thus an ethical imperative for the social sciences to eschew the various forms of militant discourse in favour of the axiological neutrality advocated by Spinoza.

In the days that followed the Israeli army's reinvasion of the West Bank in March 2002 and the resultant destruction of the embryonic elements of a sovereign Palestinian society, I, like many, sat in my office fuming, emailing with depressed friends and colleagues to express our helplessness and despair at the unbelievable injustice of it all. Besides the death and devastation, most depressing perhaps was the mediatic normalization of the very idea of a nation's military rampaging virtually unopposed—like

Genghis Khan in tanks—in another nation's cities and towns, leveling entire streets, destroying homes. It was for all of us an absurdly anachronistic form of violence: a medieval mode of warfare outfitted in modern technology.

I took it upon me to send Arab, Jewish, and other concerned friends an email that attempted to think through the nature and ramifications of this violence. While addressing the Israeli government's use of Palestinian suicide bombers (PSBs) as an excuse for transforming cities into rubble, I pointed out that to a large degree the Israeli government shared with the suicide bombers a lack of concern with the humanity of the people murdered in the course of the conflict. In a communal Us versus Them logic, the dehumanizing gaze that saw Them as a nondifferentiated entity (Israel/the Palestinians), abstracted from the particular human beings that constituted it, is often accompanied by an equally self-dehumanizing, abstracted vision of Us. I knew very well from my experience of the Lebanese civil war both as a participant and a student that when a logic of communal war prevails, neither of the warring sides really cares for the actual material human beingness of the situation. More "important" things like "communities" and "nations" are at stake. I argued that given the prevalence of that logic, "the bombs of Hamas against civilians might outrage the humanists among us for being precisely that: bombs against civilians," but what was more important for the Israeli colonialist government was that these bombs showed the Israeli Us to be vulnerable, which is also what the suicide bombers were trying to demonstrate.

The day after I sent my e-mail, I was surprised to receive a long rebuke from a colleague on the Jewish left. In an e-mail, he informed me that he was "sad to see that these days scholars speak in strangely brutal language" and that he could not "join in common cause with people who endorse this horrendous path of voluptuously violent martyrdom. I don't really want to stand alongside anybody who cheers other people, young people, along that appalling path without being prepared to follow it themselves. ... I cannot respect the political sensibilities and moral judgement of people who indulge, from positions of comfortable impunity, in this unbecoming kind of vicarious bravery—which is really a form of bad faith and moral cowardice."

The moralizing nature of the reply took me aback. I could not believe that I had become someone who endorsed the "horrendous path of voluptuously violent martyrdom," someone faced with either exploding himself in Palestine or acknowledging his moral cowardice. I wondered how my matter-of-factly stated observation about the political imaginaries behind suicide bombing, regardless of whether one agrees with it, was transformed into support for "voluptuously violent martyrdom." It was as if the moral neutrality of my statement was itself self-condemnatory.

Indeed, as I was later informed by a mutual friend, my colleague felt that the real issue was whether I "absolutely condemn" suicide bombers. Apparently it is crucial to "absolutely condemn" suicide bombers if you are going to talk about them, otherwise you become a morally suspicious person. This immediately raised an issue for me. As I only mentioned suicide bombing in relation to what I thought were the inhumane acts of violence Israel was perpetrating through its reoccupation of the West Bank, I wondered why it is that suicide bombing cannot be talked about without being condemned first. After all, we can sit and analyze in a cool manner the formidably violent colonial invasion without feeling that "absolute" moral condemnation should be a precondition or even a substitute for uttering an opinion about it. To my mind, both the Israeli invasion and the suicide bombings constitute a kind of warped postmodern pastiche associating medievally violent political affects, early modern veneration of political entities such as "the nation," and late-modern military technology. The fact that my colleague decided that only suicide bombing is *necessarily* a moral issue raised questions about the assumptions implicit in our categorization of violence and about their significance in shaping our political and analytical judgment. The polemic also raised another question that pertained to the political nature of the "condemnation imperative" and its significance for academic practices in the social sciences.

It is clearly the case that in the Western public sphere the condemnation imperative operates as a mode of censoring the attempts to provide a sociological explanation for why PSBs act the way they do. It is difficult to express any form of understanding whatsoever, even when one is indeed also condemning the practices of PSBs. Only unqualified condemnation will do. And if one tries to understand, any accompanying condemnation is deemed suspicious. A number of public figures have expressed some form of "understanding" of suicide bombers (often linking their emergence to the absence of hope among Palestinian teenagers) only to be forced to apologize for voicing such views; the most publicized cases were those of Ted Turner, former owner of CNN, and Cherie Blair, wife of the British prime minister. There is a clear political risk in trying to explain suicide bombings.[1] [...]

Are suicide bombers human beings like us?

As a testing ground for my initial question—Can one understand suicide bombers?—I used a seminar with some of my senior students to try and imagine what an anthropology of the practice of suicide bombing could be like. Primary sources consisted of a number of conversations I had with Palestinians in Australia, and secondary material was the body of available literature on suicide bombing. [...]

A student came up to me after the seminar. "I wasn't very comfortable during some parts of this talk," she said. "You've made it as if suicide bombers are ordinary human beings." This struck me as true. But isn't that what is always at stake in social explanations? This is why it is not surprising that it is often Arabs or Arab sympathizers who on the popular political market of condemnation of suicide bombers counter these populist condemnations with equally populist attempts at social explanations. In demanding or proposing a social explanation, regardless of whether the explanation is satisfactory, Arabs are demanding to be included as part of humanity. They're claiming: "We are not as weird as you think." Thus, in an open letter to President George W. Bush, the former Lebanese prime minister Selim el-Hoss asks: "Those deplorable suicidal operations which you brand as terrorism, have they not ever for a moment prompted you to ask yourself the question: why would a young boy or girl be willing to sacrifice himself or herself with utter peace of mind and full determination? ... How do you label the phenomenon of a whole people standing ready to sacrifice half its numbers in a struggle and martyrdom so that the other half will regain dignity on its own land?"[2]

While on fieldwork (working on the unrelated issue of transnational migration) in a Shi'a village in south Lebanon, a village studded with photos of young men who died fighting the Israeli occupation of Lebanon, I heard the same argument—expressed in stronger terms—from one of my informants, an educated man and a member of Hizb'allah:

Ali: The Americans pretend not to understand the suicide bombers and consider them evil. But I am sure they do. As usual, they are hypocrites. What is so strange about saying: "I am not going to let you rob me of all my humanity and all my will?" What is so strange about saying: "I'd rather kill you on my own terms and kill myself with you rather than be led to my death like a sheep on your own terms?"[3] I know that the Americans fully understand this because this is exactly what they were celebrating about the guy who downed the Philadelphia flight on September 11, the one where the hijackers failed to hit their target. Isn't that exactly what he must have said when he decided to kill himself and everyone else by bringing the plane down? Didn't he say to those hijacking him: "I'd rather kill you on my own terms and kill myself with you rather than be led to my death like a sheep on your own terms?" They made a hero out of him. The only hero of September 11. They are hypocrites, the Americans. They know as much as we do that as a human being we all have the capacity to rush enthusiastically to our death if it means dying as a dignified being.

Me [laughing]: We are all enthusiasm! (*kulluna hamas*, which also translates as we are all Hamas).

Ali [smiling]: That's right; comes a time we are all enthusiasm!

Despite its convenient "forgetting" of the more unsavory aspects of suicide bombing that were not part of the "suicide crashing" of the Philadelphia plane, this interpretation can be seen as driven by a desire to establish a "common humanity."[4] This view stands in opposition to the condemning attitude that wants to deny such a common humanity. Emanating from a kind of warring disposition toward the suicide bombers, those who can only condemn the PSBs end up sharing with them, at a very general level, the same warring logic. After all, the negation of a common humanity, in its more dramatic form as a vision of an abstract dehumanized other (where children are not perceived in their children-ness, mothers in their motherliness) is of course inherent to the practice of the Palestinian suicide bomber. Rather than losing it ourselves as we rush into condemnation, those of us driven by the ethics of social explanation will always want to ask, "What kind of social conditions must avail and what kind of history must a people have internalized to make them lose this capacity of seeing the other in his or her humanness?" This is not an easy question to ask in the West today because the West itself is rapidly losing whatever capacity it had to see the other in his or her humanness.

Social explanation and the humanity of the other

The rise and dominance of neoliberal economic policy and its substitution of the welfare state by a penal state is a well-documented and -researched phenomenon today, especially in the United States, where this penal state has become a particularly salient feature of the social structure.[5] Less documented has been the accompanying backlash against social explanations of crime. The newspapers' letters to the editor commenting on apprehended criminals are often accompanied by sarcastic "and please let's not hear about his or her deprived childhood"-type statements. There is a noticeable public division between a minority that still likes to hear or formulate some kind of social explanation and a majority that sees any social explanation as a full-blown or creeping justification aimed at depriving people of the right to seek justice through appropriate forms of punishment. More than ever, the practice of social science in this domain becomes itself the object of political struggles. Social scientists, generally proponents of social explanations, are often attacked as a privileged group sheltered from the effects of crime and therefore unable to understand the feelings of the general population.[6]

It is clear that both the zero tolerance toward crime and the zero tolerance toward the social explanation of crime are grounded in the uncertainties created by what is called globalization. The latest cycle of capitalist accumulation, the modalities of class exploitation it has made necessary, and the resulting change in the quality of work and precariousness of people's hold on their employment have all led to a general climate of insecurity in the face of the future. Increasingly, there is a sense of society's shrinking capacity to provide a good life to everyone. As a result, a defensive attitude of guarding whatever good life is left supplants the enjoyment of that good life. In this phobic culture where everything is viewed as either threatening and in need of extermination or threatened and in need of protection, there is an invasion of the order of the border. From the borders of the self to the borders of the family, friendship, neighborhood, nation, and all the way to the borders of Western civilization, everything and everywhere is perceived as a border from which a potentially threatening other can leap. Elsewhere, I have referred to this cultural tendency as *anthrax culture*—where every breath of fresh air we take becomes a threatening border.[7] It is a combination of a warring and a siege mentality, which by necessity emphasizes the eradication of a potentially menacing other.

In a war/siege culture the understanding of the other is a luxury that cannot be afforded; on the contrary, the divisions between Us and Them are further emphasized. War emphasizes the otherness of the other and divides the world between friends and enemies and good and evil. This war logic is negated in a social explanation that draws on an ethics of social determinism. By proposing that the other is fundamentally like us, social determinism suggests that given a similar history and background we might find ourselves in the other's place.[8] When we explain an act as the product of a particular history and particular social circumstances we give its perpetrators some of their humanity back. The ethics of social determinism invites us to think that we might—indeed ought to—put someone like former Yugoslav president Slobodan Milosevic and his followers on trial, but not to emphasize how different they are from us. Social determinism reminds us how depraved *we* human beings can become under certain circumstances and how much we need to work against what is worst in us. This is not a negation of responsibility but an affirmation of the importance of both the social conditions of action and the historical conditions of formation of the acting self—that is, an affirmation of Marx's everlasting dictum that "we all make history but not in conditions of our own choosing."

Social explanation is driven by an inclusionary rather than an exclusionary ethics, and as such it embodies the negation of the logic of war and becomes itself perceived as a political threat in times of war. In the war/siege society, social explanation can disrupt the way both self and society are invited to define and stabilize themselves against another that has to remain different and unknowable. Social explanation can threaten the warring self with disintegration, which is why it sometimes unleashes such passionate response. Social explanation is not merely rejected. The threat of the humanized other it carries with it is affectively feared. Thus emerges the couplet of phobias I refer to in the title of the essay: exighophobia (from the Greek *exigho*, to explain) and homoiophobia (from the Greek *homoio*, the same).[9] In this homoio–exighophobic culture anyone wishing to *know* and to inquire about the social conditions that might explain a possible rise in criminal offenses, for example, or about the social background of asylum seekers, is perceived as inherently suspect, a nuisance if not a traitor. Recently, it was revealed that the Australian government directed its bureaucrats against issuing photos that would "humanize" the refugees seeking entry to Australia. Note that while people refer to such an attitude toward refugees as xenophobia, what is really feared here is not the otherness of the other but the other's human sameness—not xenophobia but homoiophobia.

Consequently, given its warring imaginary, it is hardly surprising to see that this homoio-exighophobic cultural tendency has emerged even more strongly: first, in relation to the terrorist mass murders of September 11, 2001 and, later, in relation to the PSBs. The monstrous criminality of the September 11 events and the war climate they helped create understandably made them resistant to social explanation at a popular level. But this very resistance was used by politicians to give the homoio–exighophobic attitude a monopoly over morality. To attempt a sociopolitical explanation of the terrorists' action or to explain why those acts were supported by large sections of the Arab population was considered sacrilegious and immoral on the post-September 11 market of outrage.[10] In answering the famous question "why do they hate us?" anyone who deviated from the presidential "they hate us because they hate us," they hate "our values" and "our way of life" (i.e., they are not humans in the same way we are), was considered not outraged enough and accused of blaming the victim. This is why a group of American politicians referred to a number of critical academics as "the weak link in America's war against terrorism."[11] It is this same attitude that also shapes the "nothing ever justifies suicide bombing" discourse.

Thus in taking the side of social explanation one is clearly not inhabiting a politically neutral position. But it should also be noted that in taking the side of explanation one does not necessarily stand in opposition to the condemnations voiced by politicians. Condemnations of the type "nothing ever justifies" might well be considered useful when there is a fear of imitation. But clearly if the aim of condemnation is to stop the spread of such practices, the knowledge and the modification of the social conditions of their emergence is far more effective than the assumption that they are somehow the product of some transposable cultural or religious "state of mind" disconnected from any social situation, any social conditions, or any specific history. Suicide bombings are undoubtedly a form of social evil, but their evil is also the evil of the living conditions from which they emanate. That evil (or sinfulness) resides more in certain social conditions of life where the possibilities of a meaningful life are shrinking, rather than in the individuals trying to survive in such conditions. Seeing evil in the conditions rather than in the people is what Roy Bhaskar, following Margaret Archer, powerfully refers to as *structural sin*.[12] Some politicians might choose to portray social scientists who detect such structural sins as "on the other side," but never have these social scientists been more necessary. Now more than ever, we could all benefit from Spinoza's ethical injunction for the intellectual: "Do not deplore, do not laugh, do not hate, but understand."

Notes

1 Here is a typical example of the journalistic attempt at (not) understanding the phenomenon: "The suicide bomber's name, appropriately enough, was Mohammad al-Ghoul. Other than blind hatred, who can say what motivated this 22-year-old to detonate himself on a bus full of students on a Tuesday morning in Jerusalem?" Tony Parkinson, "Defenders of the Palestinian Cause are Running Out of Excuses," *The Age* (Melbourne), 20 June 2002.
2 Selim Hoss, "Open Letter to George Bush," *Daily Star* (Beirut), 11 April 2002.
3 This same discourse emerges in Daniel Williams's investigation of the suicide bombers. The suicide bomber Abu Aisheh was reported to have asked: "Aren't we being shot like dogs? Do you feel like a human being when the Israelis control your every move? Do you believe we have a future? If I'm going to die at their hands anyway, why shouldn't I take some of them with me?" Williams, "Young Bombers Nurtured by Despair: Among Palestinians, a Growing Attitude of Little to Live for," *The Age* (Melbourne), 25 March 2002, 10.
4 On this general theme see the excellent work of Raimond Gaita (1999), *A Common Humanity: Thinking about Love and Truth and Justice*, Melbourne: Text Publishing.
5 See Marc Mauer (1999), *Race to Incarcerate*, New York: New Press. See also Loïc Wacquant's body of work on the rise of the penal state, particularly *Les prisons de la misère*, Paris: Raisons d'Agir, 1999.
6 In Australia, academics are dismissively called "the intellectual elite." According to the populist attacks encouraged by the conservative governments, the intellectual elite are unrealistic people who are completely out of touch with the reality of so-called ordinary people.
7 Ghassan Hage, "Anthrax Politics," *Canberra Times*, 31 January 2002, 7.
8 I have derived this idea of an ethics of social determinism particularly from the work of Pierre Bourdieu. This ethics is most apparent in the collective work directed by Bourdieu (1999), *The Weight of the World: Social Suffering in Contemporary Society*, Cambridge: Polity, especially the last chapter.
9 I thank Gina Rizakos for providing a quick lesson in Greek to help me to construct the phobia terms I use in this essay.
10 I am not implying here that the social explanations presented were adequate. Nevertheless, it was not the inadequacy of the explanations that raised people's ire. It was the mere fact that an explanation was attempted.
11 Jerry L. Martin and Anne D. Neal, "Defending Civilization: How Our Universities Are Failing America and What Can Be Done about It," a report produced by the American Council of Trustees and Alumni. This group was founded by Lynne Cheney (wife of the vice president of the United States) and U.S. Senator Joseph Lieberman. The report is available online at www.goacta.org.
12 Roy Bhaskar (2000), *From East to West: Odyssey of a Soul*, London: Routledge, pp. 37, 57, 91.

32 Assessing the new bioethics

Arthur Kleinman

Arthur Kleinman (born in 1941) is a professor of medical anthropology, a discipline that he contributed to founding, at Harvard University. He has produced pioneering work on mental illness and cross-cultural psychiatry in China, where he has conducted most of his research. As a psychiatrist and anthropologist, he has promoted the trend of explanatory models of illness before foregrounding illness narratives and analysing the experience of suffering. He combines anthropological, medical, and moral approaches, notably in the three volumes he coedited entitled *Social Suffering*, *Violence and Subjectivity* and *Remaking a World*. While Arthur Kleinman has long been interested in the pain and distress of patients affected by neuropsychiatric disorders, his approach has progressively shifted from a culturalist reading, attentive to the different expressions of illness according to national historical contexts (for example, in *Patients and Healers in the Context of Culture*), to a humanist one, seeking more universal traits of the human condition (from *The Illness Narratives* onwards). His orientation towards moral questions in his later works is therefore as much the continuation of his previous research as it is a new departure.

The text presented here is simultaneously programmatic and illustrative. Using examples taken from anthropological studies, Arthur Kleinman puts forward a reflection on morality that is grounded in cultural contexts, far from the universalising and normative philosophical speculations of ethicists, which he opposes. The study of ethics depends, however, upon a method: despite all its imperfections and its fundamental uncertainty, ethnography has, in his view, all the necessary qualities to allow an understanding of moral questions, including by health-care professionals. He advocates associating fieldwork research attentive to social contexts and individual ethics with general reflection on norms and values tending towards universality. While the author underscores the inherent hesitations of such a programme, it is a change of paradigm that he puts to the reader. A legitimate field of analysis for philosophers, cognitive scientists and ethicists alike, morality could be the locus for implementing true interdisciplinarity, where the ethnographic approach could enrich philosophical debates.

Remaking the case for bioethics

For all these efforts at repair and reform, however, bioethics is confronted with an extraordinarily difficult quandary: how to reconcile the clearly immense differences in the social and personal realities of moral life with the need to apply a universal standard to those fragments of experience that can foster not only comparison and evaluation but also action.[1] For philosophers, the gulf between the universal and the particular may be regarded as an irksome and a perennial barrier; but bioethicists, like clinicians and policy implementers, simply cannot function without finding a way of relating ethical deliberation to local contexts.

The issue can be put in other terms. For almost all of us, everyday life experience in communities and networks—no matter how influenced we are by global forces of communication, commerce, and the flow of people—centers on *what is locally at stake*. What matters most in the mundane and extraordinary transpersonal details that bind and define us through relationships, work, and the close politics of a particular place is the overwhelmingly pragmatic orientation of men and women everywhere. Even the quest for transcendent meaning needs to be understood in this light. The "local" nowadays may be better understood as more like a network than a neighborhood; yet its power to engage us in what matters continues to define human affairs. There is great diversity in what is valued, to be sure; but that ordinary people, even the marginalized, are stakeholders in local worlds is what social life is about. Status, material resources, relationships of exchange, survival, identity, and transcendence are examples of the things that are sought collectively and individually. What is at stake may differ, but the human experience of pursuing such goals is empirically describable. And that is the point: empirical research can provide knowledge about local worlds of experience—knowledge that is useful, even essential, for bioethics.

There simply is no getting around the great influence of these local moral processes. Why moral? Because they consist of the contestations and compromises that actualize values both for collectives and for individuals. Indeed, the individual–collective dichotomy is overdone; within these social processes values are negotiated and reworked among others in a space that is thoroughly intersubjective.[2] Think of the adult children of a father with Alzheimer's Disease whose dementia is so severe that he cannot remember the content of his children's statements about the question of his placement in a nursing home. The experience of suffering is lodged as much in the emotions (sadness, grief, frustration) of the children as in those of their father; indeed, these emotions build on each other. The responses that lead to decisions about when and where to be institutionalized are moral engagements within this family's relationships. They are part of ongoing conversations and exchanges that began even before these adult children were born, developed in ways inseparable from their own trajectories, bled into their actual situations at a particular time, and will without question go on after their father's death. It is not individuals as isolated beings who make the choice to place a parent in a nursing home, *pace* the primal and somewhat atomistic scene favored by analytic philosophers. It is rather the person as part of a network of relations, memories, current pressures, and uncertain prospects, and constrained by interconnections and shared fate, who is the locus of moral experience. Hence moral experience is about the local processes (collective, interpersonal, subjective) that realize (enact) values in ordinary living. These processes cross the boundary of the body–self, connecting affect and cognition with cultural meanings, moral norms and collective identity with sense of self. Thus moral experience and personal experience are interfused: value with emotion.

Modeling ethics as a person's individual choices, which in turn are supposed to be based in deep, philosophically and psychologically informed reflection shaped by religious and secular standards that seek universal application, simply does not account for the social processes of moral life. Those processes illustrate how the person is located in economic, cultural, kinship, friendship, and work activities that powerfully define his or her moral horizon in ways of which he or she is likely to be only partially aware. In the end, then, ethics, once framed as models of moral reasoning championing the reflection and rational choice of autonomous individuals in quest of objective standards, risk irrelevance to the almost always uncertain circumstances and highly contextualized conditions of human experience.[3]

The irrelevance of ethics can be seen when considering universal ethical formulations of justice and equity that do not begin with the local moral conditions of poor people, those experiencing the systematic injustice of higher disease rates and fewer health-care resources because of their positioning at the bottom of local social structures of power. Dealing with issues of justice in the absence of these contextual concerns renders ethical formulations mere speculations, utopian pronouncements that are gratuitous and beside the point. Consider, for example, the fact that bioethics generally regards informed consent an overriding ethical condition of international health research—say, in vaccine trials for HIV among impoverished African villagers. Of course, few villagers are likely to be literate or possess knowledge of randomized controlled trials, placebos, or perhaps even conceptions of individual autonomy in deciding about participation in a community-wide activity. Yet even when attention is devoted by bioethicists to these issues, they demonstrate surprisingly little understanding of local cultural realities, and even less appreciation of the dire effects of the global economy in deepening villagers' poverty and suffering by means of structural-adjustment programs that tend to intensify local conditions of inequity and render most Africans without any hope of even minimal health-care services to treat AIDS. Then application of the "ethical" in the local setting of the "moral" must be highly suspect.

And yet can there be an understanding of ethics—in the sense of, at the very least, an imagination of and struggle to develop universal values—that does not seek to transcend the local? After all, local worlds—as in the recent examples of Bosnia, Kosovo, and Rwanda—can be utterly unethical.[4] How could we make the case for human rights and against genocide in such terrible instances based on something called ethics—unless ethics provides translocal values that can criticize local practices from the outside?

And this is the quandary, is it not? Bioethics requires *both* approaches: it must possess a method for accounting for local moral experience and a means of applying ethical deliberation. But it is unclear how this pairing of what so often seem like opposing approaches can be accomplished, or, for that matter, whether the combination inherently requires more than current concepts and methods can achieve. It is not only the limitations of analytic philosophy that create problems for bioethics in this regard; biomedicine's reductionistic paradigm also encourages blindness to this issue—as does the passionate commitment of certain social scientists to a rather superficial version of universal human rights. [...]

An ethnographic moment for bioethics

There are decidedly important limitations to what ethnography can achieve for bioethics. The first stems from the kind of scholarship that ethnography is. Ethnography is a backward-looking methodology. More nineteenth than twenty-first century, it starts with face-to-face engagements enabling both indirect participant observation and direct questioning with a small number of informants. And it takes time, a great deal of time: months and years, not hours, days, or even weeks. It requires rapport, trust, and intimacy. There is such a thing as rapid ethnography, especially in public health, but it is not a mainstream professional technique. And for good reason: ethnography requires the capaciousness of the book-length monograph to work out what its findings signify. It is thus an anachronistic methodology in an era of extreme space–time compression in global markets and in managed health care, or in requirements for knowledge production and intervention pressed on ethicists. Against such standards, it is seriously inefficient. Neither is it a compelling way to claim objectivity or to prove causality. But it does lend itself to laying out the social dynamics of ordinary experience in an (often) accessible manner, and it does offer a means of doing comparative analysis. In an era that is witnessing the hegemony of analyses based in economic, molecular biological, engineering, and (of course) legal framings of research questions, ethnography offers more than a certain quaint utility at getting at deeply human (real value-oriented) aspects of a wide range of subjects.

But ethnography is not something one picks up in a weekend retreat or via autodidactic readings. It is not simply a fungible methodology. It requires systematic training in anthropology (or interpretive sociology), including critical mastery of ethnographic writing and social theory; and that, too, takes time.

So how practical can it be to argue for an ethnographic moment in bioethics? In the clinical setting, the knowledge produced by this discipline seems highly appropriate for engaging the moral content both of experiences of illness, and of the professions of doctoring and nursing. That is why clinicians and clinically oriented ethicists have had an interest in ethnography. Indeed, in an earlier time I advanced an ethnographic model for caregiving itself.[5] Today, however, the dire effects on caregiving of the managerial revolution in health services and the unchallenged primacy of economic concerns, driven by the corporatization of medicine, do not encourage a sense of feasibility. Nonetheless, ethnography still seems to me appropriate as a heuristic strategy for educating medical and other health-care students about illness as human experience and about moral issues in practice. Ethnography makes unavoidable the moral requirements of doctoring, which are so easily distorted by analytic preoccupation with medicine as a business practice and caregiving as the quest for technological efficiencies. In contrast to these approaches, it describes the actual moral content of the experiences of illness and doctoring over against the sentimentalizing ideal-typical models that are now predominant.

In the complex, changing, diverse, and divisive local worlds of our era, the uneasy, divided sensibility that ethnography brings of being both within and without the flow of experience is a not inappropriate modus vivendi. The ethnographer's self-reflective criticism of her own positioning and its limitations; her hesitancy to prescribe interventions, at least until their human consequences can be better understood; her newly emergent readiness to make a commitment not just to study others, but to engage them and to witness their problems so as to be of use (based as it would be in her acutely dismayed understanding of the failure of earlier generations of field workers to do so); and her willingness to compare local processes and non-local discourse so that they can come into relation with each other—all are relevant to the thrust of argument in this paper. None of this is to make the claim that ethnography is anything like a panacea or proven preventative. Yet in the absence of any ultimate guarantee of compassion and willingness to acknowledge or respond to the suffering of others—owing to the alteration of subjectivity as worlds change—the epistemological scruples, the ontological uncertainties, and the moral sensibilities (and predicaments) of the ethnographer offer themselves up as one means, limited and unpredictable though it be, of sustaining empathy and engagement that deserves serious consideration.

That is to say, the ethnographer is "called" into the stories and lives of others by the moral process of engaged listening and by the commitment to witnessing. That call to take account of what is at stake for people becomes an instructive aspect of the ethnographer's sensibility. (Or, at least, the possibility is there for this to happen, even if it frequently does not occur.) Were this sensibility to be encouraged among ordinary men and women as a mode of moral experience (and ethical reflection), would there be the possibility of a countervailing social process in our globalized times? Could it broaden the horizon of moral imagination so as to encourage engagement with the marginal and solidarity with the afflicted? The expectation of what could be achieved would, of course, need to be more limited than these possibilities, in keeping with the modesty of an anthropological intervention that amounts to rather little when put up against the driving force of political, economic, technological, and social institutional change in our disordering epoch, or the equally dangerous political, religious, and ethnonationalist fundamentalisms that have intensified in order to resist such transformation. The only thing perhaps to recommend it is that it is the only thing I can think of that emerges from (and seems valid within) my own circumstances.

Some of us have argued for such an ethnographic moment in policy and programs directed at social suffering. The obstacles to the realization of that moment are formidable; the language of policy is so powerfully controlled by economics, decision analysis, and legal procedure that it is difficult to pry open even a small space for ethnography. Nonetheless, efforts are underway to try to produce change.[6] What I am now suggesting is that the ethnographic approach be developed more generally as a means of teaching about moral processes and examining their practical implications. How this might be accomplished in a society such as ours goes far enough beyond the limits of this exercise to suggest that it would be most prudent to break off here with merely the barest outline of this modest proposal. Yet I do think that it may well be in the sphere of applied moral theory that ethnography, notwithstanding the usual fear among ethicists about its encouragement of cultural relativism, could well hold the most promise. Such a seeming irony would be quite in keeping with the deeply human roots and consequences of ethnographic engagement. Without relinquishing my own tendency to see the future in Weberian terms as the unfolding of newer and deeper historical tragedies, I am willing to propose ethnographic sensibility as a way of living with the challenges our era has already brought us, a way that at least clarifies the magnitude and offers a means of engaging the form of that threatening future. Of course, such a change in sensibility will amount to too little too late unless it helps to usher in new political and economic policies to address the social roots of suffering.

Nonetheless, one must also admit what a complex role the ethnographer must manage. Inherent to that role, and seemingly regardless of the ethnographer's amount of experience doing fieldwork, is a set of classical structural crises that Renée Fox, among others, refers to as phase movements from over-identification with the local world, to under-identification, and finally to crises of personal identity—the consequence of the ethnographer's resocialization in different worlds and transformation of her subjectivity in situations that can be as much occasions of personal threat as occasions for psychological growth and maturation in handling values. Ethnographers often find themselves in situations that place health and life at risk. There are distinct perils and perplexities of doing ethnography. These can lead not only to distortion and even failure in the ethnographic craft, but to inner trials of the self and suffering. Ethnographers can appropriate the voices of local actors for their own purposes and can be appropriated by them. After three decades of fieldwork I have few illusions about how trying ethnography is, both as professional practice and as way of being-in-the-world. So what I am recommending is difficult and dangerous as well as uncertain in outcome, like much of ordinary social life around the world.

An ethnographic method

To bring the moral and the ethical together in the exigent setting of bioethics consultations—a rather narrow and highly focused application—I recommend consideration of a simple and admittedly limited method. Starting in the clinical setting, this ethnographic approach might exert a broader effect on bioethics as a general way of proceeding.

The ethnographer first clarifies vis-à-vis the issue at hand her own moral positioning in her lived worlds of work and domestic life. This is a mixture of self-disclosure and self-reflexivity.

The ethnographer describes the particularities of the local world she has been asked to engage. She does so by setting out three sorts of knowledge: (1) knowledge of what is locally at stake for stakeholders concerning the particular instances of health, suffering, and health care under consideration; (2) knowledge of how local parties use indigenous or global ethical framings to understand these moral processes in their own world; and (3) knowledge of how the ethnographer herself applies ethical categories to the issue at hand locally.

The ethnographer, as the instrument of interpretation and comparison, then triangulates across these different forms of knowledge to set out a framework for understanding how the intersection of moral processes and ethical discourse in this particular world defines the local human conditions of health equity and the local human consequences of health rights and responsibilities. The ethnographer should not seek a determinative understanding, which usually is illusory and can itself become an obstacle to a serviceable understanding that sustains engagement, but rather should emphasize the process of soliciting and engaging multiple perspectives as the most valid means of relating internal and external approaches.

That processual framework, with its specific implications for policies and programs, then becomes the grounds for community-wide conversations between stakeholders (e.g., laypersons and professionals), out of which will emerge an agenda for practical action. At each level, the ethnographic task is to encompass and incarnate both agonistic and antagonistic framings. It is not the ethnographer's responsibility to resolve these tensions, but rather to clarify and relate them in such a way that they can be better seen and understood and handled by participants.

The burden of responsibility placed on the ethnographer is to acknowledge and make unavoidable the engagement with alternatives that is the grounds of moral and ethical action. The limit of ethnography is that it provides no assurance or certain means of resolving this prototypical conflict. The steps I have outlined merely establish the more favorable conditions for such an outcome. Yet they also teach that "good outcomes" may not occur. This tragic sense, mixed in with the optimism of a practicable approach, is the sort of mixed knowledge ethnography can at best produce. Of course, like any useful intervention, it too can have untoward effects; and this needs to be taken into account case by case. Yet the tragic sense of the ethnographer, along with her commitment to appreciate and sustain complexity in her analytic framing of the issues at hand, may help counterbalance both excessive American optimism about how problems can be fixed and excessive reductionism of the kind of data considered to be especially relevant to policy making.[7]

Notes

1 That this question has been present from the beginning of the contemporary bioethics movement in the 1960s can be seen in a paper by one of the early formative figures in the field: James Gustafson (1965), Context versus Principles, *Harvard Theological Review*, 58: 191. That bioethicists still routinely are unable to provide useful answers can readily be seen in Ruth Macklin (1999), *Against Relativism: Cultural Diversity and the Search for Ethical Universals in Medicine*, New York: Oxford University Press. Macklin, while acknowledging cultural diversity, treats it as the anthropologist's source of unacceptable relativism, and then clears the field by making the search for universal ethical principles the only serious and supportable moral procedure. This bit of sophistry—which stereotypes and stigmatizes contextual perspectives—simply declares the problem resolved by denying that there is one. This is not an encouraging sign that bioethicists coming out of an analytic philosophy background are making much progress on this core dilemma.
2 These aspects of moral processes as social processes in local worlds are developed more fully in several of my recent publications. See Arthur Kleinman (1997), Everything that Really Matters: Social Suffering, Subjectivity, and the Remaking of Human Experience in a Disordering World, *Harvard Theological Review*, 90 (3): 315–326; and Experience and its Moral Modes: Culture, Human Conditions, and Disorder, *The Tanner Lectures on Human Values, Vol. 20*, Grethe B. Peterson (ed.), Salt Lake City, UT: University of Utah Press, 1999, pp. 355–420.
3 For example, higher-order, abstract, ethical principles like beneficence and justice tell us almost nothing about the actual moral content of most patient–doctor interactions in American society, even ones among poor patients for whom there is an unjust social distribution of health and health-care resources that precedes people's access to the clinics. These principles are simply too remote from the local grounds of experience to be of much service in actual cases, and yet at the level of the national regulatory system of policies and programs, they are obviously important.
4 Philip Gourevitch (1998), *We Wish to Inform You that Tomorrow We Will be Killed With Our Families: Stories from Rwanda*, New York: Farrar, Straus & Giroux, describes communities in Rwanda where all Hutus took part in the killing of their Tutsi neighbors and relatives; there was no internal criticism or resistance. Hence, here a translocal perspective is crucial.
5 Arthur Kleinman (1988), *The Illness Narratives: Suffering, Healing, and the Human Condition*, New York: Basic Books, Chapter 15.
6 See, for example, Robert Desjarlais et al. (1995) (eds.), *World Mental Health: Policies and Priorities in Low-Income Countries*, New York: Oxford University Press; Paul Farmer (1999), *Infections and Inequalities*, Berkeley, CA: University of California Press; and Veena Das and Arthur Kleinman (2001), Introduction, in *Remaking a World: Violence, Social Suffering, and Recovery*, Veena Das et al. (eds.), Berkeley, CA: University of California Press.
7 In closing, I had hoped to review the relationship of moral processes and ethical deliberation to religion, which also can be understood as social process (i.e., ritual and ordinary devotional practices) and institutionalized discourse (i.e., theology), and which has in the past and can in the future play a clearly crucial role in bioethics. But this proved too much for a short paper to support and so will be the subject of another essay.

Practical tensions

33 Culpability and reparation

Nandini Sundar

Nandini Sundar (born in 1967) is a professor of sociology at the Delhi School of Economics, having previously taught at Jawaharlal Nehru University and the University of Edinburgh. Her anthropological works focus on questions of inequality and environment in India, on which she has notably published *Branching Out: Joint Forest Management in India* and *Sovereigns and Subalterns: An Anthropological History of Bastar*. She has conducted ethnographical and historical research in the state of Chhattisgarh among the Adivasi, a scheduled tribe, where she developed an engaged approach around the issues of social protection, education and rights more generally, which led her to bring legal action against the government. Her reflection also concerns the development of the social sciences outside of the Western world and she was co-editor of the book *Anthropology in the East: The Founders of Indian Sociology and Anthropology*.

In the text from which extracts are presented here, Nandini Sundar examines the consequences, for a political anthropology that focuses on moral issues, of the author belonging either to a Western academic tradition or to the national scientific tradition of the country in question. In particular, regarding the rhetorical and judicial mechanisms that have developed over recent decades around forgiveness, truth, justice, reparation, and human rights more generally, she criticises the often optimistic and even self-congratulatory way to consider these innovations as the product of moral progress carried by liberal ideology without recognising its incoherency, hypocrisy and double standards. Examining the positions of the different agents in function of their cultural and historical dispositions, Nandini Sundar raises the question of anthropologists' role in the construction of an international morality.

The problem for anthropology really is that its most powerful practitioners do not yet realize that the discipline is no longer the preserve of the West but, rather, is a global phenomenon inflected by national histories of scholarship. One indication of this problem is that whereas most Western, particularly U.S., scholars claim the unmarked category "anthropologist" for themselves and "anthropology" for their discipline, those of us in the academic peripheries refer to ourselves and are referred to by our national denominations, for example, as "Indian anthropologists." When Cynthia Mahmood compares anthropologists to missionaries and justifies anthropological engagement with violence as a spiritual impulse, she ignores the fact that many non-Western anthropologists have also initiated studies of suffering, violence, or state terror.[1] The "places that anthropologists go to" or the "people that anthropologists study" have for some time now not been "foreign" but their own homes or people like themselves. Passages like the following are unlikely to endear U.S. or European anthropologists to those of us at the "ends of the earth": "Why do so many of us risk life and limb to venture to the ends of the earth, suffer enormous privation and delays of career and family, collect tropical diseases as other people collect stamps, all for salaries that often barely support us and a field whose value is barely recognized by the outside world? Reflections on our motivation, by African campfires or Arctic starlight, show it is surely not the adventure nor the intellectual curiosity alone. There is more to the ethnographic enterprise: I believe a sort of—dare I say it—spiritual impulse, that was recognized in the early days of our discipline but now lies unlabelled beneath the determined demeanours of those young students bravely going off to Palestine or to Colombia, to face new kinds of fieldwork and new kinds of dangers."[2]

Why indeed? I argue here that rather than attempting to save the souls of others, anthropologists' primary task today must be to widen public understanding of what it means to be human. This involves turning the same lens by which we examine Others on ourselves, wherever we stand in the global contours of the discipline. To do this we must put bricolage, juxtaposition, and comparison—between the "West" and the "rest"—at the heart of the ethnographic research and teaching enterprise. Although this idea was mooted at least two decades ago,[3] and hybridity is the name of the fashionable identity game, in fact very little has been done in the direction of exploring cultures refracted in the common light of globally traveling discourses of terror, war, economic rationality, or even human rights. [...]

In recent years, the world has witnessed a number of demands for the redress of historical injustices and some remarkable acceptances of culpability. Some instances have involved crimes against individual groups within a state (e.g., the U.S. government's reparations to Japanese Americans for internment during World War II, the Australian and Canadian governments' recognition of the harm done to their Native populations through forcible acts of assimilation and expropriation). Others have international dimensions, involving crimes against foreign citizens (Japanese reparations to Korean "comfort women," Clinton's "apology" for supporting the military junta in Guatemala) or crimes that have resulted in the relocation of people from one state to another (e.g., German reparations to Jews, demands for reparations for slavery). Some demands are directed by groups to institutions within their own country, such as the Native American and Canadian First Nations' demand that museums return human skeletal remains and sacred objects to them, whereas in other cases the demand for restoration of looted treasures has become a matter between two countries. In a broader perspective, the trend toward setting up truth commissions (as in Guatemala or South Africa) or war crimes tribunals (as for Rwanda or the former Yugoslavia) is equally an attempt to identify culpability and to repair social fractures. According to Marc Gibney and Erik Roxstrom, "The apology phenomenon is best viewed as part of a much larger effort at seeking, establishing, and understanding the truth, exemplified in the myriad of truth commissions that have been created throughout the world."[4]

Why have retributive justice and reparations become important at this moment in time, some half a century after the Nuremberg Trials first placed these questions on the international agenda? Several scholars have argued optimistically that the recent wave of apologies and demands for reparations signals a real change in the international political order, the emergence of a new international morality and a triumph of human rights discourse.[5] John Torpey notes that reparations have been: "an essential complement to the spread of human rights ideas. This is because reparations help to make the notion of human rights seem real and enforceable in the absence of a global police force empowered to back rights claims with armed might."[6] Laura Hein argues in the context of reparations that "the key postwar legal transformation has been the growing consensus that individuals—not just states—have standing in international law."[7] Alan Cairns talks of a "postimperial" world order in which, through the mechanism of apologies and reparations, previously voiceless people are now asserting their histories and humankind as a whole is "coming to terms with its past."[8] Even while recognizing the serious limitations of Clinton's apology to the Guatemalan people, Gibney and Roxstrom argue: "the transnational state apology serves as a special kind of truth commission in the sense that it has become the western states' vehicle for acknowledging their own involvement (or, in the case of Rwanda, non-involvement) in some of the world's horrors.[9] Finally, in his much praised account of the history of war crimes tribunals, Gary Bass argues that such proceedings are the outcome of domestic liberalism extended to international politics: "Liberal ideals make liberal states take up the cause of international justice."[10]

There have been other explanations, too, of a more sociological, historical, or psychological nature—for instance, locating the wave of reparations in the transition from authoritarianism to democracy,[11] the rise of a historical consciousness as an essential part of modernity and the emergence of many little histories that challenge the notion of a unitary nation-state and a unitary history,[12] and the loss of a transformative vision for the future and the rise of narrow ethnicities.[13] Voices like Charles Maier's, however, are minor compared with the triumphalist crescendo connecting state apologies, reparations, restitution, reconciliation, truth commissions, and international war crimes tribunals to a victory for liberal morality and "new human rights standards"[14] as institutionalized mainly in Western states. This liberal morality may be defined broadly as respect for individual life, liberty, and property.

To some extent it is true that the discourse of reparations, apologies, and the like is a marker of morality in international relations because it signals acceptance of the principle that there must be justice for wrongs committed. It is also important to note that the demand for justice—for reconciliation, reparation—and, indeed, the notion of human rights more generally have roots as deep in the non-West as in the West. When commentators reiterate the common claim that notions of rights or humane governance came from "Greek, Stoic and Christian roots"[15] or debate cultural relativism and human rights in terms of the conflict between Western values and non-Western cultures,[16] they ignore other traditions. Ultimately, however, origins do not matter. Edward Said points out that ideas (and people) travel across geographical boundaries: "What matters a great deal more than the stable identity kept current in official discourse is the contestatory force of an interpretative method whose material is the disparate but intertwined and interdependent, and above all overlapping streams of human experience."[17]

Critical to the interpretative method Said talks about are analyses of historical time and context or what certain ideologies set out to silence as much as what they promote.[18] As in any sociological study of practical morality—apart from philosophical debates over its origins in moral realism, emotivism, utilitarianism, and the like—scholars need to subject the phenomenon of reparations and its ideology to deeper excavations. As Karl Marx pointed out long ago, although bourgeois citizenship and its concomitant morality of rights was an advance over feudalism, it was not enough as long as citizenship or rights in the political community were "degraded ... to a mere means for the preservation of the so-called rights of man" or private property rights in civil society.[19]

Applied to the reparations context, until a more thorough-going transformation of national and international systems is achieved, portraying reparations claims collectively as part of a new international morality becomes part of a self-congratulatory liberal understanding that allows real and ongoing inequalities and injustices to go unchallenged. Without minimizing the justness of existing calls for reparation and the struggles of those who are making these demands, the most important effect, perhaps, of the contemporary conduct of the international discourse of restitution, public apologies, and international tribunals for war crimes has been to legitimate powerful states. The implicit message sent out by Western states is that the behavior giving rise to the need for apologies is a thing of the past as far as they are concerned and that the only present-day acts warranting prosecutions and the establishment of tribunals are those by "rogue" states, such acts often necessitating military intervention by the West. In the case of international tribunals for war crimes or of truth commissions, the predominance of First World judges or prosecutors sitting in judgment on Second or Third World criminals, while ignoring the liability of their own or allied countries for war crimes or complicity in violence, cannot but fail to reinforce this perception. If international morality is to mean something more than the self-serving prejudice of powerful states, scholars must explore the political economy of restitution claims and tribunals in a comparative perspective. One needs to ask why and how certain groups succeed in having their demands taken seriously and others do not, or why certain prosecutions of war are recognized as giving rise to war crimes whereas others are not.

Even were one to take claims to a new morality on their own terms, however, and admit that moral disagreements are possible primarily because of the existence of shared moral traditions that transcend cultures, the nature of differences here is troubling. The moral reasoning involved in reparation claims admits of several different and difficult-to-resolve issues. First, there is the question of distributive justice across time: Whereas some liberal philosophers tend to discuss this issue in terms of the responsibility of individuals for the sins of their ancestors,[20] others have pointed to the continuing disadvantage of certain groups or to the continuity in state structures as a reason for the state and not for individuals to own guilt and provide reparation.[21] The second problematic issue is that of the appropriate unit of reparation—whether entire countries, communities, or individuals.

A third problem for the anthropologist concerned with morality is the clash between new entitlements due to need or labor invested and old entitlements based on expropriation. As Maier notes, it is not immediately obvious whether "a handsome private villa that for several decades has found a new life as a kindergarten or communal facility be returned to descendants who have never seemed to need the asset."[22] Given the same basic principle, public discourse is framed very differently depending on the subjects of restitution and their relative economic and political power. Take, for example, the differences in Western media coverage and the attitude of international financial institutions when restitution involves privatization (as in Eastern Europe) versus a situation involving collectives (e.g., Australian Aboriginals) or currently disadvantaged individuals (e.g., black demands for white farms in Zimbabwe).

Even where restitution works in favor of groups who owe their continuing disadvantage to initial acts of violence, the implications for contemporary equity are not always clear: For instance, a recent domicile bill in the Indian state of Jharkhand proposed to grant priority in government recruitment to applicants whose ancestors were listed in the 1931 settlement records. This bill was struck down by the High Court but not before it became a contentious issue, with many long-term settlers and working-class immigrants claiming that their citizenship rights were being denied and indigenist advocates claiming the "historic necessity" of restoring rights to indigenous peoples. The poor are usually pitted against the poor—in the struggle for jobs, for land, and for identity; one is scarcely ever afforded the luxury of a clear class struggle.

Restitution claims also raise questions of memory and representation: how historical injustices are framed and transmitted in national history texts and popular narratives; how the symbols of a nation—for example, monuments, founding days, flags, and anthems—are implicated in previous histories of conquest and violence; and whether restitution privileges certain moments in history as against others.[23] The histories demanded by criminal trials may differ in quite significant respects from historian's histories, in which attributions of culpability may be less black and white or more evenly distributed between perpetrator and victim groups.[24] It is not clear how morality and the cause of deterrence are better served by seeing history through the prism of a courtroom trial rather than through a historian's pen. Audrey Chapman and Patrick Ball[25] also show how the "truth" that emerges from truth commissions is framed through seemingly "technical" issues like the choice of commissioners, the model and methods they employ, and the manner in which they select and present materials. In the South African case, given Archbishop Tutu's commitment to reconciliation, "by giving white victims space in hearings far beyond their proportion of statement-givers and out of proportion to their level of victimization, the TRC created the truth that the 'children' of all races suffered violations more or less equally."[26] The contribution of such "truths" to the process of healing and the cause of justice is thus debatable.[27]

Some scholars have questioned whether truth commissions or international tribunals, given their focus on individual legal responsibility, can address the issue of societal breakdowns of morality, or what Mark Osiel calls "the uncertain line between culpable and inculpable parties."[28] Some state legislation has begun to address this issue: For instance, the Rwandan Organic Law of 1996 on the prosecution of offenses for genocide or crimes against humanity distinguishes among four different categories of perpetrators—from masterminds to those who engaged only in stealing and damaging property.[29] Yet as Stef Vandeginste, Laurel Fletcher and Harvey Weinstein,[30] and others have shown, international tribunals have serious limitations in dealing with the issue of mass involvement in violence. Truth commissions assume that once ordinary people—as opposed to state leaders, top-ranking officials, and so on—learn the full horror of what was being done in their names, perpetrator remorse will be part of a national reconciliation process.[31] This assumption does not appear to be necessarily borne out, and reconciliation increasingly seems another name for impunity. Fletcher and Weinstein, who studied responses of judges and prosecutors to war crimes trials in Bosnia, found that the trials did not have the desired effect in terms of reconciliation and healing—on the contrary, "universally individuals identified their national groups as victims."[32] They also "question whether individualized guilt may contribute to a myth of collective innocence" and argue that there is a "collective nature to mass violence" that must be understood on its own terms and not in the legally permissible terms of individualized guilt and responsibility. They call, therefore, for the integration of criminal trials into "broader initiatives in rule of law, humanitarian assistance, democracy building and economic development."[33]

Equally serious, apologies for particularly egregious acts of colonialism, for example, Blair's expression of regret for England's complicity in the Irish potato famine, might falsely suggest that such acts were aberrations in an otherwise humane system.[34] Various crimes, moreover, find no mention in the growing list of acts for which recognition is demanded as crimes against humanity, among them, the bombing of Hiroshima and Nagasaki. As Justice Radhabinod Pal had noted in his dissenting judgment in the Tokyo war crimes trial: "If any indiscriminate destruction of civilian life and property is still legitimate in warfare, then, in the Pacific war, this decision to use the atom bomb is the only near approach to the directives of the German Emperor during the first world war and of the Nazi leaders during the second world war."[35] What makes the bombing of Japan even worse is that, in the words of one U.S. military historian, "The bomb was not needed to avoid an invasion of Japan and to end the war within a relatively short time. Alternatives to the bomb existed and Truman and his advisers knew it."[36]

Surely, the inscription of certain sufferings as more deserving than others cannot help in the creation of a new international morality. As Wole Soyinka notes, the redress of injustices like the 1492 edict that evicted Jews from Spain, while negating the demand for reparations for slavery on the grounds of limitation by time, seems a fresh injustice: "Justice must be made manifest either for all, or not at all."[37] But most importantly, if "reparations ... serve as a cogent critique of history and thus a potent restraint on its repetition," how does one understand the frequent replay of actions that should have belonged firmly in the past? For instance, the U.S. government apology to Japanese Americans for internment in World War II by implication suggests that the state no longer targets populations within its midst on grounds of suspect nationalism, an idea that is increasingly doubtful post-September 11, given the profiling of Muslim men.[38] Apologies for the Tuskegee experiments conceal the way in which, as Eduardo Galeano writes, "the environmental map is also a racial map. The most polluting factories and the most dangerous dumps are located in the pockets of poverty where blacks, Indians and Latinos live."[39]

To summarize, the reparations phenomenon only raises a series of moral questions that attend acts of injustice. It does not, as yet, point to anything like common or equitable international norms, unless one accepts norms that encode inequality in their very being. Much more needs to be done in the direction of a comparative political economy of claims and achievements than is currently envisaged in the literature if scholars and activists are to use this phenomenon to advance a common humanity.

Notes

1 See, for instance, Daniel, E. Valentine (1996), *Charred Lullabies: Chapters in an Anthropography of Violence*, Princeton: Princeton University Press; Das, Veena (1990), Introduction: Communities, Riots, Survivors – The South Asian Experience, in *Mirrors of Violence: Communities, Riots and Survivors in South Asia*, Das, Veena (ed.), Delhi: Oxford University Press, pp. 1–36; some of the anthropologists referred to by Sluka, Jeffrey A. (2000), Introduction: State Terror and Anthropology, in *Death Squad: The Anthropology of State Terror*, Sluka, Jeffrey (ed.), Philadelphia: University of Pennsylvania Press, p. 24.

2 Mahmood, Cynthia Keppley (2002), Anthropological Compulsions in a World in Crisis, *Anthropology Today*, 18 (3): 1.
3 Marcus, George E., and Michael M. J. Fischer (1986), *Anthropology as Cultural Critique: An Experimental Moment in the Human Sciences*, Chicago: University of Chicago Press.
4 Gibney, Marc, and Erik Roxstrom (2001), The Status of State Apologies, *Human Rights Quarterly*, 23 (4): 937.
5 Vandeginste, Stef (2003), Victims of Genocide, Crimes against Humanity, and War Crimes in Rwanda: The Legal and Institutional Framework of Their Right to Reparation, in *Politics and the Past: On Repairing Historical Injustices*, Torpey, John (ed.), Lanham, MD: Rowman and Littlefield, p. 251.
6 Torpey, John (2003), Introduction: Politics and the Past, in *Politics and the Past: On Repairing Historical Injustices*, Torpey, John (ed.), Lanham, MD: Rowman and Littlefield, p. 5.
7 Hein, Laura (2003), War Compensation: Claims against the Japanese Government and Japanese Corporations for War Crimes, in *Politics and the Past: On Repairing Historical Injustices*, Torpey, John (ed.), Lanham, MD: Rowman and Littlefield, p. 131.
8 Cairns, Alan (2003), Coming to Terms with the Past, in *Politics and the Past: On Repairing Historical Injustices*, Torpey, John (ed.), Lanham, MD: Rowman and Littlefield, p. 68.
9 Gibney and Roxstrom (2001), The Status of State Apologies, op. cit., pp. 937–938.
10 Bass, Gary Jonathan (2000), *Stay the Hand of Vengeance: The Politics of War Crimes Tribunals*, Princeton: Princeton University Press, p. 18.
11 Huntington, Samuel P. (1993), *The Third Wave: Democratization in the Late Twentieth Century*, Norman: University of Oklahoma Press.
12 Olick, Jeffrey K., and Brenda Coughlin (2003), The Politics of Regret: Analytical Frames, in *Politics and the Past: On Repairing Historical Injustices*, Torpey, John (ed.), Lanham, MD: Rowman and Littlefield, pp. 37–62.
13 Maier, Charles S. (1993), A Surfeit of Memory? Reflections on History, Melancholy and Denial, *History and Memory*, 5 (2): 136–152.
14 Gibney and Roxstrom (2001), The Status of State Apologies, op. cit., p. 915.
15 Falk, Richard (1992), Theoretical Foundations of Human Rights, in *Human Rights in the World Community*, Claude, Richard Pierre and Burns H. Weston (eds.), Philadelphia: University of Pennsylvania Press, p. 32.
16 Perry, Michael J. (1997), Are Human Rights Universal? The Relativist Challenge and Related Matters, *Human Rights Quarterly*, 19 (3): 461–509; Tesón, Fernando R. (1992), International Human Rights and Cultural Relativism, in *Human Rights in the World Community*, Claude, Richard Pierre and Burns H. Weston (eds.), Philadelphia: University of Pennsylvania Press, pp. 42–52.
17 Said, Edward (1994), *Covering Islam: How the Media and the Experts Determine How We See the Rest of the World*, New York: Pantheon Books, p. 312.
18 See, e.g., Iyer, Raghavan (1960), *Utilitarianism and All That: The Political Theory of British Imperialism in India*, St. Anthony's Papers, 8, London: Chatto & Windus; Arneil, Barbara (1996), The Wild Indian's Venison: Locke's Theory of Property and English Colonialism in America, *Political Studies*, 44 (1): 60–74.
19 Marx, Karl (1977), On the Jewish Question, in *Karl Marx: Selected Writings*, McLellan, David (ed.), Oxford: Oxford University Press, pp. 39–62.
20 See Thompson, Janna (2001), Historical Injustice and Reparation: Justifying Claims of Descendants, *Ethics*, 112: 114–135; Wheeler, Samuel C. (1997), Reparations Reconstructed, *American Philosophical Quarterly*, 34 (3): 301–318.
21 On the continuity of personnel from the Nazi state to the Federal Republic of Germany, see Perels, Joachim (1993), Those Who Refused to Go Along Left Their Country in the Lurch: The Resistance Is Also Being Reassessed in the Historikerstreit, in *Forever in the Shadow of Hitler? Original Documents of the Historikerstreit, the Controversy Concerning the Singularity of the Holocaust*, Knowlton, James and Truett Cates (eds.), Atlantic Highlands, NJ: Humanities Press, p. 252.
22 Maier, Charles S. (2003), Overcoming the Past? Narrative and Negotiation, Remembering and Reparation: Issues at the Interface of History and the Law, in *Politics and the Past: On Repairing Historical Injustices*, Torpey, John (ed.), Lanham, MD: Rowman and Littlefield, p. 297.
23 Maier (1993), A Surfeit of Memory, op. cit.; Minow, Martha (2002), *Breaking the Cycles of Hatred: Memory, Law and Repair*, Princeton: Princeton University Press; and Torpey (2003), Introduction, op. cit.

24 Arendt, Hannah (1963), *Eichmann in Jerusalem*, London: Faber and Faber; Rousso, Henry (2003), Justice, History and Memory in France: Reflections on the Papon Trial, in *Politics and the Past: On Repairing Historical Injustices*, Torpey, John (ed.), Lanham, MD: Rowman and Littlefield, pp. 277–294.
25 Chapman, Audrey R., and Patrick Ball (2001), The Truth of Truth Commissions: Comparative Lessons from Haiti, South Africa and Guatemala, *Human Rights Quarterly*, 23 (1): 1–43.
26 Chapman and Ball (2001), The Truth of Truth, op. cit., p. 40.
27 See also Osiel, Mark J. (2000), Why Prosecute? Critics of Punishment for Mass Atrocity, *Human Rights Quarterly*, 22 (1): 137; Wilson, Richard (2001), *The Politics of Truth and Reconciliation in South Africa: Legitimizing the Post-Apartheid State*, Cambridge: Cambridge University Press.
28 Osiel (2000), Why Prosecute, op. cit., pp. 125–129.
29 Vandeginste (2003), Victims of Genocide, op. cit., p. 255.
30 Fletcher, Laurel E., and Harvey M. Weinstein (2002), Violence and Social Repair: Rethinking the Contribution of Justice to Reconciliation, *Human Rights Quarterly*, 24 (3): 573–639.
31 Minow, Martha (1998), *Between Vengeance and Forgiveness: Facing History after Genocide and Mass Violence*, Boston: Beacon Press.
32 Fletcher and Weinstein (2002), Violence and Social Repair, op. cit., p. 581.
33 Fletcher and Weinstein (2002), Violence and Social Repair, op. cit., pp. 580–581.
34 Gibney and Roxstrom (2001), The Status of State Apologies, op. cit., p. 933.
35 Minear, Richard H. (1971), *Victors' Justice: The Tokyo War Crimes Trial*, Princeton: Princeton University Press, 1971, pp. 100–101.
36 Walker, J. Samuel (1995), in Alperovitz, Gar, *The Decision to Use the Atomic Bomb and the Architecture of an American Myth*, New York: Alfred Knopf, p. 7.
37 Soyinka, Wole (1999), *The Burden of Memory, the Muse of Forgiveness*, Oxford: Oxford University Press, pp. 91 and 84.
38 American Civil Liberties Union (2002), *Insatiable Appetite: The Government's Demand for New and Unnecessary Powers after September 11*. Electronic document, accessed July 1, 2003, www.aclu.org/SafeandFree/SafeandFree.cfm?ID=10623&c=207; Cole, David (2003), *Enemy Aliens: Double Standards and Constitutional Freedoms in the War on Terrorism*, New York: New Press; Lewis, Anthony (2003), Un-American Activities, *New York Review of Books*, 50 (16): 16–19.
39 Galeano, Eduardo (2000), *Upside Down: A Primer for the Looking-Glass World*, trans. by Mark Fried, New York: Metropolitan Books, p. 221; see also Kuletz, Valerie (2001), Invisible Spaces, Violent Places: Cold War Nuclear and Militarized Landscapes, in *Violent Environments*, Peluso, Nancy Lee and Michael Watts (eds.), Ithaca, NY: Cornell University Press, pp. 237–260.

34 Development and assistance

Erica Bornstein

Erica Bornstein (born in 1963) is an associate professor in anthropology at the University of Wisconsin-Milwaukee. Her research focuses on solidarity in two very different cultural contexts. In *The Spirit of Development: Protestant NGOs, Morality and Economics in Zimbabwe*, she looked at the development aid provided to African populations by two Protestant NGOs. In *Disquieting Gifts: Humanitarianism in New Delhi*, she studied the meaning of the gift in Indian society. In other words, while in both cases the question of charity was part of a religious framework, in the first one the actions taken were external, whereas in the second they were internal to the society in question. Erica Bornstein also co-edited the book *Forces of Compassion: Humanitarianism Between Ethics and Politics* with Peter Redfield.

The research she carried out in Zimbabwe, a fragment of which is presented here, considers two Christian non-governmental organisations with international programmes – World Vision and Christian Care. Their proselytising is grounded in concrete assistance provided in poor regions of the third world and they implement moral principles in the daily life of the members of the communities they help. Extending the Weberian analysis of the relationship between economy and religion, Erica Bornstein shows how Protestant ideas insinuate themselves into this development work and how this discourse is shaped by neoliberal conceptions of the individual. More specifically, she analyses the moral tensions between the suspicion raised by economic success within the local populations and the perspective of the international organisations that make this success morally acceptable.

In the work of World Vision and Christian Care, moral categories of good and evil provided an interpretive frame for economic activity. Christian development constituted categories—of the developed and the undeveloped, the "evangelized" Christian and the "unreached"—and inspired tensions over these categories. Perhaps all development, secular and religious alike,[1] makes distinctions between human beings and attempts to make new persons in the process. Development discourse is itself relational and morally charged, reconstituting the previously existing ethical ground in the lives of those who do the "developing" and those who are "being developed."[2] For employees of religious NGOs in Zimbabwe, the danger of witchcraft lurked in this morally charged ground.

In development efforts, the evil of witchcraft was framed by the goodness of Christianity; the two were bound together. Witchcraft interfered with and "retarded" development. Christian development workers simultaneously saw witchcraft in

274 *Erica Bornstein*

evolutionary terms as "backward" and acknowledged it as part of the lived present. Their trajectory was at first glance teleological, and seemed a reproduction of modernist narratives of progress and "stages" of development. With further scrutiny, however, I saw how the dichotomous categories of good and evil, and the apparent contradictions of Christianity and witchcraft, coexisted. Embedded within the development discourse of benevolent progress existed its inverse: the evil of Satan and witchcraft.

In this chapter, I examine these moral tensions from what may initially seem like two competing perspectives. First is the Zimbabwean view of morally correct economic behavior that de-emphasized the successes of individuals. My neighbor in Harare, for example, a young Zimbabwean man, explained how doing well in Zimbabwe was suspect. He said, "In the rural areas, if you are doing very well [economically] people suspect you of doing witchcraft. People will say, in response to someone's success: 'How can he be doing so well when other people are not?'" Second is the view of World Vision and Christian Care employees who attempted to make the material successes of individuals morally acceptable as they trained people to do well economically. In the development work of World Vision and Christian Care, the contradiction between these two perspectives was not resolved. Rather, it was given a discursive space for negotiation. Christian NGOs, with their explicit religious agendas, gave voice to moral forces of economic development—to teleological striving for progress, and to the malevolent forces of demon spirits. Unlike so-called "secular" agencies, religious NGOs offered a language to discuss conflicts such as jealousies and witchcraft, and they offered the possible resolution of these conflicts through Christianity.

A bookkeeper's story

At a rural economic development project in northwestern Zimbabwe an employee of World Vision was attacked by a demon. The project bookkeeper, a young man of twenty-eight, had grown up in the community that housed the development project. Elected by his neighbors and hired by World Vision, he monitored the daily activities of rural development, including the initiation of irrigation schemes, the introduction of water and sanitation programs, and the building of schools. Such examples of participation were part of progressive trends in development that were thought to move away from West-centered models and to place the directives of development in the hands of the people being developed. They were manifestations of "participation from within." One evening, while walking home from the project office, he was suddenly struck by an illness that rendered him paralyzed and unable to speak. After seeking help from doctors who could not cure him, he went to a traditional healer, a *n'anga*, who told him that an evil spirit called a *chikwambo* (pl: *zvikwambo*) had been sent to kill him. During an interview, conducted after he had recovered, I asked the bookkeeper why the *chikwambo* had tried to kill him. He explained, "Now they [community members] say, 'he is developed and he is proud of himself.' It wanted to kill me because they say, 'he is proud.'" The community had elected him the World Vision project bookkeeper. "I grew up in this community and they are the ones who voted for me," he explained. The *n'anga* told the bookkeeper that the person who sent the *chikwambo* was jealous. The bookkeeper said: "In development we are seeing a lot of things, because the first thing, it is hard to bring the community together. There are some of them who don't participate, so to bring them together you have to mobilize people. The way you mobilize the people could even make the *chikwambo* to come to you, because other people don't know they are being helped ... People say, 'He is doing such and such and we should fix him.'" This bookkeeper was grateful to have survived his encounter with a *chikwambo*. He employed the *n'anga* to kill the *chikwambo*, and he gradually recovered his speech, but the moral tensions underlying economic development remained.

The story of the bookkeeper's malady was recounted to me repeatedly on separate occasions by staff in World Vision's Zimbabwe national office in Harare. His experience was a social drama held in institutional memory, cast and recast as an emblem of the link between religion and development. His experience marked the social and spiritual dangers of economic development, as well as the appropriate (Christian) moral stance necessary to combat them. When the story was told to me by World Vision field officers, it was narrated as a straightforward series of events: the bookkeeper at the development project had been attacked by a demon; he was physically paralyzed, he found himself unable to speak; the cause was witchcraft. However, there was a subtext to this story. As a young man, the bookkeeper's status placed him in jeopardy with regard to his community. His new position incurred the jealousy of elder community members who were bypassed for the position. Months after the bookkeeper's recovery, I met with him and he offered his story. While recounting his battle with forces of change and community, he expressed a tremendous sadness. It had been a difficult ordeal and things had not become much easier afterward. [...]

When I was told about the bookkeeper's predicament by the World Vision field officer responsible for this region, she acknowledged that it had happened, but expressed concern that he had gone to a *n'anga* for assistance. God, the Christian God, was where Christian NGO workers were supposed to turn for assistance. For the Harare staff of World Vision, the bookkeeper's acts were examples of how easy it was for rural project staff to slip in belief, to fall from Christianity "back [into] traditional ways."[3] The bookkeeper was not quite "developed enough." Being developed, for the upper (urban) echelons of Christian NGOs, was like being "converted" in the colonial era: it meant being economically successful, self-sufficient, and Christian. Here Christian field workers echoed the civilizing mission of earlier eras. Yet, for the bookkeeper, *zvikwambo* (pl.) were part of a daily reality. They were a threat posed by the community, and they were precisely a product of development. Without his job as bookkeeper, he would not have inspired jealousy from the community. Without World Vision and Christianity, a *chikwambo* would not have been sent to harm him. For the bookkeeper, there was no contradiction between Christianity and his visit to a *n'anga*. A Catholic, he did not see himself as less Christian for treating his affliction with the mediation of a *n'anga*'s skills. The *n'anga* was simply able to solve the problem, and God (a Christian God) helped the *n'anga* to do that. Religion, whether Shona religion or NGO-inspired Christianity, was an integral component of development, and of a person's economic successes or failures in relation to the community in which he or she lived. [...]

The dangers of doing well

In Shona, the word for development, *budiriro*, is also the word for physical and material success. Yet, as much as Christianity in Zimbabwe carried with it implicit narratives of faith in action—trust, honesty, and benevolence—the ways development was interpreted in local contexts manifested more than a simple munificent moral outcome. Good and evil were locked in an intimate embrace in Zimbabwe. Trust and honesty implied the potential for their opposites. Desire, greed, and envy were the flip sides of moderation, generosity, and contentedness, and they coexisted, one calling upon the other through its silence.

At the time of my research in 1997, Zimbabwe's national economy was fraught with rising inflation. IMF–World Bank–state collaboration in "structural adjustment," including programs of privatization and market liberalization, polarized economic relations between individuals. Differences between wealthy and impoverished people were exaggerated to new extremes. Development took place in this context, and hailed those who were "needy" and those who must be "developed." Newspapers during my fieldwork continued to document a climate of economic hardship, and this was made clearer through the strikes and protests that spilled onto the streets daily. People struggled to feed their families in the face of rising inflation. With new wealth in Zimbabwe came new perspectives on poverty—ones that emphasized the violence and frustrations of economic inequality. In this climate of rapid economic change and increasing inequity, Christianity embraced the moral dimensions of development and made wealth more respectable. It simultaneously articulated inherent contradictions and provided solutions. In the Shona press, the weekly newspaper, *Kwayedza*, was filled with stories of people struggling to negotiate the religious and moral terrain of economic development. One article, in March of 1997, described how a dam that had recently been constructed was morally dangerous. It told of children dying while trying to cross it. The explanation given by the author was that the dam had not been made "Shona" through ancestral rituals. Since it was still "English" (the product of international development efforts), it was evil. "Good development" in this context was local, "indigenous" development. It was development from within. It was development that acknowledged local spiritual realities and the role of the supernatural, phenomena invisible to secular development agencies. My Shona tutor and research assistant helped me to read stories in the vernacular press about people rumored to have killed children in order to help their businesses. One story was about a family that owned a successful bus transport business. People in the village were certain that this family had used *muti* to become successful. The proof was in their son, who was crazy and acted like a bus, walking around making bus noises, asking people to get on like a driver. There were rumors circulating of taxis in town that talked, and said things such as "Oh, I'm tired," as if the spirits of the children killed to help the owner of the taxi business were speaking. This witchcraft accusation framed the material successes of individuals as morally suspect. [...]

In addition to sanctifying life at development projects, Christianity made business "good" in the Harare offices of Christian NGOs. In response to my asking what made NGOs Christian, people said repeatedly that it was the relationship of Christianity to trust. To be a Christian business meant to be a trustworthy business. With a Christian business, there was less likelihood of embezzlement, theft, or other evil associated with personal gain. Christian money was good money. Aside from using the life of Jesus as a motivational model for their development work, NGOs emphasized that to have money, as a Christian business, was to be able to improve one's life in order to help people. It was not associated with wealth at the expense of others (as in the case of witchcraft and *muti*). Since the objectives of Christian development were benevolent, it was benevolent prosperity. For example, an employee from the Mennonite

Economic Development Association (MEDA) explained that "the [Christian] environment at work is crucial and influential, [we have] devotions every day in the morning from 8:00 to 8:30. ... If you are living with Christ, everything becomes very simple. To be productive, [you] need teamwork, there must be peace, which is what we preach every day. The word of God tells us how to approach difficult relationships." Faith, in the work of religious NGOs in Zimbabwe, was described to me as a context, an environment of expectations, and a set of ideal principles that guided the workday world. It delineated the work of development. The topic of faith and development was difficult to discuss with people, and variable in expression. Faith was belief in a supernatural world, in the good icons of Christianity: God, Jesus, the Holy Spirit, and the evil manifestations of its challenge. The MEDA employee continued to explain the relation of Christianity to good business by emphasizing that the work of the Christian NGO should "portray the Christian element of our environment," specifically, "the ability to accept difficulties, being honest, being faithful, being considerate to other people." He said, "Money is to improve your life, not for profit, but to [create] a situation whereby you can help other people." This Christian benevolence in turn inspired others to follow Christianity. He explained, "We are doing a lot in helping the unemployed in Zimbabwe; the way we help people will also attract other people, and at the end of the day people will be interested in knowing something about Christ." The faith of Christian development was evangelical. It involved trust in a Christian business ethic, a Weberian Protestant ethic. The employee from MEDA said, "Trust, being Christian. ... the whole thing rests on faithfulness, and being trustworthy. [Good business means] no kind of cheating is expected, trust is being faithful and honest. Christianity is a kind of communication." Christianity gave principles to business, which might otherwise be seen as greedy or avaricious. "You have to be a person of principles. In business there is a lot of profit, corruption. As a Christian, before you do any transaction you use Christian principles." Christian business was good business—profitable, successful, and morally sound. Christianity, in turn, shaped business—not only the ethic of conducting oneself economically, but the industry of development as well. [...]

Before working for ZECLOF, the Zimbabwean Ecumenical Church Loan Fund, and being appointed to the governing board of Christian Care, the chairman had worked for the Zimbabwean state in a parastatal lending organization that administered small loans to facilitate post-independence development efforts, and worked very much like ZECLOF. However, there was a difference between his experience working for a church-based Christian organization and his experience with the state, which had to do with the association of Christianity with honesty in business conduct. My point here is that the capitalism advocated by development programs, when identified with Christianity, strove to release itself from an association with evil in the Zimbabwean cultural context. Whether or not it achieved these aims is not pertinent. Of significance is that discursively the tendency of capitalism to inspire greed and personal gain at the expense of others was transformed into traits of benevolence and honesty. Not only did these traits redefine economic activity, they reinforced the power of Christianity in people's lives.

Development discourse, with its cult of rational actors and its emphasis on individual progress, with its Protestant ethic inspiring and demanding work and individualism, did not simply unleash evil, like bats out of Weber's iron cage. It also did not inspire evil, as if it were some moral reaction to the conditions of development itself. Rather, development discourse carried within it the moralizing forces of both good and evil, and the language to describe it in these terms. Christian development, with its dichotomous moral categories of "good" progress and "evil" backwardness (read heathenism, traditionalism, superstition, corruption, etc.), echoed the discourse of progress articulated by missionaries in the colonial era.[4] As we have seen in the case of Christian NGOs in Zimbabwe, the evil of witchcraft was not produced by progress; it was part of the goodness of progress. It was its chorus, its counterpoint. Alongside the evil of witchcraft, the goodness of Christian business and development was articulated. Jealousy and witchcraft, and the tensions of success in Christian development, were bound together. For Christian development workers in Zimbabwe, witchcraft may have interfered with their efforts, but it also provided a space in which to discuss Christianity.

Notes

1 For development more broadly, see Introduction, in *International Development and the Social Sciences: Essays on the History and Politics of Knowledge,* Cooper, Frederick and Randall Packard (eds.), Berkeley: University of California Press, 1997, p. 18; and Pigg, Stacy Leigh (1992), Inventing Social Categories through Place: Social Representations and Development in Nepal, *Comparative Studies in Society and History,* 34: 491–513.
2 Ferguson, James (1995), From African Socialism to Scientific Capitalism: Reflections on the Legitimation Crisis in IMF-Ruled Africa, in *Debating Development Discourse: Institutional and Popular Perspectives,* Moore, David B. and Gerald J. Schmitz (eds.), New York: St Martin's.
3 Group discussion with the Christian Witness Committee, World Vision Zimbabwe, September 25, 1997, Harare.
4 Comaroff, John L., and Jean Comaroff (1997), *Of Revelation and Revolution: The Dialectics of Modernity on a South African Frontier, Vol. 2,* Chicago: University of Chicago Press.

35 Selfhood and prayer

Gregory M. Simon

Gregory M. Simon (born in 1972) has taught anthropology at the University of California. His research, largely conducted as part of a doctoral thesis entitled *Caged in on the Outside: Identity, Morality and Self in an Indonesian Islamic Community*, is at the intersection of cultural, psychological and religious anthropology. Taking a person-centred ethnographical approach, he studies the construction of moral subjectivities and the resolution of ethical conflicts among the members of a Minangkabau community of West Sumatra in Indonesia.

The text presented here is part of an anthropological tradition initiated by Talal Asad and his followers, particularly Saba Mahmood and Charles Hirschkind, which explores self-transformations in the context of prayer in the Muslim world and more widely in an approach that is attentive to the production of ethical subjects above and beyond the simple reproduction of the moral codes of a society. By questioning the concept of 'selfhood', Gregory Simon combines an analysis of moral representations with the ethnography of practices of the self. Focusing on the study of *shalat* – the five daily prayers that Muslims must respect – he thus describes the Minangkabau's conceptions of a good life, the means through which they attain it and the forms of self-realisation that they implement. In this perspective, prayer does not simply mean performing a duty; it implies moral self-transformation, purification from evil, deliverance from suffering and free submission to divine authority. But the originality of this text resides in the endeavour to not dissociate the approach of the techniques of the self from the analysis of the traditional Muslim moral systems. It reveals the conflicting values that underpin them and the contradictory expectations that result from it, such as having to conform simultaneously to the principles of social integration and the ethos of the autonomous actor, to the rules of conventional manners and the aspirations to personal success.

The field of the "moral" can be defined in a variety of ways in ethnographic work.[1] I use the term *moral* here in reference to the idea of a person, or self, that not only acts good but also is good, that realizes its purpose and achieves its proper mode of being.[2] When people evaluate the success or failure of such realization, they engage with morality. This sense of the term necessarily links moral life with broader questions about the nature of the self in the manner Charles Taylor[3] has described in tracing the development of formal conceptions of selfhood in the West. Taylor examines the various capacities that have been assigned to the self in different philosophical traditions. One of his key insights is that conceptions of the self always implicate moral questions: Given particular capacities, what should one do to achieve a valuable existence? Which capacities should be developed and which should be suppressed to achieve human value, and how should one go about doing this?

The arena of the moral in this sense goes well beyond the narrower usage described by James Laidlaw,[4] who draws from Bernard Williams and Michel Foucault in limiting "morality" to codes of conduct. The broader conception of the moral includes (as does Laidlaw's "ethics") the processes through which actors work to fashion themselves as particular kinds of persons. Morality may be an arena of conscious practice[5] in addition to habitus, of the reproduction of established social structures as well as the exercise of free choice in pushing against social structures or navigating their contradictions.[6] Beyond the issue of freedom, morality becomes a significant dimension of life whenever people are concerned with "the ultimate terms of their existence"[7] and how these terms define one's personal value and the value of others. People can experience themselves as inhabiting moral states, or failing to inhabit them, whether or not they have exercised freedom in realizing those states. Such a conception invites ethnographic exploration of the capacities of self imagined within particular cultural traditions, the practices through which they are cultivated, and the experiences of actors attempting to endow them with human value.[8]

In West Sumatra, the performance of *shalat*, the five obligatory daily prayers, is an especially rich point of engagement with self-consciously "Islamic" conceptions of the self and its moral orientations and with Islamic practices of self-formation. Shalat is one of the five fundamental practices required of every Muslim, and the only one required multiple times every day. In Bukittinggi, it is one of the most frequent topics of sermons and religious lectures, which regularly emphasize the obligation to pray, the benefits of prayer, the proper way to approach prayer, and the gravity of the sin of neglected prayer. Posters sold in the marketplace and subsequently hung on the walls of some shops and living rooms detail the tortures one will face in the afterlife for each prayer that goes unfulfilled. Learning how to recite the Koran and learning to perform shalat are the most prominent elements of a Minangkabau child's religious education. When my conversations with people turned to matters of religion, or even to the idea of being a good person, prayer usually found its way to the center of the discussion. This was often the case whether or not the person in question prayed regularly. It is through the performance of shalat that the capacities of a moral self are said to be realized. Some people claimed to me that in the absence of shalat such realization was impossible, an idea that no one discussed in connection with any other Islamic practice.

Shalat consists of a series of prescribed movements of the body carried out as an embodiment of submission to God. These movements are performed in concert with the recitation of the first sura (chapter) of the Koran, praising and declaring one's faith in and submission to God, followed by the recitation of another, usually brief Koranic passage of the worshipper's choosing. Each performance of shalat involves a series of these movements and recitations. When a person has completed the ritual, he or she may also elect to take advantage of the closeness to God achieved during prayer and ask God for more specific forgiveness or guidance in facing personal problems, but this is not considered obligatory. Shalat is sometimes performed collectively, most notably by men in mosques during the Friday noon prayer (a standard Islamic obligation for men but not for women). Going to the mosque or prayer house to perform shalat is said to strengthen its value, as it constitutes a more involved performance of piety. Most of the time, people in West Sumatra perform shalat at home or in some other private space or, perhaps, in the marketplace in a public space set up for this purpose (*musholla*). Either way, people usually perform shalat as an individual act. An optional midnight prayer, almost always performed alone, is said to be the most intensely experienced kind of shalat and is practiced especially by those faced with a difficult problem.

The ways in which people understand a moral self to be cultivated through shalat—and the ways in which they discuss, in an experience-near fashion,[9] the concept I have more abstractly termed "moral selfhood"—can best be appreciated by turning to what people told me about its significance and effects. I begin with Da Dan, a struggling petty trader in his mid-thirties. Da Dan and I sat frequently in the small, cluttered main room of his house. Recently erected in the neighborhood of Bukittinggi that Da Dan considered to be his home "village" (*kampuang*), the house was built in part from reused wooden boards and aluminum sheets. Da Dan typically spoke in a controlled, self-confident register, offering strong, thoughtful opinions punctuated by drags on a cigarette. "When Muslims pray," Da Dan told me, "pray the right way, understanding what is said, understanding prayer ... after praying they feel strong. Very strong. Without any problems. All problems disappear." For example, he elaborated, "if we pray, we won't ever be sick. Never any kind of illness at all." He explained that, when the prayer is "received" by God, "the pain disappears. Why?" he asked, rhetorically, and then answered, "The soul is freed of cares [*plong*]. Without any burden. No burden in one's life. As for myself, if I don't pray enough, [I think,] 'What's going to happen? What about tomorrow? What about the future? What about the kids? What about the household? What about the debt? What about this?' It's a lot of 'What about? What about? What about?'—those are the questions. If a person prays, it's never like that. None of that. If it's true [*betul*] prayer. Not just any prayer—no. If it's true prayer. Sometimes, you know, people pray but they still have problems in their life. It's not God's fault. Ask them, 'How are you praying?'"

There is a great deal to consider in Da Dan's comments, including the notion that prayer must be true to be effective. I concentrate here on the claim that shalat can eliminate all problems from one's life. This idea was echoed by many of my subjects, who discussed the ways that prayer allows one to realize his or her most valuable mode of being. Below, I outline three main dimensions of this realization: the mechanical realization of a clean and well-ordered self, the realization of a self that acts morally, and the realization of a self that does not suffer.

First, shalat transforms a self mechanically into one that is clean and well ordered. When I first talked about shalat with Da Palo, an underemployed skilled laborer in his fifties, he focused entirely on this kind of realization. "The benefit of prayer is so great," he began. He then referenced the required ablutions that precede the prayers: "Muslims are obligated to pray five times, right? In terms of the face alone, it gets washed every day, five times. Just to pick an example, if the face is washed all the time, it's going to be clean."

After expanding on the idea of cleanliness, he turned to the way prayer structures a person's use of time. Shalat takes place at specific times of the day, signaled by the call to prayer that echoes throughout the city. Da Palo traced out the course of an entire day for me, as structured by prayer: rising early for the dawn prayer to drink coffee and then go to work, working until the noon prayer signals a break and time to eat, working again until the afternoon prayer signals that the workday is through, going home tired and dirty from work, washing and praying again, and being with one's family until the evening prayer signals the time to eat dinner and then go to bed. He concluded, "At eight o'clock in the evening we rest, sleep, and tomorrow morning go to work again, at full strength, right? If you sleep at the appropriate time, the next morning your body will be fresh when you wake up. And that's how prayer educates human beings."

People's claims about the temporal discipline of prayer often went further than this. By embodying the regularity of prayer, people explained, they came to realize the disciplined use of time in their everyday lives. They came to know time as divisible in an orderly, productive fashion that allows human beings to fully take advantage of the opportunities provided by God, leading to greater prosperity. This notion resonates broadly in a context in which individual endeavor in a competitive marketplace is central to economic life, as I discuss below.

Of even more concern to most of the people I spoke with, however, was a second kind of realization effected by prayer: A self that prays will always act morally. Da Palo offered the common example that a person who prayed would have no desire to steal a large amount of money sitting within easy reach. This will be true, he said, as long as the prayer is not just performed, but is truly *mandirikan*, established as a genuine act of the autonomous self. *Mandirikan* conventionally translates as "establish," but it has more significant connotations. The root of the term is *diri*, meaning "self," but many forms of the word take on the meaning of "standing." Further, to be *mandiri* is to be "autonomous," to be as a freestanding self. Da Palo is thus expressing the idea that true prayer must be an autonomous expression of the self. The self must not just do prayer but become a state of prayer, a state of moral consciousness that is then carried out into the everyday world. People frequently repeated this central point to me: A person who truly prays will inhabit a moral state, always aware of the difference between right and wrong, and will never become driven by a desire to do wrong.

The realization of a self that acts morally is closely connected to a third kind of realization: that of a self that does not suffer. Ni Galeh, a widow in her mid-forties who owns a small clothing shop, described those who do not pray: "They punish themselves. Their lives are aimless. It's senseless, their talk is senseless. They can't do this or that. Yes, their thoughts are chaotic. Their souls aren't calm, their spirits aren't calm." "They get punished," she explained. "If we don't pray, we'll disturb people, we'll steal other people's things. If we pray properly … we won't feel like getting angry, won't want to steal, won't want to disturb people. Those are sins." Notice how Ni Galeh weaves together the idea that a person who does not pray will act immorally and the idea that this person will suffer. People who do not pray do bad things "and it seems right," she said. "But it's still wrong. They don't get any guidance. Their spirits aren't calm." In this state of turmoil, their immoral acts are, in her words, "out of their consciousness" [*diluar kesadaran*].

Virtually everyone I spoke with explained that praying resulted in a feeling of *tanang* (calm), a positive state associated with a lack of anxiety and a general feeling of well-being. Despite the apparent cliché, people spoke convincingly and with emotion about their experiences of *tanang*. Interpreted within a particular religious framework, the experience can be understood as "a spiritual state, but also at least partially a purely physical consequence of the prescribed regulated breathing, chanting, and rhythmic prostrations of the supplicants, which have a potent physiological effect."[10] This state of well-being may be said to extend well beyond the moment of prayer itself, until—as Da Dan claimed—a person who prays regularly literally has no problems in life at all.

The basis for all of these realizations of the moral self is the idea that, in praying, a person directly embodies submission to God. The term *Islam* itself refers to the submission to God that is the defining characteristic of moral selfhood. In this sense, the reason a person should pray is simply that God commands prayer, and, therefore, practicing prayer constitutes a moral self. However, as should be clear at this point, the way people in West Sumatra engage with prayer reaches far beyond this abstract ideology. Even if shalat is ideologically defined as a form of submission, in contrast to forms of prayer that constitute supplication,[11] shalat is not experienced purely as a "non-reciprocal" affirmation of faith. It is crucial to take into account people's concern with how the moral selfhood promised by shalat is manifested in the experience of living. People's emotional investment in shalat is rooted most deeply in the promise that a moral self can be realized through the living of a physically pure, orderly, and prosperous life; experiencing an absence of problematic immoral desires and behaviors; achieving a sense of tranquility; and attaining freedom from suffering. [...]

For the last 200 years, Minangkabau society has worked to reconcile Islam with the conceptually traditional, village-based system of social order, known as *adat* (or, in Minang, *adaik*). Adat defines properly "Minangkabau" ways of interacting, including kinship and property relations, ritual life, and etiquette. The notion of conflict between Islam and adat, usually in regard to the matrilineal kinship system at the heart of adat, is frequently discussed in West Sumatran ethnographic and historical literature,[12] but this literature often points to the significance of merging and accommodation as well as to conflict between the two frameworks. To a large degree, the idea that adat is a self-contained, well-defined set of social codes and structures, and that it can be understood as something indigenous and in tension with "Islam," was a product of Dutch colonial authorities and scholars.[13] Many "traditional" adat forms were, in fact, shaped by the colonial era.[14] However, many Minangkabau thinkers adopted this "traditional" conception of adat, attempting to define its precise outlines or considering how it should be reconciled with Islam. Although the notion of friction between the two has not disappeared, the relationship has evolved in such a way that in contemporary Bukittinggi, Islam has—at least rhetorically—become the dominant moral term, co-opting adat. Public discourse on moral life in West Sumatra today inevitably involves reference to the phrase "adaik basandi syarak, syarak basandi kitabullah," meaning "adat is based on Islamic law, Islamic law is based on the Koran" and, thus, asserting that adat itself has its most fundamental basis in Islam. (The phrase is so pervasive that it is most often simply abbreviated to "ABS SBK.") Earlier versions of the saying posited that adat was based on what was true or right, with no mention of Islam; or that adat and Islamic law were mutually constituting; or that adat was based on Islamic law, which was based on the Koran, which, in turn, was based on what was true or right. These versions appear to be totally absent from discourse in contemporary Bukittinggi. To act properly according to adat, one must, by definition, also act in an Islamic fashion.

Many elements of adat—that is, many elements of social interaction that are now identified self-consciously as characteristically "Minangkabau"—have not been erased in favor of "Islamic" social life but have, instead, been reframed by or interwoven with Islamic discourses. People use Islamic conceptions to make sense of or work through the conflicts of moral selfhood that arise in the course of everyday interactions. What I am particularly interested in here is the way that everyday interactions—especially properly Minangkabau ones—consistently communicate the notion that individual will and desire must be displaced so that the good of social integration can be realized.

One can see this ritualized in etiquette, the component of adat known as *baso-basi*, in which strong emotions and individual endeavor and consumption are displaced in favor of conventional, ritualized interactions. Merely by carrying out this etiquette, Minangkabau people demonstrate that they do not act according to inner, individual impulses but, instead, according to conventions that they have accepted as morally superior. The content of baso-basi reinforces the message of social integration. The foundation of baso-basi is simply the act of *bagaua*, socializing by being out in the community, greeting, being together with and talking to other people. This is often considered the single most telling sign of a person's overall moral status. As one man put it to me—addressing what he saw as foreign misconceptions of West Sumatra's Islamic society and the way they obviously contrasted with the social interaction we saw around us every day—"How can people be terrorists if they are able to bagaua with others?" To bagaua according to baso-basi means to properly greet others, to offer food and drink to others before consuming them, and to avoid direct expressions of disapproval, anger, longing, sorrow, or other sentiments that may cause social conflict. These sentiments are, instead, suppressed or expressed obliquely, for example, through sayings, metaphors, or allusions. [...]

For all of the emphasis in the public performance of baso-basi on displacing individual will and desire, Minangkabau culture, in fact, also greatly celebrates individual autonomy. This is seen clearly in celebrations of Minangkabau ethnic identity. For example, people repeatedly returned to the same saying to describe what they saw as Minangkabau character: "Wanting to be on top when pressed down, wanting to be outside when caged in." It refers most obviously to a desire to be free of burdens and restrictions, and people cited it often when talking to me about the proclivity of Minangkabau people for independent trade, their tendency to be particularly clever or crafty, and their refusal to passively submit to others (as, they would often say, the hierarchical Javanese do). Perhaps more tellingly, people connected the phrase, with pride, to personal stories that they told me of their own refusals to be pushed around by authorities, whether by direct resistance or, more usually, stealthy maneuverings.

"Wanting to be on top when pressed down, wanting to be outside when caged in," not only refers to a desire to be free of burdens and restrictions, however. It also refers to a desire to simultaneously bear those burdens and honor those restrictions while being free of them: that is, wanting to actually be outside while still, apparently, caged in. It references an attempt to do the seemingly impossible, managing to successfully realize the public, socially integrated part of oneself while still cultivating oneself as an autonomous actor.

The kinds of careful and indirect communication people engage in with others do not at all mean that individual desires and emotions, criticisms, and so on are devalued or dismissed as inauthentic. To the contrary, such impulses are kept out of public circulation because of their great but particular value: They make up the realm of the *paribadi*. The paribadi is the "personal": those attributes and behaviors that adhere to the individual person and should be kept apart from those parts of one's self that integrate with others. One's individual character traits are one's paribadi, but so are one's relationship with a spouse, one's mystical powers, and one's financial pursuits. When my respondents told me stories of their lives, they often stressed to me that such stories were paribadi: I was not to circulate them inside the community. These stories were not only embarrassing accounts of pain, failure, and moral lapses but also of personal success that would be sombong to talk about openly. It was these stories that people referred back to when claiming that, after months of conversations, I now understood who they really were. Far from being suppressed or devalued, the paribadi is the site of an alternate locus of the authentic self, albeit one that is, by definition, inappropriate to display openly.

Discussing daily interactions with my subjects, I came to see clearly that they felt that these interactions needed to be tightly controlled not only so that smooth integration could be maintained on a social level but also so that their own, and others', autonomy could be preserved in the process. Integration with others involves risks: that one will violate the boundaries or autonomy of another or that one will lose control of oneself if one's own boundaries are not protected. Thus, just as part of the self must be realized in relationships with others, another part of the self must be kept from being exposed too directly to such relationships.[15] For all of the concern in West Sumatra with the moral value of socializing, it is striking that people almost invariably attributed immoral behavior to the consequences of this socializing. Rather than blame immoral behaviors on the innate immoral impulses of human beings, people almost always described such behaviors as the result of interpersonal contact, regrettable social norms, or supernatural entities that corrupted what had been the innate good intentions of the individual.

All of this becomes intertwined with Islamic discourses as well. When Ibilih refused to bow down to Adam, God condemned him to eternity in hell but then gave him a reprieve: He could inhabit the world of humans until judgment day, exploiting their napasu (appetites) to draw them toward evil. There is no concept of original sin in Islam: Instead, human beings are understood to be born pure, and only through interacting with a corrupt world do they become corrupted. As human beings face the temptations and corruptions of the world, they experience the presence of Ibilih. In this view, the goal for human beings is not so much to resist innate appetites as it is to keep the world from drawing them away from the pure core of themselves: the *ati*, or emotional heart in which there exist those things that people truly feel, no matter what they may express outwardly, and their true intentions, no matter how they actually behave. In particular, the ati is where compassion (*ibo*) and faith (*iman*) reside. The ati is, at its core, good. This concern with the truth of inner being is entwined in a larger discourse that distinguishes between the *laia*, or external reality, and the *batin*, or internal, metaphysical reality. This distinction is associated with Sufi influences, especially strong in Java, that have sometimes been underappreciated in accounts of contemporary Islam in Indonesia.

In the West Sumatran context, Islamic discourses of moral selfhood are thus intertwined with Minangkabau cultural concerns about social order and integration, as realized through the conventional performance of baso-basi, but also with concerns about the value of individual autonomy and internal states. Minangkabau moral selfhood cannot be usefully essentialized as based on a particular concept or locus of the self or on one particular value or moral orientation. Rather, it is located within the particular ways that multiple and contradictory concepts of the moral self are managed, each given its own forms of expression and arenas of meaningful experience. These contradictory concepts do not form alternate models of selfhood that circulate separately in West Sumatra, creating different kinds of Minangkabau selves. Although one moral orientation may be dominant within a particular cultural sphere, such neat correlations do not always exist.[16] Successful socializing, for instance, often both realizes integration on a public level and defines and protects the realm of the paribadi (personal). The challenges this balancing poses are an integral part of moral selfhood for all Minangkabau actors and are, thus, an integral part of the nature of Islam in Minangkabau society. This observation is not surprising if one understands cultural configurations of selfhood to grow out of, rather than simply create, the processes through which people reflect on and try to make sense of the worlds in which they find themselves,[17] worlds that are often contradictory.

In his detailed intellectual history of selfhood in the West, Jerrold Seigel has argued that theorists have had to confront three major dimensions of the human self: bodily, relational (the integration of the self into larger social structures that help to constitute it), and reflective (a self-conscious agency capable of reacting to, elaborating on, or even moving against the other dimensions in creative ways).[18] He also persuasively argues that theories of the self that deny or minimize one or more of these dimensions are necessarily less satisfying than those that attempt to understand the interrelationships and tensions that exist between them. My analysis of the culture of selfhood in Minangkabau society supports this idea (although I have given less attention here to the body) from an ethnographic perspective: Like the theories of individual philosophers—if less coherently—cultural systems grow through people's attempts to think through and elaborate on these different dimensions of self and the relationships between them. Broadly speaking, the dual orientations toward integration and autonomy in Minangkabau selfhood are elaborations of a basic existential paradox in the experience of the human self: The self is undeniably constituted by its integration with the world yet undeniably autonomous as well. This tension emerges through a particular history and in particular cultural patterns of moral selfhood in West Sumatra, revolving around ways of managing, expressing, and even celebrating these conflicting dimensions of the experience of self, although never completely reconciling them.

Notes

1 Howell, Signe (1997), Introduction, in *The Ethnography of Moralities*, Howell, Signe (ed.), London: Routledge, pp. 1–22.
2 The terms *person* and *self* are not defined consistently in anthropological literature (Harris, Grace [1989], Concepts of Individual, Self, and Person in Description and Analysis, *American Anthropologist*, 91 [3]: 599–612); and their usage often overlaps, making it difficult to engage with a range of literature that uses these terms without furthering the confusion or being diverted into long exposition on definitions. Broadly, *person* is most fruitfully used to indicate the outlines of individuals' particular social and moral relationships with others and with larger social and metaphysical collectives. A "self" can better be understood as a person's living of his or her own particular personhood. I am concerned in this article with conceptions of personhood but also with the way people subjectively experience their own personhood. For the sake of simplicity, I favor the use of *selfhood* throughout the article.
3 Taylor, Charles (1989), *Sources of the Self: The Making of the Modern Identity*, Cambridge, MA: Harvard University Press.
4 Laidlaw, James (1995), *Riches and Renunciation: Religion, Economy, and Society among the Jains*, Oxford: Clarendon Press, pp. 17–21; Laidlaw, James (2002), For an Anthropology of Ethics and Freedom, *Journal of the Royal Anthropological Institute*, 8 (2): 311–332.
5 Lambek, Michael (2000), The Anthropology of Religion and the Quarrel between Poetry and Philosophy, *Current Anthropology*, 41 (3): 309–320.
6 Robbins, Joel (2007), Between Reproduction and Freedom: Morality, Value, and Radical Cultural Change, *Ethnos*, 72 (3): 293–314.
7 Parish, Steven (1994), *Moral Knowing in a Hindu Sacred City: An Exploration of Mind, Emotion, and Self*, New York: Columbia University Press, p. 290.

8 For example, Marsden, Magnus, *Living Islam: Muslim Religious Experience in Pakistan's North-West Frontier*, Cambridge: Cambridge University Press, 2005; Parish, cit. n. 9; Simon, Gregory, Caged in on the Outside: Identity, Morality, and Self in an Indonesian Islamic Community, Ph.D. dissertation, Department of Anthropology, University of California, San Diego, 2007.
9 Geertz, Clifford (1984), "From the Native's Point of View": On the Nature of Anthropological Understanding, in *Culture Theory: Essays on Mind, Self, and Emotion*, Shweder, Richard and Robert LeVine (eds.), Cambridge: Cambridge University Press, pp. 123–136.
10 Lindholm, Charles (1996), *The Islamic Middle East: An Historical Anthropology*, Cambridge, MA: Blackwell, p. 143.
11 Headley, Stephen (2000), Afterword: The Mirror in the Mosque, in Parkin, David and Stephen Headley (eds.), *Islamic Prayer Across the Indian Ocean: Inside and Outside the Mosque*, London: Routledge, pp. 213–237; Parkin, David (2000), Invocation: *Salaa, Dua, Sadaka* and the Question of Self-Determination, in Parkin, David and Stephen Headley (eds.), *Islamic Prayer Across the Indian Ocean: Inside and Outside the Mosque*, London: Routledge, pp. 137–168.
12 See, for example, Blackwood, Evelyn (2000), *Webs of Power: Women, Kin, and Community in a Sumatran Village*, Lanham, MD: Rowman and Littlefield; Sanday, Peggy (2002), *Women at the Center: Life in a Modern Matriarchy*, Ithaca, NY: Cornell University Press, 2002.
13 Kahn, Joel S. (1993), *Constituting the Minangkabau: Peasants, Culture, and Modernity in Colonial Indonesia*, Providence, RI: Berg; Hefner, Robert (2000), *Civil Islam: Muslims and Democratization in Indonesia*, Princeton, NJ: Princeton University Press.
14 Benda-Beckmann, Franz von, and Keebet von Benda-Beckmann (1985), Transformation and Change in Minangkabau, in *Change and Continuity in Minangkabau: Local, Regional, and Historical Perspectives on West Sumatra*, Thomas, Lynn L. and Franz von Benda-Beckmann (eds.), Athens: Ohio University Press, pp. 235–278; Kato, Tsuyoshi (1982), *Matriliny and Migration: Evolving Minangkabau Traditions in Indonesia*, Ithaca, NY: Cornell University Press.
15 See Wikan, Unni (1990), *Managing Turbulent Hearts: A Balinese Formula for Living*, Chicago, IL: University of Chicago Press.
16 See Robbins (2007), Between Reproduction and Freedom, op. cit.
17 See Cohen, Anthony (1994), *Self Consciousness: An Alternative Anthropology of Identity*, London: Routledge.
18 Seigel, Jerrold (2005), *The Idea of the Self: Thought and Experience in Western Europe since the Seventeenth Century*, Cambridge: Cambridge University Press.

36 Compassion and accountability

Omri Elisha

Omri Elisha (born in 1972) is an assistant professor in anthropology at Queens College, CUNY, the City University of New York. He is a specialist in the anthropology of religion and carried out a study of the Evangelical churches of Knoxville, Tennessee, focusing on the forms of social outreach engaged in by these churchgoers, who represent the Christian Right in the United States. The resulting monograph is entitled *Moral Ambition: Mobilization and Social Outreach in Evangelical Megachurches*.

 The article presented here, which received the *Cultural Horizons* Prize in 2009, examines the practice of charity among evangelical white suburban Christians from this Southern state. Testifying to a recent ideological evolution of conservative Protestantism that corresponds to what has been called 'compassionate conservatism', helping the poor, mainly from African American neighbourhoods, creates a confrontation between two principles: assistance and accountability. While the evangelical Christians are aware of this, they are often frustrated because, on the one hand, their generosity is supposed to be unconditional, but on the other, they have expectations in terms of gratitude and self-improvement on the part of the beneficiaries. Bringing together theological questions, observation of ethical practices and attention to daily emotions, Omri Elisha provides a well-balanced vision of the moral dilemmas facing the agents, showing that these emerge not from conceptual incoherencies but rather from the tensions inherent to practices that necessarily affect the implementation of morality. He thus offers a rich and detailed analysis of the well-known phenomenon of 'compassion fatigue' that can affect 'Good Samaritans' whether close to home or further afield.

As religious conservatives and secular liberals throughout the United States compete to dictate the terms of moral governance in public life, the form and meaning of civil society are continually evolving for local communities. The dismantling of federal welfare in the 1990s, for example, sparked renewed public interest in what has come to be known as "faith-based activism," a field of social engagement associated with religious charities, social service organizations, and congregations, whose concerns for the common good ostensibly transcend sectarian interests and, in the eyes of the faithful, exceed the capacities of federal welfare. Given the Protestant overtones inherent in the language of faith, it is unsurprising that the politicization of "faith-based initiatives"—which gained currency as a key component of "compassionate conservatism," a Republican platform in the 2000 elections—has been met with marked enthusiasm by conservative Protestants. The trend is viewed in an especially positive light by conservative yet socially engaged evangelicals, whose missionary interventions in civil society are predicated on the presumed failures of the welfare state and its policies of entitlement.[1]

Despite their zeal to embrace faith-based activism, many conservative church-goers encounter ethical dilemmas and frustrations as they attempt to reach across the race and class divide in their home communities. Among the predominantly white suburban churchgoers I observed while conducting fieldwork in Knoxville, Tennessee (over a period of 15 months between 1999 and 2001), one of the most commonly identified challenges of social outreach was what they called "compassion fatigue." This concept was a recurring theme over the course of my research, and its various ideological and practical connotations are ever present in the discourse of outreach mobilization that takes place in conservative evangelical congregations and faith-based organizations.

The term *compassion fatigue* commonly refers to the desensitization that occurs as a result of the shallow and formulaic manner in which humanitarian crises in remote regions of the world are represented in Western news media.[2] In the lingo of the nonprofit sector, the term is used to explain seasonal drops in charitable donations from the general public. For evangelicals, however, compassion fatigue means something rather different, although it still is meant to evoke contemplation of the relationship between one's expectations and actions or, more precisely, the gaps between one's moral ambitions and the conditions of existence that reinforce and simultaneously threaten to undermine them at every turn. When evangelicals speak of compassion fatigue, they speak of a condition of emotional exhaustion—also called "burnout"—that they attribute to frustrating experiences of being resisted or manipulated by irresponsible and unrepentant beneficiaries of charitable aid. Evangelical volunteers often cite compassion fatigue as a reason for their withdrawal, sometimes permanently, from social outreach. Socially engaged evangelicals—pastors and lay churchgoers who are identifiably committed to the mobilization of church resources for charitable or philanthropic purposes in the community at large—confront this phenomenon most directly, and so it is mainly from their perspective that I endeavor in the proceeding discussion to analyze it.

That many conservative evangelicals, especially white Southerners, remain fixated on the potential difficulties and drawbacks associated with charitable social outreach makes sense in light of the fact that their churches and denominations have maintained positions of social withdrawal over the last century, emphasizing proselytization and cultural separatism over social action (in contrast to liberal Protestant, Catholic, and African American churches with long-standing traditions of social action). But the factor that I want to highlight in this essay is that evangelical outreach activities are ambiguously defined by the twin imperatives of *compassion* and *accountability*. Compassion invokes an ideal of empathetic, unconditional benevolence, whereas accountability imposes reciprocal obligations on the part of others as a condition of continued benevolence.[3] To an outside observer it may seem that compassion fatigue is simply an inevitable outcome of an "obvious" contradiction, but such a conclusion would not take into account that evangelicals explicitly recognize the paradox of compassion and accountability and see the relationship as dialectical rather than contradictory.

White conservative evangelicals in the suburbs of Knoxville are aware that putting theology into practice is never easy, and they know that the challenges of practical theology can be especially troublesome when it comes to the ways in which suburban churchgoers interact with cultural strangers affected by conditions of poverty, distress, and marginalization (e.g., urban poor blacks, the homeless, ethnic minorities). And yet, when they do engage in social outreach, their sensitivity to the dynamics of social power often diminishes in the face of stronger cultural prejudices and religious aspirations. Their prejudices may be expressed as suspicion toward charity recipients, and their aspirations include the desire to embody "active and sacrificial compassion," a romanticized ideal of Christian charity based on a belief in the possibility of creating profound interpersonal bonds that transcend social boundaries and status hierarchies. As a result, evangelicals often overlook the degree to which the implementation of compassion and accountability reproduces conditions of "deep-lying incommensurability"[4] between those who have the power to give and those who are burdened with the obligation to reciprocate, either through return gestures or some other moral premium.

My aim here is not merely to point out ideological discrepancies or explain why suburban churchgoers encounter friction when they intervene in the lives of cultural strangers. I am interested, rather, in the conditions under which a conceptually manageable paradox becomes practically unmanageable for religious actors who uphold it (for this reason I do not address, at least not directly, the experiences of people on the receiving end of "active compassion"). Why do evangelicals have such difficulty balancing the relationship between compassion and accountability when their outreach methods assume these two concepts to be essentially compatible, even complementary? If we accept that socially engaged evangelicals earnestly operationalize compassion and accountability as a productive paradox, why should the stress of simultaneously embodying both virtues remain an impediment to their moral ambitions?

I argue that much of the difficulty stems from the fact that evangelical faith-based activism is embedded within a larger ideological framework of Christian evangelism, which, in turn, is rooted in a theology of exchange that is partially obscured by the romanticization of Christian compassion. When conservative evangelicals offer assistance and encouragement to poor and distressed people, they interpret their actions as unconditional gifts, free of the constraints of interest, debt, and power. However, their theology asserts that even the most "unconditional" gift of all (eternal salvation) is conditioned on the recipient's obligation to receive that which ultimately can never be repaid and thus remain a willing subject of divine authority. So while evangelical acts of compassion and charitable gifts are conceived as graceful gestures with "no strings attached," they invoke norms of reciprocity and indebtedness that are central to evangelical thought. The misrecognition that occurs here pertains less to the difference between interested and disinterested giving[5] so much as it betrays a deep-seated concern among evangelicals to act like God without acting like they are God. In their "moral rhetorics of charitable action,"[6] the conditions of giving are made prominent while the conditions of receiving are obscured to the point where the givers—enchanted by what Derrida calls the "madness of the impossible"[7]—are often surprised or flustered to have to manage them at all.

Furthermore, the religious precepts of compassion and accountability, as conceived by conservative evangelicals, are simultaneously consonant and at variance with prevailing social aesthetics,[8] technologies of citizenship,[9] and constructions of personhood through which populations, rich and poor alike, are produced, empowered, and governed. The postwelfare era is represented within the discourse of evangelical faith-based activism as a historic opportunity to "restore" principles of biblical compassion and theocentric accountability to a public sphere seen as long deprived of such values. Welfare privatization is viewed not only as a chance to promote intensive engagement on the part of religious actors in the arena of social services and community development but also as a chance to redefine the very essence of altruism. As with "spiritual gifts" among charismatic Protestants, charitable giving of goods and services is, among evangelicals, "linked to a Maussian concept of the gift as breaking down two forms of distinction: those differentiating persons and those distinguishing persons from objects."[10] Socially engaged evangelicals complicate individualism in the conventional sense because their methods and moral ambitions suggest a desire to collapse or transcend the boundaries of human intersubjectivity. The romanticization of compassion is among the most salient and appealing expressions of this desire. [...]

One of the peculiar ironies of charitable social outreach, especially in affluent church communities, is that well-meaning efforts are guided by expectations and preconceptions that become burdensome for everyone involved once they begin to overdetermine the way in which generosity is enacted. When charity recipients react with indifference (i.e., lack of gratitude), obstinacy, or resistance, the ideals of active compassion become harder for charity givers to rationalize and sustain. The risk of compassion fatigue is understood by socially engaged evangelicals to be especially high under such circumstances. Outreach volunteers become self-conscious that their judgment is clouded by anger or exhaustion, and they are faced with a choice either to withdraw or persevere.

What follows are two personal narratives that were gathered during recorded interviews. They demonstrate how socially engaged evangelicals experience and recall the dilemmas of social outreach. In their tone and emphasis, they closely resemble anecdotes that volunteers and activists share with one another during mobilization sessions and outreach workshops. They reveal in part the role of narrative in the construction of a religious identity based on ideals of service, perseverance, and grace. They also reveal the extent to which socially engaged evangelicals wrestle with questions of discernment and suspicion and an anxious concern to avoid bad judgment.

Stacy Miggs is a homeschooling mother of four who attends Eternal Vine Church, a popular suburban megachurch with a congregation of over 4,000.[11] Despite her self-identification as a "stay-at-home mom," she is deeply committed to her work as a volunteer outreach coordinator for her church and regularly attends meetings of the Samaritans of Knoxville. In addition to organizing outreach activities, such as group visits to nursing homes and domestic violence shelters, she spends much of her time mobilizing churchgoers to become more actively involved. Stacy considers mobilization to be by far the most challenging aspect of what she does, in part because people are busy with other priorities in their lives but also because many conservative churchgoers still feel ambivalent about social outreach. As is the case in congregations throughout the country, Stacy represents a fairly small segment of socially engaged members of her church.

Stacy has also committed herself to ministering one-on-one to women in need, and she remains dedicated to this aspect of her religious life, despite many setbacks. She spoke often of a particular relationship she once had with an alcohol and drug-abusing single mother whom she met at a homeless shelter. Upon getting to know the woman and her child, Stacy decided to become involved in their lives, at first buying them food and clothing and eventually helping them move into a new home once the mother's situation stabilized. Soon, Stacy felt the Holy Spirit urging her to get more closely involved. She realized it was incumbent on her not only to help the woman with mundane affairs but also to put her on a path toward long-term health and self-sufficiency and ultimately spiritual redemption.[12]

Stacy stepped up her investment in the relationship, gradually working herself into a position of credibility and authority so that she could take advantage of the opportunity "to impart some wisdom and offer some guidelines" in practical and spiritual matters. Over the course of a year, while the woman underwent drug treatment, Stacy and her husband (a practicing physician) contributed to her home and car expenses, using mostly their own money plus some extra funds provided by Eternal Vine Church. They also helped the woman cover the costs of day care for her daughter and night classes for herself so she could earn her GED and get a job. After all this, Stacy sadly recounted, the woman "chose to go back to the bottle, go back to the abuse": "We helped her to try to come out of this path. We tried to encourage her, we tried to help her in every way—physically, emotionally, spiritually. But she has still chosen ultimately to go back to the drugs and alcohol. Well, I don't want to enable that, and we've been enabling that. And I did not see it soon enough. If you choose that path, there's nothing we can do. So I've had to sever that tie. I *have* severed that tie."

Ending the relationship was emotionally draining for Stacy, and she thought about the situation every time she reflected on the difficulties of active compassion. While desiring to be an instrument of God's mercy and grace, she had learned to set limits and boundaries to avoid getting "burned" by people who "choose" to remain on destructive paths and refuse to accept responsibility: "I wanted to help. I wanted to see how the Lord could use me in that. But the wrong thing to me would have been to continue to pour into that relationship without any commitment there on her part. There are too many people who say, 'I need help, and I want somebody to walk this road with me,' and I'm there ready to do that. But there is an issue of responsibility and accountability on the other end."

Evangelicals who consistently engage in this kind of social outreach, as individuals or members of organized groups, often develop their own guidelines to assess the sincerity and personal accountability of those seeking or receiving help or material aid. Their guidelines are informal and reflect a combination of experience and intuition, which they confirm through prayer and consultation with other experienced volunteers and activists. They are careful to avoid practicing indiscriminate charity while at the same time they try to remain open to the everyday realities of poverty and dependency. At times, evangelicals may be so keen to avoid getting "burned" that, through misplaced suspicion or rash judgment, they will reject someone with "sincere" needs, instead of, as activists say, "erring on the side of compassion."

Steve Latham, also a member of Eternal Vine, has spent most of his professional life working for Christian nonprofits and faith-based organizations in downtown Knoxville. He deals with homeless people on a daily basis and believes strongly in the importance of balancing absolute compassion with firm standards of accountability. Steve admitted, however, that it is often hard to draw the lines between them. He described to me an occasion when he was working at a social service agency and a disheveled man, who was not one of the agency's registered clients, approached him for a handout. The man walked right into his office and announced, "I need gas money," prompting Steve, who was suspicious of the man on sight, to think to himself, "Yeah right, you need gas money. I've heard that so many times." Steve assumed that the expressed need was not genuine and the money would be used to buy drugs or alcohol. He turned the man away, claiming that he had no cash on him and could not simply give away money that belonged to the agency without proper procedures. As the man was leaving he encountered a female coworker of Steve's and managed to get money from her instead. Observing this, Steve decided to follow through on his suspicion: "I got in my car and followed him to the gas station. I said to myself, this is gonna be a test of humanity. Sure enough, he actually bought gas. The sad thing was that he was buying gas for his truck, which was such a pitiful truck that he had to pour it into the tank and then siphon it straight into the engine because the gas tank was eaten out. I realized that, even as long as I've been in the business and thinking I'm galvanized by it all, there are still hurting people."

Steve remembered his momentary lapse of Christian intuition with regret, but in his telling of the story he highlighted the positive lesson to be learned: the only way to help people in need is to have relationships with them. In relationships, sincere needs are clearly ascertained and individual accountability is either more visible or more easily inculcated. Nonetheless, as both of the stories above reveal, practicing compassion—whether in the context of a personal relationship or not—often entails the need for evangelicals to reconcile themselves with disappointments, surprises, false expectations, and errors in judgment. In the process of "incarnating" themselves into worlds of poverty and dependency, evangelicals face daunting realizations not only about the "people we serve" but also about themselves, their temperaments, and the extent of their willingness to make sacrifices in the name of compassion. [...]

To summarize the core of my argument, the problem identified by evangelicals as "compassion fatigue" is an ethical problem (thus not easily trivialized) because it reflects coexisting and conflicting layers of meaning intrinsic to evangelical thought and practice. The simultaneous influence of these layers produces both assertiveness and ambiguity among socially engaged evangelicals about exactly what it is that they are doing when they externalize the values of compassion and accountability. An ideology of the pure gift intersects with the transactional logic of redemption; ideals of benevolence and equality are mobilized through practices of "benign suspicion" and incommensurability; the pathos of compassion meets the fervor of evangelism. If the challenge facing evangelicals were simply a matter of negotiating the paradox of compassion and accountability—that is, finding the perfect balance of "tough love"—then I suspect they would have a much easier time addressing the "nerve issue" of accountability. The reality is far more complex. The discourse around compassion fatigue is performative, in that it stresses the virtues of humility, adversity, and perseverance that evangelicals value so highly, but as the ethnographic material reveals, it also reflects deep-seated tensions that impede the ambitions of churchgoers to master the elusive give-and-take of perfect grace. [...]

My concern is not merely to suggest that evangelical thought and practice are in conflict with competing ethics but, rather, to argue that *competing ethics enter into and exist within the very contours of evangelical thought and practice.* The desire among suburban evangelicals to practice perfect generosity and thereby accentuate affective rather than contractual dimensions of charitable giving is as much an effect of modern liberalism and middle-class idealism as it is a testimony to the resurgence of conservative Protestantism in public life. Their ambition to embody divine grace and their embattled sense that such ambitions are never fully realized are in some ways suggestive of nascent counterhegemonic impulses while in other ways consistent with ascendant neoliberal and neoconservative ideologies.

The expanding influence of religious conservatism in the welfare arena, where the authority of progressive secularism is no longer guaranteed, forces us to assess with care the complex motivations of religious activists and the "communities of faith" they seek to mobilize. Rather than assume that conservative evangelicals are categorically absolutist in their defense of personal responsibility and moral individualism, we must continue to identify the nuances, layers, and multiple strands that inform various missionary interventions in civil society. This is especially important given that civil society, like the public sphere as described by Talal Asad, is "a space *necessarily* (not just contingently) articulated by power. And everyone who enters it must address power's disposition of people and things, the dependence of some on the goodwill of others."[13] As evangelical activists are explicitly (and "not just contingently") concerned with issues of both power and goodwill, their struggles to make sense of the ideological intricacy of postwelfare activism merit ethnographic sensitivity as well as critical scrutiny.

Notes

1 Labels such as "conservative Protestant," "evangelical," and "fundamentalist" are often used, especially in the mass media, with little appreciation for their specificity or historical connotations. In this discussion, I follow Woodberry and Smith (Woodberry, Robert D., and Christian S. Smith [1998], Fundamentalism et al.: Conservative Protestants in America, *Annual Review of Sociology*, 24: 25–56) in using "conservative Protestant" as an umbrella category for Christians who, among other characteristics they display, "emphasize a personal relationship with Jesus Christ, believe in the importance of converting others to the faith, have a strong view of biblical authority, and believe that salvation is through Christ alone" (1998: 36). Included in this category are subgroups such as evangelicals, fundamentalists, Pentecostals, and charismatics, all of whom share similarities and crucial differences with one another. The label "evangelical" refers here to the "moderate wing" of conservative Protestantism (and its largest segment in the United States), whose cultural characteristics reflect a long tradition of evangelical Protestant revivalism, missionary zeal, and, more recently, social and political activism. Those who identify with the evangelical tradition are a diverse lot, however, and the label itself has become fluid and contested. Evangelicalism has earned tremendous popularity since the mid-20th century, when "neo-evangelicals" like Billy Graham differentiated themselves from both sectarian fundamentalism and liberal ecumenism. Today evangelicalism is as celebrated as it is maligned, and Protestants from across the ideological spectrum—including political liberals, such as Jim Wallis of *Sojourners*—lay claims to its legacies and core doctrines. I have chosen to refer to the subjects of my ethnography as "conservative evangelicals," to highlight the social and political as well as theological conservatism of the majority of pastors and churchgoers I observed during my research. In addition, I use the phrase "socially engaged evangelicals" to describe pastors and churchgoers within a largely conservative milieu who take an active role in mobilizing their fellow evangelicals to participate more widely in social and community services and faith-based organization.
2 Moeller, Susan D. (1999), *Compassion Fatigue: How the Media Sells Disease, Famine, War and Death*, New York: Routledge.
3 Bartkowski, John P., and Helen A. Regis (2003), *Charitable Choices: Religion, Race, and Poverty in the Post-Welfare Era*, New York: New York University Press.
4 Simmel, Georg (1950), *The Sociology of Georg Simmel*, New York: Free Press, p. 392.
5 Bourdieu, Pierre (1990), *The Logic of Practice*, Stanford, CA: Stanford University Press.
6 Allahyari, Rebecca Anne (2000), *Visions of Charity: Volunteer Workers and Moral Community*, Berkeley, CA: University of California Press, p. 32.

7 Derrida, Jacques (2001), *On Cosmopolitanism and Forgiveness*, London: Routledge, p. 45.
8 Brown, Peter (2005), Remembering the Poor and the Aesthetic of Society, *Journal of Interdisciplinary History*, 35 (3): 513–522.
9 Cruikshank, Barbara (1999), *The Will to Empower: Democratic Citizens and Other Subjects*, Ithaca, NY: Cornell University Press.
10 Coleman, Simon (2004), The Charismatic Gift, *Journal of the Royal Anthropological Institute*, 10 (2): 424.
11 "Megachurches" are defined as congregations with upward of 2,000 members. In theological orientation, megachurches are predominantly conservative Protestant (mostly evangelical or Pentecostal), and they are especially popular among middle-class urban and suburban professionals. Known for their organizational and aesthetic innovations as much as for their size, megachurches emerged in response to the counterculture movements of the 1960s, as charismatic young evangelists and church-growth specialists sought to develop new approaches to the ministry that would attract idealistic baby boomers who were eager to join churches with contemporary cultural relevance as well as religious enthusiasm. Today, the most influential preachers in the United States are megachurch pastors (incl. Rick Warren, Robert Schuller, Bill Hybels, Creflo Dollar, Joel Osteen, and the late Jerry Falwell). Megachurches are also productive sites of evangelical mobilization, useful for generating mass support for Christian parachurches and missionary agencies as well as building political coalitions at the grassroots.
12 Stacy's account does not refer to the woman's ethnic or religious identity, a fair indication that the woman was white and nominally Christian. White evangelicals usually rely on identity markers in their stories only when the people described are non-white or non-Christian.
13 Asad, Talal (2003), *Formations of the Secular: Christianity, Islam, Modernity*, Stanford, CA: Stanford University Press, p. 184.

Part V
Prescriptions

Introduction

Didier Fassin

Moral issues are not simply an object that anthropologists attempt to grasp in the way they would study a ritual or a therapeutic practice or an artistic performance. Far more than any other topic, they also question them in their capacity as moral subjects. Of course, subjectivity is never really absent from research: we can be disturbed by a ritual, interested by a therapeutic practice or moved by an artistic performance. More generally, the very principle of participant observation, the methodological cornerstone of the discipline, implies that the researcher is a subject interacting with a research object. In the case of morality, however, this interaction goes somewhat further, for two reasons. First, because what is being studied is of the same nature as the means used to study it: norms, values, emotions and judgements – in sum a set of cognitive and affective elements. Second, because the same tools used by those being studied are supposed to apply to those studying them: approaching the ethics of a society implies examining the ethics of the social scientist. In other words, the problem concerns both the relationship between anthropologists and the world – what moral stance do they adopt? – and the relationship of the world to anthropology – what ethical practice can we expect from the discipline?

The first question has been expressed most notably by Norbert Elias, who opposed involvement and detachment as two epistemological poles.[1] In the natural sciences, researchers can maintain distance from the object, which is external to them: an atomic particle, a chemical reaction, a genome sequence … In the humanities, however, they are always involved to some extent or another because they are intrinsically linked to their research objects, whether marriage strategies, class relations or illness representations. However, this does not mean that all anthropologists – to focus on them alone – are involved with their object to the same degree. To pursue the Eliasian reference, one could say that when anthropologists study a given group, if we learn more about them than about this group, then they are positioned on the side of involvement, whereas if they teach us more about the latter, they are rather situated on the side of detachment. The test is particularly relevant where morality is concerned. After having read an article or a book, one often knows more about the researcher's position than about the fact being analysed and the way in which people consider it. Over the last decades, moral engagement – against racism, intolerance, social injustice, Western imperialism, human rights' and women's rights' violations – has become more common in anthropology, particularly in the United States. This phenomenon, which warrants further development, is however not only quantitative but also qualitative. The partial replacement of certain research objects, such as relations of production or of domination, by others, such as the meaning of suffering or the experience of violence,[2] has reconfigured the way in which morality and politics link together.

This raises anew the question posed by Howard S. Becker: 'Whose side are we on?' The sociologist's answer is well known: 'we' are on the side of the dominated, the subordinates and the deviants. And this is not simply for the moral reason of rectifying the harm that has been done to them, but rather for the scientific reason consisting in re-establishing a truth that they can neither see nor say, because society generally only knows and recognises the interpretation of the world by those who hold both political power and symbolic authority. In this way, by looking at the point of view of those who do not master the rules of the social game and by contesting what seem to be obvious facts to those who define and apply them, researchers do more than simply listen to the voices of those who do not have access to the public space – they participate in an alternative representation of the world, one which, in a sense, unveils its hidden side.[3] This position would certainly not be accepted by all specialists in the social sciences, but it is probably fairly widely shared within anthropology. Its most radical expression came in the shape of Nancy Scheper-Hughes' famous article in which she advocates a militant anthropology, resolutely on the side of the victims and actively against the oppressors and their accomplices. Thus, she has denounced the social causes of infant mortality or the raids of death squads in Brazil as well as international organ trafficking. This approach is part of a much wider scientific programme that is sometimes referred to as critical anthropology and that particularly concerns the field of medical anthropology.[4] It has not only led to new research stances – involvement, or even activism – but it has also created new research objects – the subjectivation of the dominated, the marginalisation of the poor, the treatment of refugees and the commodification of bodies.

As generous and fascinating as this approach may be, not raising a certain number of questions, which are both theoretical – ultimately taking sides means only accounting for one part of social reality, and the ethnography of the wealthy and the powerful can be just as important to analyse the social world – and political – focusing studies on the misery of the world, and on social suffering – can mean losing sight of larger socio-economic processes. This last aspect underpins Leslie Butt's critique of what she considers to be the risk of a compassionate shift resulting in our using figures of suffering to move people rather than explaining the unequal order of the world and making people hear the voices of those in whose name we speak. More generally, it is important to ask ourselves what we gain and what we lose, from the point of view of critical thinking, when we reconfigure our objects of research in this way; when we pay more attention to wounded subjectivities, when we represent, in both senses of the word, the wretched of the earth, and when we ultimately make the anthropologist into a sort of moral hero. The question reaches far beyond the social sciences, which – due to their orientation – are involved in the wider evolution of contemporary sensibilities. The global spread of humanitarian reasoning and the politics of human rights is the most obvious sign of this. For the past three decades, we have seen an internationalisation of this dual rationale: on the one hand, moral sentiments are now present in world government from the local stage of aid for the poor to the global theatre of military interventions; on the other, calling upon universal principles has become a general necessity, whether in terms of women's rights or of transitional justice.⁵ For the social sciences, these policies pose a particular problem because they claim to call upon superior values of what is right, and those who implement them are therefore endowed with a sort of moral immunity.

The second question outlined initially refers anthropology back to its own history. The ethics of the discipline has indeed been greatly put to the test, from the French and British colonial enterprises to the United States' imperial project, and the relationship of anthropology to politics and the military are filled with episodes in which its professional deontology has been shaken. To consider only the facts concerning US anthropologists, which has proven to be the most open to debate on this sensitive subject, it is the contribution of certain scholars to war efforts that have given rise to the most intense discussions. As David Price reminds us, things began at the end of the First World War when Franz Boas denounced the spying carried out by certain ethnologists for the US army – which led to the American Anthropological Association excluding not the accused, but the accuser. Since then, all conflicts, including the low intensity wars in Latin America, have seen collusion between anthropologists and the intelligence services, the most recent example being the controversial Human Terrain System operation in Afghanistan and Iraq involving social scientists supposed to contribute their knowledge of the local populations and culture. The revelation of these practices has led to moments of crisis within the discipline.⁶ And yet when we examine closely each of these alleged deviances and discover the small number of scholars involved, sometimes for operations that did not even take place, like in the Camelot scandal, the contrast between the small scale of the affairs in question and the proportions taken by the issue can seem surprising. One way or another, these crises have been an opportunity for ethical reflection and the definition of deontological principles. Peter Pels retraces the prehistory of the resulting codes, which appeared relatively late, including elements concerning European anthropologies that have been far less studied. This prehistory is not linear, and the relationship of the discipline both to colonial subjects and colonial authorities, for example, has evolved considerably, from the moral civilising project regarding the 'natives', presupposing a certain collaboration with the white rulers, to scientific autonomy excluding any collaboration with the latter but increasingly including the notion of responsibility towards the populations.

While anthropologists were asking themselves more and more questions about their practice and attempting to define their own rules, a phenomenon with a somewhat distinct rationale was correspondingly unfolding. Following the trial against some of the actors of the Nazi genocide programme, and in particular the verdict regarding several German doctors involved in experiments on human beings, the 'Nuremberg code', as it is known, defined what should be the ethical criteria for research – particularly informed consent and absence of coercion. The principles outlined in this code were reformulated and stabilised in the 1964 Helsinki declaration on human experimentation aimed at the medical community. A revision decided upon a decade later introduced the notion of independent committees in charge of checking that these principles are respected in all research carried out. In the United States, where questions of medical ethics had become particularly sensitive after the revelation of the existence of the Tuskegee study in which several hundred African Americans suffering from syphilis were left without treatment in order to observe the natural evolution of the disease, these committees took the name of Institutional Review Boards generally designated by their acronym IRB. For a long time, the mechanism only served for research in the life sciences. However, over the last two decades, it has started to be imposed in the social sciences – first in North America, and then in Europe – on the basis that they also work with 'human subjects'. The implementation of this ethical regulation gave rise to protest from researchers and sometimes from their representative bodies, because the criteria conceived for medicine did not match the methods of the social sciences and particularly of ethnography, since, for example, the idea of getting every inhabitant of an area to sign an informed consent form in the context of participant observation would make no sense.[7] Charles L. Bosk echoes this discontent, giving a sociological analysis of the 'new bureaucracies of virtue' and their critics. The development of deontological codes, like that of the American Association of Anthropology presented here, and the spread of ethics committees, are not unrelated. The strategy generally put forward by social science bodies to resist the external control that is increasingly imposed upon them is to promote a form of internal control.

Anthropology studies society, of which anthropologists are members. The moral questions raised in the social world can therefore not be foreign to them. And the ethical issues at stake within their profession cannot leave them indifferent either. The two elements are partly linked. Anthropologists must examine the moral dimension that is necessarily an integral part of their work with lucidity and rigour, for lack of which the ethics of their research is in danger in terms of the responsibility they bear towards both the discipline they represent and the people with whom they work.

Notes

1 For Norbert Elias, involvement and detachment must be seen as two founding and necessary poles of human, and particularly scientific, activity. While the natural sciences tend to be 'detached', Elias does not deny that they are also in part determined by value judgements. Conversely, the social sciences originate in an effort to detach themselves from the structural constraint that means that researchers are 'involved' because 'the objects are also the subjects'. See Norbert Elias (1987), *Involvement and Detachment*, Oxford: Basil Blackwell, 1st German edition 1983.

2 The publication in the United States of three volumes on suffering and violence resulting from a programme funded by the Social Science Research Council was an important point in this evolution of anthropology. See Arthur Kleinman, Veena Das and Margaret Lock (eds.) (1997), *Social Suffering*, Berkeley, CA: University of California Press; Veena Das, Arthur Kleinman, Mamphela Ramphele and Pamela Reynolds (2000), *Violence and Subjectivity*, Berkeley, CA: University of California Press; and Veena Das, Arthur Kleinman, Margaret Lock, Mamphela Ramphele and Pamela Reynolds (2001), *Remaking a World: Violence, Social Suffering, and Recovery*, Berkeley, CA: University of California Press.

3 In sociology, this approach has been developed in particular by two 'schools of thought': one around Pierre Bourdieu in France, and the other around Michael Burawoy in the United States. See Pierre Bourdieu (ed.) (1999), *The Weight of the World: Social Suffering in Contemporary Society*, Oxford: Polity Press, 1st French edition 1993, and Michael Burawoy (ed.) (2000), *Global Ethnography: Forces, Connections, and Imaginations in a Postmodern World*, Berkeley, CA: University of California Press.

4 Other than Nancy Scheper-Hughes' work, that of Paul Farmer and Philippe Bourgois obviously come to mind. See in particular: Nancy Scheper-Hughes (1992), *Death Without Weeping: The Violence of Everyday Life in Brazil*, Berkeley, CA: University of California Press; Paul Farmer (2003), *Pathologies of Power: Health, Human Rights, and the New War on the Poor*, Berkeley, CA: University of California Press; Philippe Bourgois (1996), *In Search of Respect: Selling Crack in El Barrio*, Cambridge: Cambridge University Press. Among a substantial amount of literature on the subject, a collection of studies that can be considered to be part of critical and

engaged anthropology can be found in two books, the first extending across the world: Jeremy MacClancy (2002), *Exotic No More: Anthropology on the Front Lines*, Chicago, IL: The University of Chicago Press; and the other focusing more specifically on society in the United States: Hugh Gusterson and Catherine Besteman (2010), *The Insecure American: How We Got Here and What We Should Do About It*, Berkeley, CA: University of California Press. There are, however, several ways in which to consider critical anthropology, particularly from a more epistemological perspective. This is the case in the collective volume published by George Marcus (1999), *Critical Anthropology Now: Unexpected Contexts, Shifting Constituencies, Changing Agendas*, Santa Fe: School of American Research Press.

5 As well as the substantial body of literature available on these issues in the fields of international relations and international law, there are also a series of anthropological studies: on humanitarian action see Jonathan Benthall (1993), *Disasters, Relief and the Media*, London: I. B. Tauris; Didier Fassin (2010), *La Raison humanitaire: Une histoire morale du temps présent*, Paris: Hautes études-Gallimard-Seuil; Erica Bornstein and Peter Redfield (eds.) (2010), *Forces of Compassion: Humanitarianism Between Ethics and Politics*, Santa Fe: School of Advanced Research Press; and on human rights, see: Harri Englund (2006), *Prisoners of Freedom: Human Rights and the African Poor*, Berkeley, CA: University of California Press; Sally Engle Merry (2006), *Human Rights and Gender Violence: Translating International Law into Local Justice*, Chicago, IL: The University of Chicago Press; Adam Branch (2011), *Displacing Human Rights: War and Intervention in Northern Uganda*, Oxford: Oxford University Press.

6 This history is recounted in Carolyn Fluehr-Lobban (2003), *Ethics and the Profession of Anthropology: Dialogue for Ethically Conscious Practice*, Walnut Creek, CA: Altamira Press. David Price's three-volume study is the most substantial work on the important episodes of this history: (2004), *Threatening Anthropology: McCarthyism and the FBI's Surveillance of Activist Anthropologists*, Durham: Duke University Press; (2008), *Anthropological Intelligence: The Deployment and Neglect of American Anthropology in the Second World War*, and (2011), *Weaponizing Anthropology: Social Science in Service of the Militarized State*, Oakland, CA: AK Press.

7 The ethical regulation of the social sciences and more specifically the role of committees have given rise to special numbers of journals: IRBs, Bureaucratic Regulation, and Academic Freedom, *American Ethnologist*, 2006, 33 (4); Informed Consent in a Changing Environment, *Social Science & Medicine*, 2007, 65 (11); The New Bureaucracies of Virtue, *Political and Legal Anthropology Review*, 2007, 30 (2).

Moralising the world?

37 Whose side are we on?

Howard S. Becker

Howard S. Becker (born in 1928) is a sociologist of the second Chicago school. A student of Everett Hugues and the editor in chief for the journal *Social Problems* in the early 1960s, he is a leading figure of symbolic interactionism. Advocating a clear and simple written style as illustrated in his works on medical students, marijuana smokers, and jazz musicians, he developed innovative practices of participant observation. Considered the founder of labelling theory (*Outsiders*, 1963), he is also known for his contribution to the sociology of art (*Art Worlds*, 1982) and music (*Do you know...? The Jazz Repertoire in Action*, 2009).

The text presented here corresponds to the lecture Howard Becker delivered at the annual meeting of the Society for the Study of Social Problems in 1966. He proposes the notion of hierarchy of credibility to characterise the fact that authority is not distributed equally: in a given social space, the members of superordinate categories (doctors, police officers, adults, etc.) define, in a sense, the legitimate version of reality that the members of the subordinate categories (patients, delinquents, adolescents, etc.) must accept as such. By integrating deviant behaviour into a hierarchical relation of a moral type, this essay raises the sensitive issue of the researcher's stance and the resulting moral tensions. In substance, Becker shows that sociological studies always entail a certain form of engagement, linked to researchers' social affinities or political commitment, or even simply to the perspective from which they examine a problem, by approaching it from one side or the other. He notes, however, that accusations of bias are only expressed when sociologists are suspected of taking the side of the subordinates because, in doing so, they question the monopoly of truth held by the 'moral entrepreneurs'. Rather than denying the social scientist's engagement, he argues that it is preferable to address its consequences and the best way analysis can take it into account.

To have values or not to have values: the question is always with us. When sociologists undertake to study problems that have relevance to the world we live in, they find themselves caught in a crossfire. Some urge them not to take sides, to be neutral and do research that is technically correct and value free. Others tell them their work is shallow and useless if it does not express a deep commitment to a value position. This dilemma, which seems so painful to so many, actually does not exist, for one of its horns is imaginary. For it to exist, one would have to assume, as some apparently do, that it is indeed possible to do research that is uncontaminated by personal and political sympathies. I propose to argue that it is not possible and, therefore, that the question is not whether we should take sides, since we inevitably will, but rather whose side we are on.

I will begin by considering the problem of taking sides as it arises in the study of deviance. An inspection of this case will soon reveal to us features that appear in sociological research of all kinds. In the greatest variety of subject matter areas and in work done by all the different methods at our disposal, we cannot avoid taking sides, for reasons firmly based in social structure.

We may sometimes feel that studies of deviance exhibit too great a sympathy with the people studied, a sympathy reflected in the research carried out. This feeling, I suspect, is entertained off and on both by those of us who do such research and by those of us who, our work lying in other areas, only read the results. Will the research, we wonder, be distorted by that sympathy? Will it be of use in the construction of scientific theory or in the application of scientific knowledge to the practical problems of society? Or will the bias introduced by taking sides spoil it for those uses? We seldom make the feeling explicit. Instead, it appears as a lingering worry for sociological readers, who would like to be sure they can trust what they read, and a troublesome area of self-doubt for those who do the research, who would like to be sure that whatever sympathies they feel are not professionally unseemly and will not, in any case, seriously flaw their work. That the worry affects both readers and researchers indicates that it lies deeper than the superficial differences that divide sociological schools of thought, and that its roots must be sought in characteristics of society that affect us all, whatever our methodological or theoretical persuasion. If the feeling were made explicit, it would take the form of an accusation that the sympathies of the researcher have biased his work and distorted his findings. Before exploring its structural roots, let us consider what the manifest meaning of the charge might be.

It might mean that we have acquired some sympathy with the group we study sufficient to deter us from publishing those of our results which might prove damaging to them. One can imagine a liberal sociologist who set out to disprove some of the common stereotypes held about a minority group. To his dismay, his investigation reveals that some of the stereotypes are unfortunately true. In the interests of justice and liberalism, he might well be tempted, and might even succumb to the temptation, to suppress those findings, publishing with scientific candor the other results which confirmed his beliefs.

But this seems not really to be the heart of the charge, because sociologists who study deviance do not typically hide things about the people they study. They are mostly willing to grant that there is something going on that put the deviants in the position they are in, even if they are not willing to grant that it is what the people they studied were originally accused of.

A more likely meaning of the charge, I think, is this. In the course of our work and for who knows what private reasons, we fall into deep sympathy with the people we are studying, so that while the rest of the society views them as unfit in one or another respect for the deference ordinarily accorded a fellow citizen, we believe that they are at least as good as anyone else, more sinned against than sinning. Because of this, we do not give a balanced picture. We focus too much on questions whose answers show that the supposed deviant is morally in the right and the ordinary citizen morally in the wrong. We neglect to ask those questions whose answers would show that the deviant, after all, has done something pretty rotten and, indeed, pretty much deserves what he gets. In consequence, our overall assessment of the problem being studied is one-sided. What we produce is a whitewash of the deviant and a condemnation, if only by implication, of those respectable citizens who, we think, have made the deviant what he is.

It is to this version that I devote the rest of my remarks. I will look first, however, not at the truth or falsity of the charge, but rather at the circumstances in which it is typically made and felt. The sociology of knowledge cautions us to distinguish between the truth of a statement and an assessment of the circumstances under which that statement is made; though we trace an argument to its source in the interests of the person who made it, we have still not proved it false. Recognizing the point and promising to address it eventually, I shall turn to the typical situations in which the accusation of bias arises.

When do we accuse ourselves and our fellow sociologists of bias? I think an inspection of representative instances would show that the accusation arises, in one important class of cases, when the research gives credence, in any serious way, to the perspective of the subordinate group in some hierarchical relationship. In the case of deviance, the hierarchical relationship is a moral one. The superordinate parties in the relationship are those who represent the forces of approved and official morality; the subordinate parties are those who, it is alleged, have violated that morality.

Though deviance is a typical case, it is by no means the only one. Similar situations, and similar feelings that our work is biased, occur in the study of schools, hospitals, asylums and prisons, in the study of physical as well as mental illness, in the study of both "normal" and delinquent youth. In these situations, the superordinate parties are usually the official and professional authorities in charge of some important institution, while the subordinates are those who make use of the services of that institution. Thus, the police are the superordinates, drug addicts are the subordinates; professors and administrators, principals and teachers, are the superordinates, while students and pupils are the subordinates; physicians are the superordinates, their patients the subordinates.

All of these cases represent one of the typical situations in which researchers accuse themselves and are accused of bias. It is a situation in which, while conflict and tension exist in the hierarchy, the conflict has not become openly political. The conflicting segments or ranks are not organized for conflict; no one attempts to alter the shape of the hierarchy. While subordinates may complain about the treatment they receive from those above them, they do not propose to move to a position of equality with them, or to reverse positions in the hierarchy. Thus, no one proposes that addicts should make and enforce laws for policemen, that patients should prescribe for doctors, or that adolescents should give orders to adults. We can call this the *apolitical* case.

In the second case, the accusation of bias is made in a situation that is frankly political. The parties to the hierarchical relationship engage in organized conflict, attempting either to maintain or change existing relations of power and authority. Whereas in the first case subordinates are typically unorganized and thus have, as we shall see, little to fear from a researcher, subordinate parties in a political situation may have much to lose. When the situation is political, the researcher may accuse himself or be accused of bias by someone else when he gives credence to the perspective of either party to the political conflict. I leave the political for later and turn now to the problem of bias in apolitical situations.[1]

We provoke the suspicion that we are biased in favor of the subordinate parties in an apolitical arrangement when we tell the story from their point of view. We may, for instance, investigate their complaints, even though they are subordinates, about the way things are run just as though one ought to give their complaints as much credence as the statements of responsible officials. We provoke the charge when we assume, for the purposes of our research, that subordinates have as much right to be heard as superordinates, that they are as likely to be telling the truth as they see it as superordinates, that what they say about the institution has a right to be investigated and have its truth or falsity established, even though responsible officials assure us that it is unnecessary because the charges are false.

We can use the notion of a *hierarchy of credibility* to understand this phenomenon. In any system of ranked groups, participants take it as given that members of the highest group have the right to define the way things really are. In any organization, no matter what the rest of the organization chart shows, the arrows indicating the flow of information point up, thus demonstrating (at least formally) that those at the top have access to a more complete picture of what is going on than anyone else. Members of lower groups will have incomplete information, and their view of reality will be partial and distorted in consequence. Therefore, from the point of view of a well socialized participant in the system, any tale told by those at the top intrinsically deserves to be regarded as the most credible account obtainable of the organization's workings. And since, as Sumner pointed out, matters of rank and status are contained in the mores,[2] this belief has a moral quality. We are, if we are proper members of the group, morally bound to accept the definition imposed on reality by a superordinate group in preference to the definitions espoused by subordinates. (By analogy, the same argument holds for the social classes of a community.) Thus, credibility and the right to be heard are differentially distributed through the ranks of the system.

As sociologists, we provoke the charge of bias, in ourselves and others, by refusing to give credence and deference to an established status order, in which knowledge of truth and the right to be heard are not equally distributed. "Everyone knows" that responsible professionals know more about things than laymen, that police are more respectable and their words ought to be taken more seriously than those of the deviants and criminals with whom they deal. By refusing to accept the hierarchy of credibility, we express disrespect for the entire established order.

We compound our sin and further provoke charges of bias by not giving immediate attention and "equal time" to the apologies and explanations of official authority. If, for instance, we are concerned with studying the way of life inmates in a mental hospital build up for themselves, we will naturally be concerned with the constraints and conditions created by the actions of the administrators and physicians who run the hospital. But, unless we also make the administrators and physicians the object of our study (a possibility I will consider later), we will not inquire into why those conditions and constraints are present. We will not give responsible officials a chance to explain themselves and give their reasons for acting as they do, a chance to show why the complaints of inmates are not justified.

It is odd that, when we perceive bias, we usually see it in these circumstances. It is odd because it is easily ascertained that a great many more studies are biased in the direction of the interests of responsible officials than the other way around. We may accuse an occasional student of medical sociology of having given too much emphasis to the complaints of patients. But it is not obvious that most medical sociologists look at things from the point of view of the doctors? A few sociologists may be sufficiently biased in favor of youth to grant credibility to their account of how the adult world treats them. But why do we not accuse other sociologists who study youth of being biased in favor of adults? Most research on youth, after all, is clearly designed to find out why youth are so troublesome for adults, rather than asking the equally interesting sociological question: "Why do adults make so much trouble for youth?" Similarly, we accuse those who take the complaints of mental patients seriously of bias; what about those sociologists who only take seriously the complaints of physicians, families and others about mental patients?

Why this disproportion in the direction of accusations of bias? Why do we more often accuse those who are on the side of subordinates than those who are on the side of superordinates? Because, when we make the former accusation, we have, like the well socialized members of our society most of us are, accepted the hierarchy of credibility and taken over the accusation made by responsible officials.

The reason responsible officials make the accusation so frequently is precisely because they are responsible. They have been entrusted with the care and operation of one or another of our important institutions: schools, hospitals, law enforcement, or whatever. They are the ones who, by virtue of their official position and the authority that goes with it, are in a position to "do something" when things are not what they should be and, similarly, are the ones who will be held to account if they fail to "do something" or if what they do is, for whatever reason, inadequate.

Because they are responsible in this way, officials usually have to lie. That is a gross way of putting it, but not inaccurate. Officials must lie because things are seldom as they ought to be. For a great variety of reasons, well-known to sociologists, institutions are refractory. They do not perform as society would like them to. Hospitals do not cure people; prisons do not rehabilitate prisoners; schools do not educate students. Since they are supposed to, officials develop ways both of denying the failure of the institution to perform as it should and explaining those failures which cannot be hidden. An account of an institution's operation from the point of view of subordinates therefore casts doubt on the official line and may possibly expose it as a lie.[3]

For reasons that are a mirror image of those of officials, subordinates in an apolitical hierarchical relationship have no reason to complain of the bias of sociological research oriented toward the interests of superordinates. Subordinates typically are not organized in such a fashion as to be responsible for the overall operation of an institution. What happens in a school is credited or debited to the faculty and administrators; they can be identified and held to account. Even though the failure of a school may be the fault of the pupils, they are not so organized that any one of them is responsible for any failure but his own. If he does well, while others all around him flounder, cheat and steal, that is none of his affair, despite the attempt of honor codes to make it so. As long as the sociological report on his school says that every student there but one is a liar and a cheat, all the students will feel complacent, knowing they are the one exception. More likely, they will never hear of the report at all or, if they do, will reason that they will be gone before long, so what difference does it make? The lack of organization among subordinate members of an institutionalized relationship means that, having no responsibility for the group's welfare, they likewise have no complaints if someone maligns it. The sociologist who favors officialdom will be spared the accusation of bias.

And thus we see why we accuse ourselves of bias only when we take the side of the subordinate. It is because, in a situation that is not openly political, with the major issues defined as arguable, we join responsible officials and the man in the street in an unthinking acceptance of the hierarchy of credibility. We assume with them that the man at the top knows best. We do not realize that there are sides to be taken and that we are taking one of them.

The same reasoning allows us to understand why the researcher has the same worry about the effect of his sympathies on his work as his uninvolved colleague. The hierarchy of credibility is a feature of society whose existence we cannot deny, even if we disagree with its injunction to believe the man at the top. When we acquire sufficient sympathy with subordinates to see things from their perspective, we know that we are flying in the face of what "everyone knows." The knowledge gives us pause and causes us to share, however briefly, the doubt of our colleagues.

When a situation has been defined politically, the second type of case I want to discuss, matters are quite different. Subordinates have some degree of organization and, with that, spokesmen, their equivalent of responsible officials. Spokesmen, while they cannot actually be held responsible for what members of their group do, make assertions on their behalf and are held responsible for the truth of those assertions. The group engages in political activity designed to change existing hierarchical relationships and the credibility of its spokesmen directly affects its political fortunes. Credibility is not the only influence, but the group can ill-afford having the definition of reality proposed by its spokesmen discredited, for the immediate consequence will be some loss of political power.

Superordinate groups have their spokesmen too, and they are confronted with the same problem: to make statements about reality that are politically effective without being easily discredited. The political fortunes of the superordinate group—its ability to hold the status changes demanded by lower groups to a minimum—do not depend as much on credibility, for the group has other kinds of power available as well.

When we do research in a political situation we are in double jeopardy, for the spokesmen of both involved groups will be sensitive to the implications of our work. Since they propose openly conflicting definitions of reality, our statement of our problem is in itself likely to call into question and make problematic, at least for the purposes of our research, one or the other definition. And our results will do the same.

The hierarchy of credibility operates in a different way in the political situation than it does in the apolitical one. In the political situation, it is precisely one of the things at issue. Since the political struggle calls into question the legitimacy of the existing rank system, it necessarily calls into question at the same time the legitimacy of the associated judgments of credibility. Judgments of who has a right to define the nature of reality that are taken for granted in an apolitical situation become matters of argument.

Oddly enough, we are, I think, less likely to accuse ourselves and one another of bias in a political than in an apolitical situation, for at least two reasons. First, because the hierarchy of credibility has been openly called into question, we are aware that there are at least two sides to the story and so do not think it unseemly to investigate the situation from one or another of the contending points of view. We know, for instance, that we must grasp the perspectives of both the resident of Watts and of the Los Angeles policeman if we are to understand what went on in that outbreak.

Second, it is no secret that most sociologists are politically liberal to one degree or another. Our political preferences dictate the side we will be on and, since those preferences are shared by most of our colleagues, few are ready to throw the first stone or are even aware that stone-throwing is a possibility. We usually take the side of the underdog; we are for Negroes and against Fascists. We do not think anyone biased who does research designed to prove that the former are not as bad as people think or that the latter are worse. In fact, in these circumstances we are quite willing to regard the question of bias as a matter to be dealt with by the use of technical safeguards. [...]

What I have said so far is all sociology of knowledge, suggesting by whom, in what situations and for what reasons sociologists will be accused of bias and distortion. I have not yet addressed the question of the truth of the accusations, of whether our findings are distorted by our sympathy for those we study. I have implied a partial answer, namely, that there is no position from which sociological research can be done that is not biased in one or another way.

We must always look at the matter from someone's point of view. The scientist who proposes to understand society must, as Mead long ago pointed out, get into the situation enough to have a perspective on it. And it is likely that his perspective will be greatly affected by whatever positions are taken by any or all of the other participants in that varied situation. Even if his participation is limited to reading in the field, he will necessarily read the arguments of partisans of one or another side to a relationship and will thus be affected, at least, by having suggested to him what the relevant arguments and issues are. A student of medical sociology may decide that he will take neither the perspective of the patient nor the perspective of the physician, but he will necessarily take a perspective that impinges on the many questions that arise between physicians and patients; no matter what perspective he takes, his work either will take into account the attitude of subordinates, or it will not. If he fails to consider the questions they raise, he will be working on the side of the officials. If he does raise those questions seriously and does find, as he may, that there is some merit in them, he will then expose himself to the outrage of the officials and of all those sociologists who award them the top spot in the hierarchy of credibility. Almost all the topics that sociologists study, at least those that have some relation to the real world around us, are seen by society as morality plays and we shall find ourselves, willy-nilly, taking part in those plays on one side or the other.

There is another possibility. We may, in some cases, take the point of view of some third party not directly implicated in the hierarchy we are investigating. Thus, a Marxist might feel that it is not worth distinguishing between Democrats and Republicans, or between big business and big labor, in each case both groups being equally inimical to the interests of the workers. This would indeed make us neutral with respect to the two groups at hand, but would only mean that we had enlarged the scope of the political conflict to include a party not ordinarily brought in whose view the sociologist was taking.

We can never avoid taking sides. So we are left with the question of whether taking sides means that some distortion is introduced into our work so great as to make it useless. Or, less drastically, whether some distortion is introduced that must be taken into account before the results of our work can be used. I do not refer here to feeling that the picture given by the research is not "balanced," the indignation aroused by having a conventionally discredited definition of reality given priority or equality with what "everyone knows," for it is clear that we cannot avoid that. That is the problem of officials, spokesmen and interested parties, not ours. Our problem is to make sure that, whatever point of view we take, our research meets the standards of good scientific work, that our unavoidable sympathies do not render our results invalid. [...]

We can, I think, satisfy the demands of our science by always making clear the limits of what we have studied, marking the boundaries beyond which our findings cannot be safely applied. Not just the conventional disclaimer, in which we warn that we have only studied a prison in New York or California and the findings may not hold in the other forty-nine states—which is not a useful procedure anyway, since the findings may very well hold if the conditions are the same elsewhere. I refer to a more sociological disclaimer in which we say, for instance, that we have studied the prison through the eyes of the inmates and not through the eyes of the guards or other involved parties. We warn people, thus, that our study tells us only how things look from that vantage point—what kinds of objects guards are in the prisoners' world— and does not attempt to explain why guards do what they do or to absolve the guards of what may seem, from the prisoners' side, morally unacceptable behavior. This will not protect us from accusations of bias, however, for the guards will still be outraged by the unbalanced picture. If we implicitly accept the conventional hierarchy of credibility, we will feel the sting in that accusation.

Notes

1 No situation is necessarily political or apolitical. An apolitical situation can be transformed into a political one by the open rebellion of subordinate ranks, and a political situation can subside into one in which an accommodation has been reached and a new hierarchy been accepted by the participants. The categories, while analytically useful, do not represent a fixed division existing in real life.
2 William Graham Sumner (1960), Status in the Folkways, in *Folkways: A Study of the Sociological Importance of Usages, Manners, Customs, Mores, and Morals*, New York: New American Library, pp. 72–73.
3 I have stated a portion of this argument more briefly in Problems of Publication of Field Studies, in *Reflections on Community Studies*, Arthur Vidich, Joseph Bensman, and Maurice Stein (eds.), New York: John Wiley & Sons, 1964, pp. 267–284.

38 The primacy of the ethical

Nancy Scheper-Hughes

Nancy Scheper-Hughes (born in 1944) is a professor of medical anthropology at the University of California, Berkeley. Her first monograph, *Saints, Scholars, and Schizophrenics*, focused on mental health in Ireland where it generated controversy due to the bleak portrait she depicted of the disintegration of Irish rural life. Her book, *Death Without Weeping: The Violence of Everyday Life in Brazil*, has become a classic revealing the structures of inequality and forms of rationality underpinning motherhood within the context of poverty in Northeast Brazil. The collective volumes she has co-edited, *Small Wars: The Cultural Politics of Childhood*, on the mistreatment of children, and *Commodifying Bodies*, on the commodification of the human body, analyse and denounce multiple forms of violence in the contemporary world. Beyond her academic activity, Nancy Scheper-Hughes also works as an activist, notably with Organs Watch, a non-governmental organisation that combats international organ trafficking, about which she testified in court cases, documentaries, and newspapers.

The essay presented here was published in *Current Anthropology* alongside an article by Roy D'Andrade. Although they had been conceived independently, the editorial board of the journal considered that the two pieces offered opposing visions of anthropology and published them together under the title 'Objectivity and Militantism', with one defending a politically committed and morally engaged anthropology and the other calling for a positivist approach. The comments to which this dialogue gave rise illustrate the tensions running through anthropology at the time in reaction to the radical nature of criticism initiated by the linguistic and textualist turn. In a sort of anthropological *coup de force*, Nancy Scheper-Hughes proposes a transcendental and therefore universal version of ethics, which grounds the involvement of the anthropologists. For her, the ethical is 'primary' because it is not culture that produces ethics but rather ethics that produces culture, allowing human beings to live together. Thus, anthropologists resolve the existential tensions of a discipline that is defined by its approach to 'otherness', but is always challenged to go beyond it. According to Nancy Scheper-Hughes, action should replace observation, guided by higher moral principles that exceed the specificity of contexts, groups, and moments.

For much of this century cultural anthropology has been concerned with divergent rationalities, with explaining how and why various cultural others thought, reasoned, and lived-in-the-world as they did. Classical anthropological thinking and practice are best exemplified, perhaps, in the great witchcraft and rationality debates of decades past.[1] Ideally, modernist cultural anthropology liberated "truth" from its unexamined Eurocentric and Orientalist presuppositions. But the world, the objects of our study, and consequently, the uses of anthropology have changed considerably. Exploring the cultural logic of witchcraft is one thing. Documenting, as I am now, the burning or "necklacing" of accused witches, political collaborators, and other ne'er-do-wells in beleaguered South African townships—where a daily toll of "charred bodies" is a standard feature of news reports—is another. A more womanly-hearted anthropology might be concerned not only with how humans think but with how they behave toward each other, thus engaging directly with questions of ethics and power.

In South African squatter camps as in the AIDS sanatoria of Cuba and in the parched lands of Northeast Brazil, I have stumbled on a central dilemma and challenge to cultural anthropology, one that has tripped up many a fieldworker before me (for example, Renato Rosaldo in his encounters with Ilongot headhunters)[2]: In bracketing certain "Western" Enlightenment truths we hold and defend as self-evident at home in order to engage theoretically with a multiplicity of alternative truths encoded in our reified notion of culture, anthropologists may be "suspending the ethical" in our dealings with the "other," especially those whose vulnerable bodies and fragile lives are at stake. Moreover, what stake can anthropologists expect to have in current political debates in rapidly "democratizing" nations in Eastern Europe, Latin America, and Africa where newly drafted constitutions and bills of rights—and those of Brazil and South Africa are exemplary—speak to a growing global consensus ("Western," "bourgeois," "hegemonic," if you will) defending the rights of women, children, sexual minorities, the accused, and the sick against "traditional and customary law," cultural claims increasingly viewed as hostile, oppressive, and exploitative?

Framing the issue and calling the bluff

In the introduction to *Death Without Weeping*[3] I suggest that cultural relativism, read as moral relativism, is no longer appropriate to the world in which we live and that anthropology, if it is to be worth anything at all, must be ethically grounded: "If we cannot begin to think about social institutions and practices in moral or ethical terms, then anthropology strikes me as quite weak and useless." The specific instance I treat at length in *Death Without Weeping* concerns the moral thinking and social practices of poor shantytown women toward some of their small, hungry babies viewed as "wanting" to die or "needing" to die, as filling the role of "generative scapegoats"[4] and dying, like Jesus, so that others might live.

More recently, I have dealt with the impact of the AIDS epidemic on moral thinking, public policy, and the "politics of truth" in the United States, Brazil, and Cuba.[5] I suggest that more could have been done to prevent the spread of the epidemic if such standard public health measures and practices as routine testing with partner notification had not been rejected in the United States and, more generally, in the West (through the WHO global AIDS program) as politically unpalatable. I point to a lapse in moral courage by those empowered to protect the well-being of the social body and in the writings of medical anthropologists, among whom "critical" thinking seems to be suspended in the time of AIDS. Finally, in South Africa I ran headlong into a dispute with local "discipline" and "security" committees in a black squatter camp of the Western Cape, where the threat of the "necklace" and public floggings were used to keep especially young bodies in line.

In each case I have had to pause and reconsider the traditional role of the anthropologist as neutral, dispassionate, cool and rational, objective observer of the human condition: the anthropologist as "fearless spectator," to evoke Charles McCabe's (un)felicitous phrase. And I am tempted to call anthropology's bluff, to expose its artificial moral relativism and to try to imagine what forms a politically committed and morally engaged anthropology might take. [...]

The politics of representation

As writers and producers of demanding images and texts, what *do* we want from our readers? To shock? To evoke pity? To create new forms of narrative, an "aesthetic" of misery, an anthropology of suffering, an anthropological theodicy? And what of the people whose suffering and fearful accommodations to it are transformed into a public spectacle? What is our obligation to them?

Those of us who make our living observing and recording the misery of the world have a particular obligation to reflect critically on the impact of the harsh images of human suffering that we foist on the public. I think of the brutal images of fleeing Haitian boat people and the emotionally devastated family around the bedside of a dying AIDS patient with which the business magnate Benetton has assaulted us, for reasons that remain altogether unclear, and of the daily media images of horror in Bosnia, Somalia, the Middle East, and the townships of South Africa and of Sebastião Salgado's images of hunger and death in the Brazilian Northeast. To what end are we given and do we represent these images as long as the misery and the suffering continue unabated? The experience of Northeast Brazil and South Africa indicates that the more frequent and ubiquitous the images of sickness, political terror, starvation and death, burnings and hangings, the more people living the terror accept the brutality as routine, normal, even expected. The shock reaction is readily extinguished, and people everywhere seem to have an enormous capacity to absorb the hideous and go on with life and with the terror, violence, and misery as usual.

As Michael Taussig has noted, citing Walter Benjamin's analysis of the history of European fascism, it is almost impossible to be continually conscious of the state of emergency in which one lives.[6] Sooner or later one makes one's accommodations to it. The images meant to evoke shock and panic evoke only blank stares, a shrug of the shoulders, a nod—acceptance as routine and *normal* of the extraordinary state of siege under which so many live. Humans have an uncanny ability to hold terror and misery at arm's length, especially when they occur in their own community and are right before their eyes. Anthropologists do so themselves when they apply their theoretical abstractions and rhetorical figures of speech to the horrors of political violence—both wars of repression and wars of liberation—so that the suffering is aestheticized (turned into theater, viewed as "performance") and thereby minimized and denied. The new cadre of "barefoot anthropologists" that I envision must become alarmists and shock troopers—the producers of politically complicated and morally demanding texts and images capable of sinking through the layers of acceptance, complicity, and bad faith that allow the suffering and the deaths to continue without even the pained cry of recognition of Conrad's[7] evil protagonist, Kurtz: "*The horror! the horror!*"

Anthropology without borders: the postmodern critique

Ethnography has had a rough time of it lately. In the brave new world of reflexive postmodernists, when anthropologists arrive in the field everything local is said to dissolve into merged media images, transgressed boundaries, promiscuously mobile multinational industry and workers, and transnational-corporate desires and commodity fetishism. This imagined postmodern, borderless world[8] is, in fact, a Camelot of free trade that echoes the marketplace rhetoric of global capitalism, a making of the world and social science safe for "low-intensity democracy" backed by World Bank capital. The flight from the local in hot pursuit of a transnational, borderless anthropology implies a parallel flight from local engagements, local commitments, and local accountability. Once the circuits of power are seen as capillary, diffuse, global, and difficult to trace to their sources, the idea of resistance becomes meaningless. It can be either nothing or anything at all. (Have we lost our senses altogether?)

The idea of an anthropology without borders, although it has a progressive ring to it, ignores the reality of the very real borders that confront and oppress "our" anthropological subjects and encroach on our liberty as well. (The obstacles that the U.S. government puts in the way of North Americans wishing to conduct research in Cuba or establish ties with Cuban scholars are just one case in point.) These borders are as real as the passports and passbooks, the sandbagged bunkers, the armed roadblocks and barricades, and the "no-go zones" that separate hostile peoples, territories, and states. The borders confront us with the indisputable reality of electric fences, razor wire, nail-studded hand grenades, AK47s; where these are lacking, as in South African townships and squatter camps, stones and torches will do.

Having recently returned from South Africa, where both black and white tribes, Zulus and Afrikaners, were demanding enclosed and militarily defended homelands, it is difficult to relate to the whimsical postmodernist language extolling borderless worlds. The anthropology that most Cape Town Xhosa, Venda, Zulu, Afrikaner, and Muslim students want is *not* the anthropology of deconstruction and the social imaginary but the anthropology of the *really real*, in which the stakes are high, values are certain, and ethnicity (if not essentialized) is certainly essential. Here, writing against culture[9] would be writing against them, against *their* grain, against their emergent need, in a newly forming and, one hopes, democratic state, for collective self-definition and historical legitimacy—for a place in the sun.

Anthropology, it seems to me, must be there to provide the kind of deeply textured, fine-tuned narratives describing the specificity of lives lived in small and isolated places in distant homelands, in the "native yards" of sprawling townships, or in the Afrikaner farm communities of the Stellenbosch and the Boland. And we need, more than ever, to locate and train indigenous local anthropologists and organic intellectuals to work with us and to help us redefine and transform ourselves and our vexed craft.

Many younger anthropologists today, sensitized by the writings of Michel Foucault on power/knowledge, have come to think of anthropological fieldwork as a kind of invasive, disciplinary "panopticon" and the anthropological interview as similar to the medieval inquisitional confession through which church examiners extracted "truth" from their native and "heretical" peasant parishioners. One hears of anthropological observation as a hostile act that reduces our "subjects" to mere "objects" of our discriminating, incriminating, scientific gaze. Consequently, some postmodern anthropologists have given up the practice of descriptive ethnography altogether.

I am weary of these postmodernist critiques, and, given the perilous times in which we and our subjects live, I am inclined toward compromise, the practice of a "good enough" ethnography.[10] While the anthropologist is always a necessarily flawed and biased instrument of cultural translation, like every other craftsperson we can do the best we can with the limited resources we have at hand: our ability to listen and to observe carefully and with empathy and compassion. I still believe that we are best doing what we do best as ethnographers, as natural historians of people until very recently thought to have no history. And so I think of some of my anthropological subjects—in Brazil Biu, Dona Amor, little Mercea, little angel-baby that she is now; in South Africa, Sidney Kumalo and the three boys rescued in the nick of time from a mortal flogging—for whom anthropology is not a "hostile gaze" but rather an opportunity for self-expression. Seeing, listening, touching, recording can be, if done with care and sensitivity, acts of solidarity. Above all, they are the work of recognition. Not to look, not to touch, not to record can be the hostile act, an act of indifference and of turning away.

If I did not believe that ethnography could be used as a tool for critical reflection and for human liberation, what kind of perverse cynicism would keep me returning again and again to disturb the waters of Bom Jesus da Mata or to study the contradictory medical and political detention of Cubans in the Havana AIDS sanatorium? Or, more recently, to study the underbelly of political violence and terror in the makeshift mortuary chapels of Chris Hani squatter camp?[11] What draws me back to these people and places is not their exoticism and their "otherness" but the pursuit of those small spaces of convergence, recognition, and empathy that we share. Not everything dissolves into the vapor of absolute cultural difference and radical otherness. There are ways in which my Brazilian, Cuban, Irish, and South African interlocutors and I are not so radically "other" to each other. Like the peasants of Ireland and Northeast Brazil, I too instinctively make the sign of the cross when I sense danger or misfortune approaching. And like Mrs. Kumalo and so many other middle-aged women of Chris Hani squatter camp, I too wait up (till dawn if necessary) for the scrape-scrape sound of my son and daughters as, one by one, following their own life plans, they turn their keys in the latch and announce their arrival one more day from an unsafe and booby-trapped outside world.

The primacy of the ethical

The work of anthropology demands an explicit ethical orientation to "the other." In the past—and with good reason—this was interpreted as a respectful distance, a hesitancy, and a reluctance to name wrongs, to judge, to intervene, or to prescribe change, even in the face of considerable human misery. In existential philosophical terms, anthropology, like theology, implied a leap of faith to an unknown, opaque other-than-myself, before whom a kind of reverence and awe was required. The practice of anthropology was guided by a complex form of modern pessimism rooted in anthropology's tortured relationship to the colonial world and its ruthless destruction of native lands and peoples. Because of its origins as a mediator in the clash of colonial cultures and civilizations, anthropological thinking was, in a sense, radically "conservative" with respect to its "natural" suspiciousness of all projects promoting change, development, modernization, and the like. We knew how often such interventions were used against traditional, nonsecular, and communal people who stood in the way of Western cultural and economic expansion. Therefore, it was understood that anthropological work, if it was to be in the nature of an ethical project, had to be primarily transformative of the self, while putting few or no demands on "the other." The artificial and (at times) counterintuitive notion of cultural (and moral and political) relativism evolved as the sacred oath of anthropological fieldwork. As the physicians' injunction was to "do no harm," the anthropologists' injunction was (like the three monkeys of ancient China) to "see no evil, hear no evil, speak no evil" in reporting from the field.

While the first generations of cultural anthropologists were concerned with relativizing thought and reason, I have suggested that a more "womanly" anthropology might be concerned not only with how humans think but with how they behave toward each other. This would engage anthropology directly with questions of ethics. The problem remains in searching for a standard or divergent ethical standards that take into account (but do not privilege) our own "Western" cultural presuppositions.

In the shantytown of Alto do Cruzeiro in Northeast Brazil I encountered a situation in which some mothers appear to have "suspended the ethical"—compassion, empathic love, and care—in relation to some of their weak and sickly children, allowing them to die of neglect in the face of overwhelming difficulties. In the South African squatter camps of the Western Cape I stumbled upon another instance: the expressed sentiment that one less young thief or police "collaborator" makes good sense in terms of social and community hygiene. At times the shantytown or the squatter camp resembles nothing so much as a battlefield, a prison camp, or an emergency room in a crowded inner-city hospital, where an ethic of triage replaces an ethical regard for the equal value of every life. The survivor's "logic" that guides shantytown mothers' actions toward some of their weak babies is understandable. The fragility and "dangerousness" of the mother–infant relationship is an immediate and visible index of chronic scarcity, hunger, and other unmet needs. And the revolutionary logic that sees in the pressured but self-serving acts of a young police collaborator the sorcery of a scarcely human witch or devil is also understandable. But the moral and ethical issues must still give reason to pause and to doubt. How often the oppressed turn into their own oppressors or, worse still, into the oppressors of others!

Anthropologists who are privileged to witness human events close up and over time, who are privy to community secrets that are generally hidden from the view of outsiders or from historical scrutiny until much later—after the collective graves have been discovered and the body counts made—have, I believe, an ethical obligation to identify the ills in a spirit of solidarity and to follow what Gilligan has called a "womanly" ethic of care and responsibility.[12] If anthropologists deny themselves the power (because it implies a privileged position) to identify an ill or a wrong and choose to ignore (because it is not pretty) the extent to which dominated people sometimes play the role of their own executioners, they collaborate with the relations of power and silence that allow the destruction to continue.

To speak of the "primacy of the ethical" is to suggest certain transcendent, transparent, and essential, if not "precultural," first principles. Historically anthropologists have understood morality as contingent on and embedded within specific cultural assumptions about human life. But there is another philosophical position that posits "the ethical" as existing prior to culture because, as Emmanuel Levinas writes, in presupposing all meaning, ethics makes culture possible: "Morality does not belong to culture: [it] enables one to judge it."[13] Here I will tentatively and hesitantly suggest that responsibility, accountability, answerability to "the other"—the ethical as I would define it—is precultural to the extent that our human existence as social beings presupposes the presence of the other. The extreme relativist position assumes that thought, emotion, and reflexivity come into existence with words and words come into being with culture. But the generative pre-structure of language presupposes, as Sartre[14] has written, a given relationship with another subject, one that exists prior to words in the silent, preverbal "taking stock" of each other's existence. Though I veer dangerously toward what some might construe as a latent sociobiology, I cannot escape the following observation: that we are thrown into existence at all presupposes a given, implicit moral relationship to an original (m)other and she to me. "Basic strangeness"—as the psychoanalyst Maria Piers labeled the profound shock of misrecognition reported by a great many mothers in their first encounters with a newborn—is perhaps the prototype of all other alienated self–other relations, including that of the anthropologist and her overly exoticized others. Just as many women may fail to recognize a human kinship with the newborn and see it as a strange, exotic, other—a bird, a crocodile, a changeling, one to be returned to sky or water rather than adopted or claimed—so the anthropologist can view her subjects as unspeakably other, belonging to another time, another world altogether. If it is to be in the nature of an ethical project, the work of anthropology requires a different set of relationships. In minimalist terms this might be described as the difference between the anthropologist as "spectator" and the anthropologist as "witness."

Notes

1 Excellent reviews of these debates in anthropology can be found in Mohanty, Satya P. (1989), Us and Them: On the Philosophical Bases of Political Criticism, *Yale Journal of Criticism*, 2 (2): 1–31; Hollis, Martin and Steven Lukes (1982) (eds.), *Rationality and Relativism*, Cambridge: Harvard University Press; Wilson, Bryan (1985) (ed.), *Rationality*, Oxford: Oxford University Press; and Tambiah, Stanley (1990), *Magic, Science, Religion, and the Scope of Rationality*, Cambridge: Harvard University Press.
2 Rosaldo, Renato (1989), *Culture and Truth: The Remaking of Social Analysis*, Boston: Beacon Press, pp. 1–21.
3 Scheper-Hughes, Nancy (1992), *Death Without Weeping: The Violence of Everyday Life in Brazil*, Berkeley: University of California Press, p. 21.
4 Girard, René (1987), Generative Scapegoating, in *Violent Origins: Ritual Killing and Cultural Foundation*, Hamerton-Kelly, R. (ed.), Stanford: Stanford University Press, pp. 73–105.
5 Scheper-Hughes, Nancy (1994), AIDS and the Social Body, *Social Science and Medicine*, 39: 991–1003.
6 Taussig, Michael (1992), *The Nervous System*, New York: Routledge.
7 Conrad, Joseph (1910), *Heart of Darkness*, New York: Harper.
8 Appadurai, Arjun (1991), Global Ethnoscapes: Notes and Queries for a Transnational Anthropology, in *Recapturing Anthropology*, Fox, Richard (ed.), Sante Fe: School of American Research Press, pp. 191–210.
9 Here I have taken Lila Abu-Lughod's "writing against culture" (in *Recapturing Anthropology*, pp. 137–162) notion out of context, and I want to suggest that her reflections on the "abuses" of the culture concept are not incompatible with the views put forward in this paper. Culture has been invoked in many inappropriate contexts as a kind of fetish. Paul Farmer (Conflating Structural Violence and Cultural Difference. Lecture given at the Department of Anthropology, University of California, Berkeley, November 10, 1994) notes

in his recent reflections on the structure of violence that the idea of culture has often been used to obscure the social relations, political economy, and formal institutions of violence that promote and produce human suffering. Cultures do not, of course, only generate meaning in the Geertzian sense but produce legitimations for institutionalized inequality and justifications for exploitation and domination. The culture concept has been used to exaggerate and to mystify the differences between anthropologists and their subjects, as in the implicit suggestion that because they are "from different cultures, they are [also therefore] of different worlds, and of different times" (Farmer 1994: 24). This "denial of coevalness" is deeply ingrained in our discipline, exemplified each time we speak with awe of the impenetrable opacity of culture or of the incommensurability of cultural systems of thought, meaning, and practice. Here culture may actually be a disguise for an incipient or an underlying racism, a pseudo-speciation of humans into discrete types, orders, and kinds—the bell jar rather than the bell curve approach to reifying difference.

10 Scheper-Hughes (1992), *Death Without Weeping*, op. cit., p. 28.
11 Scheper-Hughes, Nancy (1994), Unpopular Justice: The Case for People's Courts, *Democracy in Action*, 8 (4): 16–20.
12 Gilligan, Carol (1982), *In a Different Voice: Psychological Theory and Women's Development*, Cambridge: Harvard University Press.
13 Levinas, Emmanuel (1987), Meaning and Sense, in *Collected Philosophical Papers*, Dordrecht: Martinus Nijhoff Publishers, p. 100.
14 Sartre, Jean-Paul (1956), *Being and Nothingness*, London: Methuen.

39 The empire of suffering

Leslie Butt

Leslie Butt (born in 1963) is a medical anthropologist whose research focuses on gender, sexuality, and reproduction. An associate professor in the Department of Pacific and Asian Studies at the University of Victoria in Canada, she has carried out research in the Highlands of Papua New Guinea on the cultural values surrounding family planning and female prostitution. Her recent work concerns AIDS, particularly as it relates to issues of female stigmatisation and conspiracy theories. She has co-edited the volume *Making Sense of AIDS: Culture, Sexuality and Power in Melanesia*.

The article 'The Suffering Stranger' is a critique of what Leslie Butt considers a recent moral trend in medical anthropology consisting in foregrounding the suffering of the poor, often through poignant narratives, as a means of mobilising the emotions of the readers and potentially their reactions. She takes as an example the collective volume *Dying for Growth*, which presents a series of studies on social inequalities in health, and, more largely, the Harvard school of medical anthropology around Paul Farmer and, at the time, Jim Yong Kim (who has since become President of the World Bank). She argues that such studies may identify themselves with global justice, but do not actually do justice to those they defend. The vignettes that serve to elicit the empathy of the audience in fact isolate these tragic life stories from their local contexts on a social, cultural and political level, and the agents represented in this way become simply the pretext for the deployment of a 'human rights culture'. For Leslie Butt, rather than helping the poor, whose voice is absent, these approaches manipulate them for a global audience and, ultimately, entrench them within the agendas of international organisations whose humanitarian goodwill is the moral counterpoint to neoliberal ideology. The essay, which obviously elicited a response from the authors of the book under fire, has the merit to question the social sciences themselves in how they contribute to the politics of compassion.

Attempts to reduce suffering through committed scholarship have a long history. Medical anthropologists, in particular, have been galvanized by the conditions they observe in the field to take an explicitly activist position on health issues. Echoing Das,[1] many ask "how we can make institutions concerned with large issues of human dignity and human rights responsive to small happenings in local communities." In consciously identifying with the powerless and poor of the world, for example, Jim Yong Kim, Joyce V. Millen, Alec Irwin and John Gershman, the editors of the volume *Dying for Growth: Global Inequality and the Health of the Poor*,[2] have taken as their mandate the task of studying, working alongside, and advocating on behalf of those living in ill-health caused by international flows of capital.

One of the most compelling, and potentially problematic, features of such recent activist scholarship is the use of personal tales to enhance descriptions of suffering. First-hand accounts help tell a human story about poverty and powerlessness. People whose stories are produced for consumption in international circles are referred to in this article as "suffering strangers." Their stories are valuable because they provide support for claims about justice and well-being. And yet, within other public contexts, anthropologists have been quick to criticize a cavalier use of images and tales. In human rights work in particular, images assimilate a broad range of experiences into a single, often gut-wrenching, emotionally charged iconic representation of an identified group—"the starving," "the displaced," or "the dying."[3] However, anthropologists have, as yet, given little attention to how such images and stories might be deployed in their own work. In taking as a case study the flagship volume, *Dying for Growth: Global Politics and the Health of the Poor* (hereafter referred to as *Dying for Growth*), this paper focuses upon the role of stories of suffering in activist scholarship. I suggest that truncated first-hand accounts do not provide a voice of human experience so much as they mask a set of assumptions about global moralities. In other words, the suffering are finally talking, but is anyone really listening? [...]

The phantom public sphere of international morality

When scholars of any stripe appeal to passion and obligation in the name of humanity, they operate in a realm that has been referred by some as the "public sphere." In its original form, Habermas saw the public sphere as "a realm of our social life in which something approaching public opinion can be formed."[4] Ideally taking the shape of an organized forum for discussing issues of potential dissent, debates conducted within this realm require a common language and sentiment. The premises for this forum clearly rely upon a set of values derived from Enlightenment principles and a presumption that one form of thinking (i.e., one that entails a rational, open debate) is superior to others.

Currently, it is unclear whether a public sphere can exist in transcultural and international realms that are enmeshed within a global economy. Some emphatically argue that they can, seeing the search for public, panhuman rational decision making as an ideal 21st century model of communication. Berman,[5] for example, argues—both optimistically and polemically—that the horrors of the past century have moved the world toward an identity that is inclusively human—a global "we." Within world "public opinion" claims to rectify inequities have a concrete role. People at the margins, for example, are learning to use their voice on the world front to further notions of collective human rights.

An opposing position dismisses claims to a universal global morality. Multiple media, for example, or interest groups in industrially advanced democracies, enact apparent displays of openness. All appear to draw from public input in the construction of moral claims. However, these ephemeral claims are elusive, more a "phantom public sphere" than a public morality in the making. As Rorty argues, a public morality is not an end achievable through some rational process—a process that assumes the existence of some form of "reason" made up of "context-free validity." There is no such thing as "natural, intrinsic relevance—relevance dictated not by the needs of any given community, but by human reason as such."[6]

If one accepts Rorty's argument, "then scholarship helps construct moral positions like reducing suffering"—positions that appear to be both rational and achievable. In fact, claims to "address inequality" or to "improve health" draw their legitimacy, and elude critical study, because they rely upon moralities that are based in the "shoulds" and the "oughts" of a very narrow, if globally dominant, contemporary worldview. I refer to this worldview as the "human rights culture." Rorty uses the concept "human rights culture"[7] to argue against any universal, rationally based idea of rights. Ideas of rights are constantly changing. I would further his point by suggesting that a dominant human rights culture propels norms in social justice scholarship within the discipline of medical anthropology. Adams,[8] among others, has signaled the problematic biases of a Western individualism and universal assumptions about subjective bodily experiences that pervade contemporary human rights claims. However, I would elaborate the complex moral grounds of the human rights culture in health advocacy by suggesting that it is also based upon assumptions pertaining to justice, difference, and action.

First, human rights culture is rooted in rational claims about justice. One example of this might be ideas about the right to a disease-free life based on rational notions of entitlement and universality. Justice is evidenced in well-being. Second, human rights culture embraces a relativist recognition of difference that is recognized as being linguistic, cultural, and economic. An example of difference would be the recognition that not everyone has a disease-free life and that unequal rates of disease can have societal causes. Third, human rights culture is a culture of action: it is about recognizing that not everyone is in the same boat. It means doing something so that "a basic economic and political structure can be created to make everyone better off while giving priority to bettering the conditions of the worst off."[9] The cultural value of eliminating inequality, within putatively universal frameworks that define standards of well-being for all, is currently very popular. And the notion of social justice as equitable access to health resources easily comes to seem universal because it is rendered more powerful through institutions—such as Partners in Health and the World Health Organization—whose collective engagement heightens a sense of shared moral identity.

The suffering stranger and other representations of human distress have a prominent role to play in strengthening the merits of current moral claims. The human rights culture depends upon being able to make some aware that others live differently. The proliferation of measurement systems—from life expectancy through to qualitative accounts of torture and mutilation—consolidate awareness of differences within a collective sentiment of "something must be done." Within this communication network, a key means of communicating comes from hearing what Rorty refers to as "sad and sentimental stories."[10] At present, sad stories, like those of the suffering strangers in *Dying for Growth*, move listeners to action within the public sphere. But the capacity of suffering-stranger stories to get readers out of their seats and on to a social justice bandwagon is accomplished not because the stories are in and of themselves morally compelling but, rather, because, in the human rights culture of the present, people presented with moral claims expect them to be in story form.

Capital justice

The appropriation of sad stories to further moral claims is an issue that not all will necessarily find problematic. When stories help redress inequities, surely the end justifies the means. For many, global concerns matter more than do local problems.

Having the poor speak is better than having them be silent. However, recent critiques have argued that those moral claims unquestioningly trumpeted by so many are, in fact, conditioned to a significant degree by the very economic systems their advocates seek to undermine. What are scholars to do if "moral universalism is an invention of the rich?"[11] What are the real roots of justice if the notions of "health equity" and "access" are rooted in neoliberal economic policies?[12] The human rights culture obtains its legitimacy from a distribution of economic resources that allows the "haves" to improve the lot of the "have nots." These concerns have been tagged as "an affordable luxury to an imperial power."[13] Miyoshi,[14] for example, places morality ploys squarely on the back of global capital. Transnational corporations, and other regulators of the flows of soft capital, destabilize political institutions such as nation-states and/or regional political systems to such an extent that they are able to lay claim to the discourse of civil society. [...]

What are the implications of these arguments for social justice scholarship? To return to the papers in *Dying for Growth*, it is unclear how truncated tales of suffering strangers can do anything other than reinforce the inseparability of NGO activism and global economic forces as well as the discourse of health that accompanies it. Worse still, the use of stories may exacerbate the problem. The authors in *Dying for Growth* work within an expanded definition of poverty. On the basis of ethnographic or field experiences, this definition includes vulnerability and insecurity measurements as well as economic status. Although it goes further than do standard definitions based on an "idolatry of economic growth,"[15] it nonetheless privileges international standards that can only concede the impacts of local-level practices or events in superficial ways. The authors' focus on "poverty" brings *Dying for Growth* into closer alignment with the international institutions whose impact they decry than it does with the poor and their alliances. The poor do not necessarily know that they are "poor"; they have to learn to think this way and to embrace a collective identity based on notions of poverty—a "cultural citizenship of the world community of poor."[16] In the concluding sections of *Dying for Growth*, the authors even facilitate the process of defining the poor in terms that closely align them with the institutions regulating human rights culture: "We urge that, in the future, the health of poor people become a central, systematic, and binding criteria [sic] according to which new policies and strategies are designed; new political and economic relations between institutions and countries are forged; and new trade and investment regimes are established ... We believe it would be possible, in most instances, to model with reasonable accuracy the health costs and benefits likely to be associated with specific policy measures and business ventures."[17]

This claim raises disturbing issues. When the editors argue for using health standards as a means to evaluate development projects because they have evidence of suffering from first-hand accounts, they help to entrench the poor within an international institutional framework already identified as being highly destructive. There is no discussion as to how the poor will control systems of evaluations or the methods used. They do not suggest that, given a choice, the poor will necessarily choose to support an internationally based model over local ones, or an internationalist mandate over ones bound more tightly with their own concerns. As Cheah[18] comments, the real key to an international civil society lies in bringing a Northern agenda into closer alignment with the requirements of the postcolonial South or, in Malkki's words, privileging neither empty "universalisms" nor chauvinistic "localisms."[19] It is not clear how internationalist social justice claims will be able to transcend the political complexities of multiple moralities on the basis of their combination of emotive appeals and diligent scholarship. However, since the human rights culture remains in the ascendant, first-hand accounts will no doubt continue to be used in evaluations in order to promote policies that run the risk of producing the opposite effects of those intended. As evaluators increasingly look for, and demand, personal accounts of suffering in order to legitimize policy evaluations, we can expect to see a proliferation of suffering-stranger voices that will, it seems inevitable, be given more and more room to speak but will be allowed to say less and less.

Toward a conscientious medical anthropology

All universalisms are dirty. And it is only dirty universalisms that will help us against the powers and agents of still dirtier ones.[20] At their best, stories of suffering strangers sketch lives of struggle that, at each turn, are affected by structural violence. Who can deny the suffering that results from the inequities implicit within tales like Sumirah's or within statistics such as: "the wealth of the three richest individuals on earth surpassed the combined annual GDP of the 48 least developed countries?"[21] Such knowledge requires humanitarian action: it is the only decent thing to do. But "decency originates in the same cultures that violate it."[22] We are far more implicated in the lives of others than can be realized by reading the stories of suffering strangers. Just because suffering appears to be universal does not free those who experience it from being exposed to the abuse and manipulation that can follow from any claim to universality. We need to think twice before allowing the suffering stranger to become further marginalized as a token qualitative addition to a dominant universalism. Furthermore, Das sounded a warning signal several years ago: suffering can too easily become "the child of the pronouncer of this discourse."[23] The suffering stranger is just such a child. She is a discursive construction that reduces global entanglements, and potentially rich human stories, to a moral model that allows for a sustained dependency between one group of people (i.e., those coded as needy) and another group of people (i.e., those coded as expert).

Maneuvering around international claims to promote effective humanitarian scholarship becomes one of social justice's trickiest challenges. The alternatives to humanitarianism, as Malkki[24] points out, are either indifference or repressive logics, neither of which is acceptable. Recognizing the placement of moral claims does not necessarily mean plunging into an abyss from which there is no place to act. Nor does it mean turning to a form of armchair globalism that is ill-equipped to engage in an activist anthropology. On the contrary, querying international interventions allows us to create a clearer framework from which to challenge old models and to conceptualize new ones. Tsing urges deeper exploration of ideologies of scale—in particular, cultural claims about globalism (such as those embedded in social justice rationales). The "relatively coherent bundles of ideas and practices"[25] that make up social justice translate and mobilize ideologies about global relations. It is up to us to ensure that these are ideas worthy of activist practice. Solutions to socioeconomic inequities may not lie in a rational model based upon normative ideals; they may, however, lie in recognizing the pitfalls of making such claims.

There are many ways to honor suffering. One way may be to withdraw from a universalizing ideal of a single global public whose needs are representable through convention-laden voices of suffering and, instead, to attend to the multiplicity of distinct and overlapping public discourses that our idealizations have screened from view.[26] A collective and engaged form of worldliness might embrace alternate discourses and their novel messages. It might also engage in a process of educating people about the use and manipulation of sentiment in the pursuit of global moral claims. Still, these are hardly new ideas. We are left with the depressing thought that there is almost certainly no sphere free from all strategic considerations. This being the case, we need to view social justice concerns within medical anthropology as a courageous move toward a new theoretical positioning. It remains to expand the parameters of study: to focus not just upon targets (multinationals, U.S. hegemony, and the like), but also to explore the nature of moral debates taking place globally and to show support for the slow move toward an accountable public sphere—one within which there might be a space for communication without domination.

Notes

1 Das, Veena (1999), Public Good, Ethics, and Everyday Life: Beyond the Boundaries of Bioethics, *Daedalus*, 128 (4): 126.
2 This book is part of the "Series in Health and Social Justice" produced by the Harvard-based Partners in Health. The mandate of Partners in Health is listed in the final section of *Dying for Growth*. It aims to work "with community-based organizations on projects designed to improve the health and well-being of people struggling against poverty ... The partner relationship is the central core of PIH and is reflected in the organizational commitment to struggle alongside vulnerable communities, and against the economic and political structures that create their poverty," Patel, H., J. Millen and E. Lyon (2000), Pragmatic Solidarity, in *Dying for Growth: Global Inequality and the Health of the Poor*, J. Y. Kim, J. Millen, A. Irwin, and J. Gershman (eds.), Monroe, ME: Common Courage, p. 420.
3 Kleinman, A. and J. Kleinman (1996), The Appeal of Experience, the Dismay of Images: Cultural Appropriations of Suffering in Our Times, *Daedalus*, 125 (1): 1–23; Malkki, L. (1997), Speechless Emissaries: Refugees, Humanitarianism, and Dehistoricization, in *Siting Culture: The Shifting Anthropological Object*, K. F. Olwig and K. Hastrup (eds.), London: Routledge, pp. 223–254; Malkki, L. (1998), Things to Come: Internationalism and Global Solidarities in the Late 1990s, *Public Culture*, 10 (2): 431–442.
4 Habermas, J. (1974), *The Structural Transformation of the Public Sphere*, Cambridge, MA: MIT Press, p. 49.
5 Berman, M. (1995), Modernism and Human Rights Near the Millennium, *Dissent* (Summer): 333–341.
6 Rorty, R. (1998), Justice as a Larger Loyalty, in *Cosmopolitics: Thinking and Feeling beyond the Nation*, B. Robbins and P. Cheah (eds.), Minnesota: University of Minnesota Press, pp. 45–58.
7 Rorty, R. (1993), Human Rights, Rationality and Sentimentality, in *On Human Rights: The Oxford Amnesty Lectures*, S. Shute and S. Hurley (eds.), New York: Basic, pp. 111–134.
8 Adams, V. (1998), Suffering the Winds of Lhasa: Politicized Bodies, Human Rights, Cultural Difference, and Humanism in Tibet, *Medical Anthropology Quarterly*, 12 (1): 74–102.
9 Lukes, Steven (1993), Five Fables about Human Rights, in *On Human Rights: The Oxford Amnesty Lectures*, S. Shute and S. Hurley (eds.), New York: Basic, pp. 19–40; see also Daniels, N., B. Kennedy, and I. Kawachi (1999), Why Justice is Good for our Health: The Social Determinants of Health Inequalities, *Daedalus*, 128 (4): 215–251; Krieger, N. (1998), A Vision of Social Justice as the Foundation of Public Health: Commemorating 150 Years of the Spirit of 1848, *American Journal of Public Health*, 88 (11): 1603; Heggenhougen, H. K. (2000), More than just "Interesting!": Anthropology, Health and Human Rights, *Social Science and Medicine*, 50: 1171–1175; Young, I. (1990), *Justice and the Politics of Difference*, Princeton: Princeton University Press.
10 Rorty, R. (1993), Human Rights, Rationality and Sentimentality, op. cit., p. 119.
11 Rorty, R. (1993), Moral Universalism and Economic Triage, *Diogenes*, 41 (1): 9.

12 Petersen, A. and D. Lupton (1996), *The New Public Health: Health and Self in the Age of Risk*, London: Sage.
13 Connery, C. (1994), Pacific Rim Discourse: The U.S. Global Imaginary in the Late Cold War Years, *Boundary 2*, 21 (1): 34; Appadurai, A. (1990), Disjuncture and Difference in the Global Cultural Economy, *Public Culture*, 2 (2): 1–24.
14 Miyoshi, M. (1993), A Borderless World? From Colonialism to Transnationalism and the Decline of the Nation-State, *Critical Inquiry*, 19: 726–751.
15 Gershman, J. and A. Irwin (2000), Getting a Grip on the Global Economy, in *Dying for Growth: Global Inequality and the Health of the Poor*, J. Y. Kim, J. Millen, A. Irwin, and J. Gershman (eds.), Monroe, ME: Common Courage, p. 42.
16 Petersen and Lupton (1996), *The New Public Health*, op. cit.
17 Millen, J., A. Irwin and J. Y. Kim (2000), Conclusion: Pessimism of the Intellect, Optimism of the Will, in *Dying for Growth: Global Inequality and the Health of the Poor*, J. Y. Kim, J. Millen, A. Irwin, and J. Gershman (eds.), Monroe, ME: Common Courage, pp. 388–389; see also pp. 8–9.
18 Cheah, P. (1998), Introduction, Part 2. The Cosmopolitical—Today, in *Cosmopolitics: Thinking and Feeling Beyond the Nation*, B. Robbins and P. Cheah (eds.), Minneapolis: University of Minnesota Press, pp. 20–41.
19 Malkki, L. (1998), Things to Come: Internationalism and Global Solidarities in the Late 1990s, *Public Culture*, 10 (2): 431–442.
20 Robbins, B. (1999), *Feeling Global: Internationalism in Distress*, New York: New York University Press.
21 Gershman and Irwin (2000), Getting a Grip on the Global Economy, op. cit., p. 14.
22 Falck, H. S. (1995), Medical Humanitarianism and Human Rights: Reflections on Doctors Without Borders and Doctors of the World, *Social Science and Medicine*, 41 (12): 1622.
23 Das, Veena (1995), *Critical Events: An Anthropological Perspective on Contemporary India*, Delhi: Oxford University Press, p. 164.
24 Malkki (1997), Speechless Emissaries, op. cit., p. 225.
25 Tsing, A. (2000), The Global Situation, *Cultural Anthropology*, 15 (3): 347.
26 Robbins (1999), *Feeling Global*, op. cit.

40 The immunity of humanitarianism

Didier Fassin

Didier Fassin (born in 1955) is a professor of social science at the Institute for Advanced Study in Princeton. He has taught at the University Paris North and is director of studies at the École des Hautes Études en Sciences Sociales. Originally a physician trained in internal medicine and public health, he later turned to the social sciences and conducted fieldwork in medical anthropology on the healing practices in Senegal and on health inequalities in Ecuador. With *When Bodies Remember*, focusing on the issues of history and memory revealed by the South African AIDS epidemic, and *The Empire of Trauma*, examining the social and political use of suffering related to violence, his research became oriented towards contemporary moral economies, the issues that permeate them, and the subjectivities they produce. *Humanitarian Reason* offers a moral history of the present through a series of ethnographies in French and non-European fields of the politics of compassion, while *Enforcing Order* forms a sort of counterpoint to this, shedding light on the policing rationale through an ethnography of law enforcement in underprivileged areas.

In this essay, Didier Fassin discusses the conditions in which an anthropology of humanitarianism is possible. It is often difficult and sometimes even considered illegitimate to study humanitarian government and its actors because representations of their mission, their intentions, and their actions are already saturated with positive moral judgements. What is suggested here is a critique that escapes the dual trap of condemnation and apologia by taking seriously the agents' capacity for reflexivity regarding their own practice, while also calling for an autonomous space to address the logics and consequences that escape them. This text is part of a wider project in political and moral anthropology that aims to grasp the meanings and tensions inherent to how moral sentiments are mobilised in the public sphere by providing an analysis that includes both the discipline and its members.

For the anthropologist the world of humanitarianism is in many ways a unique research object. First, its manifestations are so diverse and indeed contradictory that its object seems nearly impossible to apprehend. Ranging from programs for assisting Central Asians in refugee camps to Seattle street demonstrations against globalization policies, from the struggle against famine in Africa to the defense of the national social protection system in France, from non-governmental organizations decrying armed intervention to military operations justified as humanitarian, it always exceeds what we can say about it. Second, it appears saturated with discourses that often turn out to have been authored by its own agents. Regardless of whether those humanitarian workers speak in the first person or proceed by way of their authorized commentators, whether they denounce world disorders or their own errors, they themselves are the ones to circumscribe the relevant questions and define what may legitimately be said about them. Lastly—and this point follows in part from the two preceding ones—the world of humanitarianism tends to elude critical analysis. Because it is a valued good that many are seeking to appropriate for themselves by qualifying their own activities as "humanitarian" even when they are warlike and because it operates by internalizing debate on the meaning and effects of its actions, it resists to the inquiry of social sciences. It is this resistance that I am particularly interested in here, but I will also try to draw conclusions likely to improve our understanding of the "humanitarian world" itself. In other words, though I will focus on the conditions of possibility for studying the humanitarian world anthropologically, I will try to identify some of its blind spots.

"Can any and everything be laughed off?" one sometimes wonders. The recent Danish scandal known as the "caricatures of Mohammed" and the violent reactions it gave rise to in many Muslim countries remind us that the question cannot be thought of as a mere scholarly philosophical exercise—it is charged with political and moral issues. Here I will use a similar turn of phrase: not "Can any and everything be criticized?" (which would imply a normative stance) but rather "Can any and everything be submitted to critical analysis?" (implying a scientific approach). This question comes up every time we handle subjects that simultaneously involve persons trying to deal with painful situations—poverty, immigration, asylum, serious illness, childhood with AIDS, violence against women, to name only those I myself have worked on—and institutions whose mission is to help those persons. Deconstructing the obviousness of those categories, demonstrating that individuals assumed to be vulnerable also know how to use tactics for obtaining what they want, showing that the organizations or agents that take charge of them may have cynical attitudes and behavior of their own and may actually be indifferent or cruel, is an undertaking that implies upsetting a kind of compassion consensus wherein the ill fortune or distress of some and the solicitude of others are understood to harmoniously respond to each other, pressured only by the impersonal, inhuman forces of the market, bureaucracy, or globalization, these last entities being easier to condemn than humanitarian agents and their sentiments. As anthropologists we may even feel ourselves embarrassed by such empirical observations and hesitant to let them be known: in that case we practice self-censorship so as not to endanger, even abstractly or collectively, the men and women whose discourses we have collected and whose practices we have observed, fearing to betray their trust in us. We may also occasionally perceive reluctance on the part of our listeners and readers to learn about such matters, and it is not always easy in this case to know if what bothers them is the content of what we report or the very fact that we are speaking of it. Some matters would thus seem more sensitive than others. But how can we characterize them?

One thing they have in common is that they bring affects and values into play around two figures: victims, either of poverty, illness or oppression, and benefactors who assist, protect and struggle to defend them (the third figure—money-grubbing bosses, insensitive bureaucrats, cruel soldiers—is obviously easier to criticize). These two figures are linked by moral sentiments in Adam Smith's sense, beginning with "sympathy," that "emotion which we feel for the misery of others, when we either see it, or are made to conceive it in a very lively manner."[1] For Smith, this affective dimension is what underlies the moral sense as it is inscribed in agents' virtues, judgments or actions they take. Compassion and pity are not only emotions but good feelings in that they manifest attachment to others. Humanitarian government, which can indeed be defined as "the introduction of moral sentiments into the political and policy spheres,"[2] paradigmatically crystallizes the emotion-charged encounter between victims and benefactors within the many different scenes of planetary tragedy it operates on. It extends the gesture of traditional charity, or rather shifts it from near-by victims (the poor person one can see) to distant ones (victims of disaster, war, epidemics). It thus goes beyond Hannah Arendt's conceptual distinction[3] between compassion as direct attention to individual suffering and pity as abstract consideration for the suffering of the masses in that it makes possible a paradoxical form of long-distance compassion where those masses (of disaster victims, refugees, sick) become real (in tents, camps, hospitals), if only through media-delivered images. In this connection, the exercise in critical analysis that focuses on humanitarian government exemplifies the difficulties that may be encountered in any anthropological study of morally prized social activities, precisely because those activities stage persons and institutions believed to be above suspicion because they are acting for the good of individuals and groups understood to be vulnerable.

Noli me tangere—"Do not touch me," said Christ to Mary Magdalen when she extended her fingers toward him after his resurrection. It is the "untouchability" of certain actors and the values they incarnate that is of interest to me here. The Christian reference (*noli me tangere*) and the dimension of sacredness (untouchability) are central to my remarks. The humanitarian world is heir to a religious tradition of caring for the other and giving of oneself; it has become the secular expression of that tradition. As Craig Calhoun recalls,[4] Florence Nightingale and Henri Dunant led their fight for the right to treat wounded soldiers on battlefields in the name of religion, and the very choice of the name "Red Cross" and the accompanying symbol refer back to Christian imagery—the Islamic response being the Red Crescent. The "second age of humanitarian action," that of "bearing witness," presumably broke free of these religious references; many of the founders of Médecins Sans Frontières (Doctors Without Borders) and Médecins du Monde (Doctors of the World) were previously linked to either the worlds of communism or leftism rather than Catholicism or Protestantism. But in addition to the fact that the cross (a white one) has long been the emblem of the first of these humanitarian organizations and the dove, a biblical symbol, is still the emblem of the second, the concept of humanitarian work is still strongly marked by the history of western thinking on charity. Specifically, humanitarian government links up with "pastoral power" as characterized by Michel Foucault: it is exercised on "a multiplicity", that is the "flock"; it is "fundamentally beneficent" in the sense that "its only *raison d'être* is doing good"; and it is "an individualizing power" in that "the shepherd directs the whole flock, but he can only really direct it insofar as not a single sheep escapes him, and the shepherd owes everything to his flock to the extent of agreeing to sacrifice himself for its salvation."[5] This was precisely the language used by the president of Médecins Sans Frontières[6] to establish an opposition between the "cannibal ideal" of states and their armies, which, by their murderous actions, organize "the premature deaths of a part of humanity," and "the humanitarian spirit," which has taken on "the radical, arbitrary challenge of trying to succor those the society itself sacrifices" and whose responsibility is "to save as many lives as possible." This mystic salvation and sacrifice language, this moral language about absolute evil and supreme good attains here a sort of paroxysm to which many humanitarian agents would probably not subscribe. Still, a euphemized version of it may be heard daily in the offices of non-governmental organizations and on their fields of action.

Under these circumstances, how can any independent analysis be permitted—or even possible? What autonomy is left for using a moral anthropology approach to apprehend a social world that presents itself as imbued with a sort of moral supremacy—a world, therefore, that claims it need not submit to any external oversight? It is this situation, where criticism becomes critical, that interests me here. [...] The question I raise is the following: is it possible to hold a discourse that critically analyzes what humanitarian agents are doing while remaining "audible" to them? Both points are important. It is crucial to give a critical account of humanitarian action, but that critique has to be audible to those it is directed at. The difficulty of developing a critique that is both autonomous and engaged is thus twofold: the agents have to recognize themselves in what is said of the way they act, but at the same moment, they have to perceive the distance that is being established. To put it more forcefully, the critical stance I am advocating involves in my interlocutors a dual sentiment of recognition and betrayal. Criticism is both loyalty and displacement. This is why I am particularly concerned in my work to examine "where it hurts"; i.e., where an institution or group is divided, what tears it apart. This is not intellectual sadism, but a theoretical choice: in periods of conflict, in the interstices of disagreement, a certain truth gets told that would not be told otherwise. An anthropologist who attempts to grasp that truth does not usually emerge from the experience entirely intact himself: the truth-telling ordeal puts him in a difficult position too. This is not mere rhetoric. It often seems to me that the accuracy of an analysis can be measured by the discomfort it causes in both the person who produces it and the person who receives it. With regard to humanitarian organizations, neither (of course) admiring support nor (paradoxically) virulent denunciation constitutes a moment of truth; the truth will only rise toward the surface if we stick as close as possible to the action. I propose to illustrate this stance by way of two case studies. [...]

Situations of crisis

The first scene, which I have recounted in detail elsewhere,[7] takes place at Médecins Sans Frontières, an organization founded in 1971 by a small group of doctors and medical journalists. Some of them (the most renowned being Bernard Kouchner) were "veterans" of the war in Biafra. They had worked there two years earlier for the International Committee of the Red Cross, and they had experienced that organization's neutrality principle as a genuine "law of silence." On the basis of what they had learned there, they decided to refound humanitarian action on two dimensions: assisting populations and bearing witness. Three decades later, this group of friends had developed into an influential international non-governmental organization; its original French section was the largest in the French humanitarian world, with more than 400 positions in approximately 100 field missions, 1000 volunteers a year being sent to work in those missions, and a budget of approximately €150 million, raised almost exclusively from private donors, a guarantee of financial independence. Being awarded the Nobel Peace Prize in 1999 gave Médecins Sans Frontières international legitimacy and made it an actor to be reckoned with in every conflict it was present in.

It was in this context—that is, after the association had become a sort of humanitarian force or power—that the following scene took place.

In March 2003, just before the United States' air attack against Iraq, a Médecins Sans Frontières mission made up of six persons, including the president of the international bureau in charge of coordinating the 19 national sections, chose to remain in Baghdad. The decision was a source of painful tension. Two of the six were not in favor, but stayed on to show their solidarity. Some in the headquarters were against the decision, but they constituted a minority on the executive committee. The question posed during the administrative council meeting a few days later was quite simple: Why take such a heavy risk (getting caught between American bombs and Iraqi resistants) for such modest anticipated results (six volunteers alongside several hundred qualified Iraqi medical personnel spread out among the capital city's 35 hospitals)? Both the president and the director-general argued in favor of keeping the team on the scene, the understanding being that even that minimal presence would save lives. However, several members of the executive committee and administrative board had their doubts, and events proved them right. Twelve days after the first attacks by the United States and their allies, two members of the Médecins Sans Frontières team were taken hostage—the organization had not even set to work yet and there it was, paralyzed both locally and internationally. The wounded, meanwhile, began pouring into the hospitals. After eight days, the hostages were released—and revealed they had been taken hostage by Iraqi policemen. The Marines were already entering Baghdad. Traumatized by the hostage-taking, the association's head officials in Paris decided—against the recommendation of their colleagues on the scene, who were now in a position to help the local population—to close down their mission and repatriate the volunteers to France, at just the time the other two Médecins Sans Frontières sections and most of the other humanitarian organizations were getting down to work. To justify their sudden departure, it was claimed that there was no real humanitarian emergency.

The violence of the disagreement on the executive committee and later the administrative board about whether or not to stay in Iraq suggests that what was at issue was more than the technical matter of assessing the danger involved and the potential benefits. This is what I tried to explain during the debate. In fact, up against an army that was massively bombing the territory, causing high numbers of deaths in the Iraqi civilian population mostly to avoid losses of its own, the decision to remain was a courageous symbolic gesture aimed at establishing a kind of balance: by exposing themselves in this way, the humanitarian workers seemed to be showing that their lives were just as vulnerable as those of Iraqi civilians. However, this gesture revealed a twofold tension. First, the notion of symmetrical exposure of lives did not hold up to analysis: in reality, Iraqi civilians were being sacrificed whereas humanitarian agents were sacrificing themselves; one group passive victims; the other committed heroes. Second, the notion of symmetrical exposure of lives did not hold up against the facts either: the humanitarian agents were free to pull out of the ordeal, whereas the civilian population had no other option but to remain; the former could protect themselves; the latter simply had to endure. This tension is not circumstantial but structural. To reveal it is to unveil a hidden truth of humanitarian work, a sort of family secret not even mentioned by the agents when they are among themselves. The humanitarian "gift" of assistance to the suffering is founded on two untold facts. First, it is unequal in that there can be no counter-gift: recipients of humanitarian assistance cannot offer anything in return, except in the highly asymmetric form of gratitude or narratives of their distress. Second, that gift is illusory in that it cannot be a true one: those proffering assistance always protect themselves as much as they actually help, and everybody finds this normal because they are not there to lose their lives. The Iraqi scene, the spectacular exposure of organization members and the subsequent withdrawal of the team in response to the danger, thus functioned as a moment of *véridiction*.

The second scene, which I have also mentioned in another text,[8] involves Médecins du Monde, a humanitarian organization founded in 1979 out of a schism in Médecins Sans Frontières between certain founders (led by Bernard Kouchner) and a segment of the newcomers (including the president Claude Malhuret); the conflict came to a head around the question of chartering a ship to help Vietnamese boat people in the China Sea. For the first group, the point was to go save lives of civilians fleeing communist persecution, whereas for the second group, the action appeared dangerous and primarily conceived to attract media attention. One can only be struck by the parallel with the scene just analyzed, which took place 24 years later. Finding itself outvoted by the young guard, the veterans' group favoring intervention seceded and left to found a new organization: Médecins du Monde. That organization considers this episode emblematic. Its motto is "There are no good or bad victims," a reference to the presumed indifference of leftist humanitarian workers to the Vietnamese boat people because they were victims of communism. A quarter of a century later, this dissident organization has consolidated itself and operates on a budget of approximately €50 million—one-third that of the French section of Médecins Sans Frontières. Like the older organization, Médecins du Monde gives special emphasis to one of its missions, the one it has set up in the Palestinian Territories. The second scene thus concerns Médecins du Monde's presence there and unfolds in the context of the second Intifada.

When the Palestinian revolt against Israeli oppression broke out anew in September 2000 after Ariel Sharon's visit to the Esplanade of the Mosques known to Muslims as the Noble Sanctuary, Médecins du Monde had already been present for several years in Jerusalem and the Territories, namely through its surgical assistance, psychological aid and drug addiction prevention programs. The new violence led the organization to undertake new actions, particularly testifying actions, as was the case for Médecins Sans Frontières during the same period. In early 2002, it carried out a joint mission with the Fédération Internationale des Droits de l'Homme (FIDH; International Federation of Human Rights) in the city of Nablus, where a Tsahal military operation had killed 85 and wounded 289, a third of them civilians according to Palestinian hospital sources. The acts of violence committed by the Israeli army were recorded and violations of international law identified on the basis of eye-witness accounts by health professionals and services, municipal authority estimates, press articles and direct observation by members of the Médecins du Monde mission—of building destruction, for example. The fully substantiated report concluded that the state of Israel had failed to abide by the "body of international law that governs armed conflict," and called upon it to carry out the necessary investigations, punish the guilty parties and repair the damage done. Publication of the report elicited contradictory reactions within the organization, specifically on its administrative board. Some said they were satisfied with the report, which objectified war crimes and allowed for envisioning judiciary responses; others deemed it entirely one-sided and were indignant at what they considered its biased perspective. In this particularly stormy context, the decision was made to conduct another investigation, this time in Israel, to show the damage caused by Palestinian attacks. The FIDH refused to participate in this second study. The information collected came from Israeli police statistics and accounts by persons who may not all have been directly involved in the violent acts. The attacks were termed "crimes against humanity" and the neologism "democide" was coined to signify murder of civilians. In the section assessing consequences, emphasis was placed on psychic trauma, which, it was explained, affected not only direct victims but also persons exposed by way of television coverage. This report was published together with the first report, and the cover bore the association's watchword, a direct reference to its founding moment: "There are no good or bad victims."

Published in the summer of 2003, the text provoked intense internal debate and wounding accusations. Initiators of the second investigation, including the organization's acting and honorary presidents, were openly suspected of having conducted it for reasons of religious group affinity: clearly they were accused of defending Israel because they were Jews. This was a hard blow for the organization, which of course claimed to be above all partisan allegiance and to be working to promote universal ideals. But the point here is to understand the real implications of the organization's watchword about victims. We might think of the expression as amounting to a kind of founding credo not only for this non-governmental organization but for the humanitarian world as a whole. Humanitarian workers who succor civilians in conflicts are not there to choose sides—this is what differentiates them from the military, as humanitarians themselves like to recall, especially since, in the field, some organizations actually confuse sides. This presumably obvious point is nonetheless misleading. Sides *are* often chosen (humanitarian workers recently intervened in favor of the Kosovars rather than the Serbs, just as some time ago they intervened in favor of the Biafrans rather than the Nigerians and the Afghanis rather than the Soviets) while not choosing means getting involved in complicated issues. In the Israeli–Palestinian conflict, the organization's apparent neutrality has two consequences. First, it reduces agents in the conflict to the status of victims, a status they then have to conform to so as to enable humanitarian testimony to follow its expected course: in the case of the Palestinians, we agree to consider them trauma victims, not combatants or martyrs. Second, in order to more effectively claim victim equivalence, it abolishes collective and individual history: insisting on the shared experience of psychic trauma cancels out the meaning of the violence and, in this case, the historicity of Israeli occupation and oppression. This twofold impasse is revealed by publication of the second report, meant simply to "supplement" the first one.

From contradictions to aporia

I first outlined the preceding discussion—of Médecins Sans Frontières' politics of life in Iraq and Médecins du Monde's politics of victims in Palestine—with those two organizations at or near the time they were making their decisions. In other words, this critique is not being made from any retrospective heights; it was made earlier—and is made again here—in the interests of reopening dialogue with humanitarian agents. As explained, I mean to position myself on the threshold of the cave—as I did when I was on the administrative board of Médecins Sans Frontières and as I did again, in connection with the scene involving Médecins du Monde, by participating in a special issue of a journal on humanitarianism. Each of these organizations was in a crisis situation, which I tried to understand while sharing my analyses with my interlocutors. Their reactions—actually the presidents'—were sharp, probably because the distancing I was trying to manage touched on particularly sensitive points: the sacredness of life for Médecins Sans Frontières (the president's reaction was most virulent when I suggested that staying in Baghdad seemed comparable to a type of sacrifice); the issue of choosing victims for Médecins du Monde (it was when I showed how the maps of Palestine presented in the two reports differed, since the first was historical and political whereas those dimensions had entirely disappeared in the second, that the president asked the review to publish a response). Before further clarifying these two points, I would like to put forward the two levels of discussion I perceived during these crises. At the first level, humanitarian agents were debating together—inside the cave, as it were—and the issues raised did not ultimately affect the foundation on which their practices are based. At the second level, an internal foreigner came to perturb the normal dispute proceedings. He was situated on the threshold of the cave, neither truly outside nor entirely within it, and the questions he asked were troubling precisely because of this liminal position. Paradoxically, a possible third level—namely, contesting from "outside" the cave by asserting that humanitarian work can actually facilitate military action and that humanitarian agents partake of a neocolonial order—would not have shaken my interlocutors so much. They would either have rejected those accusations or even appropriated them for their own purposes, probably to call into question the work of other organizations. The idea I am putting forward here is that this liminal position is a specific one. We can now push the distinction further, bringing to light two orders of argument and confrontation.

At the first level, that of internal dispute, protagonists themselves point out the contradictions in their action; in other words, they themselves observe that the facts are running counter to their values and norms. Contradiction, then, can be thought of as "the relation that exists between affirmation and negation of one and the same piece of knowledge."[9] In the case of Médecins Sans Frontières, members' criticism of the decision to remain in Baghdad bore on the contradiction between the high level of risk incurred and the slim benefits to be expected. The organization's charter made clear to those taking action that they were there to "bring help to the population" and that they had to "measure the risks and perils of the missions they set out to accomplish." The president and director-general's reply, of course, was that lives would be saved and that the risks incurred were no greater than usual. In the case of Médecins du Monde, the suspicion that the organization leaders provoked when they decided to conduct an investigation in Israel and later to publish the report on it concerned their presumed "denominational" allegiance, as any such allegiance would contradict the "neutrality principle" that is the cornerstone of humanitarian intervention and the very condition for ensuring that such intervention remains legitimate. Obviously the accused rejected that interpretation, arguing that their moves actually reflected a return to the organization's origins; i.e., concern for all victims, regardless of side. The advantage of contradictions of the sort brought to light by the actors at the first level is that they can be uttered, demonstrated and even overcome. In Baghdad, later developments proved the accusers right: Médecins Sans Frontières picked up stakes after its kidnapped workers were returned and left without having succored a single Iraqi. The risk was shown to be real and the organization's ineffectiveness clearly demonstrated. In Palestine, conclusions were harder to reach: media support of the second report and the approval it received from Jewish organizations in France were not enough to establish that the leaders had particular affinities. Whatever the case may be, contradiction could be overcome in both these cases.

At the second level, the level of what I am calling liminal critique, an internal foreigner raises questions that reveal an aporia—an inextricable impasse. I am using the modern, strong sense of the word: aporia are "logical difficulties that cannot be gotten out of."[10] I would be tempted to rephrase that definition for anthropological aporia; in this case I would call them questions that touch on the very foundations of humanitarian action and admit of no solution given the state of the contemporary world. Contrary to contradictions, aporia are not a matter of organizational dysfunction but rather of the dysfunction intrinsic to their very functioning. For Médecins Sans Frontières (I am of course only citing this example for its general import), the aporia lie in the impossibility of actually maintaining the "equality of lives" promoted by humanitarianism. As I suggested—and above and beyond any rational risks/benefits calculation—the point of staying in Baghdad was not to sacrifice oneself but rather to recall that the lives of Westerners could be as vulnerable as the lives of Iraqis and that Westerners were morally capable of endangering themselves in order to protect Iraqis—in sum, that all lives were equally sacred. The fact is that in addition to the asymmetry of the exchange, due, as mentioned, to the fact that the victims can never offer a "counter-gift" in return for the "gift" of their benefactors, the hostage-taking revealed a vulnerability specific to such organizations, as well as a hidden truth: the lives of humanitarian workers are actually much more precious than those of local civilians—even (as was discovered then) within the organization itself. The lives of "expatriates" are valued more than those of "nationals" in matters of wages, social protection, freedom to associate, recognition—to the point where the belligerents themselves, when attacking humanitarian mission sites, always differentiate between the two, claiming ransoms for western hostages and simply killing local workers. The fact that there is a hierarchy of equally "sacred" lives represents a sort of anthropological non-sense—a fairly unbearable one. In the case of Médecins du Monde (but once again, the illustration only matters for its paradigmatic relevance), the aporia lie in the impossibility of maintaining victim equivalence as the humanitarian world claims to do. The suffering of Israelis threatened by Palestinian attacks can only be considered equivalent to the suffering of Palestinians crushed by the Israeli army if we reduce the social experiences involved to wounds and trauma—in other words, to the physical and psychic body—and eschew any grim accounting, which would quickly show a casualty ratio between the two sides of one to ten—one to one hundred in some instances. Above all, deciding to focus on suffering means deciding not to attend to either the historical dimension or the political issues of the conflict, though these too correspond to what victims are going through. More than bodies fall under bullets or bombs—though many more bodies fall on one side than the other. What fall are human beings who have not been and are not treated with equal dignity. The Palestinians experience daily oppression, humiliation, negation; this is not true of the Israelis. When the humanitarian organization forgot this, it was called to order by its own members, who spoke of injustice at the very moment their leaders explained that they were only defending all victims equally.

What I am calling anthropological aporia here concern humanitarianism precisely because it is inscribed in contemporary moral economies. The fact that lives and victims are not equal is not specific to the humanitarian world. The truths thus revealed go beyond the framework of non-governmental organizations and their volunteer workers, even if these organizations and volunteers do represent a kind of moral core in our societies and thus deserve particular attention. We therefore cannot hold these groups entirely responsible for the complex tensions and insurmountable problems they are confronted with. But we can expect them to be more clear-sighted than they often appear. Discovering that they actually partake of certain realities that they condemn and that the principles of equal lives and equivalent victims that they identify as their own cannot be realized, due to the very foundations of their action—i.e., asymmetrical, ahistorical solidarity—means that they would have to surrender a certain representation of the moral hero in our time.

Notes

1 Smith, Adam (1982), *The Theory of Moral Sentiments*, Raphael, D. D. and A. L. Macfie (eds.), Indianapolis: Liberty Fund (original edition 1789).
2 Fassin, Didier (2011), *Humanitarian Reason: A Moral History of the Present*, Berkeley: University of California Press.
3 Arendt, Hannah (1963), *On Revolution*, New York: Viking Press.
4 Calhoun, Craig (2009), The Idea of Emergency, in *Contemporary States of Emergency: The Politics of Military and Humanitarian Intervention*, Fassin, Didier and Mariella Pandolfi (eds.), New York: Zone Books, pp. 29–58.
5 Foucault, Michel (2007), *Security, Territory, Population: Lectures at the Collège de France 1977–1978*, New York: Palgrave Macmillan, pp. 126–127 (1st French edition 2004).
6 Bradol, Jean-Hervé (2003), L'ordre international cannibale et l'action humanitaire, in *À l'Ombre des Guerres Justes*, Weissman, Fabrice (ed.), Paris: Flammarion, pp. 17, 32.
7 Fassin, Didier (2007), Humanitarianism as a Politics of Life, *Public Culture*, 19 (3): 499–520.
8 Fassin, Didier (2004), La cause des victimes, *Les Temps Modernes*, 59 (627): 73–91.
9 Lalande, André (1993), *Vocabulaire technique et critique de la philosophie*, Paris: Presses universitaires de France, p. 183 (1st edition 1926).
10 Ibid., p. 69.

Codifying the discipline?

41 Anthropologists as spies

David Price

David Price (born in 1960) is a professor of anthropology at Saint Martin's University in Washington State. After having conducted ethnographic and archaeological research in Egypt, he turned to the history of anthropology and particularly the relationship between the discipline and the United States intelligence corps. While examining FBI documents in order to write about anthropologists' contribution to the war effort during the Second World War, he discovered archives revealing the harassment of anthropologists engaged in militant activity in favour of racial equality in the United States during the 1940s and 1950s. He then went on to write a trilogy on the relationship between anthropologists and the secret services. The first volume, *Threatening Anthropology*, analyses the FBI's activity against militant anthropologists under McCarthyism. The second one, *Anthropological Intelligence*, returns to the role of anthropologists during the Second World War. The final one, *Weaponizing Anthropology*, focuses on the links between anthropology and the CIA during the Cold War and the more recent use of anthropological knowledge in military doctrine.

In the essay presented here, David Price considers a famous episode in the history of American anthropology: the letter published by Franz Boas in 1919 criticising the role of researchers who had used their work as a cover for political spying during the First World War. Although the names of the researchers were not mentioned, the author of the letter called for disciplinary action against anthropologists engaged in secret activities that, according to him, put the deontology of the discipline, and even the safety of its members, in danger. But, ironically, it was the accuser who was condemned, and Franz Boas was excluded from the American Anthropological Association that he had created a few years prior. Taking this founding ordeal of the professional organisation as a starting point, David Price shows that the question of the dubious relationship between intelligence and anthropology haunts the history of the discipline in the United States, without its full implications having ever been examined. His study therefore sheds new light on the history of anthropology by questioning the relationship between research ethics and political stakes.

On December 20, 1919, under the heading "Scientists as Spies," *The Nation* published a letter by Franz Boas, the father of academic anthropology in America. Boas charged that four American anthropologists, whom he did not name, had abused their professional research positions by conducting espionage in Central America during the First World War. Boas strongly condemned their actions, writing that they had "prostituted science by using it as a cover for their activities as spies." Anthropologists spying for their country severely betrayed their science and damaged the credibility of all anthropological research, Boas wrote; a scientist who uses his research as a cover for political spying forfeits the right to be classified as a scientist.

The most significant reaction to this letter occurred ten days later at the annual meeting of the American Anthropological Association (AAA), when the association's governing council voted to censure Boas, effectively removing him from the council and pressuring him to resign from the national research council. Three out of four of the accused spies (their names, we now know, were Samuel Lothrop, Sylvanus Morley and Herbert Spinden) voted for censure; the fourth (John Mason) did not. Later Mason wrote Boas an apologetic letter explaining that he'd spied out of a sense of patriotic duty.

A variety of extraneous factors contributed to Boas's censure (chief among these being institutional rivalries, personal differences and possibly anti-Semitism). The AAA's governing council was concerned less about the accuracy of his charges than about the possibility that publicizing them might endanger the ability of others to undertake fieldwork. It accused *him* of "abuse" of his professional position for political ends.

In 1919 American anthropology avoided facing the ethical questions Boas raised about anthropologists' using their work as a cover for spying. And it has refused to face them ever since. The AAA's current code of ethics contains no specific prohibitions concerning espionage or secretive research. Some of the same anthropologists who spied during the First World War did so in the next war. During the early cold war Ruth Benedict and lesser-known colleagues worked for the RAND corporation and the Office of Naval Research. In the Vietnam War, anthropologists worked on projects with strategic military applications.

Until recently there was little investigation of either the veracity of Boas's accusation in 1919 or the ethical strength of his complaint. But FBI documents released to me under the Freedom of Information Act shed new light on both of these issues.

The FBI produced 280 pages of documents pertaining to one of the individuals Boas accused—the Harvard archeologist Samuel Lothrop. Lothrop's FBI file establishes that during the First World War he indeed spied for Naval Intelligence, performing "highly commendable" work in the Caribbean until "his identity as an Agent of Naval Intelligence became known." What is more, the Second World War saw him back in harness, serving in the Special Intelligence Service (SIS), which J. Edgar Hoover created within the FBI to undertake and coordinate all intelligence activity in Central and South America. During the war the SIS stationed approximately 350 agents throughout South America, where they collected intelligence, subverted Axis networks and at times assisted in the interruption of the flow of raw materials from Axis sources. Lothrop was stationed in Lima, Peru, where he monitored imports, exports and political developments. To maintain his cover he pretended to undertake archeological investigations.

From his arrival in Lima in mid-December 1940, Lothrop was dogged by constant worries that his communications with Washington were being intercepted by British, Peruvian, Japanese or German intelligence operatives. By August 1941 he became concerned that his lack of significant archeological progress might lead to the discovery of his true work in Peru. Lothrop reported his fears of being detected to FBI headquarters: "As regards the archaeological cover for my work in Peru, it was based on the understanding that I was to be in the country six months or less. It is wearing thin and some day somebody is going to start asking why an archaeologist spends most of his time in towns asking questions. This won't happen as soon as it might because the Rockefeller grant for research in Peru makes me a contact man between the field workers and the government."

Lothrop was referring to the Rockefeller Foundation, which financed twenty archeologists who were excavating in Peru, Chile, Colombia, Mexico, Venezuela and Central America. He also used his ties to a variety of academic and research institutions—including Harvard, the Peabody Museum, the Institute of Andean Research and the Carnegie Institute—as cover in Peru. Archeologist Gordon Willey, who worked on an Institute of Andean Research Project in Peru and had some contact with Lothrop at this time, recalled that "it was sort of widely known on the loose grapevine that Sam was carrying on some kind of espionage work, much of which seemed to be keeping his eye on German patrons of the Hotel Bolivar Bar."

In fact, Lothrop was considered a valuable agent who collected important information on Peruvian politics and leading public figures of a nature usually difficult to secure. An FBI evaluation reported that headquarters "occasionally receive[s] information of sufficient importance from Mr. Lothrop to transmit to the President." Lothrop's principal source was an assistant to the Peruvian minister of government and police. In the spring of 1944 this informant resigned his governmental position and began "working exclusively under the direction of Dr. Lothrop." In May 1944 the US Embassy reported that Lothrop's principal informant was fully aware of Lothrop's connection to the SIS and FBI. Lothrop's cover was compromised by four Peruvian investigators in the employ of his top informant. His informant had been heard bragging to the Peruvian police that he made more by working for the US Embassy than the police made working for the Peruvian government.

The FBI decided to test the reliability of Lothrop's key informant by assigning him to collect information on nonexistent events and individuals. The informant was given background information about a nonexistent upcoming anti-Jewish rally that he was to attend, including a list of specific individuals who would be present. Though the rally did not occur, the informant provided a full report on it. He also filed detailed reports on a nonexistent commemorative celebration of the bombing of Pearl Harbor held in a distant town, and on a fictitious German spy who supposedly had jumped ship in Peru.

Lothrop was instructed not to tell the informant that his duplicity had been detected; instead, he was to say he was out of funds to pay for informants. Lothrop refused to believe his informant was lying and sent a letter of resignation to J. Edgar Hoover. His resignation was accepted and he returned to the United States to resume his academic duties at Harvard's Peabody Museum and the Carnegie Institute.

What is now known about Lothrop's long career of espionage suggests that the censure of Boas by the AAA in 1919 sent a clear message to him and others that espionage under cover of science in the service of the state is acceptable. In each of the wars and military actions that followed the First World War anthropologists confronted, or more often repressed, the very issues raised by Boas in his 1919 letter to *The Nation*.

While almost every prominent living US anthropologist (including Ruth Benedict, Gregory Bateson, Clyde Kluckhohn and Margaret Mead) contributed to the Second World War war effort, they seldom did so under the false pretext of fieldwork, as Lothrop did. Without endorsing the wide variety of activities to which anthropological skills were applied in the service of the military, a fundamental ethical distinction can be made between those who (as Boas put it) "prostituted science by using it as a cover for their activities as spies" and those who did not. The Second World War did, however, stimulate frank, though muted, discussions of the propriety of anthropologists' using their knowledge of those they studied in times of war, creating conditions in which, as anthropologist Laura Thompson put it, they became "technicians for hire to the highest bidder." Although the racist tenets of Nazism were an affront to the anthropological view of the inherent equality of humankind, Boas (who died in 1942) would probably have condemned anthropologists who used science as a cover for espionage during the Second World War. Approximately half of America's anthropologists contributed to the war effort, with dozens of prominent members of the profession working for the Office of Strategic Services (OSS), Army and Navy intelligence and the Office of War Information.

In the following decades there were numerous private and public interactions between anthropologists and the intelligence community. Some anthropologists applied their skills at the CIA after its inception in 1947 and may still be doing so today. For some of them this was a logical transition from their wartime espionage work with the OSS and other organizations; others regarded the CIA as an agency concerned with gathering information to assist policy-makers rather than a secret branch of government that subverted foreign governments and waged clandestine war on the Soviet Union and its allies. Still other anthropologists unwittingly received research funding from CIA fronts like the Human Ecology Fund.

The American Anthropological Association also secretly collaborated with the CIA. In the early 1950s the AAA's executive board negotiated a secret agreement with the CIA under which agency personnel and computers were used to produce a cross-listed directory of AAA members, showing their geographical and linguistic areas of expertise along with summaries of research interests. Under this agreement the CIA kept copies of the database for its own purposes with no questions asked. And none were, if for no other reason than that the executive board had agreed to keep the arrangement a secret. What use the CIA made of this database is not known, but the relationship with the AAA was part of an established agency policy of making use of America's academic brain trust. Anthropologists' knowledge of the languages and cultures of the people inhabiting the regions of the Third World where the agency was waging its declared and undeclared wars would have been invaluable to the CIA. The extent to which this occurred is the focus of ongoing archival and FOIA research. When the CIA overthrew Jacobo Arbenz in Guatemala in 1954, an anthropologist reported, under a pseudonym, to the State Department's intelligence and research division on the political affiliations of the prisoners taken by the military in the coup.

During the Korean War linguists and ethnographers assisted America's involvement with little vocal conflict of conscience. Norwegian sociologist Johan Galtung's revelations in 1965 of Project Camelot, in which anthropologists were reported to be working on unclassified counterinsurgency programs in Latin America, ignited controversy in the AAA. During America's wars in Southeast Asia the AAA was thrown into a state of upheaval after documents purloined from the private office of UCLA anthropologist Michael Moerman revealed that several anthropologists had secretly used their ethnographic knowledge to assist the war effort.

As a result of inquiries made into these revelations, the 1971 annual meeting of the AAA became the scene of a tumultuous showdown after a fact-finding committee chaired by Margaret Mead maneuvered to create a report finding no wrongdoing on the part of the accused anthropologists. An acrimonious debate resulted in the rejection of the Mead report by the voting members of the association. As historian Eric Wakin noted in his book *Anthropology Goes to War*, this "represented an organized body of younger anthropologists rejecting the values of its elders." But the unresolved ethical issue of anthropologists spying during the First and Second World Wars provided a backdrop to the 1971 showdown. Almost two decades later during the Gulf War, proposals by conservatives in the AAA that its members assist allied efforts against Iraq provoked only minor opposition.

Today most anthropologists are still loath to acknowledge, much less study, known connections between anthropology and the intelligence community. As with any controversial topic, it is not thought to be a good "career builder." But more significant, there is a general perception that to rake over anthropology's past links, witting and unwitting, with the intelligence community could reduce opportunities for US anthropologists to conduct fieldwork in foreign nations.

In the course of research in this area I have been told by other anthropologists in no uncertain terms that to raise such questions could endanger the lives of fieldworkers around the globe. This is not a point to be taken lightly, as many anthropologists work in remote settings controlled by hostile governmental or guerrilla forces. Suspicions that one is a US intelligence agent, whether valid or not, could have fatal consequences. As Boas prophetically wrote in his original complaint against Lothrop and his cohorts, "In consequence of their acts every nation will look with distrust upon the visiting foreign investigator who wants to do honest work, suspecting sinister designs. Such action has raised a new barrier against the development of international friendly cooperation." But until US anthropology examines its past and sets rules forbidding both secret research and collaboration with intelligence agencies, these dangers will continue.

Over the past several decades the explicit condemnations of secretive research have been removed from the AAA's code of ethics—the principles of professional responsibility (PPR). In 1971 the PPR specifically declared that "no secret research, no secret reports or debriefings of any kind should be agreed to or given" by members of the AAA. By 1990 the attenuation of anthropological ethics had reached a point where anthropologists were merely "under no professional obligation to provide reports or debriefing of any kind to government officials or employees, unless they have individually and explicitly agreed to do so in the terms of employment." These changes were largely accomplished in the 1984 revision of the PPR that Gerald Berreman characterized as reflecting the new "Reaganethics" of the association: In the prevailing climate of deregulation the responsibility for ethical review was shifted from the association to individual judgments. As anthropologist Laura Nader noted, these Reagan-era changes were primarily "moves to protect academic careers ... downplaying anthropologists' paramount responsibility to those they study." The current PPR may be interpreted to mean that anthropologists don't have to be spies unless they want to or have agreed to do so in a contract. A 1995 Commission to Review the AAA Statements on Ethics declared that the committee on ethics had neither the authority nor the resources to investigate or arbitrate complaints of ethical violations and would "no longer adjudicate claims of unethical behavior and focus its efforts and resources on an ethics education program."

Members of the current ethics committee believe that even though the AAA explicitly removed language forbidding secretive research or spying, there are clauses in the current code that imply (rather than state) that such conduct should not be allowed—though without sanctions, this stricture is essentially meaningless. Archeologist Joe Watkins, chairman of the ethics committee, believes that if an anthropologist were caught spying today: "the AAA would not do anything to investigate the activity or to reprimand the individual, even if the individual had not been candid [about the true purpose of the research]. I'm not sure that there is anything the association would do as an association, but perhaps public awareness would work to keep such practitioners in line, like the Pueblo clowns' work to control the societal miscreants." Watkins is referring to Pueblo cultures' use of clowns to ridicule miscreants. Although it is debatable whether anthropologist intelligence operatives would fear sanctions imposed by the AAA, it is incongruous to argue that they would fear public ridicule more. Enforcing a ban on covert research would be difficult, but to give up on even the possibility of investigating such wrongdoing sends the wrong message to the world and to the intelligence agencies bent on recruiting anthropologists.

Many factors have contributed to the AAA's retreat from statements condemning espionage and covert research. Key among these are the century-old difficulties inherent in keeping an intrinsically diverse group of scholars aligned under the framework of a single association. A combination of atavistic and market forces has driven apart members of a field once mythically united around the holistic integration of the findings of archeology and physical, cultural and linguistic anthropology. As some "applied anthropologists" move from classroom employment to working in governmental and industrial settings, statements condemning spying have made increasing numbers of practitioners uncomfortable—and this discomfort suggests much about the nature of some applied anthropological work. The activities encompassed under the heading of applied anthropology are extremely diverse, ranging from heartfelt and underpaid activist-based research for NGOs around the world to production of secret ethnographies and time-allocation studies of industrial and blue-collar workplaces for the private consumption of management.

As increasing numbers of anthropologists find employment in corporations, anthropological research becomes not a quest for scientific truth, as in the days of Boas, but a quest for secret or proprietary data for governmental or corporate sponsors. The AAA's current stance of inaction sends the dangerous message to the underdeveloped world that the world's largest anthropological organization will take no action against anthropologists whose fieldwork is a front for espionage. As the training of anthropology graduate students becomes increasingly dependent on programs like the 1991 National Security Education Program—with its required governmental-service payback stipulations—the issue takes on increased (though seldom discussed) importance.

It is unknown whether any members of the AAA are currently engaged in espionage, but unless the scientific community takes steps to denounce such activities using the clearest possible language and providing sanctions against those who do so, we can anticipate that such actions will continue with impunity during some future crisis or war.

Many in the American Anthropological Association are frustrated with its decision neither to explicitly prohibit nor to penalize secretive government research. It is time for US anthropologists to examine the political consequences of their history and take a hard thoughtful look at Boas's complaint and the implications implicit in the association's refusal to condemn secret research and to re-enact sanctions against anthropologists engaging in espionage.

42 The moral ordeals of anthropology

Peter Pels

Peter Pels (born in 1958) is a professor of anthropology at Leiden University in the Netherlands. A specialist of colonial interactions in Africa, he has notably published *A Politics of Presence: Contacts Between Missionaries and Waluguru in Late Colonial Tanganyika* and co-edited the book *Colonial Subjects: Essays on the Practical History of Anthropology*. A substantial part of his research has focused on the history of anthropological practice, from a reflexive and critical perspective. The book *Embedding Ethics*, which he co-edited, suggests approaching ethical questions as an integral part of anthropological activity, in other words as being a matter for negotiations between different viewpoints and contradictory stakes rather than a set of rules that can be laid out a priori.

The text presented here offers a 'prehistory' of deontological codes. Peter Pels historicises the question of ethics in anthropology by showing how it was formed in the particular context of colonial relations and through a process of academic professionalisation by which the discipline endeavoured to distinguish itself from politics and the administration, though it remained dependent on both. The concern with affirming their autonomy led anthropologists to position themselves ethically on the side of their subjects (the colonised) while addressing their own community of origin (the colonisers). They could therefore not escape being caught up in contradictions that could not be resolved by deontological codes. For Peter Pels, the ethical question therefore reflects an epistemological problem, that of duplicity without malice, for which he forges the term 'duplexity'. Rejecting the idea according to which the proliferation of ethical codes would be the sign of moral progress for the social sciences, he makes an important contribution to the debate that mobilises professional organisations such as the American Anthropological Association. Published with comments from fifteen scholars from different national research cultures and deontological traditions, the essay became a classic in the field. Its historical reading, foregrounding the multiple forms of ethical relations, suggests the possibility of alternative forms of professional morality to codification.

Ethical codes have recently reemerged as a fashionable topic for anthropological discussion. The American Anthropological Association discussed the adoption of a new code of ethics for its members in November 1995, the productive phase of one of the cycles of ethical discussion that it has experienced since the late 1960s. But whereas the AAA's ethical fervour has been a regular feature of the past 30 years, it has since the early 1990s spread to a number of anthropological associations for which ethical codes have not figured prominently on the professional agenda: the Association of Social Anthropologists in Britain and the Dutch Association of Anthropologists have contemplated revisions of their codes; Swedish anthropologists have been discussing the adoption of a newly drafted one; German ethnologists have decided not to adopt a code because it would stifle their ethical discussions; the Danish development agency has commissioned research into the ethics of development research, including anthropology; and one French anthropological association has held a workshop to voice, among other things, its aversion to the U.S. model of ethical codes.

Whence this resurgence of ethical self-consciousness among anthropologists? Recent ethical discussions clearly accompany shifts in the self-understanding of anthropologists and their position in society,[1] but they do not usually address the long-term history, social position, and self-understanding of anthropology. If history is invoked in discussing anthropological ethics, it does not often go beyond the "Whiggish" acknowledgment of early-20th-century precedents of the ethical consciousness of the 1960s or the identification of (neo)colonial anthropology as morally suspect. This may be a prophylactic against the uncertainties of questioning the anthropological self-image, for a historical approach would soon indicate that the present interest in ethical codes is only one way of institutionalizing moral standards and ethical guidelines in anthropology and a very recent and fairly unusual one at that. If the history of anthropology suggests alternative institutionalizations of anthropological morals, it becomes possible to question our present conduct in the field of ethics, including the desire to have an ethical code. Hence my notion of a "prehistory" of ethical codes in anthropology—although I stress it is "a" prehistory, an interpretation based on a necessarily incomplete genealogy of anthropological morals.

Having an ethical code is a necessity in the folk epistemology of professionalism, an epistemology widely shared by anthropologists. This folk epistemology is a product of the interwar period, when the rise of the academic expert was accompanied by social scientific attempts to identify the public service of a professional intelligentsia[2] and its relative autonomy from class interests.[3] In this professional ideology, ethical codes are meant to ensure the competence and honour of the professional, that is, to help discipline the members of the profession so that its clients can trust the technical and moral quality of the service rendered.[4] This folk epistemology of autonomous corporate professions ensuring their public service has been called into question by studies of internecine warfare,[5] "conspiracies against the laity" and "commercialization,"[6] and the loss of professional autonomy.[7]

In contrast to this folk epistemology, Anglo-Saxon anthropology adopted a rather peculiar trajectory of professionalization. In accordance with 1930s professional folk epistemology, it strove to define itself in terms of technical and public service rendered to colonial administration,[8] but after the Second World War a vision of anthropology became dominant that identified this service as foreign to it. The professional ideology of "service" was marginalized as "application" in the self-image of the anthropological profession, and while both "pure" and "applied" academics were thought to be legitimately professional, extra-academic employment made one a "no longer anthropologist," as if one were to exclude general practitioners from the medical or legal profession because they *are* practitioners.

There is therefore reason to question the assumption that anthropology needs an ethical code for the same reasons that other professions say they do. Furthermore, our ethical discussion must go beyond that of the necessity for or adoption of an ethical code to inquire into the different morals of pre- and postwar, or colonial and postcolonial, anthropology's attempts to establish its academic and professional status. Given the support which anthropologists promised to colonial administration, such an inquiry inevitably ends up questioning the moral standards of European "civilizing missions" in general. It has become standard practice to "unmask" the moral standards that were crucial in legitimating both colonial rule and the anthropological profession as the surface hypocrisy of European expansionist desires and private interests. This oscillation between the notion of morality as a set of universal and impersonal standards and the critical awareness that these standards are used duplicitously to serve some particular interest is, as Alasdair MacIntyre[9] has argued, characteristic of Occidental talk about morality. I shall try to avoid this oscillation: one cannot merely discuss the morality of anthropology in terms of a set of moral standards and its subsequent betrayal by particular interests—in short, in terms of a duplicity of which anthropologists can be declared guilty. Instead, I want to argue that since the late 19th century anthropology's epistemological commitment to cultural difference has made its morals essentially *duplex*: without duplicitous intention or moral corruption, anthropologists cannot but adopt "double standards." [...]

Advocacy: truth as value in the protection of aborigines

British ethnology emerged from moral concerns. After their successes in the early 1830s, the campaigners for the abolition of slavery transferred their attention to "a corresponding effort to rescue and elevate the coloured races at large."[10] A parliamentary select committee established to investigate the suffering of the aboriginal tribes of the British settlements resulted in the founding in 1837 of the Aborigines Protection Society, the immediate predecessor of the Ethnological Society of London. The aim of the Society was "to assist in protecting the defenceless, and promoting the advancement of uncivilized Tribes." Interestingly enough, this practical aim was to be accomplished by research and its publication: by inquiry into the facts of aboriginal life and how it suffered under colonization and the collection and dissemination of these facts in a library, in a museum, and through the press. The APS exemplified a typically 19th-century attitude of British reform: that "truth" or "the facts"—provided by science—would convert the ignorant to the moral necessity of change. Natural science's "anti-conquest" declared its innocence at the same time that it proclaimed its universal hegemony. Through phrenology's "naturalizing" of human social order and the moral individual, it became a powerful bourgeois ideology.[11] In this case, truth—scientific fact—was thought to be both politically neutral and morally compelling. Truth was itself moral: fact was value.

The APS asked that "the due observation of Justice, and the protection of Rights" be extended to the native inhabitants of British settlements. Its moral community was humanity, its motto *ab uno sanguine*,[12] and its audience the (British) nation, which was expected to be ashamed of its conduct as a colonizer. It defined itself politically against "the enterprising, avaricious and powerful" and in solidarity with those who were unable to resist their encroachment.[13] This solidarity was, however, qualified by the missionary intent of the APS, which clearly saw itself as paving the way for Christian conversion. In practice, the political agenda of the APS should be seen in the light of the predominantly Nonconformist persuasion of its members, whose decades of participation in campaigns for radical reform must have made them suspicious of "the powerful." Whatever the practical politics, however, the moral community defined by the protectors of aborigines (the "one blood" of humanity) was something that only their own political community was sufficiently conscious of. According to the APS, both the powerful and the powerless needed to be missionized, although the former more about the latter than vice versa.

This emphasis on advocacy—the APS's representation of, or speaking for, the aborigines to a national audience—was to become more and more autonomous from the work of protection as such. [...]

The "dual mandate" and the epistemological duplexity of ethnographic fieldwork

In 1922, Frederick Lugard set out the duties of a 20th-century colonizing power as a balance between "material" and "moral" obligations.[14] The moral ones were directed to the "subject races" in particular, and encompassed "the training of native rulers; the delegation to them of such responsibility as they are fit to exercise; the constitution of Courts of Justice free from corruption and accessible to all; the adoption of a system of education which will assist progress without creating false ideals; the institution of free labour and of a just system of taxation; the protection of the peasant from oppression, and the preservation of their rights in land, &c." At the time, this sense of moral obligation was widespread among European colonial powers and often centered on paternalist notions of imperial "trusteeship." In France it went under the name of *mission civilisatrice*, in the Netherlands under that of "ethical policy." It generally combined an explicit commitment to "native interests" with an equally explicit definition of these interests in terms of modernization on Occidental terms. Dutch ethical policy combined paternalist control and political emancipation, concentrating on both military pacification and indigenous education. The duality of the colonial mandate can be read as an explicit and pragmatic recognition of the duplicity of Occidental moral discourse.

It is easy to unmask the ethical policies of colonialism by referring to their practical politics: in the Dutch case, an ethical colonial policy was partly a politics of weakness in the face of British jingoism or French and German chauvinism, for if one could not actually beat the imperialist competitor one might at least set an "ethical" example for him.[15] In British circles, colonial administrators had long resisted commercial powers by juxtaposing an image of impeccable administrative integrity to the base utilities of mercantile thought. Indeed, the late 19th and early 20th century often legitimated power in terms of the "white man's burden," in which considerations of natural utility or laissez-faire were attacked from the standpoint of more elevated sensibilities, just as defenders of the former found ways to unmask the latter. Yet the duality of colonial rule was more complicated than a simple affirmation or betrayal of a set of moral values. One can see this at work in Lugard's moral obligations: one "trains" native rulers, stopping short of giving them the responsibility one takes on oneself; one provides education but not "false" ideals, that is, of an education equal to the European; one protects the peasant from oppression except by "free" labour and taxation. Once Europeans engaged in the definition of "native" interests or forms of rule, they necessarily became immersed in paradox.[16] The seemingly simple formulation of the dual mandate hid a more complex entanglement, and, to make matters even more difficult, anthropology was intimately involved in producing such definitions. [...]

The duplicity of ethnographic authority has only recently become an issue for the ethics of ethnographic representation.[17] In contrast to textual duplicity, however, the duplexity of fieldwork has created problems throughout the history of anthropology. Early on, Burton was accused of betraying his "character of a European gentleman, let alone that of a Christian," in disguising himself as a Muslim in order to enter Mecca.[18] Like his betrayal of Achenese confidence, Snouck's instrumental "conversion" to Islam for his trip to Mecca raised similar doubts about his identity. It sometimes seems as if high imperial anthropologists were more explicitly concerned with the ethics of instrumentalizing identity during fieldwork than their more "professional" successors. Especially between 1925 and 1960 (the era of the emergence of "professional" fieldwork), duplicity was rarely explicitly problematized, and reflection on the dilemmas of fieldwork practice began only in the more reflexive 1960s. During earlier attempts at anthropological professionalization, the methodology of contact was much more debated than between 1925 and 1960. The coalition of anthropologists and colonial administrators that, around 1900, wanted to institutionalize anthropological training for future colonizers emphasized "tact" and "sympathy" in dealing with native peoples. Derived from a discourse of colonial servants about the practical skills required to manage the colonized, this "tact" was now redefined as intuitive anthropological knowledge.

The instrumental morality of late-19th-century fieldwork required sympathy with natives for both the acquisition of knowledge and the peaceful administration of a district. This tact and sympathy bordered on make-believe: the strategic quotation of a native proverb, the observation of the proper native etiquette, or, as Snouck advised his superiors during the Acheh War, paying lip-service to an apolitical Islam in order to counter one that seemed politically dangerous. But this was not simply a form of ethical duplicity, in which an ulterior end (order) was covered up by the means of presentation (sympathy). Early fieldwork tact was more profound than just the idea of putting on a mask: it was thought to be a necessary doubling of the identity of the ethnographer (whether humble anthropologist or administrative overlord). This epistemological doubling of identity was not yet allowed to interfere with the hierarchy of values—in fact, tact belonged to, and complicated, only the realm of means, not that of ends. But if the ends of the civilizing mission justified the means of their realization, anthropological intervention in an "other" society required a "different" means by a doubling of self and other. Tact and sympathy did not, in this period, supersede the hegemonic morality of the civilizing mission's universal truths (such as order and peaceful administration), but they added moral truths of particularity and difference to the means necessary for their realization.

The morals of representation: truth against value in the politics of professionalization

Professional anthropology inherited this problematic combination of ethical and epistemological doubling. The process of anthropological professionalization can perhaps best be understood as a bet on the latter in the hope that the problems of the former would disappear. This bet took the form of a *morality of representation*: the argument that only a disinterested, noninterventionist attitude in the field could reduce the duplexity of fieldwork and lead to an adequate knowledge of the colonized. This morality of representation was fundamental to what has become the hallmark of 20th-century anthropology: cultural critique. This critique, based on the juxtaposition of truths of difference and particularity with Western, "universal" values of mental and social order and economy, was exemplified by the work of such architects of Anglo-Saxon professional anthropology as Mead and Malinowski. In Malinowski's work, the duplicity of this morality of representation lay in subordinating the presentation of such antiphonal knowledge to another major goal: transforming the anthropologist into a welfare expert "serving" the colonial state. This was possible only by excising the "contact zone" of colonial intervention from accounts of professional conduct except where including it would set up the colonizer as a client of anthropological experts. Thus Malinowski's morality of representation was suspended between a cultural critique that sought to go beyond ethnocentric Western standards and an instrumentality of "indirect cultural control" of native life in the interests of "rationalizing" colonial administration.[19]

The professionalization of British anthropology was made possible by the selection of functionalist anthropology at the London School of Economics as the proper recipient of Rockefeller Foundation funding, at the expense of other anthropological schools. This selection was made on the basis of the claim, made by the missionary Joseph Oldham, the former administrator Lord Lugard, and the anthropologist Malinowski, that functionalism would help prevent racial conflict, particularly by endorsing and elaborating the British administrative doctrine known as indirect rule. Yet, at the same time, Rockefeller funding reduced the need to rely for support on the colonial establishment. Henceforth, LSE anthropology was free to claim professional scientific independence of the kinds of questions, research programmes, and intelligence that colonial administrations required. This shift in funding therefore perfectly fitted the erasure of the colonial context in works such as Malinowski's *Argonauts of the Western Pacific* and Radcliffe-Brown's *The Andaman Islanders*, both published in 1922, which defined the relevant social relationship of anthropology as a dyad of ethnographer and informants rather than a triad that also included colonial rule.

This was a move away from the previous generation's emphasis on tact and sympathy, while at the same time adopting its ideas about intensive fieldwork as necessary for understanding the native point of view. Instead of working with colonial ethnographers, Malinowski and Radcliffe-Brown denied them the capacity to do ethnographic research because of their "inevitable" bias.[20] After claiming this academic monopoly, Malinowski argued that only academic anthropologists could provide the adequate representations of the colonized so urgently needed by those who administered them. This 1929 essay was a "standard grant proposal"[21] meant to convince the Rockefeller Foundation that functionalism was far more useful to colonial administration than other schools of anthropology. Anthropology defined itself in this respect as a "technical service,"[22] in conformity with the professionalist ideals of social scientific welfare experts being developed at LSE at the time (by, among others, R. H. Tawney). To this complex strategy another step was added by E. E. Evans-Pritchard after the Second World War. He emphasized that any practical "service" rendered by anthropologists should be subordinate to the academic detachment and scientific goals that distinguished "pure" anthropology from its "application."[23]

Thus, the morality of representation could work out in two different ways: as a commitment to practical relevance (which was dubbed "applied" anthropology) and as ("pure") scientific detachment. Emphasizing the distinction between science and its application defined the ethnographer as an essentially academic creature, and in the same year that Evans-Pritchard published his manifesto of scientific purity that definition was made into a practical reality by the foundation of the Association of Social Anthropologists, from which the administrators, missionaries, and other non-academics of the Royal Anthropological Institute were excluded. The ASA—according to Edmund Leach, meant to "prevent the Universities from employing unqualified refugees from the disappearing Colonial Service to teach 'applied anthropology'"[24]— united the largely "amoral" and apolitical followers of Radcliffe-Brown and the more politically committed Malinowskians. Morally speaking, the hegemonic image of "pure" science foregrounded the duty to truth and scientific development, although it affirmed the value of expert anthropological knowledge to colonial administration. After the Second World War, "applied" anthropologists also emphasized the anthropologist's academic autonomy in (re)formulating issues, probably because "application" had become derivative and secondary. [...]

Commitment to the represented: truth as value in the emergence of ethical codes

Ethical codes arrived late in anthropology and played a negligible role in the professionalization of the discipline. The emergence of worries about anthropological duplicity long before these worries were codified in the 1960s and 1970s is to be explained by the desire to produce or maintain professional autonomy vis-à-vis the governments by which anthropologists were employed. In 1914 Northcote Thomas, a student of Haddon and Rivers, refused to disclose the names of his Leopard Society informants to his employer, the Sierra Leonian colonial government.[25] In 1919 Boas condemned, in the name of science, anthropologists' spying for the U.S. government in the First World War. In the early 1940s the "moral" of Malinowski's warning that anthropologists should not act as spies or *agents provocateurs* was that they should equally study the "motives, intentions, and ways of action of the European community."[26] Professional autonomy from research sponsors was also the motivation behind the first codification of ethics: in 1948, the freedom of publication for anthropologists vis-à-vis, in this case, the government was put on paper. Despite the practical involvement of anthropologists in the war effort, they soon returned to the value-freedom of "pure" science after 1945. There was little sign of a fusion of ethical and epistemological concerns until about 1965, when, especially in the U.S.A., anthropologists' capacity to represent the interests of the people studied was increasingly identified as their foremost duty.

The story of the emergence of the "first ethical code in the field" and its background in the protest against counterinsurgency research for the U.S. government in Latin America and Southeast Asia has been well told elsewhere.[27] The turning point was the outrage over Project Camelot, the social scientific research project that supported the U.S. Defense Department's counterinsurgency programme in Latin America and had to be cancelled because of the protest. The significance of this becomes apparent when we recapitulate what went before, in particular that the professionalization of anthropology was partly accomplished through the definition of a dyadic relationship between anthropologists and people studied, from which the colonial situation, its representatives, and its values had been erased. This dyadic relationship gave academics a monopoly on ethnography and created a measure of professional autonomy that turned colonizers—the foremost audience for anthropology apart from the academics—into their clients. This academicism was not attacked by the critics of the 1960s. On the contrary, they took it as the basis from which to commit themselves to the people studied. This radicalized the ethics of representation: to lay the ghosts of ethical and epistemological duplicity, anthropologists committed themselves not to the values of colonizers but to the values of the people represented.

This radical ethics of representation not only excluded administrators and missionaries from the epistemological relationship between anthropologist and people studied but also excluded them morally by defining them as a threat to the latter. The critique of value-free social science no longer simply said that objectivity was an illusory ideal that harmed anthropology's professional responsibility towards, among others, colonial administrators (as Nadel had argued in 1946) but emphasized that it could harm those studied. This turned the dyad of ethnographer and people studied into the "most important" relationship for anthropologists[28] and provided the basis on which one could think of those studied as clients. It spawned the first article of the Principles of Professional Responsibility—that "the anthropologist's paramount responsibility is to those he studies." This fear of third-party involvement in the dyadic relationship between anthropologist and informant can be related to the process of political decolonization, which was, at the time, still unfinished.

Franz Boas's 1919 protest against anthropologists' "spying" for the U.S. government in Mexico was motivated by his ties with the Mexican scientific establishment (to which his ambivalence about the war against Germany only added): he feared that "in consequence of their acts every nation will look with distrust upon the visiting foreign investigator who wants to do honest work, suspecting sinister designs."[29] Malinowski's warnings against anthropological duplicity and espionage were also made in the context of a newly arisen African nationalism,[30] and his student Jomo Kenyatta made no secret of the fact that his anthropology was directed against the duplicity of Western "pretenders to philanthropy" who claimed to "monopolise the office of interpreting [the African's] mind and speaking for him."[31] Decolonization provided a context in which the "duplicity of the West" was commented upon by Third World leaders[32] and anthropologists worried about the extent to which their work could be associated with it. The 1967 Beals committee complained that the "international" reputation of anthropologists had been damaged by anthropologists' engaging in intelligence reporting.[33]

The reputation of anthropology was indeed tarnished. Spokesmen and gatekeepers for the people studied associated anthropologists with colonial administration and Christian mission. Kwame Nkrumah was reported to possess a painting in which a colonial official, a missionary, and an anthropologist fled before a black giant breaking its bonds. Native Americans viewed anthropologists as a curse, and in independent Africa anthropology was nearly everywhere banned from the universities. This suggests that anthropologists were afraid not just of the accusation of duplicity but also of the denial of admission to the field by newly decolonized governments. Identification with the people studied and those who controlled access to them was further encouraged by anthropologists' relatively autonomous academic position, which allowed them to voice their suspicion of their colonial or neocolonial home governments.

Conclusion

One can summarize these four periods of the history of anthropology as follows: first, a morality which saw intervention among the to-be-converted on behalf of the morally superior as the end of the ethnological endeavour; second, a morality which saw intervention in other societies as necessary and ethnology as the means to do it in a morally justifiable way; third, a morality that opposed the disinterested representations of other societies by professional anthropologists to interventions by the powers that be among the colonized and said that the latter could not be efficient except by means of such representations; and fourth, an ethics that defined intervention among the people studied as unethical except when based on the anthropologist's representations of their interests. Intervention as moral end, intervention as efficient means, representation as efficient means, representation as moral end: phrasing the sequence in this way raises the question whether the 21st century will witness a return of anthropology to an earlier combination of intervention, representation, morality, or expediency or whether other factors will help to produce something novel.

Notes

1 Fluehr-Lobban, C. (1991), *Ethics and the Profession of Anthropology: Dialogue for a New Era*, Philadelphia, PA: University of Pennsylvania Press.
2 Carr-Saunders, A. M. and P. A. Wilson (1933), *The Professions*, Oxford: Clarendon Press, p. 394.
3 Mannheim, Karl (1966), *Ideology and Utopia: An Introduction to the Sociology of Knowledge*, London: Routledge & Kegan Paul, p. 137.
4 Carr-Saunders and Wilson (1933), *The Professions*, op. cit., pp. 302, 394; Taeusch, C. (1933), Professional Ethics, in *Encyclopedia of the Social Sciences*, Seligman, Edwin (ed.), New York: Macmillan, p. 472.
5 Bücher, R. and A. L. Strauss (1961), *Professions in Process*, Indianapolis, IN: Bobbs-Merrill, College Division.
6 Shaw, G. B. and C. Wright Mills, quoted in Johnson (1973), The Professions, in Hurd, G. (ed.) *Human Societies*, London: Routledge & Kegan Paul, p. 128.
7 Freidson, E. (1984), The Changing Nature of Professional Control, *Annual Review of Sociology*, 10: 1–20.
8 Malinowski, B. (1929), Practical Anthropology, *Africa*, 2: 22–38; Wilson, G. (1940), Anthropology as a Public Service, *Africa*, 13: 43–61.
9 MacIntyre, Alasdair (1984), *After Virtue: A Study in Moral Theory*, Notre Dame, IN: University of Notre Dame Press.
10 Aborigines Protection Society (1838), First annual report of the Aborigines Protection Society, London.
11 Shapin, S. (1979), Homo Phrenologicus: Anthropological Perspectives on an Historical Problem, in Barnes, B. and S. Shapin (eds.), *Natural Order: Historical Studies of Scientific Culture*, Beverly Hills, CA: Sage Publications, p. 59.
12 Motte, Standish (1840), Outline of a System of Legislation for Securing Protection to the Aboriginal Inhabitants of All Countries Colonized by Great Britain, London: John Murray, p. 1.
13 Motte (1840), Outline of a System, op. cit., p. 5.
14 Lugard, Frederick (1965 [1923]), *The Dual Mandate in British Tropical Africa*, London: Frank Cass, p. 58.
15 Locher-Scholten, E. (1981), *Ethiek in fragmenten: vijf studies over koloniaal denken en doen van Nederlanders in de Indonesische archipel 1877–1942*. HES studia historica, 5. Utrecht, HES Publishers, p. 197.
16 Pels, Peter (1996), The Pidginization of Luguru Politics: Administrative Ethnography and the Paradoxes of Indirect Rule, *American Ethnologist*, 24: 738–761.
17 See Clifford, James and George Marcus (eds.) (1986), *Writing Culture: The Poetics and Politics of Ethnography: A School of American Research Advanced Seminar*, Berkeley, CA: University of California Press.
18 Burton, Richard F. (1964 [1893]), *Personal Narrative of a Pilgrimage*, New York: Dover, p. xxi.

19 Malinowski, B. (1922), *Argonauts of the Western Pacific*, London: Routledge, pp. 517–518; (1929), Practical Anthropology, op. cit.; (1930), The Rationalization of Anthropology and Administration, *Africa*, 3: 405–423.
20 Malinowski (1922), *Argonauts of the Western Pacific*, op. cit., p. 5.
21 Cell, J. W. (1989), Lord Hailey and the Making of the African Survey, *African Affairs*, 88, n. 8.
22 Wilson, G. (1940), Anthropology as a Public Service, op. cit., p. 46.
23 Evans-Pritchard, E. E. (1946), Applied Anthropology, *Africa*, 16: 92–98.
24 Cited by Wright, S. (1995), Anthropology: Still the Uncomfortable Discipline?, in *The Future of Anthropology: Its Relevance to the Contemporary World*, Shore, C. and A. Ahmed (eds.), London: Athlone, p. 67.
25 Kuklick, Henrika (1978), The Sins of the Fathers: British Anthropology and African Colonial Administration, *Research in Sociology of Knowledge, Sciences, and Art*, I: 103.
26 Malinowski, B. (1945), *The Dynamics of Culture Change: An Inquiry into Race Relations in Africa*, New Haven, CT: Yale University Press, p. 61.
27 Fluehr-Lobban (1991), *Ethics and the Profession of Anthropology*, op. cit., pp. 20–22, 27, 239–242.
28 Jorgensen, J. G. (1971), On Ethics and Anthropology, *Current Anthropology*, 12: 321.
29 Quoted in Woodbury, Nathalie (1993) For God, Country and our Foreign Policy: (Mis)uses of Anthropological Fieldwork, *AAA Newsletter*, 34 (7): 31.
30 Malinowski (1945), *The Dynamics of Culture Change*, op. cit., pp. 60–61.
31 Kenyatta, Jomo (1965 [1938]), *Facing Mount Kenya: The Tribal Life of the Gikuyu*, New York: Vintage Books, p. xviii.
32 Rabemananjara, J. cited by Gjessing, G. (1968), The Social Responsibility of the Social Scientist, *Current Anthropology*, 9: 399.
33 Woodbury, Nathalie (1993), For God, Country and our Foreign Policy: (Mis)uses of Anthropological Fieldwork, *Anthropology News*, 34 (7): 32.

43 The new bureaucracies of virtue

Charles L. Bosk

Charles L. Bosk (born in 1948) is a professor of sociology and medical ethics at the University of Pennsylvania where he is also a member of the Center for Bioethics. Focusing on the professional cultures and personal experience of medical practitioners, he dedicated his first book, *Forgive and Remember: Managing Medical Failure*, to the extreme situations in which medicine fails. He later conducted a research on genetic counselling, which was published under the title *All God's Mistakes: Genetic Counseling in a Pediatric Hospital*. In recent years, he has developed an ethnographic approach to bioethical questions in *What Would You Do? Juggling Bioethics and Ethnography*.

His interest in bioethics has also led him to examine the controversial problem of the ethical control of scientific research, which is the subject of the article presented here. Adopting a humorous tone, he analyses the conflictive relationship between the social scientists and the Institutional Review Boards (IRBs) responsible for evaluating the ethical grounds of their studies. These administrative bodies were established in the 1970s in order to regulate research in the life sciences focusing on 'human subjects', and have since been extended to sociological and anthropological research. The increasing control they exert over scientific activities is constantly denounced by researchers as absurd and ill-suited to the realities of the field. The author's aim here is to replace such confrontations with pacified dialogue. This, however, is only possible on condition that sociological terms are used to rationalise the relationship among the research in social science, the requirement to respect a certain scientific ethic, and the introduction of administrative bodies in charge of regulating the latter. Using Weber and Merton, Charles Bosk approaches IRBs as ordinary bureaucratic organisations: since they are responsible for achieving an ideal and vague goal, namely ethically irreproachable research, their members are all the more likely to forget the ultimate aim of their work, making formal compliance with rules and procedures a goal in itself. This inevitable shift from substantive to formal rationality seems to doom the project of creating a bureaucracy of virtue to failure. But the author also casts a critical eye upon his colleagues' relationship to their own research ethics. For him, academics' outright rejection of any form of ethical control reveals both their poor reflexivity regarding their scientific practice and their reticence to become themselves objects of inquiry – which is ironically their method when they study others.

Although little is added by rehearsing one more time how the set of standardized practices that count as "ethics review" were established, a minimal account here is necessary if only to anchor the discussion that follows. The "just-so" history used to justify the formation of IRBs is a recitation of a grab bag of abuses. Originally, the reach of IRBs was limited to government-funded biomedical research. Then, gradually, their jurisdiction was extended—first, to all biomedical research in institutions that received federal funds and then to all research that involved human subjects. The ethical principles upon which review is based emerged from the Belmont Report and are codified as 45 *CFR* 46, widely referred to as "the Common Rule." The definition of what is to be reviewed—research involving human subjects—has been surprisingly resistant to precision while the scope of review has remained fixed: (1) the comprehensiveness and clarity of the consent process, and (2) the assessment of the balance of risks versus benefits relative to a community standard. The rules for the composition of panels require that each panel have a "community" member—amplifying the signal that both the assessment of the clarity of consent forms and the assessment of risk were local matters.

Often overlooked in the history that we fashion to explain the current regulatory structure are the resources that organizations are required to invest to support the enterprise of ethical review. The regulatory structure requires two types of workers: (1) local personnel who organize the process and maintain records, and (2) workers from the central rule-creating/enforcing agency familiar enough with standards to audit compliance. The new bureaucracies of virtue have a center and a periphery. The center is comprised of federal agencies charged with promulgating regulations, issuing clarifications or interpretations of regulations, and monitoring compliance with the entire structure.

The periphery is made up of the policies, personnel, and offices created to meet the demands emanating from the center. Universities needed to form offices and train administrators who aid and educate researchers, schedule IRB meetings, create agendas and distribute protocols for these meetings, record the actions taken by IRB committees at the meetings, communicate those actions to researchers in writing, help researchers respond to those writings so that rejected protocols pass muster the next time around, and document for the appropriate federal agencies that all this activity is happening within the framework of the regulations.

In large research universities in which human subjects research is conducted by faculty across multiple schools and disciplines, the administrative task required is daunting, especially because it is safe to assume that despite generous indirect cost recovery on federal grants, the administrative office is under-resourced. Lost in all this is the fact that although IRBs are committees of faculty members that deliberate on research protocols, the formal bureaucratic work and the documenting of that work on forms, filed and organized so that compliance with regulations is capable of being audited at some later date, falls to functionaries who lack the authority of faculty members.

With that bureaucratic structure in mind—faculty committees whose work is to deliberate upon the compliance of protocols with regulatory standards and administrators whose work is to organize deliberations and document their outcomes—both the focus of the chorus of complaint and its tone become more understandable. The system of IRB review is often described as a peer review system. In reality, it is faux peer review. The labor of preparing documents, communicating negative judgments to researchers, and then negotiating with outraged, disgruntled faculty thrown off schedule by niggling objections falls to personnel that faculty most likely perceive as "merely" secretarial. The standard complaints about prospective review of research fail to mention the officeholders that administer the IRB system. IRBs are spoken of as monolithic entities. Two features of the administrative structure necessary to make compliance with federal regulation deserve underscoring. First, new occupations, training programs, and career ladders provide a great deal of practical authority to the new functionaries. Second, the functionaries who staff the new bureaucracies of virtue are able to create the impression of efficiency by shifting burdens directly to researchers and their staff. Action on proposals, a measure of administrative activity, occurs when proposals are returned to researchers for reasons no more serious than incorrect font size, incorrect pagination, or other niggling matters.

The differences in status and rank between committee members, staff, and research faculty deserve more commentary and analysis than they have so far received. Before I undertake that analysis, the chorus of complaint needs a fuller characterization than I have so far provided. Although the chorus of complaint is capable of either significant expansion or compression, I reduce it to the following essential elements:

1. *The mission creep or bureaucracy run amok complaint*: The process of prospective review is unwarranted. There is no convincing evidence that the risks attached to social science research justify it. Horrible as the Nazi prison experiments were, what social science analogues exist to justify the extension of this review to social science research? We do not kill people either by design or by negligence. All we want to do is talk to people and observe them as they go about their daily routines. Where is the harm in that?

2. *The inappropriate model argument*: Even if what we did was sufficiently risky to warrant prospective review, the model that we are saddled with is so rooted in the model of the biomedical randomized clinical trial that we cannot use it sensibly. These terms are not ones that we can use to describe faithfully our procedures. As a consequence, we cannot fashion a language to talk in a realistic way about risks and benefits. The randomized clinical trial has a beginning (subjects are enrolled), a middle (subjects are assigned specific interventions [control, treatment arm a, treatment arm b]), and an end (the course of treatment is completed). To each arm of the study, there are both theoretical risks and benefits, and in most cases an empirical risk calculation is available. All that is calculable and specified in the randomized clinical trial is open-ended not only in ethnographic research but also in any research that takes place outside a controlled setting.

3. *The fetish of written consent objection*: Forms that need to be signed accompany patients through their treatment for whatever ails them. When patients are transformed into research subjects, they reasonably anticipate that written forms will be part of this transition. There is little evidence that either as patients or as research subjects, people pay much attention to these forms, read and digest them, or make judgments based on them. Patients and research subjects sign forms because they understand that the signing of forms is "an obligatory passage point." Patients and research subjects have become inured to forms; they are a necessary bother, an indispensable ritual of institutional treatment.

In the everyday settings in which ethnographers conduct their investigations, forms do not carry this meaning. In fact, very few naturally occurring activities of everyday life require written forms. For some of the populations that ethnographic researchers are especially interested, written forms carry painful historical and legal meanings that are a reminder of how duplicitous formal authority is capable of being.[1] Even when our subjects have no reason to distrust relationships whose ground rules require "a writing," the signing of written consents, at worst, destroys both the naturalness and trust upon which the gathering of ethnographic data depends and, at best, makes achieving them that much more difficult to accomplish. Finally, the notion that consent is something attested to by a signature on a form and then finished is a denial of a primary fact of all ethnographic research: consent and trust are constantly in play, always being negotiated and renegotiated.

4. *Journalists are allowed to do what we seek to do without fetters*: Journalists interview subjects on sensitive topics under conditions in which prior review or imposed institutional restraints would be seen as a violation of guarantees of the First Amendment. A nice ironic twist that is often added to the chorus of complaint is that research conducted by journalists and done with procedures that IRBs would never permit, such as faking resumés or misrepresenting their identity in interaction, becomes books that are widely used in the undergraduate curriculum.[2] Another ironic twist is that the relative freedom of inquiry provided to journalists has led ethnographers to bypass IRBs and rely on data gathered by journalists.[3]

5. *The chilling effect fear*: In our most romantic self-fashionings, we, ethnographers, fancy ourselves as possessing a tool kit of methods that permit us to speak the truth to power. For sociologists, this often means poking around the backstage of those who present themselves in front-stage settings as possessors of expert knowledge, as competent wielders of authority, or as guardians of those pious homilies that we recite to convince ourselves of our own worth as some identifiable group. We are debunkers, muttering sotto voce to point out the inevitable shortfall between ideals and actual behavior. We are fervent believers in the fact that with very little probing we can discover attitude–behavior slippage of all types. In this immodest model, our research presents risks only to entrenched institutional interests. IRBs and their equivalent in other national systems will clearly see this danger and prevent us from exploring "sensitive" topics.[4]

6. *There is no evidence that IRBs have been very successful in preventing just those abuses that they were designed to create argument*: This is a claim that, by extension, suggests how wasteful of resources is extending the jurisdiction of IRBs to ethnographic research.

The problem with the chorus of complaint is that it fails to explain the organizational logic that enabled, even encouraged, such pernicious "mission creep" or what to do about it now that it has become an inescapable part of the lived experience of ethnographic research. The task of the next few paragraphs is to explain how mission creep emerged with such little fanfare so that it appeared a "natural" development and, now that it has emerged, how we might shape a response that is more effective than mere complaint. The problem with complaint, the undeniable compensatory charm that a sputtering public moral outrage provides notwithstanding, is that it does not create a viable alternative to the status quo. Frequently, the chief recommendation of complaint is to wish the problem away, a nostalgic plea for a return to some Arcadian past when the fetters of the current regime did not exist. Moreover, public complaint has an embedded defect in that it evokes a defensive reaction: horns get locked, positions hardened, and options foreclosed. Under these conditions, change occurs slowly and painfully, if at all. […]

The chorus of complaint identifies the defects of applying prospective ethical review to ethnographic research. The analysis becomes murkier when trying to identify either the agents who promoted or the motives that inspired this expanded authority. The passive acceptance of "mission creep" by universities is not merely a social fait accompli that demands protest but also a social mystery that requires explanation. After all, prospective research review is an unfunded government mandate—one that increases the operating costs to universities of organizing a process that complies with regulatory requirements; that subjects universities, administrative staff, and researchers to new liabilities if procedures fail to identify foreseeable risks that become material; and that requires considerable uncompensated labor to carry out the review function.

The mystery of understanding the motive for extending regulatory reach and the university's passive acceptance of that overreach are partially resolved by applying the internal logic of bureaucratic processes—Mertonian goal displacement—to each of the items in the chorus of complaint. The wrongheaded extension of prospective review to ethnography, the inappropriate standards of that review modeled on the randomized clinical trial with its measurable (at least in theory) costs and benefits and its clear beginnings and endings, the requirement of written consent in circumstances where all but the most socially dim-witted recognize that such formalities undermine trust and create suspicion rather than ensure the protection of rights, and the potential of committees to act to protect entrenched political and economic interests from a close analysis of their practices are more understandable once we recognize that those who command and control the process have sanctified the means while forgetting the ends of prospective research review. Further, once we recognize the discrepancy in mission between those who order the process and those who must comply with it—completing my project versus safeguarding a vulnerable subject population—the lack of flexibility, discretion, and understanding of the special problems that some ethnographic proposals pose all become more understandable.

When we add to this the large dependence of universities on federal funds and the risk of losing them because of inadequate compliance with federal regulations, the expansion of the administrative roles for those charged with oversight of research becomes an understandable strategy and policy to minimize research risk.[5] Further, the expansion of oversight is not limited to prospective review of research; a similar expansion has occurred in the domain of audit and compliance. This expansion has all the characteristics of that of prospective research review—new formal roles, new training programs, new career ladders, an ever-expanding rule book, and, of course, pushback from those now subject to the new, more rigid oversight regimes.

When we view the extension of prospective review from the perspective of those whose actions are vilified by the voices of the chorus of complaint, we expect to find a fair amount of either bewilderment or outrage. After all, the extension from the point of view of those responsible for the operation of the new bureaucracies of virtue is an unproblematic exercise in the rules-in-use. Extending prospective review to all research involving human subjects simply treats all researchers equally. To make written consent the touchstone of review has a dual purpose: (1) the feature of bureaucratic logic that says all need be subject to the same rule is reinforced, and (2) signatures on consent forms provide documentary evidence that the rules have been followed. From the perspectives of administrative workers, the chorus of complaint is an affront to the authority of the review process, an attempt by faculty and students to assert the superiority of the research mission over the lower-order task of prospective review. The resentment of those voicing the chorus of complaint most probably meets its match in the resentment of those who are the object of the complaint.

I have taken some time to specify the social dynamic that helps to explain the reaction to extending prospective review to social science research for two reasons. First, those voicing the chorus of complaint have spent much energy explaining how the system is broken but given hardly any thought to what motivates such a flawed process. Without such thought, however accurate the chorus of complaint is, its critical thrust is unlikely to lead to change. Without acknowledging some of the bureaucratic imperatives now guiding the system, the mutual understanding that leads to constructive change is unlikely to concur.

Second, even though ethnographic research as a whole has grown increasingly self-reflexive, very little of that self-reflection finds its way in the chorus of complaint, which is almost entirely one-sided. A notable exception is found in the work of Lederman,[6] who specifies how all of the boundaries that demarcate formal research from disciplined curiosity are "fuzzy." In some critiques, the problem lies with the very idea of prospective review, which is seen to run counter to democratic values, individual freedoms, and the right to free speech. In other critiques, the problem is the practitioners of normal science who populate IRBs and who fail to possess a sympathetic understanding of the open-ended, dynamic nature of ethnographic research methods. The inability of IRB members to comprehend the research strategies of ethnographers leads to objections that reveal their ignorance rather than ones that uncover ethical problems.

Having now been on the receiving end of IRB objections that I find incomprehensible, I appreciate my colleagues' multiple frustrations. However, having also sat on the other side of the table as an NIH study section proposal reviewer and as an IRB member, I think we need to recognize that we do not always act as our own best advocates. Our frustrations with the review process itself shines through in proposals that are much vaguer about methods of inquiry than they need to be. For example, on occasion, our explanations of our methods are no fuller than "we will employ standard techniques of participant-observation." At other times, we simply state that we will gather data to provide a "thick description." There are reasons why we cannot be overly detailed about our methods. However, a reviewer might conclude quite correctly that our failure to provide greater detail than we do says something about how we regard the labor of the committee and the process of prospective review.

At the same time, many proposals fail to even entertain the idea that a risk to subjects is a possibility. It is not uncommon to find under the heading *Risks to Subjects* a single word: *none.* The single word is often an accurate descriptor. However, a little elaboration of why the researcher believes this to be so expressed in a paragraph that indicates that the researcher has at least considered possibilities defuses tensions with IRBs. Such a paragraph demonstrates that the researcher is not contemptuous of the regulatory process and is acting in good faith. I find it hard to escape the conclusion that some of our shared difficulties with IRBs are of our own making. Acknowledging this fact permits us to make a critique that has the possibility of falling upon more sympathetic ears.

Further, beyond the mission discrepancy of researchers voicing complaint and the bureaucratic officials that are at the receiving end, there are a number of other features of the chorus of complaint that strike me as at the hairy edge of incivility.[7]

First, much of the resistance to prospective research review comes from those social scientists who in other contexts advocate fuller communication with patients in both clinical and research settings. There is something unseemly about demanding from physicians and biomedical researchers because we believe them not fully trustworthy while asserting that our own motives are so beyond question that we ought by right be free of those restrictions we impose on others. Next, as we voice the chorus of complaint, we seem to forget that those who serve on IRBs are our colleagues, that their service spares us unwanted burdens, and that they deserve a civil dialogue. In general, the chorus of complaint fails to deliver this—urging resistance, noncompliance, demands for formal explanations, and asymmetrical bureaucratic engagement by memoranda. Finally, the chorus of complaint portrays the social scientist as a powerless victim; and surely, this is not an accurate characterization of the choir, whose members are a privileged, voluble strata of the labor market. If Becker is right in "Whose side are we on?" if we are to speak for those whose voices normally do not get heard, then we surely ought to be able to speak for ourselves.

If we are to speak for ourselves, if we are to make our case persuasively, then we need to base our arguments in data that support the claims that we make to professional authority based on technical expertise. We need to present an evidence-based case supported by empirical research. Ethnographers, like everyone else, are permitted to ask for privilege based on special pleadings that claim our problems are unique; and, as a result, we deserve special treatment. Like everyone else, ethnographers need to expect that such special pleadings will be met with a great deal of skepticism.

If the chorus of complaint is taken at face value, the presence of any new ethnographic research is a testament to the doggedness and persistence of researchers who refuse to allow bureaucratic silliness to deter them. We know that IRBs and their acronymic counterparts in other national systems are a bother, but we lack systematic detail about the various forms that this bother takes and how much effort is required to tame it.

We are beginning to see the development of a literature that provides narratives of four types of experiences with the prospective review process: (1) studies that researchers thought about conducting but decided not to pursue, anticipating that the difficulties gaining clearance made the game not worth the candle; (2) studies that were stalled by IRB objections, the nature of those objections, the time that was required to negotiate an understanding that allowed the study to go forward, what changes in procedures were required to satisfy the IRB, and how the process of negotiation impacted upon the eventual research; (3) studies that were proposed to IRBs to which objections were raised and for which no amount of negotiation yielded an outcome that allowed the research to go forward; and (4) studies that researchers proposed, that the IRB made modifications to, and that went forward with researchers ignoring IRB objections.

These narratives, whatever the underlying interpretive difficulties presented by a consideration of the self-motivation of their producers, have both a practical and a theoretical value. The practical benefits are many. Multiple narratives from multiple institutions are necessary to begin even the most rudimentary assessment of the chorus of complaint and, more importantly, to take the steps necessary to change the tune the chorus sings. An expanding collection of narratives that describe and analyze experiences with prospective review is essential to our understanding. Although the same formal rules apply to all institutions, we have no idea how uniform is the interpretation of those rules. There is a general suspicion of enormous variability supported by the type of anecdotal evidence gathered in random hallway exchanges at professional meetings or circulated in e-mail chains.

By continuing to collect narratives, we will be in a better position to distinguish common problems generic to the review process across institutions from those resulting from idiosyncratic local interpretations. In the generic cases, we are then in a position to separate those that might be remedied by educating better IRB members about the nature of qualitative methods or of the regulations themselves. Idiosyncratic local problems require local solutions. Further, the frequency and variety of the problems will allow us to see how much validity there is to the most general claim of the chorus of complaint: the system is so broken that it cannot be salvaged.

Notes

1 Shannon, Jennifer (2007), Informed Consent: Documenting the Intersection of Bureaucratic Regulation and Ethnographic Practice, *Political and Legal Anthropology Review*, 30 (2): 229–248.
2 Dingwall, Robert, *Confronting the Anti-Democrats: The Unethical Nature of Ethical Regulation in Social Science*. Plenary Address to BSA Medical Sociology Group Annual Conference, Edinburgh, September 2006.
3 Katz, Jack (2006), Ethical Escape Routes for Underground Ethnographers, *American Ethnologist*, 33 (4): 499–506.
4 Hamburger, Philip (May 2005), The New Censorship: Institutional Review Boards, in *The Supreme Court Review 2004*, pp. 271–354.
5 Bledsoe, Caroline, Bruce Sherrin, Nathalia Headley, Carol Heimer, Eric Kjeldgaard, James Lindgren, Jon Miller, Michael Roloff, and David Uttal (2006), Regulating Creativity: Research and Survival in the IRB Iron Cage, in *Northwestern University Law Review*.
6 Lederman, Rena (2006), The Perils of Working at Home: IRB "Mission Creep" as Context and Content for an Ethnography of Disciplinary Knowledge, *American Ethnologist*, 33 (4): 482–491, and Lederman, Rena (2007), Comparative "Research": A Modest Proposal Concerning the Object of Ethics Regulation, *Political and Legal Anthropology Review*, 30 (2): 305–327.
7 Part of my aggravation with the chorus of complaint centers on the fact that I share with my colleagues their vexations at how unnecessary the prospective review process is, how its costs outweigh its benefits, and how the dangers it represents to free inquiry are so much greater than any protection it affords to subjects. None of us is in favor of violating subjects' rights, abusing their trust, or exposing them to danger. What has probably gotten lost in this paper is how much sympathy I have for the complaints of my colleagues. What is probably clear is how frustrated I am that a set of beliefs that I share has not yet been voiced in a way that appears likely to promote change.

44 Ethical code

American Anthropological Association

The American Anthropological Association (AAA) is a US professional organisation that brings together scholars in cultural, linguistic, biological, and archaeological anthropology, in accordance with the four field structuring of the discipline which is a legacy of the Boasian paradigm. Founded in 1902, it has 11,000 members, publishes around twenty scientific journals and organises every year the discipline's largest international event. From the outset, it has been confronted with intense debate and often ideological divides concerning the deontology of the profession, particularly in contexts where the United States found itself engaged in armed conflict, from the First World War to the invasion of Afghanistan and Iraq, where researchers put their expertise at the disposal of the military and the intelligence corps. In 1976, following the denunciation by the Chilean press of Project Camelot, which intended to use scholars in Latin American social sciences as informers regarding the internal situation of their country, the AAA drew up its first deontological text: *Statement on Problems of Anthropological Research and Ethics*. Shortly thereafter, when reports were published revealing the involvement of anthropologists in military operations against the Southeast Asian communist regimes, the AAA Committee on Ethics produced its famous *Statement on Ethics: Principles of Professional Responsibility* known under the acronym PPR. This was the AAA's first deontological code and it was adopted in 1971.

Many revisions have since been made to this founding document, taking new situations and issues into account, but also in line with changes in expectations about regulation within the organisation. The new forums and discussions that went hand-in-hand with these revisions testify to the importance of the issue for anthropologists in the United States and beyond. The code lays out a set of ethical responsibilities for anthropologists towards a number of agents, from populations to governments, and including institutions and funding sources, but it stipulates that the primary responsibility should be towards the people – and animals – with whom and on whom they work. In developing a deontological code, the AAA thus demonstrates its concern with the ethical issues of the discipline while at the same time developing an approach independent from bodies such as Institutional Review Boards. Some believe, however, that the issues at stake are too complex, and the necessary responses too context-specific to be dealt with in a satisfactory fashion by a code. In 2012, a new version of the code was submitted to the members of the AAA.

Preamble

Anthropological researchers, teachers, and practitioners are members of many different communities, each with its own moral rules or codes of ethics. Anthropologists have moral obligations as members of other groups, such as the family, religion, and community, as well as the profession. They also have obligations to the scholarly discipline, to the wider society and culture, and to the human species, other species, and the environment. Furthermore, fieldworkers may develop close relationships with persons or animals with whom they work, generating an additional level of ethical considerations. In a field of such complex involvements and obligations, it is inevitable that misunderstandings, conflicts, and the need to make choices among apparently incompatible values will arise. Anthropologists are responsible for grappling with such difficulties and struggling to resolve them in ways compatible with the principles stated here. The purpose of this Code is to foster discussion and education. The American Anthropological Association (AAA) does not adjudicate claims for unethical behavior. The principles and guidelines in this Code provide the anthropologist with tools to engage in developing and maintaining an ethical framework for all anthropological work.

Introduction

Anthropology is a multidisciplinary field of science and scholarship, which includes the study of all aspects of human kind: archaeological, biological, linguistic, and sociocultural. Anthropology has roots in the natural and social sciences and in the humanities, ranging in approach from basic to applied research and to scholarly interpretation.

As the principal organization representing the breadth of anthropology, the American Anthropological Association (AAA) starts from the position that generating and appropriately utilizing knowledge (i.e., publishing, teaching, developing programs, and informing policy) of the peoples of the world, past and present, is a worthy goal; that the generation of anthropological knowledge is a dynamic process using many different and ever evolving approaches; and that for moral and practical reasons, the generation and utilization of knowledge should be achieved in an ethical manner. The mission of the American Anthropological Association is to advance all aspects of anthropological research and to foster dissemination of anthropological knowledge through publications, teaching, public education, and application. An important part of that mission is to help educate AAA members about ethical obligations and challenges involved in the generation, dissemination, and utilization of anthropological knowledge.

The purpose of this Code is to provide AAA members and other interested persons with guidelines for making ethical choices in the conduct of their anthropological work. Because anthropologists can find themselves in complex situations and subject to more than one code of ethics, the AAA Code of Ethics provides a framework, not an ironclad formula, for making decisions. Persons using the Code as a guideline for making ethical choices or for teaching are encouraged to seek out illustrative examples and appropriate case studies to enrich their knowledge base.

Anthropologists have a duty to be informed about ethical codes relating to their work, and ought periodically to receive training on current research activities and ethical issues. In addition, departments offering anthropology degrees should include and require ethical training in their curriculums.

No code or set of guidelines can anticipate unique circumstances or direct actions in specific situations. The individual anthropologist must be willing to make carefully considered ethical choices and be prepared to make clear the assumptions, facts and issues on which those choices are based. These guidelines therefore address general contexts, priorities, and relationships which should be considered in ethical decision making in anthropological work.

Research

In both proposing and carrying out research, anthropological researchers must be open about the purpose(s), potential impacts, and source(s) of support for research projects with funders, colleagues, persons studied or providing information, and with relevant parties affected by the research. Researchers must expect to utilize the results of their work in an appropriate fashion and disseminate the results through appropriate and timely activities. Research fulfilling these expectations is ethical, regardless of the source of funding (public or private) or purpose (i.e., "applied," "basic," "pure," or "proprietary").

Anthropological researchers should be alert to the danger of compromising anthropological ethics as a condition to engage in research, yet also be alert to proper demands of good citizenship or host–guest relations. Active contribution and leadership in seeking to shape public or private sector actions and policies may be as ethically justifiable as inaction, detachment, or noncooperation, depending on circumstances. Similar principles hold for anthropological researchers employed or otherwise affiliated with nonanthropological institutions, public institutions, or private enterprises.

Responsibility to people and animals with whom anthropological researchers work and whose lives and cultures they study

1. Anthropological researchers have primary ethical obligations to the people, species, and materials they study and to the people with whom they work. These obligations can supersede the goal of seeking new knowledge, and can lead to decisions not to undertake or to discontinue a research project when the primary obligation conflicts with other responsibilities, such as those owed to sponsors or clients. These ethical obligations include:

- To avoid harm or wrong, understanding that the development of knowledge can lead to change which may be positive or negative for the people or animals worked with or studied
- To respect the wellbeing of humans and nonhuman primates
- To work for the long-term conservation of the archaeological, fossil, and historical records
- To consult actively with the affected individuals or group(s), with the goal of establishing a working relationship that can be beneficial to all parties involved

2. In conducting and publishing their research, or otherwise disseminating their research results, anthropological researchers must ensure that they do not harm the safety, dignity, or privacy of the people with whom they work, conduct research, or perform other professional activities, or who might reasonably be thought to be affected by their research. Anthropological researchers working with animals must do everything in their power to ensure that the research does not harm the safety, psychological wellbeing or survival of the animals or species with which they work.

3. Anthropological researchers must determine in advance whether their hosts/providers of information wish to remain anonymous or receive recognition, and make every effort to comply with those wishes. Researchers must present to their research participants the possible impacts of the choices, and make clear that despite their best efforts, anonymity may be compromised or recognition fail to materialize.
4. Anthropological researchers should obtain in advance the informed consent of persons being studied, providing information, owning or controlling access to material being studied, or otherwise identified as having interests which might be impacted by the research. It is understood that the degree and breadth of informed consent required will depend on the nature of the project and may be affected by requirements of other codes, laws, and ethics of the country or community in which the research is pursued. Further, it is understood that the informed consent process is dynamic and continuous; the process should be initiated in the project design and continue through implementation by way of dialogue and negotiation with those studied. Researchers are responsible for identifying and complying with the various informed consent codes, laws and regulations affecting their projects. Informed consent, for the purposes of this code, does not necessarily imply or require a particular written or signed form. It is the quality of the consent, not the format, that is relevant.
5. Anthropological researchers who have developed close and enduring relationships (i.e., covenantal relationships) with either individual persons providing information or with hosts must adhere to the obligations of openness and informed consent, while carefully and respectfully negotiating the limits of the relationship.
6. While anthropologists may gain personally from their work, they must not exploit individuals, groups, animals, or cultural or biological materials. They should recognize their debt to the societies in which they work and their obligation to reciprocate with people studied in appropriate ways.

Responsibility to scholarship and science

1. Anthropological researchers must expect to encounter ethical dilemmas at every stage of their work, and must make good-faith efforts to identify potential ethical claims and conflicts in advance when preparing proposals and as projects proceed. A section raising and responding to potential ethical issues should be part of every research proposal.
2. Anthropological researchers bear responsibility for the integrity and reputation of their discipline, of scholarship, and of science. Thus, anthropological researchers are subject to the general moral rules of scientific and scholarly conduct: they should not deceive or knowingly misrepresent (i.e., fabricate evidence, falsify, and plagiarize), or attempt to prevent reporting of misconduct, or obstruct the scientific/scholarly research of others.
3. Anthropological researchers should do all they can to preserve opportunities for future fieldworkers to follow them to the field.
4. Anthropologists have a responsibility to be both honest and transparent with all stakeholders about the nature and intent of their research. They must not misrepresent their research goals, funding sources, activities, or findings.

Anthropologists should never deceive the people they are studying regarding the sponsorship, goals, methods, products, or expected impacts of their work. Deliberately misrepresenting one's research goals and impact to research subjects is a clear violation of research ethics, as is conducting clandestine research.
5. Anthropological researchers should utilize the results of their work in an appropriate fashion, and whenever possible disseminate their findings to the scientific and scholarly community.
6. Anthropological researchers should seriously consider all reasonable requests for access to their data and other research materials for purposes of research. They should also make every effort to insure preservation of their fieldwork data for use by posterity.

Responsibility to the public

1. Anthropological researchers should make the results of their research appropriately available to sponsors, students, decision makers, and other nonanthropologists. In so doing, they must be truthful; they are not only responsible for the factual content of their statements but also must consider carefully the social and political implications of the information they disseminate. They must do everything in their power to insure that such information is well understood, properly contextualized, and responsibly utilized. They should make clear the empirical bases upon which their reports stand, be candid about their qualifications and philosophical or political biases, and recognize and make clear the limits of anthropological expertise. At the same time, they must be alert to possible harm their information may cause people with whom they work or colleagues.
2. In relation with his or her own government, host governments, or sponsors of research, an anthropologist should be honest and candid. Anthropologists must not compromise their professional responsibilities and ethics and should not agree to conditions which inappropriately change the purpose, focus or intended outcomes of their research.
3. Anthropologists may choose to move beyond disseminating research results to a position of advocacy. This is an individual decision, but not an ethical responsibility.

Teaching

Responsibility to students and trainees

While adhering to ethical and legal codes governing relations between teachers/mentors and students/trainees at their educational institutions or as members of wider organizations, anthropological teachers should be particularly sensitive to the ways such codes apply in their discipline (for example, when teaching involves close contact with students/trainees in field situations). Among the widely recognized precepts which anthropological teachers, like other teachers/mentors, should follow are:

1. Teachers/mentors should conduct their programs in ways that preclude discrimination on the basis of sex, marital status, "race," social class, political convictions, disability, religion, ethnic background, national origin, sexual orientation, age, or other criteria irrelevant to academic performance.

2. Teachers'/mentors' duties include continually striving to improve their teaching/training techniques; being available and responsive to student/trainee interests; counseling students/trainees realistically regarding career opportunities; conscientiously supervising, encouraging, and supporting students'/trainees' studies; being fair, prompt, and reliable in communicating evaluations; assisting students/trainees in securing research support; and helping students/trainees when they seek professional placement.
3. Teachers/mentors should impress upon students/trainees the ethical challenges involved in every phase of anthropological work; encourage them to reflect upon this and other codes; encourage dialogue with colleagues on ethical issues; and discourage participation in ethically questionable projects.
4. Teachers/mentors should publicly acknowledge student/trainee assistance in research and preparation of their work; give appropriate credit for coauthorship to students/trainees; encourage publication of worthy student/trainee papers; and compensate students/trainees justly for their participation in all professional activities.
5. Teachers/mentors should beware of the exploitation and serious conflicts of interest which may result if they engage in sexual relations with students/trainees. They must avoid sexual liaisons with students/trainees for whose education and professional training they are in any way responsible.

Application

1. The same ethical guidelines apply to all anthropological work. That is, in both proposing and carrying out research, anthropologists must be open with funders, colleagues, persons studied or providing information, and relevant parties affected by the work about the purpose(s), potential impacts, and source(s) of support for the work. Applied anthropologists must intend and expect to utilize the results of their work appropriately (i.e., publication, teaching, program and policy development) within a reasonable time. In situations in which anthropological knowledge is applied, anthropologists bear the same responsibility to be open and candid about their skills and intentions, and monitor the effects of their work on all persons affected. Anthropologists may be involved in many types of work, frequently affecting individuals and groups with diverse and sometimes conflicting interests. The individual anthropologist must make carefully considered ethical choices and be prepared to make clear the assumptions, facts and issues on which those choices are based.
2. In all dealings with employers, persons hired to pursue anthropological research or apply anthropological knowledge should be honest about their qualifications, capabilities, and aims. Prior to making any professional commitments, they must review the purposes of prospective employers, taking into consideration the employer's past activities and future goals. In working for governmental agencies or private businesses, they should be especially careful not to promise or imply acceptance of conditions contrary to professional ethics or competing commitments.
3. Applied anthropologists, as any anthropologist, should be alert to the danger of compromising anthropological ethics as a condition for engaging in research or practice. They should also be alert to proper demands of hospitality, good citizenship and guest status. Proactive contribution and leadership in shaping

public or private sector actions and policies may be as ethically justifiable as inaction, detachment, or noncooperation, depending on circumstances.

Dissemination of results

1. The results of anthropological research are complex, subject to multiple interpretations and susceptible to differing and unintended uses. Anthropologists have an ethical obligation to consider the potential impact of both their research and the communication or dissemination of the results of their research on all directly or indirectly involved.
2. Anthropologists should not withhold research results from research participants when those results are shared with others. There are specific and limited circumstances however, where disclosure restrictions are appropriate and ethical, particularly where those restrictions serve to protect the safety, dignity or privacy of participants, protect cultural heritage or tangible or intangible cultural or intellectual property.
3. Anthropologists must weigh the intended and potential uses of their work and the impact of its distribution in determining whether limited availability of results is warranted and ethical in any given instance.

Epilogue

Anthropological research, teaching, and application, like any human actions, pose choices for which anthropologists individually and collectively bear ethical responsibility. Since anthropologists are members of a variety of groups and subject to a variety of ethical codes, choices must sometimes be made not only between the varied obligations presented in this code but also between those of this code and those incurred in other statuses or roles. This statement does not dictate choice or propose sanctions. Rather, it is designed to promote discussion and provide general guidelines for ethically responsible decisions.

Other relevant Codes of Ethics

The following list of other Codes of Ethics may be useful to anthropological researchers, teachers, and practitioners:

– *American Board of Forensic Examiners*
n.d. Code of Ethical Conduct. (American Board of Forensic Examiners, 300 South Jefferson Avenue, Suite 411, Springfield, MO 65806.)

– *American Folklore Society*
1988 Statement on Ethics: Principles of Professional Responsibility. *AFSNews* 17(1).

– *Animal Behavior Society*
1991 Guidelines for the Use of Animals in Research. *Animal Behavior* 41:183–186.

– *Archaeological Institute of America*
1991 Code of Ethics. *American Journal of Archaeology* 95:285. 1994 Code of Professional Standards. (Archaeological Institute of America, 675 Commonwealth Ave, Boston, MA 02215-1401. Supplements and expands but does not replace the earlier Code of Ethics.)

– *National Academy of Sciences*
1995 *On Being a Scientist: Responsible Conduct in Research.* 2nd edition. Washington, D.C.: National Academy Press (2121 Constitution Avenue, NW, Washington, D.C. 20418).

– *National Association for the Practice of Anthropology*
1988 Ethical Guidelines for Practitioners.

– *Sigma Xi*
1992 Sigma Xi Statement on the Use of Animals in Research. *American Scientist* 80:73–76.

– *Society for American Archaeology*
1996 Principles of Archaeological Ethics. (Society for American Archaeology, 900 Second Street, NE, Suite 12, Washington, D.C. 20002-3557.)

– *Society for Applied Anthropology*
1983 Professional and Ethical Responsibilities. (Revised 1983.)

– *Society of Professional Archaeologists*
1976 Code of Ethics, Standards of Research Performance and Institutional Standards. (Society of Professional Archaeologists, PO Box 60911, Oklahoma City, OK 73146-0911.)

– *United Nations*
1948 Universal Declaration of Human Rights. 1983 United Nations Convention on the Elimination of All Forms of Discrimination Against Women. 1987 United Nations Convention on the Rights of the Child. Forthcoming United Nations Declaration on Rights of Indigenous Peoples.

Conclusion

Towards a *hauntology* of the moral question

Samuel Lézé

> The time is out of joint.
>
> William Shakespeare, *Hamlet*

> The vast, distant and hidden land of morality – of morality as it really existed and was really lived – has to be journeyed through with quite new questions and as it were with new eyes.
>
> Friedrich Nietzsche, *On the Genealogy of Morality*

As our journey through the 'vast, distant and hidden land of morality' draws to a close, what should we take away with us? Should we focus on the contours of its geography, on its numerous and unusual landscapes, on its generous vegetation or on the rivers that continue to irrigate it? We might run the risk of finding ourselves lost. In our view, beyond the cartography that we have tried to establish, the interest of this intellectual territory actually lies in the journey itself and in the new questions that it inevitably continues to raise today. So, what general lessons can we learn from the approach of a moral anthropology, or more specifically from all these anthropological readings of the 'moral question' as outlined in the introduction to this volume?

In order to answer this question and underline its current relevance, one can distinguish three such lessons. First, there is the lesson for social anthropology: What can it gain from studying morality in a more direct fashion today? Then there is the lesson for moral philosophy: Can moral anthropology allow a new dialogue to be opened up, and if so, on what basis? And finally, there is a wider lesson to be drawn from this for everyone, because the moral question is now an issue that is aired and debated in the public sphere: How can the particular light shed on the issue by moral anthropology contribute to an understanding of the moral stakes arising in contemporary societies?

* * *

The studies focusing on morality in anthropology have a theoretical, analytical and methodological impact.

On a theoretical level, this research can be considered as providing renewed responses to a central problem in the social sciences: that of the relationship between the individual and society. It is true that recent studies in moral anthropology have not made their theoretical contributions explicit, beyond the general idea that it is now necessary to examine morality by developing a specific field of study. And yet it is more ambitious to see this as a locus for testing theories of action accounting for the social properties of contemporary societies (social transition, globalisation and individualisation). However, this means running the risk of reviving old oppositions, as certain recent debates have shown.[1] Indeed, the theoretical issue at stake is not so much knowing whether morality lies on the side of the individual or of society, on the side of freedom or of constraint, or on the side of subjectivity or formal codes, as it is of understanding the specificity of the existing social tension between morality and ethics. Studying one while feigning to ignore the other means failing to fully grasp the workings of how we regulate the relationship to the self (the meaning of existence) and others (living together), which inextricably interweave norms, values, and affects.

On an analytical level, these studies provide anthropology with the opportunity to widen and even enrich its description of the complexity of social activities. On the one hand, they immediately submerge us in the concrete and circumscribed situations in which individuals must act: whether by thinking or obeying, valuing or evaluating, encouraging or changing, persisting or providing justifications. On the other hand, they show us how the norms, values and moral affects invoked by individuals are born and mobilised in practice, whether responsibility or guilt, honour or justice, charity or caution, freedom or dignity.

On a methodological level, these studies cannot help but create a new form of reflexivity that requires fundamental overlooked issues to be made explicit: the norms, values and affects involved in our own moral relationship to our object of study. They also involve the politics of science and the moral image that the discipline has long displayed as being self-evident: tolerance and respect in the face of difference. However, the consequences of these values today raise questions: Should everything be tolerated? Indeed, an absence of judgement might result in complicity or lead to the issues at stake being depoliticised. It is therefore the implicit definition of morality that should be included in our attempts to analyse our own position. A whole range of possible kinds of indignation, indifference, and enthusiasm can give a particular tone to our research, and it is not that easy to artificially suspend them in the name of combating ethnocentrism. It is therefore worth considering them for what they are: a moral engagement.

* * *

Moral philosophy has generally considered social anthropology as an ancillary science, with theory being the remit of philosophers and empirical material that of anthropologists. In this context, which fuels misunderstandings more than it does fruitful dialogue, ethnographic descriptions seem able to contribute to the normative work of philosophers – either by providing the final word in debates between competing moral theories (that of virtue, of duty or of moral consequences) or by settling the matter of the nature of morality, as illustrated, notably, by the ever-lasting discussions regarding the theory of 'ethical relativism'.

Today something remains of this ambiguous relationship. Anthropologists may have refined their descriptions of morality, yet more often than not they retain a reflex conditioned by the history of this asymmetrical dialogue between philosophy and anthropology. It thus sometimes seems necessary to them to come down on one side or other of a particular philosophical theory of morality or to defend one in particular in order to account for their research objects. However, anthropologists would gain from putting forward an alternative form of theorising that, rather than making a priori choices between philosophical stances, would attempt to understand the situations involving moral stakes for the actors in question, that is, to apprehend the genesis and development of norms, values, and affects in context.

In this regard, moral philosophers should be credited with orienting themselves more clearly in this direction than anthropologists, as evidenced not only by certain classical texts included in our anthology but also by the more recent 'conversion' of philosophers to the contributions of describing moral stakes in situ and to the development of what we could call an 'empirical philosophy', whether 'experimental psychology' or 'fieldwork'.[2] Not satisfied by the discussion of abstract moral dilemmas, they want to look at the concrete ways in which these problems arise and how individuals face them.[3] Similarly, it is all well and good to call upon the value of autonomy in the field of mental health, but it remains to be seen what actual concrete difficulties this poses when applied to populations in difficulty, such as psychiatric patients.[4] In this perspective, the conditions are certainly ripe for the beginning of a new collaboration between philosophers and anthropologists around the moral question.

* * *

This moral question is all the more acute because each and everyone of us, anthropologists included, are plunged into the specific concerns of our time and, even more fundamentally, into a moral relationship with our time – a time in which moral points of reference seem to have been irremediably turned upside down – 'out of joint'. Should we curse this legacy of a present that has come apart at the seams and that we would be at pains to put back together again? Or should we rather do our best to analyse the gap between the world as we conceive of it and the world as we make it? The moral question can only appear in a multiple fashion, from the local to the national and international scales: at first glance, what does the Truth and Reconciliation Commission in South Africa, for example, have in common with suicide bombings in the Middle East, controversies on homosexual parenting and the wearing of the veil in France, corruption in Africa and the development of humanitarianism, the Occupy movement and the salaries of company executives, professional deontology in medicine or the fabrication of proof in the scientific world, the exemplary nature of elected representatives or the legitimacy of a just war, etc.? What do any of these things have in common? And yet in this book we put forward the hypothesis that all these expressions of the moral question make sense together, as an ensemble, and call for the contribution of the social sciences.

The task of the anthropologists, taking into consideration the historicity and the political conditions of these moral questions, could precisely be to contribute to the analysis of these contemporary concerns. On the one hand, by identifying and examining the proliferation of local sites where new values, norms, and affects incessantly emerge and develop, but also converge and disappear. On the other hand, by clarifying the main issues at stake so as to think through the nagging and yet difficult question of social changes and the resulting moral debates. It is necessary to constantly remember – no matter how heated the debate or how self-evident the arguments advanced – that the boundaries of what is desirable or intolerable never cease to shift, whether we interpret this as moral progress or regression.[5]

Finally, we should remain wary of too hasty prognoses or obituaries of our time. The fact may well be that 'God is dead', 'ideologies are over' and it is 'the end of history'. However, we have not reached the reign of anomie: on the one hand, there have never been so many demonstrations of radical moral authority (from ethical codes to religious fundamentalism of all kinds) and we should avoid seeing these as a simple 'return' to morality after a short period of laxity or liberation; on the other, there have never been so many spectres of God roaming through and haunting our current affairs in various, more or less menacing forms. Perhaps we should offer the reader a critical *hauntology*[6] to accompany our critical anthology, which would attempt to understand the reasons behind the contemporary deployment of the moral question.

Notes

1 Such as the debate held in the anthropology journal *Ethnos*, confronting an approach focused on freedom and an approach focused on the constraints faced by individuals (Robbins 2009 and Zigon 2009).
2 These expressions are taken, respectively, from the works of Annemarie Mol (2002), Fabrice Gzil (2009) and Nicolas Lechopier (2011).
3 This is notably the case of Joan Tronto (1993).
4 As suggested by Jeannette Pols (2004).
5 As shown by Didier Fassin and Patrice Bourdelais (2005).
6 Taking up Hamlet's expression referring to his father's ghost ('the time is out of joint'), Jacques Derrida (2004: 202) forges the following neologism: 'To haunt does not mean to be present, and it is necessary to introduce haunting into the very construction of a concept. Of every concept, beginning with the concepts of being and time. That is what we would be calling here a hauntology.'

References

Derrida, Jacques (2004), *Specters of Marx: The State of the Debt, the Work of Mourning and the New International*, New York: Routledge, 1st French edition 1993.
Fassin, Didier and Patrice Bourdelais (eds.) (2005), *Les Constructions de l'intolérable. Études d'anthropologie et d'histoire sur les frontières de l'espace moral*, Paris: La Découverte.
Gzil, Fabrice (2009), *La maladie d'Alzheimer: problèmes philosophiques*, Paris: PUF.
Lechopier, Nicolas (2011), *Les valeurs de la recherche. Enquête sur la protection des données personnelles en épidémiologie*, Paris: Michalon.
Mol, Annemarie (2002), *The Body Multiple: Ontology in Medical Practice*, Durham and London: Duke University Press.
Pols, Jeannette (2004), *Good Care: Enacting a Complex Ideal in Long-Term Psychiatry*, Utrecht: Trimbos-instituut.
Robbins, Joel (2009), Value, Structure, and the Range of Possibilities: A Response to Zigon, *Ethnos*, 74 (2): 277–285.
Tronto, Joan (1993), *Moral Boundaries: A Political Argument for an Ethic of Care*, New York and London: Routledge.
Zigon, Jarrett (2009), Phenomenological Anthropology and Morality: A Reply to Robbins, *Ethnos*, 74 (2): 286–288.

Index

Abelard, Pierre 127
Aborigines Protection Society 349–50
Abraham, Karl 130
Abu-Lughod, Lila 5, 156, 319–20n9; biography 173; *Dramas of Nationhood* 173; *Veiled Sentiments: Honor and Poetry in a Bedouin Society* 173; *Writing Women's Words* 173
Achebe, Chinua 219n13
Acheh War (1873-1942) 351
adat (Sumatran social order), reconciliation with Islam 283–4
adultery, social/moral attitudes to 55, 171–2, 172n7
Africa: corruption in 212–19, 375; gift-giving traditions 215–16; instability of norms 215; misuse of authority 217–18; national variations 219n2; postcolonial attitudes to anthropology 354; range of legal systems 215; solidarity networks 216–17; survival of tribal societies 246; treament of HIV/AIDS 258
The African Queen (1951) 239
agency 105; distinguished from freedom 102
AIDS epidemic 314–15, 328
Aisheh, Abu 255n3
al-Ghoul, Mohammad 255n1
al-Qaeda 120–1
Alavi, Hamza 211n10
Allport, Gordon W. 128
alternative, problem of 114–15, 117n13
altruism, in primitive societies 84–5
Alzheimer's disease 257
American Anthropological Association 299, 341–6; codes of ethics 342, 345, 347 (*see also* Principles of Professional Responsibility); collaboration with CIA 344–5; core principles 366; findings in favour of members accused of espionage 341–2, 344–5; foundation/membership 365; tacit approval of espionage 342, 343, 345–6

Ames, Roger 128
Anderson, Jon 181n7
Anscombe, Elizabeth 14; biography 33
'anthrax culture' 253
anthropologists: criticisms of approach 232–3, 316–17, 354; involvement in espionage 299, 341–6; personal engagement/subjectivity 7, 232, 239, 297–8, 300n1, 315, 317, 318
anthropology: and colonialism 234n1, 299, 349–51; comparative approach 266; ethical codes 7, 347–55, 365–72; evolution of discipline 231–4, 265–6, 317–18; hostility towards 316–17, 354; medical 321, 325–6; relationship with morality 2–8, 46–9, 279–80, 297–300, 317–19, 373–6; relationship with psychology/sociology 128–30, 132; *see also* anthropologists; cultural relativism; universalism
Apel, Karl-Otto 151
aporia, and humanitarianism 335–7
Appiah, Kwame Anthony 91n6, 149
Arbenz, Jacobo 344
Archer, Margaret 254
Arendt, Hannah 330
Aristotle 5, 14, 33, 34, 35, 88, 90, 115, 148, 150, 151, 153
Asad, Talal 5, 40, 91n3, 234n1, 279, 294
asceticism 103, 107–8, 119–20
Ashton, T. S. 202
Association of Social Anthropologists (UK) 348, 353
Austin, J. L. 14, 111, 112, 113, 114, 117n11
Australia: anti-intellectual attitudes 255n6; anti-refugee policy 254
authority, as right to be earned 175–6
Awlad `Ali community 173–80; family relationships 175; 'free' *vs.* 'tied' tribes 174, 176–7, 180n4; honour-linked values 176–8; social structures 173–5; upbringing of children 177–8, 179–80

Ba, Amadou Hampate 219*n11*
Bachelard, Gaston 157, 221, 222, 227
Bailey, Frederick George 183–4
Baktaman people 142
Balandier, Georges 8
Ball, Patrick 269
Barth, Fredrik 142
Barth, Heinrich 231
Baso-basi (Sumatran social ritual) 284
Bass, Gary 267
Bateson, Gregory 343
Beals Committee 354
Becker, Howard S. 298, 363; biography 305
Bedouin peoples 173–80; code of honour 175–80, 181*n7*; family relationships 175, 179–80; importance of bloodline 173, 177; social hierarchy 173–5; valued characteristics 177–8
Beidelman, Thomas 239
Belmont Report 358
Beloff, Max 202
Benedict, Ruth 90, 127–8, 137, 342, 343; *The Chrysanthemum and the Sword* 147*n11*; *Patterns of Culture* 147*n11*
Benedict XVI, Pope 149
Benetton 315
Benjamin, Walter 315
Bentham, Jeremy 70, 72
Berber people 156
Berman, Marshall 322
Bernoulli, Jakob 225
Berreman, Gerald 345
Berry, R. B. 133
Berry, Sara 219*n7*
Beruf (calling), concept of 64, 68*n4*
Bestemann, Catherine 300–1*n4*
Bhaskar, Roy 254
bias (alleged) 305–12; circumstances leading to allegation 307–9; impossibility of avoidance 305–6, 311–12; in political situations 310–11; towards deviants 306–7; towards subordinate parties 307–10; *see also* anthropologists: personal engagement/subjectivity
bioethics 256–62, 357; and ethnography 258–62; problems facing 256–8
Blair, Cherie 251
Blair, Tony 270
Bloom, Allan 149
Boas, Franz 3, 82, 90, 128, 137; allegations against colleagues 299, 341–2, 343–4, 345, 346, 353, 354; exclusion from AAA 7, 299, 341, 342; *The Mind of Primitive Man* 130
Bonaparte, Marie 130
Booth, Wayne 136
Borges, Jorge Luis 2
Bornstein, Erica 233; biography 273

Bosk, Charles L. 300; biography 357; *All God's Mistakes: Genetic Counseling in a Pediatric Hospital* 357; *Forgive and Remember: Managing Medical Failure* 357; *What Would You Do? Juggling Bioethics and Ethnography* 357
Bosnia *see* Yugoslavia (former)
Bouglé, Célestin 56
Bourdieu, Pierre 4, 177, 180–1*n5*, 255*n8*, 300*n3*
Bourgois, Philippe 300–1*n4*
Brazil: democratisation processes 314; poor communities 314, 317, 318
Brögger, Jan 183
Brook, Peter 239
Buddhism 106
Burawoy, Michael 300*n3*
Burma (colonial), peasant activism in 157, 210
Burton, Richard (explorer) 351
Bush, George W. 251
Butt, Leslie 298; biography 321

Caduff, Carlo 40
Caesar, C. Julius 21
Cairns, Alan 267
Calhoun, Craig 330
Camelot affair *see* Project Camelot
Canada, reparations to indigenous peoples 266
cannibalism 19–22, 137; compared to Western customs 21–2
Cantril, Hadley 128
capitalism, ethics of 65–8
Carrithers, Michael 7
Carson, John 228*n1*
Cassian 106
categorical imperative 23, 27–8, 90
Cato, M. Porcius Uticensis (Cato the Younger) 19
Cavell, Stanley 111, 112–13, 114, 117*n8*
Chakraborty, Dipesh 234*n2*
Chamfort, Nicolas 16*n1*
Chapman, Audrey 269
Charles IX of France 22
Cheah, Pheng 324
Cheney, Lynne 255*n11*
Chicago School (of sociology) 305
Childe, V. Gordon 130
children: deaths 314; developmental stages 177–8; differential treatment of boys and girls 179–80; having of, as social virtue 188; maintenance of 36–7
Christian Care 233, 273–4
Christian morality 34–5, 86; contrasted with pagan 43–5, 163, 164, 165, 170–1; criticisms 29–30

Christianity: contrasted with other faiths 106–7, 109*n16*, 285; formation of legal/moral codes 44–5; humanitarian evocations of 330–1; influence around the world 119, 142; linked to good business 276–8; methods of propagation 276–7; NGOs, operations of 273–8; philosophical adherence to 149; set against witchcraft 273–5; subgroups, imprecision of definition 294*n1*; theology *vs.* practice 289–90; in the US 288–95; *see also* Christian morality; evangelism; Pentecostalism
Chrysippus of Soli 21
CIA (Central Intelligence Agency) 344–5
Cicero, M. Tullius 19
Clarke, David L. 190n3
Clarke, Samuel 71
Clinton, Bill 266, 267
colonialism, relationship with anthropology 234*n1*, 299, 349–51
Comaroff, John/Jean 235*n6*
'compassion fatigue' 289, 293
Comte, Auguste 222
Conrad, Joseph, *Heart of Darkness* 316
conscience, nature of 187–8; *see also* guilt; remorse
consent, requirement of 258, 359–60
consequences (of behaviour), consideration of 36–7
consequentialism 120–2
Cook, James, Captain 231
Cook, John 91*n6*
Cooley, Charles 129
corruption 212–19; and culture 218–19; factors producing 213–14; and gift-giving traditions 215–16; and negotiation 215; official *vs.* practical norms 214, 219*n6*; and predatory authority figures 217; and redistributive accumulation 217–18; and solidarity networks 216–17; tacit acceptance 213–14, 219*n6*
Craig, John 225
credibility, hierarchy of 308–10; in political situations 310–11
crime, social explanations for 252–4
crowds 201–3
Cuba: AIDS sanatoria 314, 317; difficulties of work in 316
Cudworth, Ralph 71
culpability 118–20
cultural relativism 3–4, 6–7, 89, 130–1, 136–9; concerns 138; defences 138–9, 143; misconceptions regarding 136–7; rejection 127–8, 132–3, 136, 149, 314–15
cultural theory 88–9
culture of poverty 244–8; community spirit 248; defining traits 245–8; family life 247, 248; individual traits/responses 248; low levels of organisation 247–8

Dahomey people 137
D'Andrade, Roy 196, 313
Das, Veena 91*n1*, 91*n4*, 321, 325
Daston, Lorraine 157; biography 221
Daumas, Maurice 230*n26*
Davis, John 183–4
Deleuze, Gilles 29, 56–63
Denmark, ethical codes 348
deontology 118, 120–2, 299, 375; challenges to 7, 299, 341; development of codes 300, 347–55, 365; Kantian 14, 23, 56
Derrida, Jacques 114, 290, 376*n6*
deviance, studies of 306–7
Devji, Faisal 120–1
Dewey, John 82
Dicks, Henry V. 128–9
Dollar, Creflo 295*n11*
Dumont, Louis 118
Dunant, Henri 330
Duncker, Karl 133*n3*
Durkheim, Émile 3, 4, 104, 108, 131, 148, 150, 192, 208–9, 222; biography 56; influence on later thinkers 15, 88, 202; influences on 14, 23; objections to 100, 101–2; *The Division of Labour in Society* 15, 56; *The Elementary Forms of the Religious Life* 56; *Suicide* 56
Dutch Association of Anthropologists 348
duty: as formal principle 26; as motive 24–6, 61; and reverence for the law 26–7
Dworkin, Ronald 150
Dwyer, Daisy H. 181*n8*
Dying for Growth see Kim, Jim Yong

Edel, Abraham 3, 14, 108–9*n6*, 130; biography 46; *Anthropology and Ethics* 46, 47, 48; *Ethical Judgment: The Use of Science in Ethics* 46
Edel, May Mandelbaum 3, 46, 108–9*n6*
Eickelman, Dale 181*n7*
el-Hoss, Selim 251
Elias, Norbert 229*n7*, 297, 300*n1*
Elisha, Omri 91*n3*, 234; biography 288; *Moral Ambition: Mobilization and Social Outreach in Evangelical Megachurches* 288
emotion: importance in Newar culture 194–6; role in moral judgments 69–70; studies 197–8*n4*
Enlightenment values: (attempts at) global imposition 314, 322; influence on anthropology 232
espionage, involvement of anthropologists in 299, 341–6; tacit approval of AAA 342, 343

ethical relativism 141–6; problems 142–3
ethics: capitalist 65–8; codes of 7, 347–55, 365–72; descriptive vs. normative 96–7; distinguished from morality 98; individual choices vs. social processes 257–8; and judgment 111–16; in non-literate societies 97–9; relationship with behaviour 98–9; relationship with freedom 104–6, 107–8; relevance to practical experience 258; review boards 357–64; as a science 72–3; theoretical/analytical 97
ethnography 258–62; dangers of 260–1, 362; ethical review 359–62; informed consent, doctrine of 258, 359–60; relationship with bioethics 259–60, 261–2; relationship with morality 279–80, 317; risks to subjects 362; self-reflexivity 361; study methods 258–9, 261
Ethnos (journal) 376*n1*
Euripides, *Hippolytus* 117*n11*
evangelism: competing ethics within 289–90, 293–4; defined 294*n1*; 'megachurches' 295*n11*; social activism 288–94
Evans-Pritchard, E. E. 3, 75, 352–3
'exighophobia' 253–4
exogamy *see* incest

faith-based activism 288–9
Falmouth, food riots (1727) 202, 203*n4*
Falwell, Jerry 295*n11*
Farmer, Paul 300–1*n4*, 319–20*n9*, 321
Fassin, Didier 91*n1*, 235*n5*; biography 328; *The Empire of Trauma* 328; *Enforcing Order* 328; *Humanitarian Reason* 328; *When Bodies Remember* 328
father-love, in primitive societies 79
Faubion, James 40
FBI (Federal Bureau of Investigation), investigation of spying anthropologists 342–3
Feibleman, James K. 132
'felicity condition' 112, 117*n11*
feminism 91*n4*
FIDH (Fédération Internationale des Droits de l'Homme) 333–4
First World War 64, 299, 341, 342, 343, 345, 353, 365
Firth, Raymond 3, 164, 166
Fish, Stanley 136
Fiske, A. P. 146
Flaminius Nepos, C. 19
Fleck, Ludwig 221, 222, 229*n6*
Fletcher, Laurel 269–70
Florence, medieval republic 67–8
Flugel, John 128
food riots 202–3, 203*n4*, 209
Fortes, Meyer 75, 131–2; *The Web of Kinship Among the Tallensi* 172*n5*

Foucault, Michel 5, 14–15, 88, 102, 107, 224, 316, 330; biography 40; influence on later philosophers/schools 100, 280; treatment of freedom 104–6; *Discipline and Punish* 104; *The History of Sexualilty* 40
France: colonial policy 350; ethical codes 348; social/political controversies 87–8, 375
Franklin, Benjamin 65–8; *Der Amerikamüde* 68*n2*
freedom 100–8; and ethics 104–8; (lack of) anthropological treatments 100–1
Freeman, Derek 144, 147*n13*
Frege, Gottlob 222
Frenkel-Brunswik, Else 128
Friedrich, Paul 176
Fugger, Jacob 65–6

Gahuku-Gama people 155–6, 163, 164–72
Gaita, Raimond 255*n4*
Galba, P. Sulpicius 19
Galeano, Eduardo 270
Galileo Galilei, *Il Saggiatore* 225
Geertz, Clifford 90, 92*n8*, 114, 141; biography 135; *Available Light* 135; *The Interpretation of Cultures* 135; *Islam Observed* 135; *Local Knowledge* 135; *Negara* 135; *Works and Lives* 135
Gellner, Ernest 101
gender, scientific accounts of 229*n10*
Germany: reparations for historical wrongs 266
Germany,: codes of anthropological ethics 348; colonial policy 350
Gershman, John 321
Gibney, Marc 266, 267
Gilligan, Carol 91*n4*
global morality: (attempted) implementation 1–2, 314; claims for 131–2, 314, 322
globalisation, effects of 253
good/evil, concepts of 29–31; opposed to morality 33; in Zimbabwean culture 273–4, 275–6, 277–8
good will, nature of 23–4
Gourevich, Philip 262*n4*
Graham, Billy 294*n1*
Greece (Ancient): approaches to morality 44; code of honour 176
Greece (modern), codes of honour 156, 184–90; attitudes to outsiders 186–7; bad luck/moral taint (*grousouzia*) 186–7; conscience (*sinithisi*) 187–8, 189, 191*n18*; regional variations 184, 189, 190*n14*; self-regard (*egoismos*) 185–6, 189, 190*n13*; social worth (*filotimo*) 184–5, 189
Griaule, Marcel 95
Guatemala: truth commission 266; US apology to 266, 267; US intervention in 344

Guilhot, Nicolas 159*n5*
guilt: consciousness of 32; studies 198*n6*; *see also* remorse
Gustafson, James 262*n1*
Gusterson, Hugh 300–1*n4*
Guyer, Jane I. 121, 122

Habermas, Jürgen 151, 322
Haddon, Alfred C. 353
Hage, Ghassan 232–3; biography 249; *Against Paranoid Nationalism* 249; *White Nation* 249
Hales, Stephen 225
happiness, morality of 25–6
Harrington, Michael, *The Other America* 245
Hastorf, Albert 128
Hegel, Friedrich 150, 232
Heidenheimer, Arnold 219*n6*, 220*n15*
Heilbron, Johan 16*n1*
Hein, Laura 267
Helsinki Declaration (1964) 299
Herodotus 97, 137, 231
Herskovits, Melville 137, 143
Hertz, Robert 56
Herzfeld, Michael 156; biography 182; *Anthropology Through the Looking-Glass: Margins of Europe* 182; *Cultural Intimacy: Social Poetics of the Nation-State* 182; *Evicted from Eternity: The Restructuring of Modern Rome* 182; *The Social Production of Indifference: Exploring the Symbolic Roots of Western Bureaucracy* 182
Hippolyte, Jean 40
Hiroshima/Nagasaki, bombings of 33, 270
Hirschkind, Charles 91*n3*, 117*n11*, 279
Hirschman, Albert 15–16
Hitler, Adolf 136
Ho, Karen 159*n5*
Hobsbawm, Eric 201, 204*n5*
Hocking, William Ernest 133
Hogbin, H. Ian 172*n10*
Homer, *Iliad* 176
'homoiophobia' 253–4
honour, questions of: among Bedouin peoples 175–80; in Islam 156; linked to sexual behaviour 179, 183–4; in Mediterranean societies 156, 176, 183–4
Hooke, Robert 227
Hoover, J. Edgar 342, 343
Howell, Signe 108–9*n6*, 158*n1*
Hubert, Henri 56
Hull, Clark 128
human rights culture 322–3
humanitarianism 328–37, 375; (allegations of) one-sidedness 333–4; anthropological approach to 328–9, 336–7; Chritian-influenced vocabulary 330–1; problems/contradictions of 329, 332–6
Humboldt, Alexander von 231

Hume, David 13, 35
Hybels, Bill 295*n11*

Ik people 232, 239–43
incest, in primitive societies 77–8
India, controversy over citizenship issues 269
Institutional Review Boards 7, 357–64; bureaucratic structure 358–9; criticisms 359–62; 'mission creep' 359, 360–1; poor relations with scientists 362–3; resources 358; value of literature on 363–4; widening of jurisdiction 357–8, 362
intention, role in assessment of behaviour 36–7
International Labour Organization (ILO) 121–2
Iraq, international humanitarian work in 332–3, 335–6
IRBs *see* Institutional Review Boards
Irwin, Alec 321
Islam 279–86; associated with morality 180*n4*; differences with Christianity 285; discourses of selfhood 281–3, 285–6; moral debates 87–8; pretend conversions to 351; a priori rejection 149; questions of honour 156; recociliation with traditional social customs 283–4; response to alleged blasphemy 329; significance of prayer 280–3
Israel–Palestine conflict 249–54, 333–4, 335–6; *see also* suicide bombings
Italy, conceptions of honour 183–4, 189

Jains 88, 100, 108, 110*n32*; confessional practices 106–7; religious beliefs 103–4, 109*n16*
James, Wendy 234*n1*
Japan, reparations for historical wrongs 266; *see also* Hiroshima/Nagasaki, bombings of
Java, Dutch colonial policy 211*n5*
Jharkand (Indian state) 269
journalists, scope of investigation 360
judgment, criteria for exercise of 111–13
Jung, Carl Gustav 82
justice, relationship with morality 34–5, 37–8
Juvenal (D. Iunius Juvenalis) 21

Kant, Immanuel 4, 13, 102, 115, 150–1, 153; biography 23; criticisms 33; influence on later philosophers/schools 48, 56, 60–1, 90, 114, 148; *Critique of Practical Reason* 32*n2*; *Groundwork of the Metaphysic of Morals* 14, 32*n2*
Kenyatta, Jomo 354
Kepler, Johannes 227
Kessing, Felix/Marie 144
Kim, Jim Yong 321; (et al), *Dying for Growth: Global Inequality and the Health of the Poor* 321–2, 323, 324, 326*n2*

Kleinman, Arthur 233; biography 256
Kluckhohn, Clyde 47, 90, 137, 142, 343; biography 127; *Beyond the Rainbow* 127; *To the Foot of the Rainbow* 127; *Mirror for Men* 127
'kola' (gifts), traditions of 215–16
Kolb, William L. 129
Kosovo *see* Yugoslavia (former)
Kouchner, Bernard 331, 333
Kroeber, Alfred L. 131, 137
Kuhn, Thomas 136
Kürnberger, Ferdinand, *Der Amerikamüde* 65, 68*n*2
Kwakiutl people 133
Kwayedza (Zimbabwe newspaper) 276

La Rochefoucauld, François de 16*n1*
Labat, Jean-Baptiste 231
labelling theory 305
Ladd, John 4, 47, 88, 136, 142; biography 95; *Ethical Issues Relating to Life and Death* 95; *Ethical Relativism* 95
Laidlaw, James 3, 14, 40, 88, 280; biography 100; *Religion, Anthropology and Cognitive Science* 100; *Riches and Renunciation* (with Harvey Whitehouse) 100; *Ritual and Memory* (with Harvey Whitehouse) 100
Lakatos, Imre 138
Lambek, Michel 14, 89, 108*n*2; biography 111; *Ordinary Ethics* 111
Las Casas, Bartolomé de 231
Latham, Steve 292–3
Latour, Bruno 229*n*12
law(s): as basis of ethics 34–5; circumvention 78–9; as God-given 35; in primitive societies 75–81; reverence for 26–7, 28*n*2
Leach, Edmund 75
Lebanon: civil war (1975-90) 250; Israel occupation (1982-5) 251–2
Lederman, Rena 362
Leibniz, Gottfried Wilhelm 225–6
Lenau, Nikolaus 68*n*2
Lévi-Strauss, Claude 92*n8*, 131, 137; *Tristes Tropiques* 232, 234–5*n4*
Levinas, Emmanuel 319
Levy, R. 194
Lévy-Bruhl, Lucien 82
Lewis, Oscar: biography 244; *The Children of Sanchez* 244; *Five Families: Mexican Case Studies in the Culture of Poverty* 244; *La Vida: A Puerto Rican Family in the Culture of Poverty* 232, 244
lie, problem of 114–15
Lieberman, Joseph, Senator 255*n11*
Linton, Ralph 131, 132
Lipton, Michael 206
Lock, Margaret 221
locutionary/illocutionary statements 113, 115
Lothrop, Samuel 342–4, 345

Lugard, Frederick (Lord) 350, 352
Lukes, Steven 14, 90; biography 148; *Marxism and Morality* 148; *Moral Conflict and Politics* 148; *Moral Relativism* 148; *Power: A Radical View* 148
Lund, Christian 219*n*7
Luther, Martin 120
Lycurgus of Sparta 20

Macbeath, Alexander Murray 133
MacClancy, Jeremy 7, 300–1*n4*
MacIntyre, Alisdair 108*n*2, 349; *After Virtue* 33
Macklin, Ruth 262*n1*
Mahmood, Cynthia 265
Mahmood, Saba 40, 91*n3*, 117*n11*, 279
Maier, Charles 267, 268
Malhuret, Claude 333
Malinowski, Bronislaw 3, 202, 232, 234*n*3; biography 75; professional ethics 352, 353, 354; *Argonauts of the Western Pacific* 75; *Crime and Custom in Savage Society* 15, 75, 101; *Freedom and Civilisation* 101
Malkki, Liisa 324
Mandler, George 193
Mannoni, Octave 133*n10*
Marcus, George 300–1*n4*
marriage 112; and the culture of poverty 247; in primitive societies 76–7, 84; in primitive societiesnegotiations 215
Marx, Karl 267–8
Marxism 148, 156–7, 201, 205, 311; rejection 64
Maslow, Abraham 128
Mason, John 342
Mauss, Marcel 56, 131
McCabe, Charles 315
McCarthy, Joseph, Senator 341
Mead, Margaret 144, 147*n13*, 311, 343, 344–5, 352
Médecins du Monde 330, 333–6; alleged failure of impartiality 333–4, 335–6
Médecins Sans Frontières 330–3, 334–6; foundation/core values 331; members taken hostage 332–3, 335; Nobel Peace Prize (1999) 331; religiously-influenced language 330–1; scale of operations 331–2
Mediterranean peoples/cultures 182–90; conceptions of honour 91*n2*, 156, 176; *see also* Greece; Italy
'megachurches,' defined 295*n11*
Mennonite Economic Development Association (MEDA) 276–7
Merry, Sally, *Human Rights and Gender Violence* 152
Merton, Robert 221, 223, 224, 229*n8*, 357, 361
Mexico: labour activism 121–2; lower-class society 245, 248

Miggs, Stacy 291–2, 295*n12*
Mill, John Stuart 35–6, 70
Millen, Joyce V. 321
Milosevic, Slobodan 253
Minangkabau people (Sumatra) 279, 280–6; Islamic prayer observances 281–3; personal/private matters *(paribadi)* 284–6; resistance to oppression 284; ritualised social etiquette *(baso-basi)* 284; social order *(adat)*, merging with Islam 283–4
Mintz, Sidney 205
'mission creep' 359, 360–1
Miyoshi, Masao 324
Moerman, Michael 344
Mohammad, caricatures of 329
Molière, *Le Bourgeois gentilhomme* 155
Money-Kyrle, Roger 128–9
Montaigne, Michel de 16*nn1–2*, 137, 140*n4*; biography 19; 'Of Cannibals' 14, 19; *Essays* 19
Moore, Barrington 207, 208
Moore, George 35–6
Moose/Mossi people 146
moral economy 221–8; coinage of term 201, 228*n1*; corrupt 213–14, 218–19; definitions 157–8, 159*n4*, 221–2; differing usages 205, 212, 213, 221, 228*n1*; negative definitions 222–4; of science 221–2, 225–8; working-class 203
morality: codes of 43–5; definitions 41, 47–9, 87, 88–9; evolving attitudes to 1–2; individual's relationship with 41–3; practical application 46–7; problematic nature 33–4, 46–7; relationship with justice 34–5, 37–8; studies 4–8; subjective nature 69–73; *see also* anthropology; ethics; ethnography; global morality
Morley, Sylvanus 342
Morocco: codes of honour 181*n7*; stages of maturity 181*n8*
mother-right, in primitive societies 76–7, 78, 79
Murdock, George Peter 130
Myanmar *see* Burma

Nadel, Siegfried Frederick 163, 165, 170, 354
Nader, Laura 345
Native Americans: demands for reparation 266; hostility to anthropologists 354; *see also* Navajo; Winnebago
naturalism 90
Navajo (or the older form: Navaho) 4, 47, 88, 95, 96–7, 142
Nazi regime 299, 344, 359
neoliberalism 252–3
Nepal *see* Newar people
Nepali, Gopal Singh 194

Netherlands: codes of anthropological ethics 348; colonial rule/policies 283, 350
Neumann, Franz 227–8
Newar people (Nepal) 156, 191–7; concept of mind 191–2; history/economy 193–4; importance of *lajyā* (sensitivity/moral worth) 194–6
NGOs (non-governmental organisations) 271–2, 324
Nicolás Ruiz community 121–2
Nietzsche, Friedrich 14, 106, 156, 376; biography 29; influence on later philosophers/schools 100; moral stance 29, 102–4, 109*n11*; *On the Genealogy of Morality* 1, 14, 100, 373
Niger, social traditions 216, 219*n8*
Nightingale, Florence 330
Nkrumah, Kwame 354
Noll, Mark 119
Nuremberg Trials (1946) 266, 299
Nussbaum, Martha 148, 151–2

Objectivism 35–6, 39*n1*
officials: allegations against researchers 307–9; need to lie 309
Oldham, Joseph 352
Olesko, Kathryn 227–8
Olivier de Sardan, Jean-Pierre 157; biography 212; *Anthropology and Development* 212; *Everyday Corruption and the State* 212; *Les Sociétés songhay-zarma* 212
Oresme, Nicole 225
Osiel, Mark 269
Osteen, Joel 295*n11*

Pal, Radhabinod, Justice 270
Papua New Guinea 118–22, 142, 155–6, 321; rituals 113
paribadi (realm of the personal) 284–5; merging with Islamic concepts 285–6
Parish, Steven M. 156; biography 191; *Moral Knowing in a Hindu Sacred City: An Exploration of Mind, Self and Emotion* 191; *Subjectivity and Suffering in American Culture: Possible Selves* 191
Park, Mungo 231
Parsons, Talcott 129
Partners in Health 323, 326*n2*
Pascal, Blaise 109*n16*, 132, 149
peasant societies 205–10, 246; minimum-income principles 207–8; subsistence arrangements 206–7
Pels, Peter 299; biography 347; (et al), *Embedding Ethics* 347
penal state, rise of 252–3
Pentecostalism 119–21
Peristiany, J. G. 182

Petty, William 225
Philip V of Macedon 19
Piers, Maria 319
Pitt-Rivers, Julian 182, 190*n10*
Plato 20; *Laws* 44; *Republic* 44
Pocock, J. G. A. 2
Polanyi, Karl 206, 211*n2*
Polynesian peoples 139
Porter, Theodore 226
postmodernism 313
poverty: contradictory views on effects 245; as 'dehumaninsing' 239–43; descriptions of 323–5; *see also* culture of poverty
prayer *see Shalat*
Price, David 299, 301*n6*; biography 341; *Anthropological Intelligence* 341; *Threatening Anthropology* 341; *Weaponizing Anthropology* 341
Price, Richard 71
'primitive' societies 19–22, 75–81, 82–6; conflicts within 77–8, 79–81, 143–4; ideals of conduct 83; legal systems 75–7; moral criteria 53–5, 83–4; sexual morality 77–9, 171–2, 172*n7*; standards compared with West 21–2; supernatural beliefs 78–9, 84; war/peace rituals 83; Western stereotyping 82–3, 84, 97–8; *see also names of specific peoples*
principle(s), subjective *vs.* objective 28*n1*
Principles of Professional Responsibility (AAA code of ethics) 354, 365–71; academic responsibilities 368–9; application 370–1; creation 345, 365; dissemination of results 371; position on espionage 345–6; responsibilities to public 369; responsibilities towards objects of research 367–8; teaching responsibilities 369–70
Project Camelot 7, 299, 344, 353–4, 365
promises, keeping of 27–8
provincialism, dangers of 138
psychology: cross-disciplinary studies 197–8*n4*, 222–3, 228–9*n5*; philosophy of 33–4, 37; relationship with anthropology 128–9, 132, 138
Pyrrhus of Epirus, King 19
Pythagoras 71

Quetelet, Adolphe 227

Radcliffe-Brown, Alfred R. 352, 353
Radin, Paul: biography 82; *Crashing Thunder: The Autobiography of an American Indian* 82; *Primitive Man as Philosopher* 15, 82; *The Trickster: A Study in Native American Mythology* 82; *The Winnebago Tribe* 82
Rank, Otto 130
Rappaport, Roy 111, 113–14
rationalism 68, 89–90

Rawls, John 152
Read, Kenneth E. 4, 91*n2*, 155–6; biography 163; *The High Valley* 163; *Other Voices: The Style of a Male Homosexual Tavern* 163; *Return to the High Valley* 163
Reagan, Ronald 345
reason, role in moral judgments 71–2
Redfield, Robert 137, 244, 271
Reid, Thomas 71
Reingold, Nathan 228*n1*
relativism *see* cultural relativism; ethical relativism
remorse, sensation/expression of 85–6
reparation (for historical injustices) 266–70; conflicting claims 268–9; and new international morality 267–8; omissions 270; rise on international agenda 266–7; systemic flaws 269–70
ressentiment, Nietzschean concept of 29, 103
Rice, P. B. 133
ritual, nature of 113–14
Rivers, W. H. R. 353
Rizakos, Gina 255*n9*
Robbins, Joel 89, 91*n1*; biography 118; *Becoming Sinners: Christianity, Moral Torment in a Papua New Guinea Society* 118
Rockefeller Foundation 343, 352
Roheim, Geza 130, 133*n10*
Rome (Ancient), approaches to morality 44
Rorty, Richard 322–3
Rosaldo, Michelle 5, 158*n2*
Rosaldo, Renato 314
Rose, R. B. 204*n6*
Ross, W. D. 39*n1*
Rostow, W. W. 202
Rousseau, Jean-Jacques 232
Roxstrom, Erik 266, 267
Rudé, George 201
Rwanda: genocide (1994) 258, 262*n4*; Organic Law 1996 269; war crimes tribunal 266, 269
Ryle, Gilbert 135

Said, Edward 267
Salgado, Sebastião 315
Samoa 142, 143–6, 147*n13*; ethical contradictions 144–5; linguistic subtleties 144
Sartre, Jean-Paul 319
Saya San 210
Scanlon, Thomas 148, 151
Scheffler, Israel 136
Scheler, Max 29
Scheper-Hughes, Nancy 7, 298, 300–1*n4*; biography 313; *Commodifying Bodies* 313; *Death Without Weeping: The Violence of Everyday Life in Brazil* 313, 314; *Saints, Scholars, and Schizophrenics* 313; *Small Wars: The Cultural Politics of Childhood* 313

Schneider, Jane 189
Schopenhauer, Arthur 29
Schuller, Robert 295n11
Schumpeter, Joseph 206
science: ethical control of research 357; ideal of objectivity 221–2, 226–7; moral economy of 221–2, 225–8; precision measurement 227–8, 230n27; and quantification 225–8
Scott, James C. 157; biography 205; *The Moral Economy of the Peasant: Rebellion and Subsistence in Southeast Asia* 205
Second World War 163, 201, 341, 342, 343, 344, 345, 348, 352, 353; anthropologists' contribution to war effort 343–4; *see also* espionage
self: formation of 42–3; Islamic/traditional Sumatran conceptions of 281–3, 284–6; range of definitions 286n2; realisation through prayer 281–3; Western theories of 286
self-control, virtue of 177–8
Seligman, Charles 75
Sen, Amartya 148
September 11 attacks, public/governmental response to 254, 270
sexual behaviour, linked to morality 41–5; *see also* adultery; honour; marriage; 'primitive' societies
Shaffer, Simon 230n21
Shakespeare, William, *Hamlet* 1, 146, 373, 376n6
Shalat (Islamic daily prayers) 280–3; realisation of selfhood through 281–3; time/place of performance 280–1
shame, role in morality/social interaction 194–6; studies 198n6
Shapin, Steven 223, 230n21
Sharon, Ariel 333
Shils, Edward 129
Shiner, Roger 112–13
Shore, Bradd 90; biography 141; *Culture in Mind: Cognition, Culture and the Problem of Meaning* 141; *Sala'ilua, a Samoan Mystery* 141
Sidgwick, Henry 35–8, 71
Siegel, Jerrold 286
Simiand, François 56
Simon, Gregory M. 233–4; biography 279; *Caged in on the Outside: Identity, Morality and Self in an Indonesian Islamic Community* 279
sincerity 117n11
Smith, Adam 329–30
Snouck, Christiaan 351
sociology: allegations of bias 305–12; criticisms 360; political stance of researchers 310–11; relationship with anthropology 129–30, 132

Soeffner, Hans-Georg 120
Sombart, Werner 68n3
Songhay-Zarma people (Niger) 212
Sophist school 72–3
South Africa: apartheid regime 246, 248; calls for racial homelands 316; conditions in squatter communities 315, 316, 317, 318; democratisation processes 314; truth commission 266, 269, 375
Southeast Asia (colonial) 157; peasant protest 208–10; repressive nature of regime 208, 210
Soyinka, Wole 270
Speed, Shannon 121–2
Spiegel, Sam 239
spies/spying *see* espionage
Spinden, Herbert 342
Spinoza, Baruch 10, 249, 254
Staël, Madame de 16n1
Stephen, Sir James Fitzjames 70
Steward, Julian 130
Stoczkowski, Witold 7
Stoler, Ann Laura 235n6
subjectivism 72–3; (alleged) dangers of 72
subsistence: culture 207–9; insurance arrangements 206–7; as moral right 207
suffering: attempts to alleviate 321–3; impact of descriptions 321–5, 329–30; impact of images 315–16; pitfalls of attempting to alleviate 323–6
suicide bombings 232–3, 249–54; (calls for) absolute condemnation 250–1, 254, 255n1; compared with US/Israeli tactics 250, 251–2; 'humanity' of participants 251–2; motivation 251–2, 254, 255n3
Sumatra 233–4, 280–6; *see also* Minangkabau
Sundar, Nandini 233; biography 265; *Anthropology in the East: The Founders of Indian Sociology and Anthropology* 265; *Branching Out: Joint Forest Management in India* 265; *Sovereigns and Subalterns: An Anthropological History of Bastar* 265
Sweden, ethical codes 348
Sykes, Karen 91n1, 91n5

Tacitus, P. Cornelius 231
Taussig, Michael 235n6, 315
Tawney, R. H. 208, 352
Taylor, Charles 108n2, 279
Tennessee 288
Thomas, Northcote 353
Thompson, E. P. 156–7, 205, 212, 221, 228n1; biography 201; *The Making of the English Working Class* 201
Thompson, Laura 344
Thorndike, F. L. 128
Throop, Jason 91n1
Toffin, Gérard 194

Torpey, John 267
Towles, Joseph 239, 242
tribunals: doubts as to effectiveness 269–70; failings of impartiality 269
Trimborn, Hermann 130
Trobriand people 76–81, 202–3
Truman, Harry S. 33, 270
truth commissions *see* Guatemala; South Africa; tribunals
Tsembaga Maring people 113
Tsing, Anna 325
Turnbull, Colin M.: biography 239; criticisms 239; methodology 232, 239–40; *The Forest People* 239; *The Mountain People* 232, 239
Turner, Ted 251
Tuskegee experiments 270, 299–300
Tutu, Desmond, Archbishop 269
Tylor, Edward B.: biography 53; *Notes and Queries on Anthropology* 46–7, 53; *Primitive Culture* 4, 15

Uganda *see* Ik people
United Kingdom: codes of anthropological ethics 348, 349–50; colonial policy 350–1
United States: anthropologists' involvement in espionage 299, 341–6; black culture 248; capitalist ethos 65–6, 67–8; codes of professionl ethics 7, 353, 371–2 (*see also* American Anthropological Association; Principles of Professional Responsibility); health system 262$n3$; invasion of Iraq (2003) 332–3; National Security Education Program 346; 'penal state' 252–3; reparations for historical wrongs 266, 270; rhetoric on Middle East conflicts 251–2; Social Science Research Council 300$n2$; *see also* American Anthropological Association; Tennessee
universalism 6–7, 90, 129, 130–3; criticisms 152; ethical universals 131–2; *see also* global morality
utilitarianism 66, 70

Vandeginste, Stef 269
veil(s), wearing of 87–8, 375
Villegaignon, Nicolas Durand, sieur de 20

Wagner, Richard 29
Wagner, Roy 142
Wakin, Eric 345
Wallis, Jim 294$n1$
Walzer, Michael 91$n6$

war crimes tribunals *see* Rwanda; tribunals; Yugoslavia
Warren, Rick 295$n11$
Watkins, Joe 346
Watson, James D. 229$n15$
Watts riots (1965) 310
Wearmouth, R. F. 202
Weber, Max 118; biography 64; influence on later philosophers/schools 182, 202, 233, 260, 273, 357; *Economy and Society* 64; 'Politics as Vocation' 6, 15, 122; *The Protestant Ethic and the Spirit of Capitalism* 6, 15, 64
Weinstein, Harvey 269–70
Westermarck, Edward 75, 149; biography 69; *Ethical Relativity* 69, 136; *The Origin and Development of the Moral Ideas* 15, 69
Westfall, R. S. 223
White, Leslie A. 130
Whitehouse, Harvey 100
WHO (World Health Organization) 314, 323
Widlok, Thomas 91$n1$
Willey, Gordon 343
Williams, Bernard 102, 104, 105, 109–10$n20$, 280
Williams, Daniel 255$n3$
Wilson, Charles 202
Winnebago people 82–6; ideals of conduct 83; moral criteria 83–4
Wise, M. Norton 229$n11$
Wissler, Clark, *Man and Culture* 130
Wittgenstein, Ludwig 14, 33, 89, 111, 112–13, 135
Wolf, Eric 205, 206
women: correct social behaviour 179; dress 87–8; subordinate social position 175
Woodruff, Paul 128
working classes: derogatory/stereotypical views of 202–3; influence on history 201–2
World Vision 233, 273–5

Young, Allan 221
Yugoslavia (former): conflicts on 258; war crimes tribunal 266, 269–70

Zeno of Citium 21
Zigon, Jarrett 91$n1$, 91$n3$
Zimbabwe 233, 273–8; national economy 276; supernatural beliefs 273–6
Zuni people 133, 137
Zunz, Olivier 159$n5$

Made in the USA
San Bernardino, CA
05 November 2017